Yale Law Library Series in Legal History and Reference

There Is a Deep Brooding in Arkansas

The Rape Trials That Sustained Jim Crow,
and the People Who Fought It, from
Thurgood Marshall to Maya Angelou

Scott W. Stern

Yale UNIVERSITY PRESS   NEW HAVEN AND LONDON

Published with support from the Lillian Goldman Law Library, Yale Law School.

Copyright © 2025 by Scott W. Stern. All rights reserved. This book may not be reproduced, in whole or in part, including illustrations, in any form (beyond that copying permitted by Sections 107 and 108 of the U.S. Copyright Law and except by reviewers for the public press), without written permission from the publishers.

"My Arkansas" from *And Still I Rise: A Book of Poems* by Maya Angelou, copyright © 1978 by Maya Angelou. Used by permission of Random House, an imprint and division of Penguin Random House LLC. All rights reserved. And Little, Brown Book Group Limited. Reproduced with permission of the Licensor through PLSclear.

Yale University Press books may be purchased in quantity for educational, business, or promotional use. For information, please e-mail sales.press@yale.edu (U.S. office) or sales@yaleup.co.uk (U.K. office).

Set in Scala Pro type by IDS Infotech Ltd.
Printed in the United States of America.

Library of Congress Control Number: 2024939554

ISBN 978-0-300-27357-1 (hardcover : alk. paper)

A catalogue record for this book is available from the British Library.

This paper meets the requirements of ANSI/NISO Z39.48-1992 (Permanence of Paper).

10 9 8 7 6 5 4 3 2 1

To Charlie

There is a deep brooding
In Arkansas.
Old crimes like moss pend
From poplar trees.
The sullen earth
Is much too
Red for comfort.

—Maya Angelou, "My Arkansas"

Contents

Author's Note xi

Introduction 1

PART I. | DOWN SOUTH

1. The Making of a Cotton County, 1541–1927 13
2. The Law of Rape, 1820–1920s 23
3. Vigilantism and Resistance, 1899–1930s 33
4. A Jim Crow Childhood, 1930s 43

PART II. | ARRESTS

5. Bethel and Wallace, 1928 53
6. Class War, 1929–1935 62
7. Clayton and Carruthers, 1935 67
8. Mr. Freeman, Mid-1930s 82

PART III. | TRIALS

9. The Trial Begins, 1929 93
10. The Trial Begins, 1935 104

11. Pearl Testifies, 1929 112

12. Virgie Testifies, 1935 129

13. Marguerite Testifies, Mid-1930s 137

14. The Origins of an Advocate, 1908–1933 146

15. The Witnesses Testify, 1929 153

16. The Witnesses Testify, 1935 158

17. The Recovery, 1930s–1953 165

18. The Rape Docket, 1930s 176

19. Bethel and Wallace Testify, 1929 183

20. Clayton and Carruthers Testify, 1935 193

21. The Ascent, 1954–1968 201

22. The Anti-Rape Docket, 1930s 214

23. The Trial Ends, 1929 220

24. The Trial Ends, 1935 227

PART IV. | APPEALS AND DEMANDS

25. Taking Flight, 1968–1969 241

26. The Appeal, 1935–1936 252

27. Seeking Mercy, Seeking Clemency, 1929–1936 271

28. The Appeal, 1937–1939 278

29. The End, 1939 289

PART V. | AFTERLIVES

30. Maya Angelou, 1970s 303

31. Frank Bethel, 1931–1952 318

32. Mike Wallace, 1931–1983   321

33. Pearl, 1929–   323

34. Virgie, 1936–2005   325

35. Bubbles Clayton, 1939–   327

36. Jim X. Carruthers, 1939–   331

37. Thurgood Marshall, 1977   334

Epilogue   344

Notes   353

Acknowledgments   433

Index   437

Author's Note

This is a true story. Every character was real, and every event happened. All descriptions and dialogue come from archival records, legal case files, newspaper articles, letters, diaries, and secondary sources, as cited in the endnotes.

This is a book about sexual violence. Part of its purpose is to foreground the voices of the women and girls who chose to publicly testify about what happened to them in spite of extraordinary pressures against doing so. To write this book without including their words would be to erase their experiences or diminish their courage. That said, I feel it is important to warn readers that much of what these women and girls spoke about is deeply upsetting to read. This book contains *no* graphic descriptions of sexual assault, but it discusses the existence of sexual violence at length. Further, the testimony of these women and girls does not come to us unfiltered; their words were recorded by court stenographers or reported by journalists, who may have been imperfect transcribers or allowed their biases to affect the text.

As in my first book, I struggled with a number of decisions regarding terminology. First, I was torn about how to refer to the women and girls who testified in sexual assault trials. I experimented with the words "survivor," "victim," "complainant," and even "prosecutrix"—the most common term used in rape trials in the early twentieth century—and spoke about the drawbacks of each of these words with trusted teachers and friends. Ultimately, and after much thought, I chose to use the word "accuser," in part because it is the predominant term used in sexual assault trials today, and in part because of the specific historical context of the dozens of trials that are analyzed in this book. The word "accuser" is, to be sure, a contested term and a deeply imperfect choice—emphasizing the accusation and not the assault—but my hope is that it can adequately describe the reality of cases ranging from the trial of Maya Angelou's rapist to the unjust persecution of the Scottsboro Boys.

Second, I have chosen to refer to the accusers by their first names only. I have done this not out of a desire to obscure the historical record but rather in an attempt to protect the privacy of their descendants. Readers who wish to learn more about the trials analyzed in this book will be able to easily discover the accusers' full names by reading the case files or, often, the published opinions and press coverage of these trials—all identified in the endnotes. My hope was simply that if a person looked up the name of their grandmother in an internet search engine, the grandmother's testimony in a trial that surely represented one of the most traumatic moments of her life would not appear among the results. (The sole exception to this first-name rule is Maya Angelou, in part because her fame would make it fairly pointless, and in part because she herself very publicly discussed her experiences of sexual violence.)

Finally, and with reluctance, I feel I should very briefly discuss myself. I am a white man, writing about a history of violence in which the violent disproportionately looked like me. To be clear, I am not a character in this book—this is not my story—yet the biases and assumptions that accompany my particular experience of gender and race undoubtedly shaped my writing. I note my identity not to check some sort of box but rather to acknowledge my own perspective and its limitations. Further, my race and gender are not the only aspects of my identity that affected this book. As the legal scholar Patricia Williams wrote many years ago, "Since subject position is everything in my analysis of the law, you deserve to know that it's a bad morning." In my case, readers deserve to know that I wrote the bulk of this book over a bad couple of years: I wrote in the midst of a pandemic, in which the indifference or greed of those in power resulted in mass death and unfathomable suffering—and just as oppression led millions across the United States and around the world again to rise up in support of Black Lives. I also wrote it as I was becoming a lawyer. My profound frustrations with the legal system I was becoming a part of, and my deep hopes for the ongoing struggle for justice, shaped this book as well.

Readers deserve to know that I believe our criminal legal system is fundamentally violent, that it blithely deprives so many of their homes, their health, their safety, their freedom, and even their lives. This book therefore provides a history of this unjust "justice" system, which—in spite of unending struggle—remains unjust almost a century later. This book tells a story with many bad actors, but ultimately it is the story of a bad system. It is my hope that by illuminating the foundations and genealogy of that system, this book can be one small tool to aid readers who hope to dismantle it.

Introduction

Ironically, it was something of a comfort to three-year-old Marguerite Johnson when the jolting train she was riding crossed into the Jim Crow South and the passengers suddenly had to segregate themselves. Even at three she probably already understood that the society into which she'd been born saw her as inherently defective, profoundly second-class, for not just one but two reasons—her dark skin and her identity as a girl. But as soon as the train, belching smoke and lurching with each curve of the tracks, crossed a point well known to the porters, the Black passengers had to stand up and move to a section of the car separated from the whites; Marguerite and her four-year-old brother, Bailey, went with them. The writer Isabel Wilkerson would later note that trains heading south were typically "quiet and sober," unlike the liberating vehicles of the Great Migration that carried Black people north.[1] Although, years later, Marguerite did not remember much of the journey—the sights that flashed by the dusty windows or, indeed, the date and time that she left—she would recall that "things must have looked up" after the moment of segregation on her journey to the east and, more fundamentally, to the south. "Negro passengers, who always traveled with loaded lunch boxes, felt sorry for 'the poor little motherless darlings' and plied us with cold fried chicken and potato salad," she later wrote. It was this small act of humanity that welcomed Marguerite into cotton country for the first time in her life.[2]

Her journey had begun in sunny Long Beach, California—a hopeful place, if still a fairly quiet one, in 1931, two years before the catastrophic earthquake that would force the city to modernize and a decade before the wartime boom that would eventually make it one of the biggest industrial hubs in the Sunbelt. The train ride was more than 1,600 miles in all—a very long journey for two very small children to make on their own, with only the distracted conductor to watch out for them. "To Whom It May Concern," proclaimed the notes attached to their wrists, printed with their names. After the conductor got off the train in Arizona, their tickets were pinned to Bailey's inside coat pocket, and they were left alone. This was still a time when people got dressed up to take the train, women in sensible traveling dresses and men in suits and hats; even three- and four-year-olds donned their Sunday finest, especially if they were moving across the country, saying goodbye to the only home they'd ever known, irrevocably disrupting the rhythm of their young lives.

Little Marguerite and Bailey finally stepped off the train in Stamps, Arkansas. "Musty" was the word Marguerite would later use to describe it—for sprayed over everything was dirt and detritus from speeding trains like the one she had just ridden in on.[3] Stamps had sprung up from the red clay barely a generation earlier, a lumber town created to mill logs carried by the trains of the Louisiana and Arkansas Railway. It was barely three square miles, home to some 2,500 residents—a population that had been fairly constant for the last decade and would hold steady for the next eight, the town's fortunes tied to the railroad and the lumber mill. Stamps lay in the far reaches of southwestern Arkansas, built around Lake June, a small, man-made pond that had been constructed to float yellow pine logs to the mill.[4] It was home to a few stately mansions, with wraparound porches and towering trees; a smattering of shops and stores, such as the one that Marguerite's grandmother ran with great success; and a coursing undercurrent of bigotry, poverty, and violence.

"The town reacted to us as its inhabitants had reacted to all things new before our coming," Marguerite would later write. "It regarded us for a while without curiosity but with caution, and after we were seen to be harmless (and children) it closed in around us, as a real mother welcomes a stranger's child. Warmly, but not too familiarly."[5]

For most of the next decade, Marguerite would call Stamps home. It would be the site of many happy memories—a loving, tight-knit family, a modicum of prosperity eked out in a town wracked by Depression, and the place where this young girl—who would later become one of the world's best-loved writers—would learn to read Shakespeare ("my first white love") as well as a pantheon of Black writers: Paul Lawrence Dunbar, Langston Hughes, James Weldon Johnson, and W. E. B. Du Bois, at whose deathbed Marguerite would one day be present.[6] Yet many years later, in the book that would launch her into worldwide fame, Marguerite would also reveal that Stamps had been a place of deep pain. It was where she had suffered so profoundly, and so alone, that for many years she literally couldn't speak at all.

Arkansas was not the place where eight-year-old Marguerite would endure the sexual violence that would define her childhood, but it was where she would return to suffer, for years. It was also where she would return to heal. It was where she would rediscover not only the ability to speak but the ability to tell her story. And when, years later, she would begin to write about her trauma, to reclaim her history, to start to reinvent herself, she would do so using a new name: Maya Angelou.

This is a book about the journey of Marguerite to Maya, about people overcoming acts of casual, unspeakable violence only to discover the ability to speak, themselves, in the most courageous ways imaginable. But it is also a book about injustice, about the ways that their society failed girls like Marguerite, women like Maya. About how the American system of law and order—trumpeted as the greatest, fairest legal system in the world—was utterly, fundamentally unequipped to do justice when presented with cases of sexual assault. To understand this history demands listening for the voices of girls like Marguerite and women like Maya, but it also necessitates looking beyond her single life, to other cases of Jim Crow injustice. And to do that, we must move from the southwestern corner of Arkansas to the northeastern tip. From the musty mill town of Maya's memory to the most profitable cotton country in the world.

Possibly on the very day in 1931 that Marguerite Johnson was speeding toward Arkansas, two white men sat in prison near Little Rock. They were not well educated, not tall, not handsome, not rich, not socially prominent. One, a barber, had a broad, flat face and high forehead, his dark hair slicked back from a heavy brow; the other, a farmer, had a more compact face, protruding ears, and sported a bow tie for photographs. The two had been sentenced to death for sexually assaulting a young, white schoolteacher. But they were also white men, and in the Jim Crow South, so Frank Bethel and Mike Wallace had not been electrocuted.[7] Rather, in 1931, their case was on appeal, and Bethel and Wallace were residing in The Walls, at the time Arkansas's oldest state penitentiary. If from the outside The Walls resembled the grim fortress of nightmare—with crenelated turrets, imposing brick walls, and one notorious room into which flowed electricity and out of which flowed corpses—behind the heavy doors was a veritable summer garden. Petunias, zinnias, marigolds, and hundreds of other flowers, many of them bright scarlet and yellow, lined well-ordered paths; poplars and mulberry trees—both the weeping and non-weeping varieties—swayed gently in the breeze beside the lily pool; croquet was "the game of the hour" in the early 1930s, with wickets set up on a smooth stretch of green grass beside the death chamber. The food was notably good, the labor famously easy. Conditions were so pleasant in The Walls, in fact, that some prisoners seemed embarrassed to be sent there.[8]

In the handsome sandstone courthouse, gazing at the marble embellishments and occasional splashes of copper, surrounded by a handful of shops and houses and millions of acres of cotton fields, a jury of their peers—farmers and tradesmen, all white, all male—had convicted Bethel and Wallace of assault with intent to rape. This was in Blytheville, the largest city in Mississippi County, Arkansas, which at the time boasted soil so fertile and plantations so massive that it produced more cotton than any other county in the United States; in fact, the county alone produced almost 2 percent of the *entire world's* cotton.[9] It was no small matter in those days to skip a day of picking or sorting or selling to gawk at two notorious criminals, but Bethel's and Wallace's trial reportedly attracted the largest crowd ever to pack a Mississippi County courthouse, and the local papers labeled their case "one of the hardest fought legal battles here in a number of years."[10] For years, the Bethel-Wallace rape case would rock Mississippi County, becoming a subject of fervent speculation in the taverns and offices and fierce gossip in the fields, eventually forcing some of the trial's witnesses to flee the state altogether.

Five years later, herself the victim of sexual assault, Marguerite Johnson returned to Arkansas, roughly eight years old, silent, and profoundly traumatized. As, once again, she sat on the train south, watching dense pine forests and endless acres of farmland fly by the window, two other men sat in an Arkansas prison, waiting to die. Their names were Bubbles Clayton and Jim X. Carruthers, and, like Frank Bethel and Mike Wallace, they had been convicted of sexual assault in a Mississippi County courtroom. Their case too was notorious, widely discussed, and well covered in the press. But Clayton and Carruthers were Black, convicted of raping a white woman. Thus, as Marguerite returned to Arkansas, they did not idle away their hours in the leafy Walls penitentiary. They were forced to reside instead in Tucker Prison Farm, a sprawling collection of penal buildings constructed in the middle of an immense cotton plantation. In the early 1930s, the state of Arkansas spent $29.78 per month on each prisoner at the Walls compared to just $6.23 at Tucker; the average population at the Walls was just 43 while at Tucker it was 787.[11] The hundreds of men in Tucker were compelled to work hard, to raise enough crops and livestock to satisfy their hunger and enough valuable cotton to keep the prison doors open. Inmates were a source of cheap and expendable labor at the Tucker farm; shortly before Clayton and Carruthers arrived, the prisoners were instructed to replace the mules in the fields. Groups of convicts walked up and down the rows of cotton plants in "teams," tied together with rope, dragging farm equipment in their wake under the bright sun. To cut costs, other inmates—mostly poor, white men—served as guards and carried weapons, freely and indiscriminately beating their fellow convicted men, often to death. The buildings themselves were literally falling apart. "Arkansas penal farms were hellish in princip[le] and brutal in practice," wrote one historian several years later.[12]

"Guilty," proclaimed the foreman, a white man, in the same Mississippi County courthouse in which Bethel and Wallace had seen their lives change forever. But unlike Bethel and Wallace, Clayton and Carruthers were almost certainly *not* guilty of the crime for which they were forced to endure captivity and, quite possibly, death in the chair. Though Mississippi County had a substantial Black population, the jury that had sentenced the two Black men to die had been entirely white, as all Arkansas juries had been since the end of Reconstruction. The courtroom in which they had been convicted had seethed with race hate, and many of the men who had tried their hardest to lynch Clayton and Carruthers shortly after their arrest surely sat in the spectators' benches, glaring at them. No lawyer in town would take their case, and the out-of-town one who was dragooned into doing so by the judge was given woefully little time to prepare. Their conviction was so absurd that the famously overworked lawyers of the National Association for the Advancement of Colored People (NAACP) would take over their appeal. The young NAACP lawyer eventually assigned to the case, a man named Thurgood Marshall, would call their case "worse than any we have had as yet."[13]

This book contains many stories. It is a thorough and wide-ranging study of sexual assault trials in the Jim Crow South and the first study of the anti-rape activism of Maya Angelou.[14] It is the first full retelling of the Bethel-Wallace and Clayton-Carruthers rape trials, and a probing scholarly analysis of the NAACP's voluminous sexual assault docket.[15] I have chosen to braid these stories together rather than present a traditional chronology or a book of statistics. It is my hope that by weaving these stories together—and by narrating them *as stories*—I can provide a layered, impressionistic portrait of a place, a time, and a society. Jim Crow society, like all societies, contained multitudes, and I fear that the presentation of any of these narrative threads without the others would minimize the portrait of Jim Crow and its legal system that I wish to draw. Resistance accompanied repression; progress coexisted with regression; the same individual could fight for justice and promote backlash. Further, the violence of Jim Crow was inseparable from white supremacy, patriarchy, capitalism, and the legal system. I chose these particular narrative threads to highlight this inseparability. One cannot understand rape in the Jim Crow South without a thorough accounting of the plantation, the legislative chamber, the sharecropper's shack, the general store, the courtroom; likewise, one cannot understand the courtroom or the sharecropper's shack or the general store without understanding sexual violence under Jim Crow. It is my argument that rape *and* its legal adjudication were forms of violence that held this hierarchical and oppressive society together.

To tell these stories, I have drawn on Maya Angelou's newly released personal papers, held in a glass-and-brick building on Malcolm X Boulevard in Harlem; on the NAACP's mammoth archival collection at the Library of Congress; on crumbling primary documents unearthed from archives across Arkansas and the broader South; on newspaper accounts and oral histories; on books and pamphlets and family lore; and, above all, on tens of thousands of pages of trial transcripts drawn from a nearly untapped treasure trove of court records held by the University of Arkansas at Little Rock.

Over the last generation, a number of books have been published arguing powerfully that grassroots resistance to sexual violence launched the modern Civil Rights Movement, and that Black female activists so often marginalized by powerful men in their own time and observers in the future—activists like Rosa Parks, Fannie Lou Hamer, Jo Ann Robinson, and Recy Taylor—were, in fact, the true, radical leaders of a struggle so often associated with famous men.[16] This book seeks to build on this pathbreaking scholarship to provide the backstory that more clearly explains the unjust reality they were protesting against. While much of this scholarship has focused on the 1940s and 1950s, this book aims its gaze most squarely at the 1920s and 1930s—at the years before a confluence of factors made a mass movement possible. In the years before Parks investigated rape cases and Hamer, herself a survivor, glared past television cameras and declared, "I question America," countless women and girls braved stigma and ostracism, as well as threats of impoverishment and even incarceration, to bring their rapists to justice. As the twentieth century continued, they occasionally secured help from lawyers, such as the pioneering ones at the NAACP who built their reputation and their practice in no small part from their victories in sexual assault cases. Yet all too often, these women were forced to proceed on their own. The fact that they did speaks to a tradition of resistance and resilience that is every bit as worthy of remembrance and celebration as the exploits of those lawyers.

In focusing on these stories, I offer an account of the legal system in the Jim Crow South—more an intricate legal history than an intimate social history. I therefore broaden these earlier histories by revealing that Jim Crow rape trials were not dispassionate adjudications of evidence, but rather highly personal struggles over virtue and moral worth among neighbors, friends, and families. They were, at their core, community battles over social norms; the questions debated at trial were not primarily what happened and to whom, but rather who was respectable, who was promiscuous, and who had violated the ironclad mores of the Jim Crow South. In the end, these trials were battles over who deserved violence. In what should be unsurprising to even cursory students of American history, the casualties in these battles were disproportionately Black people. Race pervaded sexual assault trials as much as did questions of morality. The racial hierarchy of the Jim Crow South determined who was charged and who was on the jury; it structured what witnesses could say and how they had to present themselves; it informed how the judge instructed the jury and the verdict the jury ultimately reached. Especially after the trial was completed, race was critical in determining who deserved mercy and who deserved to die.[17]

Jim Crow rape trials were, then, also a sick form of public theater. They were like plays in which each participant knew the role he or she was expected to play, performed before a large, interested audience. Black men knew they would be asked certain questions, and they knew which answers might save their lives; white men knew how to respond to inquiries in ways that preserved their privilege and, generally, secured their continued liberty and social standing; white women knew they would face intense scrutiny, but they also knew that there were certain questions almost no lawyer would ask them; and Black women knew they enjoyed no such protection from allegations of impropriety. This knowledge shaped their behavior, and it also shaped the outcomes of the trials. The authorities could not always stop their female neighbors from bringing charges of sexual assault, but they could choreograph the trials carefully so as to preserve the race, class, and gender hierarchies on which Jim Crow society depended so tenaciously and so tenuously.[18]

In this respect, the legal system itself was complicit in the omnipresence of sexual violence in the Jim Crow South. Indeed, in this book I argue that the legal system's primary function was to adjudicate transgressions of racial, sexual, and economic hierarchies, not determine who was "innocent" and who was "guilty."[19] To a degree previously under-explored by scholars, the Jim Crow legal system relied heavily on prosecuting (or not prosecuting) rape in order to sustain an unequal society. The specific demands, requirements, and rituals of rape trials at this time rendered these trials almost uniquely incapable of delivering justice to survivors, while simultaneously serving to ensure the maintenance of Jim Crow's many intersecting forms of oppression. What's more, the precedents that emerged out of that system continue to shape sexual assault trials to this day.

In any given year in the 1920s and 1930s, there were somewhere around fifty to a hundred rape and sexual abuse prosecutions across Arkansas, surely representing only a small minority of actual assaults. Yet what is surprising is not that these trials took place rarely; what is surprising is that they took place at all. So many barriers stood in the way of survivors seeking justice following a sexual assault: stigma, familial or financial hindrances, and startlingly onerous legal requirements. The fact that there were dozens of sexual assault trials every year in Arkansas suggests that these trials had some useful function for the system of which they were a part. When we look at the stories explored here, we see that more than anything, the trials often served to reinscribe and legitimize white supremacy and a rigid gender hierarchy.[20] However, the fact that there were dozens of these trials also reveals a hidden undercurrent of resistance and resilience, for as much as trials were repetitions of strict oppressive norms, they were also sites where women could resist, protest, speak—even if their words did not change the trial's outcome.

In this book, I delve into the records of more than a hundred of these trials, but I tell the story of two of them: the prosecutions of Bethel and Wallace and of Clayton and Carruthers. These two pairs of men, one pair white and the other Black, each asserted their innocence, yet each was quickly convicted and sentenced to die. Both cases became public spectacles and media sensations. Both were appealed to higher courts, and to the court of public opinion. Yet, in the end, they would have very different outcomes.

I also seek to put Maya Angelou and the journey she described in *I Know Why the Caged Bird Sings* into broader historical context. She was one of many Black women and girls who testified against their assailants in spite of the extraordinary obstacles the Jim Crow social order put in their way. Yet she also wrote about this experience, in spite of her intense hesitation to do so. Today she is well remembered for her literary contributions, but few remember that Angelou was also once a proud member of the activist left. In fact, Angelou was more than a memoirist, a poet, a screenwriter, and a playwright; more than an internationally renowned dancer, singer, and Tony-nominated actress. She was an organizer—an associate of both Martin Luther King Jr. and Malcolm X, who had fought for years for pan-African solidarity and a free and revolutionary Ghana. Even more, with her writing, she sought to give voice to countless survivors of sexual assault who, like her, had endured years of trauma and silence. For this reason, Angelou should be understood as an anti-rape activist, one who sought not only healing for herself through her writing but also collective justice in the face of violence.[21]

Fifty years after the Bethel-Wallace and Clayton-Carruthers rape trials had faded from memory, an organizer with Take Back the Night addressed a letter to Maya Angelou's office at Wake Forest University. The organizer was writing to ask if Angelou would consider speaking at the organization's annual march and rally in Washington, D.C. "This event," the organizer typed, "takes place to support women who have experienced sexual assault and to increase community awareness surrounding this pervasive societal problem."

"To most people, you are a well-known and well-respected author," the organizer continued. "To us, and to other people who are committed to ending violence against women, you are much more."[22]

For generations, Maya Angelou's words had spoken, plainly and directly, to survivors of sexual assault—women and men and others, Black and brown and white. Her words had offered strength, vulnerability, and, above all, recognition. And though she could not be at this particular Take Back the Night rally—she would be traveling from Michigan to Virginia—she had given a voice to those who felt, as she silently had a lifetime before, alone.

But Maya Angelou was not alone. She was one of countless women who had availed themselves of the justice system, however unjust, and demanded that what happened to them be taken seriously. She was one of countless women who had refused stay silent, to subordinate her life and autonomy to men who sought to destroy her. She was one of countless women whose very survival bespoke incredible strength and resiliency. Her rapist had threatened to kill her beloved brother if she ever told anyone what he did—but, first at trial and then in books that were read by millions, she had told everyone. She also knew that not every victim could speak up as she had, and so she wrote to empower all survivors. She told a story that defied the intentional injustice of the Jim Crow legal order.

"I support the efforts of the Rape Crisis Center," she wrote back to the organizer, "and my heart is with you."[23]

Part I
Down South

1 • The Making of a Cotton County, 1541–1927

With its dense, hardwood forests and dark, murky swamps, the Arkansas Delta has long endured a forbidding reputation. A vast fertile swath of the Mississippi River Valley, the Delta—especially its northern reaches—was dotted with sucking bogs and marshes, teeming with snakes, angry insects, and, according to the rumors, outlaws. For more than half a millennium, Native Americans had resided in northeastern Arkansas, eventually moving from isolated hamlets into complex villages centered around giant pyramidal mounds, clearing the forests for corn and lumber. By the time the bearded conquistador Hernando de Soto—the first European to set foot in the Delta—arrived in 1541 in search of gold, the land that is now Mississippi County, Arkansas, was within one of the most densely populated areas in North America. Although de Soto was impressed by the walled towns and canals he came across, he and his men attacked the Native Americans and likely passed along epidemic disease. Within a year, de Soto himself was dead by fever, but Arkansas's Indigenous inhabitants enjoyed no respite. The conquistador had noted a severe, ongoing drought in the region, and this continued for a hundred years. Eventually, crops failed, wildlife fled, and men, women, and children starved.[1]

Surviving Natives relocated, and for the next two centuries northeastern Arkansas remained fairly empty. The forests began to grow again, the deer returned, and the carefully carved canals gradually collapsed, coming to resemble a massive swamp. Native Americans periodically came to hunt or seek refuge from the genocidal wars settlers were waging nearby, but none remained for long. In the winter of 1811, less than a decade after the United States acquired the Arkansas Delta as part of the Louisiana Purchase, the most destructive earthquakes in recorded American history struck in southeastern Missouri and rocked the land that is now Mississippi County. Animals fled bellowing as trees toppled, buildings disintegrated, rivers erupted in waves, and, in some places, the earth itself groaned and was ripped open. One county historian claimed it sounded "as if a thousand pieces of artillery were suddenly exploded." Thousands of quakes, including at least three that would have scored above an 8.0 on the Richter scale, devastated the region over three terrifying months; tremors could be felt as far away as New York and Boston. A dense, black vapor settled over the remade land. Many of the Cherokee then living in northeastern Arkansas saw the earthquakes as divine punishment directed at the rapacious whites, and they relocated closer to Little Rock to avoid being caught in the geological crossfire.[2]

The earliest American settlers of Mississippi County thus had "a rude beginning," wrote one local historian. Primarily hunters, fishers, and trappers, they eked out lives in one- or two-room log cabins and cooked in iron-covered pots on open fireplaces. Many lived forty to eighty miles from the nearest post office. Throughout the nineteenth century, flood waters regularly washed in to drown or bankrupt them, and even in the dry years they were not infrequently trailed by panthers or wolves. Criminals and brigands continued to seek sanctuary in the sparsely populated swampland. Still, settlers kept coming. There was potential for great profit in the fertile Delta, if one could stand the natural disasters and the seedy underbelly peeking out from the muck. New residents, as well as much-needed goods, arrived by raft, by bullet-shaped riverboats, nicknamed "Alligators," and eventually by steamboat, which quickly became the dominant mode of transportation along the mercurial Mississippi River. A few enterprising settlers began setting up plantations along the banks of the river. "More cautious men saw only danger and unpromising circumstances in those wild and earthquake-damaged lands," wrote the great historian of Arkansas, Jeannie Whayne, "and by planting their expectations in more solid ground elsewhere, they missed an opportunity that only shrewd and calculating eyes could see."[3]

Of course, not all of Mississippi County's settlers arrived by choice. Black slaves had resided in the area since at least the eighteenth century, but increasing settlement in Arkansas resulted in the forcible introduction of thousands more Black men, women, and children. Organized slave patrols began moving throughout the burgeoning towns. By the time Arkansas was admitted to the Union as a slave state in 1836, the "peculiar institution" was "firmly established," as one scholar has written. The slave population rose faster in Arkansas than in any other state, and the Delta was at the heart of this increase; by

1860, some two-thirds of the state's slave population resided there. Yet because of Mississippi County's extreme conditions—the wild swamps that had to be quickly transformed into orderly plantations—its enslaved Black inhabitants "necessarily endured the most extreme conditions confronting slaves in the American South," wrote Whayne. Thus, it was hardly a surprise that when the Civil War descended on Arkansas, Black people fled plantations in droves, with more than five thousand ultimately donning Union blue uniforms themselves to fight against their former owners.[4]

In Mississippi County, the Civil War did not end with Appomattox; for the better part of a decade after the Confederacy was crushed, the county "constituted a virtual war zone." A militia, organized by the state's Reconstruction government that sought to give tangible meaning to emancipation, battled Klansmen in the streets, while freed Black people organized and began marching by the hundreds to demand their rights. The state briefly became a military district under federal administration, and many Black men were elected to positions of power. But by the 1870s, white supremacist violence and federal timidity had resulted in a white supremacist state government and the withdrawal of federal support; many Black residents fled the county at the same time, leaving a devastating labor crisis in their wake. It would take years for Mississippi County planters to recover, and they were able to do so only by enticing tens of thousands of former slaves to move from Georgia, Alabama, Mississippi, and the Carolinas to places in the Old Southwest, including Arkansas, with propaganda, positive press, and promises of steady work and maybe even land ownership in the fertile Delta. Between 1880 and 1900, the Black population in Mississippi County more than tripled. As Whayne noted, for the first time in the county's history, Black people were a majority. Edward Bradley, who had been born a slave in Tennessee, was typical: he moved to the county in the late nineteenth century, arriving with a team and two cows after an exhausting four-day journey.[5]

These new workers found, to their horror, an unsanitary, undeveloped morass; Mississippi County was still a land of swamps. "My folks was sick all the time," recalled Bradley. "Wasn't any canals in that country, and my wife had malaria every year." He quickly moved a hundred miles away. Even for the rich whites of the planter class, malaria was a constant threat, closely trailing pneumonia and tuberculosis as a cause of death; typhoid, dysentery, and cholera likewise stalked those in the Delta as surely as did the mosquitos. Traveling doctors had to stop at virtually every house. Hundreds died, febrile and sweating.

Still, it wasn't the omnipresence of disease that motivated the planters to eventually drain the swamps. It was greed. The county was home to some of the most fecund land in the country, but 90 percent of it was subject to regular inundation. Constant flooding, weak levees (a mere twelve feet high), and a volatile river that changed its course pretty much every year made it difficult to build up massive plantations. Late in the nineteenth century, federal engineers, state levee district officials, and rich businessmen teamed up to begin draining the swamps and building better levees in earnest, funding these efforts by taxing small landholders out of existence. The working men who constructed the new levees likewise suffered tremendously in the name of progress. In times of emergency, overseers forced them to labor all night, water crashing and wind whipping around them; men who lost their footing could tumble thirty or forty feet through the darkness, down an embankment: "The horror of the situation cannot be realized even by the imagination," recorded one local journalist.

As the land in Mississippi County became drier and more arable, the price per acre skyrocketed. More small farmers lost their holdings and began working as tenants on the fields that their fathers had owned. The rich landowners joined with the lumber companies to win still more land in court. These landed gentry created private clubs to hunt for game in remaining swamplands, which had once been owned by small holders; now it was protected from these same homesteaders by hired Pinkerton guards. In Osceola, the county seat, the rich men built fine brick homes and one of the best opera houses in the South. By the end of the next century, over 90 percent of the wetlands along the Mississippi River would be gone. In their wake would remain a society shaped by volatility, labor conflict, and racial violence.[6]

Tensions rose as more swamps were emptied. Many powerful landowners, led by an up-and-coming planter, Robert E. Lee Wilson, pushed for still more drainage in Mississippi County. In fact, they sought "the largest drainage district ever organized in the United States up to that date." Every day it seemed more likely that violence would erupt. And then, on July 8, 1908, opposing bands of armed, landless men met at the Mississippi County Courthouse while the judge considered Wilson's latest drainage scheme. Someone hung a noose at the courthouse door. Wilson stationed gun-toting guards around the windows and doors. Yet the cries and threats from within the packed courthouse grew so intense that the elderly judge and attorneys retreated to chambers for three hours. Upon their return, angry members of the crowd, brandishing pistols and whiskey bottles, began shouting speeches—accusing Wilson of "stealing the homes of the poor people"—and one man called for the crowd to "hang the damned scoundrels." When the crowd advanced, the judge fled through the backdoor and into a carriage. One angry man seized the noose from the door, the mob pursued the carriage, and later that evening a band of night riders visited the judge's home to threaten violence. "That was the last term of the County Court that judge ever held," solemnly recalled one observer.[7]

When the elderly judge's successor conveniently died a few months later, planter Wilson and sixty-six "leading citizens" convinced the governor to appoint Silas Lee "S. L." Gladish, Osceola's young mayor, as his replacement until a special election could be held. That night, Gladish and several of Wilson's cronies enjoyed a steak dinner. Fearing that the special election would be close, Wilson engaged in a bit of election fraud, "voting" on behalf of his convict laborers. According to later testimony from one convicted man, the night before the election the overseer of the local jail brandished a "big whip" before the convicts and "stated that any of the convicts who failed to vote for S. L. Gladish for County and Probate Judge would at least be given ten lashes well laid on." Gladish won the election and quickly approved Wilson's drainage scheme.

As a result, the number of acres suitable for farming doubled during the first two decades of the twentieth century. Mississippi County became the single largest site of cotton production on earth. Yet even as the number of farm owner-operators doubled, the number of tenants and sharecroppers quadrupled. Numerous small homesteaders, who had grown used to the ebbs and flows of the river, lost their land. And rich planters consolidated acres into vast, feudal empires. By the 1920s, Mississippi County's own Robert E. Lee Wilson—"Boss Lee" to his friends—had become the lord of a plantation eight miles wide and twenty-seven miles long, commanding great armies of landless men, women, and children. His cronies assumed positions as judges and sheriffs and other local officials, granting him massive control over county affairs. He reportedly owned the largest plantation in the world.[8]

Somewhat unusually, Mississippi County was home to two county seats: Osceola, the largest town in the county's south, and Blytheville, the biggest city in its north. American settlers had moved into Osceola first, displacing Indigenous inhabitants in the late eighteenth and early nineteenth centuries and then, ironically, naming the town after a famous Seminole chief. It grew quickly from a small collection of log huts nestled on the banks of the Mississippi River to a village of nearly a thousand by 1900; the first railroad reached the county in 1901, the first telephone two years later, and in 1902 electricity arrived in Osceola with twenty-eight streetlamps illuminating the business district. Blytheville developed later. In about 1880, a reverend named Blythe led a group of about two hundred people to settle a square half mile of land; in 1891, shortly after they secured a post office, the town was legally incorporated; by 1902, it had just two brick buildings, no electricity or telephones, and practically no industry to speak of. Yet Blytheville grew quickly, and between 1900 and 1910, mills began opening and the town's population increased more than tenfold, from barely three hundred to well over three thousand, handily displacing Osceola as the county's biggest city. For years, it was treacherous to travel from one end of the county to the other, from Blytheville to Osceola, because of the deep, sucking mud. But circumstances began to improve when, in 1916, Blytheville constructed a sewer system, and in 1919 the town fathers paved a few intersecting roads. By the 1930s, both towns featured bustling Main Streets with shops, groceries, and packed sidewalks.[9]

Yet farming still dominated even the lives of city slickers. Cotton remained the reason for both cities' existence and thus was "the chief topic of conversation for the entire year," recorded one observer. "Many of the town's thoroughfares run into cottonfields," he wrote of Blytheville in the 1930s. "Main Street has a cotton gin at the east end and a cotton garment factory at the west end." Farmers were often in town, selling produce, buying dry goods, and meeting friends. "Sacks of feed and coops of squawking chickens are piled high outside the stores at the eastern end of Main Street. Perhaps a huge catfish, fresh-hooked from a Mississippi slough, dangles before a lunchroom."[10]

It would be easy to dismiss this heavily agrarian, rigidly white supremacist community as antiquated, stunted, backward. Yet this would be a mistake; it had, in many ways, a distinctly modern and brutally efficient economic structure—that is to say, thoroughly privatized and startlingly unequal. "Contrary to the popular image of plantation agriculture as an Old South relic," wrote the historian Story Matkin-Rawn, "the plantation system reborn from the ashes of the Civil War was far larger, lasted longer, and exported a great deal more cotton than its predecessor."[11]

In the years following the Civil War, plantation owners could no longer rely on slaves to pick cotton, leading to two related but distinct labor arrangements. Sharecroppers would work a certain allotment of a richer man's land, live in the rich man's shack, use the rich man's plow and seeds, and be paid with a third of the crop; share tenants, in contrast, worked another man's land but they had their own mules and tools and thus "owned" the crop—but owed half of it to the landowner. Share tenants had greater legal rights and tended to be white; sharecroppers had virtually no legal rights and were more often Black. But both white and Black, tenant and sharecropper, were thoroughly outmatched by the wealthy planters. Pretty much all the workers depended on advances from planter-owned stores or commissaries, with interest rates of 25 to 50 percent. They were routinely underpaid. And often they were paid not in cash but in scrip, coupons, unique metal currency, or credit, which was only good at the plantation store, and which kept workers trapped in a cycle of debt. Men, women, and children labored, even in brutal weather, under the watchful eye of overseers armed with guns and whips. Men, women, and children starved.[12]

At the same time, plantation owners could lease county convicts to work the fields for even less remuneration; convict leasing quietly continued years after Arkansas ostensibly banned the practice. And in a system that many denounced as akin to slavery, local officials routinely arrested poor people, especially poor Black people, for vague offenses like loitering or vagrancy; these unlucky souls were then charged fines they couldn't possibly pay and were forced to work off their debt on cotton plantations. To facilitate such a system, in the 1870s the powers that be passed laws increasing the economic clout of landlords and making the theft of goods worth as little as two dollars an imprisonable offense; within three years, nearly two-thirds of prisoners were confined for stealing "petty sums." By the 1930s, NAACP officials had begun hearing reports of a system in Arkansas "even worse than the usual case of leasing prisoners to private land owners," recorded a young Thurgood Marshall. "It seems that, in this case, the land owner actually 'purchases' the prisoners and works them involuntarily and under the constant threat of brutal punishment and death." Some of these men were beaten up to three times a day if they failed to pick an obscene three hundred pounds of cotton. A number of Black people held in this form of peonage escaped from Mississippi County plantations and told their stories to federal officials, but for decades little changed. "The Arkansas Delta became known as a place where people disappeared," wrote the historian Nan Woodruff.[13]

In Mississippi County, there were no jails to hold misdemeanants who owed fines. Instead, the city would "sell" them to planters or mill owners, who would house the convicts in dormitories constructed on their farms or out in the woods; as one resident later recalled, these private captors "would manacle the convicts to their beds; would take them out to work in the daytime; feed them and then back to the barracks at night."[14]

By 1930, nearly two-thirds of Arkansas farms were cultivated by tenants and sharecroppers. In eastern Arkansas in particular, just one in seven farm families actually owned the land on which they labored. In Mississippi County, the number of tenants and sharecroppers had increased nearly eightfold from 1900 to 1930, while the number of acres under cultivation nearly tripled.[15] Things got worse as the years passed and the Depression deepened. One survey from 1934 found that 99 percent of Black sharecroppers and tenants in Arkansas were in debt to their landlords. Only one in ten could see a doctor when they were ill; one in four had to carry their water at least a mile. By this time, tenants occupied somewhere between 80 to 90 percent of all farms in the Delta—"among the highest rates in the nation," noted the historian Sammy L. Morgan.[16]

For sharecroppers and tenant farmers, life was unrelenting toil. Their days began as they dragged themselves out of bed, ate a breakfast consisting of some combination of "the three M's—meal, molasses and meat" (if they ate at all), and then trudged off to the fields following the clang of a bell. There, they worked all day, men crawling on their knees amid the rows of cotton plants, women bending at the waist. "Everyone's hands swelled at the start of the season," recorded one historian, and "when they shrank again, the skin and fingers cracked, and stayed cracked until the harvest was over." For hours under the hot sun, they trudged through the rows of cotton plants, dragging denim sacks that might stretch as long as nine feet and weigh as much as one hundred pounds. At the end of the day, the workers returned to tiny, unsanitary hovels. When it rained, their shacks flooded, and with little to no furniture on which to climb, the fetid water simply pooled around them. They might own just a single piece of clothing and little else. As one observer wrote, "Along the highways and byways of Dixie they struggle—lonely figures without money, without homes and without hope. Mother, father, little ones, many of them bare-foot, they are living symbols of a civilization that failed them, a bargain that never worked. . . . They are living in a feudal system."[17]

In light of such conditions, small landholders and smaller farmers had tried to fight back for generations. Early in the twentieth century, for instance, a homesteaders' union formed in neighboring Poinsett County. But this union excluded Black farmers, and without true smallholder solidarity it was quickly crushed by the big planters. Every time Black and white sharecroppers came close to uniting in a genuine populist movement, state and local officials leaned on race-baiting and outright fraud to defeat the effort. And when Black farmers tried to form their own cooperatives to counter the growing power of the rich, white planters, they were violently repulsed. In 1889, for instance, white vigilantes in western Mississippi responded to rumors of an armed, Black uprising by killing dozens—perhaps more than a hundred—Black farmers; the planters then banned the distribution of the Black cooperative's newspaper and threatened any subsequent organizing efforts with grave violence. Two years later, in 1891, Black cotton workers in eastern Arkansas launched an ambitious strike—only to be crushed five days later when a posse of whites murdered a dozen strikers and their leader.

In the years that followed, still more Black farmers lost their land and began working as sharecroppers on newly consolidated, corporatized plantations. After cotton prices fell sharply in 1921, many Arkansas planters began pushing to eliminate rental contracts and turn all of their workers into sharecroppers. When Black tenant farmers balked, white landlords and plantation agents responded with terroristic violence. In the spring of 1923, police pulled a Black labor organizer from his car and beat him savagely; the *Osceola Times* used this as an opportunity "to once again remind the county's black community that nothing but trouble awaited them elsewhere, particularly north of Mississippi County," as Jeannie Whayne summarized. Yet in spite of the repression and loss, resistance remained a constant, as Black Arkansans continued to join nascent labor unions and strikes and populist political parties.[18]

Then came a disaster of biblical proportions. In 1927, the Mississippi River flooded, displacing more than 600,000 people across the South and inundating one-seventh of Arkansas. It was the most destructive river flood in American history, and it was terrifying. According to one Delta planter, "The 1927 flood was a torrent ten feet deep [and] the size of Rhode Island; it was thirty-six hours coming and four months going; it was deep enough to drown a man, swift enough to upset a boat, and lasting enough to cancel a crop year." For more than a day, the terror was pure and omnipresent; everyone in the Delta tried to flee by every means available: by rail, by road, even by boat. When the waters came, foaming and yellow and high, the land became terribly, deadly quiet.[19] Although, remarkably, Mississippi County's levees managed to hold the Mississippi River, they could not contain the Little River, and the resulting inundation flooded 200,000 acres (including 90,000 acres of cropland). From an economic perspective, the great flood was disastrous: in one year, the number of acres of cotton in the county fell from nearly 50,000 to fewer than 20,000. From a humanitarian perspective, it was even worse. More than 10,000 Mississippi Countians were forced to flee their homes for the cities on higher ground. In

Osceola, the refugees were sheltered in the county courthouse until they grew too numerous; they were then relocated to a handle factory and Red Cross tents.

For Black refugees, conditions were predictably much worse. Since no Black people were allowed in Red Cross camps in Mississippi County, they had to squeeze in with friends or relatives or try to survive in their leaking homes. Yet this exclusion was a silver lining: Red Cross officials elsewhere kept "black refugees virtually imprisoned in camps until signed out by the planters for whom they worked," recounted Whayne. "Planters were typically fearful of losing their laborers, and because many of their sharecroppers and tenants were in debt to them, they wanted to be sure to be in a position to collect on those debts when the time came." Just as predictably, the flood was an extinction event for many small farmers. Robert E. Lee Wilson, meanwhile, came through the flood "relatively unscathed."[20]

The Great Flood clarified what everyone already knew: Arkansas was an oligarchy. Indeed, in the aftermath of the flood the rich landholders even got to decide when to dispense Red Cross food rations, making sure not to give the workers too much to eat, lest they get any big ideas. "Nowhere was elite rule stronger than in Arkansas," wrote the historian Sammy L. Morgan. Through the influence of money, the use of violence, and the comfort with casual vote rigging, a handful of immensely wealthy Delta planter families thoroughly dominated state politics. They were the governors, the senators, the most powerful bureaucrats. These fabulously rich cotton planters ruled the region, and the state, like feudal lords, with an iron grip and a fierce adherence to white supremacy and small government. "There were only two classes," recalled the Mississippi County blues singer Billy Lee Riley. "The ones that had everything and those that didn't have anything."[21]

To say that there were separate legal systems for rich and poor would be a gross understatement. "The local Magistrates and Sheriffs all come from the planter class with the result [being that] peonage is used to recruit laborers," recorded W. E. B. Du Bois in an unpublished essay titled "The Black Belt of Arkansas."[22] Indeed, many of the largest plantations had their own penal systems. "It was the owner's own court," recalled one sharecropper. "They had a judge, a legal justice of the peace on the plantation. The plantation was actually like a state. It had its own government, and the plantation owner actually appointed the justice of the peace." If a worker were convicted in such a court, he might be sent to the planter's "own penal farm."[23] One woman who grew up in 1930s Arkansas recalled that the laws applied only to those without "pull": "To pay a traffic ticket meant you were friendless or a hick."[24]

2 • The Law of Rape, 1820–1920s

The very first reported case heard in the Territory of Arkansas was a rape case. The year was 1820, and a man named Thomas Dickinson was accused of raping his stepdaughter. Dickinson apparently argued that since the stepdaughter had become pregnant, a rape by definition could not have occurred. The jury rejected that argument and found him guilty in just twenty minutes; the judge sentenced him to be "castrated according to the law." A passing traveler was appalled, calling the punishment "barbarous," and Arkansas's territorial governor may have agreed, for he pardoned Dickinson shortly thereafter.[1]

The governor need not have worried too much—the barbarous punishment of castration was on its way out. Three years later, in 1823, Arkansas's territorial government passed a law reading simply, "If any person shall have carnal knowledge of any female, forcable [sic] and against her consent, he shall be deemed guilty of rape, and on conviction thereof, shall suffer death."[2] But this was too vague. What about assault with intent to rape? What about the sexual assault of a child? Over the next two decades, the legislature of Arkansas—newly a state—revised the rape law repeatedly, leaving the definition and punishment of rape largely unchanged but establishing separate punishments for "carnally knowing, or abusing unlawfully, any female child, under the age of puberty" and for "administer[ing] to any female any potion, substance or liquid" with the intent to incapacitate and then commit rape. The punishment for the former was five to twenty-one years' imprisonment; the punishment for the latter was death. Finally, the legislature created the crime of assault with intent to commit rape (when no "potion" was involved).

Yet when it came to this last offense, the legislature followed a trend that was becoming increasingly common across the South: it created separate punishments for white and Black men. According to the new law, when a Black man—enslaved or free—committed assault with intent to rape a white woman, the statute carried a death sentence, but a white man committing the same crime received only imprisonment of "not less than one year."[3] Such a delineation along the lines of race was unremarkable in the antebellum South. Indeed, writing in 1850 in response to the only constitutional challenge ever filed against this racial disparity, the Arkansas Supreme Court upheld the statute and construed it as the best that Black people would get: "The provision was doubtless inserted in the constitution from a feeling of humanity towards the unfortunate African race, and in order to secure them against that barbarous treatment and excessive cruelty which was practiced upon them in the earlier period of our colonial history," for example, being tortured prior to execution.[4]

The administration of the state's rape law continued to be "barbarous" by modern standards, with Black men routinely executed on the thinnest of evidence, white men routinely set free in spite of evidence, and white women routinely humiliated and disbelieved. Yet it would be a mistake to dismiss this system as entirely lawless. Indeed, as several historians have noted, in the years before the Civil War and Reconstruction, the racist idea that Black men were obsessed with raping white women was not nearly as pervasive as it would later become, and courts sometimes acquitted slaves accused of rape.[5] In a bizarre contrast to the legal system that developed after emancipation, enslaved men accused of raping white women sometimes received surprisingly fair trials.[6] In fact, as the historian Diane Miller Sommerville has shown, white women who accused Black men of rape were not always believed at this time; poorer women, women "without male protectors," and women whose sexual behavior was deemed promiscuous were sometimes dismissed as liars. In some cases, white witnesses might break ranks and testify on behalf of the accused Black man, especially if the woman's "past actions smacked of libidinous indiscretion." Even young white girls could face such scrutiny. This was all the more true in cases where white women were accusing free Black men of rape, especially those men with reputations for industriousness and deference. Further, slaveholders might intervene to save their valuable "property." Of course, none of this necessarily stopped lynch mobs from pursuing their own brand of justice, but it does complicate the picture of antebellum rape trials.[7]

Note that the statute books said nothing about the punishment for a white or a Black man who raped or attempted to rape a Black woman. That is because, before the Civil War, it was generally not considered a crime anywhere in the South; certainly, courts of law did not concern themselves with such cases.[8] Indeed, in 1859 the Mississippi Supreme Court famously reversed the rape conviction of an enslaved man accused of assaulting an enslaved child, accepting the defense's argument that "our laws recognize no marital rights as between slaves; their sexual intercourse is left to be regulated by their owners. The regulations of law, as to the white race, on the subject of sexual intercourse, do not and cannot, for obvious reasons, apply to slaves; their intercourse is promiscuous."[9] What this meant was that Black women were, in the words of legal scholar Dorothy Roberts, "innately unrapeable."[10]

Undoubtedly, there were secret sexual relationships between white women and enslaved Black men, but these are virtually impossible to find in the archive. When an enslaved man named Pleasant was accused of attempting to rape his white mistress in Arkansas in 1854, Pleasant's lawyer argued that the woman had a reputation for promiscuity and that she had willingly had sex with Pleasant. Unsurprisingly, he was found guilty and sentenced to die. On appeal, the chief justice conceded that while it was "well settled" that a woman's "character ... for unchastity" was fair game for impeachment, it simply could not be believed that a white woman would willingly yield herself "to the embraces of a negro ... unless she had sunk to the lowest degree of prostitution."[11]

From its time as a territory through the early years of statehood, Arkansas remained a frontier, with a scattered populace, few large towns, and much internecine violence. Most disputes were settled with a duel or a fight or a mob or an escape or a handshake or an exchange of property—in other words, without the partisans ever seeing the inside of a courtroom.[12] Over time, however, legal institutions and traditions took hold. Even rural places began to embrace legal procedures, making do with few lawyers and fewer resources. In the earliest days of Mississippi County, court was held at the house of a man named Peter Reeves. "It was a common thing to adjourn court to go out and kill a passing bear," recorded a county historian.[13] As more lawyers and better-trained lawyers arrived and the county constructed not one but two beautiful courthouses, the threat of vigilante violence receded to the background. Yet it never disappeared entirely. And, in the years after the Civil War, especially in cases alleging interracial rape, it returned with a vengeance.

The Civil War was more than just a political and economic cataclysm; it was a social cataclysm as well. In its aftermath, the period known as Reconstruction, white and Black people—in Arkansas, in the South, and in the nation as a whole (now that it *was* a unified whole)—had to figure out how to interact with each other in a new legal landscape of formal equality. Although historians have documented a greater level of discomfort when it came to "racial mixing on an intimate level" in the war's immediate aftermath, it took time for this to solidify and harden. Interestingly, in the years just after the war, white juries on occasion sided with Black men accused of rape by poor or less-than-respectable white women. It was a number of years before white southerners began to consistently draw a "connection between black rapes of white women and black equality with whites."[14] Southern white writers started penning popular tracts about how immoral Black men were, how animalistic their behavior was, how insatiable their sexual appetites were—and over time, this morphed into an obsession with the idea that Black men were constitutionally fixated on raping white women. If these Black men got their wish, these white writers believed, next they would demand political or economic equality, too.[15]

White supremacist terrorism likewise emerged in stages. One evening just months after Appomattox, a handful of Confederate veterans gathered in a law office in Pulaski, Tennessee, and founded the Ku Klux Klan (KKK), one of many, similar terrorist organizations springing up at this time. The Klan grew quickly across the South, like a rash or a plague, with masked members murdering Black people and pillaging Black wealth in the name of protecting white men from disfranchisement and white women from rape. The Klan "spread like wildfire" in Arkansas, wrote one historian, and a "general nature of terrorism . . . gripped the state." In 1866, a group of white terrorists near Pine Bluff set fire to a Black settlement and hanged twenty-four Black men, women, and children. In Mississippi County, Klan members "were virtually indistinguishable from roving outlaw bands." At the same time, with violence plaguing the countryside, Black and white delegates gathered in Little Rock to debate whether the new state constitution should ban interracial marriage; the press used images of Black men raping white women to rally support for the ban. One white delegate from the north, James Hinds, eventually pushed through a compromise resolution condemning but not outlawing interracial marriage; two years later, Klan terrorists assassinated Hinds. Yet for all the talk of the Klan defending white women from rape by Black men, Klan members and other white vigilantes routinely raped Black women in the years after the Civil War. This was explicitly about maintaining racial hierarchy; Klan rapists often admitted they were retaliating against the families of those who had voted the radical ticket or served in the Union army.[16]

By the early 1870s, federal troops and grassroots Black resistance had largely driven the KKK out of existence, but new forms of white supremacist violence continued to flare. Former Confederates began seeking to get back into state government—either by winning elections or, if necessary, staging outright coups. Soon, the states of Louisiana and Mississippi descended into full-scale warfare, with white supremacist guerrillas murdering Black leaders and "redeemer" militiamen massacring uniformed troops. Reconstruction officials begged the federal government to intervene, but by the middle of the decade the White House and Justice Department had given up on the South and generally allowed the Confederates to openly and bloodily retake power.[17] Arkansas was certainly not immune from the violence. In 1872, two different men—one a supporter of Reconstruction, the other a supporter of Confederate redemption—claimed to have been elected governor of Arkansas. Legal battles quickly turned into actual battles, and each ostensible governor mustered his own militia. Both sides hastily constructed fortifications throughout the state capital and began raiding gun shops and the state arsenal for arms. "Reinforcements poured into Little Rock from all directions, coming by horseback, wagon, train and boat," wrote one chronicler. Hot exchanges of words soon became actual exchanges of bullets, killing dozens, perhaps hundreds. The bloodshed ceased only in 1874 when President Ulysses S. Grant, exhausted by the fighting, intervened and threw his support to the Confederate redeemers, who sought to overturn many of the meaningful political gains toward Black-white equality in the war's aftermath. The neo-Confederate Democrats took power, immediately pushed through a new constitution, won a new election marred by paramilitary violence directed at Black voters, and entrenched their power for decades to come. Reconstruction ended, not with a bang but with a series of them.[18]

Even as white supremacists fought to retake the South, federal oversight left state legislators little choice but to eliminate the racial distinctions in their rape statutes and make them race-neutral, at least on paper. Now forced to put Black and white men on an equal legal playing field, southern authorities suddenly turned away from the death penalty and began creating more lenient penalties for men convicted of rape.[19] Arkansas bucked the trend toward leniency. In laws passed during Reconstruction, it kept the death penalty for the crime of rape or attempting to rape with the assistance of an incapacitating "potion," and it clarified that the punishment for assault with intent to commit rape was three to twenty-one years in prison.[20] Yet Arkansas fit neatly within the rest of the postbellum South in finding ways to treat Black men convicted of raping white women just as harshly as it had treated them during slavery—often more harshly. Legislators gradually realized that by granting local courts greater discretion in sentencing, they would empower judges to impose more severe sentences on Black men and lighter sentences on white men—if the white men were convicted at all.[21]

"In the past, interracial rape charges had not meant an automatic death sentence for Black men, for the class and reputation of the accuser helped determine whether the relationship had been consensual or coercive," the renowned historian of rape, Estelle B. Freedman, has written. "By the 1880s, however, southerners had begun to deny the possibility of consensual interracial unions. Soon they portrayed all African American men as a constant, and monstrous, threat to all white women." Years later, the Black scholar W. E. B. Du Bois would look back at the end of Reconstruction and lament, "The charge of rape against colored Americans was invented by the white South after Reconstruction to excuse mob violence." What the pioneering Black journalist Ida B. Wells would call the "old thread-bare lie that Negro men rape white women" had become, in Du Bois's words, "the recognized method of re-enslaving blacks." And to do this, white people across the South—poor and rich, male and female—relied on an old tactic, one they embraced in the late nineteenth century with great relish: lynching.[22]

A lynching is more than merely an extrajudicial killing, a murderous form of vigilante violence. It is a *public* execution, intended to inspire fear in a broader community; it is a threat, wielded by the powerful, to tell the marginalized what might happen to them, at any moment, if they challenge the forces of capital or whiteness or patriarchy.[23] Lynching had long been part of American life, from Colonel Charles Lynch murdering "Tory miscreants" in the eighteenth century; to vigilantes in the South and the West murdering Mexicans, Asians, and Native Americans accused of theft; to bosses' posses murdering striking workers; to mobs of family or neighbors murdering alleged rapists of all races. The method of killing might include whipping, tarring and feathering, hanging, mutilation, a barrage of bullets, or burning at the stake. In antebellum Arkansas, white men routinely lynched slaves accused of crimes in all manner of grisly ways, and the *Arkansas Gazette* often commended them for doing so—the people need not "trouble our court or juries with" escaped prisoners, the paper wrote in the 1830s; instead, "they ought to be hunted down as wild beasts and their carcasses left as food for the buzzards." But only in the years just after Reconstruction did lynching morph into "a tool of racial terror, driven in part by rape accusations." Only in the 1880s did lynching become primarily justified by the specter of the Black male rapist.[24]

Arkansas's "redeemed" white supremacist government moved quickly to politically neutralize the Black populace, using every tool and trick at its disposal. By the turn of the twentieth century, the state's white planter elite had effectively disenfranchised the entire Black population through a combination of the poll tax and the all-white Democratic primary. The number of Black men serving in the state legislature dropped from twelve, to four, to zero. Heeding the call of rural whites who were appalled to visit Little Rock and see Black residents stepping out of their "place," the legislature passed laws demanding racial segregation in trains, coach cars, toilets, hotels, restaurants, and, of course, schools. Such legal changes went hand in hand with all manner of extralegal violence, from mass murders to forced population resettlement. White farmers who had been neighbors with Black farmers for years began posting notices in the dark of night, demanding that all Black people leave town immediately; night riders enforced such orders with swift brutality, and Black stragglers were often killed. Rumors flew of an impending "race war." The map of Arkansas became dotted with sundown towns—places where Black people were not safe after dark. One scholar of Arkansas has noted that prior to this period, whites usually referred to Black people as "Negroes, colored, or darkies," but by the late 1880s, their language had become "more shrill, hostile, and snide," and "terms such as [n-word] and *coon* began to appear with frequency." And, of course, there were the lynchings. Before 1886, the number of white people lynched had always been greater than the number of Black people. This would never be true again.[25]

In the spring of 1882, in a sequence of events that illustrate the emerging new normal, a crowd of masked men broke into the jail in Butlerville, Arkansas, subdued the guards, and dragged out and hanged three Black men who had been accused of raping a white teenager. Subsequent reports suggested that the girl may have invented the story to explain why she had arrived home three hours late, but, in any event, the truth of the accusation wasn't the point; lynching had become about keeping the Black population under control. Southern law enforcement officials investigating rape allegations began focusing disproportionately—sometimes exclusively—on Black suspects. In the 1890s, amidst a cratering economy and the profusion of ever more explosive racist rhetoric, the number of lynchings reached record highs in Arkansas and the broader South.[26]

Plenty of people deemed respectable at the time openly supported, or at least rationalized, lynching. One prominent southern lawyer told the American Bar Association that the law was "too calm in its procedure" to sufficiently deter Black rapists; a student at Yale Law School wrote that the "daily terror" of Black men raping white women in the South was "the cause of most of those lynching cases.... It is to be kept down only by the severest methods. Is it too much to say that if the courts are not ready to apply these, the people will?"[27] Arkansas's own Jeff Davis—named for the Confederate president and a self-proclaimed champion of "hillbillies" and "rednecks" who became state attorney general, governor, and U.S. senator in quick succession—argued that lynching was the only sensible solution for white men in the South: "To the father, the husband, the brother, suddenly beholding the fresh marks of the brutal clutch, seeing the tender trembling flesh and listening with swelling bosom and shortening breath to the agonizing story of the frenzied victim, it is vain to plead for abstract justice or talk philosophically of the orderly vindication of law." Or, as the wife of a former congressman put it more succinctly, "I say lynch a thousand a week if necessary."[28]

Scholars have debated, for over a century, the extent to which allegations of rape *actually* motivated lynchings. The courageous journalist Ida B. Wells compiled statistics suggesting that only about a third of lynchings were even ostensibly in response to accusations of rape, and subsequent observers, including modern academics, have looked at the numbers in various states and regions and provided figures that range from 20 percent to 60 percent.[29] In an effort to protect the reputation of Black men and demonstrate the true lawlessness of southern whites, the newly founded NAACP devoted much of its energies in the early twentieth century to compiling statistics that might "explod[e] the rape myth." In one of his last essays—"Why Is the Negro Lynched?"—Frederick Douglass did likewise. Nonetheless, it is indisputable that the *symbol* of the Black male rapist motivated the sheer number of lynchings in the abstract, regardless of what motivated any particular mob in isolation. Lynching, wrote one southern columnist, was "the remedy for rape."[30]

And still, even as this epidemic of lawless violence supplanted the justice system in the turn-of-the-century South, even as the constant racialized murders led one Black Arkansan to memorably describe the Delta as the "American Congo," some semblance of legal process remained. This meant juries continued to sometimes scrutinize the behavior and morality of their female neighbors—even white female neighbors. As Diane Miller Sommerville has shown, "Not all accusations of black rape against white females resulted in lynchings." Some number went to court, and a number of these resulted in acquittals—especially when the white woman's "innocence" or "purity" could be impeached.[31]

Rape charges were not raised in a vacuum; they were raised by members of communities, well known to others in the same community. Some people were well-regarded by their neighbors, others were not. Some people were seen as morally upstanding, others were not. This mattered, and it shaped who was lynched, who was tried, and who was freed.

In part because of the secrecy and stigma surrounding sexual violence, and in part because of the prevalence of lynching, few rape cases reached the inside of a courtroom. But by the early twentieth century, the majority of sex crime prosecutions—in Arkansas and in the country at large—were for cases of statutory rape. In other words, most of the rape cases that went to trial in this era were those that involved children.

This reality was the product of a remarkably swift and successful activist campaign to change the laws in every state in the nation. Under the common law—the collected body of judicial decisions that the United States inherited from England—the "age of consent" had been ten. That is to say, nineteenth-century authorities believed that a ten-year-old was fully capable of consenting to sex. Most states had adopted statutes codifying ten as the age of consent, though a handful had chosen eight or twelve; Arkansas was unique because it did not specify a particular age but rather criminalized sex with a female child "under the age of puberty." Even when claims of abuse went to trial, nineteenth-century judges were "usually disinclined" to believe the claims of children against the protestations of adult men—especially when those men were the children's father—and medical authorities agreed, believing that children were prone to dishonesty and that no healthy man would wish to have sex with a child.

In the 1870s and 1880s, stories began appearing in the press about Black or immigrant men raping small, white children. Unsurprisingly, these stories routinely resulted in lynchings. In this climate, the elite female reformers of the Women's Christian Temperance Union and the Society for the Prevention of Cruelty to Children became determined to change age-of-consent laws. These women—many of them rich, bored, religious, college educated, and itching to find ways to participate in a political process that almost always excluded them—were motivated by new thinking about the nature of children. Whereas previously twelve was deemed a suitable age for a girl to be married, the extension of childhood through the creation of compulsory public schooling and the elimination of child labor made marrying a child off so young appear unsettling and déclassé. Further, with the news media so rife with stories of dark-skinned men forcing virginal white girls into lives of prostitution and promiscuity, the reformers wanted new tools with which to prosecute these men.[32]

Beginning in the 1880s, these elite female activists embarked on a campaign to raise the age of consent, a campaign that was breathtaking in its ambition and astounding in its quick success. Activists gathered tens of thousands of signatures and presented them to state legislatures and to Congress; they lobbied legislators, armed with charts and graphs and terrifying images; they wrote novels and articles and exposés about drugged and abused young girls, greedy and perverted old men, and, sometimes, the authorities who refused to intervene. Real-life legislators were quickly cowed. By 1900, thirty-two states had raised their ages of consent to at least fourteen; by 1920, every state but Georgia had raised its age to at least sixteen, often to eighteen.[33] Arkansas was no different. One state senator called on his colleagues to "throw every safeguard" around girls who were preyed upon by men on the lookout "for victims to indulge their brutal lusts." In 1893, the state's legislature revised its law in accordance with the national trend, writing that carnal knowledge or abuse of "any female person under the age of sixteen years" was to be punished with five to twenty-one years' imprisonment.[34]

In the wake of these statutory changes, rape trials became ever more focused on vindicating the rights of children. As Estelle B. Freedman has noted, in New York City prosecutions for sexual assault involving girls under the age of eighteen jumped from around 40 percent of all sexual abuse prosecutions at the beginning of the nineteenth century to nearly 90 percent at century's end; in one county in Iowa a full 85 percent of sexual assault charges brought between 1880 and 1910 involved girls younger than fifteen.[35] In Arkansas in the years after the law changed, statutory rape cases became an increasingly large share of the total cases of sexual assault, and by the mid-1920s there were 78 rape prosecutions in Arkansas over a two-year period, compared with 133 "carnal abuse" prosecutions.[36]

3 • Vigilantism and Resistance, 1899–1930s

As Arkansas entered the twentieth century, the epidemic of lynchings continued unabated. In the spring of 1899, a Black tenant farmer in Little River County allegedly murdered a white planter, fled to the bottomlands, and then surrendered himself to the sheriff; an angry mob overtook the farmer on his way to jail and hanged and shot him until he was dead. This was "only the first in what became a classic southern 'lynching bee,' " wrote the historian Todd E. Lewis. The white mob in Little River County quickly embarked on a killing spree, decimating the local Black community, taking at least seven—and possibly as many as twenty-three—lives. Three years later, not too far from Mississippi County, a white mob broke through the walls of the local jail with sledgehammers and seized a well-regarded Black man accused of raping and murdering a white woman. Members of the mob began impatiently chanting "burn him! burn him!" and its leaders quickly complied.[1]

It is true that lynching declined in Arkansas in the first decade of the twentieth century, but then came 1910, which was one of the bloodiest years in the state's history of white supremacist violence. Mobs of white Arkansans murdered eight Black men and one Black woman that year, with clubs and guns and rope, for alleged crimes ranging from adultery to interracial rape. For most of the next decade, Arkansas fell back into a "period of relatively few lynchings"—but still, extralegal murders continued with some frequency, and they were always, always a threat. Lynching served "not only to punish individuals accused of violating the color line," Lewis has written, "but also to terrorize the African-American community at large." A majority of Arkansas's twentieth-century lynchings occurred in the Delta. Many, though certainly not a majority, involved Black men accused of attacking or raping white women.

These lynchings were ritualistic, meant to humiliate the victims and amuse the bloodthirsty crowd. Mobs often defiled the corpses of Black victims; they often paraded dead or soon-to-be-dead men through the streets. "Apparently," recounted one historian, "in Arkansas, *Judge Lynch* remained the highest court in the land."[2]

Law enforcement officials, lawyers, and prominent professionals often had few qualms with openly taking part in the violence. "Arkansas' lynchings were not the work of secretive nightriders, though nightriding remained a problem in Arkansas," continued Lewis. Rather, lynchings were the public work of dozens or hundreds or thousands of local residents, few afraid to show their faces openly or of suffering any consequences. Indeed, in one 1907 rape case from Louisiana, the *defense* counsel told the jury: "Gentlemen of the jury, this man, a [n-word], is charged with breaking into the house of a white man in the nighttime and assaulting his wife, with the intent to rape her. Now, don't you know, if this [n-word] had committed such a crime, he never would have been brought here and tried; that he would have been lynched, and if I were there I would help pull on the rope."[3]

By the early years of the twentieth century, lynchings had become social affairs, with vendors hocking souvenirs and postcards and families in their Sunday finest bringing picnic baskets and children to take in the spectacle. And, as the historian Crystal Feimster has pointed out, contrary to popular images of sheltered southern belles, white women sometimes took the lead in lynchings. In 1892, as a "howling mob" in Arkansas was preparing to burn an alleged Black rapist alive, the white woman who accused him of rape emerged from the crowd to wield the torch and light the pyre. In the 1920s, Arkansas women drove cars that carried Black men to lynching sites and rode in cars that dragged the corpses of lynching victims through the streets. After a 1926 lynching in Mississippi County, one Black newspaper ran an editorial titled "Women in Lynch Mob: Female of the Species More Deadly Than the Male: No Race Can Rise Above Its Women."[4]

At the start of the 1920s, the Ku Klux Klan made a comeback in Arkansas and nationwide. The Klan "thrived in every part of Arkansas," wrote one historian, accumulating thousands of members and quickly seizing control of the state government in Little Rock. In Mississippi County, hundreds of men gathered at a spot known as "Blue Hole" and lit an enormous electric cross. In the early 1920s, Klan members routinely engaged in intimidation of those who violated the mores of white supremacy: as Lewis wrote, "tactics included threats sometimes accented by floggings, tarring and feathering, burning of property, and even kidnapping." But by 1923, the Arkansas Klan turned away from concerted violence and toward the "more respectable" realm of politics. "By 1924," added the historian Story Matkin-Rawn, "Klansmen had organized into a powerful faction of the Democratic Party and controlled a number of county governments." That year Tom Terral—an avowed Klan member—was elected governor. And though the Klan did not have much documented direct involvement in the recorded lynchings of Arkansas, its presence undoubtedly ratcheted up the racist rhetoric in the state.[5]

During these years of genocidal violence, many Black Arkansans learned tactics that might help them survive, such as entering a white person's house only through the backdoor, stepping off the sidewalk whenever a white pedestrian approached, walking to school in the rain rather than riding the school bus, waiting at a store until every white customer had been served, and never, ever eating with a white person. Many Black domestics shared an informal "blacklist" of households where harassment or abuse was common. In one Delta town, recounted Matkin-Rawn, white moviegoers "informed blacks that they were never allowed to laugh first in a movie, only *after* whites laughed." In order to scrape by economically, many Black Arkansans were forced to rely on white patrons—relationships that could be remarkably paternalistic. When one Black boy went to a drugstore to pick up a prescription for his mother's employer, a wealthy white doctor, the clerk called him a "[n-word]" and reduced him to tears. In response, the white doctor beat the clerk, reprimanding him, "Don't you call *my* [n-word] a [n-word]."[6]

In the face of such insults and abuse, many Black Arkansans found ways to resist, overtly and covertly. Between Reconstruction and World War I, some Black residents founded all-Black towns with names evoking their settlers' high hopes: Peace, Sweet Home, Blackville, and Little Africa, among several others. In places where Black people stayed and were subjected to white supremacist terrorism, many engaged in armed self-defense. After white assailants sought to drive the Black residents out of Lonoke County, an open letter appeared on Black-owned cabins and houses: "The time has arrived when the Negroes of Lonoke County must look out for themselves," it declared. "The law offers them no protection . . . arm yourselves and protect your lives and homes." The Black residents of Lonoke remained, armed and ready to weather decades of violence. In the town of Jericho, Black residents reportedly had a Winchester rifle in every house, the knowledge of which once forced a white posse to call off a planned attack. Finally, when armed resistance failed or proved to be impossible, many simply fled. Black farmers began migrating north during these years, leaving fallow fields and unpicked cotton plants rotting in their absence.[7]

Across the country, Black people were becoming more organized than ever in their fight for equal rights and an end to white supremacist terrorism. In 1908, after the white residents of Springfield, Illinois, were denied the chance to lynch a Black man accused of raping a "quiet, respectable young" white woman, a white mob exploded in violence against their Black neighbors, setting fire to Black businesses and beating and murdering Black passersby. It took four thousand troops to quell the riot that ensued, and in its aftermath some two thousand Black people fled Springfield. This well-publicized incident led directly to the founding, in 1909, of the National Association for the Advancement of Colored People, which immediately focused on eliminating lynchings nationwide, using a combination of litigation, lobbying, and investigative journalism. After each lynching, the Association would fly a black-and-white flag outside its national headquarters, printed with the words "A MAN WAS LYNCHED YESTERDAY."[8]

On Independence Day in 1918 a Black seamstress and Black pastor organized a mass meeting in Little Rock to found Arkansas's first NAACP branch. "The charter membership read like a roster of Little Rock's black professional class," noted Matkin-Rawn, "numerous physicians attorneys, and teachers, but not a single domestic worker, farmer, or porter." Nonetheless, larger and more heavily working-class branches soon sprang up in Pine Bluff, Fort Smith, and Jonesboro, with two branches in the Delta—in Edmondson and Grand Lake—populated almost entirely by farmers. In the years to come, these NAACP branches would face so much violence and repression that they would be temporarily snuffed out—but not before fighting for justice following the deadliest lynchings and massacres Arkansas had ever seen.[9]

Deep in the heart of the Delta, Phillips County was still hot on the last day of September in 1919. All the Black farmers crowding onto wooden benches at the Baptist church in tiny Hoop Sour, three miles north of the town of Elaine, knew that they might face retribution for attempting to organize for their rights, but they almost certainly could not have predicted just how swift and bloody and immense the white backlash would be. In Elaine, over the gruesome days that followed, a mob of white Delta residents would murder hundreds of Black men, women, and children, ultimately driving thousands of Black residents away from the county forever. Black activists all across the country would decry the pogrom, launching investigations and diatribes and demanding justice from the powers that be. For Elaine was more than a lynching, more than a massacre; it was genocide. It was, according to one contemporary source, "possibly the bloodiest racial conflict in the history of the United States," and it instantly became the lens through which Black Arkansans understood their home state and their place within it.[10]

The context for events in Elaine was a familiar one in Arkansas: stunning inequality, constant racist violence, the lust for profits coupled with white fears of Black uprising. Less than a decade before, developers had created Elaine as a home for white merchants and supervisors in the Delta. It became a prosperous, largely white island within an overwhelmingly Black township, where Black residents outnumbered whites ten-to-one and white residents were petrified by fears of Black revolt. Yet, as Matkin-Rawn has noted, "Whites' tremendous dependence on African Americans as laborers and consumers complicated their fear of being outnumbered. Of the 30,000 bales of cotton produced in Phillips County in 1909, black farmers raised 25,000." White planters and their agents knew their wealth depended on Black labor, so they kept Black farmers trapped in an endless cycle of debt and deception and sought to eliminate dissent by wielding the constant threat of white supremacist violence. Night riders might force Black tenants from their homes and mobs of white residents might murder their Black neighbors. Years before he was America's most famous Black novelist, Richard Wright moved to Elaine in 1916, where he witnessed one of Arkansas's many unrecorded lynchings.[11]

In the face of such violence, Black farmers began meeting by moonlight to figure out how they might secure adequate compensation for their cotton crops. First, they sought out a white lawyer, but armed white men nearly lynched him—twice. So they decided to join a new, secretive union—the Progressive Farmers and Household Union of America, which grew rapidly through the Arkansas Delta as more and more Black farmers signed up. The union's literature invoked the language of the Bible, a language of blood and justice. As Matkin-Rawn put it, "a people well-versed in the Book of Revelations knew that devastating hardships would precede their victory." Black veterans returning from World War I further swelled the union's ranks, intent on winning for themselves the rights they had secured for others abroad. Many Black women joined as well. The union demanded an end to Black subordination. A generation later, many of these same activists would help to form and sustain the Southern Tenant Farmers' Union. Theirs was a resistance that had begun in slave cabins and would continue in the courtrooms and farms and shop floors of Jim Crow Arkansas.[12]

But at about eleven o'clock on the night of September 30, 1919, several carloads of white vigilantes opened fire on the union meeting in Hoop Spur, spraying bullets through the church's thin walls and sending surviving Black union members fleeing for the woods. By the time the sun rose, the vigilantes had burned the church to the ground. Platoons of heavily armed white men from Elaine and surrounding towns began a rampage, looking for union members to murder. Black veterans and others fought back; many had been arming themselves for months in anticipation of such an attack. White authorities quickly called in reinforcements, claiming a horde of Black people had Elaine "surrounded." Thousands of white men arrived by horse and train and car, many from out of state; the governor sent a machine gun battalion to put down the "Negro Uprising." Together, the soldiers and the mob opened fire on Black residents, overwhelming them with their grossly superior numbers. They ransacked Black homes, hunted Black people hiding in the canebrakes, and, in one notorious incident, murdered four handcuffed Black brothers (one of them the uncle of the future playwright Lorraine Hansberry). In the midst of the violence, several Black women sacrificed their freedom or their lives so their children and husbands could escape; other Black women and girls were raped by white soldiers. A desperate exodus of Black residents began.[13]

In the days that followed, the state government issued a report claiming that the Elaine massacre was the fault of a "deliberately planned insurrection"; the union had been committed to "the killing of white people." The state's white newspapers uniformly echoed such accounts, conveying tales of Black treachery and depravity. Nearby counties banned the sale of guns and ammunition to Black purchasers. Authorities in Phillips County imprisoned perhaps a thousand Black residents in disgusting, makeshift cells in basements and schoolhouses, tortured them until they falsely confessed to all manner of crimes, and confiscated more than a million dollars of Black-picked cotton. A grand jury indicted 122 Black people and zero whites in connection with the events in Elaine. All-white juries swiftly convicted the first eleven of these men of murder. Their death sentences quickly convinced the rest of the defendants to plead guilty.[14]

In the aftermath of the genocidal violence in Phillips County, planters in nearby Mississippi County reacted with terror of a "black insurrection." The sheriff quickly dispatched a deputy to Tennessee to buy arms in anticipation of "an expected uprising," and several wealthy white residents partnered with the few wealthy Black residents to hold a community meeting at which they exhorted the county's Black population to pledge "friendship to our white friends" and, above all, to stay put. Between 1890 and 1910, the Black population of Mississippi County had more than doubled, but with the cotton plantations growing ever larger and more profitable, the wealthy planters were terrified that the county would witness an economically debilitating general exodus of Black residents seeking safety and opportunity elsewhere. The planters knew their business model relied on a massive supply of cheap, non-unionized labor. For whatever reason—the absence of the boll weevil in northeastern Arkansas, the general flight of Black people from southeastern Arkansas—Mississippi County's Black population did not decline in the aftermath of Elaine; in fact, the county's Black population increased by more than 30 percent over the course of the 1920s.[15]

Black activists—in Arkansas and nationally—responded to Elaine with an urgent, righteous fury. The pioneering Black journalist Ida B. Wells raised attention and funds with her powerful editorials and definitive investigative reports. NAACP field secretary Walter White traveled to Arkansas to investigate, using his light skin and blue eyes to pass as white and infiltrate the remnants of the mob, though he was still nearly lynched as a result. Local Black leaders liaised with the governor in an attempt to prevent further violence, publicly claiming the pogrom had been the result of "racial tensions" originating from segregation, systematic impoverishment, and "the attentions of the lower class of white people to negro women." The NAACP partnered with local leaders in fighting for the lives of the eleven Black men sentenced to death, as well as a union leader extradited to Arkansas and similarly facing the electric chair; these men became known as the "Elaine Twelve." In Washington and New York, the Association lobbied senators and Justice Department lawyers; in Arkansas, it hired a respected white lawyer to defend the unionists; all across the country, it distributed articles and pamphlets. The NAACP took the case of the Elaine Twelve all the way to the U.S. Supreme Court, resulting in *Moore v. Dempsey*, a 1923 decision credited with having "sparked the modern revolution in criminal procedure" and that established the NAACP as a legal organization to be reckoned with.[16]

On Christmas Day in 1920, Henry Lowery, a Black tenant farmer, arrived at the home of the white planter who had long held him in "virtual peonage," demanding compensation for his labor. This was in Mississippi County, just one year after Elaine and just one plantation over from the immense empire controlled by Robert E. Lee Wilson—in fact, the planter in question was

Wilson's brother-in-law. The planter's refusal to accede to Lowery's demands quickly escalated into violence, and Lowery shot the planter, his daughter, and two of his sons. Lowery fled into the night, narrowly escaping a massive lynch mob. He made it to the swamps and then to Texas, but Mississippi County authorities managed to discern his location from an intercepted letter, and two county deputies (one a longtime Wilson employee) traveled south to retrieve him. Theirs was an onerous return journey, as they had to alter their route repeatedly to avoid lynch mobs, but when they got back to Mississippi County, a crowd of five hundred was waiting. The mob allowed Lowery to see his wife and children one last time and then burned him alive. With some effort, the sheriff managed to prevent the lynchings of other Black prisoners in Osceola and Blytheville who had allegedly assisted Lowery. Of course, the sheriff should have prevented the lynching of Lowery as well, but he did not—he hid out in a Memphis hotel room instead—leading the historian Jeannie Whayne to posit planter Wilson's probable complicity. "It seems inconceivable that such a well-orchestrated public event as the Lowery lynching could have occurred virtually on Wilson's doorstep without at least his tacit approval," she wrote.[17]

Not even two months later, rumors flew through southern and eastern Arkansas of an "assault wave" by Black men against white women, and soon white people were scouring the countryside for Black suspects. The authorities captured a Black man named Emmanuel West and claimed he had raped a white woman in Little Rock. An enormous crowd—estimates range from five hundred to two thousand—gathered at the Little Rock jail and demanded that authorities relinquish West to them, but he had already been spirited out of town. Shouting "to Hell with the law," the white mob rioted, until it was finally dispersed by a combined force of police and soldiers. Little Rock remained a city on edge. Another alleged interracial rape led to another near lynching, and dozens of newly deputized police were forced to patrol the city by night to prevent violence. West's case eventually went to trial, and although his lawyer presented thirty Black alibi witnesses, he was convicted—but in a "compromise" he was sentenced only to life in prison.[18]

The early 1920s remained bloody in Arkansas, with multiple lynchings a year, and many more near misses. A slight lull in the mid-1920s ended abruptly in the spring of 1926 when a Black man in Mississippi County was accused of raping a twelve-year-old white girl. The police took the man to a warehouse, from which they "hoped they could withstand a massed assault," as one historian recounted, but an enormous mob easily overpowered the authorities. A line of more than one hundred cars drove to a nearby plantation, where the Black man was murdered—he was hanged from a tree as a fire burned him from below.[19]

White supremacist violence continued to mar the state's communities. In 1927, a mob in Little Rock seized a Black man named John Carter—accused of attacking a white mother and daughter—hanged him from a telephone poll, shot at him, and then dragged his body behind a Star Roadster through Little Rock's Black business district. "A riot by over a thousand whites ensued that lasted three hours," wrote one historian. As darkness fell, the white terrorists beat at least one passing Black man senseless and attempted to harm many others; they eventually burned Carter's body, reportedly using pews from a nearby Black church as firewood. Police officers apparently played cards amidst the riot; the sheriff of Little Rock, who sat back and watched the lynching, remarked, "I never saw a more orderly crowd of hunters in my life." The mob finally dispersed after the governor sent in troops. The trial of another Black man—a teenager, actually—led to the swift assembly of a new lynch mob demanding blood. Hundreds of deputies and national guardsmen assembled at the courthouse, but with so much violence in the air, the verdict was inescapable: the jury convicted the Black youth after just twelve minutes of deliberation; he was electrocuted on his eighteenth birthday. Shortly thereafter, many Black residents reportedly fled the city forever.[20]

Remarkably, lynchings dropped off sharply—both in Arkansas and nationally—in the late 1920s and 1930s, the result of a confluence of factors, including the decline of the Klan, campaigns of grassroots Black resistance, national media scrutiny, increased anti-lynching work by local women, what one historian called "improved law enforcement systems and procedures," and a nationwide reckoning with extralegal violence spurred by the NAACP and other national activist organizations. In all, there were nearly five hundred recorded lynchings in Arkansas and certainly many more unrecorded ones. Indeed, according to an innovative study of lynchings by the Equal Justice Initiative (EJI), between 1880 and 1940 Arkansas had the highest proportion of Black people lynched, compared with every other state in the South, largely because the massacre at Elaine. According to EJI, Phillips County, Arkansas, had the highest number of lynchings of any county in the United States. The last recorded lynching in Arkansas would occur on April 29, 1936—a Black man named Willie Kees was accused of attempting to rape a white woman not even forty miles from Blytheville; he was murdered by a mob shortly thereafter. "It is rather ironic that the last known lynching to occur in Arkansas was for the very crime that southerners erroneously used to justify lynchings," the historian Richard A. Buckelew has written. "As with most lynching cases, we will likely never know whether the victim was guilty or innocent, but that was the nature of lynching."[21]

The Arkansas branches of the NAACP floundered in the 1920s. Early in that decade, the Little Rock NAACP branch raised thousands of dollars for Emmanuel West's defense and hired a prominent white attorney, but the branch soon folded for want of committed members. It survived as long as it did only because of dedicated female leaders, none of whom received adequate credit for their efforts.[22] Story Matkin-Rawn counted seventeen attempts to establish local NAACP branches in Arkansas during these years, of which just one succeeded. Many Black activists tried, mailing crumpled dollar bills to the NAACP headquarters in New York, but memories of Elaine haunted their every move. Their activism was under constant threat by the forces of capital and white supremacy. "Mississippi County, dominated by the massive 30,000 acre R. E. L. Wilson plantation, was all but impenetrable to the NAACP," Matkin-Rawn noted.[23]

Yet the national NAACP did not neglect the Arkansas Delta, keeping the national spotlight shining brightly even as many state leaders attempted to distance themselves from the supposedly insurrectionary Black people murdered at Elaine. The NAACP sent an investigator to Mississippi County from Harlem to investigate the murder of Henry Lowery and later published his findings in a pamphlet entitled, "An American Lynching." It sent a copy to every single member of Congress, seeking to press representatives into supporting an anti-lynching bill. The Association also contributed financial assistance to the defense of Black people facing legal lynchings.[24]

The end of lynching did not, of course, mean the end of racism or the end of racist violence. As Buckelew has written of Arkansas, "The lethal sanctioning of blacks was now accomplished in a more covert fashion, as the number of black inmates and legal executions increased dramatically. Perhaps lynching had changed, but in name only." Other historians have persuasively demonstrated that "even as acts of lynching became increasingly untenable . . . violence against black men became legitimized into the routine of the courtroom." In perhaps the most famous example of the time, nine Black youths— the youngest just thirteen—were dragged off a train in Alabama in 1931 for allegedly raping two white women. The authorities managed to shield the so-called Scottsboro Boys from a lynch mob, only to railroad them in swift, public trials. Despite an astonishing dearth of evidence, all nine were quickly convicted by all-white juries, and all but the youngest was sentenced to death. In the years and decades that followed, lawyers from the NAACP and especially the Communist Party would fight valiantly to overturn their convictions.[25]

4 · A Jim Crow Childhood, 1930s

One day in the early 1980s, a bulldozer operated by the Army Corps of Engineers was cutting through the soggy bank of Arkansas's Red River when it unearthed a tombstone. The date on the stone indicated that it was from the 1910s. A team of archaeologists soon traveled to the area and discovered an "extensive" graveyard, with some 117 grave sites dating from the 1890s to the 1920s, many of them unmarked. The Army Corps had accidentally stumbled across the forgotten cemetery of a Baptist church, part of a once "thriving black community." After the Red River flooded in 1927, dumping roughly eight feet of silt onto of the cemetery, it was abandoned. The Army Corps decided to quickly reinter the remains in a cemetery two miles away. But before doing so, the Corps called in a specialist to analyze the bones, giving him just twenty-four hours per skeleton.

The specialist concluded that the remains provided "hard biological evidence for the historians that, in a sense, said the lives of rural Southern blacks were pretty terrible." The bones revealed that the health and nutrition of this population were "about as bad as it could be." The specialist surmised a 27 percent infant mortality rate and that 58 percent of children were iron deficient. Forty-once percent of child skeletons, 52 percent of adult female skeletons, and 60 percent of adult male skeletons showed signs of infection. "For an infection to impact the bone, it has to be severe and chronic," the specialist told the press. There was evidence of arthritis "from the hard labor of sharecropping," as well as rickets, scurvy, and weanling diarrhea. To the specialist, the bones revealed a history that written documents could not. This community, he told the press, "may have suffered more maladies than any others examined in recorded history."[1]

This cemetery was just a few miles west of Stamps, and it revealed conditions just a few years before Marguerite Johnson arrived in town.

When three-year-old Marguerite and her brother Bailey arrived to Stamps in 1931, they moved into the home of their paternal grandmother, Annie Henderson. An imposing woman, born in Columbia County, Arkansas, in 1877, Henderson was over six feet tall, with heavy brows and large, expressive eyes. She had a quiet speaking voice, but in church she could "shatter the windows" with her songs, recalled Marguerite. Deeply religious, thrice married, the daughter of freed slaves, Henderson rose to be a community leader in Stamps. She was the only Black woman in town whom the white residents referred to as "Mrs." "My grandmother was God to me," Marguerite later told an interviewer.[2]

Early in the twentieth century, Annie Henderson had sold lunches to factory workers in Stamps; her meat pies and cool lemonade were such a hit that she built a stand, and then a store—"Store," Marguerite would always write—located in the heart of the "Negro area" of Stamps. By the time Marguerite arrived, it was the center of Black life in town. Barbers clipped hair in the shade of the Store's porch, men bragged about how much cotton they were going to pick, and itinerant troubadours paused to play juice harps and cigar-box guitars. Everything from pig food to lightbulbs, coal to balloons, packed the shelves of the Store. Marguerite reveled in the smells and sensations: the aroma of the pickle barrel, the lusciousness of ripe fruit, the bulging sacks of corn. There was snuff from North Carolina, matches from Ohio, ribbon from New York; the whole world felt like it was in the Store. And now, into the back moved Marguerite and Bailey. They would remain there for the better part of the next decade.[3]

For the first time in her memory, Marguerite was meeting members of her extended family. Henderson—or "Momma" as her grandchildren soon took to calling her—lived with her son, their uncle Willie. Disabled since he was a child, with the left half of his face pulled down as if by a pulley, his left hand as shrunken as his right one was strong, Willie used to sit "like a giant black Z" as Marguerite told him about her day.[4] Trips to St. Louis meant encountering Marguerite's maternal grandfather, a Pullman porter with a West Indian lilt, and grandmother, a light-skinned, German-accented doyenne who "had pull with the police department."[5] And she would always vividly recall meeting Momma's mother, her great-grandmother. A tiny woman who dominated her tall daughters, Mary Wafford had been born into slavery on August 20, 1853. After slavery was abolished, she had renamed herself Kentucky—not because she was from that state, she too had been born in Arkansas—but just because she liked the sound of it. Kentucky never discussed her time in slavery, never discussed her background at all. Her great-granddaughter recalled her as the arbiter of all that was right and wrong in town; she controlled the Black community with gusto.[6]

On all four sides of her family, Marguerite was directly descended from slaves, including one great-grandmother who died in 1942 at (according to her obituary) the age of 150. Another great-grandmother was impregnated at the age of 17 by a 53-year-old white man who had once owned her as a slave. This case, and other light-skinned forebears, suggests that instances of rape may have been present in Marguerite's family tree, as they are in the family trees of many Americans whose ancestors were enslaved.[7]

Marguerite soon began attending Lafayette County Training School, the school for Black children, which, unlike the white school, possessed no tennis court, no ivy, no hedges, no fence—indeed, no lawn. It was just two buildings set on a dirt hill, surrounded by farms.[8] Every day began the same way: the students would gather in the auditorium at eight o'clock, one would recite the preamble to the Constitution in three breaths, and then the class would sing, "O Say Can You See"—or, if the adults weren't looking, "Any Bed Bugs on Me." Then, in the same key, they would sing "Lift Every Voice and Sing," the Black national anthem. "Everyone I knew, or met, knew Lift Every Voice and Sing," Marguerite recalled decades later.[9]

The teachers were imports from the Arkansas Negro colleges, forced to board with private families in a small town with no rooming houses. "If a lady teacher took company, or didn't receive any mail or cried alone in her room at night," Marguerite later wrote, "by the weeks' [sic] end even the children discussed her morality, her loneliness and her other failings."[10] Yet Marguerite was lucky to be able to attend school at all. For Black children in the area, education was perpetually precarious. Some forty miles away in Redland, the Depression so thoroughly decimated the finances of the school for Black children that in 1930 it was able to operate only two and a half months a year. Donations allowed school officials to keep the doors open for another month, and in the years that followed, relief funding enabled it to operate for seven months. In 1936, loans and tax income "again enabled the school to operate on its own resources, though on a greatly reduced scale."[11] Indeed, between 1931 and 1934 the state spent thirteen dollars per year for the education of white children, compared with just four dollars per year for Black children. White children attended an average of forty-one more days of school per year than did Black children, and only sixteen of the state's seventy-five counties provided full-time high school for Black teenagers.[12] In the face of such uncertainty, some Black children enrolled in nontraditional schools. For instance, many residents of Stamps sought a different life by learning gospel songs at all-day singing schools.[13]

The Depression was on, and Black people—across the South, and certainly in Stamps—were suffering, usually more than their white neighbors.[14] At first, the Black residents of Stamps thought the Depression was just for white people, but when the price per pound of cotton dropped from ten cents to eight, then seven, and finally five, they learned that it did not discriminate. They stopped raising hogs because, well, who had enough food even for slop? But Momma was careful with money. She spent long hours going over her books, figuring out how to run the Store when none of her customers had any money.[15] She recorded her finances in a small, cardboard notebook with "THE BODCAW BANK, STAMPS, ARK.," printed across the top.[16] And though she occasionally splurged and bought dresses at Talbot's—"We Outfit the Family!"—or entered raffles to try to win a free Ford, she was generally remarkably frugal.[17] Momma made Marguerite's and Bailey's clothing from two bolts of cloth she ordered each year from Sears, Roebuck. And while many of the town's white residents had to go on welfare, Momma managed to keep her family off relief.[18]

Late one Thursday, as Marguerite and Bailey were attending to the pigs, a white man rode up to the Store, his horse crossing the front yard.[19] He was a former sheriff, bitter and nonchalant, exuding confidence and unconcern, but his twang cut through the air. Marguerite distinctly heard him say to Momma, "Annie, tell Willie he better lay low tonight. A crazy [n-word] messed with a white lady today. Some of the boys'll be coming over here later." Then, without even waiting for Momma's response, he turned his horse and rode out of the yard, off to warn some of the other Black families he favored.

Marguerite's whole body seized with fear, dry air filling her mouth and her body feeling light. She knew what "the boys" meant. The Klan. Momma moved quickly. With the horse's thudding hooves still audible in the distance, Momma blew out the coal oil lamps and called for Bailey and Marguerite to run into the Store. She told them to remove the potatoes and the onions from their bins; Uncle Willie—the only grown Black man present—then climbed in, taking forever to lay down flat. Marguerite and Bailey then covered him with the displaced potatoes and onions. Momma fell to the floor to pray.

The Klan did not come that night—which, Marguerite would later write, was fortunate, since Willie was moaning so loudly that they surely would have found him "and just as surely lynched him."[20] Yet this episode illustrates an inescapable fact of Marguerite's childhood: in the 1930s Stamps was an exceedingly dangerous place for Black people, especially Black men accused of rape. The white residents of Stamps were so racist, people used to say, that a Black person couldn't buy vanilla ice cream except on the Fourth of July; every other day they had to make do with chocolate.[21]

To be sure, not all Black people agreed with such an assessment. "Well, the further west you went in Arkansas, the less severe, should I say, treatment one received as a result of being black," recalled one Black woman who grew up in Stamps at the same time. Not far from Texas and Louisiana, Stamps was more the Southwest than it was the South, she claimed, and "the lynchings and the cruel treatment of blacks did not occur in southwest Arkansas as it did in Mississippi and Alabama and Georgia and perhaps Carolinas."[22] If this was true, surely Mississippi County was one of the least humane places to be Black, about as far east as Stamps was west. But, in any case, this woman from Stamps, who described her Black grandfather as a "gentleman farmer" even during the Depression, was discussing a very different town from the one experienced by Marguerite Johnson.

"In Stamps, the segregation was so complete that most Black children didn't really, absolutely know what whites looked like," Marguerite later recalled. Marguerite herself didn't believe that whites were "really real."[23] In a town starkly divided by the train tracks, those residing on her side of town lived lives of crushing, desperate, vicious poverty. And, all too often, hunger.[24] Jobs became hard to come by and hard to keep, especially as pro-union and anti-union activists battled fiercely over the railroad industry in Stamps, intermittently coercing, seducing, and threatening the Black mill workers.[25] A few years before Marguerite arrived, a local woman had tried to organize an NAACP chapter in Stamps, but the effort proved too onerous.[26] And there certainly were lynchings. On March 20, 1907, two Black women, accused of "murderous assault," were lynched in Stamps.[27] A few years before Marguerite and Bailey arrived in town, a man "was hunted down for assaulting white womanhood." When he tried to escape by running into the Store, Momma and Willie hid him behind their chifforobe and then sent him on his way with provisions. In the end, though, he was apprehended. Marguerite did not describe his ultimate fate.[28]

Certain writers tend to romanticize the place where they grew up. "The back country of Arkansas is always the same, no matter which fork of the road you follow," waxed one, the daughter of a white doctor, who wished to redeem the reputation of her native state, which she felt had been unfairly lumped with hillbillies and barefoot fiddlers. "Always the narrow, rutted wagon road winds through thick woods of pine and scrub oak and sumac bushes; always past green and white cotton fields, tall waves of whispering corn—down the same valley, up the same hill, in at the gate and along the path to the weary, rain-grayed farmhouse."[29]

For Marguerite Johnson, though, the place of her childhood decidedly lacked in romance. "There is a South in this nation's blood where there is no greening," she would write. "Wisteria does not soften the landscape, sycamore trees are for hanging and cotton is a blood red tale told in shame and anger. In this land, violence is a constant season and base survival the only possible triumph. . . . The composite white 'Man' rapes Black women, kills or isolates Black men and exploits the children. Although he is nameless, he is legion and legend and his power has been near omnipotent."[30]

Marguerite would always refuse to sugarcoat her reality, but neither would she surrender to nihilism. In an undated, untitled, unfinished handwritten fragment of a play, Marguerite had a Black woman tell her granddaughter, "White folks just want to make you feel bad. . . . I thought I had taught you that." Near tears, the granddaughter asks, "But if I think about them all the time, who is going to think about me?" The grandmother pauses. "The whole world. You're on the very bottom. But you're rising. You rising."[31]

In spite of the poverty and racism and danger of Stamps, young Marguerite Johnson, the future author of such acclaim, began to learn how to write. In a blue composition book, she practiced her handwriting, printed vocabulary words—"electricity," "library," "finish"—and doodled people in hats and a fancy, black car. She worked her way through multiplication and long division and wrote letters to "My Deer dady."[32] As a school project, she compiled a scrapbook entitled, "Yesterday and Today: Arkansas History." It included sections written in careful cursive, with pictures cut out from newspapers and glued to the page, covering the state's timber and mining industries, its Native American inhabitants, and other topics. In one section, entitled, "Cotton Is King," she wrote, "Mississippi County now produces more cotton than any other county in the United States. Nowhere else in the world can better soil and climate be found for cotton."

Marguerite's teacher, Mrs. F. C. Readye, scrawled "B-" on the first page of the scrapbook, which was surely something of a disappointment, considering how hard Marguerite had evidently worked on the project.[33] Nonetheless, Marguerite's description of the state's cotton industry is revealing. Even for a child living some three hundred miles away, Mississippi County was part of her identity as an Arkansan. It was the crown jewel of the state's agricultural industry, its most profitable site of production.

It also exemplified the violence of this geography, this era, the way that the pursuit of capital and control could mark certain lives as disposable—as much as it did the forms of individual and community resistance Black people developed to survive in the midst of oppression.

Part II
Arrests

5 • Bethel and Wallace, 1928

There wasn't quite a full moon that night, but the sky in the Arkansas Delta was so big, the land so flat, that it may well have seemed full as it shone down on the arrest taking place. It was around midnight on Sunday, April 1, 1928. The weather was fair and warm, a good sign for the big planters, as well as for those who depended on the vast plantations for food and shelter. It had been a hard couple of years of cotton farming in Mississippi County, Arkansas, home to some of the world's biggest plantations and some of the world's most fertile soil. First came the flood in 1927, an inundation that decimated the county's output and momentarily threw labor relations—and the resulting social hierarchy—into chaos. Then, as 1928 began, it was just too cold, too rainy, the constant chilly downpours causing fears that seeds would not germinate and young plants would be pounded back to the ground. The soil had been as sticky as gumbo, the lush vegetation seeming riper than usual, and some no doubt feared that the rivers that meandered through the county would again burst through their levees and destroy a year's hard work. People were on edge. That spring, when one cotton hand was arrested for violating the liquor law, the judge temporarily suspended his sentence so he could remain on his farm during planting season.[1]

Yet, as Frank Bethel and Mike Wallace approached the Poplar Corner store the April night was pleasant, the moonlight bright as they walked away from their Chevrolet Coupe over dusty red earth. They were heading to a popular local hangout, a country store and filling station in tiny Poplar Corner, an unincorporated community a few miles from Manila, an island of urban life in the sea of rural abundance that was Mississippi County. The store sat at the corner of two roads, one paved and the other dirt. It was a place to get some feed or a cola or a bite to eat, with a porch where tenant farmers could while away Sunday afternoons, casually violating Prohibition. It was where struggling men might try to sell twenty-acre farms, and where baseball teams from neighboring towns could inquire about scheduling a game with the Poplar Corner nine. As the two men walked into the store, they likely passed under a single harsh bulb. A photograph from two decades earlier showed high shelves packed tight with wares, bags of grain or flour leaning on the counters, cans of paint or oats piled near the ceiling, and handsome hats hanging from hooks over the cash register.[2]

It was late when Bethel and Wallace arrived at the store, but they were hungry. They woke up J. C. Pillows, the store's proprietor, who had been sleeping in the living quarters in the backrooms. Pillows made them a couple of sandwiches and the two customers sat down to eat. They had taken only a few bites when, all of a sudden, two men burst into the store.

"I heard a racket in the store, someone talking loud, and when I heard that I figured it was a robbery or something," recalled Pillows's son, Gus, who had also been sleeping in the back. Gus got up and crept toward the main part of the store. When he reached the door, he heard Henry T. Bolin, a farmer and night marshal for the nearby town of Leachville, say "something about sticking your hands up or I will knock your damned head off." Bolin was a middle-aged white man, of medium height and medium build, with blue eyes and light brown hair. He was speaking very loudly.[3]

With Bolin was W. L. Dismukes, another Leachville marshal, who told Bethel and Wallace they were under arrest and to put their hands up. As the marshal began to handcuff them, Bethel, the taller man, kept still, but Wallace, shorter and with a more intense face, kept lowering his hands; Bolin had to order him to keep them up. Dismukes, known to friends as Bill, searched the two men, feeling and patting their bodies for guns or knives or liquor. When he didn't find anything, he and Bolin dragged the two men out to the store's porch. The Pillowses, father and son, followed, watching. They joined Bert Taylor, another police official, as well as a young woman named Pearl.

What happened next would later become a matter of some controversy. It would be undisputed that either Bethel or Wallace asked the night marshals why they were being arrested. Dismukes replied with something along the lines of, "they had committed a crime against this young lady up there," meaning Pearl. Dismukes would later claim that Bethel and Wallace replied that "they didn't know that goddamn woman and had never seen her before." The two arrested men would strenuously deny using the word "goddamn."

At some point Pearl cut in. She was visibly nervous. Her red sweater had a five- or six-inch tear on the left side; she had a big bruise on her left leg and some scratches on her right, and her face had clearly been beaten.

"Now boys," she said (according to later recollections), "I guess you believe what I said, if you had did right . . . there wouldn't have been any of this."

One of them shot back, "Now the Court will settle it, we have not mistreated you."

Bolin would later recall that he hadn't been paying much attention to what Pearl said. But her talking was too much for him. He "told her to hush."

Still hungry, the men asked the cops if they could finish eating their sandwiches before their arrest. "I told them yes," Dismukes would testify.

"They went ahead and finished their lunches after you told them what they were arrested for?" an attorney would ask the constable, disbelief plain in his phrasing.

"Yes, sir," Dismukes would reply.[4]

Even under arrest for rape, Frank Bethel and Mike Wallace were still men, still white. And, in a moment revealing of the Jim Crow social order, as well as the justice system they were soon to face, the two got to finish their midnight snack before being hauled off to jail.

Twenty-five years earlier, at about two o'clock on the morning of Sunday, July 19, 1903, a mob of white men waited patiently, fully aware that the evening would end with a lynching. A day earlier, police officers in Warren, Arkansas, had picked up the telephone—still a novel contraption—and breathlessly relayed reports of a Black rapist on the loose to all points in the southern part of the state. A "reputable white man" (as the press called him) employed at a mill about eight miles from town had reported that a young, Black coworker named Crane Green had sexually assaulted his thirteen-year-old daughter while most of the other employees were off work. Green fled, and a manhunt ensued. On Saturday morning, a posse of white men captured Green near Lanark. On the way to the county jail, the posse came upon the lynch mob, which had been waiting on the Kingsland Road. The posse handed Green over. The next morning, a farmer found his body hanging from a tree on the side of the road. "Negro Rape Fiend Suffers the Usual Penalty for His Crime," noted the *Pine Bluff Daily Graphic*, above an article claiming that the lynch mob had "quietly dispersed" after murdering Green.[5] The very next day, with the lynching of Green printed on front pages across the state of Arkansas, Frank Bethel was born.

Christened Guy Frank Bethel, he came into the world in Monette, a small Delta town one county over from Mississippi County. There are indications that Bethel was born to a family of some means—his father, John Warren Bethel, was a merchant who sold Singer sewing machines; a doctor was present at the birth, to make sure everything went smoothly and to administer silver nitrate drops in the infant's eyes. Both of his parents, John and Florence, had been born in Indiana (though Frank would later tell authorities that he didn't know of their origins), and Frank was their fourth child (of what would be six). John, Frank's father, had stopped school after the eighth grade, but it appears that he rose to become a county registrar.

Yet Frank himself would prove to be downwardly mobile. He left school after the fourth grade to become a barber, cutting hair for the farmers and other folks of the Arkansas Delta. He grew to be a fairly short, sturdy man with pale skin, black hair, and gray eyes. He married young. With his wife Gladys, he had a son, but the marriage fell apart. Few other details of his life survive before he was accused of attacking Pearl. He did not attend church. He had been vaccinated. He had slightly elevated blood pressure though was generally healthy. He smoked.[6]

If Frank Bethel came from a family with some means—his people weren't sharecroppers after all—the same cannot be said of Mike Wallace, his eventual partner in assault and arrest. Mike was born Roy Thomas Wallace on September 4, 1903, less than two months after Bethel, and also in Monette. Since Monette was home to only a few hundred residents early in the century, Wallace and Bethel had known one another since birth. "Practically since I have been big enough to know anybody I have known Frank," Wallace would recall, and records show that they attended the same small schoolhouse together. Wallace was the son of a farmer, originally from Kentucky, and a housewife, originally from the Arkansas Delta. Whereas Bethel was his parents' fourth child, Wallace was his parents' fifth, the baby. Like his father, he grew up to be a farmer.

As with Frank Bethel, little beyond these bare facts is known of Mike Wallace's early years, except for his family's evident financial insecurity. His father died when he was a young teenager, and it is unclear how his widowed mother, Minnie, supported him and his siblings after that, though hints remain that she may have mortgaged the family home. Wallace briefly moved to Colorado as an eighteen-year-old to work for the Colorado Fuel and Iron Company, probably to bring in much-needed cash. Like Bethel, Wallace had dark hair and fair skin. By the age of twenty-five, he had no wife or children. He also smoked.[7]

Neither Bethel nor Wallace had much. But they were white, a fact that would prove critical once they were accused of rape.

Men like Bethel and Wallace did not have many options when it came to fun in their tiny, rural, Delta town. There were public dances, though respectable citizens believed that only "a very rough element" defied local blue laws to attend. There were often baseball games. One wealthy man would occasionally put on fairs, with rides, concessions, bingo, hamburgers, and cotton candy. Nearby Osceola had opened a swimming pool in 1925, just off Highway 61; it had a wading pool on one end, diving boards on the other, and two towering slides—but, recollected one resident, the "legendary 'Miss Blanche' was often there to make sure that the boys and girls 'behaved properly.'" The town also was home to the famous Black pianist and singer Willie Bloom, who was popular among both Black and white residents.[8]

Still, boredom or ennui were inevitable. And so, one Sunday morning in 1928, Frank Bethel and Mike Wallace piled into a Chevrolet Coupe and went out looking for trouble.

It did not take the two men long to come across Pearl, a young schoolteacher, facing a wearisome walk home and grateful for a ride to the bus station. Yet, she would later claim, the station came and went, the two men refusing to stop the Chevrolet, insisting Pearl go riding with them. She protested; she asked to get out; she asked to drive; she began to cry. Eventually, the men pulled her from the car, and, in a forlorn area by the railroad tracks, they raped her.

Pearl would later testify that she did not know her assailants' full names, but she decided to memorize their car's license plate number—and told them so. Hearing this, Bethel walked to the front of the car, removed the front plate, and placed it near the car's rear. After the rape, the men had a bit of car trouble, giving Pearl a chance to furtively walk around the car and look for the license plates. "I didn't know at the time where I was," she would later recall, "and I thought if there was any way to have these brutes caught I am going to have them caught." Pearl scanned her surroundings, but they were nondescript and shrouded in darkness. She grabbed both license plates—front and back—and stared at them, trying to memorize their contents. But then she heard Wallace coming back around. She took one of the license plates and threw it as far as she could. This would be proof that she had been here. Wallace saw her and said, "hell's, she's reading our license number," knocking her to the ground. He grabbed the other license plate and threw it into the back of the car. But it was too late. Pearl had already thrown the first one.[9]

The two men shoved Pearl back into the car and drove back toward Leachville. After a few moments, Wallace said to Bethel, "Damn her, let's break her damn neck and leave her down here in one of these sloughs. What do you say, Frank?"

Bethel, seeing Wallace was serious, replied, "No, let's don't do that."

The Chevrolet continued on under the almost full moon. Yet just past the second turn out of Manila, shortly after they hit the paved road, the car stopped dead. Bethel got out of the car but quickly concluded he couldn't fix the car without a pair of pliers. As he walked to a house a few hundred yards away, Pearl saw an opportunity and tried to jump out of the car, but Wallace grabbed her. When Bethel returned emptyhanded—the house had no pliers—Wallace said to him, "Frank, this goddamn woman is figuring on leaving. What do you think about that?"

Bethel replied, "Hell, no, if she don't act just right we'll take her out here and do it to her again."

With Wallace still holding Pearl, Bethel tried to flag down a car. Three or four passed without stopping. Eventually, a car did stop, parking just in front of their Chevrolet. Suddenly, Pearl had her chance. She said, "I am going to get out and ride with them," and, with the other car right there, Wallace couldn't hold her or "remonstrate" her any longer. Pearl leapt out of the Chevrolet and ran up to the other car, saying, "men, let me ride."

One man replied, "lady, we can't, we are full up," but Pearl ran around to the car's other side and jumped up on the running board, opened the door, and said, "You must let me ride, I want you to take me in, these boys have been mistreating me."

The men in the car took one look at her torn clothes and bruised body, took one look at Bethel and Wallace, and let her jump in the back. Their car took off and traveled straight to Leachville. Pearl quickly located the town marshals and with them set out to look for Bethel and Wallace. Just minutes later, outside the Poplar Corner store, Pearl spotted the Chevrolet.[10]

In a land of haves and have-nots, Frank Bethel and Mike Wallace had pretty much nothing at all. And yet, even under arrest for rape with their victim standing just feet away, they were allowed to finish their sandwiches. The two young, white men simply "stood there," in the moonlight, on the porch of the store in Poplar Corner, and "ate our lunch," recalled Bethel. The police waited.

It was the middle of the night when Dismukes and Bolin drove Bethel and Wallace to the lockup in Leachville, the darkness broken during the five-mile ride with the lights or lanterns of Mississippi County residents.[11] No photographs of the Leachville lockup have survived, but it was undoubtedly a cramped, informal, uncomfortable place. In nearby Manila, recalled one local lawyer, the jail consisted of a two-room cage in the rear of City Hall, "enclosed entirely by iron bars or other metal bars. One door was used for entry into each of these sections. The door was kept locked at all times whether or not an occupant was confined in the jail."[12]

After depositing the two suspects in the lockup, officers Dismukes, Bolin, and Bert Taylor, accompanied by Pearl, got back into the Ford and returned to Poplar Corner. They continued south, passing Beauchamp Corner—another tiny, unincorporated collection of houses—passing a filling station, the railroad tracks, a ditch on the side of the road. Pearl suddenly spoke up. She said "something about there being a woods there on by the road." The group got out and walked carefully up the ditch. Pearl decided this wasn't the place.

They continued south toward Manila, passing a marble obelisk in a grassy field, a monument to an Arkansas sniper who, though the smallest man in his company, singlehandedly took out four German machine gunners during World War I. They turned west and reached a floodway. "This ain't the place," Pearl said, again.

The group turned north, crossing the ditch they'd crossed before and coming to the same railroad. This time, they turned the other direction, following the railroad. They were about a mile past Manila. It was starting to look familiar. "That's the road they carried me down," Pearl told the men. They continued west for about a quarter mile, until Pearl told them to stop. To their left was a thicket of trees; to their right was cultivated land. And there, in front of them, was the license plate.

This was evidence, strong evidence, that Pearl was telling the truth. Frank Bethel and Mike Wallace had raped her.[13]

It took barely a week for a jury to convict Bethel and Wallace. On April 10, crowds of observers squeezed into the imposing Mississippi County Courthouse, hastening up the marble staircase, packing the ornate courtroom, no doubt straining to see the two local youths accused of "having brutally assaulted a young woman school teacher," in the words of the *Arkansas Gazette*. As one attorney would later recall, it was not uncommon in Blytheville for people to crowd into the courthouse to witness murder or rape trials: "It is somewhat of an occasion and somewhat of a vacation and entertainment."

Jury selection occupied the better part of a day. Opening statements followed, with the prosecutor demanding the death penalty. Testimony started that night and continued through the next day. The observers remained the entire time. Even after the attorneys had given closing arguments, after the jury had departed the courtroom to deliberate, after sunlight had faded from the springtime sky outside, the crowd waited. In the end, they would not wait long. After just forty-five minutes, the jury returned. "Guilty," they pronounced. It was a verdict that carried the death sentence. This was "the first case in which the maximum penalty has been given in several years," the prosecutor told the press.[14]

Two days later, on April 13, Bethel and Wallace returned to the courtroom for sentencing. Was there any reason the sentence of death should not be imposed upon them, the judge asked. "We are not guilty," the two replied. The judge disagreed. He imposed the death penalty, the first time in six years an Arkansas judge had done so in a case of sexual assault. If all went according to plan, the two defendants would die in the electric chair on June 1, just seven weeks away—a typical timeline for the era. Bethel and Wallace processed the news "without outward sign of emotion," the papers reported.[15]

There followed several weeks of waiting. Sitting together in one of the "death cells" in the state penitentiary in Little Rock, Bethel and Wallace no doubt contemplated their fates. Yet outwardly, at least, the two were not worried. Even as the calendar crept closer to June 1, as the prison authorities began preparing for the double execution, the two told reporters they were "confident that the death sentence will not be carried out." They were correct. On May 28, 1928, with three days to spare, the Arkansas Supreme Court temporarily stayed their execution, after their lawyer filed an appeal alleging all manner of errors during the trial.[16]

For the next five months, the two men continued to wait. No record survives to document this period in their now-tenuous lives. Indeed, no record of their 1928 trial appears to still exist. Pearl's feelings, her actions, during this long delay are likewise lost. What we do know is that on November 5, the Arkansas Supreme Court overturned Bethel's and Wallace's convictions. According to the court, the trial judge had committed two reversible errors. First, he had permitted a physician to testify that he had examined the two defendants and that they had tested positive for a sexually transmitted infection. "This testimony did not tend to prove the crime charged, but only tended to prejudice, disgrace and humiliate them before the jury," noted the supreme court. Second, the judge had allowed the prosecution "to prove the good reputation of the prosecutrix for virtue and chastity, when her general reputation therefor had not been attacked by appellants." Because Pearl's "reputation for chastity" was not "in issue," this testimony was improper. The prosecution would have to try the two men again and not commit these errors.[17]

"Bethel and Wallace Win Chance for Life," read the front-page, banner headline in the *Blytheville Courier-News,* which had only recently begun publication. "The trial attracted widespread interest," the newspaper noted. The two men would remain behind bars for the next several months, as the state prepared for their second trial. If Bethel and Wallace wished that the interest of their neighbors would dissipate in the coming weeks, that hope would soon be dashed.[18]

6 • Class War, 1929–1935

Though it would've been impossible to predict at the time, the arrests of Bethel and Wallace came at the end of a period of relative calm in Arkansas history. In the years that followed, the state exploded in anger, fear, and radical potential. In the blink of an eye, much of Arkansas was starving, homeless, and unemployed. Compared with twenty years earlier, the income of sharecroppers fell by almost half. Literal plagues, almost biblical in their extremity, struck the state with regularity. Riots, assassinations, and virtual warfare became the norm. "Not since the one-hundred-year drought that De Soto witnessed in the mid-sixteenth century had the country seen such a disaster," wrote Jeannie Whayne.[1]

This furor and unrest form a backdrop vital for understanding Jim Crow society, its intersecting, overlapping hierarchies, and the way that the authorities, the courts, and the legal system strengthened those hierarchies. More specifically, the class warfare that erupted in the Delta during these years was inextricably linked to the arrests of Bubbles Clayton and Jim X. Carruthers. As we shall see, many believed that their persecution was simply the latest tactic adopted by powerful planters determined to divide white and Black workers, to keep all workers in their place. Certainly, it is undeniable that the rich men of the Delta, and their law enforcement allies, knew how to use the legal system to their great advantage.

First, in 1929, came the Depression. Initially, many Arkansans shrugged off Black Tuesday—the state's economy had been faltering for the better part of a decade—but within a matter of weeks it was clear that the bottom had fallen out of their financial institutions. Soon more than a hundred Arkansas banks had shut their doors, including three in Blytheville. In less than three years, nearly 40 percent of the state's laborers were out of a job. Then, beginning in the summer of 1930, the Delta was struck by a miserable, year-long drought. Months passed without rain, temperatures topped 110 degrees, and fish began turning up dead from "hot water." As a result, crops wilted in the fields, livestock keeled over, and creditors descended on big planters; many small farmers were wiped out entirely. The state lost 30 to 50 percent of its crops. The drought was followed, naturally, by widespread famine. Hunger set in. That winter, one Arkansas bluesman recorded "Starvation Blues" and crooned, "Now, I almost had a square meal the other day, but the garbage man come, and he moved the can away." The Red Cross returned to provide aid and, quickly, half the state came to depend on it. Then, in 1933, in an effort to raise the price of cotton, New Deal administrators told plantation owners to not plant—if necessary, to destroy—a third of their cotton crops; this rendered a significant chunk of the workforce superfluous, which led the planters to institute mass evictions.[2]

In the aftermath of the drought and the famine, elite planters initially opposed outside assistance, "fearing that if laborers were not facing starvation, they would not pick the surviving portion of the cotton crop for the usual fifty cents, or less, per one hundred pounds," wrote Sammy L. Morgan. Once the situation became sufficiently dire, the planters made sure "that the local committees supervising Red Cross aid in the Delta included only members with an interest in preserving the status quo: bankers, store owners, planters, and politicians. Abuses by the privileged class were endemic during the winter of 1930–31; they included diversion of supplies to plantation commissaries, profiteering by storekeepers, and the withholding of rations from those refusing to work." Some planters forced laborers to work for below-normal wages—or no wages at all—in exchange for Red Cross food; some denied help entirely to "unworthy" Black laborers. In 1933 and 1934, local elites likewise ensured that they controlled New Deal agricultural programs, further entrenching inequities and suffering. Such planter control meant that "untold numbers of families went hungry," noted Nan Woodruff.[3]

In response, thousands of Delta farmers—Black and white, tenant and cropper, male and female—began marching on local relief agencies, demanding their rations. In the bustling city of England, three hundred armed farmers assembled to demand food. "Our children are crying for food," they shouted, "and we're going to get it." They got it. In tiny Tyronza—a town not forty miles southeast of Mississippi County—five hundred unemployed men gathered at the Odd Fellows Hall to hear some socialists speak and decide what to do. In Manila, just a stone's throw from where Bethel and Wallace had been arrested, some thirty or forty hungry and jobless tenant farmers undertook a "hunger march" straight down Main Street. All the merchants barricaded or locked their stores, and the city marshal removed all the cars in anticipation of the march. "There was no incident that came out of it," recorded one Mississippi County lawyer, "but it was a very ominous threat." Black farmers across the South began sitting in, walking off plantations, refusing to work for their Red Cross rations. Rumors flew that the Communist Party was plotting a sharecroppers' union.[4]

Although most sharecroppers lived in unsanitary, unpainted, unscreened shacks. Lacking in plumbing and virtually all worldly comforts, these were the only homes they had. The Depression, the drought, and the famine cost many of them these homes; New Deal crop reductions and increased mechanization added to the problem. As Morgan noted, the epidemic of poverty allowed elite planters to increase their land holdings "at bargain rates." Since these planters were often the only source of credit for small farmers, the elites could use foreclosure to obtain tremendous acreage. One survey from 1934 found that a fifth of the land of big plantations had been acquired through foreclosure. Tens of thousands of people were evicted in northeastern Arkansas. "Members of farm families throughout the Delta recalled friends and relatives losing their land, frequently after only one missed payment."[5]

It was the evictions that finally led a young dry cleaner and a gas station operator in Tyronza to found the Southern Tenant Farmers' Union (STFU), which represented nothing less than an attempt to overthrow the social order under which the poor farmers lived, labored, and, all too often, died. After one plantation owner (a financier who lived a state away) expelled twenty-three sharecropper families in July of 1934, eleven white and seven Black men, clad in overalls, gathered in a dingy one-room schoolhouse to plan a response. One was an experienced Black activist, another the son of a Klansman. Many had been evicted themselves. Weeks earlier, the dapper northern socialist and perennial presidential candidate Norman Thomas had visited Tyronza and toured the sharecroppers' shacks, muttering "deplorable, deplorable" as he went. He had told a rapt crowd of farmers that what they needed was a sharecroppers' union. The men assembled in the schoolhouse that hot summer night, speaking under the glow of kerosene lamps, agreed. Building on decades of populist-socialist organizing, legacies of resistance going back to slave revolts and farmers' alliances, and more specifically on months of demanding jobs and relief for poor farmers, the STFU founders called for decent wages, adequate land for food and crops, an end to crippling (and illegal) rates of interest, and the right to sell cotton at market price to anyone a worker chose. Although they knew it would be hard, their union would have to unite tenants and sharecroppers, Black and white. "We colored people can't organize without you, and you white folks can't organize without us," one Black man said at the first meeting. "Aren't we all brothers and ain't God the Father of us all?"

With the help of socialist allies, the farmers drew up a constitution calling for "one big union of all agricultural workers." First they sued the planter who had evicted twenty-three families. Then they started writing letters, raising money, trying to find homes for homeless farmers, and driving dirt roads by night to recruit new members. Several bone-tired unionists drove a thousand miles to Washington, D.C., and sat in at the Department of Agriculture until the secretary agreed to send an investigator down to the Delta. The STFU spread rapidly across northeastern Arkansas and beyond, bringing fed-up farmers and entire families to union meetings in church halls, masonic lodges, and living rooms, uniting them with religious and Marxist language of suffering, freedom, and justice. Many of the most fervent and convincing organizers were preachers. "The language of the Bible was like oxygen around them," wrote one historian. The recruits were starving and angry. And because more women than men were literate, many women became significant leaders in STFU locals. Within a year, the organizers claimed to have 25,000 members across the South.[6]

Organizing poor farmers into the union wasn't always easy. "True to its name, Mississippi County had been one of the most difficult counties to penetrate and organize," recalled one of the STFU's leaders. "No section of Arkansas is more slave-ridden or barren of anything that remotely resembles what we ordinarily think of as being culture than Mississippi County." For this very reason, the sharecroppers of Mississippi County were among the first to seek a union local, but their first meeting was barely underway when a posse of planters and deputy sheriffs burst into the church and told the assembled poor, "Git and don't never come back here for we ain't goin' to have our [n-words] spoiled by no damn union." The STFU was indefatigable, however, and over the following months, through meetings behind padlocked doors and boarded up windows, Mississippi Countians organized for their liberty.[7]

The planters struck back by expelling union members—or, to be clear, those suspected of being union members—from their homes with relish. By November 1934, more than twelve hundred sharecroppers had reportedly been evicted simply for joining the STFU.[8] Several hundred more families received eviction notices in December, just as the winter cold was setting in.[9]

This mass expulsion was complemented by the start of a concerted campaign of planter-backed violence.[10]

At the same time, local authorities began arresting union organizers for distributing union literature. Many towns in northeastern Arkansas simply banned public assemblies. One mayor declared, "Anyone can speak except the radicals."[11] It would quickly become clear to members of the STFU that they were not fighting evictions or censorship or vigilante violence in isolation. In the words of Nan Woodruff, the union members soon would realize that "fighting the evictions meant combatting the terror and torture that were entrenched in plantation life."[12]

Anxiety was in the air in Blytheville, Arkansas, at the end of 1934. Over a period of several weeks, recalled one observer, "an unusual number of robberies and other crimes were committed." Many of those robbed had been young people at "petting parties" on the highways out of town. There were even reports of some rapes. The crisis peaked in December when a prominent railroad official exchanged gunfire with a would-be bandit; the official was rushed to a Blytheville hospital while the robber, reportedly shot three times, made a daring escape. After that, local and county police enhanced their surveillance of the area, desperate to capture the elusive bandits.[13]

Early in 1935, Norman Thomas returned to the Arkansas Delta. Less than fifty miles from Mississippi County, he and several STFU members came across a man, a woman, and their five children, ages four to seventeen, all white, their belongings lying on a mound of dirt next to a ditch. The family had been evicted from "their miserable shack," recorded a journalist for *The Nation*. All they had left was a rusty old bed, some broken furniture and household possessions, and a crate with two small hogs and some chickens. The children held two puppies in their arms. "Why were they evicted?" the journalist asked. It wasn't just that the father was in the STFU, though he was. It was also that the summer before, a couple of mercenaries hired by elite planters to terrorize union members had raped the couple's fourteen-year-old daughter. When the couple complained and sought to have the rapists prosecuted, the father was arrested "on a trumped-up charge of 'stealing two eggs.' " After his release from jail, hired thugs beat him savagely, and then the entire family was evicted. The rapists kept their jobs.

"Who had ever heard of a share-cropper getting the law on a riding boss for the rape of his child?" *The Nation*'s journalist asked rhetorically. "That was unpardonable." After all, the justice system was designed to work for the big planters and their agents, not against them.[14]

7 • Clayton and Carruthers, 1935

Saturday, January 12, 1935, began as an unusually warm, albeit overcast, winter's day. Excitement was in the air. Newspapers across Arkansas carried the story of an exhausted Amelia Earhart completing the first ever solo flight from Hawaii to California, and the populist firebrand Huey Long made headlines by attacking President Franklin Roosevelt and demanding that the government "share the wealth." As evening fell, the temperature dropped. A cold snap was settling on the Delta, and the possibility of chilly rains hung over the residents like the increasingly angry clouds.[1]

Clarence H. Wilson, the sheriff of Mississippi County, and his deputy Arch Lindsey were sitting in a police car stopped along Highway 61, north of Blytheville. Lindsey sat in the front; Wilson sat in the back. The two men had parked near a notorious lovers' lane not far from the Blytheville Country Club's golf course. Wilson had returned from Arizona the night before, having gone there to extradite two men facing robbery and kidnapping charges. He was notorious among "the workers and Negroes," recorded a journalist for the *Daily Worker,* "because of his brutality in 'enforcing' the law." Known to his many friends as "Big Boy," Wilson had been elected sheriff in 1932, after serving as chief deputy sheriff for four years. Before that he'd worked for planter Robert E. Lee Wilson for fifteen years.[2]

Now, he and Lindsey were parked by this lovers' lane to try to catch the bandits who had been robbing many of the "petting" couples over the last few months; there had reportedly been two holdups earlier that day. The idea, the newspapers later reported, was "that the highjackers would show up" and try to rob them—"a method that officers had been following for a number of weeks without success." This night it would have near-deadly consequences.

As Wilson and Lindsey sat in the dark, two men crept up, one on either side of their car, and aimed flashlights inside. Seeing the two lawmen within, they reportedly opened fire. Bullets exploded through the windows, and a spray of flying glass struck Wilson in the face, leaving a gash running across the bridge of his nose and causing profound damage to his eyes. The men also shot at Deputy Lindsey, but they missed, instead blasting the knob off the car's radio. Finding himself unharmed, Lindsey fired back at the two men as they disappeared into the night. According to press reports, Lindsey briefly tried to pursue them, but Wilson's injuries were too great: Lindsey abandoned his pursuit to take his boss to the hospital.[3]

The Mississippi County police had long believed that the crime wave had been the fault of Black men, and the wounding—perhaps blinding, perhaps death—of the sheriff caused an instant, racist uproar. A posse of police and hastily deputized white citizens quickly spread across the countryside, bursting into the homes of Black people and searching for guns. "I suppose they were officers," recalled one Black man whose residence was searched. "They said they were officers." Heavily armed white men set up cordons across roads leading into Blytheville. According to one press report, "an intensive search started" for the shooters; according to another, "a drag-net was thrown out."[4]

Sheriff Wilson was sped to a Baptist hospital in Memphis, where, perhaps, the doctors might be able to save his eyes. The physicians delicately tried to remove the glass, and Wilson, in tremendous pain, could not sleep. His wife would join him in Memphis two days later.

Meanwhile, rumors flew around the county about the sheriff's condition, one claiming that "he had both eyes shot out." A common question was, "Do you reckon Wilson will die?" The white people of Mississippi County wanted blood. As one lawyer later recalled, "Because of this thing that was done to the Sheriff, the popular mind became so inflamed that it was almost dangerous for negroes, as it was agreed that negroes were committing these crimes, to even appear upon the streets of the city of Blytheville."[5]

Within a matter of hours, or so went the reports, a deputy sheriff spotted a car near where Wilson had been shot. It was a big, handsome, six-cylinder Chevrolet, exuberantly curved and with a tall grille in the front. It was parked a few hundred yards from the intersection of Highway 61 and a gravel road. Finding it suspicious, the deputy sheriff broke in and searched for incriminating evidence. Although he later claimed to have found several caps and white handkerchiefs with eyeholes cut out—things robbers could have used to obscure their identities—he did not find a weapon. Nonetheless, he had the car towed to the police station.[6]

According to press reports, the car's license plate number was quickly conveyed to the state revenue department in Little Rock, which sent back the name of the car's owner: Jim X. Carruthers, a Black man. Later there would be reason to doubt the veracity of this account.[7]

In any case, Carruthers himself showed up to the police station. He was there to report that his car had been stolen. "I didn't know they were waiting for someone to come along and claim the car," Carruthers would later testify, "but I sure found out about it." The newspapers labeled his appearance "a daring move." Delighted, the police took him into custody and, as one journalist wrote, the "grilling of Carruthers was started." Such a "grilling" involved no small amount of abuse. "They started whipping me," Carruthers would recall. "When they started whipping me and beating me I was scared to tell any more." Barely a year before, three Blytheville police had been convicted of assault and battery after they forced suspects to beat each other with rubber hoses. Such a conviction was rare; such a practice was not, especially when it came to the questioning of Black suspects.[8]

In the midst of the questioning, Blytheville's chief deputy sheriff returned from Memphis, where he had traveled to take Sheriff Wilson to the hospital. The other deputies gathered around the chief deputy, eager to hear word of Wilson's condition, leaving Carruthers temporarily guarded by only one man. According to press accounts, Carruthers asked this officer for a drink, and, when the officer left the room to get the water, Carruthers escaped through a small window. "I jumped out of the window and mozeyed away from there that night," he would recall.[9]

Minutes later, the police realized what had happened. With fury, they embarked on a frantic search.

It was the afternoon of January 13, just hours after the shooting, when the men began to gather. There were about forty or fifty of them, all white, armed with pistols. They were given a description of the man they were to seek. Then they descended on "Sawdust Bottom," the Black section of Blytheville, waving their guns, invading the homes of Black people, looking for Jim X. Carruthers. One journalist at the time claimed that the search "produced many weapons of various kinds but failed to effect the capture of Carruthers."[10]

According to the account passed down through generations of the Carruthers family, the men in the posse had been standing around the town square, getting more and more worked up until they came to resemble a lynch mob. Among the houses this mob attacked was the one belonging to Jim X., his wife, Lorraine, and their young daughter, Dora. As the mob made its way through the yard and toward the Carruthers house, Lorraine and Dora fled out the back, into the woods. They had to leave their land, their animals, all their valuables. The white men seized these, and the Carruthers family would never see their property again. In just a few minutes the tenuous prosperity they had eked out of Jim Crow Arkansas had been stolen from them. Lorraine and Dora found sanctuary in the nearby home of James and Virgie Carruthers, Jim X.'s parents. Jim X., however, wasn't with them.[11]

Meanwhile, the police and their hastily deputized associates had detained a "succession of negroes," as the newspaper put it, "and questioned [them] through the night." By the morning, the police claimed that a story had emerged: Jim X. Carruthers had shot Sheriff Wilson, and his partner had been a man known as Bubbles Clayton. At the same time that a posse was tearing through Sawdust Bottom and uprooting the Carruthers household, police captured Clayton in the unincorporated Mississippi County community called Armorel and dragged him to the jail in Osceola. Clayton did not resist.

At about 5:30 p.m., the police received a tip about Carruthers's location. They pursued it, descending on what the press labeled a "negro shack," a half mile northeast of Blytheville. "He offered no resistance when a squad of about six officers crashed open front and back doors of the shack and found him, shaking and unarmed." Jim X. Carruthers too was taken to the jail in Osceola.[12]

It was there that the police would start to question the two Black men, determined to elicit a confession to the shooting of the sheriff by whatever means necessary.

Bubbles Clayton has been living in Mississippi County "all my life," he would later testify, and had "been farming all my life for different white men." Born in 1914, he was not a particularly tall man—about five feet, nine inches— or a particularly heavy or scrawny one—166 pounds. By 1934, he was farming 10.79 acres, unaware he was about to become locally notorious and, soon, nationally famous.[13]

Bubbles came from a family of farmers. His parents were Edie (also called Edith) née Mitchell and Clay Clayton of DeSoto County, Mississippi. Clay's parents had come from Georgia; the origins of Edie's parents are unknown. Edie and Clay had married on April 16, 1898, when Edie was eighteen and Clay was nineteen. According to a census taker, Clay could neither read nor write, and he rented—not owned—the land he farmed. By 1900, the couple had two children, Isabella, known as Bell, and Missouri Lucile, sometimes just called Lucile. The Clayton family disappears from the historical record until 1920, when they pop up in Mississippi County, Arkansas, where Clay is once again listed on the census as a farmer. By then, the Claytons had five children living at home, including seven-year-old Clear. Bell appears to have left home, and Lucile has gotten married.[14]

Young Bubbles (sometimes called "Bubbers"—the origin of the nickname is unclear) had attended school only until the third grade, at which time he left to start working in the fields. His was a life without much privilege, without pretty much any upward mobility at all. In his first two decades, he left few traces on the historical record, except for a brief moment in August of 1931 when he was arrested for grand larceny in Missouri and sentenced to three years at the state prison in Jefferson City. Years later, his persecutors would make much of his incarceration; he would insist he'd been wrongly convicted, a claim that is impossible to verify but quite easy to believe.[15]

Jim X. Carruthers, on the other hand, had never been arrested, a fact that hardly mattered to his persecutors. Like Bubbles, he'd been born in Mississippi in about 1914, and like Bubbles he was a farmer with (according to state records) a third-grade education. Like Bubbles, he was five feet, nine inches (though Jim X. weighed at least twenty pounds less than Bubbles). Yet unlike Bubbles, Jim X. happened to be part of a family who could trace their antecedents back remarkably far.[16]

In the late 1700s, there was a slave named Naomi; her father was named Brown (or Browne), and in time she became known as Naomi Brown. Naomi lived and labored in South Carolina, but eventually she left and settled in Chickasaw County, Mississippi. By the time emancipation came she was an older woman, but she and her husband, Samuel Carruthers, had a large family and a fierce determination to support their children through their own labor. By the time Naomi died, she had saved up enough money to leave each of her children a not insubstantial sum. One of these children was Simon Carruthers, who married a woman named Adline and had a son named James; James, born in 1869, married a woman named Kate and also had a son named James. James Carruthers the younger became a farmer, and in about 1907 he married a woman named Virgie (also spelled Vergie). By 1910, James and Virgie owned their own home and farm in Chickasaw County.

James and Virgie had a number of children, but just three survived to adulthood: U.S., the eldest; Jim X., the youngest; and Sue Willie, the only daughter.

Jim X. grew up in rural Mississippi, the son of self-reliant farmers, and soon he began making money himself by working on a nearby hog farm. At some point, when Jim X. was still young, the family relocated to Mississippi County, Arkansas, where they had relatives. While still a teenager, Jim X. marry a young woman named Lorraine America Rusk. Soon, Lorraine would give birth to their daughter Dora, named for her grandmother.

Jim X. grew up to work the land, as had his father and generations of forbearers before him. But according to his descendants, Jim X. Carruthers was ever so slightly more prosperous than most of the other Black residents of Mississippi County. Over generations, he and his family had acquired some of the trappings of wealth, including a new car, Jim X.'s handsome Chevrolet. The car was more than a status symbol—although, of course, it was that too—for it also allowed Jim X. to transport other cotton workers to plantations, for which he was compensated. To be a Black man so conspicuously successful in a Jim Crow serfdom was to be labeled a troublemaker.[17] By the first days of 1935, whether he knew it or not, Jim X. had a target on his back. Then he was arrested.

The jail in Osceola was a plain, squat, three-story brick of a building, with two doors and sixteen tall windows in the front, most lined with bars. It was the twin of the county jail in Blytheville—both had been constructed in 1924 at a cost of $50,000 each—but the one in Osceola was overseen by a "legendary" man named Mr. Gwaltney. Mr. Gwaltney carried a large set of keys, and with these he controlled who came in and who was allowed to go free. It appears that most of the people who came in were Black men. Years earlier, a newspaper report described the jail that then existed in Osceola as populated primarily by "many gentlemen of color"—"benighted sons of Ham" who "have a penchant for tossing the dice, pulling the trigger, or wielding the razor, or selling a little wine or a little beer 'for the stomach's sake,' and such like."[18]

When the police arrested Bubbles Clayton, they took him briefly to the police station in Blytheville, but after just a short time they carried him to the jail in Osceola. Yet the authorities did not put him in a cell; instead, they brought him to the front and "started whipping me," he would recall. "Mr. Arch Lindsey, Mr. Hale Jackson and Mr. Ran Miller"—all deputies—"and the jailer, and there was one more. . . . They come talked to me telling me lots of stuff and asked me didn't I do it, and they said they were going to whip me and going to take me out and shoot me full of holes." They threatened to tie him to a telephone post before they shot him. The whipping, Clayton maintained, was lacking in all mercy. But still, he refused to confess to anything.

After a while, the police grew tired and paused the beating. By this point, Clayton was laying on the floor, unable to stand up, so the police dumped cold water on him, pulled him up, and sat him in a chair. As he sat there, bruised and bloody, another prisoner—a white man—came over and said, "Just go ahead and tell them anything you want to keep them from killing you. If you don't, they are going to kill you."[19]

It was Sunday evening, about a day after the shooting, when the police brought in Jim X. Carruthers. Then they started beating him. "They uncovered my back and took a rubber hose and pulled up my clothes and one got on the ladder and put his feet on my hands and just beat me until the blood ran out," Carruthers would remember. They wanted him to admit to shooting Sheriff Wilson. "They whipped me and I said 'No' and he hit me across the head and beat me up." The cops—led by the most vicious deputy, Arch Lindsey—kicked him in the mouth until several of his teeth came out. Yet Carruthers wouldn't confess either.[20]

Late the following night, on Monday, January 14, a man arrived at the Osceola jail. He introduced himself as the prosecutor from Carruthersville, Missouri, and he told Deputy Sheriff Lindsey that a young, white woman in Missouri had reported that two Black men had raped her while she was visiting Mississippi County, Arkansas, and that he believed Clayton and Carruthers were these two Black men. The prosecutor asked Lindsey to hand them over so he could take them back to Carruthersville and charge them with rape. Lindsey refused. "I told them I couldn't do it; that the Sheriff was in the hospital and I had charges against them here," he recalled.[21]

Sheriff Wilson was lying in his hospital bed in Memphis, unable to see and wracked with pain, when he received a phone call from Lindsey. The deputy sheriff told him about the prosecutor and the young white woman, but he added something else: the prosecutor had warned him that a posse of angry white men from Missouri was on its way to Osceola, determined to lynch Clayton and Carruthers. Time was short. Cars were racing toward Mississippi County as they spoke. What did the sheriff wish for him to do, Lindsey asked. "I told him the very best we could do would be to move these boys from that jail to Tucker farm and if anything happened we would have them out of the way," Wilson would later testify.[22]

About forty men from Missouri had made it to Blytheville and were almost at Osceola when the deputies decided to act. With mere seconds to spare, the police hustled Clayton and Carruthers out of the jail under cover of darkness and into a nearby cornfield at the edge of town. They told the two prisoners to keep down, as the cars were pulling up outside of the jailhouse, and to keep out of the glare of the headlights. In the cornfield, ensconced amid tall, naked stalks of corn, the white cops told the Black men that a mob was after them.

The mob was not that easily deterred. It was the middle of the night, but the white men from Missouri were blazing through Mississippi County, determined to find, and murder, Clayton and Carruthers in response to the white woman's rape allegation. One car had apparently trailed the Black men to the cornfield. Feeling they had few other options, the deputies hurried their prisoners into a police car and sped toward Memphis. Clayton, Carruthers, and Deputy Lindsey sat wedged in the back seat, a deputy named Hale Jackson was driving, and a third deputy sat in the passenger seat.

The men from Missouri spotted the car as it drove away. They took off in hot pursuit. For twenty-five or thirty miles, the cars of the lynch mob tailed the car of the cops, driving at top speed. Clayton and Carruthers huddled in the backseat, terrified, with Clayton begging the deputies not to "let those men following us hang me." Several times, the mob's car came close. All Clayton and Carruthers could see throughout the dark chase was the sickening flash of headlights.

But the deputies managed to outrun their pursuers; about halfway to Memphis the lynch mob fell away. In its absence, the police resumed their questioning. Clayton recalled, "They kept asking me what in the hell did I want to shoot at them, I told them 'I didn't shoot at you,' and they told me, 'You are a liar.'"

Early on the morning of Tuesday, January 15, the deputies delivered their two prisoners safely to Memphis. For four days, Clayton and Carruthers remained in a prison there, and then the deputies took them back to Arkansas and to Tucker, the state prison farm. There, the two men were placed on death row, ostensibly for their own protection.

In the meantime, the press began reporting that the two had not only shot Sheriff Wilson but also had committed the spate of lovers' lane robberies, as well as "other crimes committed against women victims of hold-ups." One Missouri prosecutor began making noise about seeking to try Clayton and Carruthers himself. "The negroes are said to have admitted to an attack on a young white girl of the Holland vicinity," reported the *Blytheville Courier-News*, though they had admitted no such thing. "It was reported that the negroes held up and robbed a young couple, then attacked the girl, threatening both with guns and death." Such unsubstantiated coverage made sure that the white populace remained riled up; it also sold papers. Hoping to forestall violence, the reporters assured their readers that Clayton and Carruthers were truly out of the state, and that it would be "an imposition" on the injured sheriff were any violence to befall his assailants "during his absence from the county."[23]

The reporters also noted, in passing, that the police had arrested Jim X. Carruthers's mother, Virgie, on a charge of "receiving stolen property." Apparently, the authorities had found a car radio in her kitchen and claimed it was stolen. For weeks, possibly months, the middle-aged housewife remained behind bars, unable to pay the $1,000 bond. The newspapers reported that her hearing was repeatedly delayed; it certainly appears that the powers that be were deliberately delaying her opportunity for release. Press accounts of Virgie's travails disappear after a few articles, but her son's lawyer ultimately interceded and negotiated her discharge. Soon after her release, she and her husband, James, fled the state forever, eventually making their way two hundred miles north to the home of Jim X.'s sister, Sue Willie, in East St. Louis.[24]

The newspapers also reported breathlessly, and in more detail, on Sheriff Wilson's recovery. Within days the front pages confirmed that his eyes were improving and "out of danger." By the following week he was back at the office, although his eyes remained covered by dark-tinted glasses. He told the newspapers that he was confident that "the negro bandits who fired on him would eventually receive the death penalty."

"Not, however, he was careful to point out, for their attack on him," the paper continued, "but for more serious crimes confessed by the pair who have alleged admitted a series of 'petting party' hold-ups, mistreatment of white women, and other offenses."[25]

Yet even as Bubbles Clayton and Jim X. Carruthers were being spirited across state lines and back, narrowly avoiding a hideous death only to be delivered to death row for crimes they had never confessed to, neither had yet heard any intimation that they might be charged with rape.

January 15, 1935 was another cool, overcast day in an unsettled Mississippi County, but tempers were running hot.[26] "REMOVE NEGROES AS CROWD THREATENS," screamed a banner headline on the front page of the *Blytheville Courier-News*, recounting Clayton's and Carruthers's close call.[27] Yet the near lynching was far from the only violent moment that week. That evening—just three days after the shooting, two days after the arrest, and a day after the attempted murder—Ward Rodgers, a young, white Methodist minister and local STFU official, slender and boyish, arrived at a union hall in Marked Tree, Arkansas, not fifty miles from Blytheville. It was dark outside, but Rodgers lit up the room with a fiery speech decrying the evils of the sharecropping system, his voice booming out across a crowd of thousands. The assembled men and women had walked or ridden all day, on mules and broken-down automobiles, to get there. "It was to be a big day," recorded one STFU leader: "*It was their day.*" With the violence against union members clearly on his mind—and perhaps other violence in contemplation as well—Rodgers closed with a warning to the "respectable citizens" threatening to lynch union members: "that is a game two can play." He continued, "You know if I wanted to do so, I could lead a lynch mob to lynch any plantation owner in Poinsett County." For a moment, a shocked silence filled the room. Breath caught in throats. Then, as the STFU's founder later recalled, "about 1500 hats went up in the air." In the words of one historian, the "crowd went crazy." Rodgers was quickly arrested and charged with, among other things, blasphemy and anarchy.

The trouble with Ward Rodgers had started a few days earlier. Some of the big planters had objected to sharecroppers learning to read, write, and, especially, do arithmetic. When Rodgers visited the school superintendent and told him that "this sounded like Ku Klux ideas," the superintendent replied that "he could call it whatever he wanted but he might find himself strung up on a telephone pole, if he did not leave." Yet Rodgers would not leave. In fact, at the packed STFU meeting on January 15, Rodgers committed the unpardonable sin of referring to a Black man as "Mister." That, as much as his boast about lynching the bosses, led to his arrest that night. "We've had a pretty serious situation here," one local man told a reporter for the *New York Times*, "what with the mistering of these [n-words]." Rodgers was taken to jail in Harrisburg, then moved to Jonesboro for "safekeeping." A few days later, he received a trial before a Marked Tree justice of the peace. A jury, consisting mostly of planters, quickly convicted him.[28]

After this the STFU had to go "underground" for a while. It moved its headquarters—really just a backroom in a dry-cleaning shop—from Arkansas to Tennessee, the union officers depending on "dark nights, fast cars, and back roads to get them in and out of the state safely." In the days that followed Rodgers's arrest, plantation agents arrested, attacked, and attempted to murder numerous STFU leaders. The leaders lived, one chronicler wrote, "without sleep, without food, and often without hope—but never without faith in the ultimate triumph of their cause." The founders sent a telegram to Norman

Thomas, summarizing the mood of the county and the region in just three words: "Entire population terrorized." Henry Wallace, the left-leaning secretary of agriculture, dispatched a pioneering female attorney to sit in at Rodgers's trial. He was convicted in just fifteen minutes and sentenced to six months in prison. The attorney, meanwhile, spent weeks collecting affidavits from hundreds of Arkansas sharecroppers. Her eventual report on their oppression was so explosive that even Wallace ordered the department to bury it and do nothing. To this day, the report has never surfaced.[29]

The threat of violence was constant and terrifying that winter. One meeting of forty or fifty sharecroppers, all of them Black, began with the singing of the union song, "We Shall Not Be Moved," and ended with four or five heavily armed, very drunk white men bursting in and nearly lynching the attendees. Twenty-six union families, living not seventy-five miles from Mississippi County, were evicted. Plantation thugs threatened them with guns to try to get them to name other union members; two older Black men were beaten with leather straps because the planters believed they were members. Lynch mobs and assassins continued to pursue STFU leaders. National newspapers started writing about the "Sharecropper War" in eastern Arkansas.[30]

Still, the farmers of the Delta were not deterred. Thousands gathered for a meeting in February, where they again sang "We Shall Not Be Moved" and meant it. Union members still in Arkansas began stockpiling guns, establishing a system of mutual protection and self-defense. "We're not gonna let them . . . just come in and kill us out," one sharecropper recalled hearing other members say. "So we gon' be prepared." One union leader recalled seeing several "tough-looking white and black men, wearing overalls and jumpers, lined up against the walls" at a meeting; he worried they were there to cause trouble, but then he learned that they were there to protect the meeting, with Winchester rifles and shotguns jammed down the legs of their overalls.[31]

As winter turned to spring, the reign of terror intensified. The violence "ripped into the country like a hurricane," wrote one STFU leader. Planters and their minions declared open season on the organizers; masked men emerged from the darkness to attack union meetings; law enforcement officers frequently sanctioned the violence or even joined in themselves. They bombed and burned more churches and schoolhouses, attempted to assassinate more union leaders. Machine gun fire strafed homes, and numerous members were falsely accused of all manner of mischief and hauled off to jail. The STFU's founder recalled that he was "almost constantly engaged thereafter in getting union workers out of jail."[32] A New England ally offered to buy the STFU an armored car, decked out with a loudspeaker. "This idea was rejected in Memphis on the grounds that sending a small tank into Arkansas would be an invitation to further violence." When an armed lynch mob came to the home of one Mississippi County union member, his wife "died of fright."[33] Even as Clayton and Carruthers remained in jail, armed planter mercenaries patrolled the highways, looking for union leaders.[34]

In the midst of the violence, Norman Thomas arrived to speak in the small town of Birdsong, in Mississippi County. Dissatisfaction coursed through the county, and some five hundred people gathered to hear Thomas, most of them Black. Howard Kester, a lanky, radical preacher, climbed the steps of the church to introduce Thomas, who was white. Yet as soon as he said "ladies and gentleman," an angry, armed white man pushed his way forward and yelled, "There ain't no ladies here, and there ain't no gentleman on the platform. That God damned white-headed Yankee son-of-a-bitch can go back North where he come from." This man and thirty or forty burly allies (including, reportedly, Mississippi County sheriff Clarence Wilson) jumped up the church steps and pushed Kester and Thomas off the podium. Violence broke out as white supremacist thugs beat the largely Black crowd members. Brandishing a copy of the Bill of Rights above his head, the tall, striking Thomas found himself pushed roughly through the crowd. He was thrown into a waiting automobile and warned "never to return again."[35]

"Go on, you son of a bitch," the leader of the white mob yelled at a reporter for the Associated Press, "get the hell out of Mississippi County."[36]

This incident was followed with weeks of still more violence.[37] Clayton and Carruthers remained in jail.

It was revealing when, that spring, one band of planter-backed vigilantes began wearing armbands decorated with an insignia that was soon to become notorious: a swastika.[38]

Death row at the Tucker Prison Farm was foul, ominous, and small. It consisted of four cramped cells, organized in what one lawyer called "a kind of oblong cage . . . one, two, three, four . . . in a line," isolated from the rest of the sprawling penal plantation and providing a lonely, last waystation for men condemned to die. When Bubbles Clayton and Jim X. Carruthers arrived there in January 1935, several of the cells were occupied; the two Black men would have seen other death row inmates, Black and white, staring warily back at them, these newcomers in their midst. In one cell resided a white lawyer, Mark Shank, said to have murdered his wife and two children with poison; in another were Frank Barnes and his sons, white men who had reportedly murdered a Blytheville taxi driver; in a third cell was Ed Johnson, a Black man who had allegedly slashed his wife's throat. And in the last cell, at the end of the short hall, was a Black man named Green Phillips, convicted of murdering a railroad agent and captured by Sheriff Clarence Wilson. It was into this last cell, with Phillips, that Clayton and Carruthers were thrown. The cell had three beds and not much else.[39]

For weeks, Clayton and Carruthers remained on death row awaiting trial, alone but for the condemned men and the parade of sightseers who came by regularly to gawk at the violent criminals of Arkansas. Clayton and Carruthers usually just ignored the sightseers. So, at first, they didn't pay too much attention when Sheriff Wilson, Deputy Sheriff Arch Lindsey, and a young white man and woman walked onto death row one day in March 1935. Two sharply divergent accounts of the interaction have survived.[40]

According to Clayton and Carruthers, shortly before Wilson, Lindsey, and the young man and woman arrived, the superintendent of Tucker had rushed in and ordered Green Phillips out of the shared cell. The superintendent told him to go in Ed Johnson's cell, get into Johnson's bed, and cover himself with the covers: "Get in there and keep your head covered," he barked.

That left Clayton and Carruthers alone in their cell. The visitors from Blytheville came in. "Bubbles, what is the matter with your hand?" asked Lindsey.

"That is where you fastened the handcuffs too tight," Clayton responded.

"Get up, Jim X., come here," said Wilson.

"Come here, Jim X.," echoed Lindsey.

Jim X. did as commanded.

"You are getting fat," the sheriff added.

After that, Clayton and Carruthers just stood there, in their cell, as the visitors stared at them. After about three minutes, the unknown man and woman left; Wilson and Lindsey conferred for a moment, said some hostile things to the prisoners, and then asked the man and woman to come back in a second time. They stayed for another while, and then the visitors left.[41]

According to the police, this interaction happened differently. Wilson and Lindsey had driven a young man, Wiley Bryant, and a young woman named Virgie to Tucker and walked them to death row, but they hadn't gone into the cell block with them. Instead, the superintendent had instructed the couple to "pick out the negroes" and cautioned them to pick carefully. In this version of events, neither Wilson nor Lindsey said anything, certainly not the two prisoners' names, and neither gestured toward the two. Wiley and Virgie simply stood there, staring at Clayton and Carruthers—who were wearing blue overalls and blue jackets—for a handful of minutes. And then they left.

"If my memory serves me right, there wasn't a word spoken until they walked out and then I went back and talked to Bubbles and I think Clarence did," Lindsey claimed. "I talked to both of them. If there was a word passed, I don't remember it until after this couple walked out."

As Virgie and Wiley exited death row, Wilson would recall, "the girl whispered to me as she went out the ones in the far cell are the ones who attacked her. None of us indicated which cell they were in."[42]

This brief interaction would thus take on considerable significance, because Virgie and Wiley had been brought to Tucker that day with the express intention of identifying the two Black men who had allegedly assaulted Wiley and raped Virgie. It mattered, therefore, whether the two policemen had shaped, guided, or outright directed the identification.

"None of us indicated which cell they were in," Wilson would later insist.[43]

"There had previously been a third Negro in the cell with them but he had been taken out, placed in another cell and forced to get in bed and cover up his head, so that there could be no possibility of mistaken identity when Sheriff Lindsey brought the two prosecuting witnesses to make the identification," Clayton's and Carruthers's lawyers would counter.[44]

Further, Clayton and Carruthers would insist that this identification was the police making good on a threat from months before. While the deputies were beating Clayton that night in Osceola, he would claim, "they kept telling me that they were going to bring a white woman to identify me. I said 'bring her on here, then. There isn't any one can identify me, I have been with these white folks, and I was born there, raised here, and I know how to get along with them.' "[45] In other words, if the police couldn't pin the shooting of Wilson on them, they would pin this other crime on them.

In the days, weeks, and months that followed, the rape trial of Bubbles Clayton and Jim X. Carruthers would generate ravenous media interest, resulting in thousands of stories, dwarfing even the extensive coverage of the trial of Frank Bethel and Mike Wallace. Among these many pieces, one stands out for connecting the violence inside the courts and prisons to the roiling tensions without. The *Daily Worker* would run a lengthy article denouncing the charges against the "two young Negro cotton pickers" as a "frame-up." They were accused of rape because "this is the one way that remains for the planters to terrorize the share-croppers, both black and white, who are banding together in the Southern Tenant Farmers Union," claimed the *Worker.* "This town of 4,000 is in the heart of the cotton region of Arkansas and the plantation owners have used every tactic to smash the union but have failed."

The planter class was "frightened," the *Worker* continued with obvious glee. "A year ago there was little or no organization; today ninety per cent of the croppers and wage workers are members of the Southern Tenant Farmers Union. A year ago not a single copy of the Daily Worker was sold in Blytheville; today workers and farmers buy a hundred copies a week."

Alarmed at this wave of resistance, the planters and their allies in government were using the law to intimidate workers, to create an example, to issue a warning. In the words of the *Worker,* "Thus it is that Clayton and Carruthers are incarcerated in the Tucker Farm penitentiary waiting to drag their weary feet along the last mile to death."

But all was not lost, not yet. The *Worker* demanded that its readers send in money to support "these two innocent cotton pickers." Clayton and Carruthers "will soon die unless their defense is broadened and the case is brought to the attention of great numbers of workers."[46] If the workers of the world—or at least the county—would unite behind their defense, perhaps these two Black men had a chance.

8 • Mr. Freeman, Mid-1930s

For a long time, Marguerite Johnson assumed that her parents were dead. Why else would they have abandoned her, left her and Bailey in Stamps while they got to live in "a heaven called California," where the sun shone all the time and you could have all the oranges you could eat? When, one Christmas, presents arrived from their parents in Long Beach, Marguerite and Bailey were crushed; their parents were not dead after all. "The gifts opened the door to questions that neither of us wanted to ask," Marguerite later wrote. "Why did they send us away? and What did we do so wrong?"[1]

A year later, their father, Bailey Johnson Sr., arrived in Stamps with no advance notice. He just pulled up to the Store one morning in a freshly scrubbed gray de Soto, sending the entire household into an uproar. For seven-year-old Marguerite, her entire world "humpty-dumptied, never to be put back together again."

Marguerite was astounded by her father's bigness—he was tall and broad and muscular, packed into too tight clothing, "blindingly handsome." Over six feet tall and weighing in at some two hundred pounds, Bailey Sr. was indeed a large man, dark in complexion, with what his daughter later remembered as overly proper, "school principal" English and a "smile as slick as brilliantine." He was Momma's son, born in Stamps in 1897, a resident of this small Arkansas town until World War I expanded his horizons forever. On December 4, 1917, just months after the United States entered the Great War, twenty-year-old Bailey—a private in a Black unit—had departed from Hoboken, New Jersey, aboard a ship named for George Washington, heading to France. According to his daughter, he had run away from home to enlist. Two years later, a battle-hardened corporal with a fake French accent, Bailey returned stateside.[2]

According to later chroniclers, Bailey Johnson, though a "son of the rural South," could no longer abide the "South's blatant, violent oppression," so sometime in the early 1920s he left, "one among the legions of Black migrants drawn north . . . in search of a better life." Bailey made his way to St. Louis, one of tens of thousands of Black refugees who, together, doubled the city's Black population between the world wars. It was there that the dashing former soldier met Vivian Baxter, the eldest child in a large, boisterous family.

Vivian was born in 1912, and, when she met Bailey in 1924, she was just twelve years old. In later recollections, Marguerite would describe Vivian as "tough"—picking fights with the roughest boys in the neighborhood, climbing the tallest trees, joining her brothers (known locally as the "Bad Baxters") as they beat up those who crossed them. Yet Marguerite did not address their age gap—startling, and unlawful, by modern standards. She wrote, simply, that her father and mother "were unable to restrain themselves. They fell in love while Vivian's brothers walked around him threateningly." Eventually, Vivian told them to "lay off," and, in spite of her parents' concerns that she was marrying a southerner who was neither a doctor nor a lawyer, the two soon wed.[3]

In 1927, Vivian would give birth to her first child, Bailey Johnson Jr. The next year, on April 4, 1928, Marguerite was born. Shortly thereafter, the young Johnson family would make their way west, to Long Beach, California. There, Bailey Sr. would find a job as a doorman at a nice hotel. Later chroniclers—including Marguerite herself—would suggest that the problems in the Johnson marriage sprang up after their move to California, but there is reason to believe tensions had arisen earlier. In the spring of 1930, shortly before moving to California, Vivian, Marguerite, and Bailey Jr. were recorded as living in Vivian's parents' house on Hickory Street; Bailey Sr. appears to have been living several blocks away.

In any case, their marriage was not long for the world. "My parents soon proved to each other that they couldn't stay together," Marguerite would later write. "They were matches and gasoline. They even argued about how they were to break up. Neither wanted the responsibility of taking care of two toddlers. They separated and sent me and Bailey to my father's mother in Arkansas."[4] But four years later, when Marguerite was seven years old, her father returned to Stamps, and reentered her life.

For three weeks, the residents of Stamps stopped by the Store to gawk at Bailey Johnson Sr., the prodigal son returned. He was so handsome, he spoke so properly; many probably assumed, as Marguerite did, that he was rich and lived in a castle out in California. (He was a doorman at the Breakers Hotel in Santa Monica.) Each day Marguerite was terrified that he would leave and return to California. When he finally announced that he was, she felt relieved; the silent threat would hang over her no longer. But then he said he would take her and Bailey Jr. with him. The joy of it shot through Marguerite like electricity, followed later by terrible self-doubt.

Wearing clothes Momma had sewn just days earlier, Marguerite sat in the back of the car, boxed in by her father's leather suitcases and her own cardboard boxes, as they drove north. Bailey bonded with their father, his namesake, while Marguerite stewed in the back. Soon, her father revealed that they were actually going to St. Louis, to see the children's mother, Vivian, who had returned to that city to live with her family. Marguerite was terrified: suppose her mother didn't like her?

Marguerite would later describe their arrival in St. Louis in her most vivid prose. The city was "a new kind of hot and a new kind of dirty." She compared it to hell, with her father the "delivering devil." Her mother, on the other hand, she compared to "a hurricane in its perfect power. Or the climbing, falling colors of a rainbow." Her mother's beauty "literally assailed me." Sitting in her grandparents' over-furnished living room, Marguerite thought Vivian was the most stunning woman she'd ever seen. She wore lipstick. She danced. When Bailey Sr. departed for California a few days later, Marguerite was neither happy nor sad. He was a stranger, and he was leaving them with more strangers.[5]

In response to white fears of an influx of Black migrants, municipal officials and real estate brokers in St. Louis had forced Black people into a handful of neighborhoods, where most of the available housing was in tiny, cramped apartments, lacking indoor toilets, running water, and even ovens. Poverty and crime were rampant; young Marguerite witnessed gambling and prostitution and learned the names of the men on the street corner who ran numbers, sold lottery tickets, and dispensed whiskey. But Black St. Louis was also "rich in decency and generous in support," wrote the historian Walter Johnson; it was where Black people "turned segregation into congregation," wrote another historian, Earl Lewis. When Marguerite enrolled in the shockingly grand Toussaint L'Overture Grammar School, Johnson noted, the future comedian Dick Gregory was coming of age on the other side of town; the entertainer Josephine Baker was developing her routine; Chuck Berry and Miles Davis were starting to make music; James "Cool Papa" Bell was learning baseball;

and Sonny Liston, the future boxer and another Arkansas native, would soon arrive in town.[6]

Marguerite and Bailey got to know their tough, young uncles, and some months later they moved in with Vivian. "Mother's boyfriend, Mr. Freeman, lived with us, or we lived with him (I never knew which)," Marguerite would later write. "He was a Southern, too, and big."[7]

In St Louis, Marguerite often had nightmares. She would wake up sweating. On particularly bad nights, her mother would take her into the big bed she shared with Mr. Freeman. After many such nights, Marguerite grew accustomed to the arrangement. But one morning after Vivian left early to run an errand, Marguerite woke up to Mr. Freeman molesting her. His heart was beating so fast that she was afraid he might die—and then she would never get free from under him.

Afterward, he asked her if she loved her brother, Bailey. "Yes," Marguerite replied. "If you ever tell anybody what we did, I'll have to kill Bailey," Mr. Freeman said.

In the months that followed, Mr. Freeman stopped speaking to her. Then, one Saturday in spring, he raped her. Marguerite was eight-years-old. Mr. Freeman turned the radio up too loud. "If you scream, I'm gonna kill you. And if you tell, I'm gonna kill Bailey," he told her.

Marguerite passed out, convinced she had died. She had not. Yet as that weekend progressed, she began to wish she would die. She was sweating and terrified. When Bailey tried to change her bedclothes, he dislodged the stained panties she had hidden under her mattress. Her mother took Marguerite to the hospital. Bailey asked her who had hurt her. "When I explained that I couldn't tell because the man would kill him, Bailey said knowingly, 'He can't kill me. I won't let him.' And of course I believed him. Bailey didn't lie to me. So I told him."[8]

Although young Marguerite certainly did not know it, sexual violence enacted against Black women and girls had gone unpunished for centuries. This was true of violence perpetrated by white men, and—as in Marguerite's case—violence perpetrated by Black men.

In the decades before the Civil War, white men routinely raped enslaved women and suffered no legal or social consequences for doing so. Though this reality has been obscured and deliberately clouded by selective recordkeeping and the passage of time, scholars have looked to census records and noted the undeniably high rate of mixed-race births in the South—a rate that *grew* as the country hurtled toward the Civil War. Even more compelling evidence can be found in writings from the time. "Southern women often marry a man knowing that he is the father of many little slaves," wrote Harriet Jacobs, who had herself escaped from slavery in part to escape her master's sexual aggression, in 1861. Indeed, as the historian Darlene Clark Hine noted, "Virtually every known nineteenth-century female slave narrative contains a reference to, at some juncture, the ever present threat and reality of rape." Abolitionists made much of this fact. They labeled the South "one vast brothel" or "one great Sodom," and when a young William Lloyd Garrison was asked, "How should you like to have a black man marry your daughter?" he replied that "slaveholders generally should be the last persons to affect fastidiousness on that point; for they seem to be enamoured with amalgamation." Perhaps James Baldwin put it best a century later when he told a white southerner in a televised debate, "You're not worried about me marrying your daughter. You're worried about me marrying your *wife's* daughter. I've been marrying your daughter ever since the days of slavery."[9]

Emancipation did not end the sexual violence white men inflicted on Black women. "If anything," wrote the historian Laura Edwards, "emancipation heightened the vulnerability of African American women to violence at the hands of white men, who used rape and other ritualized forms of sexual abuse to limit black women's freedom and to reinscribe antebellum racial hierarchies." Rape remained a politically, economically, and socially useful tool for white supremacists, a threat to maintain the profitably oppressive status quo on a day-to-day basis. Klansmen regularly raped Black women, as did these women's white neighbors—a phenomenon that was often covered up or ignored by government officials at the time. Again, these white men suffered few consequences for their actions. Although rape statutes became technically race-neutral in the years after the Civil War, practically speaking Black women still "had no hope of recourse through the legal system."[10]

The legal system likewise offered little refuge to Black women and girls enduring sexual violence at the hands of Black men. "Black women's literature is full of the pain of frequent assault, not only by a racist patriarchy, but also by black men," the writer Audre Lorde has noted. Yet relatively few such incidents survive in the existing documentary record, much less led to prosecutions.[11] Meanwhile, white authorities seized on cases of Black men raping Black women or girls to "prove" the supposed innate immorality of Black people and justify the necessity of lynching. In fact, white intellectuals argued that Black men's purported propensity for rape was *the fault* of Black women—that "the sexual laxness of plantation women as a class" led Black men to lack any understanding of sexual boundaries or limits.[12] Even some Black male leaders blamed Black women for crimes committed by Black men.[13] And, as the sociologist Patricia Hill Collins has noted, these leaders proposed as a solution the installation of "a Black male patriarchy in which Black men would protect 'their' women from sexual assault," which "inadvertently supported ideas about women's bodies and sexuality as men's property."[14]

In response to the indifference or hostility of authorities, Black women began waging what the historian Estelle Freedman has called "a counteroffensive," launching an audacious campaign against their own sexual victimization by white, as well as Black, men. Although they could not vote, many Black women vocally demanded intervention from the federal government; they testified in court; they reported rapes to the authorities; they powerfully asserted their sexual respectability in the face of a culture that marginalized and belittled them. From the poor Black mother filing charges against a white attempted rapist in North Carolina in 1869 to the remarkable Black journalist Ida B. Wells decrying the "wholesale contemptuous defamation of [Black] women," the counteroffensive spanned the spectra of age, class, and geography. "We poor colored women wage-earners in the South are fighting a terrible battle," wrote one Black nurse in 1912. "On the one hand, we are assailed by white men, and, on the other hand, we are assailed by black men, who should be our natural protectors." Alone on the battlefield, many Black women used all the weapons at their disposal to protect themselves—literally, if necessary.[15]

The journalist Wells—born into slavery in Mississippi, freed in infancy, orphaned at sixteen—used her own newspaper, the *Memphis Free Speech and Headlight,* to challenge the very foundations of Jim Crow society, marshaling statistics and reportage to disprove the claim that Black-on-white rape caused most lynchings, and suggesting that "the focus and attention placed on the alleged black rapist masked the rape of black women." As the historian Crystal Feimster has noted, "Wells drew no distinctions between white men who raped black women and those who lynched black men"—to her, fighting for Black men necessitated advocating for Black women. Wells's blazing editorials eventually led a lynch mob to scour the streets of Memphis for her, ultimately destroying her offices when they discovered that she was out of town. Yet Wells—later Wells-Barnett—would not stop writing. Indeed, during the last decade of the nineteenth century, she joined other female activists in the anti-lynching and Black clubwomen movements to campaign for the rights and sexual autonomy of Black women. These well-to-do Black women founded organizations and wrote letters and articles, decrying any who impugned the respectability of Black women. They held conferences and conventions and lobbied for raising the age of consent in many states in an effort to protect Black girls from predatory white men. White female activists often built on the work of Black women—and took credit for their earlier successes, as well.[16]

While Black activists understandably shied from highlighting cases of Black men raping Black women or girls—worried about reinforcing cultural scripts that already depicted rape as "the Negro crime"—some broke even this taboo and spoke out about intraracial sexual violence too. As multiple historians have documented, Black women increasingly turned to courts and accused Black men of sexual assault in the late nineteenth and early twentieth centuries. They also turned increasingly to Black-run newspapers, which began reporting on intraracial sexual violence, albeit usually "within the context of white men's improprieties." Estelle Freedman recounted one article in the *Afro-American*, narrating a group of Black men making "vulgar insinuations" toward a passing Black girl and then a white man, having observed the incident, following the girl and making an "indecent proposal." "Naturally," the article intoned, "when he saw the men of her own race insulted her, he felt he too could do so with impunity."[17]

Through such means, prominent, educated, Black activists broke the conspiracy of silence that had long shrouded sexual violence. Yet these same activists frequently attempted to appeal to the better angels of the white public by drawing a distinction between the "higher" and "lower" classes of Black people, contrasting "the beastly men who assaulted women and the better sort of blacks who condemned them." Although they did not blame poor Black women for their own victimization, they nonetheless sought to "uplift" the poorer segments of the Black populace in order to convince the white public that they too deserved legal protection. At the heart of their campaigns was the relentless promotion of "chastity" within the Black community—which, as the historian Deborah Gray White has noted, unwittingly "placed the burden of sexual exploitation and social improvement on the shoulders of the victim." Such tactics rankled more radical Black activists, like Wells herself; after just a few years, she broke with Black clubwomen and found common cause with organizations more in sync with her confrontational politics. She argued that Black people would never achieve true freedom with "uplift"—what they needed was power and, if necessary, force. Wells wrote that "a Winchester rifle should have a place of honor in every black home for the protection which the law refused to give."[18]

More than a century later, Marguerite—writing under her chosen name of Maya Angelou—would pen a poem about the "ancestors" who had opened doors for her, had endowed her with the ability to fight for freedom and justice. They reached out to her, lifted her, urged her on, provided strength. Harriet Tubman and Ida B. Wells, she wrote in one line, left her their "courage."[19]

Marginalized, ignored, and often abused, Black women nonetheless fought against violence and oppression in the early years of the twentieth century. Marguerite's mother resisted poverty and the strictures of respectability by dealing poker after working hours ended; Marguerite's grandmother resisted white supremacist terrorism by hiding Black men in her home even as lynch mobs pursued them.

In Arkansas, as in the nation as a whole, Black women did much of the invisible labor that made resistance to white supremacy possible. Black women helped found the Little Rock NAACP, and one Black woman almost single-handedly kept it afloat into the 1920s. Black women were active in the Arkansas branches of the Universal Negro Improvement Association (UNIA), Marcus Garvey's liberationist organization; one Black woman in Blytheville encouraged young people to join the organization in order to protect themselves from "unscrupulous employers." Black women in Little Rock founded a Young Women's Christian Association chapter to make life more bearable for Black girls. And, drawing on a long history of Black female labor radicalism, many Black women became significant leaders in the Southern Tenant Farmers Union. Black female sharecroppers had a unique set of burdens—they might rise as early as four in the morning, spend their days consumed with domestic and agricultural labor, and be responsible for virtually all the childcare—so they used their involvement in the STFU to advocate for themselves and their intersecting needs as laborers, Black citizens, and women.[20]

Occasionally these women used the machinery of the legal system. In the central Arkansas town of Malvern in 1922, a woman named Callie Henry sold her house to raise the money to hire an attorney. She wished to sue the city and county for $10,000 for failing to protect her mentally disabled brother, who had been lynched while in police custody. Although her suit failed, it attracted national attention, and just a few years later a Little Rock woman won a $600 judgment after she was arrested and jailed over a fare dispute with a streetcar conductor.[21]

Yet it would be a grave mistake to claim that these organizations and lawsuits constituted the *extent* of Black resistance to white supremacy during these years. As the historian Robin D. G. Kelley has argued, there exists a "hidden history" of subtle yet powerful Black resistance to oppression and violence in the early twentieth century. In North Carolina tobacco factories, Black female laborers often broke out in song, in violation of company rules; on

Alabama buses, Black riders sometimes rang the bell to stop but then did not get off, in protest of a racist driver; in urban factories, Black female workers often staged "incipient strikes, quitting or threatening to quit just before important social affairs to be hosted by their employers." According to Kelley, "These daily, unorganized, evasive, seemingly spontaneous actions form an important yet neglected part of African-American political history." Like concentration camp inmates constructing Nazi firearms that jammed or misfired, this resistance was meant to be invisible. Thus, by informing each other of white men to avoid; by walking the extra mile to protect each other with numbers; by braving stigma to report an assault to the authorities or testify in court, Black women *were* resisting the sexual violence of the Jim Crow South.[22]

Sometimes the resistance of Black women manifested in ways so deliberately undetectable that they might not strike modern observers as resistance. The historian Darlene Clark Hine has argued that "rape and the threat of rape influenced the development of a culture of dissemblance among Black women. By dissemblance I mean the behavior and attitudes of Black women that created the appearance of openness and disclosure but actually shielded the truth of their inner lives and selves from their oppressors." Hine has also argued that the omnipresent threat of rape led many Black women to leave the South and embark on the Great Migration northward. The scholar Saidiya Hartman, meanwhile, has traced such "acts of everyday resistance" to enslaved Black people committing small, solo acts of sabotage against their white masters. In another publication, Hartman has described the hidden resistance of Black women as "revolution in a minor key."[23]

At the same time, resistance was hard, and resistance had consequences. Not everyone was equipped to resist. At least, not in recognizable ways. And not always right away.

Standing at the side of Marguerite's hospital bed, Bailey cried until she began to cry too. He then told their mother's mother—the German-accented doyenne with pull in the police department—what Mr. Freeman had done. "Mr. Freeman was arrested," Marguerite later wrote, "and was spared the awful wrath of my pistol-whipping uncles."

For some time, Marguerite remained in her hospital room—a wonderful place where her relatives visited her, bringing candy and flowers and fruit, and where Bailey was sometimes able to sneak in and read to her, for hours.[24] Yet she could not stay there forever. Mr. Freeman's trial was coming up, and Marguerite would have to testify.

Part III
Trials

9 • The Trial Begins, 1929

The sky was cloudy overhead as Frank Bethel and Mike Wallace walked into the Mississippi County Courthouse on Wednesday, April 10, 1929. The city of Blytheville bustled around them. Most of the public buildings were clustered close to the courthouse, on Walnut Street, and that morning workers made their way under the maples, poplars, oaks, and black locusts to city hall and the federal building, or a block south to the thrumming commercial thoroughfare that was Main Street. It was on Main Street that they might buy groceries and dry goods, sell produce, visit a hamburger or barbecue stand, find a farming tool, or see a Western at one of the motion picture theaters. Still another block south was Ash Street, where most of Blytheville's Black residents did their shopping and trading, and farther south still were the shipping and industrial plants, the gins, the gasoline depots, and the train tracks. The forecasts were predicting a "colder" day, but it was still pretty warm that Wednesday—in the mid-seventies. Barely a hundred miles away, a tornado was brewing that would take dozens of lives, but in Blytheville there was little precipitation in sight.[1]

Flanked by guards, the two men walked up the concrete paths, past the shrubs, bushes, and spring-green grass and into the courthouse, which was less than a decade old. Built in the Colonial Revival style, it was three and a half stories of brown brick and pale sandstone, with limestone pilasters and tall, handsome windows. Over the main entrance hung a delicate, wrought-iron balcony; green ceramic tiles were visible atop the pyramidal roof. Walking inside, Bethel and Wallace strode through the imposing, two-story foyer— decked out with ornate white marble—past the copper trim and brass flourishes, and up the marble staircase. They entered the courtroom, itself another "ornate" room, as an observer later noted, "with mahogany window trims and terra-cotta tile floors."[2] In this genteel setting, the two would be tried—again—for rape. If convicted, they would face the death penalty.

The spring term for the criminal court was shaping up to be a busy one. Twenty-one people, including Bethel and Wallace, were set to face trial; four of these defendants were charged with first-degree murder, two were charged with assault with intent to murder, and, in a case of great interest to the small cabal of county attorneys, one local lawyer was battling disbarment proceedings for allegedly embezzling thousands of dollars of his clients' money. It was an unusually "heavy" docket, noted the newspapers—but there was little doubt that Judge G. E. Keck was up to the job.[3]

An enterprising man in his early forties, Grover Elias Keck welcomed the more than fifty potential jurors to his courtroom. Born, raised, and educated in Tennessee, Judge Keck had moved to Arkansas almost two decades earlier, and since then he'd built up quite the reputation. First, he'd married Miss Nannie Boyles, a descendant of two of the oldest pioneer families in the county. Then, he'd squeaked out a hairbreadth victory in the 1916 election for county judge, in spite of his opponent's illegal machinations. In the years that followed, Keck worked to help the county get out of debt for the first time in its history; he oversaw ever-heavier criminal court dockets with ease; he masterminded the construction and financing of the very courthouse in which he sat. Elevated from the position of county judge to circuit judge in 1922, Keck experienced few setbacks on his road to power and popularity, other than a frightening two-week hiatus when he came down with typhoid fever.[4]

In an Arkansas county courthouse, the judge exercised an extraordinary amount of power: he disbursed resources for building roads and maintaining infrastructure; he managed all the county's employees; he assessed the county's taxes; he controlled the lives of the county's poor, minors, and orphans; and he administered the endlessly flexible vagrancy laws. One local judge from nearby North Carolina considered himself "the most important and powerful officer in the state," because he was the only "officer in the state who can sentence a man to death." And, noted the historian Story Matkin-Rawn, the judge might also serve as an influential landlord, further cementing his authority over the lives of his tenants. Another scholar called the position "the closest thing to an uncrowned king that the American Political system had to offer."[5]

Judge Keck's courtroom was packed that Wednesday morning. Spectators crowded the benches, straining to catch a sight of the two defendants. It was, the *Arkansas Gazette* reported, "one of the largest audiences ever assembled in the local courtroom."[6]

Toward the front of the room, no doubt exuding confidence and no small amount of imperiousness, was the prosecutor that day, S. L. Gladish, the very man whom—twenty years earlier—Robert E. Lee Wilson had installed as county judge. Born to a poor family and raised on a farm in Missouri, Gladish had finished his law course in 1902 and moved to Osceola with exactly fifty borrowed dollars in his pocket. Yet he had prospered quickly in the Delta, joining the Masons and other fraternal orders and getting elected mayor less than a decade after his arrival. His judgeship followed, and then several elections as county prosecutor; he lost the 1922 race for circuit judge to Keck but remained a local grandee. In the courtroom, Gladish had an imposing visage, with light hair combed back to reveal a high forehead, protruding ears, and intense, deep-set eyes.[7]

Yet Gladish remained, figuratively and literally, in the debt of Mississippi County's wealthiest planter. Even a quarter century after Wilson had engineered Gladish's initial appointment to the bench, the two men kept in close contact, and from surviving correspondence it's clear that Gladish often owed Wilson money. "We feel that we have been just as nice to you as you could possibl[y] ask," one of Wilson's representatives would write to the former mayor and judge a few years after the Bethel and Wallace trial, "and must now insist that you let us have check [sic] for this balance."[8] The distinguished prosecutor was—though he never would have admitted it—a bought man. He was a servant to the powerful planter interests that so dominated Arkansas politics and society. And part of being a cog in this well-oiled machine meant imposing discipline and punishing those whose misdeeds would cast a shadow on the delicate Jim Crow social order on which cotton production depended.

Sitting at the prosecutor's table in the courthouse over which he had once presided, Gladish likely glanced across the aisle to survey the competition. He was facing not one but three defense attorneys, but Gladish was probably not too worried about the first two. O. H. Hurst was a bit over forty, an attorney in Monette, and although he had some experience with criminal law—having served as both a deputy prosecutor and a defense attorney—he did not possess the gravitas that Gladish had.[9] Hurst's partner, W. A. Jackson, was about the same age and level of prominence.[10] Yet Gladish's eyes may have lingered on the third lawyer at the defense table, because the chief defense counsel, E. E. Alexander, was one of the most prominent lawyers in the county.

Fair and slender, with a Roman nose and a thick head of dark hair, Alexander had always been a man in a hurry.[11] Christened Edward Everett—after the famous Harvard orator—E. E. was the son of a Carolina farmer, born in Missouri, educated in military academies, schooled in the law in Tennessee. In about 1908, twenty-five or twenty-six years old and not long out of law school, Alexander was passing through the town of Benton, Arkansas, when he stopped in to visit the local circuit court on a whim. He "liked the looks of things," a journalist recounted years later, and immediately asked for—and received—admission to practice law in Arkansas.[12] Alexander moved to Blytheville, established a thriving legal practice, and soon was running for the state legislature. In 1914, at thirty-two and just six years after arriving in Arkansas, he was elected to represent Mississippi County in the state house; one year later, the political bosses were urging him to run for Arkansas secretary of state. Alexander decided, instead, to put his name forward for state senate, a post he won in 1916. The next year, he ran to be president pro tempore of the senate, widely viewed as the third most powerful office in the state. And while he didn't win, Alexander dispensed his endorsement to another senator with care. As a reward he was appointed chairman of a new senate committee on roads and highways. Roads were Alexander's passion. He wanted to drain the ditches and blanket the rural parts of the state with pavement. He was a progressive, and progress came on four wheels.[13]

By 1919, widely seen as one of the most productive, prolific, and powerful state senators, Alexander decided to make his next move. After flirting briefly with a run for U.S. Senate, he settled on a race for the U.S. House of Representatives. The race became heated—first there were three candidates, then five—and though observers assumed it would be close, Alexander ended up suffering a resounding loss. He suffered another as the manager of a doomed gubernatorial campaign. But Alexander regrouped, ran for the state house again, and won in 1924. Never one to rest on his laurels, he quickly put his name forward for speaker. And though he didn't win, he remained in the legislature; by 1929 he'd become a stalwart in the state house, a champion of roads, canny enough to bite the bullet and vote for women's suffrage in spite of his expressed misgivings.[14]

Even as he climbed the rungs of power in Little Rock, Alexander remained a popular and visible presence back home in Mississippi County. He established a reputation as the county's premier fisherman and hunter; he served as deputy grand exalted ruler of the local lodge of the Elks. He also kept his day job and continued appearing in the county courthouses in Osceola and Blytheville on a regular basis, even occasionally stepping in as deputy prosecuting attorney when an extra prosecutor was needed. True to his namesake, he was widely seen as an expert orator as well as one of the best criminal attorneys in the northeastern part of the state.[15] And now he was representing Frank Bethel and Mike Wallace, charged with rape.

It wasn't uncommon in 1929 for lawyers to handle a range of legal matters—criminal and civil, property and estates, wills and taxes. They often jumped back and forth between prosecution and defense. Few southern lawyers specialized, which at least kept things interesting. A young man might graduate from law school, find a room to rent, and literally hang out a shingle; an uncle or a neighbor might give him some law books or loan him a secretary. He could charge only a pittance—perhaps fifteen dollars a case—and initially cases weren't easy to come by. Rent was twenty-five or thirty dollars a month. The lucky graduates went to firms—and a firm was considered large if it had five lawyers. One of the hallmarks of small-town, early twentieth-century law practice in the U.S. was the camaraderie it generated among most lawyers; they often worked out of the same building, just a few hundred feet from the courthouse, and they depended on each other, sometimes referring cases to a colleague who was in the midst of a dry spell.[16]

In other words, all the lawyers—and Judge Keck, too—knew each other very well. And all of them knew quite well how distinctive rape trials were.

"Mr. Griffin," called out S. L. Gladish, "you have heard the case stated, do you know anything about the facts?"

"No, sir," responded W. C. Griffin.

"You live near Manila?"

"Yes, sir."

"Do you know either one of the Defendants?"

"No, sir."

"Do you know anything about the facts?" Gladish pressed.

"Nothing," Griffin responded. Well, "only what I have heard."[17]

W. C. Griffin was a big man. He was a little over five feet, eight inches tall and built thick; a decade later, a government official would record his weight at two hundred pounds. He had gray eyes, brown hair, and a light complexion. Griffin, sometimes called "Dobe," was a tenant farmer; he rented a house on a dirt road and did not own a radio set. Although he had not attended school, he claimed to be able to read and write. He had been born in Mississippi County in 1882 and lived there all his life. Half a century after the trial, nearing one hundred years of age, he would die there.[18]

But on April 10, 1929, Griffin, along with several dozen of his neighbors, was in the Mississippi County Courthouse to be considered as a potential juror in the rape trial of Bethel and Wallace. A few weeks earlier, they had been officially summoned to the criminal court by one of the sheriff's deputies; their names, as petit jurors, were printed in the newspaper.[19] Scanning this list of names, an observer would have noted that the prospective jurors were all male; they were also all white. Under state law, jurors were selected from registered voters, but although Arkansas women had achieved suffrage in 1919 and won the right to serve on juries in 1921, jury commissioners usually "simply failed to call their names" until the 1940s. Black Arkansans were likewise almost always excluded from juries until the 1940s. Thus, the crowd of potential jurors at the courthouse that day looked a lot like W. C. Griffin.[20]

After confirming that Griffin had not made up his mind about guilt or innocence and had no scruples with capital punishment, Gladish told Judge Keck he would accept him. E. E. Alexander then took over the questioning, setting out to determine if Griffin would be acceptable to the defendants. According to one local journalist, Gladish had been "content to do little questioning," while Alexander "interrogated" the prospective jurors. The defense attorney asked if the farmer had heard "anyone tell about" the case?

"Well, I have hear[d] so many different stories, I have heard a right smart talk."

"Did you ever express any opinion about the guilt or innocence of these Defendants?"

"Well, not exactly."

"Well, I don't know just exactly how to interpret that answer. 'Not exactly.' I just want to know if you did express your opinion?"

"Well, sometimes I would hear it one way and sometimes I would hear it the other, and I would just see both sides."

"So at times though, at times in the presence of others you have expressed your opinion, haven't you?"

"Well, yes, sir, in some instances."[21]

Griffin's responses gestured at the elephant in the room: the Bethel-Wallace trial was notorious in Mississippi County. It was a topic of idle gossip, furtive conversation, regular speculation. The talk was sufficient that a man such as Griffin might hear arguments for both sides and even change his mind as to guilt or innocence.

Griffin assured Alexander that his opinion had never been "firm" and he was still openminded. Alexander told Judge Keck, "We'll take him."

"Good," replied the judge.[22]

They broke for lunch. Immediately after court reconvened, prosecutor Gladish told the judge that he had changed his mind; he asked the court to excuse W. C. Griffin. Under Arkansas law, jurors could be excused for "good cause." But it was not obvious what that cause might be here, and Gladish did not elaborate. Rather, he was using one of the "peremptory challenges" he was permitted by law; using such a challenge, he could strike prospective jurors for any reason or no reason at all. State law ensured each side three peremptory challenges, but, probably because of the extraordinary nature of this case, Judge Keck had allotted the defense twenty peremptory challenges and the prosecution ten.

The judge granted Gladish's request with respect to Griffin. Perhaps the prosecutor thought he could do better.[23]

In Jim Crow rape trials, prospective jurors were routinely asked if they knew the defendants, had made up their minds, knew any of the witnesses, or had "any conscientious scruples against capital punishment." On that Wednesday, the first day of the Bethel-Wallace trial, several prospective jurors were dismissed for having firm ideological objections to capital punishment or for having formed an opinion they could not disregard. Many others, like Griffin, who'd merely heard rumors and who knew some witnesses but said this would not bias them were not excused. In another trial, in 1922—before which the white defendants were nearly lynched—the court had to excuse 138 of 173 potential jurors examined, "for cause." In still another trial, also in 1922, allegations of jury bias led the defense attorney to question a juror about whether one of his daughters had ever "ran away from home with a man," and whether another daughter had borne a child out of wedlock.[24]

The jurors, like the witnesses and lawyers and defendants, were members of a small, tight-knit community. No one harbored any illusion that prospective jurors would *not* have heard about an explosive case. But it was also far from unheard of for potential jurors to fail to disclose close relationships with the accuser or with the accused, or firm opinions, or personal grudges; both sides had to draw on their own knowledge of community relations to root out biased men.[25] The lawyers could not waste their challenges seeking blank slates; they were just looking for men who seemed openminded enough, or closeminded in just the right way.

Normally, the list of jurors summoned by the deputies weeks ahead of time would have yielded enough men to fill the jury box. But the Bethel-Wallace trial was shaping up to be one of the most controversial in county history, so Judge Keck ordered that the sheriff dispatch his men to summon some additional, "special" jurors. At about four o'clock the day before the trial began, deputies approached men on their farms and at their homes, informing them that their services were needed the next day at the Mississippi County Courthouse.[26]

One such man was Mose Smith. A middle-aged white man of medium height and build, with brown hair and eyes, Smith was yet another farmer. Yet he was slightly more prosperous than most; he owned his own fairly valuable home, where he lived with several generations of family members. Smith resided in the small community of Yarbro, in the northernmost reaches of the county, just a few thousand feet from the Missouri state line. He served as secretary of the Yarbro school board.[27] His questioning followed the usual format.

"You say you never heard the case discussed at all," E. E. Alexander asked.

"Only in a casual way and from newspapers," Smith replied. "That's all I have heard of the case at all."

"Did you ever express any opinion about the case?"

"No, sir."

"You have no opinion now?"

"No, sir."

The questioning continued for several minutes. "It doesn't prejudice you against a man simply because he is charged with the crime of Rape?" Judge Keck asked.

"No, sir."

"Alright, go ahead."

After a few more questions, the prosecution and defense would both accept farmer Smith. "Have a seat Mose," Alexander said to him.[28]

A few farmers later, the jury was complete. Judge Keck "admonished the[m] as Provided by the Statute," and the jurors were seated.[29] In the days to come, they would elect Mose Smith as their foreman.

The process of voir dire—selecting a jury—had taken most of the day; it was three by the time the lawyers finished. Now the true battle could begin.[30]

It was afternoon, the sun high overhead and attempting to break through the canopy of clouds outside, as prosecutor Virgil Greene launched into his opening statement. The jury was seated, and the courtroom was still packed even hours after voir dire, with spectators outnumbering the chairs and spilling into the aisles. Greene, one of S. L. Gladish's colleagues in the prosecutor's office, gave a stirring recitation of the night of April 1, 1928, frequently returning to the peroration, "She will tell you . . ."

But Greene also admitted he couldn't remember all of the facts of the case. He conceded he might be getting Frank Bethel and Mike Wallace confused—"if I don't get the two mixed," he said at one point, "they are just about the same." And, whether because of rhetorical abandon or simple lack of care, Greene repeatedly made editorial comments that drew objections from E. E. Alexander, the defense attorney, as when the prosecutor labeled Bethel and Wallace "two foul fellows."[31]

As he pressed on, Greene told the jurors what Pearl would tell them; he described the ditch where Bethel and Wallace had allegedly raped her; he mentioned her torn clothing. "The testimony will show further that her undergarments, her bloomers and her undergarments was literally ripped off her." But, he continued, "We will not be able to introduce that clothing in testimony here before you because the janitor—"[32]

Once again, Alexander sprang to his feet and objected. "We object, if the Court please, to them remarking on the absence of clothing. If they ain't got them."

"We have got a right to show what became of them," Greene insisted.

Judge Keck agreed and overruled the objection.

"That the janitor of the Courthouse burned the clothing in the furnace of the courthouse basement, but the testimony will show that her clothing, just as I told you, was literally ripped off of her."[33]

Greene continued talking for quite some time. Despite his moments of carelessness or forgetfulness, he made sure to emphasize not only the violence of the defendants' actions but also their broader immorality. He described Pearl crying; he mentioned Wallace's "foul mouth" and insinuated that he had previously attempted to rape a fifteen- or sixteen-year-old girl; he quoted the defendants saying "Goddamn" and calling Pearl a "slut"; he mentioned Bethel or Wallace, one of them, beating Pearl with his fists as she resisted.

The whole time, Alexander kept objecting. Initially inclined to overrule the defense objections, Judge Keck eventually began sustaining them as Greene started mentioning things that he had already ruled off-limits. After he began losing the objections, Greene finished up quickly. "When we have laid these facts before you gentlemen, as I tell you, that we will bring them before you, then we will come to you in good faith and ask you to visit the extreme penalty of the law on these two defendants for the awful crime that it will be shown that they have committed."[34]

Then Greene sat down.

Now it was Alexander's turn. He knew he had his work cut out for him.

"Gentlemen," he began, "this is a case, the like of which, I guess, you have never been called upon to sit in judgment as a Juror. The State has undertaken to tell you the testimony that it will adduce in her behalf and I shall undertake to tell you substantially upon what the defense rests."

He told a strikingly different story. Pearl had brazenly climbed in their laps during the drive, he claimed, in front of all their neighbors! "They drove through Leachville, broad open daylight, and this *saintly* woman," he said, sarcastically, "that they are telling you about in the car with two men whom she had never known before . . . submitted to their embraces." Pearl could have left the car at any point, he insisted, but she did not. "While one of the boys was driving the other one began to proposition her and the testimony will be, gentlemen, and I dare her to deny it, that she told him that she had a little trouble like that once before and had to go to the hospital for a long time and she couldn't afford to take any chances and he told her, I will protect you, I will use a protector." Alexander could not bring himself to name a prophylactic. "You gentlemen know what I am talking about. There are ladies here."

Bethel would swear that they had not raped her "with God as his witness," Alexander continued. "Of course, I do not know how that license plate got out of the car," he added, "but I have got a good idea about how it got out, but anyway she got back in the car." Alexander simply could not believe that Pearl would get back in the car with two men who had raped her. "I don't know whether she wanted to be raped again or what in the name of God she wanted, but she got back in the car with two rapers who had ravished her in the same way according to her testimony."

The defense attorney asked the jurors to draw their own conclusions, to decide whether they believed Pearl or Bethel and Wallace. "In my twenty years of experience as a lawyer I have always respected womanhood, I have always shielded her when it was to my client's interest to expose them," he concluded. "I think it is part of every lawyer, every citizen to give to womanhood the arm of protection and bestow upon her that chivalry that any woman is entitled to, no matter what depth she may have fallen, but in this case they are standing upon the rights of my client. . . . I am telling you gentlemen in this case, that as God is my witness and lets me live, and with the help of my associate counsel in this case, I am going to offer you the character of woman, this woman."[35]

By the time Alexander finished, it was 4:20 p.m. Judge Keck decided it was too late to begin the testimony. After beseeching the jurors not to allow "any casual remark that might be made by any irresponsible man on the outside" to influence their thinking, he adjourned court for the day.[36]

The first day of the trial was over. The jurors and lawyers made their ways home. Late that evening, all across northeastern Arkansas, a series of devastating tornados ripped through small towns and rural communities, destroying hundreds—maybe thousands—of structures and taking at least fifty lives. "It is probably 90 miles from one side of the storm area to the other," recorded the *Arkansas Gazette*, "and each of the storms traveled from the southwest to the northeast, dipping down into the farm communities as if a gigantic hand had reached from the skies to snatch off farm buildings." But, inexplicably, Blytheville was spared.[37]

The next day, Pearl would be the first witness to testify.

10 • The Trial Begins, 1935

Six years later, the Mississippi County Courthouse was as crowded as it had ever been as the judge gaveled it to order. It was Monday, April 8, 1935. Farmers and merchants packed the seats and overflowed into the aisles, prompting the judge to order them repeatedly to keep the aisles clear. Sheriff's deputies milled about. Outside it was unseasonably cold, but inside the press of bodies surely kept the courtroom warm, perhaps even stifling. The throng that day was overwhelmingly white, though some individuals would later claim that there had been a handful of Black people in the gallery. As the lawyers took their places toward the front, the assembled masses shifted and murmured and craned their necks to try and catch a glimpse of the two defendants, Bubbles Clayton and Jim X. Carruthers, two Black men on trial for rape.[1]

Sitting at the front of the courtroom was not Judge G. E. Keck, but a different circuit judge, Neil Killough. A tall man with dark hair and steely, deep-set eyes, Killough had first been elected judge fairly recently, in 1930. Born in 1894, he was the son of some privilege, having attended Vanderbilt for law school before moving smoothly into his father's law firm in Cross County, Arkansas, which he and his brother took over after their father's death in 1924; only eight months in France during World War I disrupted his seamless legal career. In addition to practicing law, Killough acquired substantial farm holdings in nearby Cross County and was elected mayor of Wynne, Cross County's largest city, in 1928. From there he moved on to a circuit judgeship, quickly impressing crowds of court watchers with his ability to clear dockets quickly. The *Osceola Times* wrote approvingly of the "snap and vigor" with which he judged. Many observers were doubtless relieved to see Killough on the bench this April morning, for just a month before he had been seriously ill in a Memphis hospital; S. L. Gladish had been forced to act as judge in his stead.[2]

Seated at the counsel's table, facing Judge Killough, was a young man with protruding ears and a high forehead—Denver L. Dudley, the county's ambitious, short, still fairly new prosecutor. The son of a prominent judge, Dudley had won his seat three years earlier by attacking Gladish, his predecessor and opponent, as ineffective, and Virgil Greene, his other opponent, as simply dumb. Dudley's tenure of late had been dominated by the chaos stirred up by the Southern Tenant Farmers Union and the planter-backed vigilantes; he and the sheriffs of northeastern Arkansas were struggling to cool local tempers. Now he was prosecuting the most explosive case of his career—an interracial rape case that had stirred up his constituents. He had to win.[3]

Sitting opposite him was Arthur L. Adams, the bald, bespectacled defense attorney. Known to sport a bow tie on occasion, Adams was tall, slender, and a few years older than Dudley.[4] Next to Adams were his clients, Clayton and Carruthers, who had recently been driven back to Blytheville from Tucker, the state prison farm. They would spend the next several nights in the Blytheville jail and the next several days in the Blytheville courthouse.[5]

Clayton and Carruthers must have sensed the crowd's hostility. The white men and women there to watch their trial were seething with anger and hatred. "Feeling ran high in the community," reported the *Osceola Times* before insisting that "no violence was offered the two men." Yet violence remained a constant threat as the trial began. As one local carpenter would recall years later, the atmosphere at the trial was "full of violence; if these boys wasn't stuck I don't know what would have happened."[6]

One week earlier, on April 1, in the very same courtroom, the grand jury had issued indictments charging Clayton and Carruthers with rape and assault with intent to kill. This meant that prosecutors had persuaded a group of white, male Arkansans, selected from the voter rolls, that there was probable cause to believe the two men had committed these crimes, and now they could face trial. "So far no counsel has appeared for the negroes," reported the *Blytheville Courier-News*, "and the court will probably have to appoint attorneys." On the day the indictments were issued, by sheer coincidence, Arthur Adams was in town to represent the Jonesboro Coca-Cola Company in a minor dispute that had landed in Mississippi County criminal court. He had read of the Clayton-Carruthers "affair" in the newspapers but knew nothing else—"in other words, I could have qualified as a juror." He became the two men's lawyer.[7]

Born in Indiana, the son of a Connecticut transplant, Adams had a more cosmopolitan background than most other lawyers in the county; he had been elected Phi Beta Kappa at De Pauw University before receiving his law degree from the University of Chicago. He had been practicing law in Arkansas for a quarter of a century. Although he may have been more liberal than many of his peers, he should not be confused for any sort of radical; years later, Adams would become prominent across Arkansas for promoting "states' rights" and opposing the federal civil rights program. He had practiced in Blytheville from the spring of 1914 until 1920, when he moved a county away to Jonesboro. During his years in Mississippi County he had handled a lot of criminal cases. He was a longtime acquaintance of E. E. Alexander.[8]

Judge Killough knew Adams from his years in Blytheville, and that Monday he called him to the bench. The judge wanted an experienced lawyer to represent the two Black men, but no lawyer in the county was willing to take the case. Killough told Adams about "the condition of the mind of the people" in Mississippi County; the judge felt he had to look beyond the county for help. Would Adams do him this favor—would he would represent Clayton and Carruthers? Always eager to please a judge, Adams agreed, but inside he was apprehensive; he had an ongoing case that demanded he be in Little Rock two days a week and took up most of the rest of his time as well. He knew how riled up most of the townspeople were. And besides, he had mere days to prepare. He could have filed for a continuance, seeking to delay the trial, but Judge Killough asked him not to do so, telling him that the case must be tried as soon as possible, because of the "very high" feeling in town.[9]

Later that same day, Adams traveled to the prison and met with Clayton and Carruthers. The three men spoke for about an hour, with Clayton and Carruthers telling their side of the story and who should be witnesses. "I think I spent enough time with them to get fixed in my mind my theory of the defense," Adams later recalled. As he had to go to Little Rock the next day, it wasn't until the day after—just five days before trial—that he was able to seek out and confer with any of the potential witnesses.

Immediately, Adams ran into problems. Two of Clayton's and Carruthers's key witnesses were out of town, and several others were hard to find; the urgency undoubtedly exacerbated Adams's disorientation, stemming from a lack of familiarity with the Black parts of town. He eventually located a couple of witnesses who he was "absolutely sure" would provide alibis for the defendants, but then they "evaporated somehow," undoubtedly afraid to testify. Adams would later recall that he "did experience a great deal of difficulty in my investigations, I had to do it really single handed with what help the colored people could give me. I could not call on any white folks to help me in that investigation."[10]

As the clock ticked down and the trial approached, Adams was anxious—he'd been able to devote only about three days to preparation—but he also felt he'd done his best under the circumstances. Nonetheless, he had a daunting task ahead of him, and surely his former neighbors were not pleased. Days before the trial started, the *Courier-News* wrote that it was "generally understood" around town that Adams would represent the defendants. "I had the whole case on my shoulders from the standpoint of the defense," Adams later recalled, "whereas the prosecution necessarily had assistance."[11]

With the trial of Clayton and Carruthers fast approaching, Arthur Adams quickly settled on a plan for their defense. It had taken only a day or two of investigating for him to conclude that it was his professional duty to file for a change of venue; he had no choice, given "public feeling." Under Arkansas law, it was not easy to change venue in criminal cases—it could be done only if the judge determined "that the minds of the inhabitants of the county . . . are so prejudiced against the defendant that a fair and impartial trial can not be had therein." To prove this, Adams needed to gather affidavits from the townspeople, attesting to the violent mood coursing through Mississippi County. But this was easier said than done.[12]

For days, Adams traveled through Mississippi County, spiraling out from Blytheville as far as the town of Armorel to the east and the settlements to the west; he did not go beyond the Mississippi River to his east or the Little River to his west, but this was a span of nearly a dozen miles. And he talked to so many people—to harried sharecroppers and hurried urbanites, to white farmers and Black farmers, to foes and to friends. But it soon became clear to him that it would be impossible to secure the affidavits he wanted. Adams wished to find residents who would attest to the angry atmosphere in town, who would confirm that Clayton and Carruthers simply could not get a fair trial in Mississippi County. But the Black people were afraid to sign an affidavit for fear of retribution, and the white people just refused. After days of searching, Adams found one white man willing to put his signature at the bottom of the affidavit—a white man "scorned in town as 'a Negro lover,' " reported one journalist—but "I just could not find the seconds, anybody who would make the second support affidavit to that petition." Over and over, the white people he spoke with told him they'd be "embarrassed" to sign such an affidavit, or else they looked at him with a "curious smile" and said, "Certainly, they will get a fair trial."[13]

Adams filed the motion asking Judge Killough to move the trial to Adams's adopted hometown of Jonesboro, where, perhaps, the news reports that

Clayton and Carruthers "did, over a period of time, systematically and with premeditation, assault, hi-jack and rape a number of white girls" had not permeated the public consciousness. Adams claimed that "threats, intimidation and disorder prevailed" in Mississippi County, and "that lynching of said defendants had been discussed." Adams told the judge in open court that many citizens agreed with him privately but would not say so publicly. Judge Killough was unmoved. He denied the motion; the trial would stay in Blytheville.[14]

Undoubtedly, being stuck in Mississippi County was a source of great concern for the two defendants. Undoubtedly, they had grown up hearing stories or whispers of an episode from two decades earlier, in Elaine—just a few counties south of Mississippi County—which illustrated just how much danger they were in.

Their trial began as scheduled on Monday, April 8. Toward the front of the courtroom, next to the rail by the jury box, sat Arch Lindsey, one of Mississippi County's most vicious deputy sheriffs. It was Lindsey who had been in the car with Clarence Wilson the night the sheriff was shot. It was Lindsey who had beaten and abused Clayton and Carruthers following their arrests, threatening to murder the former and kicking the latter in the mouth until several of his teeth came out. And it was Lindsey who had retrieved the two defendants from Tucker prison and delivered them to the courthouse in Blytheville. "I brought the prisoners in," he would later recall. A white man in his forties, of medium height and build, with a crop of thinning, graying hair, Lindsey would haunt the courtroom for the entirety of the trial, no doubt hoping for one particular outcome.[15]

As chief deputy, Lindsey was in charge of the several other officers stationed throughout the courthouse that day. And with violence in the air, he had no choice but to be vigilant—the powerful men of the county were apparently determined that Clayton and Carruthers face trial, not a lynch mob. That morning Judge Killough called Lindsey into his chambers to discuss the potential for disorder or disturbance during the proceedings. Lindsey told the judge of rumors he'd heard of men from Missouri coming down to commit murder. Killough would later recall Lindsey remarking, "They are not going to lynch these [n-words]. I don't care whether there is anything to it or not, we have got these reports and we are going to take precautions." According to his recollection, Killough replied, "Yes, they are wise precautions to take, and I am glad you did take them whether anybody is coming down here or not, but be prepared in case they do come."[16]

It is easy to doubt Killough's account of this conversation, but, regardless of the details, it attests to a broader truth about Jim Crow rape trials with Black defendants: murderous violence was always a threat, which meant that a visible law enforcement presence was almost always necessary to prevent a skirmish or, far worse, a lynching. At the trial of two Black men charged with rape in Arkansas two years later, the courtroom was "packed with tense spectators" and the defendants were guarded by the sheriff and five deputies. At the trial of Freeling Daniels, another Black Arkansan charged with rape, the governor dispatched national guardsmen to patrol the courtroom and grounds in full regalia "after mob violence had been threatened"; one unit from Texarkana and another from Hope were on the scene, a total of sixty-one men, reinforced by twenty-one armed ex-service men.[17]

None of this is meant to deny the reality that law enforcement officials often participated in, or even led, lynch mobs—but often they prevented extralegal violence. They did this for a reason. With the white community so riled up, there was little doubt that Clayton and Carruthers would be convicted. The trial would thus serve to legitimate the Jim Crow social order—and mete out the punishment that the mob wanted. The purpose of law enforcement officers being present at the trials of Black defendants, in other words, was to prop up a fundamentally lawless, violent, white supremacist social order.

In contrast to the Bethel-Wallace trial six years before, jury selection in the Clayton-Carruthers trial happened swiftly and without much incident. "Only three challenges were made for cause and the jury was chosen from the first 18 men examined," reported one journalist. When defense counsel Adams asked prospective jurors if they'd ever heard of the case, they all said no. When he asked if they'd "ever had any trouble with Negroes," they all, again, said no.

Adams was not naïve—he almost certainly understood that the jurors were lying. But he did not wish to provoke the anger of the crowd. "I was really trying to the best of my ability, the situation that confronted me, to effectively defend these boys at that time," he would later insist, a touch defensively. "I really felt that a motion of that sort would be merely a technical matter which would rather prejudice the minds of the people" and would not "do me any good in that actual trial." Besides, he had lived in Blytheville for years and genuinely thought he and his clients had gotten "a very good jury." He knew several of the men on the jury very well. He'd been neighbors with Frank Webb; he'd even roomed with Charles Gray for a time, and their relations had always been "most cordial."[18]

Unbeknownst to many in the crowd, Judge Killough and prosecutor Denver Dudley had conferred privately with Adams in the judge's chambers about whether or not the defense attorney would challenge the makeup of the jury. As a result of communist lawyers' efforts on behalf of the Scottsboro Boys—the nine Black teenagers accused of raping two white women on a train in Alabama in 1931, nearly lynched and swiftly convicted by an all-white jury, before an all-white audience—the Supreme Court had recently ruled that the continuous and systematic exclusion of Black people from criminal juries had denied several of the defendants equal protection of law and thus violated their Fourteenth Amendment rights. The judge and prosecutor wanted to know if Adams would invoke this case to challenge the all-white juror pool in the Clayton-Carruthers case—if he would make a "Scottsboro motion." They discussed the matter at length.

By 1935, the year of the Clayton-Carruthers trial, the Scottsboro Boys were famous, the facts of their case well known, and all of the lawyers present could undoubtedly see the parallels between the nine rail-hopping Black teenagers railroaded in Scottsboro and the two young Black sharecroppers facing rape charges in Arkansas. Both groups had initially been accused of other crimes—the Scottsboro Boys were arrested for allegedly fighting white rail passengers, Clayton and Carruthers were captured for allegedly shooting white lawmen. In both cases, lynch mobs had very nearly murdered the suspects before any trials could take place; in both cases, poor white women had given authorities sufficient legal ammunition to stage swift, public show trials, ostentatious performances of law and order; in both cases, the judges had to dragoon reluctant, out-of-state white attorneys to step in and stand for the defendants. Any southern lawyer could recount what had happened next to the Scottsboro Boys—the appeals, the landmark Supreme Court reversal, the retrials, the white accuser's recantation, the convictions in spite of this recantation, the second Supreme Court appeal, the headlines. No one wanted another Scottsboro case in Arkansas. Yet in a decision that would come back to haunt him, Adams decided not to bring such a challenge.[19]

"I just told the Judge, 'I'll be damned if I'll file a Scottsboro motion,' " Adams later recalled. "It would have had no practical value and would have caused a riot."[20]

More than a third of the population of Mississippi County was Black, but no Black person had been on a jury roll in fifty years. "They have been systematically excluded from the jury," one Black attorney would write.[21] Years later, a minister would list the various Black people who were indisputably qualified to sit on the jury: Dr. B. E. Robinson, the dentist; H. H. Thornton, the druggist; Lon Moore, a planter; L. W. Haraway, a teacher; numerous physicians, preachers, and others.[22] But it was no use. The legal custom was too engrained, the threat of violence too pressing and constant. Adams had surrendered to what he'd felt was inevitable: an all-white jury deciding whether two Black men were guilty of rape.

11 • Pearl Testifies, 1929

It was nine o'clock on the morning of Thursday, April 11, 1929, when Pearl finally took the stand in the rape trial of Frank Bethel and Mike Wallace, whom she accused of assaulting her. For a full day, the trial had consisted of the procedural posturing of the lawyers—choosing a jury, making opening statements, trading barrages of objections. But now, at last, Pearl would have her day in court. Outside, it was another pleasant day, cool and clear, no tornados in sight as Blytheville roused itself for business. Inside, the young white schoolteacher approached the witness stand to testify.[1]

Virgil Greene, one of the assistant prosecutors, started by asking her name. She responded in a soft voice.

"Speak out, Miss Pearl, clear so the Jury can hear you," he told her. "How old are you?"

"I am twenty-four years old now," she replied, a bit more strongly.

"Where do you live?"

"I am living now near Leachville."

In a series of quick, brief questions, Greene established the basics of Pearl's life. She was, reported the local paper, a "pretty young school marm" who related her story in "a tremulous but determined voice." Her initial testimony was straightforward and uncontroversial. Lawyer Greene had to get these inquiries out of the way before he could ask her what happened that day back in 1928.[2]

Catherine Pearl was born on October 28, 1904, in the tiny town of Powhatan, a smattering of houses and farms two counties over from Mississippi County, along the glistening Black River. Nicknamed "Kitty" or "Kittie" at a young age, Pearl spent the first several years of her life with her Missouri-born father, John, her Tennessee-born mother, Kittie, and her older sister, Dolly. John was a schoolteacher, and one wonders if it was his influence that ultimately led Pearl to pursue that same calling. A photo of Pearl as a toddler shows a round-faced, light-haired child in a capacious white gown, her face furrowed with concern and blurred by motion.

Hers was not a tranquil childhood. Pearl's sister died in the cold, early days of 1915, when Pearl was a mere ten years old; just a few years later, her father died as well. By the time Pearl was fifteen, in 1920, she and her mother were living with her mother's half brother as poor relations, a hundred miles to the west of her birthplace. Still, life went on. While she was a young woman, Pearl went to college in Jonesboro and, just eighteen years old, became a teacher; she soon accepted a job in Mississippi County. On July 4, 1925, at the age of twenty-one, she married a man named Onus, another Arkansas-born twenty-one-year-old. A year or so later, Pearl gave birth to their son, christened Barton Earl. Yet her marriage quickly deteriorated. By August of 1926, she and Onus were separated. Even as she taught in Mississippi County, Onus moved several counties to the west—where he lived, Pearl would testify, "when he is at home."[3]

By 1928, Pearl was twenty-four years old, living apart from her husband, boarding two miles northwest of Leachville with a young farmer and his wife. Her mother, Kittie, was living a few miles away with Pearl's toddler son. To support herself, Pearl was a teacher at a small schoolhouse in Leachville.[4] It was difficult work. Teachers might be responsible for a whole range of subjects and a whole range of ages, and they were expected to liberally dispense whippings and paddlings, teaching "to the tune of a hickory stick." Multiple grades were crammed into single rooms, with some students sitting on the floor and others perched atop their Rex jelly lunch boxes. In nearby Osceola, the high school was far from any houses, surrounded by "barren" land (critics accused the school board of sticking it "out in the country"); in Manila, another small town, there were just four or five students per grade; in tiny Shady Bend, one seventeen-year-old was initially hired to teach all eight grades. Mississippi County students from this time recalled one longtime teacher as "a typical spinster"—a fastidious, middle-aged woman, peering through spectacles to track her charges' every move—and another as taking slow students into her home, teaching them the finer points of arithmetic or grammar on her front porch. Attendance was variable, higher early in the term and dropping precipitously during cotton-picking season; students walked miles to get there, or else rode on unheated buses. Most boys wore overalls; many were barefoot. Teachers like Pearl could expect to earn a respectable income—eighty-four dollars a month if they were white, sixty dollars a month if they were Black—even though Arkansas ranked "dead last" in the nation in per capita educational spending.[5]

Life for most young white women like Pearl was not easy—but then again, it had never been easy. In the eighteenth century, one visiting European commented of Arkansas women, "they did all the work except hunting." In the nineteenth century, the white women of the Arkansas Delta occupied a position precariously situated on the razor's edge, between prosperity and poverty, liberty and servitude, life and death. The historian Elizabeth Anne Payne pointed to a particularly poignant diary entry from one Delta woman, recorded on June 24, 1864: "This day four years ago our darling little Sallie died, and our little Lou was born." This was the reality of motherhood in this time and place; in spite of herbal remedies, skilled midwives, and even the use of benevolent witchcraft, the Delta's maternal mortality rate was twice as high as in northern states. Thousands of women perished from hemorrhaging or tetanus. "Virtually every nineteenth-century Delta cemetery held the graves of husbands buried between two wives," Payne wrote, "one who died in childbirth and the other who became the stepmother of his children." Ironically, the mortality rate likely would have been higher had more Delta women been able to afford professional doctors; common practices of the time included bloodletting and even placing leeches on the vagina to diminish bleeding.[6]

As women like Pearl entered the twentieth century, life was changing, albeit slowly. Elite women had been pushing for suffrage since the 1860s, but the movement did not broaden and bear fruit until half a century later. More formal courtship routines were giving rise to furtive group parties, which might lead to games like "fishin' for love" or "spin the bottle" or "spin the bucket lid," which might in turn lead to one-on-one dating. Women married young, perhaps receiving some setting hens as a wedding present. Sewing machines and steam pressure cookers and other contraptions were easing household labor, and farm wives began encountering consumer goods for the first time. Some even began sharing the burden of cooking with neighbors, trading weeks to free up time. More women also began working in mills and factories, though a state law limited them to nine hours a day, six days a week—a moderate schedule by the standards of the time.[7]

Violence, including sexual violence, was a part of these women's lives—largely unacknowledged, often unquestioned, yet never uncontested. In spite of the shame, the stigma, the social ostracism, many women—Pearl included—demanded that they be treated as full people before the law. In the big cities up north and out west, female activists were crusading against "mashers"—rapists—but such a movement was not yet possible in Arkansas.[8]

One day in the spring of 1928, Pearl was visiting her mother and son, a couple miles southwest of Leachville, just off Highway 18—what locals called "the gravel road"—where they were living at the time. She'd traveled to her mother's place that morning, stayed all day, and around four thirty or five, she left. It was a "warm sunshiny day," she would later recall, and Pearl decided to walk home. She lived only a few miles away, and the roads—freshly paved or rough, red dirt—were not yet battlegrounds for socialist union members and planter-backed sheriff's deputies.

She was wearing a red sweater, made of heavy knit yarn, and a black hat, walking north up the left shoulder of Highway 18, when two young men, driving a Chevrolet Coupe, pulled up just ahead of her and asked if she wanted a ride.[9]

"Did you see this fellow sitting over here," the prosecutor Virgil Green asked Pearl, a year later, pointing across the courtroom at Frank Bethel.
"Yes, sir."
"Do you know what his name is?"
"I know now," she replied, a touch dryly.
"What is his name?"
"Frank Bethel."
"Did he tell you that day that Frank Bethel was his name?"
"No, sir, he said his name was George something . . . George Cruze."
"George," who was driving, asked her if she wanted a ride, she testified.
"What did you tell them, if anything?"
"I said, 'Well, I am tired.'"
One of the men got out of the car and Pearl got in.[10]

Climbing appreciatively into the Chevrolet Coupe that sunny, spring day in 1928, Pearl thought vaguely that Mike Wallace—the shorter man, fair-skinned, with a thick mop of dark hair—resembled a boy named Morgan she had known at the Agricultural and Mechanical College in Jonesboro. Pearl had spent one normal term and three summer terms at the college, and she told Wallace that he looked like her acquaintance. Wallace, sitting in the passenger seat, replied that he had gone to Jonesboro while Pearl was there, but that he was not Morgan. The men asked her who she was, and she replied that her name was Pearl and she was a schoolteacher. She tried to make conversation, asking about students they might have known in common as the Chevrolet traveled slowly down the gravel road.

According to Pearl's testimony, Bethel and Wallace soon pulled over, about a mile and a-half south of Leachville. They were having car troubles, they told Pearl. One of the men got out and began fiddling around under the hood. It didn't take long to get the car started again, and they continued, pretty slowly, toward town, driving through the country twilight. Pearl told them she would get out at the Leachville bus station on Main Street.

The Chevrolet reached the bus station, slowed slightly, but then turned the corner and kept going.

"I get out here," Pearl said.

"Oh no, you don't get out, you can go driving," the men replied.

Pearl told them she had to get out, that it was getting late, that she had to get back to the house where she boarded. She had left her mother's in time to get back before dark. But the two men just treated her objections like a joke; they'd get her back home soon enough, they told her, over her continued protests.

The Chevrolet turned east, toward the A. B. Jones Grocery Company, and continued onto the paved road. Pearl tried another tactic, asking if she could drive; the two men ignored her. They kept driving east, for four or five miles, until they reached the Poplar Corner store, a crowd of loafers sitting on its porch. They pulled up a little past the store, and Pearl thought perhaps they were going to turn around. But the taller man—the one who called himself "George"—just got out, bought a pack of cigarettes, and returned to the car. Wallace got behind the wheel. They drove on.

The car turned south toward Manila, and Pearl insisted that she must go back. Wallace told her that they had to make a stop first, that it wouldn't take long but that they were going to another nearby village, Etowah, to pick up his wife, who had been visiting with her sister. Pearl was confused; Etowah was in the other direction, she told them.

"Oh no," they replied, it wasn't.

They insisted that Etowah was close by, just on the other side of the floodway. They drove through Manila, past a marble obelisk, a little faster now. The men took some swigs from a flask of whiskey; Wallace said he couldn't drink around his wife, so he had to do it now. He tried to get Pearl to drink too, holding the flask to her lips, but she refused. The sun was beginning to set.[11]

"Up to that time, Miss Pearl, had either of these young men said or done anything that was offensive?"

Virgil Greene stood before Pearl, who was sitting in the witness stand, staring out at the packed courtroom.

"Well," Pearl replied, "on the way down there after we had left, after we left the gravel road, between Manila and Etowah they made some rude remarks and their language wasn't what it should have been, and they tried to put their hands on me, but they hadn't made any indecent proposals."

"And which one of them did that?"

"Well, it was mostly Bethel then because Wallace was driving, but he put in his share of the remarks that were made."

Pearl testified that Wallace stopped the car near a house that was just off the road; he said he was going to go find his wife. Wallace got out, marched up to the front of a house, and spoke to a man for a couple of minutes, leaving her and Bethel—"George"—alone in the car.

"Something was said by Mr. Alexander in his opening statement to the Jury," Greene said, "that during that time you were sitting in Bethel's lap? Is that true?"

"That is not true," Pearl said.

"And that Bethel was embracing you and fondling over you, is that true?"

"If he had his hands about me, or if there was any commotion going on, I was trying to keep him from feeling around me."[12]

In her answers to these questions, Pearl was insisting that she had *not* violated the prevailing moral code of this time and place by voluntarily flirting with, exchanging embraces with, a man who was not her husband. Such insistences were virtually always demanded of women accusing men of rape in the Jim Crow South. To be sure, some women were asked about inconsistencies in their testimony or openly accused of lying. Underage girls in particular were questioned aggressively—bullied, really—about whether they were mistaken. But as a plethora of trial records show, when sexual assault survivors were questioned on the stand—and especially when they were cross-examined—the questioning usually hinged on their alleged promiscuity or immorality.[13]

The most common tactic for the defense was to accuse the woman making the accusation of promiscuity. It was routine for a defense attorney to ask questions that implied that a woman had several lovers, or that she dated many men, or that she "ha[d] been going out driving at night considerably ... [w]ith men," or that she "kept company" with various "sweethearts."[14] At the 1936 trial of Bill DeVoe, for example, a white man accused of assault with intent to rape, the accuser was questioned at length about whether she played with boys in the backyard. Through these questions, the defense attorney implied that she may have been sexually active with "the boys at school." She was eight years old.[15]

In "carnal abuse cases" like the DeVoe case—those with underage accusers—the girl's chastity or promiscuity should not have come up at trial at all. "It is a well-established doctrine," wrote the Arkansas Supreme Court in 1922, "that in prosecutions for carnal abuse, the prosecutrix being under the age of consent [i.e., sixteen years old], her illicit relations with other men, showing want of chastity, are immaterial, because in such a prosecution the chastity of the victim is not in issue and testimony tending to prove specific acts of sexual intercourse with others than the accused is not relevant."[16] However, this did not stop defense attorneys from frequently asking questions meant to imply that such girls were promiscuous.[17] "Who else has been keeping company with you?" a defense attorney asked a white girl named Bessie (sixteen at trial) in 1925. Since the defendant in this trial admitted that he'd had sex with Bessie (starting when she was fourteen or fifteen), this question (and the several that followed) should not have been permitted.[18] In another trial, a fourteen-year-old white girl was asked whether she'd gone to a man's house and "stay[ed] there without the lights on for as much as 30 minutes" and whether she "ever le[ft] the school [to] go riding with any of the boys at school?"[19]

Defense attorneys also asked women questions designed to depict them as lacking in respectability. Frances, a nurse who was assaulted by two men, was asked aggressively about how much alcohol she drank when she was with them.[20] Another woman was forced to admit that on the night of the assault she'd gone out on a date without the permission of her father.[21] Yet another woman was asked about how much she had danced after her assault, and whether she had danced with her assailant.[22] In 1921, a woman named Irene was asked whether she had told a group of people that "they could 'kiss your ass,'" and "that you didn't give shit what they thought."[23] In 1929, a woman named Daisy was subject to a particularly galling cross-examination. She was accused of "run[ning her] husband off," prostituting her daughter, having sex in exchange for food or money or shoes, and having sex with married men. "Wasn't your conduct so bad your neighbors came in there to visit you and asked you to stop it and if you didn't, they would have to report you to court?" the defense attorney asked. "It didn't happen," Daisy replied.[24]

Even prosecutors—who had a tactical interest in defending the women making accusations—sometimes asked questions that seemed to serve no purpose other than shaming the victims. "The defendant is married?" one prosecutor asked a sixteen-year-old named Thelma.

"Yes, sir." she responded.

"You knew that he was married when you ran away with him?"

"Yes, sir."[25]

Interestingly, such humiliating questioning appears not to have been as prevalent in at least some places outside of the Jim Crow South. In her study of rape prosecutions in mid-century Chicago, the historian Dawn Rae Flood noted that attorneys in the 1930s and 1940s typically avoided harsh probes into accusers' personal lives—"at least," that is, "until African American rape victims began appearing in court more regularly during the mid-1950s." In fact, before the 1960s attorneys questioning white accusers in Chicago were reluctant to imply that the women sold sex or otherwise transgressed bourgeois sexual norms, and few judges allowed defense scrutiny into accusers' sexual histories. Although misogynist, invasive questioning was certainly not confined to the Jim Crow South, it may have been more prevalent there in the early twentieth century precisely because of the rigidity of the racial, gender, and economic hierarchies structuring southern society.[26]

"You and Mr. Woods were rather intimate friends, weren't you?"

Defense attorney E. E. Alexander stood before Pearl, several minutes into what the newspapers would call a "long and strenuous" cross-examination.

"Not anymore than he was my employer," Pearl replied.

"Did you ever go riding with him at night?"

"I never went riding with him," Pearl said. "I have possibly been in the car with him." She insisted that she had only been in the car with him "on business."

"Ever ride out in the country with him at night?"

"No, sir."

"Honest?"

"Not that I remember of."

"He didn't call for you at your house daylight and night too?" Alexander pressed.

"He's called for me a number of times and taken me to work," Pearl said, "because I lived upon the east side of town."

"He was a married man?"

"I suppose he is."

"You would know, wouldn't you?" Alexander asked.

"I suppose he is," Pearl replied, unshaken.[27]

The questioning about "Mr. Woods" continued in this fashion for some time. Alexander's goal was clear to everyone in the courtroom: he wanted to paint Pearl as promiscuous, and therefore untrustworthy, a woman who would have no scruples about being in a car, at night, with two men not her husband.

Such a woman might lie about being raped, Alexander's logic went; sex with such a woman could not be considered rape by dint of her promiscuity.

Throughout his cross-examination, Alexander implied that Pearl had committed adultery with this Mr. Woods, the owner of a wood supply company who had employed her for some stenographic work, that she had moved repeatedly during her years in Leachville—because of "unfriendly feeling" with the boarders and a "misunderstanding with the boys that run the hotel"—and even that she was "a drinking woman."[28]

Why had she asked the officers who arrested Bethel and Wallace to smell her breath for alcohol? Alexander inquired. "With my clothes in the condition they were and everything I thought maybe they would believe I was on a wild party," Pearl replied, "but I don't know why else I asked them."[29]

None of this should have been relevant.

The sun was sinking behind the horizon as Mike Wallace returned to the Chevrolet, that evening in the spring of 1928. He climbed into the car and got back on the road toward Manila, visibly angry and letting loose a stream of vulgarities. Pearl heard him say something about his wife double-crossing him; he cursed her, cursed women in general. His words became more and more profane.

"To think, after driving all the way down there with a hard on, and for her to be gone," Wallace exploded.

Bethel added that he was in the "same condition." He then turned to Pearl. "Do you think you can relieve us any?"

"You are mistaken in the woman," she said, alarmed.

"Hell, what do you think we have brought you out for?" Bethel asked. "That is certainly what we brought you for."

Pearl began to cry. She had to escape from this car. She moved forward quickly and managed to get her foot on the brake pedal, but Bethel grabbed her and wrenched her back, wrapping his arms tightly around her face. Pearl squirmed loose and managed to get one door open, extending her legs out and screaming as loudly as she could. "Help, help, I want out, and Lord have mercy, why don't somebody help me?" But it was no use. Bethel dragged her back in, cursing and telling her to shut up, ripping her red sweater as he grabbed her. Besides, the car was moving too fast to safely jump out. A jump surely would have killed her, Pearl thought.[30]

She managed to convince them to pull over just past the Poplar Corner store and get her a soft drink. With the car idling on the right side of the road and Bethel in the store, Pearl thought about running away, but Wallace grabbed her hands and told her that if she tried to run, they'd kill her. A few minutes later Bethel returned, and Pearl took two or three swallows of the drink he'd gotten her, but she wasn't thirsty. The men drove on, down toward the floodway, through the deepening darkness, through some sparsely settled woodlands. Eventually, Bethel told Wallace, "Hell, turn across here, cut across here." Pearl was crying and pleading, but they continued to ignore her. The car turned and followed the railroad tracks, bouncing along a very old road. Finally, in a deserted area, Wallace eased the car to a stop.

"This car is not dead," Pearl said.

"Hell, it is too," Wallace shot back, "and it won't go another step."

The men pulled Pearl from the car, telling her to hush as she begged them to let her go; she promised them she wouldn't tell; she told them she had a baby at home; she asked if they had sisters, and how would they like their sisters to be in such a situation as this? The two men ignored her pleas. Wallace pushed her from behind, and, lifting her bodily, he and Bethel threw her to the ground. For the next two or three hours, the two men raped her repeatedly. "It seemed like years," Pearl later recalled.[31]

"At that time did you resist them all you could and all that was in your power?" Greene asked Pearl, a year later.

"Yes, sir," she responded, her voice echoing across the mahogany-lined courtroom. "I resisted all I could, and also they threatened to shoot me."

Did Bethel or Wallace "strike" her? Greene asked a moment later.

Both of them did, Pearl replied. They smacked her face and scratched her leg and struck her very hard with a stick, leaving bruises that did not go away for months. After they finished raping her, she could not get up; they thought she had fainted.

"Did you resist him all that you knew how?" Greene asked again.

"I resisted him all that I knew how, but I was exhausted then."[32]

The testimony of women like Pearl was critical in rape trials; indeed, survivors of sexual assault nearly always testified first. Their testimony was essential to prove that a rape had taken place, and their words were needed to fulfill the three requirements demanded by Arkansas rape law: that the rape had been forcible, that the woman had resisted, and that penetration had been complete.

Throughout much of the nineteenth century, most medical and legal authorities agreed that it was impossible for a healthy adult woman to be raped.

Such a woman could only truly be raped if she were drugged, outnumbered, disabled, or subjected to extreme physical force. In the absence of these circumstances, physicians and judges concluded, the sex must have been consensual. This consensus began to fracture by the last quarter of the nineteenth century, yet as late as 1917, one physician could write (in a widely cited essay) that rape is a "physical impossibility" so long as a woman "remains conscious." Well into the twentieth century, grand juries consistently dismissed rape charges brought by women who had been threatened into submission but not physically subdued.[33] The Arkansas Supreme Court had long held that "[f]orce is an essential element in the crime of rape," but by the 1920s it had refined this requirement somewhat: "It is necessary for the jury to find that the accused intended to use whatever force was necessary to overcome the prosecuting witness and have sexual intercourse with her, and that he intended to use as much force as would be necessary to accomplish that purpose and overcome her resistance."[34]

In early twentieth-century rape trials, the question of force came up often. In the trial of a white man named Tug Terrell in 1927, for instance, the accuser noted (at the urging of the prosecutor) that she did not lay down voluntarily: "I just laid down on it; but it was all forced upon me. I was out, out of the car and out there in the woods by myself with five men, and there is no woman living that can stand up and fight five men."[35] In some trials, the prosecution made sure to ask about the accuser's physical injuries. "Were you hurt in some way?" the prosecutor asked the accuser in the 1925 trial of Bill Snetzer, white, charged with assault with intent to rape.

"Yes; I had two ribs that were fractured; and I had bruises all over me; my face scratched and my neck scratched, where he [defendant] had scratched me."

"Any other bruises about you?" the prosecutor asked.

"My body was bruised. I had bruises back there, two or three on my back. My knee was bruised and my leg was bruised where he beat me."[36]

This was a common strategy, given the force requirement in proving that rape had taken place. As Brian Donovan noted in his study of sex crimes prosecutions in New York, "Successful rape prosecutions typically involved situations where the defendant subjected the victim to serious physical injury."[37]

Questions about force usually came up on direct or redirect; cross-examinations more often focused on resistance. Yet force did sometimes arise in questioning from the defense, in ways that now seem absurd. In the trial of Snetzer, for instance, Snetzer's defense attorney asked the (white) accuser, "How long did he choke you?"

She responded, "He choked me until my tongue was out."

"How far out?"

"I didn't measure it."[38]

The resistance requirement appears equally absurd in retrospect. Throughout the nineteenth century, and even into the twentieth century, many rape laws had demanded that women who accused men of sexual assault be able to prove that they had fought back with all their might. By the 1920s and 1930s, these extreme requirements had faded (though certainly not disappeared), but courts (including Arkansas courts) continued to demand that women have resisted as much as could be reasonably expected, and throughout the entirety of the assault.[39]

Questions of resistance often dominated the accuser's direct testimony. "I was resisting and fighting all I could and said God have mercy on me, don't let this man over power me," testified one Black woman named Ruth in 1926.[40] Other women, such as Maxine (white, in 1925), went into more detail: "I tried to get them to let me go and they wouldn't let me. I fought with them and tried to get loose from them. . . . I scuffled and screamed." After one of her assailants put his hand over her mouth to stifle her, "I bit his hand but he kept it on there. I kept trying to scream."[41] Many other women recalled screaming, or trying to scream; on cross-examination, they might be asked about how much or how loudly they had screamed, or about why other people in the area hadn't heard them scream. Questions like these were meant to imply that they had not resisted *enough*.[42]

This was frequently the defense's principal strategy on cross-examination. Defense attorneys routinely implied that women had not fought back with sufficient force.[43] "Why didn't you scratch him?" one white accuser was asked in 1929.

"I did all I could."

The attorney pressed further: "Why didn't you hit him in the face?"

"I just fought with my hands and did everything I could to get away."[44]

Such questioning often bordered on the sarcastic. "You hadn't learned how to break his hold then even the third time?" one white woman was asked in 1928.[45]

"Minnie, did you cry out or holler when he told you to go out there in the woods with him?" asked another defense attorney in 1932.

"No, sir."

"Did you at any time cry out or holler?"

"No, sir."

"You just did what he told you to do?"

"Yes, sir."

"What do you weigh, Minnie?"

"I weigh 115."
"A hundred and fifteen pounds?"
"Yes, sir."
"You are a well developed girl, are you not?"
"Yes, sir."
"Strong and healthy."
"Yes, sir."

The implication was clear: the defense meant to suggest that Minnie, who was just thirteen years old (and white), could have—should have—exhibited more resistance.[46]

The prosecution later recalled Minnie and asked her why she didn't resist more strongly. "I was afraid he would hit me," she replied, referring to the Black defendant.[47]

This response exemplifies another hallmark of accusers' testimony regarding resistance: many stated that their resistance was stymied by fear for their safety or their lives. "Did you resist it? Did you holler or did you try to holler?" one defense attorney asked a white accuser on cross-examination in 1927.

"I started to and he told me not to. He started to pick up a gun," she replied. Then he told her he'd kill her.[48]

Other accusers gave nearly identical testimony. Such threats were apparently so common that one white woman testified in 1927 that she didn't holler "[b]ecause I was scared to; I was afraid to put up much fight because I have heard of all these kinds of cases of boys just killing a girl and throwing her out somewhere and she would never live to come back and report it to the officers."[49]

Arkansas courts recognized this as a valid exception to the resistance demand. A woman need not be "compelled to continue her resistance as long as she was conscious or had strength to offer any resistance, without regard to the effect of this resistance on her safety," wrote the state supreme court in 1924. "If, for instance, appellant's conduct had induced the fear that an outcry would cost her her life, she was not required to thus imperil her life or safety."[50]

Yet the fear that accusers reported feeling was not only fear of violence or loss of life. In the 1927 rape trial of a white man named Dock Sanders, the fourteen-year-old white accuser testified that Sanders told her "he would do it again . . . if I told."

"What did he say he would do if you told?"
"Make me have a baby."
"Make you have what?"
"A baby."

Later, on cross-examination, she was asked why she didn't "tell anybody out there what had occurred?" She replied, "He told me if I told the next time he would not use a rubber."[51] Thus, not only violence but also the prospect of forced pregnancy—in a society where unmarried motherhood was enormously stigmatized and burdensome—was wielded as a threat to silence survivors.

In addition to the requirements of force and resistance in proving rape, Arkansas law specified that there had to be "[p]roof of actual penetration."[52] And though one state supreme court opinion from 1910 clarified that the hymen did not have to be broken, the requirement that there actually had been penetrative intercourse was often a veritable obsession in these trials, bordering on the voyeuristic. Many women were asked at length about whether there was "complete" or "full" intercourse, or whether "[h]e actually penetrated your body."[53] One defense attorney even asked, "Did it enter your body? In other words did it go in?"

"Yes sir," the woman replied.

"How far?" he pressed.

"I don't know."[54]

Such questioning was likely meant to shame or humiliate—to exact social punishment against women making public what happened behind closed doors, thereby disturbing a patriarchal social order—as much as it was to fulfill a legal requirement.

"Now," E. E. Alexander asked Pearl, "you made no outcry in Manila, did you?"

"No, sir," Pearl replied.

"You made no effort to get out, no demonstration whatever, but continued to go on down somewhere you didn't even know where you were going?"

The questioning continued in this manner for some time.

"Why did you not make some outcry, or appeal?" Alexander asked.

"Because I didn't think they were going to do anything wrong to me," Pearl said.

"You didn't want to create a scene, did you?"

"No, I didn't, nor anybody else would have."

"But you were willing to risk yourself with those men rather than cry out for help after they had refused to let you out and let you stop at any place along the road, didn't you?"

"Sir?" Pearl asked.

"I think you understood my question, didn't you?" Alexander said.

"Well, it was so long I didn't quite understand what you want me to say."

And there was the point. The questioning was about what Alexander wanted her to say. For minute upon painful minute, the defense attorney asked Pearl why she hadn't made an outcry, why she hadn't tried harder to escape, why she hadn't called to one of the people walking along the streets of Manila or Leachville.

"You say you tried to get out of the car?"

"Yes, sir."

"You just feebly struggled?"

"It was feeble compared to his strength."

Why didn't she make more of an effort to get out of the car? Didn't she sit on Frank Bethel's lap? What if someone said she had? Didn't she let Bethel kiss her? Did the men really threaten to kill her? Really? Did she actually see a gun? Did she?[55]

At one point, one of the defendants leaned forward and whispered a few words to another defense counsel. They had "listened attentively" throughout Pearl's testimony, staring at her.[56]

"Why didn't you make them stop?" E. E. Alexander asked Pearl at another point in his interminable cross-examination.

"I did try to make them stop," she shot back.

"Why didn't you do anything further when you saw they weren't going to stop? Why didn't you holler help?"

"You wouldn't holler for help," she said.

Yes, he would've, Alexander insisted. "Why didn't you?"

"Because I didn't want to create a scene and cause a lot of gossip."[57]

Pearl's last answer gestures at another truth of sexual assault in this time and place. Women who were raped often faced consequences for reporting the assault—consequences that could be dire indeed.

Women who were publicly branded as "impure" could become stigmatized or ostracized for their supposed lack of chastity; this might make it much harder for them to find a husband (which was often their primary means of ensuring economic security).[58] Women could even be incarcerated for reporting a rape. On the stand, many young women and girls mentioned that, after reporting what happened to them, they were taken to a reform school or detention home, where they were placed in the custody of probation officers. Likewise, in New York in 1926, the authorities did this to an eleven-year-old Billie Holiday—the future jazz singer—after a neighbor raped her.[59] In theory, this was supposed to be for the girls' protection and health, but in reality it was a form of discipline. Such facilities were often coldly regimented and exposed female inmates to corporal punishment and even eugenic sterilization.[60] Reform schools were so unpleasant and punitive that some rapists even threatened their victims with being sent there. "What did he say to you about telling it?" one prosecutor asked a twelve-year-old white girl named Edna in 1927.

"He told me not to," she replied. "He said I would be sent to the reform school."[61]

It is true that in the press women did retain some privacy. Only in very rare trials did newspaper coverage disclose the identity of the accuser, revealing a notable and gendered restraint on the part of southern journalists. Yet trials were nonetheless public spectacles, and it is likely that many (if not most) of their neighbors were aware of women's testimony, and thus the fact that they had been raped. Indeed, their neighbors likely attended the trials. "What the country has lacked in public religious spectacle we have replaced with public narratives of crime, justice, and redemption," wrote the legal scholar David J. Gottlieb. "A century before we became addicted to simulated spectacles of triumph, tragedy, life, and death in movie theaters and sports arenas, we sought out the real thing in criminal trials and executions. These legal proceedings were often the most widely-attended public events in the community."[62]

In their testimony, some accusers spoke openly of their profound fear of appearing publicly. One white sixteen-year-old named Opal, for instance, told the jury in 1928 she "was scared" and admitted to making false statements in an earlier proceeding because "he was out and he knew where I lived.... He was out and not in jail and I was afraid he would come around to my house."[63] Other women and girls testified only because their families demanded that they do so; sometimes, these family members hired private religious organizations to track down daughters living away from home and outside the bonds of matrimony, to compel them to return home to testify. One white fifteen-year-old named Mattie, testifying in Mississippi County just three years before Pearl, had to be tracked down by a deputy and forced to take the stand against her will.[64]

The fact that some women and girls testified voluntarily, in spite of the many risks of outing themselves publicly as rape survivors, reveals a remarkable undercurrent of resistance to patriarchal violence. And, often, their testimony evinced a desire to reclaim their own reputations.[65] One white woman named Gale, for instance, testifying in 1925 recounted her assailant asking her, "Don't you ever jazz?" (with jazz being an early twentieth-century euphemism for sex).

"No, I don't jazz," she recalled answering.

"Don't you do it for money?"

"No, I don't do it for money."

"What are you anyway?"

"I am just a nice lady that is all you can say."[66]

Another white woman was asked (in 1915), "As a matter of fact, did he have intercourse with you?"

"Do you have the least idea I would sit up here and say he did when he didn't?" she shot back.

"Answer my question," replied the defense attorney. "I don't want to argue with you."

"I am just ready for argument," she said. "Sure, he did."[67]

Yet another white woman was asked (in 1942), "Did he start to try to kiss you?" to which she answered:

"Yes, sir."

"You resented that?"

"Yes, sir."

"You fought back?"

"Yes, sir."

"That makes you mad?"

"Naturally, it did."

"You had no respect for him because you resented it and you asked him to let you alone?"

"Yes, I had more respect for myself."[68]

For her part, Pearl was resolute that she had thrown the men's license plate, even as she acknowledged that she could no longer remember all the details of the rape. "I couldn't remember which boy took off the license plates," she told Alexander, "but as sure as I am sitting here they got that because I have lived that thing over a thousand times."[69]

12 • Virgie Testifies, 1935

All eyes turned to the young white woman as she made her way toward the witness stand. This was the pivotal moment, everyone knew. Virgie, the accuser, was about to testify against Bubbles Clayton and Jim X. Carruthers.

No description of the courtroom survives from this cool spring day in 1935. But it is easy to get some sense of the scene from recordings of other, similar trials at the time. One scholar described the "air" in one courtroom as "charged with an undercurrent of tension and there is a feeling of suspense, as if some exciting incident may occur at any moment." A newspaper described another courtroom as "literally bristling with armed highway patrolmen and sheriff's officers." Most observers noted how *theatrical* these trials were, with each participant carefully playing a part, following movements rigidly choreographed by Jim Crow society. The British writer Rebecca West famously called interracial trials in the Jim Crow South "operas," while the civil rights attorney Robert L. Carter compared these trials to "public theater."[1]

A decade after the Clayton-Carruthers rape trial, the NAACP sent an investigator to observe an interracial rape trial in Mississippi, and the atmosphere may have been similar to that of the trial of Clayton and Carruthers. The investigator described entering a large, circular courtroom, not too crowded, but with "scores of men moving about, talking and smoking long cigars" in front of the bar. "It was easy to pick out the lawyers, police officials, and the local constabulary with guns bulging on their hips." The sole person of color in front of the bar was the defendant. The all-white, all-male jury filed in, and then the accuser took the witness stand. The young white woman "sat easily in the witness chair; she was pretty in a colorless sort of way, of sturdy build, had fair hair and a clear skin conspicuously devoid of any makeup," recorded the investigator. "In low tones, with an all-out Southern accent, she told her version of what had happened..."[2]

Virgie was born on July 6, 1915, in Dyersburg, Tennessee, a bustling hub of railroads and commerce just across the Mississippi River from Mississippi County, Arkansas, hemmed in by rich cotton fields and even richer timber forests. Just months after Virgie's birth, a twenty-two-year-old Black man, born and raised in Mississippi County, was accused of choking and raping a young white woman on the side of the road, a few miles outside of Dyersburg. He was taken to the jail in Dyersburg but a white mob quickly assembled, intent on lynching him, and the local sheriff hastily removed him to Memphis. The Black man was swiftly tried, convicted, and sentenced to die, becoming the first person executed by electric chair in the state of Tennessee, though not before supposedly confessing to another rape back in Mississippi County.

In this town, Dyersburg, where a lynch mob could gather with such speed, little Virgie took her first steps. When she was seventeen months old, her parents—Gertrude and J. D., a railroad laborer—moved to Mississippi County, where she would spend most of her childhood. Just months after Virgie and her family left town, another young Black man was accused of raping a white woman in Dyersburg. This time, the lynch mob that assembled succeeded in forcing the authorities at the jail to surrender the suspect. The crowd of thousands tortured the man mercilessly, blinding him with irons, castrating him, and finally burning him at the stake. Among those watching was a trembling eleven-year-old newsboy who, a generation later, would dedicate his life to racial and economic justice and help to found the STFU.[3]

Virgie's formative years were spent in a series of rented homes near Blytheville. Her family did not have much: her father began working on the county's massive cotton plantations, her mother gave birth to three more children, and Virgie herself left school after the fourth grade to start working. She and her family were living in the county during the explosive Bethel-Wallace rape trial and likely followed its progress. When Virgie was about seventeen, in the early 1930s, her family moved to Missouri, but she returned to Mississippi County with some frequency. In the summer of 1932, she married a man named Bob, who lived fifteen miles to the east of Blytheville; in the summer of 1933, she and Bob separated; in the summer of 1934, she was back in Blytheville, working at the canning factory on Ash Street. Even as militant sharecroppers and sheriff's deputies came to blows across the region, Virgie was eager for companionship as well as economic stability, so she began going on dates with local men. In about October 1934 she became reacquainted with a young white man named Wiley Bryant.[4]

Wiley and Virgie had first met as children fifteen years earlier; they played together in the rural land east of Blytheville. They fell out of touch when she moved away but became reacquainted after she moved back to town. Wiley Bryant was twenty-three years old, and although he was not a rich man—he was a farmer, from a family of farmers—he owned his own car and his family owned (not rented) their home. He began visiting Virgie at the house where she was staying. They started going on dates, alone in his car, driving around town and sometimes even out of town. In the last days of 1934, they made plans to get together for yet another date.[5]

Bryant arrived at Virgie's place early on the evening of December 21, 1934, pulling up in his two-door Ford sedan. It was already dark outside, with the moon periodically peeking out from behind the curtain of clouds. Across Mississippi County, residents were preparing for Christmas; local pastors were hosting yuletide celebrations, their homes decked out with ferns, evergreen, and candles, and many others were beginning to decorate their trees. Virgie got in the car and she and Bryant set off on their date, first traveling up the gravel road that turned off Main Street, going past the Fairfield place, and then turning around at the school and doubling back, heading north. Sometime around eight or eight thirty, they stopped at Sawyers graveyard, about a mile and a half southeast of Blytheville. It was a treeless stretch of land. They parked on the side of the wide road at the edge of a ditch, near the sprouting weeds, and turned off the car's lights.

Just what they were doing in this parked car, by the graveyard, on this cloudy December evening, should have been irrelevant, though it certainly wouldn't be to future lawyers and jurors. According to their later recollections, Bryant and Virgie were sitting there, "just talking," for about forty-five minutes, Bryant with his arm around Virgie's shoulders, when two masked men approached from behind, one on either side of the car. "Stick them up!" one of the men yelled. There was no hesitation in his voice. They stuck them up. The masked men then screamed at Virgie and Bryant to get out of the car. Terrified, the two leapt out of the right side of the Ford as one of the men fired a shot into the left side, the bullet smashing into the car door just below the handle.

In Virgie and Bryant's telling, the two men shone flashlights in their faces, blinding Virgie so that she was unable to get a good look at them. The men wore white handkerchiefs over their faces and caps over their heads, further obscuring their identities. One of the masked men struck Bryant on the head with his flashlight; Bryant fell back against Virgie, who stumbled. As the larger of the two men held them at gunpoint, the smaller masked man searched Bryant for weapons. Then, taking his own gun and pressing it into Bryant's back, the smaller man forced him into the ditch by the side of the road. The larger man, meanwhile, turned his gun on Virgie. He told her to get into the car. According to her later testimony, she hesitated. Why should she get in the car, she asked. If she didn't, he replied, he would kill her.

"If I get in the car will you kill me?"

"No, if you will get in the car."

The larger man turned the front seat down and told Virgie to get in the back. He climbed in after her and, she would testify, raped her.

"This act was done forcibly and against my will," a summary of her testimony in a legal brief would later read, "under no circumstances would I have considered it."[6]

"What did he say?" the prosecutor, Denver Dudley, asked Virgie. "It may be embarrassing; I want you to tell the jury."

Arthur Adams, the defense attorney, stood to object, his height contrasting sharply with Dudley's shorter stature.

After a bit of wrangling before Judge Neil Killough, Dudley was allowed to ask his question again. "Now," he said to Virgie, "just tell the jury what it was he said to you down there, while the act of intercourse was going on, just tell them what he said."

"Well," she replied, "he asked me which was the best, a white man or colored man. I didn't answer."[7]

In trials like this one—with a white woman accusing a Black man or boy of sexual assault—much of the testimony on direct examination mirrored that in trials with white defendants. Prosecutors still had to establish that a sexual assault took place, that it was forcible, that there was resistance, and that the attack was "complete."[8] But white women in these trials often added details that served to make the Black men look less respectable. For instance, multiple white women testified that their alleged Black assailants used "vulgar" language.[9] Such women also clearly attempted to reclaim their position in the Jim Crow racial hierarchy through the use of racial epithets that, whether conscious of not, put their own whiteness into high relief (and served to rebut likely rumors of miscegenation). Thus, a white girl named Ada recounted in 1926 that she had told her alleged assailant, William Cutts, "he better go on and shut up his black mouth."¹⁰ Another white accuser, in 1949, recalled calling her attacker a "dirty black devil."¹¹ Virgie herself always referred to Clayton and Carruthers as "these boys."¹²

Prosecutors regularly brought up the defendant's race or took care to emphasize it—in an effort to underscore that such sex could not have been consensual. In the trial of William Cutts, for instance, the prosecutor frequently referred to the defendant as "the negro," and engaged in this exchange with Ada:

"When he got hold you got badly scared?"

"Yes, sir; if anything grabs you right now it scares you."

"Especially a boy like that."¹³

Prosecutors also emphasized the whiteness and innocence of the accusers. For example, in the state's brief, Ada was described as "a little white girl," and the prosecutor asked questions that highlighted that she was picking flowers with her eight-year-old friend at the time of the assault.¹⁴ In a trial in 1918, meanwhile, the prosecutor casually referred to the defendant as "the [n-word]."¹⁵

For scholars assessing sexual assault trials nearly a century later, interracial ones are particularly fraught. Norms of gender and race were often contested and reinforced in ways that must be carefully parsed and understood in their proper context. These trials simply must be approached more skeptically than those in which white women accused white men of rape. As the historian Lisa Lindquist Dorr has written, "Trials themselves were public performances in which white juries usually, though not always, acted out their role as the protectors of white women, adhering to a script of sexual and racial ideologies made familiar through southern rhetoric. Most accused black men were convicted, but they were not necessarily guilty."¹⁶

That spring day in 1935, Virgie testified that both masked men—the larger one and the smaller one—had raped her in turn. She said that while the men were assaulting her, they pulled up their masks, and the glare of the headlights of passing cars, or the glow of the moonlight, illuminated their faces. There was no doubt in her mind, she told the men of the jury, that Clayton and Carruthers were these two men: Clayton the larger one, Carruthers the smaller one. Virgie testified that after the two had raped her, Clayton suggested killing her and Bryant, but Carruthers would not agree to the idea. Rather, the two masked men told her and Bryant to wait fifteen or twenty minutes before leaving—that they were going to walk into town to catch a freight train, and if Virgie and Bryant passed them before they got to the railroad, they would kill them. Virgie and Bryant waited five minutes before leaving; they drove north, turned left toward a corn field, and then continued into town, where they immediately sought out the police.[17]

Tall and thin, a pair of spectacles adorning his bald head, Arthur Adams rose for his cross-examination. When did Virgie separate from her husband? the defense attorney asked. Was she just separated or was she divorced? Whom did she live with after they separated? When did she start going on dates with other men? When did she start going on dates with Wiley Bryant? What did they do together on these dates? What were they doing at the cemetery that night?

How did she know that Clayton and Carruthers were the two men who attacked her? he wanted to know. Wasn't it dark that night? Wasn't she blinded by the flashlights? Weren't they wearing masks? Was she aware that her identification of Clayton and Carruthers might cost them their lives? Why hadn't she screamed?[18]

At the interracial rape trial in Mississippi attended by an NAACP investigator in 1944, the investigator noted that the accuser answered "more sharply" on cross-examination. "Why hadn't she screamed? Because the man said he'd kill her. . . . Why hadn't she made an outcry? Because she was crying. No, she had not said, at the previous hearing, those words the defense attorney read. What had she said? She didn't remember. But did she remember the facts? Thereupon [she] flared up self-righteously: 'I never told a lie in my life!' Toward the close of her questioning by the defense attorney, her answers alternated 'I don't remember' and 'I was crying,' which were safe if often senseless replies."[19]

In trials with a white woman accusing a Black man of sexual assault, the accusers' whiteness did not completely insulate them from dangerous insinuations on cross-examination. The accusers were still asked the questions most female accusers were asked, ones designed to imply that they were promiscuous or that they had not adequately resisted.[20] Nonetheless, for white women these questions were far less probing than they were when the accusers were Black women. This accords with the work of Lisa Lindquist Dorr. After studying 288 "cases of black-on-white rape in Virginia" between 1900 and 1960, she concluded, "Many white women who accused black men of rape faced the same distrust and suspicion that confronted women who raised charges of sexual assault by white men." However, "white women in these cases escaped scrutiny into their sexual history or reputation at trial."[21]

Was Virgie lying? Such a question matters a great deal, yet it is fraught, and it is difficult to answer almost a century later. Certainly, Virgie could have been raped by two masked men that dark night in December and been mistaken about the identity of her attackers; certainly, she could have been raped but then lied deliberately about the identity of her attackers because Sheriff Wilson or Deputy Lindsey or someone else asked her to do so. As the jurors and spectators would soon hear, Clayton and Carruthers had powerful evidence that they could not have attacked her that night.

In order to understand Virgie's testimony, and the possibility that she may have been lying, it's useful to think about the precarious position of women accusers in this moment, even if they were white.

Many people at the time claimed that the accusers in sexual assault trials were motivated by money. Numerous witnesses testified that the mother or the father of an accuser had approached the defendant (either directly or through an intermediary) to ask for money in exchange for the charges disappearing.[22] In the 1936 trial of a white man named Bill DeVoe, for instance, DeVoe's mother testified that the white accuser's mother told her that "it cost her a lot to cure the little girl [of the sexually transmitted infection, allegedly transmitted to her by DeVoe], and she didn't want to get [DeVoe] in trouble and wouldn't have him arrested if I would pay the doctor bill of $150."[23] Such arrangements were closely related to revenge. One defense witness claimed in a 1938 trial that the (white) accuser's mother had said something to the effect of "she was going to get rid of her husband if she had to frame him and put him in the penitentiary."[24]

Witness testimony in carnal abuse cases further reveal allegations of attempted bribery or extortion. In several cases, witnesses alleged that either the accuser or her family demanded money to make the prosecution go away.[25] "Immediately before or immediately after the warrant was out, did you send anyone to talk to Johnny [the alleged assailant]?" a defense attorney asked one girl's father in 1935.

"No sir," he replied.

"Did you say if he would give you some money it would stop?"

He denied it.

"You say you didn't send anyone to Johnny to see if he would give you money and get it quiet?"[26]

In several other cases, it appears that the accuser had borne a child and the defendant had failed to provide financial support or failed to fulfill a promise to marry his child's mother.[27]

And witnesses weren't the only ones making these claims. One (white) accuser recalled in 1940 that her assailants "tried to buy me off, offered me a dollar and I said 'no.' "[28] A (white) defendant in another trial (in 1925) claimed that the accuser's father and brother were trying to coerce money from him, while a defense attorney in yet another trial (in 1929) asked the (white) defendant, "Didn't you have your mother and Mrs. Cox go see Daisy [the accuser] and offer her twenty-five dollars if she would drop this prosecution against you?"[29]

The veracity of these allegations is often unknowable. But their very existence attests to the familiarity jurors would have had with these kinds of private wrangling and negotiations, even if just as rumor. In carnal abuse cases, in particular, there would have been considerable motivation for the families of teenage girls who had borne children by older men to obtain either financial support from these men or a promise of marriage. Whether these motivations led to extortion is impossible to say, and it would be problematic to speculate. Nonetheless, this testimony underscores the precarious positions in which pregnant or unmarried women or girls would have found themselves—and the awareness members of the jury would have had of this precarity.

Indeed, evidence indicates that some poor white women, burdened with bad reputations, accused Black men of sexual violence in attempts to safeguard or reclaim their own insecure positions in the racial, sexual, and economic hierarchies. For instance, the two white women who accused the Scottsboro Boys of rape both appeared to fear that they themselves could be arrested for traveling across state lines for an "immoral purpose"—both had records for vagrancy, and one had served time for adultery. As the historian Glenda Gilmore has written, the two "must have quickly recognized their stark choices. They could either go to jail or claim to be victims. They cried rape."[30] Likewise, Dorr has noted several instances of white women accusing Black men of rape to cover up their own premarital or extramarital affairs—especially affairs *with* Black men—as well as examples of a white community "com[ing] together and us[ing] a charge of rape to exile an unpopular black man."[31]

Just what all this means for Virgie is uncertain. She was poor; she was separated from her husband; she was alone in a car with another man. Economically, socially, probably physically, she was vulnerable. But Virgie also had her whiteness, a valuable if unstable form of capital, a chip to play. Perhaps nothing clarifies the injustice of Jim Crow more than the fact that so many possibilities are thinkable—collusion, coercion, desperation. Undeniably, her testimony was useful to the injured sheriff, his ambitious deputy, and the big planters eager to maintain control of a restive labor force and still avoid the unwanted attention a lynching might bring.

13 • Marguerite Testifies, Mid-1930s

The courtroom was packed as the trial of Mr. Freeman began. It was a typically hot St. Louis day, sometime in 1935, 1936, or 1937. The usual courthouse contingent was present, plus the gamblers in their pinstripe suits, their "makeup-deep" accompaniment, and a number of acquaintances of Marguerite's mother's mother. "Some people even stood behind the churchlike benches in the rear," Marguerite later recalled. She sat with her mother and uncles—Bailey couldn't be there—and periodically Mr. Freeman swiveled in his chair at the defense table, to "look empty threats" at Marguerite.

Now eight years old, Marguerite settled into the witness stand. She was wearing her mother's navy coat with brass buttons.

"What was the defendant wearing?" asked Mr. Freeman's lawyer.

"I don't know," Marguerite replied.

"You mean to say this man raped you and you don't know what he was wearing?" the lawyer asked her. In Marguerite's memory, he "snickered as if I had raped Mr. Freeman." "Do you know if you were raped?"[1]

Courtrooms and witness stands could be intimidating places for children, especially those contending with trauma and threats. Sometimes, children simply refused to speak. A decade earlier, in Arkansas, a Black girl named Rebecca testifying against her alleged assailant before the grand jury initially refused to answer questions. "Did he ever have any improper relations with you?" asked the prosecutor.

"I am not going to tell you," Rebecca replied.

"Why won't you tell?"

"I don't want to."

"Did he tell you not to?"

"No, I don't want to."

The questioning continued like this for some time. But then, at trial, Rebecca did testify—at great length. It emerged that her assailant had cajoled and threatened her into silence.[2]

Mr. Freeman had threatened Marguerite. But Bailey had told her that he would not let Mr. Freeman kill him. Marguerite trusted Bailey. As a gust of laughter escaped the courtroom audience, following the defense attorney's insulting question, Marguerite felt glad for her mother's coat, a "friend" in this "strange and unfriendly place."

"Was that the first time the accused touched you?" Mr. Freeman's lawyer asked Marguerite.

"The question stopped me," she later recalled. "Mr. Freeman had surely done something very wrong, but I was convinced that I had helped him to do it. I didn't want to lie, but the lawyer wouldn't let me think, so I used silence as a retreat."[3]

Exceedingly few sexual assault cases with Black victims went to trial. In fact, for the most part only two categories of cases with Black accusers have survived in the archive: the first—the majority—involved assaults against Black children, and the second involved assaults against unusually prominent Black women. Typical of the second was the prosecution of a white man named James Whitaker who was accused of raping an educated Black woman named Ruth in Monroe County. Ruth was a teacher and a social worker—she "assist[ed] the County superintendent in educational work among the negroes ... visit[ing] the county schools and help[ing] the teachers in methods of teaching ... help[ing] the boys and girls throughout the community to be better home makers and better house keepers." Quite unusually, after Whitaker was convicted, the newspaper didn't print Ruth's race.[4]

In some rape cases involving Black girls, the prosecutors attempted to use their questioning to imply that the girls came from prominent or otherwise respectable families, in an effort to generate sympathy for the accusers among members of all-white juries. In one case, the prosecutor asked questions that led the fifteen-year-old accuser to testify that she had attended school and even played the piano; in his opening statement, the prosecutor characterized her father as "a hard working man." In another, the prosecutor put the girl's mother on the stand and asked her a series of repetitive questions that revealed that she was the wife of the pastor of a sizeable church.[5]

Of course, not all Black sexual assault survivors were considered "ideal" by the white authorities, and this was reflected in the cases that did or did not make it to trial: those without an "ideal" victim rarely reached a courtroom. Yet occasionally a case did get before the jury involving a Black woman who had, allegedly, strayed from conventional sexual mores. In one 1922 case in which a Black man had allegedly raped a married Black woman who lived in a tenant house on a plantation, much of the defense argument centered around the woman's supposed vocation. The defendant's lawyer claimed that she was "a common prostitute that he"—the defendant—"had been using ever since she was 13 years old," and that she "was a degenerate and operating a rendezvous for crap shooters and drunken negroes." Such an argument was more than what modern readers might call "slut-shaming"—though it was that. It also sought to exploit pernicious stereotypes about Black female sexuality, namely, hypersexuality, wantonness, and a predilection for prostitution.[6]

In part because of the pervasiveness of these stereotypes, most sexual assault prosecutions with a Black accuser involved crimes against children. Examining a slightly earlier period, the historian Estelle Freedman concluded that the relative "willingness to bring charges for intraracial assaults upon young black victims reflects a pattern in which age mattered in the successful prosecution of rape. . . . The press and the courts may have been more sympathetic to young women, whether black or white, in this era of increased concern about preserving childhood innocence." The flip side of this concern about childhood innocence, however, was a disregard of those deemed insufficiently innocent, those allegedly lacking in purity or chastity. And, as Freedman has noted, "African American girls had to be younger than their white counterparts to be identified in the press as victims of rape." Black girls "lost that innocence at a younger age, the press implied, making them more vulnerable not only to assault but also to courtroom claims that they had consented to sex."[7]

"Did the accused try to touch you before the time he or rather you say he raped you?" Mr. Freeman's lawyer asked Marguerite.

Again, his question was met with silence. "I couldn't say yes and tell them how he had loved me once for a few minutes," Marguerite later reflected. "My uncles would kill me and Grandmother Baxter would stop speaking, as she often did when she was angry. And all those people in the court would stone me as they had stoned the harlot in the Bible. And Mother, who thought I was such a good girl, would be so disappointed. But most important, there was Bailey. I had kept a big secret from him."[8]

These feelings—fear, shame, dread—were not at all unusual for Black girls suffering the trauma of sexual assault in the Jim Crow South. Subsequent scholars have documented the almost universal post-traumatic stress suffered by sexual assault survivors, especially Black women and girls in the Jim Crow South.[9]

Undoubtedly, the questions posed at trial could exacerbate this trauma. Often, the questions that Black women and girls were asked on the stand were identical to those asked of white women and girls: Did they resist? Did they resist *enough*? Were they "actually raped"? "I was resisting and fighting all I could," testified one Black woman in 1926, "and said God have mercy on me, don't let this man over power me, what do you want, turn me loose, you low down thug, I plead with him and begged all the time, I said what do you want, he said you know what I want don't you, I said do you want my money, I said don't kill me for my money . . ."[10]

Sometimes, though, the questioning gestured—intentionally or unintentionally—to racist dynamics in Jim Crow society. For instance, in 1950 Mable, a thirteen-year-old girl, was asked questions that revealed that she went to school only part time; during cotton-picking season, there was no school for Black children. During such times she had to pick cotton in the fields with the rest of her family.[11]

And often, the questioning was more explicitly racist. In 1919 Aurelia, a sixteen-year-old girl from Prairie County, was asked on cross-examination about "other negro boys" she went out with: how old they were and whether one of them "gave you $10.00 to put it on the defendant here."[12]

Everyone in every Jim Crow courtroom was aware that all-white juries did not, as a rule, value Black lives or Black bodily autonomy. This was illustrated most clearly in the 1922 trial of a Black man named Otis Cauley, accused of raping a Black woman named Sallie. In his closing statement, the prosecutor told the jury that Cauley "should be convicted in order to protect the white women of the State from such assaults, and that if he was turned loose our wives and sisters and daughters would be in danger of such assaults by the defendant." Cauley's attorney later recalled immediately noticing the jurors—white men—suddenly sit up straight and stare intently at the prosecutor. "In some of their faces it could be distinguished that their blood began to boil." This was, after all, telling the jurors that "if they turned this negro loose, he would transfer his operations to the white race and that our wives, sisters and daughters would be in danger of the same kind of attacks by the defendant." Such a statement implicitly valued the safety of white women over the safety of Black women.[13]

Even Cauley's lawyer—a white man—made astoundingly racist and gendered arguments in seeking to save his client's life. He worried about the "dangerous precedent" the prosecutor's statement would set: "What chance will a negro have who (as practically all of this class do, and always have done and always will do), after fooling a prostitute of his own race, and trying to get away without paying her, gets arrested for rape?" He sought to distinguish his case from another, which the prosecution relied on, involving a Black man convicted of raping a white woman. In that case, argued the defense attorney, statements such as the prosecutor's were relevant. But in this case, the defendant "had only bilked a negro prostitute who he had used for many years. He had never invaded the white race, but the jury were made to believe that if they didn't convict him, he would do that." This statement made clear that, to so many in Jim Crow society, only men's freedom and white women's safety mattered; the freedom or safety of Black women never entered the legal system's equations.[14]

Summoning racist ideas laden with centuries of history, Cauley's attorney continued: "This court may not know it, but if every negro who is guilty of the same act that the proof in this case develops, is to be sent to the penitentiary, few will be left in the south. Negroes, it is true, are to be tried under the same laws as the whites, but convicting them under charges of immoral conduct among themselves does not afford protection to colored society or improve their morals because there is no foundation in the race upon which morality can be built. There are exceptions, of course, but I am discussing the regular 'plantation [n-word],' the kind the defendant and the prosecuting witness are; the kind who are essential to the cotton plantations of the South. It is not, and should not be the policy of our courts to hold the negro race to high moral standards as between the members of the race. It can't be done, and to attempt it would deplete the Southern plantation of their valuable labor." This attorney was *explicitly* arguing that rape cases involving Black perpetrators and Black victims were not the province of the legal system—or, if they were, that Black people should be judged using different standards. And such a disparity was justified by the need to maintain a sufficient labor pool for the plantations.[15]

Courts embraced the same racist stereotypes. "What has been said by some of our courts about an unchaste female being a comparatively rare exception is no doubt true where the population is composed largely of the Caucasian race," noted a Florida Supreme Court decision in 1918, "but we would blind ourselves to actual conditions if we adopted this rule where another race that is largely immoral constitutes an appreciable part of the population."[16]

In carnal abuse prosecutions (such as that of Mr. Freeman), where adult men were accused by young girls under the age of consent, the accusers were almost always asked questions meant to establish their "competency" to testify in the first place. Yet even these questions were inquiries into morality. In his study of sexual assault cases involving children in New York City, Stephen Robertson noted that in the early twentieth century, girls—some as young as five—frequently testified at trial, and judges and lawyers routinely grilled them about their families, their schooling, and what would happen to them if they lied.[17] The same was true in Jim Crow Arkansas. Virtually every young accuser (white and Black) who testified in a carnal abuse case was asked some version of "Do you know what happens to little girls that don't tell the truth?" Nearly all responded "Go to the bad man," "Go to the bad place," or "Go to hell."[18]

Such questioning, designed to prove that accusers or other young witnesses were competent to testify, inevitably instilled fear in these children. Occasionally judges took measures to limit this fear. When a ten-year-old white girl named Dorothy first tried to testify against her assailant in 1935, she became visibly frightened and answered "I don't know" to almost every question. Later, the judge cleared the courtroom for her to testify again. However, such mercy was rare, and more often children were left to tell their story before an imposing room of strangers, as Marguerite Johnson was.[19]

From his examination of New York cases, Robertson found that prosecutors had to walk a fine line in the questions they asked and the testimony they solicited. On the one hand, they had to "clearly establish that the offense had taken place." But, on the other hand, they did not want the young girls to appear to be too knowledgeable about sex, which might tar them as promiscuous. Robertson found that prosecutors "sought to negotiate that tension, first, by asking leading questions that provided girls with language that was appropriate, yet still had a clear meaning for jurors, and, second, by convincing judges to allow girls to point to the parts of the body that they referred to in their testimony." The girls, in turn, "typically testified vaguely that the defendant 'did something to me' or 'done bad,' or else they used the more descriptive, but sexually inexplicit, phrases 'he took out his thing and put it in me' or 'he put his privates in my privates.'"[20]

This vagueness was often present in the Arkansas trials. Most young accusers claimed that the defendant "hurt me real bad," or "started doing it," or used some other euphemism.[21] "Do you know what your private parts are, your sexual organs?" a prosecutor asked a white thirteen-year-old accuser in 1938.

"No sir."

"Where did he put this part he took out of his pants, what part of your body did he put it on or in."

"Down in my front part."[22]

Much of this questioning was quite leading. "Did you walk under the bridge with him honey?" was a typical question. Sometimes judges even tacitly permitted it. "Avoid leading questions," a judge instructed the prosecutor in one such trial, before adding, "Of course this is a young witness." In another trial, the defense attorney even objected to the judge asking his own leading questions.[23]

The girls' physical size and appearance was also emphasized at trial. "I will just ask the court to let this child stand up," one lawyer said in 1929 of a white six-year-old named Martha, who had been permitted to testify, "for you to observe her size and apparent underweight for a child of her age, her angelic innocence and those other physical facts, in determining her maturity."[24]

The other distinctive aspect of carnal abuse trials was that, unlike in rape or attempted rape cases, the prosecution did not have to prove force or resistance. Rather, Arkansas statute demanded proof only of a man "carnally knowing, or unlawfully abusing, any female person under the age of sixteen years."[25] In an age when most children were not born in hospitals, and formal birth certificates were still a relative rarity, witness testimony often devolved into conflicting accounts of whether an alleged victim was just under or just over the age of sixteen. Dueling school records and family Bibles were frequently summoned.[26]

The primary questions posed to underage accusers after establishing competency, then, were whether intercourse had taken place and how old they were when it did. Defense attorneys often pressed them on whether they were *really* underage at the time they had sex.[27] The broader defense strategy on cross often seemed to be pointing out inconsistencies in the accusers' testimony, apparently in order to paint them as generally untrustworthy.[28] Yet in the face of such questioning, some girls responded with defiance. A white accuser named Opal, for instance, replied in 1928 to the question "You have made a different statement about this matter?" with the answer "I certainly have."

"Have you not made a statement that you had no such improper relations with him?"

"Yes."

"And you now state that you did have such relations with him?"

"Yes."

"Which statement is correct?"

"The one I just said."

"Why did you make the other statement?"

"Because I was scared."

"Which statement do you mean to say you were scared when you made it, when you had relations with him, or when you had not?"

"I wasn't scared when I made any statement, I was scared because he was out and he knew where I lived."[29]

"Marguerite, answer the question," demanded Mr. Freeman's attorney. "Did the accused touch you before the occasion on which you claim he raped you?"[30]

All eyes turned to Marguerite.

Notably, the surviving testimony of some Black women and girls reveals acts of resistance—acts made all the more stunning by the oppressive context of the Jim Crow social order. Mable, the thirteen-year-old Black girl, had done as Pearl had and used the defendants' license plate against them; she'd had the presence of mind to memorize their license plate number and then tell it to her mother, which resulted in the arrest and prosecution of her assailants. And Sallie—the Black woman whom Otis Cauley's attorney had labeled a prostitute—testified that immediately after he raped her, she managed to get ahold of her gun, and then she chased him quite a distance.[31]

The act of testifying, on its own, must be understood as extraordinary resistance in a society that so comprehensively marginalized Black women and girls.

Faced with the lawyer's question, Marguerite answered, "No." Everyone in the courtroom had expected it, she believed. But the lie caught in her throat; she could not get air. "How I despised the man for making me lie," she later recalled. Crying, she screamed out loud, "Ole, mean, dirty thing you. Dirty old thing." The prosecutor quickly ushered her off the stand.

Ultimately, Mr. Freeman was convicted, but he received a sentence of just one year and one day, likely reflecting the scant value the justice system and predominantly white juries placed on Black girls' lives and well-being. "Black men typically received shorter prison terms for intraracial than for interracial rape," Estelle Freedman has noted of the late nineteenth century, "for even when black women won convictions, doubts about their chastity influenced sentencing."[32]

Yet, in this case, Mr. Freeman would never even serve his meager sentence. Instead, he would be found murdered.

14 • The Origins of an Advocate, 1908–1933

The Bethel-Wallace trial. The Clayton-Carruthers trial. The Freeman trial. It would be easy, in focusing on these legal battles, to develop tunnel vision, to stare too intensely at just the stories at the heart of this book. But as pretty much all the lawyers in these trials were well aware, there were other, major rape trials during these years. Together, these rape trials would revolutionize American law and American society, leading directly to modern criminal procedure protections and the modern model of the "civil rights lawyer."

When it came time for William and Norma Marshall of Baltimore, Maryland, to name their baby boy, on July 2, 1908, they decided to christen him "Thoroughgood," after his uncle, who shared that unusual name (another uncle was named "Fearless"), and his grandfather, a former slave called "Thorney Good." The rest of his grandparents were already free by the time a southern militia fired on Fort Sumter, launching the Civil War, which in turn caused enough confusion for young Thorney Good to escape to Baltimore. There, after serving in the U.S. army, Good founded what would become the largest Black-owned grocery store in town; not too far away, a Black man named Isaiah Williams, another veteran, was also opening a chain of grocery stores. Their children—a railroad porter and schoolteacher, respectively—were members of the tight-knit Black bourgeoisie, and before long they would have children of their own. It was thus with the fruits of two Black-owned groceries that young Thoroughgood—who soon decided he preferred the shorter "Thurgood"—would be raised to adulthood. His was a politically active household, in an integrated neighborhood, in a city and a country dominated by white supremacist oppression.[1]

The very same summer that Thurgood Marshall entered the world, a rape allegation led to a lynching, which in turn would lead to the founding of the NAACP. The boy and the Association would come of age together. As Marshall began to read, write, and debate in a home that inculcated in him a sharp sense of humor and a deep pride in his race, the NAACP began tentatively to involve itself in litigation, inaugurating its work in this realm by petitioning the governor of New Jersey to pardon a Black farmworker who had shot a sheriff who had invaded his home in the dead of night, seeking to enforce an "agricultural contract" that was akin to slavery.[2] As Marshall enrolled first in the segregated but locally prominent School Number 103, then in the dilapidated and deeply inadequate Colored High School, the NAACP created an official Legal Redress Committee, which for its first two decades was led and staffed by elite, white lawyers—those who could represent the victims of mob violence or appeal flagrant denials of liberty without worrying that they would be run out of town.[3] As Marshall, a strong if occasionally rebellious student, enrolled at Lincoln University—the "Black Princeton"—already intent on being a lawyer, the NAACP, defiant but not radical, challenged race discrimination in the civil service, in educational institutions, in public accommodations, and especially in residential housing.[4]

Marshall began college in the autumn of 1925, having labored for months in a too-tight uniform as a railroad-car waiter to be able to afford it. Perhaps in an effort to set himself apart from his honor-student older brother, Aubrey—then a senior at Lincoln—Thurgood quickly became known for his pranks, his card games, his "inventive use of curse words," and he was soon suspended. Fellow classmate Langston Hughes described him as "rough and ready, loud and wrong, good natured and uncouth." Eventually, though, he became a more dedicated student, not coincidentally around the time he started dating Vivian "Buster" Burey—a student at the nearby University of Pennsylvania—and just as his political sensibility was awakening. Still, the part of college that seemed to excite him most was the debate club, and even as a freshman he made it onto the varsity team, traveling to Boston to debate the realities of race relations with students from Harvard. Yet, even in such rarified environs, he could not forget his social position; he later described himself as "the most uncomfortable son of a bitch in the world" when he was seated next to a white woman at the Harvard Club.[5]

After graduating from Lincoln in 1930, Marshall knew his next stop would be law school, but he also knew he could not apply to the University of Maryland School of Law in his hometown of Baltimore, for it did not admit Black students. So he enrolled instead at the law school of Howard University, another prominent, historically Black institution. In many respects, it was not an attractive proposition: Howard's law school lacked accreditation; Marshall's mother had to pawn her engagement and wedding rings in order for him to afford to go; to get there, Marshall had to wake up at five each morning to catch a train to Washington, D.C. But Howard had something no other law school possessed, and this would ultimately change Thurgood Marshall's life: Charles Hamilton Houston, its new dean.[6]

Houston was nothing short of brilliant, and everyone knew it. He had been born in Washington, D.C. in 1895, the son of a lawyer and grandson of slaves, and sped through Amherst College—graduating at nineteen as its valedictorian—and then Harvard Law School, where he became the first Black editor on the *Harvard Law Review*. He quickly obtained an additional pair of graduate degrees and began teaching at Howard in 1924; just five years later the university's trustees would make him the dean. Houston quickly set about reforming the law school, in an effort to gain accreditation and create a training ground for elite Black lawyers. He began strongly discouraging part-time or night students and frankly told Marshall's class that he would take pleasure in flunking two-thirds of them. He replaced many of the school's part-time white professors with full-time Black ones, providing a striking contrast to Lincoln, which had an almost exclusively white faculty when Marshall had attended. The Depression was on, and Marshall knew he would have to leave his collegiate pranking behind if he were to make it through Houston's rigorous program. He devoted himself to his studies, and soon he was the top student in his class—a ranking that secured him a job in the law library and a chance to work closely with Houston.[7]

These were heady times for the budding Black legal elite. Walter White had just taken over at the NAACP, and, responding to dissatisfaction from within and without, he began turning the Association away from its near-exclusive reliance on white lawyers, elevating a number of Black lawyers to work in the national office. At the same time, civil rights activists were in an uproar over the Scottsboro Boys, the nine Black youths wrongly accused of raping two white women in Alabama in 1931. Initially, the NAACP and other members of the Black bourgeoisie were reluctant to get involved on the Scottsboro Boys' behalf, to potentially "identify the Association with a gang of mass rapists unless they were reasonably certain the boys were innocent," as one historian put it. The Association was especially reluctant after the communist-affiliated International Labor Defense (ILD) swiftly dispatched attorneys and organizers to represent the Boys and organize the community, for it was less than two decades since the first Red Scare had conflated communism with criminal sedition. But after the NAACP was inundated with inquiries about the case, White hurriedly hired local lawyers for the Boys. Over the next several months, the NAACP and ILD battled fiercely for control of the Scottsboro Boys' case, badmouthing the other side to the Boys' families and even sending dueling lawyers to try to get the others excluded in court. The Association and the communists disagreed vehemently on whether to hold rallies and demonstrations in addition to representing the Boys legally; the ILD was in favor, whereas the NAACP worried it would get "these lads murdered." In the end, the NAACP lost the support of the Boys and their families and was forced to withdraw. It was a bitter defeat, casting a shadow on White's early tenure atop the NAACP and leaving the communists to lead the struggle that would become the defining narrative through which the NAACP's lawyers—and much of the nation—would interpret Black-on-white rape cases. Many of the rape cases the Association would take on in the 1930s and after—including, eventually, the Clayton-Carruthers case—were explicitly compared to Scottsboro, which had become a byword for Jim Crow injustice.[8]

Scottsboro had another lasting effect on the NAACP. It established what would become the Association's go-to defense strategy in interracial rape cases where white women accused Black men: impugning the ostensible victims' character in order to cast doubt on their allegations. From the start, the ILD had fixated on the two white women's promiscuity, venereal disease, and past sexual histories. In the retrials, ILD attorneys attempted to humiliate the two women, investigators dug into their pasts, and even the prosecutor regarded them as "women of a very low type." Similarly, in the NAACP's annual report for 1931, Association officials wrote, "Of the girls, one had a police record and the other was of low intelligence." This strategy would quickly become standard in the NAACP's work on rape cases—including, eventually, the Clayton-Carruthers case.[9] It fit well with the misogynist framing already present in the laws of rape.

Thurgood Marshall undoubtedly kept close track of the Scottsboro case. Indeed, because of his job in the law library, Marshall often had considerable time to do research: "I didn't have nothing to do but read law," he remembered. "Sometimes we'd take the rape cases and read all the rape cases." His dedication to legal research caught the attention of Howard's professors, and soon one—William Hastie, who would one day be appointed the first Black federal judge—asked for Marshall's help in the case of a Black man who sought to challenge his exclusion from the University of North Carolina's School of Pharmacy. Dean Houston, too, noticed the bright young man, and soon he was treating Marshall and the few remaining students in his class "as if they were partners in an elite black law firm." Houston brought Marshall with him to a meeting of the National Bar Association—which had been founded a few years before, after the American Bar Association refused to admit Black lawyers—and introduced him to many of the leading civil rights lawyers of the day. And then, during Marshall's final semester in law school, Houston asked for his help on a murder case, one in which a Black man was accused of killing two white women.[10]

It did not take long after the January 1932 murders of Agnes Boeing Ilsley—a white member of the "fox-hunting set" in Middleburg, Virginia— and her maid, Mina Bruckner, also white, for the community's suspicion and wrath to descend on a young Black man, George Crawford. But it took a year to the day for the proper authorities to find him, in Boston. Not long after the powers that be in Virginia announced their intention to extradite Crawford, the case came to the attention of Walter White, "Mr. NAACP" himself. White immediately saw the case's potential, not just because it could be used to challenge the constitutionality of all-white grand juries but also because of the similarities between Crawford's predicament and the ongoing Scottsboro controversy. White was desperate that the ILD not scoop the NAACP, as it had with Scottsboro, and sign Crawford as a client. Quickly, he wrote to Charles Hamilton Houston, asking him to take charge of this "most difficult situation"—without compensation, of course, as the Association was "absolutely strapped." Long an admirer of the ILD's bold tactics, Houston asked White if perhaps the communists might be better for Crawford, but White hastily dismissed such concerns. With some trepidation, then, Houston acquiesced, quickly planning a trip to Virginia to investigate the matter himself.[11]

Houston knew he would need assistance with the legal research, and so he turned to Howard's star student, Thurgood Marshall. Almost immediately, he dispatched the twenty-five-year-old law student to Howard's library to dig up supportive precedent. In the weeks that followed, Marshall assisted Houston and other, more senior legal minds in strategizing Crawford's defense.[12]

The law student and the law school dean would develop a close if contentious relationship. Houston often fretted about the folksy and vivacious Marshall, breaking up the younger man's craps games and trying to limit his partying. "His only crime," Marshall later reflected of his teacher, "was he ate too much. He didn't drink, didn't carouse, he just worked. He was a workaholic that's what killed him." Marshall worked hard, of course, but Houston worked nonstop, in his office at Howard or in the study of his tony Washington home, just a few doors down from Marshall's former college classmate, Langston Hughes. Now, Houston and Marshall had to unite their disparate styles, all in an effort to save a Black man from legal—or illegal—lynching. "Well we all worked, we had good arguments," Marshall would recall of their early collaborations. "You know Charlie was always the boss there was never any trouble but we had real good solid arguments and we weren't too polite. I know you would go out and work all week or two weeks on a particular section of a brief and bring it in and pass it around the group and sometimes you would get the following reply: Are you really that stupid or are you putting on? That's the kind of way we talked to each other."[13]

For six months, Crawford's attorneys battled the Virginia authorities in federal court, eventually taking the case up to the Supreme Court. In the end, Virginia prevailed, and Crawford was extradited to Leesburg late that fall.

When it came time for the NAACP to appoint local counsel to appear at trial in Virginia, Houston insisted that "Crawford could be defended by all Negro counsel." The nation's most prominent civil rights advocates, Black and white, including Walter White, felt strongly that there *had* to be white counsel at the table—to appease the lynch-mad Virginians—but Houston would not be moved; having only Black lawyers at the defense table "would mark a turning point in the legal history of the Negro," he wrote. Reluctantly, White agreed.[14]

At trial, Houston—tall and grand and unflappably dignified—was nothing short of dazzling, and, even though he had gradually begun to believe Crawford was actually guilty, Houston nonetheless convinced the Virginia jury to spare his client's life, sentencing him to life in prison instead. Although communist critics were deeply displeased that Houston did not appeal the exclusion of Black people from the grand jury, activists at the time and academics in the future have agreed that the case represented a milestone, demonstrating to a nation that a Black lawyer could excel in a southern courtroom. Walter White was thrilled by Houston's performance, and though he'd originally planned to indict the Jim Crow justice system for railroading Crawford, he changed his public posture to instead emphasize Houston's historic achievement.[15]

In the aftermath of the Crawford case, White began relying on Charles Hamilton Houston (and other Black lawyers) more and more. That fall, Houston began working on other NAACP cases, and within a year he had moved to New York to become the Association's "special counsel," its principal attorney. Soon, he would begin compiling a crack team of young Black lawyers. It was the height of the Depression, but the Association's membership had soared past 100,000, and excitement was in the air. "Never before . . . have our branches in all sections of the country, North and South, East and West exhibited such a militant, alert, fighting spirit," wrote one young NAACP official.[16]

Contrary to some accounts, Thurgood Marshall had missed the Crawford trial; he had been organizing an economic boycott in Baltimore at the time. But he had closely tracked its progress, and the stakes of the legal research he had done thrilled him. He graduated from Howard on a monstrously hot June day, the top-ranked of the mere handful of students that had made it through Houston's demanding curriculum. Even in the midst of his alcohol- and cigar-fueled graduation revelries, Marshall did not lose sight of the lesson he had learned in the Crawford case: he would not merely be a lawyer, but a "social engineer," precisely as Houston had trained him. "That was our purpose in life."[17]

15 • The Witnesses Testify, 1929

It was still morning on April 11, 1929, when Pearl was allowed to leave the witness stand. The next witness called to rise before the crowd, to walk across the terra-cotta floor tiles, and to take the stand was W. L. Dismukes, a constable for the town of Leachville. Virgil Greene, one of S. L. Gladish's assistants in the prosecutor's office, rose to question him.

The questioning started off simply enough. Greene asked the constable about arresting Frank Bethel and Mike Wallace, about taking them to jail, about searching the clearing in the woods for the tossed license plate. About finding it. Such testimony served a clear legal purpose: establishing the facts, verifying Pearl's story. But just a few minutes passed before Dismukes's story veered into matters of morality. The witness recalled that, upon being arrested, the two men had said "they didn't know that goddam woman and had never seen her before."[1]

Although political opponents would later dismiss him as far from the sharpest lawyer in town, Virgil Greene was not stupid. Born in rural Indiana in 1871, he'd attended Georgetown University and Indiana University Law School, moving to Mississippi County shortly thereafter to follow his brother into practice. Although too old to be drafted in World War I, he'd volunteered to serve with the American Red Cross, leaving the war with the rank of captain. A heavy-set man with a fairly full head of hair, a Mason and a Methodist, he'd become deputy prosecuting attorney under Gladish in 1926.[2]

Greene knew that the defendants' use of the word "goddamn" would have an effect on the jury. This testimony, unrelated to the questions of force, resistance, or other statutory requirements to prove rape, was nonetheless vital to show that the defendants had transgressed the bounds of respectability.

At noon, they broke for lunch. When they returned, defense attorney E. E. Alexander, who had begun his cross-examination shortly before the break, likewise turned quickly to propriety.

Did the constable smell Pearl's breath for alcohol, he asked Dismukes.[3]

Did Pearl "have much company while she was at your house," he asked Ida Culp, the young woman who ran the boardinghouse where Pearl stayed in Leachville, some minutes later.

"No, sir."

"Never went riding with anybody?"

"No, sir."

"Nobody ever called on her, no gentlemen friends?"

"Not that I remember of."[4]

These inquiries were utterly irrelevant to the question of whether Bethel and Wallace had raped Pearl, but everyone knew that they were highly important. This was because, at this time, witnesses in rape trials often testified not primarily so that they could establish particular facts, but rather so they could establish or impugn the morality of the accuser and the accused.

It was around twilight, one spring evening in 1928, when R. A. West saw the Chevrolet Coupe speed by. West, a middle-aged farmer who had lived in the area for some twenty years, was traveling south in his Ford, the sun falling behind the horizon, when he saw the Coupe approaching. At first he assumed it was a bunch of drunks, so he moved to the right to give the Coupe a wide berth. But then, as the Chevrolet passed him, West heard someone holler, "My god, won't you help me?" or something to that effect. Looking at the car, he saw two men and a woman inside; it seemed to him that the man that wasn't driving had his hand over the hand of the woman. The woman was wearing a red sweater. It was Pearl.[5]

"You don't know whether it was a man or woman hollered?"

E. E. Alexander was getting into the rhythm of his cross-examination, the slim, handsome attorney staring at the Missouri-born cotton farmer.

"No, sir," West replied.

"Or what they said?"

"No, I didn't even consider what they said."

"And you don't know who it was in the car?"

"No, sir."

In Jim Crow rape trials, many cross-examinations began this way—with simple inquiries into the facts, the defense attorney trying to poke holes in the story the prosecution was beginning to tell. But quickly, inevitably, they would morph into referenda on sexual promiscuity.

"Now was the girl in the middle or sitting on one side?" Alexander asked West.

"Well, she was apparently in the middle or partially on one of them's lap."

"You didn't see any struggling or anything like that going on?"

"I didn't pay attention. It was just about that quick."

"It might have been that they were holding each other's hands?"

"It might have been."[6]

With West and several other witnesses, Alexander was determined to show that Pearl had not screamed, or hollered, or cried, or otherwise attempted to escape.[7] This was important to the defense case as it hinged, in part, on proving that Pearl had not adequately "resisted"—a statutory requirement. Yet it was also important because Alexander wished to imply to the jury that Pearl was promiscuous—and thus the kind of woman who might *willingly* sit in the lap of a man not her husband or have extramarital sex with two men in a ditch.

Arkansas case law at the time made clear that evidence regarding an accuser's sexual behavior was admissible, but only for certain purposes. Evidence of a woman's "reputation for chastity" could be introduced, the state supreme court held in 1909, but only to "show her consent, and so no rape," not to impugn her credibility more broadly. "The reason for admitting evidence concerning her chastity is that a jury might more readily infer assent to the intercourse in an unchaste woman than in a virtuous one." The court later clarified that the prosecution could introduce "evidence of her reputation for chastity" only to rebut the defense's "evidence of reputation for unchastity."[8]

In practice, however, the line between showing consent and shaking credibility was blurry, and witnesses invoked women's "unchastity" with abandon. It was common for defense witnesses to testify that an accuser's reputation for morality was "bad."[9] For example, after the defense attorney questioned a white accuser named Daisy in a 1929 trial, he paraded forth sixteen witnesses who each testified that she had a bad reputation as far as virtue and chastity were concerned. In another trial, a defense witness accused the accuser of being a prostitute. In response, the prosecution called the sheriff to testify that he'd searched the accuser's bag and found no money; the accuser herself was then recalled and said the accused men had not offered her any money and "I would not have taken [it] if they had."

Such rebuttal witnesses were not uncommon. In Daisy's case, the prosecution called a neighbor of hers named G. S. Clark to testify that he'd never observed any immoral conduct by Daisy or her daughters. The defense pushback to these rebuttal witnesses could be brutal, however. "What color is [Daisy's] hair?" the defense attorney asked Clark.

"Dark."

"What color is [Daisy's] baby's hair?"

"Light hair."

"It is very much like you isn't it."

"No sir. It looks more like you."

"You sleep in the same room with her?"

"Yes sir."

"Sleep in the same bed."

"No sir."[10]

The most extreme example of witnesses attempting to impugn a woman by accusing her of promiscuity can be found in the 1927 seduction trial of Guy Taylor. Since, as the state supreme court put it, "Actual personal chastity on the part of the woman was necessary to make out the crime of the defendant" in a seduction case, Taylor's attorneys brought in several men, each of whom testified that they'd had sex with the woman.[11]

In the Mississippi County Courthouse, this strategy to damage Pearl's reputation began in earnest as soon as the prosecution rested and the defense began to make its case. For the next hour or so, a bevy of white men traipsed to and from the witness stand, each giving essentially the same testimony. They had been at the Poplar Corner store that day—hanging out on the porch or trading their wares or out front boxing with their friends—and they had seen Bethel, Wallace, and Pearl pull up in the Chevrolet. They had seen Pearl sitting in one of the men's laps; they had not seen her try to escape; she had made no "outcry." These defense witnesses differed fairly substantially on which of the men—Bethel or Wallace—had bought the cigarettes, and what time the car had arrived at the store, but they were in agreement on Pearl's lack of apparent discomfort or desire to get away.[12]

A number of other witnesses—all white men—testified that they had seen Pearl and the defendants drive by on the road, laughing and having a good time, or "loving up a bit," or else Pearl had cheerfully waved out the window and called, "Hello there."[13]

"If there had been an effort made by this woman to get out of that car and got her, part of her body, the lower limbs out of the car, and had been pulled back in the car could you and would you likely have noticed it?" Alexander asked one witness.

"Well, I expect I would."[14]

There was both a legal and a tactical point to this parade of witnesses. Legally, this testimony was meant to convince the jury that Pearl had not resisted; tactically, this testimony was meant to convince the jury that she wanted to have sex with the men. Sometimes, the men's testimony betrayed casual sexism. "She was nervous?" S. L. Gladish asked one witness toward the end of the trial.

"Well, seemed to be, yes, sir."

"Excited?"

"Seemed to be." The witness then continued, "Ever had a woman rattle at you?"

"It's been a while."

"Well, I have."[15]

On cross-examination, Gladish and Greene often attempted to impugn these witnesses' credibility, implying that they were friends with one of the defendants or inquiring into the state of *their* marriages.[16] But they also sought to use their questioning to paint Bethel and Wallace in an unflattering light for conduct quite unrelated to their alleged assault. In their questioning, Gladish and Greene repeatedly alluded to Bethel's previous arrest for violating the liquor law and asked whether the two men had alcohol on them that night.[17]

In other Arkansas rape trials, this type of questioning was typical; many witnesses testified to the morality or immorality of the defendant. Often the prosecution would bring in four or five witnesses to claim that the alleged rapist's reputation for morality was "bad."[18] The defense would, in turn, call witnesses to counter that his reputation for morality was "good."[19] While much of this testimony was brief—just a few background inquiries and then a specific question about whether the defendant's reputation for morality was good or bad—sometimes witnesses went into more detail.[20] In a number of cases, women testified that the defendant was so upstanding that they trusted him around their young daughters.[21] None of this testimony was strictly relevant. But it was vital to these trials nonetheless, because so much witness testimony was about trying to convince the jurors of the immorality of one side or another.

16 • The Witnesses Testify, 1935

"You didn't see any part of his face, did you?"

Arthur Adams, defense attorney for Bubbles Clayton and Jim X. Carruthers, stared at Wiley Bryant, the young farmer who was with Virgie on the night in question. Surely the crowd was bristling with anticipation, the packed bodies warming the courtroom despite of the chill outside. Armed deputies were stationed throughout the room. Tension was in the air.

"No, sir," Bryant replied.

"Didn't see that mouth of his, could you?"

"No, sir."

"And didn't see that kinky head of his, either, did you?"

"No, sir; I didn't."

"You didn't see that flat nose and mouth of this little boy, did you?"

"No, I didn't."

"You couldn't?"

"No, sir; I couldn't."[1]

Almost a century later, we can only wonder how Clayton and Carruthers must have felt to hear their own defense attorney casually use such racist tropes. It was mere minutes into the testimony of Wiley Bryant, the first witness to follow Virgie on the witness stand, and already their racial identities were being explicitly litigated. And, as they watched and listened—forced to remain impassive—Clayton and Carruthers surely knew that the racist questioning and testimony was far from over.

Yet Clayton and Carruthers may well have known—or certainly suspected— that a reliance on these racist tropes was an ordinary part of interracial Jim Crow rape trials. At the trial of a Black man named Willie Martin in 1926, for instance, one prosecution witness recalled seeing the defendant walk in front of his sister's house before the assault and claimed, "He was watching the house and I knew my sister was alone." This invoked the postbellum racist myth that Black men were sexual threats to white women. Another witness identified Martin by testifying, "In my opinion, that is the man I saw; the reason I say so is that he was very black; he looks like the [n-word]; I could not describe his face because I was not close enough."[2]

Unsurprisingly, prosecutors egged on such testimony. After the mother of one Black defendant testified in 1926 that she always made sure to watch when "strange children come around," the prosecutor clarified, "You watch that boy when little white girls come around, do you?" Another prosecutor, in 1932, repeatedly asked a witness if he recalled seeing "a darkey" or "a strange darkey."[3] Even defense attorneys invoked racist tropes, though they apparently did so to underscore the notion that Black people were interchangeable, and thus white prosecution witnesses might be mistaken in identifying the defendant. "Did he walk like any other negro looking over his back shoulder?" one defense attorney asked an eyewitness on cross-examination in 1936. "Aint there hundreds of negroes walk along about the same way?" he continued.[4]

Race was thus a tool wielded by both prosecution and defense. For the prosecution, the invocation of racist tropes served to remind the judge and the jury of their duty to uphold white supremacy; for the defense, reliance on racist tropes served to reassure everyone present that the defense was not seeking to undermine the racial hierarchy but simply to operate within it. By implying that all Black people walked alike, for instance, the defense attorney sought to exculpate his client even while potentially incriminating any other member of his client's race.

Wiley Bryant testified about knowing Virgie since childhood, about going out with her and driving her to the graveyard that night, about the clouds in the sky and the moon peeking from behind, about being set upon by two masked men, one large and one small, about being struck over the head with a flashlight and dragged into a ditch, about fearing for his life. He constantly referred to "the big negro" and "the little negro," calling them both "boys." He admitted that he had not "worked with negroes a whole lot," but he was certain of his identification of them. He claimed that Clayton "talked like any other negro."[5]

On cross-examination, Adams pressed him on why he hadn't yelled and what he had *actually* seen. "Did you hear them say anything about this young lady at all?" he asked.

"No, sir; I did not," Bryant replied.

"And you saw yourself nothing that occurred to her?"

"No, sir."

"If anything did occur to her?" Adams pressed.

Bryant refused to answer.[6]

Adams also pressed him on the state of Virgie's marriage. Had Bryant known whether Virgie was divorced when he started going out on dates with her? Did Virgie say anything about being married at the time? Did Bryant know her husband? Had he seen him recently? Such questions were obviously meant to impugn Bryant's morality, to make the upstanding men of the jury distrust this lothario in their midst.[7]

After Bryant came Arch Lindsey, the deputy sheriff, taking the young farmer's place on the witness stand. Lindsey would have been a familiar sight to the jurors, not merely because he was a well-known lawman in town but also because he was supervising the other deputies stationed throughout the courthouse that day, determined to prevent a lynching in spite of his own personal predilection for racist violence. With thinning gray hair and floppy ears and jowls, often photographed wearing a fedora, Lindsey looked like a typical southern deputy sheriff. A native of Paducah, Kentucky, he had begun working for the Blytheville Police Department in 1920; in the decade and a half that followed, he'd become locally famous for destroying more whiskey stills than any other cop in town.[8]

In his testimony that day, the deputy sheriff did not mention beating Clayton and Carruthers within an inch of their lives shortly after arresting them; perhaps that much was simply implied. Rather, he spent virtually all his brief time on the stand describing taking Virgie and Bryant to death row so the two could identify Clayton and Carruthers as the rapists. He resolutely denied instructing or guiding Virgie and Bryant to pick these two specific men; they had picked the two of their own accord, he maintained, and he had stayed outside. Then, the deputy sheriff stepped down and resumed his job of guarding the courtroom.[9]

And with just the testimony of Virgie and these two witnesses—Bryant and Lindsey—the prosecution rested.

In later filings to the court, Clayton's and Carruthers's defense team would point out that the prosecution had called no medical expert to testify to any examination of Virgie—"and obviously no such examination was ever made." The defense would write that the prosecution had given no "evidence as to her physical condition. . . . There was no evidence introduced of any after effects of the 'double rape'; no emotional or mental disturbance and no physical laceration, pain or suffering."[10]

The defense pointed this out because, at the time, medical testimony was very common in Jim Crow rape trials. The primary reason medical professionals (mostly doctors, but some nurses and health officers) testified in forcible sexual assault trials was to establish that sex (or sexual assault) had taken place or had not taken place. "There is no question but what she had been penetrated; no question whatever," went typical testimony.[11] They could also provide scientifically informed eyewitness testimony. One physician testified in 1935 that he examined the defendant, who was covered in blood, and the defendant "told me that his wife was menstr[u]ating was where he got the blood[.] I examined her and found that she was not menstr[u]ating."[12]

In sexual assault cases involving children, medical testimony often focused on whether the rape as described was physically possible.[13] Some questions were more insulting. If a girl had truly been raped wouldn't she have cried, one lawyer asked in another 1927 trial. Then the judge weighed in: "Don't you know as a matter of fact, Doctor, that the girls of today with the violent exercise that they undertake and hoeing cotton, climbing fences, running and playing, sutting sprouts and doing different things, that is, taking different violent exercises, in a measure destroys the hymen?"

"No, sir," the doctor replied. "No sir."

The judge asked whether it was true that "any woman who had gone through the process of intercourse" would be in "a very nervous condition?"

"Well it would depend a whole lot on whether it would be a legitimate or illegitimate intercourse," said the doctor.

"And it would depend on the temperament of the person?"

"Yes sir."

"Some can withstand more punishment than others, cannot they, Doctor?"

"The word punishment, I don't know whether that would apply to legitimate intercourse."

"Cannot one person stand more punishment in illegitimate intercourse than another?"

"If sexual intercourse is held between the male and female, if it is where both parties are willing and both parties assist in the manipulation of things, I do not consider that there would be much punishment about it."

"What [e]ffect does fear have on the nervous system?"

"It is owing to the person. Some persons will get very excited; others will not show it at all."

"As I understand, fear in some people would develop a highly excited condition?"

"Yes."

Eventually, the judge asked what would be the effect of a twenty-three-year-old man of his size raping a thirteen-year-old girl of her size? The physician responded that it would vary. Surely this testimony was mortifying and degrading for the thirteen-year-old accuser, as well as others present.[14]

This exchange reveals another purpose of medical testimony: it was a vehicle for men (nearly always members of the same communities as the accusers) to shame women and girls through insinuation for their sexual behavior. "There was evidence that she had had intercourse lots of times," testified one physician.[15]

"You thought she was suffering with a venereal disease?" a defense attorney asked another physician on cross-examination. There was no obvious tactical purpose to this question other than to castigate the accuser (and the physician admitted he had been "of that opinion," though he later learned he was "mistaken," rendering it even less relevant). In the trial of a white man named J. G. Cabe, where the accuser was just fourteen, a doctor testified that he found "[e]vidence of extreme foul odor with a discharge from the vagina field" and that he believed this odor was caused by "uncleanliness."[16]

Such discussions of "uncleanliness" and being "dirty" were, at this time, inescapably linked in the public mind to venereal disease, deviant women, and eugenic concerns about certain individuals being unfit to reproduce.[17] And evidence of venereal disease often played a key role in forcible assault trials involving children. The transmission of syphilis or gonorrhea could be a crucial piece of evidence supporting an allegation that intercourse had taken place, and, as historian Stephen Robertson has shown, this evidence was much more common in cases involving young accusers.[18] In the case of Dan Durham, a white man accused of raping six-year-old, white Martha Sue, for instance, one physician testified in 1929 that Durham had gonorrhea while two physicians testified that Martha Sue had the same infection. Faced with this apparent evidence of intercourse, defense attorneys often attempted creative dodges on cross-examination. One physician was asked whether or not Martha Sue could have contracted her gonorrhea "from using a toilet seat or from the use of a towel?"

He responded, "I couldn't say that. I have always thought that maybe you could contract it in a toilet some way, but I have always had an idea that there had to be two there."[19]

Medical testimony in rape trials with Black defendants often functioned in a particular way. The defense would attempt to introduce expert testimony indicating that the defendant was mentally incompetent. The prosecutor, in turn, would counter by asking whether all Black people were not equally incompetent—a question the physicians either answered in the affirmative or qualified in such a way as to reinforce racist and eugenic stereotypes. "Doctor, did you find him any different mentally than the ordinary negro of his age and his raising and his training?" was a typical question. The defendant was just an "average cotton field negro," meaning he was "of a low grade of mentality," was a typical answer. Thus, these trials functioned to validate race science in the public square; no accuser's testimony challenged the prevailing notion of racial difference. Indeed, it was the defendants who introduced and tried to achieve salvation through this testimony.[20]

It is notable that even physicians testifying on behalf of Black defendants denigrated the intelligence of all Black people in their testimony. Nonetheless, this can once again be read as a survival strategy on the part of the defendants—it would have done them no favors with an all-white jury to trouble the racial hierarchy and openly assert their equality.

A young Black man named Willie Manuel walked to the witness stand. He was the first person to testify for the defense, other than Bubbles Clayton himself. He was supposed to be the first of several alibi witnesses who could show that Clayton and Carruthers could not have assaulted Bryant or raped Virgie that night the previous winter.

But Manuel ended up testifying for just a moment. He didn't remember exactly where he'd been on December 21, 1934, he claimed. He didn't have any specific recollections of that specific evening. It had been so long ago.[21]

Arthur Adams hastily ushered Manuel off the stand. The defense attorney had surely seen this coming; from his days of traveling around the county to find witnesses to sign affidavits on his clients' behalf, he knew that many Black people were terrified of publicly standing with Clayton or Carruthers for fear of retribution. There were a number of clear alibi witnesses who had refused to testify at all. But Willie Manuel was not the defense's only option; Adams quickly moved on.[22]

The next defense witness to walk past the packed courtroom crowd, easing past the limbs overflowing into the aisles, was a Black woman named Myrtle Dodson. Born in 1908 or 1910, Myrtle had left school after the sixth grade and married by sixteen; she worked as a laundress and lived on West Cleveland

Street, just a quick walk from the courthouse.[23] Unlike Willie Manuel, she was not intimidated. She told the jurors that at about eleven on the evening of December 21, 1934, she, Jim X., Bubbles, and a number of other Black folks—including Evelyn Boyon, Lucien Taylor, Tommy Anderson, Elma Dodson, and Katie Carruthers—had piled into Jim X.'s car and driven to the state line. They were just driving around. They were gone for about an hour and a half, returning around midnight or one in the morning, and they had stayed together the whole time.[24]

After Myrtle Dodson came Evelyn Boyon, and then Lucien Taylor. Both testified as Dodson had—that all of them had been together that evening. That they were just playing cards and driving through the countryside. That they had left around eleven and stayed together. That Willie Manuel had been with them too.

On cross-examination, prosecutor Denver Dudley attempted to poke holes in their story—did they remember exactly what they had done the night after? What about in the hours before they drove to the Missouri state line? How well did they really know Jim X. or Bubbles? Did either of the defendants have guns with them that night?

"Tell the jury whether you had a conversation with Bubbles that night, in which he told you that he had shot a sheriff and had to leave town," Dudley said to Evelyn Boyon on cross. Arthur Adams immediately objected, and Judge Killough sustained the objection.[25]

The defense witnesses were committed to their testimony but ready to admit what they did not recall, insistent but not defiant; in a courtroom packed with angry white neighbors, the Black witnesses knew there could be deadly consequences if they were defiant. Nonetheless, their testimony in the face of such violence—just months after their neighbors had assembled into a lynch mob seeking to murder Clayton and Carruthers—constituted an act of remarkable courage.

The prosecution could not let this alibi testimony stand. After the final defense witness finished testifying, Dudley called Eddie B. David to the stand. David was the deputy sheriff who claimed to have found Carruthers's six-cylinder Chevrolet on a gravel road a few hundred yards from where the sheriff was shot. He also claimed to have found caps, hoods, and white handkerchiefs within—perfect for two men intent on disguising themselves.

On cross-examination, Adams asked where these items were now. David replied that he had taken them to the police stations, but that he no longer knew where they were. Conveniently, they had been lost.[26]

17 • The Recovery, 1930s–1953

Shortly after the trial of Mr. Freeman ended, Marguerite was playing Monopoly with Bailey on the floor of her grandmother's home, attempting to sublimate her shame. She was not playing well, she later recalled, because she was consumed with guilt for having "lied"—both by omission to Bailey and on the witness stand, when she answered "no" to the question of whether Mr. Freeman had touched her.

Suddenly there was a sound. It was the doorbell. Since their grandmother was busy in the kitchen, Bailey answered the door to a tall, white policeman. "Had they found out about the lie?" Marguerite thought frantically. "Maybe the policeman was coming to put me in jail because I had sworn on the Bible that everything I said would be the truth, the whole truth, so help me, God." To Marguerite, the policeman looked so tall and so white.

"Mrs. Baxter," he said to Marguerite's grandmother, "I thought you ought to know. Freeman's been found dead on the lot behind the slaughterhouse."

Wiping her hands on a dish towel, Grandmother Baxter spoke softly in her German-accented English. "Poor man. Do they know who did it?"

"Seems like he was dropped there. Some say he was kicked to death," the policeman replied.

Grandmother Baxter thanked him, delicately adding, "maybe it's better this way." The policeman left a moment later.[1]

Marguerite's whole world was ripped open as guilt consumed her. "He was gone," she thought, "and a man was dead because I lied. . . . Obviously I had forfeited my place in heaven forever, and I was as gutless as the doll I had ripped to pieces years ago. Even Christ Himself turned His back on Satan. Wouldn't He turn His back on me?" She could feel "evilness" flowing through her, ready to escape the moment she opened her mouth, so she clamped her teeth shut.

Grandmother Baxter turned to Marguerite and Bailey: "You didn't hear a thing," she told them. "I never want to hear this situation nor that evil man's name mentioned in my house again. I mean that." She began baking an apple strudel in celebration.

Bailey looked frightened. But Marguerite was beyond scared. She believed that if she talked to anyone else, "that person might die too." Her words, her mere breath, was dangerous. Wracked with guilt and self-loathing, she made a decision: "I had to stop talking."

She would hardly say a word for the next five years.[2]

Although Marguerite may not have known it, Mr. Freeman's fate was far from unique. As the sociologists E. M. Beck and Stewart E. Tolnay have noted, between 1882 and 1930 almost 150 Black people in the South were lynched by "mobs that were integrated or composed entirely of African Americans." The states of Arkansas, Mississippi, and Louisiana account for more than 60 percent of these "black-on-black lynching incidents," with most of the lynchings occurring in the Mississippi Delta, in places with high Black populations. Most of the victims of these intraracial lynchings were accused of "serious crimes"—46 percent of murder, 26 percent of rape or incest. In 1892, for instance, a Black man in Desha County, Arkansas, was accused of raping his seven-year-old stepdaughter. After he was arrested, a mob of Black men overpowered the local constable, dragged the man to a nearby cotton gin, and hanged him.

This relatively unknown historical phenomenon attests to the hidden forms of agency that Black southerners claimed in the era of Jim Crow, as well as their profound mistrust of the judicial process. In cases of sexual assault, Beck and Tolnay have written, "The formal justice system clearly overlooked or dealt relatively leniently with crimes against black victims. Perhaps black mobs took matters into their own hands because they had little confidence that the white-dominated justice system would mete out punishment that was swift enough or severe enough to satisfy them."[3]

In the first few weeks after Marguerite stopped talking, her family accepted her behavior as "a post-rape, post-hospital affliction" (though no one would mention the word "rape" or the experience in her grandmother's house). Yet after a doctor pronounced her "healed," and she still did not begin talking,

Marguerite's family grew upset. Why wasn't she back on the sidewalks playing handball? "When I refused to be the child they knew and accepted me to be, I was called impudent and my muteness sullenness," she recalled. She was punished, she was beaten, and still she did not start speaking again.[4]

"Brutally traumatized by rape and emotional betrayal," the scholar Suzette A. Henke has written of Marguerite, she "responds by constructing a wall of protective silence around her imperilled ego." According to Henke, Marguerite "exhibits the classic symptoms of post-traumatic stress disorder."[5]

Unsure what else to do, her St. Louis relatives decided to send Marguerite, as well as Bailey, back to her grandmother Annie Henderson, back to Stamps. Bailey was crushed, sad to be leaving his mother. Marguerite was simply impassive.[6]

The year was 1936 or 1937. Franklin Delano Roosevelt was president, the Southern Tenant Farmers Union was making headlines across Arkansas, and Clayton and Carruthers sat on death row. A photographer named Dorothea Lange was capturing images of Dust Bowl migrants, homeless and unemployed. Tornados, heat waves, and floods were wracking the nation. An Atlanta housewife named Margaret Mitchell was reveling in the success of her pro-Confederate epic novel, *Gone with the Wind,* and the new chancellor of Germany, Adolf Hitler, was sending troops into the Rhineland.

Marguerite probably knew little of this. Stamps was exactly as still and barren and safe as she had wanted, although she had not known she'd wanted it. There was none of St. Louis's noise or activity or loud family gatherings, only silent lanes and lonely houses and dirt yards. "Nothing more could happen, for in Stamps nothing happened," she would reflect. She remained silent.[7]

Shortly after Marguerite arrived back in Stamps, Momma was braiding her hair. The older woman told the young girl, "Sister, Momma don't care if these people say you must be an idiot, or you must be a moron, 'cause you can't talk. Momma don't care. Momma know when you and the good lord get ready, Sister, you gonna be a preacher and you gonna be a teacher and you gonna teach all over this world."[8]

For a year, Marguerite did not speak, even as Bailey regaled the residents of Stamps with the wonders of the big city to the north. His tales of tremendous watermelons and indoor toilets and Frigidaires enraptured listeners for whom news events usually included, in Marguerite's telling, "droughts, floods, lynchings, and deaths." Bailey was the only person Marguerite could speak to, even a little, and though he was many inches shorter than she was, he protected her. Years later, she would recall in a poem their silent walks and quiet talks, her brother protecting the reticent girl from prying adults. The citizens of Stamps did not understand her silence, but they seemed to forgive her for it.[9]

But then Marguerite became acquainted with Beulah Flowers, a woman she would call "the aristocrat of Black Stamps." Graceful and refined, smiling often but laughing rarely, "very, very Black, and very, very beautiful," Mrs. Flowers would soon take Marguerite under her wing and help her regain the ability to speak. "She was one of the few gentlewomen I have ever known," Marguerite would later write, "and has remained throughout my life the measure of what a human being can be."[10]

Beulah Sampson was born in Clow, Arkansas, in 1883, the daughter of former slaves. She attended the local public schools in Clow, then Clow Seminary, an elite preparatory school. She received her teacher's license in 1902 and taught in the public schools in Hempstead County, ultimately completing her own education at Clow Seminary—renamed Bowen Seminary—in 1909. That year she married Alonzo Flowers—the son of a distinguished Black family—and in 1909 they moved to Stamps, settling into a roomy house with a broad porch. By the time Marguerite arrived back in town, Mrs. Flowers had taught children in school; taught adults gardening, poultry farming, canning, and health care; and opened a store and funeral home with her husband. A few years later, she and her son Harold would organize the Committee on Negro Organizations to "spearhead the fight for equal justice and educational opportunities for blacks in Arkansas," one descendant would write.[11] Decades later, when Marguerite wrote a memoir of this period, she wrote Mrs. Flowers's first name as Bertha, not Beulah, "simply because I did not want to intrude upon her privacy."[12]

One summer afternoon, after Mrs. Flowers bought several paper sacks of groceries from the Store, she asked Momma if Marguerite could carry them to her home. For Marguerite, this invitation felt like winning a million dollars. Desperate to make a good impression, she put on one of her school dresses to accompany Mrs. Flowers to her house. "Now, don't you look nice," the older woman said to the silent girl.

As they walked back together along the rock road, passing farms and houses, Mrs. Flowers said to Marguerite, "I hear you're doing very good school work, Marguerite, but that it's all written. The teachers report that they have trouble getting you to talk in class." Marguerite could not answer, but she hung on Mrs. Flowers's exquisite diction and pronunciation.

"Now no one is going to make you talk—possibly no one can," Mrs. Flowers continued. "But bear in mind, language is man's way of communicating with his fellow man and it is language alone which separates him from the lower animals. Your grandmother says you read a lot. Every chance you get."[13] (One day, Marguerite would tell an interviewer, "I was always a reader and I read out of self-defense, out of loneliness."[14])

"That's good, but not good enough," Mrs. Flowers went on. "Words mean more than what is set down on paper. It takes the human voice to infuse them with the shades of meaning." Marguerite instantly decided to memorize this last statement. "It seemed so valid and poetic," she would later write.

When they arrived at Mrs. Flowers's house, cool and dim and comfortable, the older woman gave Marguerite some tea cookies and iced lemonade, and the two began what they would eventually call Marguerite's "lessons in living." Sitting there, at Mrs. Flowers's kitchen table, Marguerite was introduced, for the first time in her life, to poetry, to lyricism. Mrs. Flowers read the opening lines of *A Tale of Two Cities* in her educated, melodic voice, the phrases cascading gently like notes of music.

"How do you like that?" she asked Marguerite after a while.

Marguerite knew a response was expected. And, with the flavor of cookies still on her tongue and the words of poetry still in her ears, she said, "Yes, ma'am."

She had finally spoken.

"It was the least I could do," she would later reflect, "but it was also the most."

After that, Mrs. Flowers gave Marguerite a book of poetry and asked her to memorize one for her. "Next time you pay me a visit, I want you to recite," she told Marguerite.

With Mrs. Flowers's patient tutelage, Marguerite began to enter "into the private lives of strangers, and to share their joys and fears." She learned to love the language, the rhythm; Dickens brought tears to her eyes. During her five years of silence, Marguerite read every book in the Black school library. Eventually, she began to speak again. *She was liked.* The attention made all the difference in the world. She was liked "not as Mrs. Henderson's grandchild or Bailey's sister but for just being Marguerite Johnson." As she would one day tell an interviewer, "Mrs. Flowers gave me back my voice."[15]

Many years later, Marguerite would write an essay for the nation's most respected newspaper, titled, "For Years We Hated Ourselves." It was an account of what scholars now call inherited trauma—how the effects of "African enslavement" were passed down through the generations until "Blacks were immersed in cocoons of self-revilement." They hated themselves, and each other, for being Black. The trauma Marguerite had endured, which had forced her to silence herself and hate herself for so long, was not a direct result of slavery—it was the result of an act of violence by a Black man. But the society in which Marguerite lived, and the legal system that adjudicated the violence done to her, was structured in so many ways by the forces of whiteness and patriarchy and brutal capitalism, all shaped in various ways by chattel slavery. For years Marguerite, who had inherited all the lessons society told about girls who had "bad things" done to them, hated herself. But literature and kindness helped her begin to feel like her own person again.[16]

Not long after Marguerite finished eighth grade, Momma announced that she was taking her to California. She was getting older, and it was time for Marguerite and Bailey to be with their parents. Momma traded some groceries for a reduction in train fare and decided Marguerite would go a month before Bailey. Marguerite had never been apart from Bailey for so long, and she was going to miss Uncle Willie and her friends. She wouldn't have to miss Mrs. Flowers, though, for the older woman had given her a gift that would accompany her all her life: a love of reading.[17]

After spending several months in Los Angeles, Marguerite and Bailey accompanied their mother to Oakland, where they lived with her extended family (since uprooted from St. Louis) in a dingy apartment. The United States declared war on Japan. Marguerite ran home from the movies in terror of being bombed, but her mother's mother told her not to worry; Franklin Roosevelt "knew what he was doing." Soon, her mother married a well-to-do businessman, and they moved into his fourteen-room San Francisco house. Their neighborhood had been a heavily Japanese area, but Marguerite began noticing that the Japanese people were disappearing—sent, unbeknownst to her, to concentration camps in the desert by that same President Roosevelt—and Black people, many of them fellow southern migrants, moved in, transforming the area into "San Francisco's Harlem" in just a few months.[18]

After a brief, unhappy period at a local school for girls, Marguerite enrolled in George Washington High School, sixty blocks from the Black neighborhood. She stuck out at this school; not only was she one of just three Black students, but at fourteen she was six feet tall, wearing size 11 shoes. Surrounded by confident, privileged white students, she no longer felt like the most brilliant student in class. "I didn't have very many friends," she would tell students at George Washington three decades later, "but I always had a love for books. Many young people have terrible insecurities so I just tried to find myself through books."[19]

A quest for self-discovery marked Marguerite's life during World War II. She visited her father in San Diego, but a bitter fight with his new girlfriend led to Marguerite contemplating suicide and ultimately spending weeks on the streets, sleeping in abandoned cars. Upon her return to San Francisco, she decided to leave school and become a conductor on one of the city's famous trolleys, ultimately becoming San Francisco's first Black conductor. After a semester of riding up and down the city's hills in her smart blue serge uniform, she felt more independent—she had her own clothes and bank account—and reenrolled in school, though she often skipped class to wander the city. She also began to try to figure out her own sexual identity, which is mysterious and somewhat frightening to many young people but may have been additionally daunting to her as a survivor of childhood sexual assault. "What I needed was a boyfriend," she thought to herself. "A boyfriend would clarify my position to the world and, even more important, to myself. A boyfriend's acceptance of me would guide me into that strange and exotic land of frills and femininity."[20]

"Among my associates, there were no takers," she continued. So she selected a handsome young man who lived up the hill, walked up to him, and said, "Hey. Would you like to have a sexual intercourse with me?" Stunned, he agreed, and they had an awkward tryst. "He may have sensed that he had been used," she would later reflect. "Thanks to Mr. Freeman nine years before, I had no pain of entry to endure, and because of the absence of romantic involvement neither of us felt much had happened." Yet a few weeks later, feeling like the world was ending, Marguerite discovered she was pregnant. Bailey, by then overseas in the Merchant Marine, advised her by letter not to tell their mother, so she hid her pregnancy and graduated high school at the age of seventeen, two days after V-E Day. That evening, she left a letter on her stepfather's bed: "Dear Parents, I am sorry to bring this disgrace on the family, but I am pregnant. Marguerite." Her feelings about sex, sexuality, and pregnancy were inextricably tied up with shame, but her mother stood by her in her matter-of-fact way. Marguerite's son, christened Clyde Bailey Johnson (and later called Guy), was born on September 8, 1945.[21]

Marguerite's "disgrace" could've had more than just social implications; at this time and place, it could even have had legal implications. Thousands of women in San Francisco and across California during World War II were arrested and held by the police for nothing more than suspicion of promiscuity or nonmarital sex. Such "morals" policing was one way that racial divisions were enforced; in San Francisco, one white woman was detained simply for being in the presence of "a colored man." A few years later in Berkeley, police stopped a Black woman trying to catch a taxi and asked her, "What have you been doing with your big black belly?" They detained her and held in jail for three days before releasing her with no charges.[22]

"The Black female is assaulted in her tender years by all those common forces of nature at the same time that she is caught in the tripartite crossfire of masculine prejudice, white illogical hate and Black lack of power," Marguerite would write years later. "The fact that the adult American Negro female emerges a formidable character is often met with amazement, distaste and even belligerence. It is seldom accepted as an inevitable outcome of the struggle won by survivors and deserves respect if not enthusiastic acceptance."[23]

For Marguerite Johnson, World War II ended with a grand celebration all across San Francisco. Gamblers shook hands with shoeshine boys; everyone was smiling. "I thought if war did not include killing, I'd like to see one every year," she would later reflect. For many Black people, the war had been a path to temporary economic prosperity. Still, the American system of racial apartheid remained. "Thus, we lived through a major war. The question in the ghettos was, Can we make it through a minor peace?" For her part, Marguerite would write, "I was seventeen, very old, embarrassingly young, with a son of two months, and I still lived with my mother and stepfather."[24]

In the months after the birth of her son, Marguerite "tussled with my future." She became a cook, rented her own room, began dating and learning to enjoy her body and the pleasure sex could bring. "My previous brushes with sex had been just that. Brushes," she would write. "One violent. The other indifferent, and now I found myself in the hands and arms of a tender man." That man left to return to his girlfriend. Bailey suggested she head to Los Angeles or San Diego. Her mother told her, "Be the best of anything you get into. If you want to be a whore, it's your life. Be a damn good one." Marguerite received a chilly reception from family in Los Angeles, so she continued south to San Diego with her baby, Guy, in tow.[25]

"Are you in the life?" a large Black woman known as Mother Cleo asked Marguerite shortly after her arrival in San Diego.

"I beg pardon?"

"The life. You turn tricks?"

Marguerite was appalled. "No. I do not."

"Well, you surely look like a trickster," Mother Cleo replied. "Your face and everything."

"Well, I assure you, I'm not a whore. I have worked as a chef," Marguerite said, haughtily.

"Well," Mother Cleo said, looking at her as if she were lying.

Marguerite started working as a waitress at a night club, but soon two queer sex workers befriended her (or, in Marguerite's possibly prejudiced depiction, attempted to seduce or even rape her), and she proposed that she become their procurer. By the age of eighteen, she would write, "I had ended up with two whores and a whorehouse." For several months, she managed their business, which she found easy and pleasant enough, buying herself a pale green Chrysler convertible with cash. But soon, fearing the "vice squad" might come for her, Marguerite abandoned the car and took Guy and fled to Stamps and to Momma. Her visit would not last long. She found that she could not abide the violence and the depredations of the Jim Crow South any longer. Momma did not think she was safe in Arkansas. Marguerite returned to California, where a relationship with L. D., a married older man, led to her briefly working as a sex worker herself, using the name Sugar. Years later, she would write with frank bitterness but with no shame of her "great slide down into the slimy world of mortal sin." Soon, however, Guy's babysitter attempted to kidnap him, Marguerite realized that L. D. was exploiting her, and she returned to San Francisco. "At home," she would write, "life stumbled on." Bailey told her he never wanted her to be "a whore" again. She briefly found a job as a chauffeur in Oakland but then lost it. Survival seemed to elude her. "My strength had fallen away from me," she would write. "For the first time in my life I sat down defenseless to await life's next assault."[26]

Marguerite would survive. But during this period, her freedom was perhaps more precarious than even she knew. For decades, San Diego authorities had been detaining thousands of women suspected of prostitution or simply promiscuous sex; the city had even enforced an archaic ordinance banning young women from attending public dances without a chaperone. Many women arrested on such "morals" charges were forcibly examined for sexually transmitted infections, and those who tested positive could be incarcerated for weeks or for months without due process.[27] Marguerite certainly had an awareness of the risks. She would later write that she had been scared of inadvertently putting "the vice squad on my trail," and she would recount the words of one sex worker—"a damn good one"—who told Marguerite that she had raked in money on the streets but couldn't do that work anymore because she was getting "busted" too many times—two or three times a week.[28]

It is illustrative to compare Marguerite's luck to the unlucky case of Martha Louise White—a biracial woman from Tennessee who spent much of her childhood living in Mississippi County, Arkansas, before moving to California in the 1940s. There she was arrested repeatedly for "disorderly conduct," "vagrancy," and suspicion of having a venereal disease. These arrests set her down a path of stigma and limited employment prospects that ultimately resulted in her having few options other than to defraud a state welfare system; under the name Linda Taylor, she became known nationwide as the "welfare queen."[29] Marguerite's circumstances also mirror those of another Black rape survivor around this time—and another future singer and celebrity. After being released from the reform home to which the authorities had consigned her after she'd been raped, a young Billie Holiday found herself excluded from the mainstream economy and began working in a brothel, briefly turning to sex work herself. Following a police raid on the brothel in 1929, the fourteen-year-old was sentenced to four months in the workhouse, a sentence that was a month longer than the one received by the man who had raped her three years before.[30]

For Marguerite, life continued. A job at a record shop in San Francisco introduced Marguerite to the "world of music," and life began to shimmer "with beautiful colors" as she lost afternoons to the songs of Charlie Parker, Max Roach, Dizzy Gillespie, and so many others. A handsome, white customer at the record shop, Enistasious "Tosh" Angelos, became Marguerite's boyfriend, and then her husband, and he asked her to quit her job. "At last I was a housewife," she would write. "I cooked well-balanced meals and molded fabulous jello desserts." Tosh was a good provider, and Marguerite "found as much enjoyment in our marital bed as he." Yet problems soon developed in the Angelos household. Tosh was a fervent atheist, and Marguerite found that her faith mattered to her. One day, after a few years of marriage, Tosh told her, "I think I'm just tired of being married." Marguerite finished cleaning the kitchen and then sat down, a sense of loss suddenly suffocating her. She had been everything the women's magazines said a wife should be; what had she done wrong? She worried that their separation would confirm her family's predictions: "Again, a white man had taken a Black woman's body and left her hopeless, helpless and alone." Her anguish soon turned to rage. She would show him. "I was no helpless biddy to be beckoned, then belittled. He was tired of marriage; all right, I would leave him."[31]

While they were married, Tosh had encouraged Marguerite to dance, and she had traveled to New York to train with Pearl Primus, one of the pioneers of integrating African dance into an American context. Before that, she had studied at night at a communist dance school when she was a teenager, and she had danced semi-professionally, if intermittently, in the years since. After her marriage dissolved in 1953, Marguerite began dancing again in earnest, finding a job six nights a week at the Garden of Allah, a San Francisco strip club reeking of beer and disinfectant. Six feet tall, dressed in sequins and feathers, the only Black dancer at the club, Marguerite began attracting attention. She was recruited to perform at San Francisco's famous Purple Onion cabaret club, and other performers encouraged her to incorporate singing into her act. She had only ever sung at church in Stamps—one journalist would claim that her repertoire at the time was little more than "Go Down Moses"— but she decided to start singing calypso.[32]

The staff of the Purple Onion told Marguerite she needed a different name—something more exotic, more glamorous. They considered various options from mythology, from literature, from Hollywood, but none seemed to work. Then Marguerite mentioned that her brother, Bailey, used to call her "My sister," which he had shortened to "My," which transformed to "Maya." Maya was perfect. "Maya what?" one of the singers asked. They decided to transform her married name, Angelos, into something less Italian- or Spanish-sounding; it would be Angelou. Maya Angelou. They toasted her transformation with wine.

Though she privately wondered if the new name would ever feel quite right, Maya Angelou was ready for her debut.[33]

18 • The Rape Docket, 1930s

Two weeks after graduating from law school, Thurgood Marshall sat for the bar exam in Maryland. He had turned down the opportunity traditionally offered to Howard's top law graduate—to study for an advanced degree at Harvard—because he was itching to sue the Jim Crow establishment (and make some money). At the end of that summer, Charles Hamilton Houston asked Marshall to accompany him on a trip through the Deep South, where Houston sought to document the disparities between Black and white schools. Marshall acquiesced, and their bond strengthened as the two tall lawyers drove down to New Orleans, snacking on fruit, the younger man appalled by his first visit to the region. As Marshall's biographer Larry S. Gibson noted, on this trip "Dean" and "Marshall" became "Charlie" and "Thurgood." Not long after returning to Baltimore, Marshall learned that he had passed the bar exam; he was officially admitted to the bar on October 11, 1933. A week later, Maryland was home to a lynching; a crowd of thousands broke into a Somerset County jail and murdered a Black man accused of attacking an elderly white woman. A little more than a week after that, the twenty-five-year-old lawyer accompanied Houston and several other Black attorneys to personally confront the state's governor about the atrocity. Marshall, never one to stay silent even though he was often the youngest man in the room, demanded of the governor, "Is there an investigation taking place within the state police department?" The governor refused to answer.[1]

Marshall hung out his own shingle, taking up professional residence in a claustrophobic room on the sixth floor of a downtown Baltimore office building, lit by a borrowed lamp and furnished with a borrowed rug. Initially, the young lawyer had trouble finding paying clients, and in his first year of practice he lost $3,500. Propitiously, Marshall's early difficulties left time for him to join his mentor, Houston, on more NAACP fact-finding trips through the South. Eventually, though, his practice picked up, and Marshall was thrown into the criminal defense of a number of Black men charged with murder. Following the advice Houston had drilled into him, Marshall was determined to be twice as good, twice as meticulous, twice as prepared as the white lawyers. Soon Marshall's skill with traversing the white-dominated legal system and arguing before all-white juries further impressed the NAACP, and as 1933 passed into 1934 the Association began turning to the young lawyer for assistance with Maryland civil rights work.[2]

Even as Thurgood Marshall was beginning what some were predicting would be a storied legal career, Charles Hamilton Houston—a professor and dean and certified workaholic—was being pulled deeper and deeper into the cause of civil rights lawyering. Soon he had relocated to New York to take over the NAACP's legal department. The cash-strapped Association could afford to pay Houston only a few hundred dollars a month, and the Harvard-educated law school dean was forced to live in a room at the Harlem YMCA.[3]

Among Houston's first cases for the NAACP following his defense of George Crawford were a string of highly publicized interracial rape cases. First, there was Willie Peterson, a Black man accused of raping and murdering two white girls in Alabama in 1931, even as Scottsboro was an ongoing national spectacle. Although he did not match the description of the alleged rapist, Peterson had been arrested and then almost murdered in his jail cell. Throughout two contentious trials (the first ended with a hung jury), Walter White had fought doggedly with the ILD for control of Peterson's representation, believing a successful defense would "materially affect public opinion and really show up the I.L.D. in their handling of the Scottsboro cases." Days later, he found himself fantasizing about the NAACP acquitting Peterson while the ILD bungled the Scottsboro cases—"There is nothing that would be more effective in showing colored people and the country at large the soundness of our criticism of the I.L.D."[4] Eventually, the NAACP wrested control of the Peterson case from the communists, and White turned to Houston. The NAACP's new chief lawyer traveled to Alabama to investigate the case personally. He quickly settled on a less combative strategy than many of the Association's critics favored, believing that he might be able to convince the courts or the governor to show mercy if he "appealed to a sense of fairness and justice among southern whites and their own interest in maintaining civil order." The

Association was terrified of how an execution would reflect on its advocacy and worried it would tip the scales in favor of the communists. The governor did ultimately commute Peterson's death sentence to life in prison, but the ILD (as well as Peterson's family) was irate that the Association pushed only for clemency and not for freedom, especially after the NAACP agreed to have Black people barred from the clemency hearings. Peterson died in prison shortly thereafter.[5]

Houston next took on the case of Jess Hollins, a poor Black man in Oklahoma who was dragged from his bed to jail, where he was coerced into confessing to raping a white woman with whom he'd been having a consensual affair; his trial lasted just an hour before he was sentenced to die. Once again, the ILD and NAACP fought bitterly for control of "Oklahoma's 'Scottsboro' Case," and once again the Association managed to secure the case, believing this was their chance to score a great victory and, in so doing, expose the communist duplicity.[6] As before, White turned to Houston, and the Association's chief lawyer appealed Hollins's conviction all the way to the U.S. Supreme Court. Not only had Black people been excluded from the jury, but the prosecutors had made remarkably prejudicial and inflammatory statements, about "defenseless little white girls" like "your girls or mine" being "assaulted by some Negro." Houston's appeal resulted in *Hollins v. Oklahoma,* what one historian called the "first significant Supreme Court victory by a Black attorney representing the NAACP." The court unanimously affirmed the principle— first established in the Scottsboro case—that the systematic exclusion of Black people from a jury was a violation of the Constitution's equal protection guarantee. (The court did not mention the racist comments.) In years to come, the court would repeatedly rely on *Hollins* to construct a powerful common law bulwark against jury discrimination. The victory did not, however, mean much to Hollins, who was convicted and sentenced to life in prison at his retrial; he would die behind bars in 1950. Swamped with responsibilities, Houston had been too busy to continue representation himself.[7]

The Peterson and Hollins cases were the Association's best-known rape cases during these years, but they were far from its only rape cases. Houston and other NAACP lawyers took on dozens of cases of interracial rape in the early 1930s, either advising local branches or assuming the mantle of representation themselves. Under Houston's leadership, the NAACP's legal department had matured and expanded. Houston had quickly built up the national office's staff and developed a national network of lawyers and investigators to implement a broad legal attack on Jim Crow injustice. He had also remade the legal department in his ideological image. Houston believed that the NAACP could achieve change only by "slowly building precedents to support equality"; radical action or moving too fast would be counterproductive. In the face of ever-increasing calls for assistance, the Association announced that it would aid only in matters that would "establish a precedent for the benefit of Negroes in general."[8] In practice, this meant taking on a lot of cases on behalf of Black men accused of rape by white women—a lot more than in years previous. Examined collectively, these cases exemplify a strategy that became the dominant script following Scottsboro: the lawyers focused on the women's promiscuity.

In the Hollins retrial, for instance, the NAACP's defense focused on the accuser's morality; they found several Black witnesses willing to testify that she "had frequented Negro dance halls and did not have a good reputation among area residents." The prosecution struck back, claiming that the accuser was "as pure as any woman in Oklahoma" and that for any Black man to have sex with her was to "rob her of the most precious thing God Almighty gave her." After Hollins was again convicted and again granted a new trial, local NAACP allies continued to dig up evidence of the white woman's "low reputation."[9] In the Peterson case, one NAACP ally wrote to White, "There is something inherently incredible in saying that one man could rape a tolerably athletic young woman in the presence of two other young women who were perfectly able-bodied." For his part, White repeated a rumor implying (euphemistically) that the women had been killed for "being out there for purposes other than the ones which they have stated."[10]

In the NAACP's immense docket of rape cases, one can see the origins of the strategy Houston and Marshall would eventually rely on when representing Clayton and Carruthers years later.

From the beginning of its legal work, the NAACP had focused disproportionately on rape cases, an area that soon became its bread and butter, constituting many of the Association's best-known triumphs, hardest-fought defeats, and most bitterly contested battles. Even before the Association became known for litigating, it had focused on countering false rape allegations against Black men in its forays with the press and Hollywood, as well as in its anti-lynching work.[11] But after failing to force an anti-lynching bill through Congress, the Association began attempting to "explode the rape myth"—that Black men habitually rape white women—by convincing courts that these Black men were innocent. At first, the national office took mainly a back-seat role as local branches led the defense of Black men from Minnesota to West Virginia to Arkansas who had been accused of raping white women and nearly lynched as a result (with local NAACP officials occasionally chafing at perceived national office disinterest or inaction). By the early 1930s, local branches were still often in the lead, but the national office was litigating more and more. The legal strategy that emerged in these cases too was, as one historian put it, to focus on "evidence of female duplicity."[12]

A typical case from this period was that of Luther Collins. After a white woman in Houston claimed a "yellow negro, about five feet ten inches tall" had raped her, the police quickly arrested Collins, who was "six feet five inches tall." The Houston NAACP branch fought ferociously on Collins's behalf, gathering money and support—as well as affidavits impugning the white woman's character. Collins was eventually set free, and the press labeled his accuser "a white woman of ill repute."[13] Walter White wrote to a Houston official, "History has been made in nailing these so-called 'rape lies' as you express it and every Negro in the United States owes you a vote of thanks." Years before, White had written that white women routinely "raised charges of rape by Negroes to cover their own misdeeds or when hysterical, or excited by newspaper or other reports of alleged attacks upon other women." Thus White was undoubtedly pleased to report "a growing scepticism regarding charges by women of rape or attempted rape."[14]

As the 1930s continued, the NAACP was inundated with letters pleading for help in rape cases. Some came from relatives or churches, but many came from the defendants themselves, often telling horrifying stories of poverty and abuse: "I am 24 years old. Have a baby going on 4 years old. My father is dead and my mother is getting old and she is poor and can't do nothing for myself," wrote one man. He continued: "Before my trial they would take me out of my cell and beat me unmerciful trying to get me to say I was the boy that committed the crime but I say no I don't know what you are talking about. They almost beat me to death but I prayed so and ask the Lord to help and take care of me. . . . Colored people down here is treated like dogs in a case like this. And there is nothing they can do for theirself. So I want you all to hurry and do something for me before it is too late."[15]

During these years, the national office under Houston began developing a system for responding to this flood of pleading inquiries. Upon receiving a request for aid, the national NAACP would typically reach out to branch offices to investigate "whether or not it is the type of case which our association can handle." In general, the Association wanted to intervene only in cases involving innocent men. Branch lawyers would speak with relatives and do research to determine "whether there has been a probable miscarriage of justice" and "whether the Association should be officially interested," before making a recommendation. Sometimes the national office dispatched its own investigators, and sometimes, if the men had not yet been convicted, local branches would dispatch lawyers to assist in their defense. "It is quite unfortunate that in nearly all types of cases of this kind the parties do not find out about our Association until they are in their extremities and have exhausted whatever meager resources that [they] have," wrote one local activist. "Nevertheless, we feel that we ought to look into such matters in order to prevent, if we can, any flagrant miscarriage of justice."[16]

By 1934, the NAACP's docket of rape cases was starting to impress observers. That summer, the *Atlanta Daily World* ran a lengthy account of the Association's many victories on behalf of Black men and concluded, "Thanks to the efforts of the N.A.A.C.P., Negroes accused of raping white women are not always lynched or sentenced to death."[17]

As more and more letters detailing rape cases streamed into NAACP headquarters, Thurgood Marshall became one of the many local lawyers to whom Charles Hamilton Houston turned for assistance. Initially, the national NAACP office had turned to the fairly new lawyer for background research, as in 1934 when Walter White asked him to compile statistics on rape in Baltimore, broken down by race. Such statistics would "be used in the fight for the passage of the [federal] Anti-lynching Bill," White wrote, as the Association was "very anxious to bring the figures up to date for the purpose of nailing once again the notion that most lynchings are for rape."[18] Soon, however, the NAACP needed more active assistance.

Just days after Marshall sent White the rape statistics, a reverend active in the local NAACP branch approached the young attorney and asked him to investigate the arrest of a Black man named William Carter. A white woman in Frederick City, Maryland, had been sexually assaulted at about 9:45 p.m. on Halloween night, and the police had quickly arrested a Black teenager and attempted to beat a confession out of him. When, a week later, it became clear that they had the wrong person, the police had arrested Carter, another Black man, whom many in the Black community believed to be "feeble minded." After two days of questioning and, apparently, abuse, Carter had confessed. Members of the Black community worried he was being "railroaded." Rumors of an impending lynching swirled. Marshall mulled over Carter's case for a day, discussing the situation with other civil rights activists. They agreed, Marshall later recounted in a brief memorandum to the national NAACP office, "that the case should at least be looked into."[19]

The very next day, Marshall drove fifty miles to the west, in his ramshackle 1929 Ford, to Frederick. He was there to speak with members of the local community, but on arriving he discovered pure pandemonium, with cops rounding up Black men seemingly at random. Sweating through his shirt, Marshall tracked down the prosecutor, the local judge, the first suspect, and a number of witnesses. Initially it appeared that he had discovered an alibi witness, but soon the alibi fell through. In addition, local Black physicians "declined to say that Carter was insane," he recorded. When Marshall returned to Frederick a few days later, Carter's lawyer told him that his client "had freely confessed on several occasions and had admitted his guilt." Marshall decided not to become more directly involved in Carter's representation. But still, at the NAACP's behest, he sat in the back of the courtroom as Carter's case was tried before three judges (an ordinary procedure at the time in cases involving the death penalty). "In the one-day trial," wrote Marshall's biographer Larry Gibson, "the prosecution called thirteen witnesses and the defense rested after only twelve minutes, nine of which were used for Carter's confession on the stand." Based on this pittance of a defense, some subsequent scholars have questioned Carter's guilt. Yet it was hardly a surprise when Carter was convicted, though it was a genuine shock that he received not death but a life sentence.[20]

Throughout the Carter saga, Marshall had kept Houston and White abreast of his actions, typing some memos himself even though he was "tired as hell, and of course my girl has gone for the day." After the trial, he wrote to his former mentor that Carter was "guilty as the devil." Local NAACP officials decided they didn't want his involvement widely known for fear the ILD might use it against them. For his part, Marshall felt he had wasted time and money and had gained little for his labor. "In fact," concluded Gibson, "he had gained much more in credibility, contacts, geographical reach, and experience." Another Marshall biographer, Juan Williams, wrote that this case allowed Marshall to "become known to judges around the state as the eyes and ears of Maryland's NAACP." The Carter matter also reflected Marshall's—and the NAACP's—longstanding conviction that interracial rape cases were a prime battleground for the contestation of civil rights. Fittingly, it would be far from the last interracial rape case that Marshall would investigate on behalf of the NAACP.[21]

19 • Bethel and Wallace Testify, 1929

The sun was beginning to sink to the west, golden rays slanting through the tall windows and lengthening the shadows extending across the courtroom's tile floors, as Mike Wallace approached the witness stand. It was, still, April 11, 1929, in Blytheville. Ordinarily, court would have recessed this late on a Thursday. But Judge Keck wanted to complete the trial as soon as possible, preferably before the court term ended the next day, and so he authorized a special evening session.[1]

Wallace would not have stood out in a crowd. He was of average height, of average weight, with a fair complexion, small mouth, small nose, and unexceptional brown hair. Photographs reveal his only arresting quality to have been his eyes—deep set, gray, and intense.[2] For most of the trial, he and Frank Bethel had sat silently behind their lawyers, just inside the bar railing, next to "their gray haired mothers," as one local reporter noted. Wallace settled into the witness stand at the front of the courtroom.

"Now Mike," E. E. Alexander began, "I want you to address your remarks to the furthest juror on this Jury so they can all hear you. Talk in a distinct voice, loud enough for them to hear you. You are one of the Defendants in this case?"

"Yes, sir."

In the deft manner of a courtroom veteran, Alexander asked a handful of routine questions to establish the essentials: Wallace's age (twenty-five), residence (nearby Monette), marital status (unmarried), relationship with Bethel (lifelong friendship). It appears that in spite of his lawyer's admonition, Wallace answered these initial inquiries too quietly, for at one point the jurors requested that the witness's chair be moved closer to the jury box; there, a wall lamp made his features glow.

With his pro forma inquiries out of the way, and with Wallace properly situated and lit, Alexander quickly embarked on the true mission of his questioning—not just of Wallace but also of Bethel, who would assume the stand shortly after his co-defendant: assassinating Pearl's character.[3]

In Wallace's and Bethel's telling, according to their testimony, this is what happened that cool, comfortable Sunday, April 1, 1928.[4]

Early that morning, Wallace first came across his old friend Bethel outside the barber shop where the latter worked. As the day progressed, Wallace ran into Bethel several more times; small-town life in the Delta could be intimate—or claustrophobic, depending on one's perspective or mood. Sometime that afternoon, Bethel and Wallace made plans to meet up with a woman Wallace was dating, who lived in the village of Etowah, a couple dozen miles away. At around four or four thirty, the two men piled into Bethel's Chevrolet Coupe and set off.[5]

As they drove east on Highway 18, in the direction of Manila, they spotted a young woman in a red sweater and black hat. Bethel and Wallace would later claim that they had stopped on the side of the road—mechanical troubles—and Pearl had approached them. According to their story, Bethel was outside of the car, working on the stopped-up gasoline tank (or maybe it was the vacuum tank—the two men were inconsistent on this point). He looked up from behind the hood of the car and asked Pearl if she would like a ride. She agreed. "I have been walking and I am tired and hot," Wallace recalled her saying.

Bethel told her to go around to the other side and climb in. A moment later, mechanical troubles temporarily at bay, the three drove off. They were traveling at what was an average speed in those days, twenty or twenty-five miles per hour. The top of the car was up; it had become a beautiful, sunny day.

Wallace would later claim that they had told Pearl they were going to pick up his girlfriend at Etowah, and she agreed to join: "She said if you will get back by nine o'clock I don't care if I do go." She never asked to return home, they testified. She never asked them to stop.[6]

"Up to that time had she made any effort to get out of the car or make any outcry or plead with you boys to turn back with her?" Alexander asked.

"No, sir," Wallace replied, "she didn't have no right to say anything."

"Why?"

"Because we hadn't made no proposals of any kind."[7]

It was Pearl, Wallace and Bethel both testified, who decided to instigate physical contact, by sitting in Wallace's lap and then starting to "love me up"—putting her arms around him and kissing him. Shortly thereafter, they claimed, she moved over to Bethel's lap.[8]

"That was rather unusual for two strangers to be in the car with a strange girl, didn't it strike you at the time?" prosecutor S. L. Gladish would ask Bethel on cross-examination, attempting to challenge their characterization of Pearl.

"No, sir," Bethel would reply.

"And you weren't annoyed by it?"—Pearl sitting in his lap, that is.

"No, sir."

"You thought it alright?"

"I had seen it happen before."

"Where?"

"You see it happen very often."

"With what kind of a girl?"

"I don't know whether you would say that kind of girl," Bethel replied, carefully.

"With a perfect stranger?"

"Yes, sir."

"Where did it happen?"

"Well, you can go most anywhere you want to and she will sit, ride in your lap if she is"—he invoked the same phrase—"that kind of woman."

"What kind of woman?"

"Well, I don't know what you would call it."

"What would you call it?"

"Well, she is not straight."[9]

In the 1920s, and in this context, these words did not refer to queer sexuality. They meant, rather, that Pearl had strayed from the path of conventional morality. For a man to accuse a woman of not being morally "straight" was a serious charge. It told the men of the jury that they should not believe anything "that kind of woman" said.

"Did you think she was starting the party a little bit early?" Gladish pressed Bethel.

"Well, I don't know, anyhow she was starting," he replied.

"Did it shock you?"

"Nothing never shocked me."

"You were expecting it??" (The transcript included two question marks, possibly indicating the audible skepticism in Gladish's question.)

"No, I wasn't expecting it, but I had seen things like that happen."
"But you were surprised?"
"Yes, sir, I was surprised where she was a school teacher."[10]

In other words, he would not have expected a schoolteacher to be "that kind of woman." But, he was telling the jury, she was. Her dress was "short as they wear them these days," Wallace testified, and she pulled her undergarments "off herself." Bethel asked her about sex, he testified, only because "she acted like she was hot"—that is, aroused and eager.[11]

This tactic was exceedingly common in other rape trials from this time. Obviously, defendants used their testimony to deny the charges against them.[12] But many used their testimony to impugn the character of their accusers. Many accused the women of being promiscuous, or of being prostitutes, or of being too comfortable around Black men, often with shocking frankness.[13]

Even in carnal abuse trials—those involving minor victims—defendants often invoked the accusers' supposed immorality.[14] "I had always thought a lot of her until I found [out] what kind of girl she was," a white man named J. C. Young testified in 1920 regarding his white teenaged accuser. He claimed to have dated her until "I saw [her] and a man walking along down by the side of the building, and when I saw her I commenced to wonder what she could be doing out at that time of the night at that place with a man."[15]

Another defendant, also white, was asked in 1929, "You could look at her and tell she was only a child?" and responded, "I could not tell it; she had on overalls down to her feet and had on a lot of rouge and had a lipstick and stuff on." A little later, he testified, "Anybody looking at them would think they were eighteen or twenty year old girls." (The girl in question, also white, was fourteen.)[16]

The testimony of Mike Wallace and Frank Bethel continued for much of the evening, the two men answering question after question after question as the sun disappeared from the sky. Wallace "stuck steadfastly to his story," one local reporter related. Bethel, by contrast, "did not fare quite as well on cross examination but his story was told in a plain manner."[17]

"Well, after we drove on a little way," Wallace told the jurors on direct examination. "Frank said something to her about intercourse and she says, No, I can't do that, and he says, why, and she says, to tell the truth about it, I had intercourse with a fellow one time and it caused me to have to lay in the hospital about forty days"—a possible reference to an abortion followed by complications—"and he assured her he had a rubber to protect her from disease or becoming pregnant."[18]

"We drove on a piece further," Bethel added, "and I asked her again, it didn't seem to have no effect on her, and so I asked her again and this time she said she would have intercourse with me if I would, if I had a rubber and would use it." Bethel told Wallace to stop the car, but Pearl said no, they were on a public road. "She said, let's go on until we can get on some off road." It was after dark, around seven or seven thirty in the evening, when they pulled off the road to have sex.[19]

The two men claimed that Bethel and Pearl had sex first; Wallace waited by the car until Bethel returned and told him that Pearl "said for you to come there quick."

Wallace gesticulated with his body to show the jurors how Pearl was sitting on the ground—"her bloomers sitting down there something like this"—and claimed that she said to him, "Hurry up, let's get this over with, my aunt will raise hell with me for it being so late, it's late now." So, Wallace continued, "We hurried as fast as we could and got the business over with."

"Did you beat or bruise her?" Alexander asked.

"I did not."

"Did you slap her?"

"No, sir."

"Threaten to kill her?"

"No, sir."

"Or curse her?"

"I did not."

"Hit her with a stick on the side of the head?"

"No, sir."

"Or on the leg?"

"No, sir."

The direct examination continued in this fashion for some time.

"Did you use any force, violence or threats in order to accomplish your purpose?"

"No, sir."

"Alright, you got through, which—but first, did she make any protest of any sort or any resistance?"

"No, sir."

"Object at all?"

"No, sir, she didn't."[20]

This was important, legally, for the defense to establish. Resistance was a legal requirement, and if Pearl didn't adequately resist, the defense argued, there could be no rape.

In this same vein, both men also emphasized that Pearl had more than enough opportunities to get away. Indeed, Alexander asked Wallace, "Was there anything to keep her from escaping or running if she wanted to?"

"No, sir."[21]

"Now Frank," Alexander asked Bethel, "during the drive, from the time she got into the car and got back tell the Jury whether or not you were constantly meeting cars and being passed by cars and passed other cars?"

"Yes, sir," Bethel replied, "it was a Sunday afternoon, later Sunday afternoon, and we passed lots of cars, met lots of cars and passed cars."

"Did you see people walking along the roads and in towns and see folks sitting out on the front porches and all?"

"Yes, sir."[22]

If Pearl had actually resisted, this line of argument implied, she could have alerted any of these passersby. Bizarrely, this argument ignored the fact that this was precisely what Pearl eventually did.

"What kind of party?" Gladish repeated. He was staring at Frank Bethel, the barber, another unremarkably sized white man with dark hair and gray eyes. Bethel had the more open face of the two defendants, with a high forehead, thick brows, and a small scar just above his upper lip. Gladish was asking him, for the fourth time, what kind of party he and Wallace had been planning to have that evening.[23]

"A loving party," Bethel finally replied.

"Did you tell her what kind of party you expected to have?"

"No, sir."[24]

Gladish's cross-examination was proceeding along a familiar avenue. Much of his questioning, everyone in the courtroom could expect, was designed to show that it was the defendants—and not Pearl—who were immoral. It was they, not she, who should not be trusted.

"Where did you live at the time?" Gladish asked Bethel a moment later.

"I lived in Monette."

"Where did your wife live?"

"I believe she was in Memphis at that time."

"How long had you been separated from her?"

"Well, something like two or three years."

"And have you lived with her since then?"

"No, sir."

"How long did you live with her after you were married?"

"Well, I don't remember just exactly."[25]

A married man planning a loving party—a man separated from his wife since who even knew how long—this man could not be expected to conform his behavior to the standards of society.

This method of cross-examination was also common in rape trials of this era. Just as women's stories were routinely challenged by defense attorneys, so too were men's. Although accusers faced many more challenges due to the stringent legal definition of rape (and stridently sexist assumptions and norms), prosecuting attorneys often strove to show that it was male defendants who were the immoral ones. Surprisingly, perhaps, prosecutors routinely brought up the defendants' supposed promiscuity as a means of impeaching their credibility.[26] "With how many different women have you had sexual intercourse?" the prosecutor asked a white man named Clarence Bryney, at another rape trial in 1929.[27]

"I have had it with several," Bryney replied.
"How many?"
"Four or five."
"How many different times in your life?"
"I couldn't keep account of that."
"When did you start in with such behavior?"
"That wasn't behavior."
"When did you start in misbehaving?"

Eventually Bryney admitted that he sometimes paid for sex; the highest price he'd ever paid was two dollars. The prosecutor then asked Bryney's co-defendant identical questions.[28]

In other cases, such questioning even turned sarcastic. "Howard, you go out with quite a few girls, don't you?" a prosecutor asked another white defendant in 1942.

"Well, not many."
"Those who do go out with you assume the attitude that they will do what you want them to or walk back in, don't you?"
"No, sir."
"Did you ever make a girl walk home?" (This was likely a reference to a man expelling a woman from a car if she refused to engage in sexual activity.)
"No, sir, I never made one walk home."

A few minutes later: "You are one of these high-steppers, aren't you, you go out with a lot of girls and you try them all out and do your best to have intercourse with them?"

"No, sir."

"You don't do that?"

"No, sir."[29]

It is important to note that such questioning served a different purpose than when similar questions were directed at women. For women, to be accused of promiscuity was to imply that they deserved to be raped, or in fact could not be (due to an assumption of consent); for men, to be accused of promiscuity was to imply that they were dissolute characters, not to be trusted—not on the stand and certainly not around young women.

Defendants were also accused of other violations of the prevailing social order for similar reasons. For instance, in the trial of two white men, John Davis and C. F. Johnson, multiple witnesses testified (irrelevantly) that Davis had donned the accuser's "princess slip"—"a woman's undergarment"—and the prosecutor spent more time establishing that the defendants had brought in a Black man to have sex with the accuser than that the defendants had raped the accuser themselves.[30] In a trial for carnal abuse, the prosecutor's cross-examination of the defendant began, "You say you love little children?"[31]

Yet such questioning was occasionally hampered by the strict standards of morality that governed the language of the courtroom. Sometimes, the prosecutor used such abstract euphemisms for penis, vagina, or sex that the defendant seemed to misunderstand their meaning.

"You are the man that completed the arrangements?" Gladish asked Bethel late that evening.

"I don't quite understand that."

"You completed the arrangements with her?" Gladish repeated, apparently struggling to find alternative words.

"I was the first one that had intercourse with her," Bethel responded.[32]

During Jim Crow rape trials, it was also quite common for defendants to be asked about their prior criminal history.[33] In one case in 1926, a white defendant (accused of raping a Black woman) was forced to admit that he had accidentally shot a woman. "You have been in trouble all your life haven't you?" the prosecutor asked him. "No, sir." he responded. "Didn't you shoot another negro last fall?" "Yes, sir."[34] Other defendants were asked about how often they were drunk, or whether they used "vulgar" language, or whether they were "fussing around and raising the Dickens."[35] The purpose of such questioning was obvious; as one prosecutor said outright in response to an objection, "I want to show his immoral tendency."[36]

"Have you ever been convicted of a crime of this sort before?" Alexander asked Wallace.

"No, sir."

"Have you ever paid a fine of this nature?" Alexander tried.

"Not that kind of case."

"Have you ever been convicted of a crime of this sort and settled it by paying a fine?" Alexander asked a moment later.

"I haven't been convicted of rape."

"Have you been convicted of assaulting a girl?"

"I have been convicted of kissing a girl."

"What did it cost you?"

"Twenty-five dollars."[37]

This type of questioning continued all evening. Were the two men drinking alcohol? ("I didn't take no drink.") Do you drink? ("Yes, sir.") When did they first make an "indecent proposition" to Pearl? ("I never made an indecent proposition.") Did they use the word "goddamn"? Had Bethel ever been convicted of a crime? ("Well, I have been convicted of misdemeanors.") What was he convicted of? ("Well, I don't know—maybe shooting craps or getting drunk or fighting.")[38] But the most damning such questioning focused on Wallace's crimes.

"Where were you arrested and convicted of assaulting a girl once before?" Gladish continued.

"I wasn't arrested and convicted of assaulting a girl."

"Where did you pay a fine?"

"In Lake City, Arkansas."

"That was for kissing a girl?" Gladish asked a moment later.

"Yes, sir."

Was this for "keeping a little girl out all night"?

Well, Wallace "was out with girls all night. I was out in a car in a party." And he was tried and convicted "for kissing her." But "I don't know how old she was. I wasn't with her and didn't know much about her. I was with another girl."[39]

For Bethel and Wallace, then, their trial was their chance not just to win their freedom but also to reclaim their position and their standing in the Jim Crow social hierarchy. Yet first they would have to rebut the testimony of Pearl and the dozens of witnesses put forth by the state. In the end, the testimony that was the hardest to deny was Pearl's claim about throwing their license plate. Why would she have done that if she had consented to the sex?

The two men testified that the license plate had come loose about two weeks earlier, when one of the screws affixing it to the car disappeared. For a while, Bethel had tried securing it to the car with baling wire, but the wire must have broken, and the license plate was banging around as they drove. So, after the two had sex with Pearl, Bethel took the plate off and put it in the car.[40]

Did Pearl grab the license plate when she got back in the car? Gladish asked Bethel.

"She never bothered with the license that I knew anything about."

"They found one down there, didn't they?"

"I don't know."[41]

The defendants' testimony with respect to the thrown license plate came to border on obstinacy, or willful ignorance.

"Do you know why she threw your license number down there?" Gladish asked Wallace.

"I don't know that it was thrown there."

"You don't know that that is true?"

"No, sir."

"You know it now, don't you?"

"I do not."

"You have heard her testify, haven't you?"

"Yes, sir."

"It was gone?"

"I don't know."[42]

20 • Clayton and Carruthers Testify, 1935

Bubbles Clayton approached the witness stand. A stocky Black man of average height, he wore a white shirt.[1] Every eye was upon him; men in overalls and women in long dresses packing the ornate room, filling the chairs, spilling into the aisles, surely straining their necks to stare him down. "Well, the courtroom was crowded at all times," Clayton's lawyer, Arthur Adams, would recall. "The size of the crowd was large, as far as that is concerned."[2]

It was getting late in the day, on Monday, April 8, 1935, but the mood in the courtroom was undoubtedly electric. One wonders what must have gone through Clayton's mind as he surveyed the throng. "When a negro goes into court," wrote a sociologist in 1941, "he goes with the consciousness that the whole courtroom process is in the hands of the 'opposite race'—white judges, white jurors, white attorneys, white guards, white everything, except perhaps some of the witnesses and spectators."[3]

Arthur Adams extricated his long body from his chair at the defense table and rose. He began, as so many direct examinations did, with the basics. Clayton was twenty-one years old. He lived "here in town," where he had been raised. He had been farming his whole life. "I have made crops for the past two or three years," he testified, succinctly. "I made some money."[4]

This was the story that Bubbles Clayton told:

At about six o'clock on the evening of Friday, December 21, 1934, in the twilight of another Blytheville workweek, Clayton arrived at the house of a friend. He was wearing trousers, a checked shirt, and a sweater. It was a crowded get-together: Clayton was there with the woman he was dating at the time; Jim X. Carruthers was there with "his girl," along with a man named

Lucient and "his girl," Tom Anderson and "his girl," Willie Manuel, Jack Harris, Herbert Love, and some others. Some of the assembled people did not know each other well. Clayton and Carruthers, for instance, had only become acquainted in the fall of 1934, not long before Christmas, not long before they would be accused of a crime that would change their lives forever.

The group played cards and danced until, perhaps, ten o'clock, when Clayton decided it was time to head home. He got back to his house and got in bed. Suddenly, Herbert Love and some of the other acquaintances from that night burst in; they told him they wanted to head over to Missouri and get some whiskey. Grumbling, perhaps, Clayton put his clothing back on and hopped in the car, seven other souls squeezed in beside him. Jim X., the owner of the packed car, drove through the night. The group bought a pint of whiskey and a quart of wine, and the party continued. Clayton got back to Blytheville after midnight; he brought some wine home with him.[5]

That Friday was also the day that two Black men allegedly raped Virgie near a graveyard in Blytheville. Did Clayton have anything to do with that? Adams asked him on direct examination.

"It is not true that I was one of the boys who attacked this girl on the night of December 21," Clayton insisted. He recounted the story of his evening, not shying from the card playing or the dancing or the liquor. He told the jurors of his arrest, of the police officers beating and torturing him, how they brought Virgie and Wiley Bryant in to identify him, how they fastened his handcuffs so tightly that they injured his hand.[6]

Clayton's co-defendant, Jim X. Carruthers, told a similar story on direct examination. "I am nineteen years old," he began. He'd lived in Blytheville for three or four years, having worked out in the country before that. He picked cotton.[7]

Carruthers also wore a white shirt on the witness stand. His testimony began sometime after Clayton's, on Tuesday, April 9, 1935. Carruthers was dark-skinned and boyishly handsome, with heavy brows and big eyes. In the sole surviving photograph of him, he stares into the camera with a grim resignation.[8]

This was the story that Jim X. Carruthers told:

A few weeks after the December party, Carruthers was passing his evening on Ash Street, which was the heart of the business district for Blytheville's Black residents. It was about seven thirty or eight on Saturday, January 12,

1935, and Carruthers was shooting some pool. Earlier that evening an acquaintance of his named Charles approached him and asked if Carruthers would take him to the nearby village of Armorel. Charles told Carruthers that "if he was lucky we would get some whiskey and get drunk." Carruthers told him all right, "come to pool room and get me when you get ready."

After Carruthers had been at the pool hall for some time, Charles arrived. Carruthers was in the middle of a game, so Charles volunteered to take the six-cylinder Chevrolet and put a couple gallons of gas in it. "I told him all right, hurry back," Carruthers later recalled. Charles did not.[9]

After scouring Ash Street for his acquaintance and his car, Carruthers tracked down another acquaintance, Henry Johnson, who agreed to look for the car with him. Johnson took Carruthers down near the oil mill, where Charles lived, but the car wasn't there. "I went by home thinking maybe he missed me on Ash Street," Carruthers recalled, but Charles wasn't there either. Carruthers returned to Ash Street, but it was "getting kinda late," so Johnson decided it was time to quit. Apparently feeling desperate, Carruthers offered to pay Johnson to drive him to the state line. No luck. By the time Carruthers returned home, it was around midnight. A man named Sam Wilson was sitting on his porch.

Wilson told Carruthers that he'd gotten his car from Charles but had abandoned it on a hard-surface road some distance away. Carruthers asked Wilson whom he had left the car with. "Nobody," replied Wilson. "I got in a shooting scrape."

Wilson told Carruthers to go look for the car—"and then is when I went to the police station and told them the car had been stolen," Carruthers later testified. It was about one in the morning when he arrived. He showed up and spoke with the desk sergeant, Charley Short, completely unaware that he was the most wanted man in the county. The sheriff had been shot just a few hours before.[10]

"I will ask you for the purpose of contradicting you," Denver Dudley, the prosecutor, said to Carruthers, "didn't you go to the police station and tell Mr. Short your car had been stolen, and he asked you when it had been stolen and you told him that night, that when you and your girl were parked up there two negroes came along and ran you out and stole your car; didn't you tell Mr. Charley that night when you came over there claiming that car?"

Dudley was shorter and younger than Adams, a study in contrasts. He stared at Carruthers, certain he had caught him in a lie.

"Yes sir, I told him something like that," Carruthers admitted. "I told him I was out on the oil mill road and I was robbed, that was not the truth. I don't know what happened that night." He insisted he didn't know who had shot at Sheriff Wilson and Deputy Sheriff Lindsey. "I knew who had taken my car." He had lied to the police out of fear. "I told them that because I was scared to tell any more. They started beating me."[11]

For hours, over two days, Dudley would cross-examine both Clayton and Carruthers. His questioning was aggressive and relentless.

At one point, Clayton was narrating the night that the Mississippi County deputies had hidden him out in a cornfield and then driven him across state lines, in a last-second attempt to stop a posse from Missouri from lynching him and Carruthers. "I sure did beg them not to let them hang me," he recalled. Yet, even as they drove desperately into the night, with the car of their pursuers nearly catching up, the officers kept demanding that Clayton confess. "They kept asking me what in the hell did you want to shoot at us," he testified. Clayton kept denying his role in the shooting of Sheriff Wilson, and the police kept calling him a "liar." "He kept saying it and kept saying it and kept saying it and had my hands in handcuffs. You see where the handcuffs cut into my wrists."

Clayton indicated his wrists.

"You are a mistreated negro, now, we know that," prosecutor Dudley said, with sarcasm.

"Had me handcuffed and whipped me," Clayton continued.

"You are a negro man and in there charged with shooting the sheriff of this county, who had his deputy with him, Mr. Lindsey, you knew that, didn't you, charged with shooting the law?" Dudley asked a moment later.

Adams objected. "This isn't the charge in this lawsuit," he insisted. Judge Killough let Clayton answer anyway.

"I don't know no more than what they told me," Clayton replied, but he insisted that the deputies "started whipping me and telling me you done so and so. . . . I didn't do nothing and they whipped me, and whipped, and have done whipped me until I couldn't stand up."[12]

This kind of testimony was common in interracial rape trials. Much of Black defendants' testimony focused on their fear and their suffering. For instance, one defendant named Freeling Daniels admitted in his 1932 trial that he told one authority that he "did make an assault on this girl," but he said so only because "I was scared . . . I thought they might hurt me."[13]

The purpose of this testimony was to present to a jury of white men an unfamiliar image—that of an unthreatening Black man, one who knows his place. It was a survival strategy for Black defendants. And it was tied to another common strategy: insisting on their respectability.[14] Clayton: "I wanted them to drive fast and I want to tell you the reason why, I know I wasn't guilty of it and I never had no reason to get whipped up. I make a good hard honest living."[15] Carruthers: "The last man I worked for was Mr. Marvin Robinson, I picked cotton for him last year. I have worked every crop year for the past several years."[16]

Clayton and Carruthers were following a script often used by Black men unjustly accused of rape. In one trial from 1926, the Black defendant, William Cutts, made sure to couch his testimony in the most polite, deferential terms: "I stumbled and fell, and jumped up and said, 'Oh, 'scuse me,' and went and got a drink of water and went back. . . . [S]he said 'get out of the way.' I said 'Scuse me, I didn't mean no harm.' "[17] Still another Black defendant, Emmanuel West, testifying in 1921, mentioned that he was the leader of his church's choir and said that he had assisted the investigating officers in every way he could.[18]

The purpose of this testimony was for the defendants to convince the jurors that they were not a threat—to the jurors' white wives, white daughters, white sisters, white supremacist social order.[19]

In response to such insistences, it was quite common—routine, really—for prosecutors to accuse Black defendants of all manner of crimes, both related and unrelated to the rape charges against them. These were *not* trustworthy, deferential Black men, the prosecutors sought to convince the jurors; these were exactly the Black men that white men in the Jim Crow South would expect to see charged with rape.

Was Carruthers aware that the deputies had found guns in his car? Dudley asked. He was not. Did he know how many they had found? He did not. What about that big .45-caliber pistol, which the police found wedged under the upholstery of the back seat?

"The big 45 had been in there about one year," Carruthers admitted. "It stayed in the car, I guess it was mine." But he had gotten it "from a white fellow, it wouldn't shoot. I forgot to take it up to the shop and get it fixed up."[20]

"Part of your occupation has been stealing, hasn't it?" Dudley asked Clayton, early in his cross-examination. "You hijacked Mr. Frank and Miss Hutchins on November 18th and shot her, didn't you?"

"No sir, I did not," Clayton replied. "I don't know Miss Hutchins."

"You shot her in the arm, didn't you?" Dudley pressed.

"No sir, I did not."

"Did you say you never steal?"

"No sir, I haven't stolen nothing in my life."

"They sent you to the penitentiary in Missouri for stealing?"

"I never stole it myself."

"You are never guilty of anything they charge you with?" Dudley asked, with great sarcasm.

"But I was with the boy that got it," Clayton continued, attempting to clarify. "I didn't take it myself."

"You served a time in the Missouri penitentiary for it anyhow?"

"Yes sir."

"When was it you served that term?"

"It was in '31."

"After you were arrested and in custody, did you not tell the officers on a number of occasions where the stolen articles were which they could find, and which they recovered and sent back to the owners?"

Finally, Judge Killough intervened. "Let me see you gentlemen for a moment," he said to the two lawyers. Adams and Dudley approached the bench. After the three men conferred for a moment, Killough sustained an objection from Adams, and Dudley temporarily moved on.[21]

But much of the prosecutor's strategy was focused on convincing the jury that Clayton and Carruthers were guilty of the series of carjackings and assaults that had haunted Mississippi County in the winter of 1934, and he simply could not stop himself from returning to these questions. "Bubbles, you know they had a big lot of robberies down here about the time of this happening, didn't they, and before it?" Dudley asked at one point.[22] The prosecutor especially had to bring up the shooting of Sheriff Wilson, for which Clayton and Carruthers had initially been arrested and tortured.

"You heard about Mr. Wilson being shot in the eye," Dudley said to Clayton a few minutes after the judge admonished him to cut it out. "You didn't do it, of course, did you? Were you guilty of shooting Mr. Wilson?"

"No sir," Clayton replied. "I is not guilty."

"You were somewhere else at that time?"

"Yes sir."

"You are positively not guilty of that?"

"I am not guilty of it."[23]

These cross-examinations were, obviously, substantially more hostile than the cross-examination of Bethel and Wallace, even though the latter were also accused of unrelated crimes. One journalist dryly labeled Dudley's cross a "rigorous examination" of the two defendants, "about other offenses."[24]

"You know Mr. Lewis Wilson, don't you?" Dudley asked Clayton.

"No sir."

"I will ask you if you did not stick him up, and then tell Mr. Lindsey where he could find his watch and other stuff?"

"I did not."

Belatedly, Adams objected.

"I did not," Clayton repeated.

"I object to that," Adams told Judge Killough. "Mr. Dudley has announced he is trying to lay a basis for impeachment but it occurs to me instead that it is trying to get into the record an alleged confession of something, and probably something not connected with this lawsuit."

"Whether or not he committed other offenses goes to his credibility," piped up one of Dudley's fellow prosecutors.

One can almost hear Judge Killough's sigh. "He has denied it," the judge intoned, overruling Adams's objection.[25]

"Did you tell Mr. Rainmiller where they could find Mr. Lewis Wilson's watch that had been stolen?" Dudley later asked Carruthers. "Did you tell Mr. Rainmiller where he would find Mr. Atkins' radio?" In fact, didn't Carruthers tell this officer, Rainmiller, about "sixteen different robberies?"[26]

Occasionally, however, in the face of such accusations, Black defendants insisted on their innocence in stark, almost confrontational terms. "Tell the jury what happened," directed the attorney of William Cutts, on trial in 1926. "Didn't nothing happen," Cutts replied.[27]

"Was it last term or the term of court before last, we convicted you of larceny?" Dudley asked Clayton, that Monday night in Mississippi County.

"That was something I wasn't guilty of," Clayton responded. "You just convicted me for something I wasn't guilty of. They picked up the right boy and fined him for the same thing. They fined him for the same thing and sent him to the county farm."[28]

The sun was setting. The cross-examinations had gone on for some time. Dudley approached the witness stand, where Jim X. Carruthers still sat. The prosecutor carried with him a crumpled mask.

"That is not my cap, I didn't know that it was found in my car," Carruthers insisted. "I don't know that the two handkerchiefs with eyes cut in them was found in my car."

At Dudley's insistence, Carruthers put on the mask.

"That does not fit me, it is not Bubbles['s mask] that I know of," Carruthers averred. "I know it was not in my car."[29]

But the jurors had now seen him in the mask.

21 • The Ascent, 1954–1968

In the years after assuming a dashing new name, Maya Angelou established herself as an internationally celebrated dancer, singer, activist, and writer. Her success was so swift and so total that it would eventually be a point of curiosity that she had grown up in so marginal a place as Stamps, Arkansas. Yet her art, her activism, her literary accomplishments—all were part of a remarkable feat of recovery that had begun back in Stamps, in Momma's Store and Mrs. Flowers's house, in the secondhand books consumed by the silent child. And, in all her work, including, eventually, the massively popular story of her rape and her recovery, Angelou never lost sight of where she'd come from or what she'd overcome.

Armed with a calypso act, Angelou suddenly had explosive momentum. "Popularity was an intoxicant," she later wrote, "and I swayed drunkenly for months." In the early days of 1954, newspapers began carrying advertisements with her name in them, then the newspapers began asking for interviews ("I gave them in an ersatz accent"), then television and radio too. Soon Angelou had agreed to take on a role in the traveling cast of *Porgy and Bess,* and she embarked on a whirlwind tour of Italy, France, Egypt, Israel, Greece, and Soviet Yugoslavia. "For the first time," wrote later biographers, "she was experiencing life as a Black person in societies free of the segregation and institutionalized racism that polluted America."[1] Upon returning to the United States, her calypso career took off in earnest, and she started touring domestically. An article in the storied *Chicago Defender* in 1957 reported: "Maya Angelou, 'Miss Calypso,' a very tall (six-footer) gal, with an unusual voice has invaded our town, giving out with songs that are exotic, salty and intriguing.

... This new face, out this way, has made an impressive debut, and is peerless in her field, singing things like 'Since Me Man Has Done Gone and Went,' 'Calypso Blues,' and others. I must hear her again."[2]

Angelou also had literary ambitions. "I began to write," she later recalled. "At first I limited myself to short sketches, then to song lyrics, then I dared short stories." An author friend read some of her work and invited her to come to New York and join the Harlem Writers Guild, a salon of Black artists that, at various times, included Audre Lorde, James Baldwin, and Paule Marshall. Sitting in a Brooklyn brownstone in 1959, her heart pounding and her palms slick with sweat, Angelou workshopped her writing with the group for the first time. The group reacted coolly to her draft, but she found the experience invigorating; she had to do better, to learn more. "I had to try," she would write. "If I ended in defeat, at least I would be trying. Trying to overcome was black people's honorable tradition." To make ends meet, she found a job singing at a Lower East Side club, but she was miserable. "People I admired were doing important things"—Lorraine Hansberry had a play on Broadway; Harry Belafonte was using his music to protest injustice; James Baldwin was lacerating white society with his fiery essays. Meanwhile, she was getting heckled at the Apollo.[3]

But then, at a packed church in Harlem, accompanied by her friend, the comedian Godfrey Cambridge—one of the "prettiest" men she had ever seen, his skin "the color of rich black dirt along the Arkansas River"—Angelou attended a fundraiser for the Southern Christian Leadership Conference (SCLC). The preachers who would later form the pantheon of civil rights clergy—Wyatt Walker, Fred Shuttlesworth, Ralph Abernathy—spoke about justice and courage and God's wrath, and then Martin Luther King Jr. stepped to the podium. The audience erupted in roars; King had just been released from jail. He spoke that night with a prophetic cadence. Tears slid down Godfrey's face. Angelou was simply stunned. She later told an interviewer that she was "hypnotized by his art of vocal persuasion." King spoke of nonviolence, an idea Angelou later stated was "absolutely what I had been waiting for. I had lived around so much violence, and been myself violated, and when Reverend King came and said, 'We can change the world with nonviolence,' it was like pouring water on a parched desert."

"So what's next?" Godfrey asked Angelou afterward, sitting on a bench overlooking the Hudson River. "What are we going to do about it?"

They would not go down south and expose themselves to "some cracker sheriff," but surely they had to do something. Angelou had an idea—perhaps they could get some actors and singers and dancers and hold a fundraiser?[4]

In the SCLC offices in the heart of Harlem, Angelou met with the legendary activist Bayard Rustin and pitched her idea. Rustin liked it, and the "Cabaret for Freedom" came together quickly. The show premiered in the fall of 1960, recurring every Sunday night for a number of weeks at the famous Village Gate night club. New York's Black literary scene was "intrigued," and Harlem's *Amsterdam News* called the show "witty, provocative and off-beat." The audience often included Sidney Poitier, Zero Mostel, and Max Roach, and performances ranged from readings of the poetry of Langston Hughes to recitations of Nigeria's liberation song. Every cast member and every person in the audience stood for "Lift Every Voice and Sing."[5]

In a memoir written decades later, Angelou claimed that after the high of the Cabaret, life returned to normal for many of its performers; they trudged back to dreary day jobs or no job at all, and she herself was "broke again." She spent a few weeks singing at a club in Chicago before Bayard Rustin called her into the SCLC's offices and told her that he and his comrades had been so impressed with the success of the Cabaret that they wanted her to take over Rustin's job, to leave her calypso career and become the SCLC's New York coordinator. Angelou was deeply torn but she eventually accepted the job and was quickly swept up in the civil rights struggle. "The period was absolutely intoxicating," she later remembered. Yet other evidence suggests that Angelou had joined the SCLC months before the Cabaret premiered. A number of letters in the Martin Luther King Jr. Papers show SCLC staff referring to her as the New York coordinator at least a month before the Cabaret was first performed. This suggests that perhaps she was more determined to enter the Civil Rights Movement than she later portrayed, or simply that she had impressed the SCLC staff even before the Cabaret debuted. In any event, she was in the struggle now.[6]

Over the year that followed, Angelou threw herself into her work. She found volunteer and organizing opportunities for eager young people; she liaised with philanthropists; she organized a fundraising performance at Carnegie Hall featuring Frank Sinatra, Dean Martin, Sammy Davis Jr., Tony Bennett, and Nipsey Russell. She carried a briefcase and pored over legal documents on the subway. "The weeks ran together, the days raced," she wrote of that time. Martin Luther King was moving from city to city, jail to jail, and Malcolm X was astounding audiences across the country. Protests erupted outside her office in Harlem; Black nationalists and Black Muslims were on every street corner. Angelou later reflected that ordinary people began displaying "Afro pride," donning African clothes, finally seeing Africans on television for the first time, "looking lovely and regal and speaking English better than white Americans."

When she finally met Dr. King, she was surprised by his youth and his shortness; he asked respectfully about her childhood in Stamps, about her family. When she told him that Bailey was doing time in Sing Sing for selling stolen goods, King replied with sympathy, "That's why we must fight and win. We must save the Baileys of the world. And Maya, never stop loving him. Never give up on him. Never deny him. And remember, he is freer than those who hold him behind bars."

Interestingly—for Angelou was an ardent admirer of Dr. King—she later wrote that she disagreed with his sentiment. "Redemptive suffering had always been the part of Martin's argument that I found difficult to accept. I had seen distress fester souls and bend peoples' bodies out of shape, but I had yet to see anyone redeemed from pain, by pain." It is a revealing passage.[7]

Not long thereafter she resigned from SCLC. Two white men had been hired and had begun assuming some of her responsibilities; one official later told Angelou the men had been hired because "it was always assumed that she would resume her career as a performer." But Angelou felt she had to continue as an activist. So she helped to found the Cultural Association for Women of African Heritage and, as its director, helped to organize a protest against the CIA-backed coup in the Congo and the assassination of its left-leaning president, Patrice Lumumba. "Murderers. Killers. Assassins," she yelled in the chamber of the United Nations General Assembly. Newspapers reported on the "mob" of Black "women agitators" breaking into the Security Council's chamber and squaring off with "judo trained guards," resulting in dozens of injuries. Conservative Black leaders denounced their "ugly demonstration."[8]

Meanwhile, an acquaintance asked Angelou to do a reading of a new play, *The Blacks* by the white, radical French playwright, Jean Genet. The deeply controversial play, which had premiered in France three years earlier, was meant to lampoon racial stereotypes and a racist society. It was a kind of inverted minstrel show, with Black actors in whiteface reenacting an interracial rape and murder trial. Angelou took the manuscript home and read it, finding its language "tortuous and mythical," its politics naïve, and ultimately dismissing it as "a white foreigner's idea of a people he did not understand." It was only with reluctance that she agreed to appear in its American premiere. Angelou was to play the "White Queen," a role for which she wore a white mask. To her surprise, it was a role she came to enjoy: "I used the White Queen to ridicule mean white women and brutal white men who had too often injured me and mine." The play was such a "cruel parody of white society" that Angelou was certain it would flop, but *The Blacks* became, somewhat surprisingly, a legendary show. Its cast included not just Maya Angelou but such then-fairly unknown talents as Cicely Tyson, James Earl Jones, and Lou Gossett Jr. The *New York Times* called it "weird" but also "brilliantly sardonic" and "one of the most original and stimulating" plays on offer. One article years later would describe Angelou's part in the play as "her first big break."[9]

It was while Angelou was performing in *The Blacks* that she started becoming friends with the man she would one day consider her brother: James Baldwin. The two had met briefly when Angelou was in Paris, touring with *Porgy and Bess,* and they had been reunited in the Harlem Writers Guild, but they truly became friends while she was rehearsing Genet's play. Baldwin, the boy preacher from Harlem who had become a righteous, gay essayist and critic, happened to be back from Paris at the time; he had seen *The Blacks* in the original French and liked it, so he came to their rehearsals and "laughed loudly and approvingly." He and Angelou began talking often. "We discussed courage, human rights, God and justice," she later recalled. "We talked about black folks and love, about white folks and fear." Eventually, Baldwin took Angelou to meet his many siblings, "and when he took me to Mother Baldwin [he] said: 'Just what you don't need, another daughter, but here she is.' "

In the years to come, Angelou would begin to refer to Baldwin as her "favorite writer," and she would confide much of her pain and sorrow in him.[10] Baldwin relied on Angelou too, trusting her with his fears and his anxieties, concluding one missive, "No one will believe that I wanted children."[11]

All around the United States, Angelou saw activists pushing for change: Robert F. Williams arming Black activists in North Carolina; Stokely Carmichael and others founding the Student Nonviolent Coordinating Committee; white and Black students risking their lives on the Freedom Rides. But she also believed that the struggle against white supremacy was international. Thus, when a man she was dating—a Black South African freedom fighter whom most acquaintances believed to be her husband—asked her to move with him to Cairo, she agreed.[12]

The first time Angelou had visited the African continent was in the 1950s when she was traveling with the cast of *Porgy and Bess*. She would never forget standing on the deck of the Greek ship bringing the American actors from

Piraeus to Alexandria and gazing, fascinated, at Egypt. One of the ship's officers had turned to her and said, "Miss Angelou, what is your impression of your native continent?" Angelou was taken aback. "It hadn't occurred to her," a journalist later recounted, "that this was what lay, spectacularly, before her. All she had been thinking about, excitedly, was that little Maya of Stamps, Ark., was about to see the pyramids."[13]

Now she was returning, years later, an accomplished performer and an activist. In an interview marking her "farewell" to the stage, she told the *San Francisco Chronicle* that Africa was the "land of my soul" and that she wanted "to do what I can myself to educate, liberate, the women of Africa." Her romantic relationship was dissolving, so she began working at a new magazine, the *Arab Observer,* one of the only English-language publications in the Middle East at the time. It was there that Angelou would learn journalism and the art of persuasive writing. After her relationship ended, she and her son moved to Ghana.[14]

Ghana thrilled her—the fashionable clothes, the revolutionary hope. The country had achieved independence from Britain just five years before, and its president, Kwame Nkrumah, was a charismatic socialist leader, building schools and roads and a welfare system. "We were Black Americans in West Africa," Angelou would reflect, "where for the first time in our lives the color of our skin was accepted as correct and normal." Years later, she told a journalist, "The first time I ever felt at home was in Ghana."[15] Angelou immediately fell in with the community of ambitious, impassioned Black ex-pats she came to call the "Revolutionist Returnees." They included Julian Mayfield, a respected writer and actor who had been forced to flee after what Angelou called "an encounter with the CIA and the FBI"; Vicki Garvin, a union organizer; and Alice Windom, a lawyer and scholar. Soon her son was settled into life at the university and Garvin, Windom, and Angelou moved into a pretty three-bedroom bungalow together. "At last life was getting itself in joint," Angelou would write.[16]

She began to wear African clothes and to speak African languages, including Ghana's Fanti and her ex's Xhosa. She started writing for the *Ghanaian Times,* then appearing on-air for Radio Ghana, and finally appearing in leading roles on stage at the National Theatre. She dated periodically, in spite of her ex's belated protestations of love and reconciliation. (By 1967, he had remarried.) She danced and drank beer and discussed ideas with the Revolutionist Returnees. She drove her Fiat "into the bush" and explored villages with vendor-lined streets and the Cape Coast, though she avoided visiting Elmina Castle, hub of the slave trade in centuries past.[17]

During the years she spent in Africa, Angelou's politics were as radical as they would ever be. She had long been a critic of American society, possibly pushed left by her son. Indeed, in the mid-1950s she'd been called into his school because he said he'd rather go to jail than join the U.S. military. At a meeting with the teachers, he said, "Just because U.S. Steel wants to sell more steel, I shouldn't go and kill some baby Koreans who never did anything to me." Later, he attended antinuclear rallies and spoke to her of his wonder at seeing Soviet opposition to capitalism. Around this time, Angelou attended a pro-Castro rally, later invoking a saying common in the Black community: "Wasn't no Communist country that put my grandpappa in slavery. Wasn't no Communist lynched my poppa or raped my mamma." Her first story was accepted for publication in the Cuban journal *Revolución*.[18]

In Egypt—under the hopeful, anti-imperial, pan-Arab socialism of President Gamal Abdel Nasser—and in Ghana—under the revolutionary, postcolonial Nkrumah government—Angelou moved even further to the left. In a representative article from this period, she asked why "the countries which have chartered a definite course toward Socialism and are aptly carrying out those plans, come in for such libelious [sic] attacks from the Western Press. And further, why do those reactionary forces within a progressive developing country receive financial as well as political encouragement from Western government. Or simply, why is the Western clique of nations so hostile to Ghana and other Socialist tending countries. . . . And why do those governments openly finance a violent opposition to the established order?" In another, she wrote, "Certain Afro-American leaders are aware that Capitalism will never solve its own crises, since they are brought about by Capitalism for Capitalism's gain. Hence the many demonstrations, mass-movements, picket lines, protests, walk-outs, and sit-ins that have tended to fill the American newspapers are intended to bring about an equable legislation and the subsequent implementation of that legislation."[19]

Angelou's journalistic range was tremendous. She wrote straightforward news articles on the March on Washington and the Civil Rights Movement, making sure to emphasize the radical activism of Malcolm X, but she also penned less overtly political articles like, "Le Theatre Africain," written in French. She wrote many articles with titles like "Women in the Public Eye," "Women and Ghana's Moral Code," "Women as Educators," and "Women as Preventive First-Aiders," passionately advocating the active participation of women in the new nation's public life. Sometimes her zeal for Ghana's future ventured into more authoritarian prescriptions: in one draft, she wrote, "In a Socialist country, bent on consolidating a relatively new revolution, vice [and] corruption are more than practices per[pe]tuated by greedy elements within the society, but are levers which counter-revolutionary forces and neo-colonials will pry the public away from its ideals. Ghana, faced with the man[i]fold problems of development, education, budget balancing, and staying out of the clutches of the cold war, is forced to also recognize and eliminate the grafters, drifters and idlers with in the country. No country serious about its progress can afford to follow a lenient moral code."[20]

She appears to have become so invested in life in Ghana that she periodically fell out of touch with her family in America. In mid-1963, her brother Bailey wrote a letter to President John F. Kennedy, inquiring into the whereabouts and welfare of his sister, "Maya Angelo Make," whom he hadn't heard from in several months. He seemed a little worried that harm may have come to her. (He also thanked Kennedy for his work on civil rights.) Months later, Bailey's inquiry made its way to the American consulate in Ghana, and the vice consul wrote to Angelou asking her to "drop me a line so that I may tell your sister"—he thought Bailey was a woman—"that you are all right." When Angelou finally did get back in touch with Bailey, he was tremendously relieved and told her, "I did raise a certain amount of hell with the State Department here and in Washington about your whereabouts and welfare."[21]

In August of 1963, just days before the March on Washington back in the United States, the Revolutionist Returnees gathered at the home of Julian Mayfield to dig into a fresh package of spicy American pork sausages. They had been debating the latest essays of James Baldwin and lamenting the diminishing health of W. E. B. Du Bois, the ninety-five-year-old civil rights icon who had moved to Ghana a few years earlier at Nkrumah's invitation and become a Ghanaian citizen. When Mayfield mentioned King's planned march, the group reflexively mocked the idea. "We were brave revolutionaries, not pussyfooting nonviolent cowards," Angelou later wrote, summing up the mood. "Of course, none of us, save Julian, had even been close to bloody violence, and not one of us had spent an hour in jail for our political beliefs." Angelou, for her part, stayed quiet on the subject of King, not wanting to remind her radical friends of her association with him—but she too had grown dissatisfied with King's adamantly nonviolent approach.

In spite of their skepticism, the group unanimously agreed that "although we were radicals, as Black Americans we should support our people in the States." They would hold their own march, this one on the American embassy; they would hold up placards and see if local students might want to join their picketing. As Alice Windom wrote in a letter shortly thereafter, they decided "it would not simply express our sympathy and support for the Washington March, but would make an independent statement against American racialism and imperialism. Also, our consciousness of the connection between the Afro-American and the African freedom movements would be stressed."[22]

According to Windom's contemporaneous letter, Angelou had been at Du Bois's house for lunch that day, and it was she who apparently told the group "that the Old Man had suffered an attack, vaguely described as a 'chill,' and needed medical attention." According to Angelou's later recollection, she heard about Du Bois's condition from Mayfield's wife, Ana Livia. In any case, Du Bois's health worsened as the day of the march approached. He grew quiet. The march was to start at seven on the morning of August 28, but since Washington, D.C., was seven hours behind Accra, the Revolutionist Returnees decided to start their march at midnight on August 27. The night before, they gathered at Mayfield's house to plan and party, and Angelou sang for the group. The next evening, as midnight neared, they assembled to make signs and placards; her son and a group of Ghanaian friends were present. Mere minutes before they were to start marching, Mayfield arrived and informed the Returnees, in a flat voice, that Du Bois was dead.

In Angelou's recollection, Mayfield said, "I don't think we should inform everyone, but you all should know," to which Windom replied, "Well, what timing. He had a full and useful life and I think we should tell everybody. They'll feel more like marching." Windom, in contrast, recalled Mayfield saying, "We've got some running around to do."[23]

The Returnees fanned out and told the marchers the sad news. All became solemn, and there was little talking as they marched to the embassy bearing their placards and torches. In Washington, there was a moment of silence in honor of Du Bois, whose works Angelou had read as a lonely girl in Stamps thirty years earlier. Suddenly, in Angelou's recollection, someone whose voice she didn't recognize began singing, "Oh oh, Freedom, oh oh, Freedom, oh oh, Freedom over me. And before I'll be a slave, I'll be buried in my grave. And go home to my God. And be free."

A driving rain began to fall as the sun rose. "God weeps?" Angelou asked.

"Of course not," someone replied. "It is the way the spirits welcome a great soul to the land of the dead. They wash it first."[24]

Several months after the march on Accra, Malcolm X arrived in Ghana as part of a world tour during the summer of 1964 that, famously, included a visit to Mecca. Angelou would recall that he arrived midday and made his way to the Mayfields' house, where the Revolutionist Returnees packed the living room to pay homage. They were impressed that he had come alone, with no entourage. Angelou later described him as "America's Molotov cocktail, thrown upon the White hope that all Black Americans would follow the nonviolent tenets of Dr. Martin Luther King." She found his poise and his political vision enthralling. Along with Windom, Shirley Graham Du Bois, and several others, Angelou fought to arrange a meeting for Malcolm with President Nkrumah, who was nervous about possibly alienating American leaders by meeting with the visitor.

Angelou had previously met Malcolm in New York in 1961, after she organized the protest at the U.N. that resulted in fervent denunciations from Black and white leaders alike. After the press blamed the protest on the Nation of Islam, Angelou sought out Malcolm and asked for his approval but he would not give it; he believed change would come not from shouting at the U.N., but rather from "separat[ing] ourselves from the white man." Angelou was crushed, but this experience strengthened her resolve to make a positive impression when Malcolm visited Accra three years later. Ghanaian interest in seeing Malcolm "mushroomed and snowballed" to such an extent, wrote Windom, that she, Angelou, and several others hurriedly organized an ad hoc Malcolm X Committee. Angelou found his visit to be simply electrifying. Malcolm, for his part, enjoyed his time in Ghana so much that he mused in his diary about relocating to Africa permanently, though he encountered some skepticism from Nkrumah as well as from a visiting Muhammad Ali. He noted in his diary that, as he was leaving, "Maya took the bus right up to the plane."[25]

In the weeks and months that followed, Malcolm and Angelou struck up a warm correspondence. On June 1, he wrote to thank her for her "generous support while I was in Ghana" and added, "The true reason for my splitting from the Muslim movement is being told here in the states so don't be shocked when you hear it. It will be exactly as I explained it to you." Angelou confided in him her frustration at the dismissive way that many African leaders treated her: "If I, plain Maya Angelou, went to that conference, no matter how sincere and eloquent I was, I would command very little attention from those people who would be more comfortable if certain demands were not made on them."

"Malcolm," she concluded her letter, "I'm sure that we have not had a leader like you since the dear <u>dead</u> days of Frederick Douglass. Take care of your self and know that <u>we</u> certainly those in Accra, are with you, for you and love you."[26]

By the end of 1964, Malcolm was asking Angelou to return to the United States to become a coordinator for the Organization of Afro-American Unity, a pan-Africanist group he had founded with the intention of uniting Black people around the world in the struggle for freedom. Angelou was torn about leaving her friends and leaving Ghana, where for the first time in her life she had not been "threatened by racial hate." She later told an audience, "I had a beautiful life in Ghana. . . . I would have loved to have stayed there and relaxed under the palm trees. But I began asking myself: 'Maya, you say that you want change, but how far are you willing to go in order to achieve it?' " She also privately considered the devolving political climate in Ghana, where "antigovernment forces were aligning themselves at that very moment to bring down the regime of Kwame Nkrumah." In the end, as she would reflect in her memoir, "my people's struggle came first." She decided to return to the United States to work with Malcolm in the fight against white supremacy.[27]

Standing in the airport in New York one Friday early in 1965, surrounded by the discomfiting clamor of American voices, Angelou found a telephone booth and dialed Malcolm's number. "Maya, so you finally got here," he said. He offered to pick her up, but she said no; she wanted to visit her mother and brother in San Francisco for a month before starting work. Malcolm mentioned a recent attempt on his life. "You believe that, Maya?" he asked.

"I said yes," she later recalled, "but I found it hard to do so. 'I'll call you next week when I get my bearings,' " she told him.

Two days later, on a golden morning in San Francisco, Angelou got a call from Ivonne, an old friend. "Maya, girl, why did you come home?" Ivonne asked in a cheerless voice. "Why did you come back to this crazy place?"

"I came back because I think I have something to do," she replied.

"These Negroes are crazy here. I mean, really crazy. Otherwise, why would they have just killed that man in New York."

Stunned, Angelou laid the phone down on the table and walked straight back to her bedroom and locked the door. She didn't have to ask; she knew who "that man in New York" was. Malcolm X was dead.[28]

In the months after Malcolm's assassination, Angelou became profoundly depressed and felt utterly directionless. She briefly resumed her singing career but soon came to believe she lacked the drive or talent to succeed. She thought about returning to New York, but that was too close to the site of Malcolm's murder. Instead she relocated to Los Angeles and took a job going door-to-door in scorching heat, doing market research in the Watts neighborhood, speaking with Black women about their lives and the products that made these lives easier. "Black females," she later reflected, "know by the time they are ten years old that the world is not much concerned with the quality of their lives or even their lives at all." She could see this in their eyes and hear it in their voices, especially when many of these women invited her into their homes. Their resilience impressed her. It was in Watts, in August of 1965, Angelou witnessed the historic uprising of young Black people, men and women. She was very nearly seized by policemen wearing gas masks and found herself wishing to be arrested. "There is a riot in town today, started last night," she wrote to old friends. "Police brutality brought it on." When, several months later, Kwame Nkrumah was overthrown in a (possibly CIA-backed) coup, sending Ghana down a repressive, anticommunist path, Angelou knew she could never return: "My experience there was so precious that I don't want to risk spoiling it."[29]

She turned, more and more, to writing—the "only pleasant thing" in her life, as she wrote in the midst of the Watts uprising. She tried her hand at a play titled *All Day Long,* about a day in the life of a poor thirteen-year-old Black boy, but found no producer willing to take a gamble on a play about race in the aftermath of Watts. She had more luck with several other plays, which were produced in small venues, and soon she began lecturing about race in assembly halls and on television. She left Los Angeles for New York, moved into a brand-new building on Central Park West, and returned to the Harlem Writers Guild. She applied for a job at the *Saturday Review* but was snubbed by the white editorial staff—for being, in her words, "just another colored girl out of my place." Yet she received encouragement from her friends. "You are a beautiful writer and a beautiful woman," Malcolm had written in his last letter to her.[30]

She wrote still more, including a piece indicting mainstream newspapers for embracing stereotypes about Black looters and rioters, and a review of the poetry of Gwendolyn Brooks. In her review, she wrote: "Miss Brooks refuses to hand hold, to coddle, to pretend. She is a great poet which means she loves. She is greatly angry. A great poet who is greatly angry is a force not to be reckoned with. Always the poet calls to her companions and opponents to meet her on the jousting field and have at life's inequities. There are few who dare to meet her there. I wish I did." In her own poetry, Angelou was experimenting with darker themes. Throughout the 1950s and 1960s, in small notebooks and on scattered pieces of scrap paper, she started and stopped poems about isolation, abuse, and heartbreak.[31]

One day in 1968, Angelou accompanied Baldwin and several other friends to hear Martin Luther King speak in honor of what would have been the hundredth birthday of W. E. B. Du Bois. Afterward, King approached her and asked her, "What are you doing now?" She told him she was writing a play.

"Can you put a bookmark on a page and give me one month of your time?" he asked her. He wanted her to travel the country and speak to Black preachers about his Poor People's Campaign. "I need you, Maya," he said. He joked that not many Black preachers could resist "a good-looking woman with a good idea." And besides, "when anyone accuses me of just being nonviolent, I can say, 'Well, I don't know. I've got Maya Angelou back with me.'"

With some trepidation, Angelou agreed to help. She would start after her birthday.[32]

22 • The Anti-Rape Docket, 1930s

Almost exactly six months after he had first traveled to Frederick, Maryland, to investigate an interracial rape case at the behest of the NAACP, Thurgood Marshall returned for the same purpose. It was a fair day late in the spring of 1935, at nearly the same time that a pair of lawyers in Arkansas were doing legal battle over the fate of Bubbles Clayton and Jim X. Carruthers. But, noted the legal scholar Kenneth Mack, for Marshall in Frederick "something had changed." The young, Black attorney was now well known to the local legal community. He was well respected. The lawyers and judges in town rushed to convince Marshall that this had been a fair trial, that it was no legal lynching.[1]

The new troubles in Frederick had begun when two Black men allegedly attacked a pair of white high school students, knocking out the male student with the butt of a revolver before holding a knife to the female student's throat and raping her. One of the men, Alexander Jones, was quickly apprehended, tried, and convicted in a trial that Black newspapers condemned as a kangaroo court; Jones's own lawyers thanked the judge for sentencing their client to death, the *Baltimore Afro-American* reported. A nationwide manhunt commenced for Jones's alleged accomplice, James Poindexter, who was captured in Pittsburgh several months later. Even as authorities made plans to "safeguard Poindexter from possible mob violence" after transporting him to Frederick, Poindexter himself penned an open letter to the *Pittsburgh Courier* asserting his innocence, proclaiming "all I want is fairness," and exhorting the NAACP to take his case. The Association did not heed his call, and Poindexter was swiftly sentenced to die. Yet Poindexter refused to give up. In careful cursive, he begged the NAACP "to send one of your lawyers to investigate my case" and try to win him a new trial on appeal. He was "charged with attacking a white girl" but wished to "prove myself innocent."[2]

"My dear Mr. Poindexter," Houston wrote in response to this desperate missive. "I have your letter of May 17, 1935, asking me to come to Baltimore to interview you. While I appreciate the fact that this is a matter of life or death for you, I am in such a position that I can not physically handle your case. I am referring the matter to Mr. Thurgood Marshall, an attorney in Baltimore, with a request that he call to see you at his earliest convenience."[3]

Two weeks later, an NAACP administrator wrote to Marshall, asking him to "go out and talk to" Poindexter, to "see if there is anything in the case that warrants our intervention. I might add that we are refraining from entering cases now where the record does not seem to be in good shape, because we simply haven't the money to fight out doubtful cases. To tell the truth, we haven't the money to fight any kind of case, but there are some that we cannot refuse." In other words, the NAACP was swamped, which was precisely why its leaders were attempting to outsource as much legal work as they could.[4]

The very next day, an obliging Marshall drove to Frederick to investigate the docket and interview two of the judges who had heard Poindexter's case—the same judges who had heard the case of William Carter six months earlier. The judges spoke "very freely and frankly" to the young lawyer, insisting that Poindexter had a fair trial, that he was ably represented. Marshall found no cause to disagree. He interviewed Poindexter himself, who, Marshall noted, "did not deny his guilt to me yet maintained that he had not had a fair trial." Marshall recommended to the NAACP that it not get involved, as he believed there was no question of guilt and no constitutional issue. Marshall did, however, agree to write to the governor, asking for Poindexter's death sentence to be commuted to life in prison.[5]

The NAACP leaders were, once again, pleased with Marshall's performance, and they continued to refer cases to the young lawyer. Activists across Maryland were starting to notice too, and labor leaders, neighbors, and friends were soon beating a path to Marshall's door. He quickly became a leader in Black lawyers' associations at the state and national level. He was still poor, but he was taking on precisely the kind of work Charles Hamilton Houston had dreamed his students would do.[6] Over the following year, as part of what one biographer called "an impressive string of victories in lower-profile capital cases," Marshall represented two more Black men accused of rape. He won acquittals in both cases.[7]

Even as Thurgood Marshall, Charles Hamilton Houston, and the growing network of extraordinary NAACP-affiliated lawyers were representing Black men in numerous rape trials, a parallel movement was, at turns, thriving, struggling, and organizing. In its first years, the NAACP had largely excluded Ida B. Wells, preferring to marginalize her anti-rape activism rather than contend with her radical ideas.[8] Nonetheless, by the late 1910s and throughout the 1920s, a strategy emerged that both helped individual Black women and raised the Association's profile. Local branches of the NAACP began urging law enforcement officials to prosecute the white assailants of Black women, which often entailed hiring investigators to dig up evidence and hiring local white lawyers to assist the prosecutors. It also entailed defending the women's reputations against allegations of sexual impropriety.

The work on behalf of Black female rape survivors generally originated with local activists at local branches, not at the national office. In Charleston, South Carolina, for instance, the branch successfully demanded that law enforcement officials arrest and prosecute a white man accused of attempting to rape a ten-year-old Black girl (though he was not convicted). A decade later, a Black domestic servant named Irene accused a white man of raping her after she answered an inquiry for a job as a maid; the local NAACP branch hired an attorney to advocate on Irene's behalf at trial, and, after the judge dismissed charges against the white man, despite considerable evidence of his guilt, the NAACP successfully pressured the prosecutor's office to reopen charges against him. In at least one case, however, the national office took the lead. After ten white men gang-raped a fourteen-year-old Black girl named Ruby in 1926, the national office advocated prominently for the men's prosecution, hired an attorney to assist the district attorney, funded Ruby's mother's travel from Virginia to New York for the trial, and paid for detectives "to secure all possible evidence" against the men.[9]

In a revealing reflection of the NAACP's own tactics in defending Black men, which often involved trying to damage the reputations of the white women accusing them, defense attorneys in these cases nearly always attempted to impugn the Black women's sexual propriety. In the prosecution of Irene's white assailant, for instance, the defense's principal strategy was to invoke "stereotypes of black female sexuality to undermine [Irene's] claim," noted the historian Theresa Napson-Williams. The defense attorney implied that she was a prostitute, that she was a degenerate, and that her promiscuity had broken up her marriage. In the wake of such questioning, and in spite of considerable evidence of the white man's guilt, the jury acquitted him. In the trial of one of Ruby's assailants, the defense attorney (and newspapers) seized on evidence that the girl was "bad"—she sometimes misbehaved and may have been sexually promiscuous—and used these intimations to secure an acquittal for their white male clients.[10]

In response to this strategy of targeting Black women's virtue, the NAACP routinely asserted these women's respectability as a way of attesting to the veracity of their testimony. A local branch in Virginia spent thousands of dollars defending the reputations of "two colored women, of excellent repute," and a branch in New Orleans, protesting the rape and murder of a fourteen-year-old Black girl named Hattie, depicted Hattie as a "virtuous girl who chose to work honestly for a living, rather than throw herself away in the slums of the city."[11]

The NAACP's advocacy on behalf of Black women during this era almost always came in the form of pushing for the prosecution of their assailants. But the Association could have done more: it could have made *legal* arguments on their behalf, challenging the sexist laws governing sexual assault. Such a judgment is not ahistorical—some individuals implicitly raised it at the time. In the trial of the assailants of Ruby, for instance, the attorney hired by the NAACP informed the national office of the challenges of securing a conviction: New York law at the time demanded "strict proof of actual penetration" and explicitly stated that every element of the crime had to be corroborated by evidence other than the woman's testimony. After the state did indeed fail to secure a conviction, the attorney attributed this failure in part to the inability to firmly establish penetration and corroboration. As Napson-Williams has noted, "The NAACP believed that its organization and the State of New York did everything possible to win the case." Yet Napson-Williams argues that the Association could have gone further: "The NAACP could have challenged the bias against black women and black women rape victims that was evident in the legal proceedings. It could have challenged prevailing rape laws that [proved to be] inadequate for a fair and successful prosecution. Most importantly, the NAACP failed to launch a systematic crusade against the daily sexual violence that black females endured because they did not see Ruby . . . as a representative"—that is to say, "ideal"—"victim of it." Specifically, the NAACP could have challenged the penetration and corroboration requirements that so obviously hindered the prosecution of Ruby's assailants. Indeed, the Association itself noted in a press release that "the provisions of the New York Law governing rape" made it "virtually impossible to prove rape."[12]

It is clear, however, that NAACP officials resented calls from women to challenge these discriminatory laws. When, for instance, Althea Hart, a sixteen-year-old Black girl, wrote to *The Crisis* in the wake of the rape and murder of

Hattie, requesting the national NAACP's assistance and arguing that "far too many of our people have suffered the same injustices as this girl and the same thing will continue if our people doesn't stand behind us and fight for the best results," the local NAACP branch was miffed by her presumption. The branch president dismissed her for daring to "sit supinely by and whine for somebody else to do something. . . . Rest assured we are looking after this case and will continue to fight, even without the help of Miss Althea Hart and her kind." And, perhaps more important, at least one NAACP official avowedly believed in parts of these laws. In his book recounting his undercover lynching investigations, Walter White noted approvingly that New York "requires corroboration, direct or circumstantial; the unsupported word of a woman is not sufficient," depicting this legal standard as a useful protection to ensure Black men's safety.[13]

As the NAACP grew and matured in the early 1930s, the tension at the heart of its rape docket remained. The Association—led by local branches—often did assist Black women who had been raped by white men, by urging the police to investigate, the grand jury to indict, the prosecution to commence, or by simply "watching the case" to make sure the authorities were truly trying to secure a conviction. In 1936, the New Jersey Conference of NAACP Branches held a special session—with representatives from all twenty-three branches, as well as Thurgood Marshall, present—calling for the prosecution of the nephew of a white justice of the peace, who had kidnapped and raped a Black woman.[14] Still, this advocacy was dwarfed by the Association's defense of Black men accused of rape. Staff from the national office rarely demanded prosecutions themselves—in notable contrast to cases where alleged Black rapists had been lynched—although the national office often provided advice and occasionally provided money to the local branches. The centrality of defending Black women's virtue remained. "I have learned from a very reliable source that an attempt will be made to whitewash this case for reports already are current that Mrs. McDonald is a woman of questionable character, etc," one branch official in Brooklyn wrote to Walter White. "The simple fact is that she is a colored woman and Orlando is a white man. I personally know her to be of most exemplary character."[15]

Observers came to note the double standard to which Black and white rapists were held. "Last week a middle-aged white man, accused and convicted of raping an eight-year-old Negro girl, was sentenced to twenty years in prison," ran an editorial in the *Louisiana Weekly* in the mid-1930s. "We know full well had the attacker been a Negro, and the attacked a white child, details of another lynching orgy would have been broadcast to a not-so-calloused world." A few years later, a local activist wrote to Marshall about another case: "Even if he should be guilty he has not had fair trials, and too the penalty is far in excess of what is given to whites in similar cases: Several rape cases have occurred in this county since this case and nothing or little has been done simply because the parties were white."[16]

In the face of this double standard, many Black women through the decades would critique the NAACP and its male leaders for failing to engage more often in anti-rape work. "We colored women are tired of such things," one Black woman wrote to the NAACP's president some years later, referring to the unpunished rapes of Black women, "and seems like all the money we pay in organizations doesn't remedy the matter." As the historian Danielle L. McGuire has noted, in the mid-1940s, the branch secretary of the Montgomery, Alabama, NAACP—Rosa Parks—would investigate the rape of a young Black woman named Recy Taylor, helping to turn her case into a national sensation. Black female activists also demanded that white rapists be prosecuted outside of the NAACP's structure; in the early 1950s, for instance, a group of Black women in Jackson, Mississippi, organized the Negro Womanhood Defense Committee to demand the prosecution of a white man who had raped a Black fourteen-year-old.[17]

In the 1930s, these latter incidents were still years away, but the dissatisfaction that would give rise to them—the "things" that "colored women are tired of"—were accumulating, regular indignities that demanded fierce, unrelenting, and unremunerated resistance. Lone figures, among them young Althea Hart, voiced protests that survive in the archive—and that, collectively, begin to resemble a movement in waiting. It seems likely that young Thurgood Marshall heard rumblings of this dissatisfaction in the early and mid-1930s. But surviving correspondence makes clear that he did not hear it from NAACP higher-ups.

23 • The Trial Ends, 1929

"Gentlemen," boomed Judge Keck, "the Defendants, Frank Bethel and Mike Wallace were indicted by separate indictments. Both indictments were returned at the April term, 1928, of this court and filed in open Court on the 8th day of April, 1928. Each indictment charges the crime of Rape."

It was late in the afternoon on Friday, April 12, 1929, the last day of the term for the Chickasawba District of the Mississippi County Court. Judge Keck was determined that the jurors reach their verdict before the end of the work week. Earlier in the day, prosecutor Gladish and defense attorney Alexander had made their closing arguments. All that was left was for the judge to instruct the jury.

"Rape is the carnal knowledge of a female forcibly and against her will," Judge Keck told the jurors. "The punishment for Rape is death by electrocution, or at the option of the Jury, imprisonment in the State Penitentiary for the period of their natural lives." The jurors could also find the defendants guilty of simple assault, which, the judge continued, carried a sentence not of death or imprisonment, but a fine of no more than $100. Finally, there was assault with intent to rape; this carried a sentence of three to twenty-one years behind bars.

Judge Keck reviewed the force and resistance elements of rape. "The proof must show, beyond a reasonable doubt, that the female did not consent and that her resistance was not a mere pretense, but was in good faith," he told the jurors. The term "force" should be interpreted according to "its ordinary acceptation. I mean by it, common physical force," but extreme intimidation could be "equivalent to force." If the accuser "voluntarily consented or yielded at any time before the entrance of the vagina it is not Rape." She must have used "all the means within her power, consistent with her safety, to have prevented the act."

Then, perhaps a bit cryptically, he added, "You may take into consideration the conduct of the Prosecutrix toward the Defendants, together with the other facts and circumstances in the case, in arriving at a verdict." What precisely Judge Keck meant by this is unclear. But it certainly seems that he was inviting the jurors to scrutinize Pearl's behavior—whether during the encounter or before—to determine whether she was acting like a woman who *deserved* the jurors' vindication.

A few moments later, at the request of the defense, Keck told the jurors, "You are further instructed that if you have a reasonable doubt as to the degree of the crime you should find the defendants guilty of the lesser crime."

And, with that, the jury was instructed. The twelve jurors stood up and walked across the tiled floor, retiring to the small, out-of-the-way room where they would reach their verdict.[1]

It could have gotten much uglier. A judge's instructions to the jury constituted the single most contested part of rape trials in Jim Crow Arkansas. Defense attorneys frequently objected to particular instructions or requested other instructions; the degree to which judges acceded varied wildly. Though the purpose of such instructions was to lay out the elements of the crime—what the prosecution had to prove, how they had to prove it, and what was permissible for a jury to consider—the contests over jury instructions usually came down to how much the jury could consider an accuser's or a defendant's alleged immorality.

All such jury instructions contained some discussion of the elements of the crime. The judge would define force for the jurors, as well as resistance.[2] ("It is the duty of the woman who is assaulted, in the protection of her chastity, to resist such assault," one judge intoned.)[3] When instructions turned—as they almost invariably did—to matters of morality, judges generally told the jurors that evidence of immorality could not be introduced to cast doubt on whether a woman was raped, but it could be introduced to cast doubt on her credibility.[4] Jurors could consider the morality of the defendant "for the sole purpose of your consideration as to whether it is probable that a man of such reputation and character would commit such a crime."[5] In another trial years later, the judge instructed the jury that the "charge of rape is, in its nature, a most serious one, likely to create a strong prejudice against the accused. It is a charge easy to make and hard to disprove. On this account you should bear in mind the difficulty of defending against such charge."[6]

Judges sometimes allowed the jury to consider the accuser's alleged immorality when determining sentencing. In one case of alleged carnal abuse in 1942, the judge instructed the jurors, "You may also consider whether or not the actions of the prosecutrix . . . were such as to invite and entice the defendant to have sexual relations with her, in considering the question of punishment."[7]

It was about four thirty when the twelve white men of the jury settled into the deliberation room. Six of them—Spencer Bunch, W. H. Patterson, Wash Thompson, J. H. Young, A. D. Tolen, and Mose Smith—were farmers; Harry Atkins was a gas salesman; L. A. Fowler, a car salesman; E. B. Lyman was the manager of a local cotton oil mill company; the newspaper did not list occupations for the remaining two, W. J. Bryals and A. C. Neeley.

For nearly two hours, they debated the defendants' fates. None of the jurors really believed either might be innocent, but they were bitterly divided over the penalty the pair should receive. When deliberations began, one juror advocated a ten- to fifteen-year sentence; five favored life imprisonment; one juror championed the death penalty; and the others were apparently undecided. There commenced repeated rounds of debate, interspersed with ten or fifteen ballots, but still they could not agree. At around six thirty the judge agreed to give the deadlocked jurors a break, and they were taken out to dinner.[8]

Stalemates were not at all uncommon, and many rape trial juries initially told the judge they could not reach a verdict. It was the judge's job to exhort them to keep going.[9] And indeed, after the jurors returned from dinner that night in Blytheville, Judge Keck "admonished them to make every effort to arrive at a verdict," reported one local journalist, "pointing out that the trial had been exceedingly expensive to the county and that a retrial of the case was to be avoided if possible."

For another hour, the jurors continued to debate. But perhaps the judge had been persuasive, because a few minutes after nine that evening, they returned to the courtroom with a verdict. Mose Smith, the foreman, handed a slip of paper to Harvey Morris, the deputy clerk of the court, who read it aloud.

The two defendants were guilty, he told the large and expectant crowd—but of assault with intent to rape, not rape itself. Armed with the option of sentencing Bethel and Wallace to somewhere between three and twenty-one years, the jurors had chosen a number in the middle. The two defendants, recounted the local press, were "out of the shadow of the electric chair but are confronted by sentences of 18 years in the state penitentiary."

Judge Keck polled the jurors; each responded with his concurrence. The large crowd made "no demonstration," reported the *Blytheville Courier-News*, and Bethel and Wallace "displayed neither dismay nor relief as the sentence was announced." The calm of the courtroom and the blankness of their faces obscured the fact that the two had been both damned and saved.[10]

The day after the trial, Judge Keck sentenced the two defendants to the eighteen years recommended by the jury. Yet, remarkably, Bethel and Wallace were not immediately hauled off to the dreaded state penitentiary in Tucker, where they had resided since their arrest more than a year earlier. Instead, their attorney had negotiated their release on bond while their appeals were pursued. Three relatives of Mike Wallace—C. A. Wallace, J. D. Wallace, and T. R. Wallace—signed a pair of $10,000 bonds, and the two were freed from state custody. They would remain at liberty for more than six months.[11]

Life carried on. The first Academy Awards were given out at a small, private ceremony in Los Angeles that took just fifteen minutes; the leaders of many of the world's nations signed a pact in Paris that attempted to outlaw war; China and the Soviet Union skirmished over control of a railway; the first Grand Prix Formula One race was held in Monaco; a British high court considering a Canadian appeal ruled, for the first time, that women were legal persons; the stock market crashed, the roaring twenties came to an end, and the Great Depression began.

E. E. Alexander embarked on the arduous process of appealing his clients' convictions. First, he filed a motion for a new trial. The verdict was contrary to the law, he argued, and also contrary to the evidence; the court should have declared a number of potential jurors incompetent instead of forcing the defense to waste peremptory challenges on them; the court should have rebuked the prosecutor and deputy prosecutor for making an array of allegedly prejudicial statements. The court denied the motion. Alexander sought relief from the higher courts of the state.[12]

In Mississippi County, another cotton-picking season came and went. Summer passed into autumn. The county government found itself deep in debt, in large part because of the hundreds of dollars it had been forced to spend prosecuting Bethel and Wallace. The two of them, meanwhile, remained at home. Just how they spent their time is unclear, but it is certain that Mike Wallace had time during this interregnum to get married. He wed Elly Julia Meurer—a twenty-two-year-old white woman from the nearby town of Bunney—on April 27, 1929, barely two weeks after the groom had been found guilty of assault with intent to rape. One wonders who in the county would marry such a notorious resident, but perhaps his crime didn't seem so notorious to local women after all.[13]

Bethel and Wallace were presumably pariahs to some degree, but they were also, in every meaningful sense, free.

One wonders how their neighbors reacted when, one day that summer, Frank Bethel's younger brother Fred was arrested for sexually assaulting a thirteen-year-old girl. It was a warm day in June when the twenty-three-year-old Fred entered the home of a Monette junk dealer, apparently to return a shirt he had borrowed from the junk dealer's brother. He discovered that neither the junk dealer nor his brother was home, but the dealer's "pretty 13 year old daughter" was there alone. The details of what happened next are unclear, but Fred Bethel quickly fled town. Reporting on the attack, the newspapers identified him as the brother of a man sentenced to eighteen years "on a similar charge."[14]

Finally, on Monday, November 18, 1929, the authorities carried Bethel and Wallace off to prison. Alexander's attempts to overturn their convictions had not borne fruit—though he would keep trying—and it was time for the state to enforce its sentence. A deputy sheriff and champion marksman from Leachville was tasked with delivering the two to the state penitentiary in Little Rock. "When the prison gates closed on Bethel and Wallace yesterday," reported the *Blytheville Courier-News*, "the end of one of the most hotly contested legal battles in the history of Mississippi county's criminal courts was reached."[15]

Sitting in the deputy's car, approaching the penitentiary, Bethel and Wallace may have experienced a jolt of dread. They were being taken to The Walls, at the time the state's oldest functioning prison. It resembled nothing so much as a medieval fortress, with high brick bulwarks, a striking crenelated gate, and even turrets overlooking the lawn. Here the two men were supposed to remain, for nearly two decades.[16]

The authorities in Little Rock had constructed the state's first prison in 1842, not long after Arkansas was admitted to the Union. It was meant to be a rehabilitative alternative to the public whippings and small, ad hoc jails in existence at the time. The original site of the penitentiary was a forest not far from the state capital; fresh brick structures housed the officers' quarters, the four guard towers, the workshop, and the "bare cells" that could contain some

300 inmates. Each guard carried a "needle gun," named after its long, pointy shell.[17] In its first seven years, the penitentiary housed 112 prisoners, identified in one report as "109 white males, one Indian, one free Negro and one white female." Of these, 7 died behind bars and 20 escaped from custody—a number so alarming that it convinced the legislature to pay for an encircling wall.[18]

As one chronicler of the prison's early history wrote, "Strange and remarkable incidents appeared in the face of its old walls." In 1846, just four years after the prison opened, an inmate uprising destroyed the main building and nearly resulted in a mass escape; only the intervention of other prisoners, assigned to defend the doors, stopped the rebellion's leader, who was cut down while holding a knife in one hand and a pistol in the other. During the 1850s, the prison held escaped slaves until their owners could retrieve them; during the Civil War, it held Union prisoners. After the Union reclaimed the state, one military superintendent noted that the exterior walls were "in good shape," but the cells were "in bad condition," with leaking roofs, broken locks, lost keys, rusty iron gratings, and cell walls "greatly damaged by prisoners digging through."[19]

In 1899, the old penitentiary's "life was brought to an abrupt end" when the legislature decided to build a new state capitol on the spot where the prison then stood. Inmates destroyed the very site of their incarceration and used some of the salvaged bricks to construct the walls for the capitol building. Five miles to the southwest, a new prison opened. This one, popularly called "The Walls," was where Bethel and Wallace would one day be taken. It was the home to a power plant that provided electricity to every state building in Little Rock; it was also home to the electric chair.[20]

Upon being delivered to The Walls, men were photographed, fingerprinted, and "given a suit of stripes." A man incarcerated in The Walls a generation earlier than Bethel and Wallace recalled receiving a rough, short haircut and a close shave upon arrival. He described the other inmates as "the poorest and sickliest number of men that I ever saw . . . there was no color of blood in their faces; some very old and feeble; some badly crippled." Dozens might die every month. Every day, the men were rudely woken at five in the morning. They were marched, two by two, to the dining room for breakfast, where there were two tables, each one hundred feet long, one for white inmates and one for Black inmates. The provisions were awful and measly, the coffee just "stuff they called coffee," and no one was allowed to speak at all. Those inmates with money could buy better food; otherwise, they went hungry. (Those inmates with money could also buy underwear; otherwise, they went without.) At the sound of a whistle, the men dragged themselves off to hard physical labor. The one constant was the violence: the warden would beat the men, humiliate them, whip them bloody with a strap "made of the thickest of harness leather."[21]

By the late 1920s, however, The Walls was a far gentler prison. It was more of a waystation, really, a place for convicts to stay until they could be taken by train or truck to one of the larger "prison farms" to do labor and make the state some money. The few dozen men who remained at The Walls full time could enjoy poker games and "soft jobs"—unlike the back-breaking field work they might endure in the prison farms—and "good meals on holidays." The warden transformed the "bare ground of the stockade" into an exceedingly "pleasant" garden: a "park with wide grassy plots, flower bordered paths and poplar trees swaying in the breeze." The *Arkansas Gazette* claimed The Walls's lily pool could "challenge any in the city for beauty of planting and design."[22]

Most of the details of Bethel's and Wallace's incarceration have disappeared in the intervening decades. But the fact that they were allowed to stay in the relative comfort of The Walls almost certainly gestures to the good favor in which the authorities held these two convicted sexual assailants.[23] For instance, at the same time that Bethel and Wallace were incarcerated in The Walls, its warden told the press that a wealthy dentist, convicted of murder, would likely be allowed to stay at The Walls because "he is adapted" more to work in the tailor shop or the barber shop at The Walls than "our cotton fields at Tucker farm."[24] Another inmate of The Walls from this time later recalled that it was "where the prisoners who had any political pull stayed."[25] This was the site for preferred prisoners—which Bethel and Wallace apparently were.

As many in Mississippi County would soon realize, although Bethel and Wallace were neither wealthy nor prominent, they clearly had powerful supporters. And perhaps someone within the penitentiary administration simply didn't think the crime for which they had been incarcerated was all that bad.

24 • The Trial Ends, 1935

It was late in the day on Tuesday, April 9, 1935, when Arthur Adams turned to the jury in the trial of Clayton and Carruthers, ready to begin his closing argument. He stared at the twelve white men. Some of them did not stare back. Adams was dismayed to realize that one juror was reading the newspaper—the newspaper that contained accounts of this very trial! Hastily, the deputies removed the paper, and Judge Killough admonished the juror—who, to the judge, seemed "a little embarrassed." A reporter later asked Arch Lindsey about this irregularity. "Well," the deputy sheriff replied, "the evidence was all in."

Adams began to speak, but he had not gotten far when one juror suddenly stood up. "Wait a minute," said Ike Miller, the juror who would soon be elected foreman. To Adams's astonishment, Miller walked across the courtroom and told Judge Killough that he wished to ask him a private question. Once again, this was highly irregular. The judge declined, and Miller made his way back to the jury box.[1]

Adams launched once more into his closing argument. The state of Arkansas just hadn't presented enough evidence to merit a conviction, he told the jurors; they should consider the case on merits alone. Adams begged the jurors to lay aside their prejudices. He knew this case was liable to enflame their passions, but he exhorted the jury to think on the gross inadequacy of the evidence, especially regarding the identification of his clients.

Adams was trying to appeal to reason. The prosecution, in contrast, openly tried to stir emotions in its closing arguments. It was the responsibility of the jurors, Denver Dudley thundered, to "protect southern womanhood."

By the time the lawyers finished speaking, it was six o'clock. Judge Killough excused the jurors for supper but told them to return by seven thirty. The sky was growing darker, the shadows cast by the maples, poplars, and oaks growing longer. An hour and a half later, sated, the jurors filed back in and resumed their seats.[2]

"Gentlemen of the jury," intoned the judge, "the defendant, Bubbles Clayton, and the defendant, James X. Caruthers, have each of them been indicted by the Grand Jury of this County . . . with the crime of rape." The jurors were to be "the sole and exclusive judges of the weight of the evidence and of the credibility of the witnesses." It was up to them, he said, to "arrive at your verdicts of guilt or of innocence." The state had to prove guilt "beyond a reasonable doubt," which was a "sane and proper provision of the law and is designed to shield and protect innocent persons from conviction, but is designed in no case to permit one who is guilty to escape just punishment." The statutory punishment for rape, he told the jury, was "death by electrocution," but a subsequent statute gave the jury "the power and at its option of fixing life imprisonment."[3]

Judge Killough did not mention race in his jury instructions, which was not at all unusual. Race did sometimes come up in jury instructions—but very sparingly. In the 1932 trial of a Black man named Freeling Daniels, for instance, the defense attorney requested that the judge instruct, "In the consideration of your verdict you should not be influenced in any way by the fact that the defendant in this case is a negro and the prosecuting witness is a white girl." The judge refused. In contrast, after the prosecutor in the 1926 trial of William Cutts stated in his closing remarks, "a negro has no right to put his hand on a white woman," the judge sustained a defense objection and instructed: "Gentlemen of the jury you must not consider that remark at all. You must decide this case solely on the law and the evidence and nothing else at all." Such legal formalities were largely for show; everyone in every Jim Crow courtroom well understood the rules governing their society.[4]

By the early twentieth century, many southern courts had developed "special doctrinal rules [for] Black defendants accused of rape or attempted rape of white women," noted the legal scholar Jennifer Wriggins. "One such rule allowed juries to consider the race of the defendant and the victim in drawing factual conclusions as to the defendant's intent in attempted rape cases. If the accused was Black and the victim white, the jury was entitled to draw the inference, based on race alone, that he intended to rape her." The fact that Judge Killough did not instruct the jurors as to these doctrinal rules did not mean they wouldn't draw this inference nonetheless.[5]

At the conclusion of Judge Killough's instructions, the twelve jurors retired to the small jury room. There, they began to debate whether Clayton and Carruthers should live or die.

For the next three hours, tension filled the mahogany-lined courtroom. The jurors were off somewhere, speaking, considering, deliberating, and the lawyers and spectators and defendants could do nothing but wait. Seconds ticked by.

At about ten thirty the twelve white men trooped back into the courtroom. The foreman addressed the judge, informing him that they were "in hopeless disagreement." They wanted to take a break, go home and get some sleep, and return for further deliberations the next day.

Judge Killough told the jurors to remain in their box and retired to his chambers with Adams and Dudley. The three began to discuss the advisability of acceding to the jury's request. Suddenly, Sheriff Wilson burst into the room. "Judge," he told Killough, "I will never get those Negroes back to the jail across that yard if you let that jury go home." In other words, he was telling the judge that he couldn't assure the defendants' safety from the mob of spectators.

In Adams's recounting, this was enough to sway Judge Killough. Returning to the courtroom with the two lawyers, Judge Killough told the jurors that he was denying their request. He "had no reason for supposing that any other jury of this county or any other county is going to be any more competent or capable of deciding this problem than you gentlemen." The jury would have to return to the jury room, exhausted as they were, and do their duty.[6]

For the next twenty or thirty minutes, the jurors continued to deliberate. The main question, jurors later claimed, was not whether Clayton and Carruthers were guilty. "We believed her," the foreman later told a reporter. "Why, she wouldn't have lied with her parents looking on and a thousand people in the court room. Those Negroes were lucky the Sheriff saved them from being lynched." Rather, the question was whether the defendants should be sentenced to life in prison or to death. A single juror held out for life imprisonment even as the jurors took vote after vote, until finally he gave in.

At roughly eleven o'clock, the jury returned to the courtroom. "Guilty," they told the judge. They recommended the penalty of death. Judge Killough, who had privately told former judge Keck that he did not relish sentencing anyone to the electric chair, immediately acceded, pronouncing the sentence of death by electrocution on the two Black men. The judge set their date of death as May 17—barely a month away.[7]

Just days after the verdict came down, Osceola was engulfed in a dust storm—the first in its recorded history—which didn't abate until late in the afternoon. As with the tornados that marked the start of the Bethel-Wallace trial, the symbolism here is hard to resist. The swirling dust that obscured the small town was almost like a biblical plague; the deeply religious inhabitants could easily have believed they were being suffocated, like sinners in the hands of an angry god.[8]

Viewed from a certain angle, the death penalties faced by Clayton and Carruthers were surprising; viewed from another, they were utterly expected. Jim Crow juries were by and large merciful when it came to accused rapists. This mercy is notable. It quite possibly reveals a skepticism that sexual assault, and especially carnal abuse, should truly be so criminalized. But this mercy was also fickle. Certain defendants—those involved in the most brutal or gruesome rapes, those who were socially disruptive, and those who were not white—were largely deprived of it.

In dozens of cases, defendants who had been charged with rape were instead convicted of either assault with intent to rape—as Bethel and Wallace had been—or carnal abuse. Men who received these verdicts were spared the harsher available penalties and were sentenced often to just a few years, or even a single one. Even those convicted of rape were routinely sentenced to life imprisonment rather than death.[9]

Yet there were two exceptions to this broadly merciful trend. The first was Black men. In Arkansas trials involving Black defendants, nearly all resulted in rape convictions and death sentences; a rare exception was William Cutts, who was just thirteen years old and accused only of talking "ugly" to a twelve-year-old white girl and tearing her bloomers. He was sentenced to three years in "the negro boys' Industrial school." This pattern held far beyond Arkansas. In Florida, for instance, between 1940 and 1964, fifty-four men were sentenced to death for rape: six white and forty-eight Black; in Virginia, fifty-two Black men and zero white men were executed for rape between 1909 and 1949.[10]

The second exception involved those convicted of particularly violent rapes. Consider, for instance, two rare white men sentenced to death. One had violently raped an eleven-year-old, and the other had abducted a ten-year-old and raped her within earshot of several distraught neighbors. Two white men sentenced to twenty-one years for assault with intent to rape had violently assaulted a ten-year-old and thirteen-year-old, respectively, and a white man sentenced to twenty-one years for carnal abuse had raped his thirteen-year-old daughter. In fact, it was quite rare for white men to be sentenced to more than five years for carnal abuse, and these cases too were notably vicious.

It appears that these men—either through their violence or their alleged transgression of the racial order—had committed such monstrous violations of the tacit Jim Crow code of justice that they needed to pay with their lives or with decades behind bars. Men who had sex with underage girls, or who were perceived as using less violence, did not.[11]

Dutifully, Arthur Adams filed a motion for a new trial. He was not optimistic. Honestly, the only surprising thing about the verdict was that it had taken the jury so long to reach it. In a similar case, one defense attorney noted, the jurors "remained out just long enough to smoke a cigarette and returned with the death penalty." In the trial of two Black men, Theo Thomas and Frank Buster, accused of rape a few years later, the jurors required just seven minutes to reach their verdict. The two men were sentenced to die in spite of the presence of an "elderly Negro" on the jury, perhaps the first Black man to serve on an Arkansas jury in decades. At another rape trial, in Alabama, a crowd of 500 white spectators erupted in cheers after a jury pronounced the Black defendant guilty; the jurors had deliberated for just thirty minutes.[12]

Nonetheless, Adams had to do his duty. He raised every potential trial error he could think of, from procedural flaws in his clients' indictments (the indictments were not properly signed or filed) to the judge's denial of his motion for a change of venue to the gross insufficiency of the state's evidence. Yet Adams spent the most space in his motion pointing out the problems with the jury deliberations. "The defendants were prejudiced thereby as all jurors were exhausted and the hour was late at night and as a result the jury returned a verdict about 11 p.m. or shortly thereafter," he wrote. "This verdict was in effect brought about by duress and the court erred in granting the request of the foreman made on the return of the jury to the court room at about 10:30 p.m." Further, when Ike Miller, the foreman, told the judge "that the jury was in disagreement regarding the punishment," it was "in effect a disclosure of what took place in the jury room and was prejudicial error for which the court should have declared a mistrial and discharged the jury."[13]

Adams mentioned only in passing the "conditions and feelings then existing generally at Blytheville," but he did not discuss the mob atmosphere within the courtroom. Nor did he mention the attempts to lynch his clients, or the violence perpetrated against his clients by the very men who were to guard them in the courtroom, or the exclusion of Black people from the courtroom, or—perhaps most important—the exclusion of Black people from the jury rolls. In contrast, the attorney for Charles Hamm—another Black man accused of rape—argued in a motion for a new trial a decade later that "the charge being heinous in character and alleged to have been perpetrated against a comely, young white woman 19 years of age, and the defendant being a powerful young negro," the verdict was clearly "the result of passion and prejudice."

Adams signed the bottom of the four-page document in his neat cursive. Judge Killough promptly overruled it.[14]

With their trial over and their date of execution looming, Clayton and Carruthers were led from the courtroom back to the county jail in Blytheville. For five days, they stayed in the jail. On the sixth day, they were taken to Tucker Prison Farm. There, they would remain—condemned—for, it seemed likely, the rest of their lives.[15]

Tucker was a vast plantation, roughly 4,500 acres of fields and lawns and swampland surrounding squat, decrepit buildings. A narrow bayou could be glimpsed from some of the cells, but, mostly, gazing out from behind iron bars, the prisoners would have seen seemingly endless rows of cotton plants, delicate white bolls quivering on spindly brown stalks. One survey undertaken around this time determined that the inmates at Tucker were held in frame buildings "obsolete in design and construction, and in such bad condition that even extensive repairs would not make them either sanitary or satisfactory for housing purposes." The water supply was "inadequate," the fire hazards "grave," and the prison itself was overcrowded. Whipping remained the regular punishment; cruelty was the norm. Forty men at a time would have to cram into the showers, which one inmate noted was "also a place to urinate." The prison offered no religious services, no vocational training, no athletic equipment, no library. Instead, it demanded unremitting labor.[16]

In the aftermath of the Civil War, wealthy white planters in the South suddenly found themselves without a bonded workforce, and they moved swiftly to transform enslavement into a legally acceptable form. Elite planters were obsessed with "the search for a substitute for slavery," commented one historian. This obviously resulted in the emergence of debt peonage and sharecropper farming, but it also became "convict leasing"—that is, renting out the labor of imprisoned individuals to the highest bidder, with no payment to the convict and no way for the convict to refuse. This was "the middle ground between slavery and freedom," wrote another historian, not quite chattel slavery but a very far cry from freedom.[17]

Convict leasing emerged in Arkansas just two years after Appomattox, when a manufacturing firm purchased the right to exploit the state's inmates for fifteen years. The state terminated the firm's lease nine years early, however, after officials discovered rampant corruption. Undeterred, authorities began leasing prisoner labor to other upstart capitalists, sending men to work in brickyards and timber camps and coal mines and on the ever-expanding railways. The prison population increased sixfold between 1874 and 1882, ensuring the profitability of the convict-lease system; this expansion was enabled by astoundingly punitive laws, such as the Arkansas Larceny Act of 1875, which established the penalty for the theft of just two dollars at one to five years.

Working conditions for these leased inmates were predictably vile. Legislative reform in the 1880s—passed in the wake of a measles outbreak that killed a fifth of the prison population—sought to protect the inmates, limiting their workdays to ten hours, mandating the presence of a penitentiary physician, and ensuring them "sufficient good and wholesome food," but conditions barely improved. Populist politicians and left-leaning labor unions began railing against the convict-lease system, condemning it as equivalent to slavery, which was hardly a distant memory. Convict labor became a major issue in the 1892 elections, and the legislators tried again to reform the system, again failing dismally. Life for convict laborers remained nasty, brutish, and short—or sometimes, maybe even worse, long. One prisoner from this time described the men returning from a railroad labor camp: "Worked, beaten and starved to death, one of these men showed me where he had been whipped. He had sores on him as large as my hand. . . . They work in rain and mud, then lay down at night with their wet clothes on and try to sleep. Often in the winter time when the weather was cold I have known them to lay down at night with their clothes frozen stiff with ice." A leased convict worked until he could stand it no longer—"then he has to lay down and die."[18]

By the early 1910s, with more than 90 percent of the state's convicts working outside of penitentiary walls and fresh scandals popping up almost daily, the situation had become politically untenable. Governor George Washington Donaghey, a progressive and a former cowboy, fought and threatened and ultimately forced through a bill outlawing convict leasing, winning the praise of Teddy Roosevelt and Eugene V. Debs in the process. But still, the state legislature knew that the convicts represented too attractive a source of labor; rehabilitation required work, and someone might as well profit from that work. So, in 1902, with the writing on the wall, the state opened a prison farm on an immense cotton plantation in the Delta; it came to be called Cummins. Fourteen years later, with convict leasing dead and gone, the state opened another, smaller prison farm, this one fifty miles closer to Little Rock; it came to be called Tucker. It turned out that forcing the convicts to labor for the benefit of the state was hardly any better than forcing them to labor for the benefit of private parties. "Penitentiary conditions in Arkansas are a disgrace," admitted another governor.[19]

A significant part of the problem was the "Arkansas system" of guarding the inmates. To save money, the state empowered certain prisoners to guard other prisoners. (To save still more money, the state replaced virtually all prison employees—the mechanics, clerks, bookkeepers, and briefly even the mules—with convict labor.) Armed with Winchester rifles or double-barreled shotguns and a pack of bloodhounds, these inmate-guards, called "trusties," were known to be ruthless and cruel. "The practice gave trusty guards not only the authority to watch over fellow inmates," wrote one historian, "but to kill inmates for personal reasons." Between February 1933 and July 1934, trusties killed fourteen of their fellow inmates, and they beat and bloodied countless others. The abuse was so bad that one inmate, sentenced to die in the electric chair at Tucker, told a state commission, "I wish it was tonight." In 1936, with Clayton and Carruthers behind bars, there were 164 trusties working at Tucker and Cummins, virtually all of them white.[20]

One newspaper article from this time described the Arkansas system with pride, repeating the warden's claim that it saved money, improved morale, prevented escapes, and encouraged greater productivity. A visiting prison official from Texas was "absolutely dumbfounded to see hundreds of convicts, Negroes and white men, at work in the fields under the watchful eyes of other convicts. Except for the deputy warden in charge of each camp, there was not a 'free' guard on the farms." But another paper decried "the weaknesses and evils in a system whereby a convicted murderer serving a life term is entrusted with a penitentiary truck and goes after felons in various county seats to take them back to prison. He has a big pistol strapped on his hip and he is boss. Several murders have been committed at Tucker Farm by those trusties."[21]

In the summer of 1933, two years before Clayton and Carruthers were convicted of rape, The Walls was closed for good, its last remaining prisoners transferred to Tucker. At least one newspaper editorialized against this move, arguing that the penitentiary should be moved back to Little Rock—"where it belongs." The paper predicted this would soon happen, "and all this money will have been thrown away. However, that is characteristic of Arkansas." In the meantime, at least, Tucker became the "headquarters" of the state prison system, the place where the records, equipment, and electric chair were relocated. Tucker became the primary site for the state's white prisoners, and Cummins was largely for Black prisoners, but death row stayed at Tucker, and that was where Clayton and Carruthers were sent.[22]

Racism was pervasive within the Arkansas penal system. Former inmates recalled that Black men in particular were subjected to gruesome violence, whipped multiple times a day or chained to a post and left to bake in the hot sun. They were also overrepresented. A survey of prisoners from 1927 revealed that white prisoners constituted a bare majority, but by 1936 "more than half" of the inmates were Black—"about twice the ratio of Blacks to whites in Arkansas." One white prisoner later reflected that "fifty percent of the negro convicts there should never have been sent to the Penitentiary," that most were railroaded or intimidated by prosecutors. Statistically, white inmates were much more likely to have been convicted of larceny or liquor law violations; Black inmates were more likely to have been convicted of violent crimes, though this does not mean they actually committed these crimes at a higher rate. Prisoners were also, as a rule, poor. More than a quarter of all prisoners were illiterate, and only 1 in 125 had attended college; a majority farmed for a living.[23]

A newspaper article from 1930 claimed that the warden was "especially" well-liked by Black inmates. "When he visits the various camps where they are stationed, he is greeted on all sides by grinning African faces and friendly shouts of 'Howdy, Cap'n Tod. How you is? You sho' looking well dese days.'"[24] This racist fantasy aside, life behind bars was almost complete misery for Black prisoners. The NAACP investigated a case in which guards in one Arkansas jail beat a Black man so viciously that he died—and the authorities didn't even inform his family of his death.[25] Black female inmates, in particular, lived with a constant fear of sexual violence from the guards and warden.[26]

Arriving back at Tucker that day in the spring of 1935, Clayton and Carruthers would have been led to the office to have their photographs and fingerprints taken. They would have been issued overalls and jumpers, along with heavy work shoes. They would have been taken to their sleeping quarters, possibly the Stockade, which housed about three hundred men in one big room—so many men that there weren't enough beds, that two steel bunks were dragged in and placed side by side and three men were forced to wedge themselves onto two bunks, the one in the middle resting on the uncomfortable seam, some of the newer prisoners sleeping on the floor without even the comfort of a blanket to stay warm. They would have awoken to the sight of their own blood, smeared over the sheets where, rolling in their sleep, they had mashed the bedbugs that infested Tucker. They would have risen before daylight for a breakfast that one inmate later claimed "looked like wall-paper paste and tasted about the same." They would have wolfed down their food before lining up on the front yard, even in driving rain. They would have gotten their work assignments—probably the same cotton picking they had known for years, but this time without even a pittance of pay. They would have worked up to fourteen hours a day, not allowed to talk lest a trusty wielding a bull-hide whip might hear them.[27]

They would have done all of this—except they were death row inmates, and none of the usual rules applied for death row inmates. Condemned men were held in a wing of their own, cramped and unpleasant, off to the side. The details of their captivity are mostly gone.

As Clayton and Carruthers sat in their cell—struggling to accustom their minds to the rapidly dwindling timeline of their lives, perhaps thinking through the long-shot appeals that remained to them—the Arkansas Delta was exploding.

In the early months of 1935, the Southern Tenant Farmers Union had been forced underground by the assaults and arsons and assassination attempts spearheaded by the big planters and their thugs. The federal government refused to intervene. The courts refused to intervene. Feeling confident in the rush of a repressive summer, the big planters announced that they were cutting wages for the season from sixty cents per hundred pounds of cotton to just forty cents. The STFU's leaders returned to the Arkansas Delta, and, traveling by night, they strategized with their locals. Ultimately, the union members voted 11,186 to 450 in favor of a strike.[28]

One morning, late in the summer, sharecroppers across three Delta counties awoke to find handbills tacked to their porches and barn doors and fences, instructing everyone to stay out of the fields until wages reached one dollar per hundred pounds. Union organizers had begun distributing these at precisely eleven the night before, easing cars through the countryside and pulling into the woods when authorities got too close, not finishing until three in the morning. "It wasn't no easy job," recalled one Black, female organizer. "White folks thought it was a plane that distributed fliers." Many a plantation boss angrily demanded, "Where did these things come from?" Many tenant farmers didn't even know what a strike was, but they trusted the union organizers who had visited cabins under cover of darkness. The STFU leaders spread a rumor that scab pickers in another county had gotten killed for returning to the cotton fields. Sharecroppers had to decide which side they were on.

The announcement of the strike initially amused many planters, eliciting scorn from those who did not believe these unlettered unionists would forego their measly wages as well as federal relief, which was not available to those who refused to work. But on the day the strike began "a strange emptiness hung over the cotton fields." Thousands of tenant farmers and sharecroppers stayed in their cabins. Across Crittenden, Cross, Poinsett, St. Francis, and Mississippi Counties, the strike was dominant. Soon the arrests began, as deputy sheriffs angrily invaded the cabins and dragged the strikers out. But the strikers had been told not to resist arrest; the goal was to pack the jails. "Fill every jail in Arkansas but don't pick cotton until cotton prices are met," was the message they had heard. Soon the jails were packed. Still, the cotton remained unpicked.[29]

On the sixth day, the planters offered the union sixty-five cents per hundred pounds. The union held fast at a dollar. State labor officials visited the region and could find just five workers picking cotton; thousands were home, or else out fishing. The planters escalated their violence. "Two strikers were beaten with axe handles," wrote the historian Nan Woodruff, "others were evicted, arrested for vagrancy, and beaten." Yet the union did not bend. Finally, on the tenth day, the planters offered seventy-five cents per hundred pounds, and the tenant farmers and sharecroppers decided this was a victory. In some places, they got a dollar. They returned to the fields, triumphant.

"In thousands of cabins in the cotton country men received a new light," wrote one of the STFU's leaders. "They were no longer powerless. . . . These disinherited men have their ears to the wind, their eyes fixed on the far horizons where freedom and plenty await them. Today they march with firm feet toward it; tomorrow with firm hands they will seize it. *To the disinherited belongs the future.*"[30]

In such a revolutionary moment, in such a radical region, perhaps Clayton and Carruthers—or their allies—might be able to seize power and secure freedom as well. That summer and fall the impossible seemed impossible no longer.

Part IV
Appeals and Demands

25 • Taking Flight, 1968–1969

The date was April 4, 1968, and Maya Angelou's Upper West Side apartment smelled delicious. She had been cooking all day: Texas chili (no beans), baked ham and candied yams, rice and peas, macaroni and cheese, and a pineapple upside-down cake. That evening marked her fortieth birthday, and she was having a party: the Harlem Writers Guild was coming over, along with other friends and the regulars from her local pub. The ice buckets were out; the daffodils were "perky." Then the telephone rang.

"Maya?" came the voice on the other end. It was Dolly McPherson, a friend of hers.

"Yes?"

"Have you listened to the radio or television?"

"No."

"Maya, please don't turn either of them on. And don't answer the phone. Give me your word."

A few minutes later, McPherson was at her doorstep, looking ghastly. "Martin Luther King was shot," she said. "Maya, he's dead."

For a moment, Angelou could not comprehend what was happening. She had just seen King, just agreed to help with his Poor People's Campaign. Suddenly, she had to get out of her apartment. Accompanied by a neighbor, she walked into Harlem, where an uprising was beginning. Yet in Angelou's eyes, this was different from Watts, which had been about anger; this was about deep sadness. She could hear screams, discordant thuds, and, everywhere, strangers hugging and crying and asking one another, "Why? Why?"[1]

For weeks afterward, everything was drab and dull. Angelou isolated herself in her apartment, depressed and silent and alone until James Baldwin finally convinced her to accompany him to a small dinner party. "You have to get out of here," he told her. "Get dressed. I'm taking you somewhere."

That somewhere turned out to be the comfortable New York apartment of the cartoonist Jules Feiffer and the photographer and writer Judy Feiffer. Over glasses of Scotch, they talked about their childhoods and laughed late into the night. When it was Angelou's turn to share, she regaled the group with tales of growing up Black in Stamps, trying to find humor in the slights she had experienced.

You know how we survived slavery? Baldwin asked her on the street outside afterward. "We put surviving into our poems and into our songs."[2]

The next morning, Judy Feiffer called Robert Loomis, an editor at Random House, and told him he should get the poet Maya Angelou to write a book. (Angelou's recollections would later diverge about whether Baldwin and the Feiffers had first broached the subject of a memoir with her the night before.) Loomis dutifully called Angelou several days later, asking if she'd like to write an autobiography. Angelou flatly told him no, she was too busy, and, besides, she was a poet. Loomis said fine, politely ending the call, but Angelou was later sure he talked to Baldwin afterward, to figure out a next move. When Loomis called again a little later, he told her that perhaps it was better she didn't try to write an autobiography, since it was the most difficult art form. Angelou could never resist a challenge. "Well, maybe I will try it," she told Loomis. "I'll start tomorrow."

Or, as she put it in another recounting of this conversation, "At that moment I looked up at him and shouted 'STAND BACK!'"[3]

At the end of her sixth memoir, written decades later, Angelou would recall traveling to Stockton, California, to see her mother and while there deciding that if she did write this book, she would have to "examine the quality in the human spirit that continues to rise despite the slings and arrows of outrageous fortune. Rise out of physical pain and the psychological cruelties. Rise from being victims of rape and abuse and abandonment for the determination to be no victim of any kind." Sitting there, in her mother's kitchen, thinking of a poem she had heard in her mute days in Arkansas about heading for higher ground, she wrote the first line of the book that would become *I Know Why the Caged Bird Sings*: "What are you looking at me for? I didn't come to stay."[4]

Yet Angelou's thought process when it came to starting her first memoir may have not been so straightforward. In an interview she gave in 1972, she reflected that she'd "lived so many lives" in her forty-odd years on earth: "First I thought I'd relate my five years in Africa during the 60's. Being black, female, non-Muslim, non-Arab, six feet tall and American made for some interesting experiences. But then, I thought, there isn't enough written for black girls in America that says, listen, you might encounter defeats but must never be defeated. One would say of my life—born loser—had to be: from a broken family, raped at eight, unwed mother at sixteen. I wanted to show that it's a fact but it's not the truth."[5]

"I can say, honestly, that I don't believe a day has passed that I haven't thought about it, in something I do, in my own sexuality, in my own practices," she would tell another interviewer years later. "So I thought to myself, 'You write so that perhaps people who hadn't raped anybody yet might be discouraged, people who had might be informed, people who have not been raped might understand something, and people who have been raped might forgive themselves. That's why I wrote about the rape."[6]

True to this dawning realization, the many handwritten drafts that survive in Angelou's papers show a writer experimenting with several potential narrative arcs. For instance, she wrote pages and pages about selling sex in San Diego and Stockton and about her burgeoning sexuality while in San Francisco; none of these passages made it into *Caged Bird*, though she borrowed liberally from them for later memoirs. She wrote more about coming of age in San Francisco, becoming a musician and learning to dance; those passages would eventually be condensed or eliminated.[7] It does appear that her decision to focus on her childhood—and on her rape—was not immediate. And she undoubtedly made many decisions about what to cut and what to include based on her desire to craft a fairly neat narrative of overcoming specific trauma. On a scrap of paper titled "Perspectus" she sketched out the barest of outlines of coming into her own in Arkansas. One section she intended to include was "Sex again enters my life by observation of Uncle Willie in the act." Yet this does not resemble any episode she ultimately included in *Caged Bird*.[8]

When asked years later about how she selected the events to include, Angelou replied "Some events stood out in my mind more than others. Some, though, were never recorded because they were so bad or so painful, that there was no way to write about them honestly and artistically without making them melodramatic. They would have taken the book off its course."[9] And its course, it became clear, was a story of childhood, of Jim Crow, of family love, and also, undeniably and ultimately, a story about rape. "Carefully disguised in layers of narrative," comments the critic and biographer Linda Wagner-Martin, "the rape of the character of little Marguerite takes control as the core of the autobiography."[10]

Yet this same story was also one of a Black girl in the Jim Crow South overcoming breathtaking racism and a specific act of sexual violence. "All my work, my life, everything is about survival," Angelou remarked in the same interview. "All my work is meant to say, 'You may encounter many defeats, but you must not be defeated.' In fact, the encountering may be the very experience which creates the vitality and the power to endure."[11]

Although she may have started writing her memoir while in California, Angelou wrote much of it in London. One journalist would record that she did this "because 'the British treat all foreigners with benign neglect' and the detached atmosphere helped her to deal with painful childhood memories."[12] She apparently moved around London quite a bit. In November 1968 she wrote to her friend Dolly McPherson that she was "happy, happy" staying in a hotel in the north of the city, occupying a tiny room with a communal bathroom by day, learning darts and drinking beer in the downstairs pub by night.[13] Barely two weeks later, though, she was staying in a well-heeled part of central London.[14] One of the notebooks that contain her handwritten drafts includes a residential address in the Golders Green neighborhood, a suburban, historically Jewish area.[15]

Angelou always began her writing in longhand, transcribing it on the typewriter later. She wrote on yellow legal pads and stenographer pads and forty-nine-cent spiral notebooks. Her drafts were mostly page after page of neat cursive, occasionally with doodles or phone numbers scrawled on them. As she began to combine her scenes and refine her structure, she started cutting up various pages and pasting or stapling paragraphs together, forming new pages.[16] After she finished a particular section—say, twelve or fourteen pages—she would read it over again, to find "what its rhythm is. 'Cause everything in the universe has a rhythm. . . . And once I hear the rhythm of the piece, then I try to find out what are the salient points that I must make in the piece. And then it begins to take shape."[17]

For her, writing was hard work. In various articles and interviews she would compare it to physical labor—even to the labor of pregnancy. "The new book is a-borning," she would write to Baldwin in 1973, "and every 24 hours I'm certain that it's going to be a breach birth—false labor pains (and real ones), dropped placenta, broken water . . . oh Hell, why do I go on when you know the symptoms so much more painfully and productive than I?"[18] Especially after she decided to write about such a traumatic part of life, the process of writing *Caged Bird* became a sometimes painful one. "I had to entrance and enchant myself back into those times, you see," she told an interviewer shortly after the book came out. "I had to go down, down, down to that very time so that I could smell it and touch it once again."[19] She realized that there were some parts of her childhood about which she had total recall—"the smells, sounds, the color of the sun, for instance"—but others that were "just blocked out." She had not visited Stamps for twenty years, and she would not return even as she described the town in so much detail. "While I was writing the book, I stayed half drunk in the afternoon and cried all night."[20]

In the years that followed, many journalists would ask Angelou about her particular writing process, and her answers articulate a consistent desire for solitude and freedom from distraction. She would tell these interviewers, "When I'm working on a book, when I'm writing, I work about 16 hours a day. I just lock myself up. I walk, bathe, and work. . . . For me to do any writing involves the blotting out of everything else in the world." She would rip out the phone cords, close the blinds—"I can't even have the intrusion of sunlight"— and sever less important relationships, ruthlessly telling closer friends not to call or visit for months at a time. While writing in her house in California, she would take gardening breaks, go for walks, or clean the house, but this was part of her process as well, allowing her to recharge and "keep my thoughts together." When away from her house, she would isolate herself in a hotel room—often the "meanest, grimmest old" hotel she could find, free of the art and beloved objects of her home. She would lie across a made-up bed, propped up on an elbow, and try to write longhand—not even allowing the hotel staff in to change the sheets. Accompanying her into isolation would be a couple of dictionaries, a thesaurus, coffee, cigarettes, alcohol, a deck of cards or crossword puzzle, and a Bible. The last item served to inspire her language, to make it as powerful, rhythmic, and musical as scripture.[21]

Angelou would later laugh at the idea that she was a "natural born writer." "I am not!" she would insist to an interviewer. "I agonized over that book; I cried; I sweated! There's nothing easy about writing. And now my publisher wants a sequel," she groaned. "I think they want me to become a black Proust!"[22]

As Angelou moved from draft to draft—from handwritten passages to typed pages—her descriptions of her childhood in Stamps and St. Louis remained largely the same, but certain details did change. For instance, she altered names repeatedly, likely out of a desire to protect the identities of real people. In one early draft, the reverend in Stamps was referred to as "Howard

Freeman." In another draft, he was "J. C. Thomas." Finally, in the published version of *Caged Bird*, he would become "Howard Thomas."[23]

Even in her earliest drafts, her mother's boyfriend—Angelou's assailant—was called "Mr. Freeman." Remarkably, her descriptions of his assaults of her—from her first handwritten pages—remained fairly consistent; her descriptions of Mr. Freeman's trial also stayed largely the same. The only significant changes were that she added more descriptive language to the pages that were ultimately published, rounding out her imagery, making it both more graphic and more lyrical. For instance, her early draft did not contain the line "even the senses are torn apart," nor did it contain the line "the child gives, because the body can, and the mind of the violator cannot."[24]

Most of all, Angelou was interested in conveying the truth of her own experience. She readily admitted to interviewers that she would sometimes "overstate the facts" or "fiddle with the facts" or employ composite characters, but she would insist that in the most essential sense "the work is true."[25] This distinction between facts and truth is vital to Angelou's work in *Caged Bird*—and to the story she was telling about sexual assault in the Jim Crow South. "I submit that there's a world of difference between truth and fact," Angelou would write years later. "Fact tells us the data: the numbers, the places where, the people who, and the times when. But facts can obscure the truth. Because I write about a time when real people were alive—I mean, it's not as if that is a time which I can create out of the full complement of my imagination—I have to get back to the facts. But then I have to do something else in order to tell the truth of the matter."[26]

And, as the scholar Mary Jane Lupton has noted, "What frequently goes unsaid when discussing the so-called truth in the history of African American autobiography is that in many instances the truth has been censored or hidden out of the need for self-protection." Black autobiographers during the centuries of slavery often "had to restrain or disguise their opinions" and even change names or details to protect themselves or family from retribution.[27] Angelou would not have feared retribution from Mr. Freeman—he was dead—but she may have feared ridicule or disbelief or the social stigma of outing herself as a survivor of sexual assault. In this context, the fact that her memoir was so open about what happened to her must be understood as an act of courage and also an act of resistance—resistance to a racist and sexist society that insisted on silencing women and girls like her.

As she was writing, Angelou made many decisions, large and small, that would confound or astound or simply captivate the scholars of the future. Almost two hundred pages into *Caged Bird*, for instance, Angelou mentions that during middle school she had memorized "the whole of *The Rape of Lucrece*."[28]

This brief reference would eventually pique the interest of a number of scholars. Several noted how Angelou apparently drew considerable inspiration from *The Rape of Lucrece*, a lengthy narrative poem by William Shakespeare. But, crucially, Angelou subverted *Lucrece*, choosing to frame her story as one of victimization and resilience rather than one of only victimization. In *Lucrece*—a disturbing narrative account of a Roman soldier raping a comrade's wife, who takes her own life shortly thereafter—the victim believes that the assault has effectively ruined her body, a situation she can remedy only with her suicide. In *Caged Bird*, Angelou initially feels ruined as well—she wishes to die and wishes to be white—but soon she regains pride in her race, regains her voice, and begins to recover. Whereas Shakespeare's Lucrece could not overcome her own feelings of ruination, Angelou's Maya could; where Shakespeare's titular character succumbed to a society that countenanced sexist violence, Angelou's protagonist "celebrates" her own "body and words," the scholar Mary Vermillion has argued, and "critiques the rape and racial oppression she suffers."[29]

According to Vermillion, rape in *Caged Bird* "primarily represents the black girl's difficulties in controlling, understanding, and respecting both her body and her words . . . both rape and the dominant white culture's definitions of beauty disempower the black women's body and self-expression."[30] By linking sexual violence to white supremacy, Angelou highlighted the intersection of the systems of oppression that shaped her childhood. As the scholar Mildred R. Mickle has argued, "She wrote to exorcise society's reticence to face the ugly truth of the victimization of individuals not only through racism but also through sexual abuse."[31] Another scholar, Christine Froula, added that Maya's act of memorizing *Lucrece* was an emergence "from her literal silence into a literary one. Fitting her voice to Shakespeare's words, she writes safe limits around the exclamations of her wounded tongue." Nonetheless, with the very act of writing *Caged Bird*, Angelou reclaims her own voice "by telling the prohibited story."[32]

Over time, the book's title transformed. Working titles appear to have included "Rich Blacks and Powhytrash," "Rich [N-words] and Powhytrash," "Just Let Me Know the Rules of the Game," and "The Caged Bird Sings." Eventually, of course, it became *I Know Why the Caged Bird Sings*.[33]

Angelou borrowed this title from a poem by Paul Laurence Dunbar. The son of slaves, Dunbar had become an internationally renowned playwright and poet before dying at age thirty-three. Maya later told an interviewer that

Dunbar and William Shakespeare were "two men who probably formed my writing ambition more than any others." She loved "the rhythm and sweetness of Dunbar's dialect verse." Angelou's friend, the jazz singer and activist Abbey Lincoln, recommended that Angelou consider a line from Dunbar's poem, "Sympathy," for her memoir:

> I know why the caged bird sings, ah me,
> When his wing is bruised and his bosom sore,—
> When he beats his bars and he would be free;
> It is not a carol of joy or glee,
> But a prayer that he sends from his heart's deep core,
> But a plea, that upward to Heaven he flings—
> I know why the caged bird sings![34]

For generations, scholars have written about this particular choice. They have noted that Angelou often returned to the symbol of a caged bird in her writing, and it often signified a chained slave.[35] One scholar focused on the image of the "cage," which is an effective metaphor for the social strictures of Jim Crow, and another commented that "the act of singing serves a cathartic purpose in that the songs give pleasure and make life within the cage bearable."[36] Myra K. McMurry has pointed out that the Angelou's song actually went beyond Dunbar's poem: "Dunbar's caged bird sings from the frustration of imprisonment; its song is a prayer. Angelou's caged bird sings also from frustration, but in doing so discovers the song transforms the cage from a prison that denies selfhood to a vehicle of self-realization."[37]

For her part, Angelou later told an interviewer, "I think that was a bit of naivete or braggadocio for me to say I *know* why the caged bird sings!" But she added that, to her, the quotation was obviously about freedom—and about the literal act of singing, as well. "And you have to sing. You have to," she said. "The black people created the greatest music in the United States during the most horrifying of experiences—the experience of slavery. And in enduring atrocities that would break our hearts if we really, really started to look at them. And out of that time people created a music that is sung all over the world."[38]

After she had written three chapters, Angelou sent them to her editor, Robert Loomis, at Random House. Loomis looked at them and suggested a number of changes. Angelou took the pages home and worked on other things for the next six months. Finally, her friend Sam Floyd—a writer, scholar, and close friend of Baldwin's—asked her, "Whatever happened to those three chapters of that book you were going to do for Random House?"

She replied, "I'm not going to make the changes he"—Loomis—"wants."

Floyd said, "Why don't you get back to your manuscript and continue to write it. Promise me you will."

Angelou promised she would. She phoned Loomis. He asked, "Have you made those changes?"

"No," she said, "and I can't make them."

"Then you want me to see if we can get a contract on this."

About a week later, he told her that Random House would go ahead with the book according to her vision.[39]

For years, Angelou had been resistant to white editors who wanted to fundamentally change her writing. "The writing and all of that goes well," she had written in a letter from 1964. "I have had some difficulty however, because the great white fathers who, naturally must be the ones to publish my novel, are proving to be a bit of a pain in the ass. They want me to make many changes that I absolutely cannot see. Why hell, I am not about to tell somebody's else [sic] story, especially the white man's version; and you had better believe that this is making them excrete green apples!"[40]

She also felt that too many writers, even Black writers, failed to address their work to "the oppressed people themselves." The two writers that had done the best were Malcolm X and Frantz Fanon, but neither "had total success."[41] "Your analysis of our peoples tendency to talk over the head of the masses in a language that is too far above and beyond them is certainly true," Malcolm had written to her shortly before his death in 1965. "You can communicate because you have plenty of (soul) and you always keep your feet firmly rooted on the ground. This is what makes you, you."[42]

Angelou believed that Black women had a special responsibility to write books about Black women, to correct the historical insults and elisions.[43] "The black American female has nursed a nation of strangers—literally. And has remained compassionate," she would tell an interviewer a few years later. "This, to me, is survival. She is strong. And she is inclusive, as opposed to exclusive. She has included all the rest of humanity in her life and has often been excluded from their lives. I'm very impressed with her. I mean, if I were a Swede, or a Laplander or a Chinese, I would read about the black American woman and think: 'Jesus!' " She erupted with laughter. "This is incredible!" She paused, and her voice softened. "Incredible . . ."[44]

Angelou wanted to communicate this story of survival, of resilience, to the masses. And doing this meant neither ignoring the hardships nor fixating on them in a way that pathologized herself or her subjects. Shortly after *Caged Bird* came out, she was asked, "Do you feel bitterness about the black experience?" She replied, "Well, there is a propensity on the part of whites to regard the black experience as just one long siege of misery. As I've said, a sociologist might look at my early life and conclude I was a born loser. Broken home. Raped when very young. Illegitimate child. And so on. It would follow that this would be viewed as a life of misery if that was all there was. But that is never all there is. There was great love in my life. Great support. A lot of laughter. A lot of companionship. And so there has been for millions of black people. But the sociologists and psychologists and all those other ologists so rarely ever see this because they don't want to see it."[45]

Throughout 1968 and 1969, Angelou continued to revise and refine her manuscript. She spent much of her time in London, but she had a number of pressing commitments that sometimes required her to return stateside. Toward the end of 1968, she was the keynote speaker at an "exploration of femininity by and for the Afro-American woman" at St. Peter's AME Church in Minneapolis. A vinyl record of her poetry from the last fifteen years—"The Poetry of Maya Angelou"—was released during this period, as was her off-Broadway play, *In the Presence of Mine Enemies,* as well as the Sidney Poitier film *For the Love of Ivy,* for which she had written a song for B. B. King. She spent much of 1968 working on a ten-hour series for National Education Television titled, "Black, Blues, Black!" It was a remarkable revisionist history lesson on Black American life, starting in Africa, with Angelou serving as instructor. In the summer of 1969, she traveled with friends to Paris, and then on to Algiers, to attend the now iconic Pan-African Cultural Festival, which was a celebration of a revolutionary, postcolonial Africa; there she apparently saw Stokely Carmichael, Miriam Makeba, and Eldridge Cleaver, among others.[46]

At the same time, the United States and the broader world were being rocked by ever more insistent demands for civil and human rights. In France, what had begun as a student protest became a mass strike of ten million workers, nearly overthrowing the government in the process; protests spread to Mexico and Germany, Yugoslavia and England, Poland and Pakistan. In the United States, civil rights activists sought to enforce their newly won right to equal housing; in the aftermath of Martin Luther King's assassination, Black people rose up against state violence in more than a hundred cities; at the 1968 Democratic National

Convention in Chicago, thousands of young people battled the police in the streets, chanting, "The whole world is watching." In 1969, a group of trans women, drag queens, sex workers, hustlers, and queer people—many of them people of color—fought back against police harassment at the Stonewall Inn in New York, launching still more open and sweeping movements for liberation.

Angelou's writing—its radical openness, its willingness to expose the ugliest, most personal aspects of oppression—was unquestionably informed by these uprisings happening all around her, all around the world.[47] Yet it was also almost certainly shaped by a different movement that began in New York in 1969. That February and March, first at a legislative hearing and then at a church in Greenwich Village, a dozen feminist activists stood up and told stunned audiences about their experiences having abortions. This tactic, which became known as the "speak-out," spread across the country in 1969 and 1970. By 1971 radical feminists in New York were holding a "speak-out" about their sexual assaults. This moment, in the late 1960s and early 1970s, was one when women were beginning to speak publicly about parts of their lives that had so long been shrouded in euphemism, secrecy, and shame. Angelou's memoir must be understood as part of this movement.[48]

It must also be understood as part of even older movements. Over time, Angelou came to see her autobiography as part of "a tradition established by Frederick Douglass—the slave narrative—speaking in the first-person singular, talking about the first-person plural, always saying *I* meaning *we*," she would later reflect. "And what a responsibility!" Generations of scholars have charted an astoundingly wide variety of influences that shaped Angelou's crafting of *Caged Bird*, from sermons and ghost stories to the Civil Rights Movement and the blues. She drew from all these sources yet created something new, and newly vulnerable.[49]

Almost two years after she had started *Caged Bird*, Angelou was a guest at the house of Sonia Orwell, the widow of George Orwell, when she met another guest, the muckraking writer and activist Jessica Mitford. The two women—one the white daughter of English aristocracy, the other a Black child of the segregated American South—instantly hit it off in the grand drawing room; and Angelou soon showed her parts of her manuscript. Mitford was impressed. The next morning at the breakfast table she began to read it aloud, affecting her best approximation of a southern accent. The two continued reading it together the rest of the day and late into the night. "It was so fascinating," Mitford recalled. Angelou felt the book was ready for the world.[50]

26 • The Appeal, 1935–1936

On a cold, clear Friday, not long after the Clayton-Carruthers trial had concluded, Thurgood Marshall traveled forty miles south from Baltimore to a rural Maryland community that, until quite recently, had hardly ever seen a Black lawyer. A few months earlier, Marshall had personally integrated the county's courtrooms, appearing first on behalf of a young Black man charged with murder, and then again at the trial of a white police officer who had shot and killed a young Black man. Now, Marshall was back in Prince George's County, dispatched yet again by the NAACP to investigate accusations of interracial rape that the newspapers would soon label Maryland's "Scottsboro" case. Perhaps he was dimly aware that this would be what the legal scholar Kenneth Mack has noted was one of Marshall's "last significant cases before his evident skill and effectiveness resulted in a move to New York to work full time for the NAACP."[1]

A few weeks earlier, at about six thirty in the evening, the white "dining room matron" at a penal reformatory for Black boys screamed. A guard and the institution's superintendent rushed to her third-floor quarters and discovered her lying on the floor of her bathroom, dazed and bruised. Within a day, four Black youths held at the institution—ranging in age from sixteen to twenty—were arrested for attempted rape. The four were held incommunicado for five days, until reporters at the *Baltimore Afro-American* discovered their plight and alerted the NAACP. The NAACP, in turn, turned to Marshall. As had long ago become his routine, the young lawyer dropped everything, hopped in his car, and drove to the site of the crime, interviewing the suspects, the witnesses, and the police. All four Black youths had solid, credible alibis. By now Marshall had established such strong relationships with the local lawyers that, according to Mack, "they now received him, unevenly of course and with many remaining slights, but recognizably as a brother." Marshall was able to broker a deal, and soon he and the white state's attorney were holding a joint press conference, announcing that the four Black youths would quickly be released.

Back in Baltimore, Marshall typed up his usual report to the NAACP, concluding that this investigation "convinces me that it pays to look into these matters . . . and that the people in authority in the Counties will realize that at least one group is constantly watching for the protection of the Negro's rights. This, I believe, tends to keep them in line."[2]

Several months earlier, in the spring of 1935—as Bubbles Clayton and Jim X. Carruthers sat behind bars at Tucker, awaiting trial—a letter had arrived at 69 Fifth Avenue in New York City, the office building that was home to the NAACP. Printed in neat cursive on a small scrap of lined paper, the letter was addressed to "The National Association."

"Dear Sir," it began. "Just a fin line to let you and all know what is my trouble my name is Spencer Clayton and I wont you and all to help me with my Brother his name is Bubber Clayton and the other boy said to have been with him his name is Jim X Caruthers they whip and knock them around and made them own things and I wont you to help me all you can they trial will be in april but I don't know the day and I am sending you a piece of the clipping from the paper so you can read it your self I am a Poor Boy and do all you can for me." Spencer printed his return address and signed the note, "Clayton."[3]

This letter appears to have been the first the NAACP heard of Clayton or Carruthers. At the time it was written, their trial was still weeks away, and the two had no lawyer. In fact, the men had not yet been charged with rape. Thurgood Marshall was still in private practice.

A month passed. Spencer received no reply. An all-white jury convicted Clayton and Carruthers, and the pair was sentenced to die. On April 15, the NAACP received a second letter about the case. "I am mailing herein a letter that I received today from Lawyer Arthur L. Adams of Jonesboro, Arkansas, and hope you will give it such consideration as you deem best," Scipio A. Jones, a Black civil rights lawyer in Little Rock, wrote to NAACP executive secretary Walter White. "I do not know anything about the case except what I have read in the papers, and what is contained in this letter."[4]

Adams had written to Jones at the request of Carruthers's father, James. "The father was in the office last night," Adams recounted. "He is exceeding anxious that an appeal be prosecuted." Adams assured Jones that he had done his best with the case, and, frankly, he didn't think there'd been any error, but his client's father had asked if there might be "some welfare society" that could assist him with the appeal (and defray its cost). So Adams was reaching out to Jones.[5]

On April 25—less than a month before Clayton's and Carruthers's scheduled execution date of May 17—the NAACP's young assistant secretary, Roy Wilkins, replied to Jones. "With reference to the Blytheville cases, our financial situation is so poor, as you realize, that we cannot assist in these cases," he wrote. "We are writing Attorney Adams that we regret that our funds will not permit us to take over any additional cases."[6] A few weeks later, on May 13, Wilkins wrote to Spencer Clayton, with a "belated acknowledgment" of his letter and a polite but terse apology for being unable to help.[7]

Back in Mississippi County, however, an insurgency was brewing. The verdict just didn't sit right with the small community of prominent Black professionals—the doctors and lawyers and merchants—as well as, apparently, several white acquaintances. "Conservative men and women," the president of the Little Rock NAACP branch would later recall, "who live in Blytheville where the trial was held, and have known the boys for many years, expressed a strong belief in their innocence." Several of these prominent individuals brought the matter to the attention of the Little Rock NAACP. The branch decided to investigate; its president asked a white lawyer, John R. Thompson, to travel to Blytheville, obtain a copy of the trial transcript, and ask around about the case. Thompson's findings shook the Little Rock branch. "That evidence indicates that this is another Scottsboro case and one that challenges the manhood and the womanhood of Arkansas," the president would write. Mississippi County's Black community swung into action.

They decided to launch an informal "Caruthers-Clayton defense committee" and fund an appeal. Assisted by the Little Rock NAACP branch (as well as, possibly, the ILD), these individuals hired Thompson to prepare the case for the state supreme court. Thompson, in turn, worked with Arthur Adams to make an emergency request to the court and to the governor, seeking a stay of execution to allow them enough time to perfect the appeal. Remarkably, this request worked; perhaps the presence of not just one but two white attorneys was convincing. On May 13—just four days before the scheduled execution—the governor granted a thirty-day stay. Possibly unaware of this, an Arkansas Supreme Court justice named Edgar L. McHaney did likewise. Armed with stays of execution from two branches of government, Clayton and Carruthers had a temporary reprieve. Their defenders decided to hire yet another lawyer, John A. Hibbler, to prepare the brief.[8]

Hibbler was a prominent member of the Arkansas bar, but, unlike Adams or Thompson, he was Black. He'd been born in the Delta in 1878 and attended public school, then private school, then Arkansas Baptist College. After serving as a teacher, principal, and college professor in quick succession, Hibbler decided to become a lawyer. He also became an outspoken Black Republican, and throughout the 1910s and 1920s he bitterly fought the increasing efforts of the party of Lincoln to allow only white members. (He found time to sue the Democratic Party as well in what proved to be a landmark voting rights effort.) In the wake of the Elaine massacre, Hibbler joined with many of the state's small coterie of Black lawyers to form a defense committee for the condemned sharecroppers and assist in their representation; Hibbler personally interviewed a number of witnesses at the penitentiary. A few years later, he became an early member of the Little Rock branch of the NAACP and spearheaded its voting rights litigation. Hibbler was no radical, more prone to politics of respectability than of revolution; he'd come of age speaking to Baptist audiences on the need for young Black people to pull themselves up by their bootstraps. Still, he was a trailblazer, a fighter, and a professional. Now he was fighting for two more sharecroppers, wrongfully condemned by the white authorities.[9]

Throughout the summer of 1935, Hibbler worked furiously on a brief to the state supreme court. The Little Rock NAACP branch, meanwhile, began rallying the Black bourgeoisie—at meetings and church services—to raise enough money to save "these boys from an undeserved death in the electric chair." In the less tony parts of the state, sharecroppers and farm laborers dug pennies out of pockets; the STFU local in Blytheville contributed nine dollars. These efforts, in turn, led to entreaties to national civil rights figures, such as Roger Baldwin (founder and head of the American Civil Liberties Union) and Carol King (founder of the International Labor Defense and well-known labor radical). Baldwin demurred; King leapt into action, writing to Charles Hamilton Houston, "How would you like to try knocking out that brief with me and both of us going on as counsel for the appellants?"[10]

Likely concerned that communist lawyers could once again take over a publicity-generating case, Houston and the national NAACP agreed to get involved. Neither he nor King were terribly impressed with Hibbler's brief, Houston wrote to the Little Rock branch president at the beginning of September. So they decided to draft a supplemental brief themselves, focusing primarily on the prosecutor's "prejudicial error" of "accusing and questioning them as to other entirely distinct and unrelated crimes." The evidence of rape, they wrote, "is so full of holes and missing links that no jury which respected its oath could find the defendants guilty beyond a reasonable doubt, without the introduction of extraneous, irrelevant matters tending to inflame passion and prejudice." The jury, they concluded, had convicted due to "a feeling that the defendants were 'bad Negros.' " Houston also offered to dispatch a lawyer from New York to argue the case before the Arkansas Supreme Court, if that would be helpful. "I would appreciate your immediate advi[c]e," he wrote, "because the time is running short."[11]

Early on Sunday, September 15, 1935, the local NAACP president received ten copies of the supplemental brief—a joint effort by the NAACP and ILD, Houston wrote to Walter White—and Hibbler filed it the very next morning.[12]

In a letter accompanying the supplemental brief, Houston suggested that the Little Rock lawyers get in touch with "Judge Jones," to advise them as to next steps. This would prove to be one of Houston's most lasting contributions to the effort to save Clayton and Carruthers. A short, portly, courtly man, perpetually sporting a bow tie and gold pocket watch, Scipio Africanus Jones was Arkansas's most prominent Black lawyer, his fame and notoriety dwarfing even that of his friend and ally John Hibbler. He was the lawyer whom Arthur Adams had contacted first, following the trial, when he sought to get in touch with the NAACP. And by the end of October, Jones was actively involved in the fight to free Clayton and Carruthers.[13]

By the time he joined the defense team, Jones had already lived a remarkable life. He had been born a slave in 1863 or 1864, even as the owners of his mother, Jemmima, were on the lam, trying to escape the advancing Union troops. Rumors swirled around the wartime baby, christened Scipio, hinting that his father may have been a white man—which, in turn, hinted at sexual assault. Freedom came to Jones a year later, and the young boy grew up in the town of Tulip, a once thriving Arkansas metropolis (not terribly far from Stamps) that fell into disrepair following the war. Jones learned both to pick cotton and to read (the only one of his brothers to do so), and eventually the former enabled him to continue the latter at a series of colleges in Little Rock (although he was so poor that he was at times homeless). Following his graduation, Jones became a public school teacher. After being turned away from the all-white state law school, he talked his way into reading law in the offices of prominent Little Rock attorneys. Jones passed the oral bar exam in 1889, becoming a member of the state's tiny fraternity of Black lawyers. He quickly gained acclaim for his success in representing Black fraternal organizations and business associations, endearing himself to the Black bourgeoisie and eventually securing a fine home and a chauffeur-driven Cadillac. He was well-liked by the white establishment, too, and befriended the governor. But he also represented less well-off Black individuals, challenged railroad segregation, and repeatedly appealed the existence of all-white juries throughout the 1900s and 1910s. He became so widely respected that he eventually, albeit only briefly, served as a judge in Little Rock.

Jones came to the attention of national civil rights figures when, in 1919, he joined with John Hibbler and others in the defense of the Elaine Twelve. "For four years," one Black newspaperman wrote at the time, "he travelled and investigated and studied and plead[ed]"—but during all that time, "the Judge has maintained his poise." Jones became a veritable folk hero to many when he wrote the briefs that allowed the sharecroppers to prevail before the U.S. Supreme Court. In the years that followed, Jones continued to fight for civil rights, although, as one of his most dedicated biographers wrote decades ago, his "views" on the subject were paradoxical. To maintain his friendly rapport with white powerbrokers and white jurors, Jones conducted himself deferentially, even obsequiously, and he collaborated with Booker T. Washington on a mission of paternalistic racial uplift; yet he also did not hesitate to challenge the convict-lease system, the all-white primary, and eventually even educational segregation. In 1932, Jones politely but firmly threatened to sue Mississippi County's biggest planter, Robert E. Lee Wilson, for "damages based on alleged acts of peonage." ("This is not true," Wilson replied tersely. "You can take any steps that you see fit.") Three years later, racism and violence in Mississippi County again became a part of Jones's life.[14]

Now armed with a first-rate legal team—including Jones, then the most successful Black appellate litigator in the state's history—Clayton and Carruthers could finally mount a real challenge in the Arkansas Supreme Court. And, at virtually the same moment that fall, their case became a national sensation.

For months, the only newspaper outside of Arkansas that routinely mentioned the case was the communist *Daily Worker*, which undertook a dogged effort to raise awareness and funds.[15] Then, in August and September, stories began appearing in such prominent Black newspapers as the *Cleveland Call and Post* and the Wichita-based *Negro Star*. The true breakthrough occurred on September 28, when the renowned *Pittsburgh Courier* ran the banner headline: "Arkansas Youths Face Legal Lynching." The catchier phrase appeared in the subheading: "Second Scottsboro Case Looms as Appeal Goes to Supreme Court." In the days and weeks that followed, Black newspapers in Atlanta, in Baltimore, in the North and in the South, began covering the story, broadcasting the injustice in the Delta to thousands of readers. Nearly all repeated the *Courier*'s explosive charge that this was another Scottsboro.[16]

Meanwhile, Thurgood Marshall's legal practice was hurting. He may have established a solid reputation among the lawyers and laypeople in Baltimore, but his work for the NAACP was taking up more and more of his time, and the few, small cases he had rarely paid (at least not on time). He began contemplating an exit strategy. Marshall inquired about teaching at his alma mater, Howard Law School, but either Houston's lack of support or a faction of the faculty opposed to Houston and anyone associated with the dean quickly stymied that effort. When a left-leaning political organization attempted to draft the young lawyer into running for Congress, Marshall was, according to biographer Juan Williams, "seriously interested," but friends eventually talked him out of that idea as well.[17]

And still, he was being pulled ever deeper into the NAACP's orbit. At the same time that an elite cohort of lawyers was assembling to defend Clayton and Carruthers in Arkansas, Marshall and Houston were litigating a pathbreaking antidiscrimination suit against the University of Maryland School of Law, a case one of his biographers would call "the first major school desegregation victory in the nation . . . a case that historians now regard as the first step on the road to *Brown v. Board of Education*."[18]

All through the spring, summer, and autumn of 1935, as Houston peripatetically advised the Arkansas lawyers on their appeal, he and Marshall prosecuted this suit.[19] Just as Marshall and Houston were furiously preparing for their Maryland appeal, the Clayton-Carruthers appeal was finally set to be heard before the Arkansas Supreme Court. For weeks, Houston had been planning to go to Little Rock to argue the Clayton-Carruthers case himself, but on November 1 he decided he was simply too busy.[20] Ultimately, no one would argue the case before the Arkansas Supreme Court. Five days before oral arguments, the clerk of the court called Scipio Jones to tell him that the state supreme court would simply receive the briefs but hear no presentations from advocates.[21]

Instead, the decision would come down to wisdom or whim of the justices—and, in the end, to the judgment of one enigmatic justice in particular.

Edgar Lafayette McHaney was a large man with a large nose and large forehead and crisp, white hair, parted down the center. For nearly a decade, he had been an associate justice on the Arkansas Supreme Court. It was he who had granted Clayton and Carruthers a stay of execution six months before. And it was he who was now tasked with mulling over their fate.

McHaney was a striver. In fact, but for the color of his skin, his story strikingly mirrored those of John Hibbler and Scipio Jones. Young Edgar had been born on a farm in western Tennessee, perhaps an hour or two by car from Mississippi County. After attending rural public schools and graduating from state college in Tennessee, he worked as a teacher and principal in Arkansas for a number of years before moving to Little Rock to accept a post as a clerk in the office of the Arkansas secretary of state. At the same time, he enrolled in night law school. He became known as an ambitious, extroverted, and well-connected young man. But whereas other such strivers, like Hibbler and Jones, had been limited by the strictures of Jim Crow society, McHaney endured no such impediment.

In April 1904, just two months before his graduation, McHaney married a popular society belle in an elaborate ceremony that the *Arkansas Democrat* called "one of the social events of the season." The *Democrat* noted that "all predict that he has a most brilliant future."[22] Upon graduation, McHaney joined the firm of George Murphy, a former state attorney general and noted trial attorney. Theirs was a well-regarded if ordinary Little Rock legal practice—until the Elaine massacre in 1919. In its aftermath, at the request of another well-connected Little Rock lawyer, McHaney traveled to Elaine to try to secure the release of Black unionists arrested on trumped-up charges. He failed, but he and Murphy joined Hibbler, Jones, and other Black attorneys in the defense of the Elaine Twelve. Though McHaney grumbled about how much the defense was costing him, he remained a part of a legal team seeking to challenge the exclusion of Black people from Jim Crow juries; it was no small act of courage at the time.

In May 1920, as they were waiting on their latest appeal, McHaney and Murphy traveled to New York to ask the NAACP for additional funds for the appeals. The NAACP wrote out a check for $5,000, believing that McHaney's political connections and white skin made up for his frequent requests for more money. Back in Arkansas, McHaney and Jones prepared a last-minute petition seeking to stay the executions, which they filed with an iconoclastic judge named John Martineau in Pulaski Chancery Court. Seven years earlier, Martineau had granted a similar last-second order to stay an execution—and the Arkansas Supreme Court had given him what the journalist Robert Whitaker called "a good verbal spanking"—and now, continued

Whitaker, "Jones and McHaney, standing before Chancellor Martineau at 3:00 p.m., were asking him to do it again." Martineau granted their petition. Jones and McHaney then sought to persuade the state supreme court to uphold Martineau's order. The court refused, "spanking" both Martineau and McHaney in the process. When the NAACP turned down McHaney's request for another $5,000 a few months later, a week before the scheduled electrocutions, McHaney resigned, stunning and disheartening Jones and the NAACP. "These Arkansas cases are no longer mere legal cases," NAACP secretary James Weldon Johnson told Jones. "These constitute a fight for common justice and humanity ... the monetary consideration ought to be secondary." Though McHaney's resignation was at least partly for show, and he remained involved to some extent, Jones finished the last appeals largely on his own, eventually taking them all the way to the U.S. Supreme Court and winning.[23]

Now Jones was back, bringing another desperate appeal to the Arkansas Supreme Court, again arguing that the exclusion of Black people from a criminal jury impermissibly violated Black defendants' constitutional rights. This time, however, Jones's position was strengthened considerably by the Supreme Court's decision in the case of the Elaine defendants, *Moore v. Dempsey*, which he himself had appealed. And this time, he was appealing directly to his old comrade in arms, Edgar McHaney.

In spite of his involvement in the controversial Elaine cases, the well-connected McHaney won election to the Arkansas legislature in 1921. He chose not to run for reelection two years later, thinking he stood no chance at the peak of the Klan's popularity in Arkansas. A few years later, in 1927, however, then-governor John Martineau appointed McHaney to the Arkansas Supreme Court. Not long thereafter, Scipio Jones and John Hibber brought an appeal to the court, challenging the exclusion of Black people from Democratic primary elections in the state. Less than a decade had passed since the civil rights lawyers and McHaney had been on the same side, but in this case McHaney ruled against his former allies, writing that because the discrimination was perpetrated by the Democratic Party, and not the State of Arkansas, no constitutional rights had been violated. Thus, with both trepidation and hope, Jones and Hibbler appealed Clayton's and Carruthers's case to McHaney and the rest of the state supreme court in the fall of 1935.[24]

McHaney's thought process is, sadly, lost to history. All that is known is its conclusion: on Monday, November 18, he ruled against the defendants. The trial court had not erred in seating an all-white jury, McHaney wrote, because Arthur Adams had neglected to raise the issue at trial; the trial court had not erred in refusing to change venue, McHaney continued, because Arthur Adams had not presented sufficient evidence that such a change was needed; the trial court had not erred in permitting the prosecutor to question the defendants "on other unrelated crimes," McHaney concluded, because the questions related "to actual guilt or guilty knowledge and not to indictments or mere accusations." The evidence against Clayton and Carruthers, the justice wrote, "is quite substantial, and we must permit the verdict and judgment to stand."[25]

Scipio Jones dashed off a quick note to Charles Hamilton Houston: "Just a line to say that the Clayton and Corruthers [sic] cases were affirmed by the Supreme Court this morning," he wrote. The NAACP received the message two days later, and it was quickly passed around the New York office. Executive secretary Walter White scrawled "OK" on it. Someone referred it to assistant secretary Roy Wilkins for a press release, but, for some reason, Wilkins wrote, "advise against story on this."[26]

Yet for the advocates in Arkansas, the fight was hardly over. On the day the decision came down, Hibbler met with the members of the Carruthers-Clayton defense committee. These distinguished individuals weighed whether to appeal the ruling to the U.S. Supreme Court. Ultimately, they decided to file a motion for rehearing before the state supreme court, in effect asking McHaney to take another look. Houston was bearish on their chances, but the indefatigable communist lawyer, Carol King, enthusiastically contributed research for the new brief. The day after receiving her language, Hibbler filed a new petition and brief with the Arkansas Supreme Court. Then, for weeks, he and Jones—and their clients—waited.[27]

Meanwhile, the press coverage of the case grew. The *Pittsburgh Courier* and *Afro-American* ran blistering articles condemning McHaney's decision. Newspapers from Baton Rouge to Birmingham to Beaumont, from Missouri to New York, covered the appellate loss. The *Daily Worker* connected the pair's defeat in court to a broader "wave of barbaric lynch frenzy" that was "sweeping the South."[28]

On January 20, 1936, a cold and clear Monday in Little Rock—the very same day that the king of England died, muttering "God damn you," an ocean away—Justice McHaney again rejected Clayton's and Carruthers's petition. Although the appellants made "a very strong argument that we erred in holding there was substantial evidence to support the verdict," he wrote, this "was a question of fact for the jury, and it is the settled rule of this court, announced in hundreds of decisions, that it is not our province to set aside the verdict of the jury supported by substantial evidence. We think the evidence is substantial, direct and positive, and was a question for the jury's determination and not ours." And, based upon this simple and rather circular assertion, he concluded, "The petition for rehearing is therefore denied."[29]

Nothing about Justice McHaney's opinion was terribly remarkable. Most decisions of the Arkansas Supreme Court in rape cases were fairly terse and dismissive; some justices evidently did not want to dwell on these cases. "Details are too revolting," wrote one justice a few years later."[30]

On appeal, virtually every rape defendant in Arkansas argued as Clayton and Carruthers did, that the verdict was contrary to the evidence. A number of other defendants made an argument that might seem odd by modern standards: they essentially argued that if they had wanted to rape the accuser, they could have, and the fact that they did not rape her indicated that they had no intent to rape her (a necessary element of assault with intent to rape).[31] Other appeals invoked the supposed immorality or promiscuity of the accuser.[32] "The whole testimony indicates that [she] is a girl of bad character and reputation, and no attempt is made to show otherwise," read one brief.[33]

Black defendants did make some distinctive arguments, even as they also made some familiar—even regressive—ones. Unlike most of their white counterparts, several Black defendants claimed that their trials represented a violation of their "constitutional rights."[34] Clayton and Carruthers, for example, argued that they "were denied the privileges and immunities guaranteed them under the Constitution of the United States, the rights of a trial by a jury of their peers in that no negroes were on the [jury and that] this was discrimination against them on account of their race and color and a violation of the Fourteenth Amendment to the Constitution of the United States and a denial of their rights under the 'due process clause' thereof."[35]

At the same time as they were making these arguments about race discrimination, however, some Black defendants also relied on the same tropes regarding morality and promiscuity that white defendants did. Clayton and Carruthers, for instance, invoked the English jurist Matthew Hale's infamous comment that rape "is an accusation easily to be made" and noted that Virgie "was living separate from her husband, and kept company with other men." They invoked another legal theorist who wrote that it was the "duty" of a "woman injured" to "obtain prompt medical advice; and the omission to do so, in cases of alleged rape, is a fact which subjects the prosecution to discredit." They cited court decisions holding that a woman who "made no violent outcry" and "no complaint of the injury for several days, are circumstances strongly in favor of the assumption of the prisoner's innocence." They argued all of this in the brief written by Carol King and Charles Hamilton Houston. Such arguments are consistent with what the historian Lisa Lindquist Dorr found in her study of Black-on-white rape cases in Virginia—namely, that although Black defendants could not often raise the accuser's alleged promiscuity or immorality at trial, they could—and often did—raise them after trial.[36]

Indeed, defendants were far from the only parties to invoke an accuser's supposed promiscuity. In covering Clayton's and Carruthers's case, the *Daily Worker* claimed that Virgie was "known to be of loose habits." Even the justices of the Arkansas Supreme Court issued decisions with moralistic language: "We think the evidence amply sufficient to support the verdict and judgment, and that her sad experience should serve as a warning to other 19 year old virtuous girls, as she was, not to take a chance at late hours of the night by riding alone with a young man who is a mere acquaintance."[37]

Scarcely had the Arkansas Supreme Court rejected Clayton's and Carruthers's petition for rehearing when their relentless lawyer, John A. Hibbler, began to figure out the next move. They could appeal to a federal district court with a petition for a writ of habeas corpus, he thought to himself, or they could seek to be heard in the U.S. Supreme Court. Either way, they would have to move quickly; surely the state was going to try to electrocute his clients as soon as possible.

But a problem remained, the same one that so vexed Edgar McHaney a generation earlier. "The main point now," Hibbler wrote to the NAACP, "is, Mr. Houston, money." Appealing to a federal district court would cost money; appealing to the Supreme Court would cost money. Because Hibbler was now partnering not just with Scipio Jones but also with Lewis Rhoton, an aged but esteemed white criminal attorney who had long been sympathetic to the cause of civil rights, he needed at least $250 to pay Rhoton's fee. The local NAACP branch and the churches were doing their best, but it wasn't enough.[38]

More than two weeks passed. Hibbler appeared in person before the state supreme court to ask for another thirty-day stay, so he could continue the appeals. The case raised important constitutional arguments in light of the Scottsboro precedent, he argued. The justices agreed. Next, Hibbler and Jones decided to take their case to the federal district court, not to the U.S. Supreme Court, apparently in large part because the federal judge who would hear the habeas corpus proceeding, John Martineau, had, a generation earlier, been the county chancellor who stayed the execution of the Elaine Twelve. (Martineau had also served as governor; recall that it was he who had appointed McHaney to the state's highest bench.) Houston, who had been traveling on Association business in the Midwest, finally replied on February 7, offering advice and praise but no money. Carol King, in contrast, sent Hibbler a check for fifty dollars, which, he wrote, "is an answer to my prayer." With that fifty dollars, Hibbler could hire a private detective to go into Mississippi County and "secure the proper affidavits from white and colored citizens to attach to my petition for writ of habeas corpus." Hibbler was working hard, striving to get his petitions, affidavits, and exhibits in order so that he could mail them off that week. The stay of execution was for only thirty days, after all.[39]

In spite of the time pressure and financial constraints, it appears that Hibbler managed to appeal his clients' case in time. And then, for most of 1936, nothing happened. Clayton and Carruthers remained at Tucker, their appeal pending in the federal district court in Little Rock. Hibbler, Jones, Houston, and all the rest worked on other matters. In Blytheville, one journalist noted, the case was still much discussed—and inevitably "referred to as 'those Negroes who shot the Sheriff.'"[40] At one point that spring, the state supreme court—fed up with the delay—issued an order directing the governor to execute the two men post haste. The officials at Tucker eagerly began readying the electric chair, but Judge Martineau issued an order halting the execution until he could hear their appeal. A hearing was scheduled, but then Rhoton, the elderly white defense attorney, died, further delaying the matter.[41] Journalists continued to be interested in what was now widely known as Arkansas's Scottsboro case; a leftist writer for the *St. Louis Post-Dispatch* traveled to Mississippi County to do an investigation and exposé.[42] The lawyers continued to need money. The national NAACP office continued to demur. At one point, Carol King got on the phone to harangue assistant secretary Roy Wilkins, exhorting him to wire Hibbler $150; Wilkins assured her that the case was a worthy one, but that the Association just didn't have the money.[43]

Toward the end of November, Judge Martineau finally scheduled a new date for the hearing. It would be at ten o'clock on Thursday, December 10.[44]

Thurgood Marshall needed money. All through the spring and summer of 1936, his financial straits had only gotten more serious: his office was bleeding cash, his father had lost his job, his mother wasn't working, his wife, Buster, was working only sporadically, creditors were calling, clients weren't paying, and the NAACP cases just kept coming. Marshall was, one biographer has commented, "flat broke." Writing to Houston, he inquired into the "possibility" of the NAACP "helping me out through here . . . if I could be assured of enough to tide me over, then in return, I could do more on these cases." There was, of course, no money to be had. Yet even as Marshall sweated over his failing legal practice, even as he was forced to take on a night job, keeping records for a Baltimore clinic that treated sexually transmitted infections, he still managed to impress. Late that summer, he gave a passionate speech to the NAACP's annual conference that prompted a flood of new members and donations.[45]

It was apparently this speech that enabled Houston, a month later, to convince Walter White that the NAACP's national office needed another lawyer, and that Marshall was their man. Houston insisted in a letter to Marshall that the younger man stop trying to do multiple jobs at once and focus instead, wholly and completely, on civil rights work. His appointment would be for six months, at $200 a month. Marshall accepted almost immediately. "I will be indebted to you and Charlie for a long time to come for many reasons," he wrote to White, "one of which is that I have an opportunity now to do what I have always dreamed of doing!" He and Buster temporarily moved in with his aunt and uncle in their Harlem apartment. His appointment was covered in the Black press.[46]

Marshall's work as a full-time NAACP attorney was much the same as it had been previously, and he continued using the courts to fight for equality within the Maryland school system. In mid-November, with delays still plaguing the Clayton-Carruthers appeal, Marshall appeared before the Maryland Court of Appeals to argue, on behalf of Donald Murray, against race discrimination in the state's flagship law school. For weeks thereafter, Marshall anxiously awaited a ruling, determined not to file "any new race-related lawsuit" until the decision was announced.[47] In the meantime, he assisted with other matters at the NAACP's Fifth Avenue office—such as responding to a request for financial assistance from Arkansas.

"We regret that the defense fund of the Association is exhausted, and that, as a matter of fact, there is a large deficit in this fund," Marshall wrote to the Little Rock NAACP branch president at the end of November. "For this reason, it is impossible for us to assist in many worthy cases all over the country that are constantly being brought to our attention."[48]

This letter appears to have been Thurgood Marshall's first involvement in the matter of Bubbles Clayton and Jim X. Carruthers. It would not be his last.

Meanwhile, labor unrest and brutal capitalist violence were still turning the cotton bolls red all across Arkansas. The STFU's success in the 1935 strike had generated an outpouring of national support, but the big planters soon struck back. Early in 1936, one landowner evicted nearly a hundred sharecroppers; the homeless farmers set up a tent colony, but the authorities targeted them for especial savagery, even throwing dynamite into their camp. Undeterred, the STFU called for another strike that spring, demanding an increase from the hard-won 75 cents per day to $1.25. "Long lines of men, women, and children marched ten feet apart down the roads along the cotton fields," recounted the historian Nan Woodruff. From a distance, they resembled a wave of thousands. Traveling bands of picketers stormed the countryside along the back-roads, "calling the stooped laborers to drop their hoes and join the strike." Many did. The strike in the spring of 1936 was, another historian has written, "the most audacious and all-inclusive strike ever called among farm laborers in the South, and one of the least well supported."

This time the planters were ready. Mobs, led by sheriff's deputies, unleashed an unparalleled reign of terror, beating and even murdering union members. "There's going to be another Elaine massacre," one deputy announced, breaking up a union meeting at a church, "only the next time we'll kill the whites as well as the [n-words]." The authorities arrested numerous sharecroppers and tenant farmers and sent them to what union leaders called "Concentration Camps," work colonies where they were forced to pick cotton at gunpoint. Militiamen "mounted machine guns at key crossroads," Woodruff wrote, "to protect the workers' 'right' to chop cotton." By the fall, the strike was over, killed as much by weeks without rain as by planter ferocity; deputies were indicted for "aiding and abetting in holding in slavery," but still, the violence and debt peonage continued. "The members had suffered tremendously during the strike," Woodruff concluded. "Several had lost their lives, and the group had little to show for the pain that many had endured."[49]

Some saw connections between the fight for the union and the fight for Arkansas's Scottsboro defendants. "Clayton and Caruthers are innocent," the *Daily Worker* proclaimed:

> There is not a scintilla of evidence against them. But they are sentenced to die because it is necessary to smash the Southern Tenant Farmers' Union. The union is becoming too strong. It is threatening to cut into the enormous profits of the planters; profits squeezed from the sharecropper, the most exploited worker in America. The sharecropper is organizing; in the face of terror and bullets he is organizing. Last Fall black and white cotton workers won a strike together, which doubled their wages.

So the word went out: destroy the union. Two '[n-words]' were chosen to serve as an example to the Negro who thinks he's as good as a white man. It doesn't matter that the colored boys, chosen by chance, were not members of the S.T.F.U. That's a minor point. Any two '[n-words]' will do, and so Clayton and Caruthers were arrested and charged with shooting Sheriff Wilson of Blytheville, a town of 4,000 in the heart of the Arkansas cotton country. Wilson is the labor hating official who helped drive Norman Thomas out of the state last Spring.

There was just "one last resort," the *Daily Worker* told its readers: a Hail Mary appeal in court.[50]

"May it please your Honor," John A. Hibbler began, "this is a petition on behalf of Jim X. Caruthers and Bubbles Clayton."[51]

The round-faced, middle-aged attorney stood before Judge John E. Martineau, five years Hibbler's senior and adorned with the flowing black robes that signified his elite position. Also with Hibbler that Thursday in December 1936, were Scipio Africanus Jones and Charles Hamilton Houston, having come all the way from New York. Opposing these three Black lawyers were a pair of white assistant Arkansas attorneys general. Behind the bar sat more than a dozen witnesses, a number of journalists, prosecutor Denver L. Dudley, sheriff's deputy Arch Lindsey, and, bound in handcuffs and chains, Clayton and Carruthers themselves. It was probably their first time outside of Tucker in many months.[52]

Perhaps some in the audience recalled that the pair's last appeal had been rejected on the day King Edward VII had died and noted that it was another significant day in English history: King Edward VIII declared that he was renouncing the throne, abdicating to marry Wallis Simpson, an American divorcee.

The lawyers for the defendants were feeling cautiously optimistic. They thought that recent U.S. Supreme Court case law was on their side, especially the Scottsboro decision that had been championed by the ILD. They believed that Judge Martineau, well-liked by civil rights advocates for his role in the Elaine travails, "has shown a fine attitude, and has all but said that he would like to grant our petition," a Little Rock NAACP official reflected. And they noted that Martineau had just found a Delta planter guilty of enslaving Black farmers—suspected union members who had been forced to labor on a plantation in the midst of the STFU's strike. Martineau was about the best judge they could hope for. In addition, the lawyers had been busy for weeks, securing affidavits from eight white and four Black Blythevillians, all attesting to the "mob spirit" in town and the habitual exclusion of Black people from criminal juries.[53]

But the lawyers from the attorney general's office had been investigating too. Ever since the summer, assistants had been traveling from Little Rock to Mississippi County to question "local negroes," hoping to find some to rebut the charges of mob atmosphere. By whatever means they used, they succeeded; the state showed up that day with more witnesses than the defense.[54]

After quickly dispatching with a procedural objection from the state, Judge Martineau turned his attention to Hibbler. For the next several minutes, the civil rights attorney spoke uninterrupted about how his clients had been "denied the right to a trial." The Blytheville courtroom had been dominated by bloodthirsty pressures, he argued, and "negroes have been systematically excluded from the jury for the last half of a century" despite a third of the county's population being Black. He reviewed the shooting of Sheriff Wilson, the mob violence that followed, the arrest and abuse of Clayton and Carruthers, Virgie's belated identification of them on death row, and finally their trial itself. "Negroes were afraid to come to the trial," he told the judge, and all manner of irregularities had occurred while Arthur Adams was speaking, including the sheriff bursting into the judge's chambers and telling him that he could not guarantee the defendants' safety if they were acquitted.

"Which goes to show, Judge, the condition of the minds of the people while this trial was going on," Hibbler continued. "And if it were not dominated by mob violence, then I fail to understand what that word means." His clients, he concluded, had been denied their constitutional rights, confirmed in the Scottsboro case.[55]

A lawyer for the state arose to make his opening argument. Hibbler, he told the court, was attempting to "re-try the case." When Judge Martineau told him, in effect, to get on with it, the assistant attorney general noted that Adams had not raised the exclusion of Black jurors while the trial was still ongoing, something that he said was necessary for Hibbler to be able to properly raise it now.

"You do not deny the truth of the allegation?" Martineau asked. "You claim that inasmuch as it was not raised at the trial it could not be raised in this proceeding?"

"That is it, your Honor, yes sir."[56]

Arthur Adams was sworn in as a witness, and Hibbler asked him why he had not made a "Scottsboro motion"—why he had not challenged the exclusion of Black people from the jury. Adams replied that, honestly, he felt it was a decent jury; he knew some of its members. He also felt "that a motion of that sort would be merely a technical matter which would rather prejudice the minds of the people rather than do me any good in that actual trial."

Unsatisfied with this equivocating answer, Hibbler pressed on. "Did you not further think Mr. Adams, that had you done so, that the boys might have been lynched?"

"Well now, I hardly would want to go that far," Adams replied, carefully, but he acknowledged that "it would at least arouse the prejudice in the minds of the people generally if I made that motion."

"And the result might have been that the mob would have taken charge of the boys?" Hibbler asked.

"Well, that would be possible."[57]

The questioning of Arthur Adams revealed the uncomfortable position he occupied in the Jim Crow hierarchy: ensconced within the white supremacist professional class but tentatively flirting with acknowledging the humanity of his Black neighbors. The difficulty of straddling these poles shaped his answers in ways that sometimes made him sound remarkably naïve.[58]

"I want to say this," he announced at one point. "I went into the defense of that suit, and I had two defenses, either one of which seemed to me then pretty convincing; one was, the alibi defense, and I really thought at the inception of that suit that would be established pretty conclusively; the other was, that I did not think the prosecuting witness would identify these boys as the boys."[59]

According to one journalist, Judge Martineau was listening "intently" throughout the entirety of the lawyer's testimony.[60]

After Adams stepped down, Bubbles Clayton moved to the front of the courtroom. He was sworn in as a witness. But then he was not permitted to say a word on his own behalf. Instead, Judge Martineau began asking the lawyers a series of procedural questions. After a few minutes of verbal sparring, the judge told Hibbler and Jones that he was going to halt the hearing. He instructed them to apply for permission from the state supreme court to seek a special writ from the trial court in Blytheville. Although it had long since disappeared in the English courts from which it arose, a writ of error coram nobis would give the court the chance to correct a significant error in its original judgment. Only after the state courts had considered this application, Judge Martineau told the lawyers, could he properly hear the case.[61]

That evening, the newspapers reported that Judge Martineau had "abruptly terminated" the hearing, that he had "refused to take action," that he had granted

Clayton and Carruthers "additional respite."[62] In an editorial entitled, "The Law's Delays," the *Blytheville Courier-News* condemned the judge's decision: "The wheels of justice grind slowly whenever the defendant in a criminal case has the means to invoke all possible legal resources for escaping or delaying punishment." The newspaper decried this "prolonged process" as "intolerable."[63]

Shortly after the hearing concluded, a small crowd of Black men walked over to John Hibbler's office in the Mosaic Temple Building in Little Rock. They included an undertaker, a school principal, and the bootblack for a white barbershop; all had been subpoenaed to testify that day, but none had gotten the chance. The three men told Hibbler that, before the hearing that day, they had spoken with the assistant attorney general, telling him not to call them to testify "because they could not do him any good."

Later that evening, Hibbler recounted this meeting to Jones and Houston during a meeting in Jones's fine home. The three lawyers discussed the future of the case. Inevitably, the talk turned to money. The fees for the witnesses (only one of whom had testified) came to seventy-five dollars, but Hibbler told Houston he only had twenty-five dollars on hand. Speaking on behalf of the NAACP, Houston told him, "This is not our responsibility." In fact, Houston told Hibbler that the NAACP would not remain involved in the case unless the Little Rock attorneys more responsibly managed the money that was being raised on Clayton's and Carruthers's behalf. Hibbler promised to handle this immediately.[64]

The next day, Houston drove out of Arkansas, heading north toward St. Louis. On his way, he passed through Blytheville and paused to speak to a pair of Black doctors. "I told Drs. Roberts and Keith that Mr. Hibbler had stated that the Negro witnesses had come to his office after court adjourned and assured him that they were not going to testify against Clayton and Caruthers," Houston wrote in a memorandum for the NAACP, "but the doctors were sceptical. I tried to impress on the doctors the necessity of arousing public opinion in behalf of the case and conducting a campaign for a defense fund."[65]

In other words, there was still hope, still a chance to achieve justice, if only they would fight for it.

Houston drove on.

27 • Seeking Mercy, Seeking Clemency, 1929–1936

One Monday not long after Bethel and Wallace were sentenced to prison, Alexander and their other attorneys appealed their convictions. This was (and remains) the standard next step after a rape conviction and the denial of a motion for a new trial. The lawyers' nine-page brief on behalf of Bethel and Wallace covered all the usual ground for such appeals—that the verdict was contrary to the evidence, that it was contrary to the law, that there were all manner of procedural errors.[1] Such arguments almost never persuaded the Arkansas Supreme Court to reverse.[2]

Yet the lawyers also raised the argument that was among the most likely to prevail on appeal: that the prosecutor had made prejudicial remarks.[3] "When the Prosecuting Attorney, Judge S.L. Gladish, the brilliant, and influential man that he was and is in Mississippi County and the State of Arkansas, for that matter, told the jury that the defendants had barely escaped mob execution," they wrote, this denied their clients a "fair and impartial trial." It was their contention that Gladish—this brilliant and influential man—"should have been severely rebuked and told in the presence of the jury that he had no right to make such an argument, instead of the court merely saying that the argument was improper." Further, Virgil Greene, one of Gladish's deputy prosecutors, had made a prejudicial opening statement—recall that he called the defendants "foul fellows"—and, according to the defendants' lawyers, "every word of [this statement] was a flame of fire burning under a pot of oil, making ready for the boiling of the defendants." They argued that "it should have been stopped by the learned trial judge, by a reprimand if possible and with a jail sentence if necessary." They continued in this vein at length.[4]

Throughout the summer and fall of 1929—even as Bethel and Wallace remained at home, even as Bethel's brother committed his own sexual assault—the justices of the Arkansas Supreme Court considered these arguments.[5] Among the solons was one of the court's newest members, Edgar L. McHaney. Years before he contemplated Clayton's and Carruthers's appeal, and years after his role in the appeal of the Elaine Twelve, McHaney pondered this petition from Mississippi County. This was undoubtedly a hopeful fact for Bethel and Wallace, for it was he who had written the opinion overturning their first conviction more than a year previously. Perhaps their lawyer had informed them of another incident from McHaney's past—when, as a young lawyer, he had appealed the case of a southwestern Arkansas man convicted of carnal abuse. The underage girl with whom McHaney's client had commenced a sexual relationship had become pregnant, and at the client's trial another of his lawyers had sought to interrogate the accuser about her sexual "conduct" and other men she had allegedly slept with. The trial judge had refused, and McHaney argued on appeal that this was a reversible error. The Arkansas Supreme Court agreed.[6]

Yet on November 4, 1929, the Arkansas Supreme Court rejected Bethel's and Wallace's appeal. In an opinion written by McHaney the court noted, "It is well settled that trial courts have a wide discretion in the supervision of trials before them, including matters pertaining to opening statements, and this court will not reverse unless a manifest abuse of discretion is shown." McHaney concluded Bethel and Wallace's appeal had "no merit."[7]

That morning, a banner headline appeared on the front page of the *Blytheville Courier-News:* "Bethel and Wallace Must Serve Terms."[8]

Two weeks later, their appeals exhausted, Bethel and Wallace had no choice but to report to The Walls.

For the next several years, the two men spent their days and nights incarcerated in the towering penitentiary in Little Rock, far from their homes and friends and wives. The details of their incarceration do not survive, this absence a result of policies both deliberate and negligent that have erased nearly all the quotidian specifics of caging in American history. Surprisingly, though, one obscure record does provide a glimpse, a single quick look, at Wallace's time in prison. It is highly revealing.

A couple years after Bethel and Wallace disappeared into the penitentiary, a moonshiner named Elmer Mikel, the son of a socialist union miner, arrived at The Walls. He had been arrested for bootlegging and sentenced to five years behind bars, but he was pleased to be sent to The Walls; he later admitted that he knew it was the prison for favored inmates. Instead of the punishing labor endured by inmates at Tucker or Cummins, Mikel spent most of the nine months prior to his parole repairing the fine Little Rock homes of the state's politicians. He and his fellow inmates remodeled the warden's house; they fixed the long bridge leading to a night club owned by the warden's son-in-law; they constructed a new home by a lake for the governor's secretary.

It was while Mikel was helping to clear out the farm of a politically connected doctor that he came across a trusty named Mike Wallace. By this time, the penitentiary had abandoned the striped uniforms, so most prisoners wore overalls and jumpers; but Wallace, as a trusty, wore khaki clothes. Wallace "handed me a double-barreled shotgun and announced that I was now one of the Shotgun Guards," Mikel recalled. "He told me that I was supposed to shoot anyone who started to run or stepped out of line." Wallace was a "Long Line Rider," a full trusty, the boss of the Shotgun Guards and a whole line of convicts. "His word is the law."[9]

Clearly, Wallace was a privileged prisoner, probably both of them were, within the rarified walls of The Walls. Why was he so privileged? Neither he nor Bethel were rich or powerful or particularly well-connected. It could have been luck or the intervention of their influential lawyer, E. E. Alexander. It could even indicate other powerful allies—a possibility made all the more intriguing by the next part of Bethel's and Wallace's stories.

Their trials were over, their appeals done. Their only chance to leave The Walls while they were still young men was to seek mercy from the governor.

Though the odds were long, executive clemency was far from a far-fetched proposition in Jim Crow Arkansas. In part this was because overcrowding had long been a huge problem at the state's prisons. In 1934, for instance, there were approximately 1,700 men behind bars at Tucker. "We are out of clothing and shoes and nothing to buy them with," wrote the superintendent, suggesting that the Parole Board release every eligible inmate with a "clear record" in order to make more room in the prison. This group included some 250 men.[10] By 1935, the superintendent reported that he had "the largest number of men ever confined in the Arkansas Penitentiary," a total of 1,914, perhaps 350 or 400 more than it could comfortably hold. The superintendent also noted in 1935 that about 80 men had received furloughs over the past Christmas, and 352 men had been paroled over the last nine months.[11] Surviving archival records make clear that men convicted of sexual assaults were routinely granted furloughs of multiple months.[12]

Early in the twentieth century, obtaining clemency was an orderly affair. George Washington Donaghey—Arkansas's progressive governor from 1909 to 1913—liked to set aside a certain day each month, "say the 20th of each month," as "pardon day." Anyone who came in seeking clemency on any other day could file their papers with the governor's secretary. When pardon day arrived, the governor would go to the reception room in the north side of the capitol building and personally converse with each applicant.[13] Clemency was widely available; Donaghey's successor, George Washington Hays, pardoned nearly four hundred individuals over his four years in office.[14]

By the 1920s, however, clemency had become a hot-button political issue in Arkansas. In 1925, when the determined Klansman Tom Terral became governor, he proudly refused to grant any pardons or commutations at all, even for men facing the electric chair.[15] In spite of Terral's avowed opposition to the pardon power, his use of furloughs soon came under fire, and in 1926 John Martineau—another a candidate in the governor's race (and later the federal judge assigned to Clayton's and Carruthers's case)—employed Willie Horton-style newspaper advertisements trying to yoke Terral to supposedly dangerous criminals granted furloughs, including one convicted of assault with intent to rape.[16] Pardons and furloughs remained contentious in the years that followed, and by the mid-1930s, Governor J. M. Futrell agonized over whether allowing early release might represent a political liability. "We must avoid those cases that are liable to cause a vicious back fire," Futrell wrote to the former warden of The Walls in 1934. "Where feeling is strong against a convict who has been guilty of an atrocious murder, I know that he should not go back in that community."[17] He was "getting wet feet on these pardons," he wrote to another acquaintance earlier that year. "I may be called unsympathetic, but this pardon business is loaded with dynamite."[18]

Nonetheless, when Frank Bethel and Mike Wallace applied for a pardon, Governor Futrell was apparently in a generous mood.

Bethel's and Wallace's path to a pardon began in the summer of 1930, not even eighteen months after being convicted of assault. On August 23, the *Blytheville Courier-News* informed readers that the "two Mississippi County youths, once under sentence of death and now serving 18 years each on statutory charges were granted 90-day furloughs yesterday by Governor Parnell, Futrell's predecessor."[19] While these furloughs were not unusually long, they were longer than many. Tucker's superintendent at the time considered short furloughs—"from 5 to 10 days"—to be optimal for "our best convicts," since "that gives them ample time to visit with their relatives and not time enough to hunt up their old associates."[20] The *Courier-News* briefly recounted the facts of their case and reported that their "petitions for clemency contained recommendations from the sheriff of Mississippi county, and other citizens, it is stated." The sheriff, the article concluded, was "out of the city today and could not be reached," and his office refused to confirm his support for the two convicted rapists.[21]

How had Bethel and Wallace gotten out so quickly? Apparently, their defense attorney—E. E. Alexander—had championed their cause. By this time, to obtain a temporary furlough, an indefinite furlough, or a pardon, prisoners had to make a formal application to the governor; to obtain parole, they had to make a formal application to the five-man Penitentiary Board, though the governor had considerable influence over the board's decisions.[22] Before granting furlough or clemency, governors typically required written endorsements from the prosecutor who tried the case and the judge who heard it.[23] Those wishing to apply for parole had to wait until after they had served a third of their sentence.[24] It also took some money to apply for relief—the Penitentiary Board required those seeking parole to post a $100 bond to indemnify the state against loss, which, E. E. Alexander later wrote, is "a severe hardship on many a poor boy."[25] Some evidence suggests Black people were sometimes charged a higher bond.[26]

It wasn't uncommon for prisoners seeking clemency to receive recommendations from the judge, the prosecutor, the sheriff, the warden, and a small army of "responsible citizens."[27] One murderer was granted an indefinite furlough after "three or four hundred responsible citizens" signed a petition on his behalf.[28] In nearby Alabama, two white men who had raped a Black girl were supposed to serve ten years in prison, but they simply did not. Local NAACP officials could not figure out how they got out, but they wrote, "One evil part of it is the prosecutor and defence attorney are in the same family."[29] In Arkansas, individuals also wrote to the governor or the Penitentiary Board themselves to plead their case. "i am treat mity bad hear . . . cain I work for some wone else[?] I am having a hard time hear I am mistreated I dont wont [to] st[a]y hear," wrote one man in 1929.[30] Another wrote pleading that he had sick relatives who needed his help.[31]

Community support was certainly not unprecedented for convicted white rapists. Just weeks after Leon Fanning and Paul Clark, two white men, were sentenced to three years for assault with intent to rape, the judge attached to their case, as well as the sheriff, country treasurer, state representative, and dozens of other prominent people (men as well as women) had written to the governor recommending clemency for the men. "It is our opinion that if these boys did need correction that conviction alone would have more affect to correct them, than serving a sentence in the Arkansas penitentiary, whatever wrong has been done if any, has been forceably called to their attention, and in our opinion from their past reputation, it would service a better purpose [to suspend their sentences] than to incarcerate them in the penitentiary," read the petition. Within a matter of months, Fanning and Clark had secured a full pardon.[32]

Prosecutors, sheriffs, and prominent citizens often invoked a prisoner's sterling reputation or particular need. The sheriff of Mississippi County, for instance, once wrote to the governor asking that a man recently convicted of perjury be allowed to go home. "I don't feel that he should be made to suffer for I really dont think he was guilty," he wrote. "He has always born a good reputation. He is a hard worker, sober and faithful to his employer. . . . It will soon be time to start another crop and we need many more just such farmers as he is in this county."[33] Meanwhile, one woman wrote to the governor asking for clemency for her son, who was "on the county farm for hiten his wife but I know as every one Down here you wood say she ant no wife at all."[34] Similarly, the lieutenant governor would later write to the governor to make the argument for relief for "a colored boy . . . convicted in 1933 of a rape on a little girl"—"it looks to me," he continued, "that it might have been the other way around."[35] In fact, it was not uncommon for men convicted of rape to invoke the supposedly low reputations of their accusers while seeking executive clemency.[36]

Bethel's and Wallace's petitions appear to no longer be in Governor Parnell's papers. One wonders what their lawyer and the sheriff may have written on their behalf—about them, or about Pearl.

For ninety days, Bethel and Wallace were allowed to return to Manila, to revisit old haunts and see old friends and foes. But in late November 1930, in spite of Alexander's best efforts to obtain "indefinite furloughs" for them, they had to return to Tucker. Governor Parnell had declined to extend their furloughs.[37]

Alexander kept pushing for their release, and in March 1931, the two were granted six-month furloughs. "Dispatches from Little Rock yesterday said that the governor's proclamation, placed on public file 12 days after the men were released, said that nine members of the trial jury, the prosecuting attorney, sheriff and responsible citizens had recommended that clemency be granted," reported the *Arkansas Gazette*. No doubt this proved to be controversial back home, as Sheriff W. W. Shaver and prosecutor S. L. Gladish hastily issued statements denying that they had recommended clemency.[38] Yet they may well have been lying. Perhaps it is telling that after their six-month furloughs expired, Bethel and Wallace were granted indefinite furloughs.[39]

In 1932, J. M. Futrell was elected governor, which—given Futrell's tough stance on clemency—might have doomed Bethel's and Wallace's quest for full pardons and the restoration of their good names. Futrell quickly intimated to the press "that few pardons will be granted during his administration, and few other acts of clemency such as furloughs, have been recorded so far."[40] A year into his administration, he admitted that he had made a mistake in granting five furloughs, including one to a man who had reportedly murdered a municipal official in the town of Marshall while out on furlough, which was widely reported and surely further soured Futrell on clemency.[41]

Nonetheless, Futrell wasn't quite as rigid as he seemed. "Contrary to a statement made by Gov. J. M. Futrell several days ago that no clemency would be granted convicts for the Christmas holidays, it was learned today that 20 were granted furloughs of four days each," reported the *Blytheville Courier-News* on its front page on December 27, 1933. "In the group were seven convicted of murder, three of whom were under life sentences." Three of the men were from Mississippi County.[42]

Perhaps Bethel and Wallace read this and were emboldened.

On September 18, 1934, Governor Futrell granted Mike Wallace a "complete pardon and restoration of citizenship," ending what the *Blytheville Courier-News* called "one of the hardest fought legal battles here in a number of years."

"The proclamation of the governor recited that the pardon was granted on recommendation of Trial Judge G. E. Keck, of Blytheville, and Prosecuting Attorney Denver L. Dudley of Jonesboro," the paper reported.[43] The prosecutor and the judge had recommended *pardons*.

The moment a prisoner receives a pardon is inescapably a memorable one. For Arkansas prisoners, it could also be a violent one. One formerly incarcerated Arkansan wrote in 1912 about watching another inmate receiving a pardon: before the warden would let him leave, the man was told he had to remove his pants, lay down, and submit to a brutal beating.[44] Wallace, though, was already outside the prison walls and thus beyond the reach of any punitive prison authorities.

Frank Bethel received his pardon on August 15, 1936.[45]

Three hours away, Bubbles Clayton and Jim X. Carruthers remained, behind bars in Tucker, condemned to die.

28 • The Appeal, 1937–1939

As 1935 passed into 1936, and then 1937, as months in a prison became years of a life, as white rapists were routinely released on furlough or even pardoned, Clayton and Carruthers remained on death row at Tucker. Their time there mostly eludes present efforts at reconstruction, the historical record stymied by an insistent and officially enforced silence. Yet, like Bethel and Wallace, they can be glimpsed, momentarily, by chance. It is a revealing sight.

Early one Friday, a thirty-five-year-old white man named Frank Dobbs—repeatedly called "a shiftless ne'er do-well" in the pages of the *Arkansas Gazette*—was led to the electric chair, his execution the government's vengeance for a brutal stabbing, murder, and arson. Photographed wearing the torn overalls of a laborer or farmer, Dobbs had a heavy brow and powerful build. As he sat strapped in Old Sparky, his demise imminent, probably the last sounds he heard were the faint notes of "When the Saints Go Marching On." According to the *Gazette*, Dobbs had requested that "four Negro prisoners in 'death row' " sing the hymn as he died. To the end, he showed no fear. Just before he was taken away, Dobbs realized that his laundry would be returned after his death, so, noted the *Gazette*, "He bequeathed his handkerchiefs to Bubbles Clayton, a Negro awaiting execution for criminal assault in Mississippi county."[1]

It is impossible to know how Clayton and Carruthers spent their days on death row, how they stayed sane amidst the darkness and the despair. But this episode gestures to the solidarity they apparently fostered with other condemned men, white and Black. With no other choices and little hope, they allied with the men around them—even attempting to ease the passage of their doomed comrades with the singing of a hymn.

In the aftermath of Judge Martineau's ruling, the attorneys for the defendants scrambled to figure out just how a writ of error coram nobis worked. Houston dove into the research on this ancient, obscure writ, but he was "not so well" that winter, and it took him several weeks to send John Hibbler and Scipio Jones a draft petition.[2] Meanwhile, in the first days of 1937, the Mississippi River flooded. Thousands were forced to flee their homes, and Arkansas's governor ordered 955 inmates from Tucker and Cummins to attempt to repair the levees. Hundreds of men, most of them Black, were loaded into box cars, sent to Memphis, and then placed on barges and floated down the perilous Mississippi, past debris and ravaged houseboats, to the Mellwood levee. It is possible, though unlikely, that death row inmates were among them.[3]

On Monday, January 18, 1937, the Arkansas Supreme Court denied the defendants permission to seek a writ of error coram nobis in the Mississippi Circuit Court. Hibbler, then suffering from the flu, was not surprised by the ruling, and he and Jones quickly filed papers to return the case to federal court.[4]

Once again, the gears of the federal judiciary turned with maddening slowness. Deferrals, delays, postponements piled up. Almost nine months passed before Houston checked in to inquire: "What is the status of the Clayton and Carruthers cases?" he wrote. Hibbler replied that there was to be a hearing in a few weeks, but then it too was pushed back. "Another Delay in Condemned Negroes' Case," read the frustrated headline in the *Arkansas Gazette*.[5]

Back home in Mississippi County, those with money continued to try to crush the farmers' union with every means at their disposal. When organizers called for another strike, Nan Woodruff has written, "the planters launched a counteroffensive designed to destroy the STFU once and for all." Mississippi County, where organizing was especially hot, bore the brunt of this violence. One night, forty planters and riding bosses, led by the manager of Robert E. Lee Wilson's plantation, broke up a union meeting with force, destroying the furniture and scattering the farmers. The Blytheville Chamber of Commerce offered a fifty-dollar reward for the arrest of any "labor agitator," and local judges sentenced scores of these agitators to convict labor farms. When union lawyers tried to secure their freedom, judges refused to accept bond and planters even assaulted the lawyers; when union lawyers then invoked the collusion between planters and judges, federal prosecutors refused to press charges. "Apparently pursuing such cases under the Fourteenth Amendment due process clause was out of the question in the American Congo," commented Woodruff. A subsequent strike attempt led planters to drive wages *down* from seventy-five to sixty cents in retaliation, and Mississippi County authorities sentenced a Black union official and two elderly members of her family to multiple years in prison just for distributing leaflets. Other union members fled the county, fearing for their lives. "This violence continued until the union was finally forced to stop organizing in 1938," recounted the historian James D. Ross. "By then the union was a shell of itself, having been defeated by violence, coercion, and intimidation. Faced with violent suppression, men and women packed up their meager belongings and left the cotton lands."[6]

Up in New York, Thurgood Marshall had hit the ground running, launching himself headfirst into the NAACP's legal work. In the first year after Marshall joined the Association full time, the NAACP was again engaged in an all-out fight for a federal anti-lynching bill, with Houston and White testifying before the Senate, invoking the statistic that only a sixth of lynchings had even allegedly been justified by rape. For a time, this effort distracted from the NAACP's legal work: "We are all up in the air at the present time on the Anti-lynching Bill," Marshall wrote to an acquaintance in 1937, "and I doubt whether [Houston] will be able to take care of the matters you mention until he returns to the office." But, as before, the Association, faced with staunch southern opposition, could not push the bill over the finish line.[7] Marshall busied himself by consulting on the many inquiries that streamed into NAACP headquarters from Black men accused of all manner of crimes, including some accused of rape. Sometimes Marshall or another lawyer in the national office provided legal assistance or helped in fundraising for these cases, but other times Marshall and Houston felt they could do more good by devoting their energies to lobbying for executive clemency.[8]

Finally, shortly after 1937 passed into 1938, a new federal hearing for the Clayton and Carruthers case was scheduled—for early March. Up until just days before it was to be held, Hibbler and Jones expected Houston to join them in Little Rock, as he had at the last federal hearing more than a year earlier. But Houston eventually informed the Arkansans that his presence would be "absolutely impossible." He was just too busy scaling the NAACP's other mountains of work. He also may have been distracted by drama at home; his first marriage had just dissolved, and, only a few months after obtaining a Nevada divorce, he had remarried. Nonetheless, Houston wrote to Hibbler, "You have my heart-felt sympathy and interest. We hope that you will be able to get a writ and save the boys."[9]

It was a cool, cloudy morning in Little Rock, on Wednesday, March 9, 1938, as a small crowd of lawyers and witnesses traipsed into the federal district courthouse.[10] This moment had been a subject of speculation for quite some time. The repeated delays had been grating to many Mississippi Countians, and a U.S. marshal, carrying a stack of subpoenas, had been seen throughout Blytheville over the last several days, summoning townsfolk to appear for the hearing in the state capital. The witnesses' names had been printed on the front page of the *Blytheville Courier-News*, and they had duly shown up to court the day before, only to be told there was one final delay, and they should return on Wednesday. Thus, it was likely with some mix of indignation, trepidation, and fascination that the witnesses arrived at the inquiry that would determine whether Clayton and Carruthers would live or die.[11]

Once again, Hibbler and Jones were there to represent the two defendants; this time they were joined not by Charles Hamilton Houston but by Joseph R. Booker, another member of the small but mighty Black Arkansas bar. Booker had a résumé at least as sparkling as those of Hibbler or Jones; he had been born in 1893, in Helena—the site that would become infamous for the Elaine massacre a quarter century later. After gaining degrees from Arkansas Baptist College (where his father served as president) and, remarkably, Northwestern University Law School, Booker joined the U.S. Army for the final days of World War I. He had barely returned to civilian life when he was drafted into the defense of the Elaine Twelve. Over the decade and a half that followed, he joined the NAACP, founded one of the state's most powerful Black law firms, and frequently worked with Jones and Hibbler to challenge segregation and discrimination across Arkansas.[12]

At this hearing, however, the three Black lawyers were appearing not before their erstwhile ally Judge Martineau but before Thomas C. Trimble III, a well-connected small-town lawyer who had practiced at his family firm in Lonoke until Martineau's death the year before.[13]

For the next several hours, more than a dozen witnesses testified to the atmosphere at Clayton's and Carruthers's trial, nearly three years past. First, for the defendants, came a pair of longtime Blytheville residents and an African Methodist Episcopal minister from Arkadelphia. All attested to the "mob spirit" that prevailed at the trial, as well as to the total exclusion of Black people from Mississippi County juries. On cross-examination, the state's lawyers got them to admit that they could recall no specific threats of hanging and that they weren't sure whether Clayton and Carruthers had paid their taxes (which would have gotten them on the voter rolls, and thus the jury lists), but the state scored no killing blows. The *Courier-News*, however, noted that one of the witnesses was "active in labor union activities," which certainly could have colored the perceptions of him.[14]

The state countered with a dozen witnesses, all of whom claimed that the trial seemed to have been "fair and impartial," "orderly conducted," or "quiet." One resident testified, "Not a thing in the world caused my fears to be aroused in regard to the safety of the prisoners." The state found an elderly Black man to testify that the trial was free of threats, as well as a reporter for the *Courier-News*, who testified that he didn't print anything that would have influenced anyone's mind. Two jurors from the trial testified to their total impartiality and the absence of drama. Deputy sheriff Arch Lindsey and Sheriff Clarence Wilson both testified, the latter denying having made "the statement that unless they reached a verdict that night I couldn't get the defendants back across the line." Hibbler felt that the defense attorneys did well in forcing the state's witnesses to admit to "an atmosphere of mob domination during the trial" on cross-examination. And, as he later wrote to Houston, "all made splendid witnesses for the Petitioners on the points that no Negroes had been on the juries in 40 years."[15]

Perhaps the state's most important witness was Neil Killough, the judge from the original trial. He began by genially acknowledging that his memory had faded a bit over the past three years. But he "took particular pains to have everything a matter of record that was said in regard to the jury," he insisted. "Naturally, my desire was to give them a fair trial," Killough continued. Hence his appointment of Adams, one of the most respected attorneys in the region. As to the moments of controversy, Judge Killough emphasized that they were not big deals, or that he hardly even remembered them. Hibbler had no questions for the former judge, who, to his mind, had already been a fairly good witness for their side, having confirmed "two of the strongest points that we contended for": that one of the jurors was reading a newspaper during a trial and that another left the jury box to speak to the sheriff.[16]

After Judge Killough, the state rested its case. Judge Trimble adjourned the court for lunch. At two o'clock, as the witnesses and spectators returned to their seats, sated, there was likely some commotion when Clayton and Carruthers arrived. Finally, they would be allowed to testify in federal court.[17]

Clayton took the stand first. It was, quite possibly, only his second time outside of Tucker since his conviction (the first being the last, aborted federal hearing). This day, he did not speak long. But he testified powerfully to the abuse from Arch Lindsey and several other deputies, whom he identified by name. "They were all whipping me," he told the audience. When Hibbler asked him to elaborate on the violence, Clayton replied, "I have scars all over my body. There is one right there and one right there"—he gestured at his wrists—"that is where the handcuffs—that is where they put handcuffs on me and there is a scar right there and right there on the wrist."

Perhaps tellingly, the assistant state attorney general began his cross-examination by asking about the shooting of Sheriff Wilson, not the rape of Virgie. "Yes, sir, they wanted me to confess to shooting Mr. Wilson," Clayton replied, "that is what they first started whipping me about, and then after that—after they got to whipping me they got to wanting me to confess to a whole lot of stuff. They did whip me unmercifully. In spite of that I have never confessed." The lawyer for the state finished up quickly.[18]

Carruthers took the stand next. He too testified to the extreme abuse, to Arch Lindsey wielding a rubber hose and beating him with it until blood ran down his back. "Yes sir, I have plenty of scars," he said, "on my leg I have a knot; on my leg that was four inches long, scars on my head and my teeth out where he kicked me in the mouth; while I was there they kicked these teeth out." Once again, the state had few follow-ups.[19]

After Carruthers stepped down, both sides rested, and Judge Trimble addressed the lawyers. According to the *Courier-News*, he declared "that the negroes' cases had already been involved in litigation too long [and] indicated that his decision would be announced within a few days." He told Hibbler, Jones, and Booker that they had just five days to file briefs for his consideration. They did so immediately. And then they settled in, once more, to wait.[20]

Barely a week after the hearing, as Clayton and Carruthers were waiting for Judge Trimble's ruling, a reporter for the *Courier-News* visited them in their cell. It was the execution day for two other residents of Tucker's death row, and the reporter apparently wanted to see how their neighbors, Clayton and Carruthers, were coping with the latest execution.

"Three years of life in the shadow of the electric chair, during which they have watched several others enter the death chamber through the 'little green door' have failed to make the routine more acceptable to Jim X. Carruthers and Bubbles Clayton," the unnamed reporter wrote for a story on the paper's front page.

> Clayton and Carruthers and two other young negroes paced their adjoining cells ceaselessly back and forth across the center of their ample quarters as Lester Brockelhurst, "crime tourist," walked through the little door at dawn yesterday morning, never to return. Back and forth they stepped, their tread as rhythmic and effortless as the endless weaving and turning of cages of lions or tigers.[21]

The reporter's language—referring to their quarters as "ample," comparing the men to wild beasts—was patently offensive. It also reflected a perverse interest the residents of Mississippi County clearly still retained for the two men, who hadn't set foot in the county in years.

> The pacing negroes stopped short and stared at the little door as the voice of Bruckelhurst rose faintly in the death chamber. They could not distinguish the words, only the condemned man's overtones as he made his final statement to witnesses and guards.
>
> Then the negroes' eyes turned toward Newt Sims with a long, mournful regard as the Traskwood, Ark, wife slayer made ready to follow Brockelhurst through the little door. Sims walked erect and called an unemotional goodbye to the negroes as he went down the barred corridor and stepped effortlessly through the death chamber door.

The reporter's melodramatic tone aside, the anguish Clayton and Carruthers were experiencing clearly shines through. The terror must have been unthinkable. But, of course, this was precisely the point of these rituals—the last meal, the last words, the slow walk.

> The cell block was still. The negroes watched the rough blank door in thunderous silence. They said nothing. Then they resumed their steady, rhythmic pacing.
>
> Then a large black ambulance drew up behind the death house. And the negroes were left to wonder who of their group would be the next to walk through the little door.[22]

Yet Clayton and Carruthers also had one reason to hope—their pending appeal.

Not even two weeks later, Judge Trimble rejected their petition. He would not grant them a writ of habeas corpus. "Evidence fails to show petitioners were prejudiced because there were no Negroes on the jury," the judge wrote, absurdly, noting Arthur Adams's failure to raise the Scottsboro motion and adding that Adams "did not refrain because of fear of mob violence either for himself or defendants." Hibbler immediately announced his intention to appeal the case all the way up to the U.S. Supreme Court.[23]

Black newspapers across the country sounded the alarm, alerting readers to the judge's ruling and to the imminent appeal. "Almost Same as Scottsboro," blared the headline in New York's *Amsterdam News*. In Arkansas, the headlines were more subdued.[24]

The next step for Hibbler, Jones, and Booker was to file an appeal with the U.S. Court of Appeals for the Eighth Circuit, the federal appellate court covering Arkansas and much of the Midwest. (The only court higher was the Supreme Court.) Judge Trimble gave the lawyers ninety days to perfect their appeal, but it took them just a few to do so. Then they and their clients settled in, once more, for the long haul.[25]

In the months that followed, the lawyers continued to fight about—what else?—money. The amount the Arkansas lawyers were out of pocket, they wrote to Thurgood Marshall, attaching an itemized list of expenses, was an "embarrassment." When the national official turned them down, the correspondence became more heated, letters beginning to strain the bounds of cordiality. With the appeal pending, local NAACP officials exhorted national officials to contribute $500 for a fight that could reach the Supreme Court, arguing (perhaps threatening), "It would be the worst kind of advertisement if it were noised about that the great NAACP had abandoned a case on account of lack of funds." National officials shot back, "We appreciate the spirit of the Branch in not giving up, but there is no use spending $500.00 for further court proceedings unless there is an intelligent fighting chance of obtaining a reversal. There are so many problems, so many pressing and overwhelming problems for the Negroes in the United States, that we cannot afford to use up money simply to convince the authorities that we have courage. We can prove courage in other ways." ("We do not think in the light of the Scottsboro case . . . that we are on such thin ice," Hibbler wrote to Marshall later that day. Houston wrote back that he still had his doubts.) In desperation, Hibbler, Jones, and Booker wrote to the manager of the Black boxing champion Joe Louis, asking for his assistance with fundraising. The manager regretfully declined.[26]

Such fights over money were a hallmark of the NAACP's multitudinous rape cases from this era. Local branches almost always requested additional funds to finance a defense or appeal; the national office almost always pleaded poverty in response. "Our defense fund is exhausted and this office is unable to make any contributions to criminal cases at this time," Marshall wrote to one West Virginia lawyer. "We have had so many cases in the past year in the Supreme Court and other courts that our defense fund is exhausted," he wrote a few months later. "The only way we have been able to handle criminal cases for the last three months has been by raising money in the local communities where the cases have been tried." Marshall, Houston, or another national office attorney often found himself begging local officials to try to fundraise on their own, but local branches routinely pleaded peril. "It would be suicidal to undertake to raise money here," wrote one official from Mississippi. "It would get out and a race issue would then be created." Such money troubles could endanger the Association's cases. In one case, a local lawyer hired by the national office refused to file an appeal until he received a check for fifty dollars.[27]

During the spring and summer of 1938, Houston began stepping back from his position as head of the NAACP's legal work. He wished to remain involved in Association activities but also to return to Washington, D.C., to help run his father's law firm. Plus, he wanted more independence; he wrote to his father that he had always felt he was "much more of an outside man than an inside man." This left his protégé—barely thirty years old and slightly unsure of himself—to take over as the NAACP's chief lawyer.[28]

It was thus during this time that Thurgood Marshall started to get more involved in the Clayton-Carruthers case. It was to him that the Arkansas attorneys began addressing their strategizing missives and plaintive appeals for money. "I am sorry to have to write you again in reference to the financial strait in which I find myself," Hibbler wrote to Marshall, late summer of 1938. "I have done everything possible to raise this money, but the local committees have completely fallen down, and the meetings that I might go to for aid, such as church organizations, will not meet in Arkansas until October and November, hence that will be too late." Hibbler had enough money to pay for the briefs, he wrote to Marshall, but not the $190 it would take to print the record and send it to the Eighth Circuit in Omaha. "Please do what you can, Mr. Marshall, at once for I think we have waged too great a battle and have stayed the electrocution too long to fall down on our appeal to the Circuit Court of appeal which seems to be what will happen if we cannot get this financial aid at once."[29] If Marshall replied, his letter does not survive in the archive.

The Arkansas attorneys found money from other sources. The General Conference of the Colored Methodist Episcopal Church contributed $164, and the Clayton-Carruthers Defense Committee remained active in Mississippi County. At the same time, the students and staff at the small, radical Commonwealth College, in Mena, Arkansas—which was closely allied with the STFU—began loudly fundraising for Clayton and Carruthers. That spring, students at the college released a one-act play—entitled *We Are Not Alone*—which was a dramatization of "the Blytheville case." It depicted the two defendants on Tucker's death row, assailed by a bigoted jailer, insisting on their innocence even in the face of a threatened lynching. "We're innocent! You can't kill innocent men!" Carruthers told the jailer. "Who's gonna stop it?" the jailer retorted. Later, after a lawyer comes to visit the two men in jail, they beg him to "tell the people on the outside about us. Tell them if they don't help us they're just as good as pulling the switch on us." The short script closed with an exhortation from the students of Commonwealth College, directing readers to "USE THIS PLAY! Produce it. Tell the people of Arkansas about the case. Read it in your local union meetings, in your tra[d]es councils, in your churches. . . . Time is short. Help the Negro people to secure justice for themselves by freeing the innocent Blytheville boys."[30]

On Wednesday, December 14, 1938, Hibbler and Booker appeared in person before a three-judge panel at the circuit courthouse in St. Louis. The two Black men faced the three white judges, one from South Dakota, one from Minnesota, and one from Nebraska. The lawyers told the judges that Black people had been "systematically and arbitrarily" excluded from jury service in Mississippi County for more than forty years, and that the trial was "dominated by a spirit of mob violence." The lawyer for the state countered that "the trial judge had used Negroes on juries in other cases" and denied that any "mob spirit" was present. "Two Arkansas Negro Rapists' Appeal Heard," read the headline in the *Arkansas Gazette*.[31]

Two months later, the Eighth Circuit rejected Clayton's and Carruthers's appeal. The esteemed judges relied on the testimony of Arthur Adams—that he was not "affected or disturbed by any thought of mob influence"—and Judge Killough—that he possessed an "earnest purpose to accord the accused a fair and impartial trial"—but seemed to place little weight on the defendants' federal court statements. And although there was "substantial evidence that negroes had been systematically and intentionally excluded" from Mississippi County juries, the judges stated that this did not matter, as Arthur Adams had deliberately declined to object or invoke the Scottsboro decision.[32]

Only one viable path remained: to the U.S. Supreme Court.[33]

With just a few weeks to perfect their appeal, the lawyers had to hurry. A flurry of telegrams and letters whizzed up and down the eastern United States that spring of 1939. Because of the time crunch, Thurgood Marshall and the lawyers in Little Rock had to work independently on the petition for a writ of certiorari (the legal path into the nation's highest court), and Marshall then had to rush to unite their efforts and get the petition to Washington, D.C., in time.[34]

By early May, it was becoming clear that while the lawyers might be able to finish their petition within the allotted time period, the state of Arkansas could seek to carry out the execution before the case could be heard. Hastily, Marshall and other NAACP attorneys sought a stay of execution from the Supreme Court. On May 13, Justice Pierce Butler granted their request. To many observers, this might have been a surprising development. The son of Irish Catholic immigrants who had fled the Great Famine, Butler had been a controversial pick when he was nominated to the court in 1922, both because of his Catholicism and because of his violent opposition to "radical" professors teaching at the state university in Minnesota, where he lived. Even after his confirmation he had remained controversial, becoming an outspoken opponent of the New Deal as one of the "Four Horsemen" whose presence on the court made Franklin Roosevelt's early presidency so difficult. Yet Butler also had an independent, perhaps even libertarian, streak, and he was unafraid to dissent alone. He was the only justice to dissent from the notorious 1927 decision of *Buck v. Bell*, which upheld the constitutionality of forcibly sterilizing the "feeble-minded," and he was the only justice to dissent from *Palko v. Connecticut*, a case from 1937 in which the court upheld the conviction of a man for first-degree murder even though he had already been convicted of second-degree murder for the same crime.[35]

Because of Butler's largesse, the lawyers had twelve extra days. Their strenuous efforts continued. "Working on Clayton-Caruthers case," Marshall wrote to Walter White on May 18. "This one is worse than any we have had as yet." Finally, on May 24, they filed their petition before the Supreme Court, relying on the equal protection and due process guarantees of the Fourteenth Amendment, as well as the precedents set in the Scottsboro and Elaine Twelve cases. They also sought leave to proceed "in forma pauperis"—that is, without paying the usual fees—claiming that their clients "are ignorant, bearly [sic] able to read and write, and totally destitute; that their occupation was farming before their arrest, in which they were able to earn their living as sharecroppers; that they have no savings, no property or assets whatsoever, and that no member of their families have property or assets out of which the costs of this proceeding could be paid. That they are wholly dependent upon the gratuitous charity for any assistance for defending themselves in this cause." (For Carruthers, at least, this was probably truer of his lawyer than of him.)[36]

The NAACP attorneys were confident that the court would decide whether to hear the case or not within the next eleven days, before its summer adjournment. Once again, they and their clients were forced to wait.[37]

29 • The End, 1939

The sun was just starting to set, the light fading behind the handsome redbrick buildings of Howard Law School, as Leon A. Ransom prepared to send his telegram. It was shortly after five on the afternoon of June 5, 1939, and Ransom—a brilliant young law professor, who sported a trim mustache and small circular eyeglasses—composed his message tersely to convey the extreme urgency of the situation (and, perhaps, to save a little money at the telegraph office). Ransom had begun assisting on the Clayton-Carruthers case a few months earlier, lending his expertise to Marshall—who considered the scholar to be the "most knowledgeable guy of the whole [NAACP] crew"—and for the next few weeks it would consume his waking hours, as it already had Marshall's.[1] And while "Andy," as he was known to his friends, sometimes playfully addressed the younger Thurgood as "No Good," now he wrote to Marshall without even the courtesy of a salutation.[2]

"Carruthers certiorari denied," his telegram read. "How about rehearing? Mandate issues immediately. Must act. Write special delivery. Andy."[3]

This was crushing news. Marshall, Ransom, and their colleagues at the NAACP Legal Defense Fund had been cautiously optimistic about their chances in the Supreme Court. "Attorneys here think that the brief you fellows got up there for presentation of case to Supreme Court, is as good as could be," the NAACP's director of branches had written to Marshall after a nighttime discussion of the case.[4] Clayton's and Carruthers's local attorneys too were caught off guard. "I was surprised to get that news," John A. Hibbler wrote to Ransom, "as I had read your petition and brief with so much satisfaction that I was convinced that the Court would review it."[5]

The lawyers hastily began casting about for what to do next. Few options remained to them—but, as Ransom had pointed out, they had to act. "If you think of any other or further thing that can be done please do it," Hibbler wrote to Marshall a week later. "We shall, as a last resort, see if we can get the governor of this state to commute their sentences."[6]

Thurgood Marshall was a busy man. Hibbler's letter went, for the moment, unanswered, as the NAACP's special counsel was on a quick swing through southeastern Virginia, planning a case on behalf of a Norfolk schoolteacher challenging her exclusion from local schools on account of her race. On Friday, June 16, Marshall caught a Pullman train to Petersburg and then on to Washington, D.C., where he conferred with Ransom about the Clayton-Carruthers matter. After that he tried to catch a few hours of sleep in the jolting lower berth of another Pullman back to New York City. On Saturday morning he rose, spent eighty cents on some breakfast, and caught a taxi to the NAACP's office at 69 Fifth Avenue.[7]

"Returned from conference [with Ransom in] Washington on Clayton-Carruthers case," he telegraphed Hibbler shortly after his return to the office. "Suggest you immediately proceed to seek commutation of sentence. Rehearing practically impossible. Advise if we can help in any way on commutation."[8]

Officials in the governor's office knew a commutation request was coming, and they moved quickly to head it off at the pass. After Scipio A. Jones gave an interview to the press stating that their only remaining move was to beg the governor for executive clemency, Arkansas's attorney general immediately went to see the governor and implored him to set the date of electrocution as soon as possible. If the state were to succeed in killing Clayton and Carruthers, with so much unwanted attention shining on its death chamber, it had to move fast. Governor Carl E. Bailey agreed, set the date of execution as June 30, and then fled to New York City to attend the "Arkansas Day" celebrations at the 1939 World's Fair in Flushing Meadows.[9]

The June 30 date posed a problem for the lawyers. "He will not be back in the state until July," Hibbler wrote to Marshall on June 21 (nine days before the scheduled execution). "The Lt. Governor, Bob Bailey, has made a rule that he will not grant any clemencies unless it is at the suggestion of the Governor while the Governor is out of the state." Hibbler continued with a plea: "I have said all of this to say that if by any means Governor Bailey could be reached thru your office while he is in New York and induced to grant a stay of 30 or 60 days until he can hear from Arkansas people why he should commute the sentences to life imprisonment, that would be a victory. I do not know what means you may be able to do this, but you are so resourceful I thought it might be possible."[10]

That same day, Hibbler, Jones, and John R. Booker met with the lieutenant governor to exhort him to delay the execution. Perhaps they knew that Lieutenant Governor Bailey often intervened to protect convicted men from facing consequences until the governor returned to town.[11] This time, he refused. Hibbler sent a hurried telegram to the governor's hotel in New York, "kindly asking" him to instruct the lieutenant governor to halt the execution, since there simply was not enough time for them to prepare any further legal actions. It appears he never received a reply.[12]

Carl Bailey was proving to be a hard man to pin down. Not only was he occupied with the World's Fair—the most lavish, expensive, over-the-top fair in thirty years, attracting an eventual 44 million attendees—but he also hoped to secure a loan of $140 million to upgrade Arkansas's highways, turning the state into a modern hub for business and commerce. Bailey gave a speech to New York financiers at the gilded Bankers Club, trying to entice them into investing by claiming that 99 percent of Arkansas residents "are of American origin." He then traveled to a reception in his honor at the Waldorf-Astoria Hotel, where 132 past and present Arkansans praised the state's progress. Bailey probably attended the screening of a short film at the fair, *Life in Arkansas*, and he gave a four-minute radio address entitled, "Arkansas and Its Possibilities." The day Hibbler sent his telegram, Bailey was apparently spending time with his wife and daughter, who had traveled to New York for Arkansas Day, along with three hundred fellow Arkansans—all of whom, the *Gazette* reported, "had the time of their lives."[13]

The next morning, on Thursday, June 22, Thurgood Marshall took matters into his own hands. At ten, he called the Waldorf-Astoria Hotel and was informed that Governor Bailey wasn't staying there. Next he called the World's Fair itself, where someone told him that Bailey was staying at the Governor Clinton Hotel, a thirty-two-story Italianate pile down the block from Penn Station. Marshall rang the Governor Clinton and reached the governor's secretary, who told him that Bailey was asleep at the moment. An hour later, Marshall called back and was put through to the governor himself. The southern governor told the civil rights lawyer "that he was very busy and that I should call again at 6 p.m." Bailey spent the day meeting with still more New York bankers, desperate to pin down the $140 million he'd come to town to secure. Just how Marshall spent the rest of the day is unclear, but it's likely that he spent it on edge.[14]

At six, Marshall called Bailey's room again, only to be told that the governor was still meeting with the bankers and could not be disturbed. "Advised that he would call me after the conference." Marshall waited for nearly two hours, and, hearing nothing, called back. "I was told that he had rushed out to a meeting and that I should call again at 10 o'clock on Friday, June 23," Marshall recorded, masking any frustration he felt with the minimalism of his memo.[15]

The next morning, ten o'clock came and went, and though Marshall still didn't reach the governor, he did find some cause to be hopeful: "Talked to Governor Bailey's secretary who said that Governor was at a conference someplace on Wall street and that it would be practically impossible to get an appointment with him. I explained in detail the case and the necessity of a conference. I was informed that the Governor would return to Arkansas before June 30. I requested a hearing for clemency in Arkansas at some time prior to June 30. The Governor's secretary told me the Governor would hold a hearing before June 30." An hour later, Marshall typed up the last day's happenings in a hasty memo that ended on a note of uncertainty: Bailey's secretary promised to talk the governor at lunch, and if Marshall didn't hear back from him by two thirty, it would be safe for Marshall to telegraph "the people in Arkansas" telling them the good news.[16]

Three hours passed and Marshall heard nothing. He dispatched a telegram and a letter to Hibbler: "You should immediately start working in preparation for the hearing," Marshall wrote. "I would suggest that you restrict the people attending the hearing, in addition to you and the other lawyers, to very conservative and influential citizens. I would get as many Ministers as possible because the whole question now is a matter of pleading for justice rather [than] demanding justice."[17]

Early the next morning Marshall departed for Norfolk, driving west through the Holland Tunnel and then south toward Virginia, where he had to attend to other business.[18] Hibbler and the other Arkansas lawyers immediately got to work on the upcoming hearing. The NAACP issued a hurried press release, trumpeting Bailey's commitment to grant Clayton and Carruthers a "full hearing," probably hoping to put public pressure on the governor to keep his word. Interestingly, the press release stated that the two men were "awaiting execution on a four-year-old charge of shooting a Mississippi county sheriff"—it did not mention that they had actually been convicted and sentenced to die for supposedly raping a white woman. This was likely intended to gin up more public support for the two black men.[19]

One week remained before the scheduled day of execution.

Governor Carl E. Bailey, the poor son of a logger and hardware salesman in Bernie, Missouri, was never supposed to be in this position. Though headstrong and ambitious, he'd struggled as a shoe factory worker in St. Louis, a railroad brakeman in Texas, and a café operator in Campbell, Missouri, before attending Chillicothe Business College, only to drop out when he ran out of money. He had to work a series of odd jobs to support himself as he read law, but in 1926 Bailey finally managed to enter politics—a state away, in Arkansas—becoming deputy prosecuting attorney for Pulaski and Perry Counties. After assuming the role of prosecutor in his own right five years later, he first won statewide interest by leading the charge against the disgraced former head of a banking empire, now deeply unpopular in the midst of the Depression. After a dramatic trial, Bailey managed to secure a guilty verdict and a sentence of one year in prison, but the banker was pardoned before he ever set foot behind bars. One wonders if this experience predisposed Bailey against the kind of executive clemency Clayton's and Carruthers's attorneys were so desperately seeking.

Although his prosecution of the banker had earned him many enemies in state politics, Bailey positioned himself as an outsider and in 1934 ran an insurgent race for state attorney general against Hal N. Norwood, a popular incumbent. In splashy newspaper advertisements, Norwood tried to brand Bailey as soft on crime, noting that of the seven cases of rape he'd tried as prosecutor in 1931 and 1932, all had been dismissed. Nonetheless, when the election results came in, Bailey had won by 12,000 votes. "It was a spectacular feat that experienced politicians considered impossible," wrote the historian Donald Holley. As attorney general, Bailey battled the governor, J. M. Futrell, and made headlines by publicly refusing a $50,000 bribe from the mobster Lucky Luciano, who was fighting extradition from Little Rock back to New York. In 1936, Bailey ran a long-shot race for governor, once again as an outsider. Though he was still fighting to be seen as adequately tough on crime, and though he polled at only 32 percent in the primary, Bailey managed to win yet another upset, triumphing by fewer than 4,000 votes.[20]

By the time Thurgood Marshall began appealing to Bailey for mercy for Clayton and Carruthers, the governor had been waging battle with enemies in the legislature nonstop for three years, having triumphed in a punishing reelection campaign in 1938 but also seeing his popularity start to wane in 1939. He had entered the governor's mansion as a critic of the state's prison system, having labeled it "a social cancer and a relic of barbarism," but would he really be willing to hand his opponents so much ammunition by pardoning two such notorious men?[21]

With the clock ticking down, Bailey was the Blytheville boys' only chance.

Late on the evening of Tuesday, June 27, disaster struck. Barely two days remained for the lawyers to convince Governor Bailey to grant Clayton and

Carruthers clemency, and the lawyers had just gotten word that the governor was blowing them off.

"Governor Bailey did not grant us hearing while here," Hibbler telegraphed Thurgood Marshall in New York. Apparently, the governor had left for New York the day before: he had lied to them. "We are turning again to Lieutenant Governor Bob Bailey." They were truly desperate now.[22]

In his haste, Hibbler had forgotten that Marshall wasn't at the NAACP headquarters in New York; he was in Virginia. Marshall didn't receive Hibbler's telegram for more than twelve precious hours.[23] Yet as soon as he did, he swung into action. "All principles of fair play and justice point to the granting of a hearing to these two men when their lives are at stake," Marshall wired to Bailey's room in the Governor Clinton Hotel at 11:45 a.m. on Wednesday, June 28. "Would appreciate being advised whether hearing will be granted before June 30 or that a stay of execution may be granted pending hearing."[24] Then, sitting in the NAACP's Virginia headquarters in Richmond, Marshall waited for a reply.

Hours passed. Marshall spent forty-five cents for lunch, seventy-five cents for dinner, and another seventy-five cents for supper. He instructed Catherine Freeland, an assistant in the New York office, to call the Governor Clinton Hotel and see if Bailey was there. If he was not, he continued, call "the World's Fair and ask where he is, and wire me his address." Marshall spent the day calling "every important hotel" in New York. At ten that night, still having received no reply, Marshall sent a telegram to Charles Irvin of the Amalgamated Clothing Workers Union, telling him how to learn more about Clayton's and Carruthers's case. A. Philip Randolph, the distinguished labor leader and civil rights activist, had told Marshall that Irvin would be willing to send a telegram to Bailey, urging him to stay the execution, and at this point it was all hands on deck.[25]

At 9:40 a.m. the next morning, Catherine Freeland sent Marshall a brief telegram. No one knew where Bailey was. He wasn't at the Governor Clinton Hotel. Their contact at the World's Fair suggested they try Perylon Hall there, where a governors' luncheon was being served at 1:00 p.m. Lunchtime came and went. Still no luck.[26]

Late that evening—on June 29, with just hours remaining—Marshall wired Hibbler in Little Rock. "Called long distance to New York," he wrote. "Call pending all day. Just informed Governor Bailey not in New York but in Arkansas."[27]

They'd been duped. And now, perhaps, it was too late.

Seeking clemency for two Black men convicted of rape had always been a tall order. To be sure, many Black people did receive some form of gubernatorial mercy in those days, usually when their supporters could successfully exploit the paternalistic tendencies of those in power. For example, a pastor from Magnolia wrote to the governor, asking him to parole his "negro" cook, who had been caught "making some kind of an intoxicating drink. She has paid more than the cost of this fine. She like all other poor negroes is having a hard time to live." The pastor called his cook "a very faithful servant" and asked for her to be pardoned.[28] A petition requesting clemency for a man named Nathan Clayton labeled him "an ignorant negro" and added, "His family needs him for crop purposes."[29] A few years later, a man wrote on behalf of a "Darky," requesting furlough because "this negro's family need him at home to support them."[30]

Paternalism was far from the most troubling element of the clemency system as it applied to Black people. Although Arkansas had eliminated convict leasing in the early 1910s, a system continued at least into the 1930s whereby the governor often secured the parole of certain Black prisoners and then effectively gave them to wealthy white friends of his to do labor.[31] For instance, in 1929 the governor wrote to the superintendent of Tucker on behalf of a former member of the Penitentiary Board who "wants to get a negro woman," adding, "I will be glad to see him taken care of with a good cook if you have one."[32] In another letter, he referred a "Mrs. M. L. Sigman, of Monticello" to the superintendent, asking if he could "select for her a good negro woman for a cook,"[33] and in still another one he mentioned "a very close personal and political friend of the Governor [who] is very anxious to secure a yard boy from the Farm. . . . He does not care if he is a middle-aged man."[34]

Sometimes, prominent citizens wrote to the governor directly, asking for a "negro woman to stay around our home here in DeWitt and work for us and we will look after her, etc." or complaining about a delay in receiving the Black man he wanted.[35] And, as Bailey's son recalled in an oral history interview some eight decades later, one of the "perks" of his father being governor was that "you could have as many, as much household help as you wanted from the penitentiary." His family "nearly always had either a man to work in the yard or a lady to work in the house."[36] Such a practice would continue into the 1980s, when Arkansas First Lady Hillary Clinton acquiesced to continuing this "longstanding tradition, which kept down costs." She and Bill, she later wrote, "became friendly with a few of them, African-American men in their thirties who had already served twelve to eighteen years of their sentences."[37]

Such options were not available for Clayton and Carruthers, even if they'd been willing to accept them. Black men accused of rape (much less convicted of rape) rarely received mercy. It seems likely that the Blytheville boys' lawyers knew about the case of Theo Thomas and Frank Carter, two Black men who had been sentenced to death a couple years after Clayton and Carruthers, for supposedly raping a white woman in a ditch. After their appeals failed, some people close to them began seeking relief from the governor. On June 23, 1938, Carter's mother even traveled to Little Rock in hopes of securing a short stay from Governor Bailey, so that her son could prepare an appeal to the U.S. Supreme Court. But the governor was out of town at a tomato festival. Thomas and Carter died in the electric chair, not even six months after they were convicted.[38]

That said, Clayton and Carruthers did have something that Thomas and Carter did not: powerful friends.

Through the efforts of supporters who had been trying to publicize their case—the next Scottsboro—for years, Clayton and Carruthers had won the support of prominent Democratic politician Brooks Hayes and Carl Bailey's intimate advisor, Beloit Taylor, as well as middle-class groups, such as the YWCA and ACLU, and radical groups, such as the Communist Party and the International Labor Defense. In a telegram to Bailey on June 23, the president of the International Ladies' Garment Workers Union charged, on behalf of 260,000 workers, that Clayton's and Carruthers's execution "would be viewed as a terrible blot upon American justice and sense of fair play in [the] state of Arkansas."[39]

Among the most vociferous supporters of the Blytheville boys was the Joint Action Committee of Commonwealth College, a ragtag group established at the short-lived leftist (albeit nonintegrated) college in Mena, Arkansas, run at the time by the socialist reverend Claude C. Williams, aka "the preaching hillbilly." With just thirteen days remaining before June 30, the Joint Action Committee swung into action, wiring the leaders of the NAACP, National Negro Congress, Southern Conference on Human Welfare, and more than a dozen labor leaders and progressives across the south. "We must look to one another for instantaneous action to preserve Democratic processes of justice in South," the committee telegraphed. "Defeat would be tragedy for progressive cause." David Beardsley, the college's executive secretary, then forwarded the telegram to the NAACP's Walter White and begged him, "Please act upon it. Help us and others define to ourselves our own part in this fight for life and justice. And, in the name of humanity, ACT!"[40]

Even as they were fighting for Clayton's and Carruthers's lives, Marshall and the NAACP leaders also fought to ensure that they received adequate credit. Marshall was particularly incensed that the Communist Party claimed to have pushed the NAACP to act in the first place. (In fact, the ILD had pushed the NAACP to act in the first place, and given the ILD's overlap with the Communist Party, this claim was not so far-fetched.) Walter White, meanwhile, replied to David Beardsley, "It might have been helpful to you in sending out your appeal had you known that the N.A.A.C.P. has been fighting the Clayton and Carruthers case for four years."[41]

Marshall wanted to make sure that the governor's New York accommodations weren't inundated by correspondence from cranks and communists, which he could easily dismiss. "Be certain that only persons with influence wire Bailey," he wrote to Hibbler on June 22.[42] Charles Irvin of the Amalgamated Clothing Workers Union also worried "that the sending of telegram of protest from radical and northern group"—his group—"to tory-democratic Bailey [might] do more harm than good," and asked Marshall for direction.[43]

Nonetheless, as the moment of execution ticked nearer, "hundreds of requests had poured into his [Bob Bailey's] office at the capitol in Little Rock, urging him to stay the execution," reported the *Gazette*. "They came from every section of the country. Many of the letters and telegrams contained identical wording. Several demanded the acting governor delay the execution and purported to refer to new evidence, unjust trials and proof of innocence." Yet Bob Bailey still refused to intervene, continued the *Gazette*, "saying any delay was a matter for the regular governor."[44]

Finally, Friday, June 30, 1939. A warm, cloudy day at Tucker Prison Farm—and execution day for Bubbles Clayton and Jim X. Carruthers. "Prison hounds bayed mournfully in the yard outside the little frame execution chamber," wrote a reporter for the Associated Press.[45]

Ten minutes before they were set to die, Clayton was pacing nervously around his death row cell. He insisted to the reporters who were within earshot that he was not guilty. Neither he nor Carruthers had been able to sleep the night before; rather, they had kept a five-hour vigil, intoning "amens" as the prison's chaplain read passages from the Bible.

Carruthers was the first of the condemned men led to the electric chair. Spectators sat in chairs behind a railing that circled the chair. Guards pulled straps over his arms, a hood over his face, and a gauze crown soaked in water over his head—the better to conduct electricity. A few minutes later, he was followed by Clayton, who was reportedly smoking a cigar as he entered the execution chamber. He kept it in his mouth "until it was removed by a guard as he started to pray."[46]

Electrocution was a terrifying way to go. Recounting the botched 1946 execution of Willie Francis, the journalist Gilbert King wrote, "Gagged with the leather band, Willie sat in darkness now, the deafening noise of the engine amplifying his terror." After a prison official pulled the switch, "Willie's hands immediately clenched into fists. His body tensed, then stretched, as the first currents of electricity began to surge into him. He groaned audibly. He strained against the leather straps. He writhed in his agony." The condemned man's body contorted as the electricity coursed through him. "His lips swelled gruesomely, their flesh puffing out from the slit in the leather mask. His nose got flattened. Just thirty seconds into the electrocution, Willie's body, involuntarily jumping and seizing, convulsed under the current. The heavy, oaken death chair began to rock and slide across the floor before angling away from the witnesses, aghast at what they were seeing."

Remarkably, the generator failed that day. With what he thought was his dying breath, a masked and gagged Willie Francis cried, "I AM N-N-NOT DYING!" And he didn't. But his was a very rare stroke of luck.[47]

Bubbles Clayton was pronounced dead ten minutes after Jim X. Carruthers. His last words, reported the *Chicago Defender,* were, "Have mercy on my mother and father and my loved ones and may I meet them in heaven."[48]

After Clayton and Carruthers were executed, a third Black man, Sylvester Williams, age twenty, was led to the electric chair. Just a month before, Williams had pleaded guilty to raping and murdering a farm girl near Altheimer, "sinking her body into a bayou with iron weights after the crime." Several spectators left to make room for the victim's father, young sister, and four brothers, who sat and watched as the guards tied Williams down and pumped electricity through his body.

As the three men were being executed, Joel Carson—a twenty-eight-year-old white man who had been scheduled to die with the rest, but who had gained a last-second respite from a federal court—paced his cell. "After it was over," wrote a journalist for the *Arkansas Gazette,* "he said to one of the State Police who witnessed the affair: 'Well I guess you are sorry I didn't go with them, like all the rest of those people who have been coming in here. Well, you see I didn't.' Carson nibbled on an apple given him shortly before the execution by one of the condemned men."

"Following the execution," the *Gazette* journalist continued, Assistant Superintendent Lee Henslee "told of an incident which might have gained a stay of execution for Williams, had it not been for quick work by Jefferson county officials."

"He said that Tuesday night Williams told prison officials that although he was at the scene of the crime, another Negro killed the girls. He named the Negro. Officials checked the story, and found it to be false," reported the *Gazette*. According to the journalist, Williams later admitted "that Clayton and Carruthers had suggested it to him as means of gaining a stay of execution."

It is unclear if this story can be believed. The reporters had their own agendas. As John Hibbler later wrote to Thurgood Marshall, "It is our information that they went to their graves protesting their innocence, which was the report of the *Arkansas Gazette* our local morning paper. The evening paper, the *Arkansas Democrat,* however, came out with the report or statement that one of the boy's [sic], Jim X. Carruthers, confessed to his guilt just before the cap was pulled over his eyes."

By the next day, the story had solidified into accepted wisdom. On July 1, the *Gazette* reported that as the straps were being tightened on Carruthers's arms, Assistant Superintendent Henslee asked him, "Are you guilty of the crime with which you are charged?"

"Yes sir, I'm guilty, Cap'n," he supposedly replied without hesitation, "and I want to pray for forgiveness for all my sins."

"Asked who was with him at the time of the crime, he replied: 'Cap'n, I've told my part of it. I ain't got nothing more to say.'"

"He then offered a brief prayer just before the current was applied."[49]

Lieutenant Governor Bob Bailey—who, the Associated Press reported, "turned a deaf ear to scores of pleas within and without the state that he stay the execution" until Governor Carl Bailey could return—told the *Gazette* he was relieved to hear that Carruthers had confessed at last. "There was a tremendous amount of pressure on me and I did very little sleeping last night for pondering the case, but I couldn't see my way clear to take any action," he said on the evening of June 30. "I don't mind admitting that confession was a relief to me."[50]

But Hibbler doubted the veracity of this whole account. "We have not been able to find any body who heard the confession," he wrote to Marshall. "They stated that a number of persons were present, but it is our conviction that this was something said to give the Governor a way out, for in the same issue of the *Arkansas Democrat* the Lt. Governor, Bob Bailey, came out with an expression stating that his conscience was eased because of the purported confession."[51]

Such overwrought or even fabricated reports were common in southern newspapers whenever Black men were executed for rape. For instance, the *Nashville News* described Willie Martin, a Black man convicted of raping and murdering a white woman in 1926, as a "big negro" and claimed that he admitted culpability at the last moment (rendering his words in dialect).[52] When Freeling Daniels, a Black man convicted of raping a thirteen-year-old white girl in 1932, was electrocuted, the *Arkansas Gazette* reported that his last request was a pack of cigarettes; according to the newspaper, he "spent several hours last night gazing into a haze of smoke."[53]

A week after the electrocutions, Hibbler sent Marshall a letter. "It seems to me that it is fitting and proper that I should give you this letter as a resume [sic] of the final chapter here in the Clayton-Carruthers matter," he wrote. "Governor Bailey came back to Arkansas on Sunday, June 25 and stayed thru Monday, June 26, but kept himself secluded, notwithstanding we used every human force to connect with him; he very skillfully and stubbornly evaded us and all of those who we were able to interest in interceding in the interest of a stay for Clayton-Carruthers. He left at 6:00 p.m. Monday, June 26 for Washington."[54]

The governor had lied to them. He had apparently gone to great lengths to deceive the lawyers and thus ensure Clayton's and Carruthers's deaths. Bailey's subterfuge had been so successful that major Black newspapers had even run stories—about the governor's intention to give the defendants a hearing—a day *after* the execution. Weeks later, Marshall wrote to the governor, politely demanding an explanation, and Bailey replied that he had so hoped to be back in Arkansas in time, but it had simply proven to be impossible. Hibbler dismissed this "evasive" letter as emblematic of Bailey's status as "too much of a political coward to stand up and do the right thing at the right time," while Marshall wrote that Bailey's conduct would redound "to the everlasting disgrace and shame to the governors of the United States."[55]

Still, Hibbler found a small silver lining. "We succeeded in interesting the best white people of Arkansas, and Little Rock white ministers, Rabbis, politicians and a number of men who were said to be close to Governor Bailey," he wrote. "All of these people tried to get him on the telephone while here and sent telegrams to him in Washington and New York. . . . Let me thank you personally, and for associate counsel, for the earnest and zealous help rendered in this case. I still think that the fight that we put up was worthwhile, and even tho we did not save the boys' lives, we have caused all of Arkansas and other states to take notice that they cannot, under the guise of law, lynch people without a protest."[56]

Part V
Afterlives

30 • Maya Angelou, 1970s

By the time *I Know Why the Caged Bird Sings* was released in February 1970, the buzz about it had been building for some time. Newspaper stories about Angelou's other work had been teasing the book for years; both *Ebony* and *Harper's* ran excerpts, marking perhaps the first time *Harper's* had paid for the work of a Black author. In the days after it hit shelves, *Caged Bird* became an instant hit, immediately securing a spot on the *New York Times* bestseller list. The Book of the Month Club announced it as a special spring 1970 selection. And Angelou became—and would forever remain—an international celebrity.[1]

Throughout the early weeks of 1970, she was inundated with requests for interviews, speeches, and new work. Just how she felt about this instant success is difficult to discern. Angelou told one interviewer, "I was surprised at first. It was really thrilling," but she told another, "I knew when I was writing it, it would be a success."[2]

The media couldn't get enough of Angelou, reveling in the accomplishment of a Black female literary sensation in language that sometimes exoticized her and frequently discussed her appearance. The writer of one article described her as "seductively soft-spoken with full lips that are quick to smile." Another claimed she had "the grace of an African queen. Wearing an exotic ankle-length costume inspired by the women of Ghana, she is stately and charming." Still another called her "perhaps one of the most beautiful women in the world. Her smile is such that when it appears, there is no darkness anywhere about. She has the ability to make an entire room come alive with her warmth." Ironically, Angelou herself frequently deprecated her looks, once telling a journalist, "My looks don't fit the current fashion in terms of feminine beauty. I am a woman who is black and lonely."[3]

The reviews of *Caged Bird* were widespread and rapturous. *Newsweek* called the book "more than a tour de force of language or the story of childhood suffering: it quietly and gracefully portrays and pays tribute to the courage, dignity and endurance of the small, rural Southern black community in which she spent most of the early years of the 1930s." The *Courier-Journal & Times* in Louisville, Kentucky, called it "a poignant human document that is also an important contribution to American letters." The *New York Times* reviewed *Caged Bird* together with a memoir by the boxer Sugar Ray Robinson. It misstated Angelou's birth name as "Marguerita Johnson" but called the book "a carefully wrought, simultaneously touching and comic memoir of a black girl's slow and clumsy growth." Somewhat remarkably for the time, many reviews were open and explicit about the book's contents; the review in the *Chicago Daily News* began, "Maya Angelou was a rape victim at 8."[4]

Yet many of the reviewers betrayed their own racial politics, seeing in *Caged Bird* confirmation of what white writers hoped to see from Black literature. The *Greensboro News* noted of Angelou's suffering, "Like so many Negro children she was subjected to abuse not only from the white world but also from a disintegrated family structure." The *Toledo Blade* wrote approvingly that *Caged Bird* "is not propaganda nor a history of the blacks nor, most blessedly, sociology." And *San Francisco Magazine* added: "Maya Angelou goes beyond Eldridge Cleaver and Malcolm X with whom she might be compared in the sense that her pride in being black is a positive and communicable force rather than inducement for separatism or for hate. Her blackness is secondary to her humanity."[5]

Angelou herself often framed the book in universalist terms. "I tell it through the black experience, of course, because that's my experience. But I don't like it narrowed to just black womanhood or black manhood. I have a Jewish friend who's lived primarily in New York and Chicago and she says the book took her back to her childhood. That's the kind of meaning I want the book to have." She explained in another interview that this universality was the result of the book's evolution over the course of her writing: "I wrote it because I thought it was important for black girls to know something about what it's like to grow up. There aren't many books on the subject for them. Louisa May Alcott is not relevant. Then I got into it and I realized that to tell the truth I had to write for something larger than just the black girl. I accepted that I was writing for middle-aged Chinese women and young Jewish boys with braces on their teeth and, really, for anyone who is or was in a cage."[6]

At the same time, Angelou refused to sublimate her Blackness, her left politics, or her pride in both. She told one interviewer that she believed her life story had "universal" appeal but that "when I see, it is through the eyes of black women." She told another interviewer: "I like Jesse Jackson; I like what he says. I'm impressed with Shirley Chisholm. I think what the Black Panthers are doing on the West Coast is really remarkable—Bobby Seale and Huey Newton. Bobby's going to run for Mayor of Oakland. What they're trying to do to eliminate prisons is to set up community controls. It sounds like a drop in the bucket, a drop in the sea, but it's very revolutionary as far as I can see."[7]

Caged Bird remained on the bestseller list for the better part of four months (and it has never gone out of print). Its initial paperback print run was an astounding 350,000 copies. Soon *Caged Bird* was nominated for the 1970 National Book Award. The fact that it didn't win, commented one reporter, "bothers its authoress not a whit, but it did inspire something akin to a wildly loyal cult for which she serves as accessible goddess. That she likes."[8]

The press commented often on how rare it was for a Black woman to achieve such stunning success. A number of articles identified Angelou as "the first black woman to make the best seller lists," a narrative her publisher aggressively promoted but one that she told the press was "no compliment." "There are plenty of fine books that deserve that recognition," Angelou told the interviewer, "from Alice Childress' 'Like One of the Family' to those of Paule Marshall, Rosa Guy, Louise Meriwether and Sarah Wright. None of them were written specifically for the black market. But either their editors don't believe enough in the black writer's work or they didn't know how to promote it right." Sometimes these reporters' questions appeared to betray racist biases. In one interview, Angelou was asked if it were professionally advantageous to her to be a Black woman. The interviewer then mentioned the Black prisoner George Jackson and asked, "How many of your black friends have been convicts?"[9]

Undoubtedly, some of the most important plaudits for *Caged Bird* came from Angelou's friends. The Harlem Writers Guild threw her a book party. Alice Windom wrote to her from Ghana to tell her that the Revolutionist Returnees were raving about it. James Baldwin contributed a blurb for the advertisements: "This testimony from a black sister marks the beginning of a new era in the minds and hearts and lives of all black men and women." The blurb was drawn from a powerful letter Baldwin had written to Angelou's editor, Robert Loomis, in which he noted that he could not "remember when I've had a more difficult time conveying what a book means to me. Rare indeed is the book which, in its utter purity, both intimidates and liberates the reader—and also indicts a nation. I Know Why The Caged Bird Sings liberates the reader—whosoever will—into life simply because Maya confronts her own life with a such a moving wonder [sic], such a luminous dignity." To Baldwin, Angelou's book was itself literally a world event: "it marks the end of an era of a way of thought and a way of life and death in these yet-to-be United States."[10]

Yet not everyone was pleased with Maya Angelou's memoir. One former resident of Stamps, the musician Barbara Wright-Pryor, recalled in an oral history interview that many people in Stamps were "not very happy" with Angelou after *Caged Bird* hit shelves. Wright-Pryor, herself Black, claimed that "blacks and whites alike . . . the entire town was just so angry and dismayed with how they had been portrayed, how their town had been portrayed to the world." Wright-Pryor further contended (in, perhaps, a bizarrely blasé manner) that Angelou had exaggerated the violence in Stamps: "As far as any racial conflicts and lynchings and drownings and killing somebody and throwing them in the pond, or Lake June, as it was called, mother said there was no such thing. The only body that she remembers being pulled out of"—Wright-Pryor laughed—"Lake June or the pond there in Stamps, Arkansas, was of a black man who was killed by a black man who caught him with his wife, and everybody knew the story, but in the book, various bodies were pulled out of the pond, it was all fictionalized." Finally, Wright-Pryor claimed that she had family who had known Angelou in the 1930s and remembered her "very vividly," and they did not recall her being unable to speak.[11]

Other residents of Stamps told the press that they barely remembered Angelou. A reporter from the *Arkansas Gazette* visited the town in the summer of 1970 and found "considerable talk about the book" but few specific comments beyond a vague resentment among some white residents. The town's state legislator—a well-to-do white woman—told the reporter that Angelou's "people are well respected in Stamps," adding, "We have never had any trouble with our colored citizens in Stamps." By this point, Momma had died and an aging Uncle Willie was running the Store. The reporter quoted him as saying, "I wouldn't have put that in if I was her—about the whites being that mean." Of course, Uncle Willie still had to interact with the town's white residents on a daily basis. He noted that "Marguerite" had not been back in years.[12]

It is important to give space to these other voices from Stamps, but their claims are slightly beside the point. What was important to Angelou's millions of readers was how she drew from her childhood in Stamps a powerful message of resiliency and resistance and Black female personhood, one she shared in powerful prose.

One frigid night in 1985, as Angelou was traveling around the country to promote *And Still I Rise,* an hour-long PBS special featuring a conversation between herself and the historian Nell Irvin Painter, she gave a talk to a crowd of admirers in Colorado. It was a Friday, and after Angelou finished, a woman named Lee Stanfield came up and introduced herself. Stanfield was an activist from Wyoming; she had driven a hundred miles to hear Angelou's speech, which she'd found thrilling. And now she was asking the famous author if she might be willing to speak to a national conference of anti-rape activists and survivors of sexual assault. "Write to me soon, right away," Angelou replied, "and tell me what you are wishing will happen if I come to speak."

"The 'wish' is still a potential of sorts," Stanfield wrote to "Ms Angelou, magical woman" a few days later: "We want to feel something which has not really happened for/to us yet as an organization of people working in the anti-rape movement. Much more than improving technical skills, we are aiming this next time to create a space/place for personal discovery & healing & belly-laughing . . . for truth-saying & ritual & sharing (not merely comparing) women's culturexperiences."[13]

Stanfield was inviting Angelou to be the keynote speaker at the seventh annual conference of the National Coalition Against Sexual Assault, to be held in Knoxville, Kentucky, six months later. The National Coalition was an independent network of rape crisis centers and other groups and individuals providing services to rape survivors. It had emerged from the societal upheaval of the 1960s and 1970s, and like many second wave feminist organizations, it had struggled with providing equitable access for activists of color and disabled activists. Yet many recognized that the National Coalition was making a genuine and concerted effort to include Black women, to recognize that their experience with sexual assault was distinct and worthy of note. To that end, Stanfield informed Angelou that they were opening that year's conference with a Women of Color Institute.[14]

"I have found out, along with reading your prose and your poetry and then especially after hearing you the other night," Stanfield wrote, "that you are a human being who has opened herself up to feelings like rage and loss—but that you have managed to move beyond being angry and alone. You are a healer as well as a poet."[15]

Perhaps because of the sheer quantity of correspondence with which she was routinely inundated, Angelou did not see Stanfield's letter for some months. Late in June she scrawled a response on her fine stationery. "I look forward to being with you and other exciting friends in Knoxville," she wrote. "I shall try to come early to spend a little time enjoying everybody and everything."[16]

The conference was held at the Hyatt Regency in Knoxville from July 31 to August 3; its theme was "Transcending Barriers: Bridges to the Future." At eight thirty on the final night, Angelou gave her keynote address. Unfortunately, no copy of her speech survives, and press coverage of the event was quite limited.[17] Yet her invitation to this event, and her decision to attend, are significant, for they gesture toward a greater understanding of just how meaningful Angelou and her work was for anti-rape activists and how much *Caged Bird* became a touchstone text in their movement.

"I'd never heard of another Black woman, young girl, who had been raped," recalled a sexual abuse survivor from Kosciusko, Mississippi, named Oprah Winfrey. "So I read those words and thought, 'Somebody knows who I am.' "[18]

The story at the heart of *Caged Bird* resonated even a world away. Initially, British publishers were not interested in releasing a British edition, believing, in the words of a chronicler decades later, "that British people wouldn't care about a young black girl growing up in the American south in the 1930s." Eventually, however, Angelou appeared on a British talk show. When she recounted the story of her rape, her muteness, and her recovery, the "TV switchboards were jammed; the reviews and features that followed were stunning. Maya was beamed straight into British hearts." After that, *Caged Bird* became a runaway hit in the U.K.[19]

In the weeks and months after *Caged Bird* was released to the public, Angelou suddenly had more work than she knew what to do with. She was invited to the University of Kansas to be a poet in residence. Columbia Pictures asked her to adapt *The Autobiography of Malcolm X* for screen, teaming her up with the actor and director (and her old friend) James Earl Jones. She was asked to write a profile of the singer Nina Simone for *Redbook*. She began writing a movie called *Georgia, Georgia*, about a Black American singer falling in love with a white Vietnam War deserter in Sweden; the film was released in 1972, and one newspaper called Angelou "the first black woman to both write and direct feature length films." In 1971, she released a volume of poetry, *Give Me a Cool Drink of Water 'fore I Diiie*, which cemented her literary stardom and was nominated for a Pulitzer Prize. In his blurb, Baldwin wrote, "You will hear the regal woman; the mischievous street girl; you will hear the price of a black woman's survival and you will hear of her generosity routed in specific experiences." Two years later, Angelou made her Broadway acting debut in *Look Away*, a two-woman show about Mary Todd Lincoln and her Black maid; the show closed almost immediately, but Angelou was roundly praised by the critics and nominated for a Tony Award.[20]

Still, even as an international phenomenon, Angelou continued to encounter the racism endemic in American society. She tried to write a film version of *The Autobiography of Malcolm X* that would do its subject justice and humanize him, but the attitude of Columbia Pictures "could be summed up by one executive who said, 'I don't know if anybody really wants a story about a colored man right now. But I wouldn't mind if you can make it into something like *Guess Who's Coming to Dinner*.' So there was nothing to talk about, really." She dropped the project. Around the same time, she was on her way to Yale University to accept the prestigious Chubb Fellowship; the only seat available on the crowded bus from New York to New Haven was next to a ragged, unkempt white woman. "Blacks have a race memory, buried behind their kneecaps, of how to act when sitting beside a hostile seat partner," Angelou later wrote. She attempted to stay still and silent, but the woman turned to her and said, "I want to tell you something. I'm from Virginia and my pappy never hated you people." Angelou was speechless. "I hope this won't hurt your feelings," the woman continued, "but I had a colored mammy." Nodding her head, she continued. "And she loved me. More than her own children. Used to enjoy playing with my hair. I was blond then." Angelou realized that this woman did not see her as a human being. The woman continued talking, discussing how Black men constantly lusted after her—she "was always just one bed away from being raped"—even as older Black women loved her and younger Black women envied her. As she told Angelou this "most outrageous series of lies," Angelou dutifully wrote them down, seething, perhaps already planning to turn the incident into an essay titled "The Black Woman as Legend."[21]

Despite her success, these were difficult times for Angelou. In 1971, her friend Jessica Mitford wrote to her, "I was so sorry to hear of your troubles—am longing to see you, but don't know when/where you are," though it's unclear what exactly Mitford was referring to. The next year, Angelou told a journalist about her periodic depression: "I never win the depressions, but I survive. A really bad evening can take me right out. The end of a love affair really takes me out. When it's over I'm dying and desperately lonely. I try to think of what I'm going to get out of it. What song? What story? What poem? The last one brought me three good poems out of a large number I wrote. I'll be drawing on that for a long time." A year after that, Angelou added, "I'm often asked: 'How did you *escape* it all: the poverty, the rape at an early age, a broken home, growing up black in the South?' My natural response is to say: 'How the hell do you know I *did* escape? You won't know what demons I wrestle with.' "[22] A decade later, a Black writer named bell hooks echoed this sentiment, noting, "White feminists tended to romanticize the black female experience . . . They ignore the reality that to be strong in the face of oppression is not the same as overcoming oppression."[23]

Yet during these years, Angelou also found strength in the lasting relationships—the solidarity—she established with other Black female authors and activists. In 1971, shortly after Toni Morrison's first novel—*The Bluest Eye*, another book about a young Black girl surviving sexual violence—was released, Angelou wrote to the author, " 'The Bluest Eye' is just closed and while your magic is living here around me, I'm obliged to write to you. Your book is so great, your perception so deep and clear and your poetry—oh your poetry. While reading, no, better, being in your book, I was entranced yet conscious, hypnotized yet aware. Now that's magic." Angelou's letter gestures explicitly at how much she identified with Morrison's protagonist: "You led me down my own years, gave me back visions which had glanced off my mind, forgotten skipping stones which had sank in a long ago pond." Many years later, in another letter to Morrison, she wrote, "I love Beloved and I love you for knowing all that about Love, and loss and Life." Angelou would also send Maxine Waters a beautiful flower arrangement for her birthday, visit Angela Davis in prison, and exchange cordial letters with Alice Walker and Coretta Scott King.[24]

Caged Bird was published at the beginning of what some have called "the 'renaissance' of black women writers." Morrison and Walker, as well as Toni Cade Bambara, Lucille Clifton, Nikki Giovanni, June Jordan, Audre Lorde, Louise Meriwether, Sonia Sanchez, and many others were beginning to find an audience. Angelou's book marked what the scholar Dolly A. McPherson called "the beginning of a new era in the consciousness of Black men and women." Another scholar, Sondra O'Neale, argued that the book "bridged the gap between life and art, a step that is essential if Black women are to be deservedly credited with the mammoth and creative feat of noneffacing survival."[25]

Angelou's pride in the accomplishments of this new generation of Black women authors was tied to her pride in Blackness and the broader Black community. In the 1970s, she attended the funeral of George Jackson, a Black incarcerated activist, and was deeply moved; she wrote about how meaningful Jackson was for a "young black girl," a "middle aged black nurse," and an "old, earth black lady," closing her article, "Power to the People." Around the same time, one interviewer noted that Angelou was "preparing to write the script for a television movie based on the life of civil rights activist Fannie Lou Hamer." Decades later, Angelou wrote a poem in honor of Johnetta Cole, the new Black female president of Bennett College. The poem, titled "I'm on My Journey Now," included lines narrating the accomplishments of dozens of Black leaders, from Mary McLeod Bethune to Frederick Douglass, from Martin Luther King Jr. to Malcolm X.[26]

At the same time, Angelou had no patience for those who would mythologize Blackness or Black suffering. "I do not wish to be called 'Momma' by men old enough to be my fathers," she wrote in "The Black Woman as Legend." "I do not accept willingly the expectation that I will always be kind and cheerful (even Aunt Jemima's smile is painted on). I am not flattered by the idea that I stay ever ready and lusting for a man's sexual attention (I get headaches, too). I do not accept the belief that I am so strong that being the most raped, most assaulted and the most burglarized does not destroy me."

"I am a breathing, hoping, living human being," she concluded. "I need work, shelter, food, love and respect. I will not willingly accept less."[27]

In the years after *I Know Why the Caged Bird Sings* became a literary classic, Angelou continued writing about sexual assault, finding space to do so in her poetry. In her poem, "Men," for instance, she depicted the constancy of sexual violence, portraying all men as a potential threat to the teenage girl in the poem. In another poem, "No No No No," she obliquely depicted a sexual violation, and in "Now Sheba Sings the Song," an illustrated poem released many years later, she wrote of her protagonist's body sparking a "frenzy" in "small men." As the scholar Yasmin Y. DeGout has argued, "By creating a community of listeners of witnesses, those who share in the pain or trauma of the speaker, such pieces undertake the healing process by creating a community of healers—those whose acknowledgement of the pain of the speaker allows healing to occur."[28]

Angelou also, to some extent, revised her own explanation as to why she had written about her sexual assault in the memoir. In 1972, she told an interviewer that Black men "talk about change when what they really mean, I think, is . . . to take over the positions of power white men have." Angelou wished to "clear the air in black America because, as I see it, that's what needs to be done. I'm going to write in 'Caged Bird' about all those black men with their fists balled up who talk about nation-buildin' time then go home to rape their nieces and step-daughters and teen-age girls who don't know beans about life. I'm goin' to tell it, because rape and incest are rife in the black community."[29] Years later, she told an interviewer that a "number of people" had asked her why she'd written about intraracial rape in *Caged Bird*—"I wanted people to see that the man was not totally an ogre. The hard thing about writing or directing or producing is to make sure one doesn't make the negative person totally negative. I try to tell the truth and preserve it in all artistic forms." She wished to humanize Mr. Freeman even as she depicted the violence he had inflicted on her—violence that, she maintained, was all too common.[30]

In 1987, Angelou told an interviewer about the "process by which she was able to forgive the man who raped her." This process involved "seeing the man. I don't mean physically seeing him. But trying to understand how really sick and alone that man was. I don't mean that I condone at all. But to try to understand is always healing." Still, she added, "there's not been a day since the rape 50 years ago during which I have not thought of it." This was especially true in her romantic relationships. It had been "very complicated, very confusing" for her to "get beyond distrust" of men, and she still didn't "feel as comfortable with huge men." But she strove to "get beyond the distrust every other day, every other hour."[31]

During these years, Angelou had a complex relationship with the women's liberation movement. She told one interviewer that she respected the movement, respected its leaders—"like Gloria Steinem and Germaine Greer and Betty Friedan," as well as Black women's rights activists like Florynce Kennedy and Shirley Chisholm—but that she didn't "have the energy to lend to it, directly, because I'm operating in another area." She told interviewers that too many white women were complicit in racist oppression, that too many were allowing white men to place them "on pedestals" by encouraging "the idea that she was a delicate, faint little creature who had to be soft and who had to be taken care of." The problem with pedestals, Angelou continued, is that "you can be knocked off so easily." She wished that white women were "working for the liberation of all" and forming stronger alliances with activists of color. "White women are protesting against staying at home and being homemakers," she told yet another interviewer, "but that's what black women would love to do." Black women often had more pressing problems. Still, in spite of her skepticism, in 1977 Angelou gave the opening declaration at the National Women's Conference in Houston. Six years later, she marched arm-in-arm with Gloria Steinem at the twentieth anniversary of the 1963 March on Washington.[32]

In the early 1970s, Angelou moved to a house in the wine country of northern California, an area that, she wrote to Alice Windom, often reminded her of West Africa. She became a visiting professor at California State University at Sacramento, which she enjoyed greatly, "successfully shielding my ignorance with many knowing and long looks."[33]

Angelou continued to look for love and for pleasure, marrying a white British sculptor, scholar, and artist named Paul du Feu, who had been briefly married to Germaine Greer. Paul—tall and handsome, a natty dresser and former nude model—sent Angelou silly birthday cards and addressed letters to her, "Dear sweet darling beautiful witty Maya." Angelou often told interviewers about enjoying romance and sex; the interviewers often wanted to talk about why she was not married to a Black man. "I think that we both, in ways that are not as different as they may seem, have been victimised by the theology of our age; or, to put it another way, everyone's sexuality, which involves one's relation to oneself and to others, which is one's only hope of freedom, and the only key to it, is, at least, compromised and, at worst, blasted by the mercantile-puritan ethic," James Baldwin wrote to her around the time she met Paul. "For, if one's forbidden to fuck (or to find any pleasure in it) one can assuredly never learn to make love." Paul and Maya divorced a decade later.[34]

In the years that followed, she wrote often for theaters and television networks and movie studios. She appeared in Alex Haley's Black family epic *Roots*, playing an elderly midwife, modeling her portrayal after Momma.[35] She met a young Black television anchor named Oprah Winfrey, and the two formed a lasting and productive friendship. Eventually, Angelou fulfilled a lifelong goal of directing a feature film, *Down in the Delta*, about an older Black woman sending her children and grandchildren back south to Mississippi. She kept writing—poetry, music, eventually greeting cards. In 1993, she read a poem at the inauguration of President Bill Clinton—wearing, the critic Kate Kellaway noted, "a coat with brass buttons, a strange reminder of the eight-year-old Maya Angelou who stood in a courtroom, terrified at the sight of the man who had raped her." This reading rocketed Angelou ever higher into the stratosphere of fame, resulting in endless requests for speeches and work. As one journalist aptly wrote of Angelou in the early 1970s, "Her energy is nonstop."[36]

And then there were the autobiographies. In the forty-three years following the publication of *Caged Bird*, Angelou wrote six more autobiographical volumes, five collectively covering the years between 1944 (the end of the period chronicled in *Caged Bird*) and 1968 (the year she began writing *Caged Bird*), and the sixth a more general reflection on her relationship with her mother. These autobiographies constitute more than a thousand pages of personal prose, almost all of it about her first forty years, the period in her life before she was an international celebrity. Angelou later told an interviewer that she hoped a thesis ran through her autobiographical work: "We may encounter many defeats, but we must not be defeated."[37]

Over all the years that she was writing about her early life, Angelou's editor remained Robert Loomis at Random House. A decade after *Caged Bird* was released, she acknowledged to an interviewer that their relationship had become "pretty famous in publishing," and that she might have been able to get far more money elsewhere, but that she "wouldn't leave Bob Loomis for a million dollars or ten." She needed an editor "who respects me and understands what I want to do." That was Loomis.[38]

But their relationship appears to have had its rough patches, especially early on. In 1973, Angelou's friend Mitford wrote to her, "What a perfectly foul time you seem to be having—I am sorry also v. puzzled, as I thought yr. editor was crazy about your book." The source of the tension is unclear. Perhaps it had to do with Angelou's decision to write frankly and explicitly about her experiences running a brothel or about selling sex herself in *Gather Together in My Name*, the second volume of her autobiographies, covering the years 1944 to 1948. Angelou later told the press that she had been concerned and conflicted about whether to do this and how readers would react. Notably, Angelou decided to write about these experiences, in spite of her concerns, in the early 1970s, at the exact moment when a powerful and vocal sex workers' rights movement was rising all across the country—but most strongly in the Bay Area, where she lived (and, indeed, which was funded by a radical church she attended). In any event, by the time *Gather Together* was released in 1974, it received glowing reviews and remained on the bestseller lists for six weeks, a fact about which Mitford was "ELATED." As she wrote to Angelou, "How truly smashing and deserved." Most commentators agreed, though the controversial critic John McWhorter wrote that in *Gather Together*, Angelou's once-radical "honesty begins to look more and more formulaic" and that she failed to fully interrogate or explicate her journey into sex work.[39]

Next came *Singin' and Swingin' and Gettin' Merry Like Christmas* in 1976 (covering 1949 to 1955), *The Heart of a Woman* in 1981 (covering 1957 to 1962), and *All God's Children Need Traveling Shoes* in 1986 (covering 1962 to 1965). Two more volumes—*A Song Flung Up to Heaven* in 2002 (covering 1965 to 1968) and *Mom & Me & Mom* in 2013—would follow several decades later, as Angelou was in the twilight of her career. Angelou's friend from Ghana, Alice Windom, later claimed in an oral history interview that Random House "really didn't push" *All God's Children* "because it's the one that has the most appeal for black folk." It was, after all, the biography that dealt with her Africa years, with her deep admiration for Malcolm X and her deep commitment to revolutionary pan-Africanism. "Her other, the other volumes of her autobiography have been neutral, racially neutral, and they have spoken very directly to women of all races," Windom recalled. *All God's Children* was too proudly Black, too strident. "Random House even had the nerve to issue a boxed set of her books for one Christmas, and they omitted that volume. They, they put, published all the other volumes of the autobiography, and a volume or two of poetry, and omitted *All God's Children Need Traveling Shoes*. But that's the book that tells about our time."[40]

At roughly the same time—during the 1980s, during the rise of the religious right and the Reagan presidency—many schools, from Alabama to Arizona, Minnesota to Maine, started banning *Caged Bird*. The American Library Association ranked Angelou among its top three "most challenged authors." Some critics, such as the Alabama State Textbook Committee, claimed that it promoted "bitterness and hatred against whites," and many others were offended by the graphic rape scenes—claiming they raised "sexual issues without giving them 'moral resolution.' " A mother in Maryland argued that *Caged Bird* should be banned because it is "sexually explicit, racially divisive and too graphic about lesbianism." Such challenges continued for decades.[41]

Throughout the 1970s, Angelou worked diligently on adapting *Caged Bird* to the silver screen. She kept interviewers vaguely apprised of her progress, telling one that she wanted to avoid "any gimmicks" and that she hoped to get her old friends Cicely Tyson and Roscoe Lee Browne to star in it. Yet her hopes for it were never quite realized. The film finally came out—as a TV movie—in 1979, with Constance Good playing Marguerite, Esther Rolle playing Momma, and Madge Sinclair playing Mrs. Flowers. It was quite faithful to the book, with one notable exception: it omitted Mr. Freeman's rape trial, one of the most complex, harrowing, and arguably empowering moments in the memoir. Reviews were mixed. The *Los Angeles Times* called it "one of those terribly uneven efforts that fail in totality but contain enough keyholes of insight and towering moments to make it worthwhile viewing." Future biographers would note that "Maya was often forced to watch her screenplays handed over to White male directors," and though Angelou wrote the screenplay, "she was excluded from many of the artistic decisions. The resulting film was a pale imitation of the original work."[42]

"I really loved all the Stamps part, scenery etc., and thought the girl who played Maya was jolly good (the boy who played Bailey not all that good, a bit wooden)," Mitford wrote to Angelou with tact. "I did not like the portrayal of Vivian Baxter, which came off v. superficial & not the V. Baxter I know. I suppose, however, that if I didn't know you I'd have taken it all in stride? I do believe that for the vast majority of viewers the whole film must have been enormously positive in the sense that so much of Maya & her particular vision of Black family life does come off so well."[43]

In the decades after *Caged Bird* was released and Angelou became a celebrity, her politics evolved markedly, shifting away from the more radical commitments of her youth and toward a more accommodating liberalism. Whereas Angelou had denounced American capitalism in fiery terms in the mid-1960s, by the early 1970s she was writing more critically of communism. Around the same time a reporter at the *Chicago Daily News* recounted, "Miss Angelou's faith in America is strong. She described her country's character as 'built on the conviction, "yes, I can." ' " In 1976 President Gerald Ford appointed Angelou—who had once been so critical of the American state, with its fetish for overthrowing left-leaning and postcolonial governments—to a committee to help plan ways to celebrate the country's bicentennial, an event her friend Alice Windom disdainfully called "America's 200th deathday." This transformation reflected Angelou's growing wealth and cultural cachet; the scholar and journalist Gary Younge would eventually note that her name and image appeared on "everything from bookends to pillows and mugs to wallhanging. . . . The pain of her early years, and the wisdom she has derived from it, has been commodified. It seems a long way from Malcolm X." By 1991 Angelou was even supporting the conservative Supreme Court nominee Clarence Thomas.[44]

Yet this evolution also moved Angelou beyond some of the reflexive cultural conservatism of her younger years. In 1974, she told an interviewer she didn't take her son to Europe with her when she was in *Porgy and Bess* because "I knew it wouldn't be good for him. Most of the male principals in the company were flamboyant homosexuals. . . . And I wondered how that would affect an eight-year-old boy." But she also began to defend Black gay men—especially her friend James Baldwin—and by the 1990s she was a strong supporter of gay rights. In 2009, years before most mainstream Democratic politicians, she was supporting the fight for same-sex marriage.[45]

And even as her political convictions changed, Angelou retained the radical vulnerability so notable in her autobiographical writings. She wrote about her own experiences with sexual violence, bigotry, sex work, loneliness, and despair. She refused to whitewash her identity as a Black woman. And she sought to model survival to others. "One of the first things that a young person must internalize, deep down in the blood and bones, is the understanding that although he may encounter many defeats, he must not be defeated," she told an interviewer in 1977. Rather, one must learn to "bite the bullet as it is shot into one's mouth, to bite it and stop it before it tears a hole in one's throat. One must learn to care for oneself first, so that one can then dare to care for someone else. That's what it takes to make the caged bird sing."[46]

31 • Frank Bethel, 1931–1952

Frank Bethel was a free man.

By March 1931 he was out of prison on a lengthy furlough; by October 1931 that furlough had become indefinite. In addition, he was newly single. Back in August 1930, immediately after he returned home to Monette on furlough, Frank and his wife, Gladys, had petitioned the chancery court for a divorce. The two had married five years before, when she was eighteen and he was twenty-one, but clearly their union had not been what the teenaged Gladys had expected: her husband had been incarcerated for almost half of the marriage. On the divorce petition the cause of divorce was listed as "Indignities." The divorce was immediately granted, which was surely a relief to Gladys, though she received no alimony to support her in raising the couple's young son.[1]

Further, by the time the governor formally granted Frank Bethel a full pardon in 1936, the former prisoner was already living far from Arkansas. A 1934 city directory lists Bethel as living with a new wife in Flint, Michigan. Frank's occupation is listed as auto worker. Apparently he had fled Arkansas not long after securing his release from prison and started a wholly new life. He had left his ex-wife and son back in Arkansas, as well as the rest of his family.[2]

One wonders what exactly Frank Bethel was fleeing from. His name had been splashed across the newspapers, and hundreds had seen him sentenced to death. His case was famous. Indeed, there are hints that his son's name was changed from Frank Bethel Jr. to John Junior Bethel. Most likely, Frank was notorious.[3]

Yet his notoriety in Arkansas did not follow him to Michigan. He easily found a job, as well as a new wife. Flossie Gambill was six years younger than her new husband; she had been born just twenty-five miles from him, in

Jonesboro, Arkansas, though it is unclear if they met before moving north. It is likewise unclear what she knew of Frank's past. She had relocated to Flint while her future husband was still incarcerated—quite possibly before he was incarcerated—to work as a domestic. The two ex-Arkansans married in Flint sometime between 1932 and 1934.[4]

Even as Frank established a new life in Michigan, his family remained in Arkansas. His ex-wife, Gladys, may have struggled to support herself. In 1930, with Frank still incarcerated, a census taker encountered the couple's son living with one of Frank's brothers, without Gladys. The same was still true in 1940, with Frank Sr. years out of prison and his son—listed as "Jackie"—fourteen years old. Frank's son appears once more in the documentary record during these years: in 1937, he and two other boys from Monette were arrested for committing several burglaries. Two of the boys were sent to the state industrial school, but, the newspaper recorded, "Frank Bethel Jr., 11 was released providing he return to his parents in Michigan."[5]

This was not the Bethel family's only scrape with the Arkansas justice system. In 1932, Frank's younger brother Fred—who, recall, had previously been arrested for sexual assault—was charged with assault with intent to kill. He had apparently gotten into a fight with another man in a Monette pool hall over a gambling debt, which ended when Fred slashed the man's head with a knife. The newspaper noted he was the "brother of Frank Bethel who was once sentenced to die in the electric chair." Fred was eventually able to strike a bargain with the prosecutor, agreeing to plead guilty in exchange for a sentence of just eight months.[6]

Years passed. Fred joined his brother and relocated to Flint for some time, though he would eventually return to Monette. Frank's other brothers stayed put.[7] Frank himself remained employed, in Flint, though perhaps not too gainfully, for he and Flossie moved houses every few years. As the United States entered World War II, Frank was working for Chevrolet, and then Buick, two of the many car companies growing unthinkably rich producing trucks and planes for the military and convertibles and sports cars for the exploding middle class. By 1947, though, he had returned to his original profession: cutting hair. He spent the next five years as a barber. On December 6, 1952, Frank Bethel died at the age of forty-nine, apparently at a hospital in Detroit. He was buried beneath a squat tombstone in Evergreen Cemetery, near Flint. Three decades later, Flossie joined him.[8]

Frank's only child—Frank Jr., or Jackie, or John, as he ultimately came to be known—eventually relocated to Detroit. He served in the U.S. Navy during

World War II. He then moved to Twinsburg, Ohio, where he worked as a tool and diemaker for Chrysler for twenty-two years. He joined a Christian church, a Masonic lodge, and his United Auto Workers local. He acquired the nickname "Honest John." He married late, in 1971, and died early, in 1990.[9] By all appearances, John was able to escape his father's name, his father's family, and his family's reputation.

32 • Mike Wallace, 1931–1983

The details of Mike Wallace's life are fewer and farther between than those of Frank Bethel's. But he too was free.

Upon his release from The Walls in 1931, Mike returned home to Monette, where he apparently settled into an unremarkable life with his new wife, Elly. A census taker in 1940 encountered the two living in a $1,500 home that they owned, with Mike's occupation listed, predictably, as "Farming." Mike's mother still lived nearby; his father was long dead. For the rest of his life, Mike appears to have gone by his birth name—Roy, or Roy Thomas, or simply R.T. This is the only evidence of an attempt to escape any notoriety he might have endured from his years in the courtroom and in the penitentiary. When a local man received a death sentence for murder in 1934, the *Blytheville Courier-News* noted, "It was the first time since Frank Bethel and Mike Wallace were given the death sentence in April, 1928, that a verdict calling for the supreme penalty was read in the courthouse here. Bethel and Wallace were sentenced to electrocution but were eventually freed." Soon, though, even the newspapers ceased to mention his name.[1]

In contrast, the trial's other major players remained public figures. E. E. Alexander, for instance, continued his successful criminal practice, representing such notorious clients as a mother charged with drowning her newborn infant. He briefly tried returning to politics, challenging the area's congressman in 1934, but a defeat sent him back to his law office. By 1936, Alexander was the longest continuously practicing attorney in Mississippi County. Four years later, he was dead, following what the newspaper called "a brief illness."

He was just fifty-nine. The *Courier-News* lauded his success in "famous cases of Mississippi County" and "his brilliance as a courtroom orator."[2]

Judge G. E. Keck stayed on the circuit bench until his retirement in 1944. For the next dozen years, he resumed private law practice, serving for some time as president of the Blytheville Bar Association and continuing to work until shortly before his death, at the age of seventy-one, in 1958. The *Courier-News* memorialized him as a "beloved Blytheville lawyer and judge."[3]

Prosecutor S. L. Gladish traveled, perhaps, the rockiest road of these big Blytheville attorneys. Just a few years after leaving the post of prosecutor in 1932, he ran for county judge and soon became involved in a very public re-election scandal; it certainly appeared that Gladish and his longtime financial backer, Robert E. Lee Wilson, were conspiring to suppress votes. Thus shrouded in controversy, Gladish quietly completed his term and then returned again to private practice. His final years were not happy ones. In 1953, a building he owned in Osceola, worth an estimated $250,000, burned to the ground; the next year, his wife died at the age of seventy-three; Gladish himself succumbed the year after that. He was eighty years old.[4]

Mike Wallace—now known as Roy—outlived them all. He spent the half century following his release and pardon as a moderately prosperous and apparently unfamous farmer (and, for a time, furniture salesman) in and around Monette, dying at the age of seventy-nine in 1983. Elly—Mike's wife for fifty-three years—died in 1995, just past her eighty-eighth birthday. They appear to have left behind no children.[5] Wallace was not eulogized in the *Courier-News*, as the attorneys were, but neither was he condemned. Instead, he simply went unmentioned.

33 • Pearl, 1929–

Of all this book's characters, Pearl disappears most completely from the historical record in the final years of her life. Perhaps that was by design.

The first years, following Bethel's and Wallace's trials, are easy enough to track. Recall that she had been teaching school in Leachville at the time of the assault, having recently separated from her husband. By 1930, a year after the second trial, Pearl had returned to Black River, Arkansas, to the home of her older brother. It is unclear if her four-year-old son, Barton, was living with her at this time; he is not listed among the household on the census, but neither is he listed as living at the home of his father, Onus (who was then a resident of the Arkansas State Hospital for Nervous Diseases), or with Pearl's parents.[1]

Thereafter the records become vaguer and sparser. In 1932, while still in Arkansas, Pearl married a young man whose residence was listed as Los Angeles. Perhaps following him, perhaps fleeing him, she then left Arkansas, apparently for good. She traveled west, as millions of other southerners were doing, looking for opportunity in the burgeoning Sun Belt even as her home state was ravaged by the Depression and the winds of the Dust Bowl. In 1943, her second marriage apparently over, she wed again, to a tall, fair Latvian émigré named Arnold, in Reno, Nevada. A few years later, the two were living in Oakland, California, where Arnold was working as a painter-contractor. For a time, Pearl found work as a bookkeeper. Barton, meanwhile, had grown into a ruddy, strapping young man of nineteen and was living in Oakland following his discharge from the U.S. Navy. Sometime after 1950, Pearl returned to Reno.

Her third marriage lasted until the mid-1960s, when it dissolved either because of death or divorce, for Arnold remarried in Arizona in 1968. Records show that Barton lived until 1999, leaving behind several children, some still living. But of Pearl, virtually nothing. She simply is gone.[2]

For a time, I sought to find her, to figure out how she spent her final years and, indeed, to discover when and where she died. I dug and dug; I hired a professional genealogist, who found Pearl's relatives, but not her. In early 2020, I wrote letters to several of her descendants, asking if they would be willing "to share any memories you have, or family stories you've heard, about Pearl."

"I know a fair amount about her genealogy and the trial," I added, "but I don't know much about her personally, her family, her subsequent life, etc. She strikes me as a courageous person, and I'd like for her to be remembered in that way. I completely understand if you do not wish to speak with me—if this dredges up painful memories or because you don't know who I am. From the research I've conducted so far, it seems to me that Pearl was mistreated by many in the media and legal establishment in the 1920s."

I received no reply. If any conclusion can be drawn from the relative absence of records, it seems that after such trauma and humiliation, Pearl was able to successfully start a new life, taking a new last name and moving to a new place, thousands of miles from the Arkansas Delta.

34 • Virgie, 1936–2005

Back in December of 1936, within days of Bubbles Clayton and Jim X. Carruthers's long-awaited first hearing in federal district court, Virgie got married. She was twenty-one years old, and her new husband, a young man named Henry, was the same age. Henry was a short, stout man, blond-haired and blue-eyed, another son of precariously situated Delta farmers. He did not have much education, having left school around when Virgie did, after the fourth grade. Nor did he have a sterling reputation, having divorced his first wife just weeks before marrying Virgie. But he offered a stability that was undoubtedly important to a young woman about whom gossip flew.[1]

"Accusers of black men benefited enormously from their status as whites, and a white woman's word was usually enough to convict the black man she accused," the historian Lisa Lindquist Dorr noted in her monumental study of white women accusing Black men of rape in Jim Crow Virginia. But a "guilty verdict did not guarantee a woman's place in the sheltered arena of white womanhood. Indeed, her credibility and innocence remained only as long as she conformed to social standards. For the victim the trial was never over."[2] For Virgie, already separated from one husband, known to be dating around—indeed, alone in a car with a date at the time she was allegedly raped—remarriage was undoubtedly a gambit for respectability.

Few records of Virgie's and Henry's life together survive. At one point, the two moved to Little Rock, but it appears that they lived most of their marriage in and around the Delta. Henry worked as a trucker; Virgie kept house. Their family grew. On February 22, 1997, Henry died, at the age of eighty-one, following sixty years of marriage. "Dont know much to say, except I miss him so much, but I have no regrets," Virgie wrote to a relative six days later. "I did all I could for him as long as I had him. I feel he is in a much better place. And I will meet him again some day." Virgie herself died at the age of eighty-nine in 2005. At the time of her death, she had six grandchildren, thirteen great-grandchildren, and six great-great-grandchildren.[3]

35 • Bubbles Clayton, 1939–

Several weeks after the execution of Clayton and Carruthers in 1939, a newspaper in Nebraska reported that "Progressives" across the country were in an uproar over "outrages against the Negro people in two southern states." The first was Florida, where white police officers had tortured "two Negro youths." The second was in Arkansas, where "two other youths, allegedly framed on charges of rape, were legally lynched."

"Torture of Youths, Draw Nationwide Protests," read the headline of the Omaha paper.[1]

Just what the anonymous author was referring to is unclear, as no other records of these protests survive. Yet this piece gestures tantalizingly to the rising anger over injustice that was birthing what we now refer to as the Civil Rights Movement. Occurrences such as the Montgomery Bus Boycott and the March on Washington did not emerge out of nowhere; they were the products of a rage and a quest for justice that had been germinating for centuries. The "legal lynching" of Clayton and Carruthers was one more cobblestone on the blood-soaked road toward freedom.

No record remains of what happened to the remains of Clear "Bubbles" Clayton. It is possible that his family claimed his body after the execution, that they buried him in a private grave in Mississippi County, or even in the state of Mississippi, where he was born. But it is also possible that his family was unable to retrieve his body. In such cases, the authorities at Tucker often had other inmates drag the condemned man's lifeless remains out of the electric chair, place them in a wicker basket, carry the basket to a hearse, and then have the hearse drive the body to a local medical school. Other electrocuted men were buried in packed, shallow pits on a hill overlooking a grove of pine trees, not far from the prison. This crowded, haphazard place was the final indignity Jim Crow authorities could inflict on men sentenced to die.[2]

Bubbles's family moved around quite a lot during these years, probably attesting to some degree of financial insecurity. Whereas in 1920, census takers encountered his parents, Clay and Edie, in Mississippi County, by 1930 they were renting a home across the Mississippi River in Pemiscot County, Missouri, and by 1940—just months after their son's execution—they were in Phillips County, Arkansas, the site of the Elaine massacre. All these locales were deep in cotton country, and in each Clay and Edie were living near their son Clarence, Bubbles's brother.[3]

What happened to Clay and Edie following 1950 is unclear, as are most details of their lives before this year. Many of their descendants ultimately left the Delta, following the well-trodden paths of the Great Migration to Chicago and St. Louis and Detroit. Clarence Clayton lived until 1989, when he died in southern Illinois as quite an old man. He had taught school in Missouri and Illinois and been the pastor at churches throughout the region, attaining numerous leadership positions within the Baptist church; he had served in the army in World War II. Clarence's obituary concluded, "Eight brothers and two sisters also preceded him in death." Remarkably, no number of children anywhere near this high were ever listed as living with Clay and Edie during the years in question. Most likely, several of their children—Bubbles's siblings—did not survive childhood. Clarence's obituary also noted that he was a member of the NAACP.[4]

The afterlives of the other major players of the Clayton-Carruthers trial are far better documented. Sheriff Clarence Wilson, for instance, died just six years later, in 1945, at the age of fifty-three. He had suffered from debilitating "heart trouble" for some time, though in the years after the execution he was healthy enough to remain politically active and even served briefly as a county judge. His longtime deputy, Arch Lindsey, also succumbed to heart disease, a decade later. To the end of his life, Lindsey had remained a police officer—as well as, apparently, a violent racist. Indeed, the sixty-four-year-old Lindsey suffered his fatal heart attack while "scuffling" with three Black men he had spotted—their car supposedly "swerving back and forth"—while he was out for a drive with his wife in 1955. He and Wilson were buried in the same Blytheville cemetery.[5]

Justice Edgar McHaney died on May 24, 1948, leaving his money to his wife, his shotgun to one son, his fishing tackle to a second son, his watch to a third son, and his law books to "any one or more of his sons who become lawyers before his death." The *Arkansas Democrat* called him "a liberal as that word is defined by men who believe that while we should lift our eyes to the stars, we should keep our feet on the ground." One of his colleagues on the Arkansas Supreme Court told the press, "No man tried harder or with greater success to do justice to litigants, rich and poor alike. His sympathies were always for those who appeared to be oppressed." Well, perhaps. It is worth noting that McHaney wrote the state supreme court opinion preserving the all-white primary for years to come. Maybe it is also worth noting that one of his sons served as a prosecutor at the Nuremberg trials.[6]

Clayton's and Carruthers's first attorney, Arthur Adams, died just weeks after McHaney. Ironically, he was in the midst of challenging McHaney for a seat on the Arkansas Supreme Court at the time, Adams collapsing after a political rally just hours before the polls opened. The Associated Press noted in an obituary that he was a supporter of Arkansas's "civil rights program, opposing President Truman and his civil rights proposals. He was instrumental in calling the first meeting of the States' Righters in Jackson, Miss., protesting the nomination of Truman." The obituary did not mention his role in defending Clayton and Carruthers.[7]

By the time McHaney and Adams died, Scipio Africanus Jones had been gone for years. He died not even four years after Clayton and Carruthers, in 1943, at roughly eighty years of age (his precise birth date has never been known). The *Arkansas Gazette*—which had once instructed readers not to vote for him for school board, decrying the dangers of having a Black man in such a position—eulogized Jones as "one of Arkansas's best known Negroes and recognized throughout the United States as a leader for his race." Born a slave, he had died a rich man and early civil rights icon.[8]

The lawyer most responsible for Clayton's and Carruthers's years-long survival, John A. Hibbler, outlived the others. Indeed, he outlived several of his children before dying at the age of eighty-four, amidst the Civil Rights Movement. A year after his death, in 1963, his nephew, Al Hibbler—an orphan whom John had raised—made headlines when he was arrested by the Birmingham police, protesting discrimination in that city. By this time Al Hibbler was nationally known as a blind baritone singer with an unusually versatile voice, equally comfortable in the blues or "songbook standards." He had risen from Little Rock clubs and come to fame as part of Duke Ellington's band, but following his civil rights activity many labels were afraid to sign him. This obstacle stymied his career, but, in the spirit of his uncle, he continued to perform sporadically into the 1990s, his "vibrato as over-the-top as ever," reported the *New York Times*.⁹

Writing in 2005, the historian Sammy L. Morgan noted that the "patterns established and strengthened" in the Arkansas Delta "during the mid-twentieth century have proven remarkably persistent. More than seventy years since the beginning of the New Deal, forty years after President Lyndon Johnson launched his Great Society, the region continues to be rural, agricultural and poor." Mississippi County had been bleeding residents for decades, the houses of tenants and small owners disappearing from the countryside, entire farming communities devastated. "Sixty years of pursuing low-paying, nonunionized jobs have produced a region still struggling with poverty," Morgan concluded.¹⁰

But there is another legacy of the Delta—a legacy of organizing and of resistance. By 1940, the STFU had lost more than 90 percent of its members, but despite tremendous odds the union had survived the vicious crackdown of the late 1930s and quietly spread throughout much of the South, continuing to call for "a redistribution of the land and cooperative farming projects." By the end of World War II, its remaining members had changed its name to the National Farm Labor Union (NFLU) and turned their focus to California. One of the NFLU's first extended strikes in the late 1940s—at the immense DiGiorgio Fruit Corporation farms near Bakersfield—helped to inspire a young man named Cesar Chavez, picking cotton near Corcoran, to join the NFLU and begin organizing farm workers himself. Meanwhile, back in Arkansas, former STFU local leaders became important organizers for the state's first rural NAACP branches and regional Student Nonviolent Coordinating Committee (SNCC) field offices.¹¹ As one union historian wrote, half a century ago:

> Today you can hardly find anyone in the Arkansas Delta who once belonged to the Southern Tenant Farmers' Union. But, on a warm and silent night, if you stop your car on the shoulder of Highway 63 near Marked Tree, if you can hear with your whole being, listen:
> From that clump of oaks and sycamores where a ramshackle old Negro church used to stand, could you hear the rich rhythmic voices distantly singing—
>
> The Union is a-marching,
> We shall not be moved . . .¹²

36 • Jim X. Carruthers, 1939–

In 1939, in the days following Clayton's and Carruthers's execution, newspapers across the country ran stories about their deaths. An Associated Press report repeated the inaccurate tale about Carruthers confessing in the last moments of his life, and so newspapers from Nevada to Pennsylvania, Texas to Washington, D.C., spread that story. Even the *St. Louis Post-Dispatch,* which had reported so courageously on the case, as well as the *Chicago Defender* and *Atlanta Daily World,* two of the most important Black newspapers in the country, uncritically carried the story of the confession.[1]

One wonders if Jim X. Carruthers's family read these accounts. Recall that a white supremacist mob had chased Carruthers's family off their land in 1935. Jim X.'s young wife, Lorraine, and her young daughter, Dora, had been forced to flee to the home of her in-laws, James and Virgie Carruthers, their wealth and land lost to the horde. James and Virgie, meanwhile, had sought refuge in the East St. Louis home of Jim X.'s sister, Sue Willie, who had used knowledge she gained working on hog farms back in Mississippi to open the first Black-owned barbeque pit in the Illinois city. It was a celebrated establishment, well known to Black motorists, and Sue Willie made so much money from it that she bought a number of rowhouses and rented them out.[2]

Dora Carruthers was eight years old when the state of Arkansas electrocuted her father. In the years that followed, she came of age surrounded by friends and family, apparently spending some time in the Mississippi County home of her mother's parents, who had remained, before eventually relocating to Aliquippa, Pennsylvania.[3] There she found work for the Jones & Laughlin steel mill; her family prospered. Dora's mother, Lorraine, moved to Toledo, Ohio, and then to Chicago. As Dora grew older and had children, and then grandchildren, of her own, Lorraine—whom descendants called "Toota"—frequently came to visit, especially in the summers. In contrast to her level-headed daughter, Toota loved to dance, to play cards and pinochle. A tiny woman with an irrepressible spirit, she always brought presents when she visited Aliquippa. She died in 2006 at ninety-two years of age. Her daughter, Dora, also lived a long life, succumbing suddenly in 2017.

Dora had married a man named Roosevelt Barden, and they in turn had eight children, including Roosevelt Jr. One of Roosevelt Jr.'s children was the future Trina Nicholson, born in Aliquippa some three decades after her great-grandfather, Jim X. Carruthers, died. Along with her Aunt Gail Terry, Trina became the keeper of her family's history. Gail possessed a trunk full of documents, with papers going back to the days of slavery, and Trina did extensive genealogical research of her own. She also grew up hearing stories of the great-grandfather who was legally lynched by the Jim Crow establishment. Trina credits his death by electrocution with her lifelong fear of electricity, a reluctance to plug in anything.[4]

It was Trina whom I contacted in early 2020. When we first spoke, I was sitting at the rickety desk in what had to be one of the worst motel rooms in Little Rock. For the second time in a year, I had traveled to Arkansas to learn more about her family, but, ironically, Trina's ancestors had departed decades before, settling not far from my own family, in western Pennsylvania. Trina herself had moved to Alabama. Thus, our conversation took place over the phone.

We spoke for more than an hour that evening. I was tired from a day of archival research but speaking with her was invigorating, for Trina and her relatives had discovered and preserved so much about their family. (I even learned that Trina had named her daughter after Maya Angelou.) Only at the end of our conversation did I ask her the seemingly simply question that had puzzled me for years: why them? Of all the Black farmers in this rural county in the Jim Crow South, why had Clayton and Carruthers been framed by the police in the first place? Trina seemed genuinely surprised that I hadn't figured it out yet.

It was the car.[5]

Even all these decades later, Jim X. Carruthers's grand, six-cylinder Chevrolet remains memorable. It was a fine car, big, curved, with good tires and a menacing grill. It had cost $349 or so, a considerable sum in the Delta of the 1930s.[6] Few other Black people in Mississippi County owned so nice a car; crucially, few white people did either.

It was his car that led the authorities to target Carruthers, generations of descendants have believed. It was his car that led directly to Carruthers's arrest and prosecution. It was his car that led to the arrest of his mother.

There is considerable evidence to support this hypothesis. Trina Nicholson grew up hearing that Sheriff Wilson tried to obtain the title to the car to pay for his medical bills. This precisely mirrors Carruthers's testimony at trial, where he told the jurors of a visit Wilson made to death row at Tucker, to try to convince Carruthers to sign a bill of sale, signing the car over to Wilson, "to go on his doctor and hospital bills."

"I did not do it," Carruthers testified.[7]

At trial, the prosecutor, Denver Dudley, devoted a bizarrely large amount of his cross-examination to questions about the car. How had Carruthers afforded such a nice and expensive car, he wanted to know? Did he pay for it in installments or all at once? How did he pay for the gasoline and the oil? Clearly, the car rankled the authorities. Carruthers's answers to these questions were nonplussed. "I got money from my mama and sister to help pay for it," he replied. He paid in monthly installments, contributing the money he earned picking and chopping cotton.[8]

According to family members, who entrusted their stories to Trina, Sheriff Wilson even petitioned Judge Killough to get the judge to sign the car over to the lawman. The judge was sympathetic, but Arthur Adams intervened, claiming he'd already gotten the car to pay his legal bills. This enraged Sheriff Wilson, which is why he went out and arrested Carruthers's mother, Virgie, and held her in prison for weeks on trumped up charges. Only when it became clear that Virgie couldn't sign away her son's fine car did the authorities release her.[9]

The details of this story are not exactly verifiable, but every time the Carruthers family's oral tradition can be compared to the written records, the two match precisely. Without the family's extraordinary historical memory and prodigious research efforts, the story of the travails of Clayton and Carruthers would not be as rich or as complete as it is today. The car is the best answer we have to the question of why the authorities were so determined to convict these particular Black men—first of the attempted murder of the sheriff and later of rape. One of them had become too conspicuously prosperous, his success an affront to the Jim Crow economic and social order, his shining car a claim that, to many, was intolerable.

37 • Thurgood Marshall, 1977

It was ten o'clock on Monday morning, March 28, 1977, and Justice Thurgood Marshall was sitting in his imposing chair, behind an imposing table, within the imposing Supreme Court building, staring at two white attorneys who were about to speak. It was the first time either attorney had argued before the Supreme Court, and surely both were at least a little nervous. Marshall, for his part, had been a member of the court for almost a decade; for the court's first Black justice, this morning's argument was almost routine.

The first attorney rose. "Mr. Chief Justice and may it please the court," he began, using the opening words dictated by custom. "I am David Kendall and I represent petitioner Ehrlich Anthony Coker, who has been condemned by the State of Georgia to be electrocuted for the crime of rape."[1]

Kendall then quickly recounted Coker's disturbing story—his client had barely begun serving three life sentences (for rape and murder) when he escaped from custody, broke into a nearby home, and raped a sixteen-year-old housewife. Coker was quickly arrested, again tried for rape, and sentenced to die by electrocution under a Georgia rape statute that provided penalties for rape ranging from one year in prison to death.

The justices soon began peppering Kendall with their typical barrage of questions. Justice Marshall stayed silent. The lawyer for the state of Georgia, assistant state attorney general B. Dean Grindle Jr., rose to speak. Marshall still stayed silent. It wasn't until thirty-five minutes into the oral arguments, as Grindle was discussing "aggravating circumstances"—which, under Georgia law, had to be present for death to be imposed—that Marshall finally asked his first question.

"General Grindle," he boomed, "is there any statute or anything else that says what standard shall be used to decide whether it is aggravated or not?"

Grindle stammered that the standard was contained in state law, directing the justice to the proper place in the Georgia Code. Marshall asked a few follow-ups, about the proper page number in the Georgia statute book, and then fell silent again. Other than a quick question of clarification twenty minutes later, he remained silent for the rest of the oral arguments in Coker's case.[2]

It is impossible to know what was going through Marshall's head that day, but it seems likely that he went into court with his mind already made up. After all, he had vastly more experience than any of his colleagues with the ins and outs of southern rape cases. Furthermore, he had personally helped craft the very legal strategy that undergirded Coker's appeal.

Back in 1939, just a few months after the execution of Clayton and Carruthers, the Internal Revenue Service ruled that the NAACP—as an organization engaged in lobbying (for an anti-lynching law)—would have to pay taxes on the contributions it received in support of its high-profile cases. This decision prompted Marshall to set up a new, separate, legal branch of the NAACP with no involvement in lobbying. Thus, on March 20, 1940, the NAACP Legal Defense and Educational Fund (LDF) came into existence. By this point, Charles Hamilton Houston had departed the NAACP's formal hierarchy, so Marshall became LDF's first director-counsel.[3] In this role, he had general authority over the NAACP's vast menu of litigation. But he also frequently traveled to litigate personally, especially for explosive criminal trials. Not long after becoming LDF director, for instance, Marshall traveled to Connecticut to defend a Black chauffeur accused of rape by a white socialite, a case that generated ravenous press attention, especially after Marshall helped to secure an acquittal.[4]

A year later, in 1941, the United States entered World War II, and NAACP membership skyrocketed. Nearly a million Black men and women entered the U.S. military, and soon NAACP investigators were being called on to halt instances of Jim Crow injustice.[5] Just days after the Japanese attacked Pearl Harbor, a lieutenant at a training camp in eastern Pennsylvania announced that he would consider any "relations" between Black men and white women to be rape and thus punishable by death, necessitating an immediate NAACP protest and resulting in a hasty revocation.[6] This episode proved to be a harbinger; it quickly became clear that Black soldiers and sailors were wildly overrepresented in military courts martial, especially for rape.[7] Interracial rape cases became an even more important part of LDF's docket. The Association was inundated with pleas from Black soldiers and sailors—from France to Guam to Australia—facing court martial or punishment for allegedly assaulting white women. "Dear sur i am in trouble and i need your help i have ben sentious to deth," wrote a soldier in Germany with the memorable name of Earnest Shakespeare.[8] One young NAACP lawyer (an army veteran) was assigned the task of triaging the increasing flood of missives from condemned Black servicemen, a task that instantly consumed his waking hours.[9]

With Marshall at the helm, LDF won numerous appeals for mercy or outright reversal, often highlighting improper procedure or violations of due process.[10] Yet the Association continued to make frequent use of the gendered arguments it had relied on in years past, seizing on the narrative that crystallized after Scottsboro and deploying many stereotypes about promiscuity and veracity. In many cases, for instance, the Association's strategy centered on impugning a woman's believability by calling her a "prostitute." As the NAACP claimed in a brief, the exchange of sex for money was evidence of consent, and, further, the Association could find no case "in Anglo American jurisprudence in which a conviction of rape has been permitted when payment had been offered and accepted on the spot."[11] Other NAACP lawyers labeled such women "hysterical." In one memo, LDF attorney Constance Baker Motley wrote that "the character of the victim was so low that one can hardly conceive of her offering any resistance at all to sexual intercourse."[12]

Marshall himself took on perhaps the most infamous of the military cases. In 1942, three Black soldiers stationed at Camp Claiborne in Louisiana were charged with raping a white woman. Initially Marshall doubted their innocence—until, that is, he discovered that the white woman had an infectious case of gonorrhea, but the Black soldiers were not infected. Marshall took the soldiers' case all the way to the Supreme Court—his first appearance before that body—and got their convictions thrown out on technical grounds. Marshall then represented them at their court martial, where they were convicted and sentenced to death, yet because of NAACP lobbying, President Roosevelt commuted their sentences to life a year later, and a year after that they were paroled.[13]

In the years following World War II, the letters continued to stream in to NAACP offices, begging for legal help. Sisters wrote on behalf of brothers, fathers on behalf of sons, churches on behalf of congregants.[14] The NAACP's expertise in rape cases became a matter of common knowledge: "Knowing your interest in cases of this kind I suggest you investigate," wrote one man, attaching a clipping. "If the man is actually guilty of rape, why you can drop it like a hot potato on a piece of dry ice. I don't know the fellow [but to] me this case looks fishy."[15] Stretched perpetually thin, the national office usually forwarded such pleas to local branch offices, which in turn continued to plead for financial support.[16] Marshall was stretched to the breaking point, overworked and feeling guilty that he could not do more in more cases.[17] Yet particularly compelling facts sometimes convinced Marshall to personally undertake representation, as in the case of Mack Ingram—a Black sharecropper charged with assault with intent to rape for looking at a seventeen-year-old white girl in a "leering" manner from seventy feet away—and Ozzie Jones—a Black man charged with raping a white woman in spite of the fact that he'd recently been circumcised and his penis was thus "stitched and swollen" at the time.[18]

Perhaps the most famous rape case Marshall took on was that of the "Groveland Boys"—three Black youths wrongly accused of raping a white woman in 1949.[19] Eventually, this case and the other, carefully selected rape cases that Marshall brought to the Supreme Court in the 1940s and 1950s succeeded in broadening and deepening the criminal procedure precedents set by rape cases in the 1930s. These cases entrenched the right to counsel, the right to remain silent, the right to a trial free from mob violence or influence, the right to not have a coerced confession used against oneself, and the right to a jury of one's peers selected without discrimination. By the time President John F. Kennedy appointed Marshall to a federal appellate judgeship in 1961, the NAACP's rape docket had changed the face of U.S. law.[20]

It was in the years following World War II that Marshall and LDF began to use these rape cases to try to secure one additional right: the right to be free from capital punishment. In the late 1940s, as they were assisting with the representation of seven Black men in Virginia sentenced to death for allegedly raping a white woman, Association attorneys started to embrace a novel tactic—one that would have a profound impact on American law (and on the case of Ehrlich Coker). Following the lead of more radical lawyers in the Civil Rights Congress, they helped to compile *statistical evidence* of the extent to which the death penalty was applied discriminatorily against Black men. Drawing on the Association's long experience of marshalling statistics in its anti-lynching work—indeed, this had been one of Marshall's first freelance tasks for the NAACP—these lawyers showed that Black men were many times more likely to be executed for rape than were white men. Marshall was actively involved in the formation of this strategy. And although these statistics were insufficient to save the seven defendants in Virginia (who were executed in

1951), other attorneys began to use the statistical data to argue for the end of the death penalty.[21] When, in 1963, Supreme Court Justice Arthur Goldberg wrote a brief dissent asking whether capital punishment might be unconstitutional, LDF seized the moment. "His opinion signaled that the time to launch the effort had arrived," Jack Greenberg, Marshall's successor as head of LDF, remembered. "Shortly afterward, I announced to the board that we would launch a full-scale attack on capital punishment for rape. By mid-decade, we had seventeen cases."[22]

The attorneys at LDF quickly dispatched students to every county in the South to compile updated, authoritative statistics on the imposition of capital punishment for rape. The earliest test case to use these statistics was on behalf of William Maxwell, a Black man sentenced to death for rape in Arkansas. Throughout the 1960s, Maxwell's attorneys repeatedly appealed his case to the Supreme Court, but the justices refused to rule on the merits of the case. Meanwhile, Thurgood Marshall continued his steady ascent through the federal government, leaving his circuit judgeship in 1965 to become U.S. solicitor general—the lawyer who represents the federal government before the Supreme Court. In 1967, President Lyndon Johnson nominated Marshall to join the court himself. He soon became its first Black justice.[23]

Undoubtedly, though, he was keeping tabs on his former civil rights colleagues. The same year that Marshall joined the court, LDF attorneys won stays of execution in class action suits on behalf of death row prisoners in Florida and California. The next year LDF held the first national conference on capital punishment. Meanwhile, the NAACP continued attacking the death penalty on multiple fronts, soon expanding its mandate to represent alleged murderers as well as rapists. In 1971, LDF brought three death penalty cases to the Supreme Court, and allies brought a fourth. As Greenberg recalled, "By then we represented more than half of the 640-plus defendants on death row." They argued in front of their former colleague, Marshall. Several of the defendants in LDF's capital cases before the court that term were almost certainly guilty, and the details in one rape case were so horrifying that several LDF secretaries "refused to type the briefs because they thought he should be executed," recounted Greenberg.[24]

Nonetheless, on June 29, 1972, the Supreme Court decided *Furman v. Georgia*, which consolidated LDF's death penalty cases, declaring by a vote of five-to-four that capital punishment was *unconstitutional* as applied nationwide. The justices could not agree on a legal rationale, however, so—in a highly unusual development—each member of the court wrote separately. Marshall was one of just two justices to conclude that the death penalty was unconstitutional per se, and he was one of just two justices to invoke the statistics documenting capital punishment's extraordinary racial disparity.[25] The plurality of the justices left open the possibility that capital punishment could be applied constitutionally. Many scholars have noted that this fractured opinion would eventually weaken and destroy *Furman*.[26] Yet, notably, prior scholars have not appreciated the extent to which *Furman* built on many decades of NAACP representation of Black men accused of rape. Indeed, although *Furman* did not much discuss the key issues addressed in most of the NAACP's rape cases—right to counsel, jury composition, coerced confession—Justice William O. Douglas cited the example of one NAACP rape case to support the proposition that discretionary capital punishment statutes are unconstitutional, and Justice William J. Brennan cited the Scottsboro Boys case to support the proposition that death cases are different from all other cases, especially when it comes to the right to counsel.[27]

In the years after *Furman*, public opinion swung sharply in favor of the death penalty; dozens of states began looking for ways to create capital punishment schemes in line with the court's decision. In 1976 the Supreme Court revived the death penalty—so long as its application was guided by standards—by another five-to-four vote, in *Gregg v. Georgia*. Justice Marshall had tried to convince his colleagues to go the other way, recounting "stories in the judges' conferences about his own experience defending poor black men in front of all-white juries," wrote his biographer Juan Williams. "He talked about being the only one of the justices ever to have defended a client in a death penalty case." But it was no use, and Marshall dissented categorically. "The decision was more than a defeat," continued Williams. "It signaled a new isolation for Marshall." The court was drifting rightward, and Marshall eventually came to see *Gregg* as "the instant he lost touch with the Court." He read his dissent aloud in open court, then went home and suffered two mild heart attacks. Nonetheless, between *Furman* and *Gregg*, as states were altering their death penalty statutes, nearly all declined to resuscitate capital punishment for rape. This was the context in which Marshall and the other justices heard arguments in *Coker*.[28]

Indeed, Marshall was undoubtedly aware that Coker's lawyer, David Kendall—a white man who had registered Black voters in Mississippi during Freedom Summer—was an LDF lawyer. The NAACP was so determined to destroy the death penalty that it had taken on the case of Ehrlich Coker, a white man, to do it. And though the Association had submitted several petitions to the Supreme Court that term on behalf of Black men facing the death penalty for rape, the court had chosen to hear only the case of Coker—the only white man in the bunch. "Yet the LDF did not hesitate to take the case forward," recounted the historian Catherine Jacquet. The Association knew it had to be the organization to bring this issue before the court because, as Kendall later recalled, "we had many, many, many years of experience in litigating the issue." And, Jacquet has added, "racial discrimination would still be a central piece of the challenge."[29]

The statistical evidence first compiled by the NAACP featured prominently in the oral arguments in *Coker*. First, Kendall highlighted the fact that "the death penalty for rape comes to this Court with a notorious and unsavory reputation for racial discrimination." He noted that 90 percent of the people executed for rape since 1930 were Black; in Georgia over this period, fifty-eight Black men had been executed for rape compared to just three white men. Almost an hour later, Kendall returned to this point, adding that his team had included the legislative history of Georgia's rape statute in its brief and concluded that the statute was apparently "designed after the Civil War to punish Black defendants who commit the crime of rape against white victims." His client may be white, he argued, but the clear racist intent *and* effect of this rape statute added to its plain unconstitutionality.[30]

This argument was powerful, and long overdue, but it reflects an uncomfortable truth: "major efforts became focused largely on black men," Jacquet has argued. "Although racial justice activists by no means completely abandoned black women rape victims, local campaigns on their behalf began to wane in the mid-1960s. While national movement leaders did at times speak out about white male violence against black women and NAACP lawyers defended black women who took their cases to court, the NAACP did not pursue a legal strategy for supporting black rape victims writ large." This reality likewise arrived with decades of precedent: spurred on by largely unsung grassroots activists, the NAACP had long advocated for Black female rape survivors but never as consistently or as centrally as it had advocated for Black male defendants accused of raping white women. Jacquet has pointed to the LDF campaign against the death penalty (initially for rapists, and later more broadly) as "put[ting] the needs of black men at the center of the antiracist legal discourse."[31]

Two days after oral arguments in *Coker*, on March 30, 1977, the justices met around a table in Chief Justice Warren Burger's conference room to discuss the case. By tradition, Burger spoke first, followed by the other justices, in order of seniority. Brennan, the liberal lion, spoke after the chief; then Potter Stewart, then Byron White, and then Thurgood Marshall. Just what Marshall said has been lost to history, but surely his words carried no small amount of gravitas—he had, after all, worked on capital rape cases for decades.[32]

Over the course of the justices' deliberations, it quickly became clear that a sizeable majority were in favor of declaring capital punishment for rape unconstitutional. Once again, however, they could not agree on a rationale. Ultimately, Justice Byron White—who had been appointed to the court because of his strong record in the realm of civil rights—was chosen to write the plurality opinion for himself and three of his colleagues. His opinion concluded that "a sentence of death is grossly disproportionate and excessive punishment for the crime of rape," guided largely by the fact that so many states had eliminated the death penalty for rape, and also because, in terms of "moral depravity," rape "does not compare with murder." White did not mention race, an omission that, Jacquet has argued, "seems particularly striking, given the centrality of racial discrimination to the petitioner's claim." Chief Justice Burger, joined by Justice William Rehnquist—who as a young man had sought to persuade the court to rule *against* Marshall in *Brown v. Board*—dissented, largely on the ground that states should be able to determine their own laws in this area. Justice Marshall and Justice Brennan both wrote separately to reiterate their opposition to the death penalty under any circumstances.[33]

No record of Marshall's thinking survives in his archival papers, but the concurring opinion he ultimately wrote was remarkably short and to the point. In *Furman*, he wrote, he had "set forth at some length" his views on capital punishment. "The death penalty, I concluded, is a cruel and unusual punishment prohibited by the Eighth and Fourteenth Amendments. That continues to be my view."[34] The terseness of his opinion in *Coker* risks masking the depth of his thinking on this subject, and the wealth of his experience.

More revealing archival material survives in the records of Marshall's colleague, Justice Harry Blackmun. As an appellate judge in Minnesota, Blackmun had repeatedly heard the NAACP's argument that the death penalty was unconstitutionally discriminatory. Indeed, he was one of the judges that had first rejected the NAACP's statistical evidence, in the Association's first rape case making use of the numbers, that of William Maxwell of Arkansas. "We are not yet ready to condemn and upset the result reached in every case of a negro rape defendant in the State of Arkansas on the basis of broad theories of social and statistical injustice," read Blackmun's dismissive published opinion.[35] His private correspondence reveals a more conflicted man: "I am frank to say that this case, like many of its Arkansas predecessors, has given me difficulty and is bothersome," he wrote to his fellow judges, attaching his draft opinion. "I am fairly convinced that, over the years, justice in these interracial rape cases in the South has been something less than equal; yet I am persuaded by the record here that inequality for Maxwell has not been demonstrated, or even established on a prima facie basis." In even more private notes, written for himself, Blackmun was frank about why he believed southern justice had been so unequal: "To the white person interracial rape is abhorrent. Rape which is not interracial is less so and there the element of consent seems more readily accepted."[36]

Ultimately, Blackmun joined Justice White's plurality opinion in *Coker*, declining to go as far as Marshall (or Brennan) in repudiating the death penalty categorically. But Blackmun had not been thinking about this issue for nearly as long as Marshall had. In the years to come, he would keep thinking about it, keep struggling with it; his views would continue to evolve, informed in no small part by the growing body of statistical evidence of race discrimination in all aspects of capital punishment.[37]

In the days after the court announced its decision in *Coker*, numerous women's groups praised the ruling. "We never advocated more severe penalties," read a statement released by Women Against Rape. Rather, WAR and other women's groups hoped to see a greater number of rapists prosecuted, something they thought might be more likely if a penalty deemed "too severe" were off the table. And, as one attorney with the ACLU's Women's Rights Project told the press, the "whole idea of the death penalty for rape has been an outgrowth of Southern concern about rape by black men of white women. It has been completely wrong."[38]

Yet in the weeks that followed, the justices were inundated with letters from angry individuals, irate that the court "could have made such a decision that affects so much the lives of innocent women and children," as one woman wrote from Florida. "I have never championed women's lib, never felt that the Supreme Court should have a woman member purely because of her sex. Today I changed my mind," wrote another woman from Texas. "What possible, conceivable constitutional right could nine (or, in this case, seven) men have to so arrogantly rule on something which cannot, really, affect them directly. How dare you even think that you are able to do so." The tension between the responses of these women and the responses of the women's rights organizations gestures to a broader cultural divide on matters of crime and punishment and sex and, undeniably, race.[39]

For the rest of his time on the court, Thurgood Marshall continued to fight against the death penalty, but this struggle proved to be in vain. With *Furman* undone, *Coker* would be one of the court's lasting legacies in the field of capital punishment, but it would not go much further. In 1991, after twenty-four years on the nation's highest bench, an increasingly unwell Marshall announced his retirement. He died just two years later, in 1993. A year after that, his former colleague, Harry Blackmun, finally reached an intellectual position Marshall had attained through years of advocacy. "From this day forward, I no longer shall tinker with the machinery of death," the eighty-four-year-old justice wrote (assisted by a now-famous law clerk, the future scholar of race and injustice Michelle Alexander). "For more than 20 years I have endeavored—indeed, I have struggled—along with a majority of this Court, to develop procedural and substantive rules that would lend more than the mere appearance of fairness to the death penalty endeavor. Rather than continue to coddle the Court's delusion that the desired level of fairness has been achieved and the need for regulation eviscerated, I feel morally and intellectually obligated simply to concede that the death penalty experiment has failed."[40]

Of course, Marshall had witnessed the failure of that experiment—the failure of the justice system itself—decades earlier, in the appeal of Clayton and Carruthers, and in so many other cases.

Epilogue

"Thank you, thank you, thank you," Maya Angelou typed, "for being, for being on the spot when I needed you and for being my friend."

It was June 16, 1976, a blisteringly hot summer day in northern California. Angelou was writing a letter to Daisy Bates, a legendary Arkansas activist. "I don't believe I am exaggerating when I tell you that I would not have gotten through the recent Arkansas experience had you not been all three of the above things," she continued. "Life may provide me the opportunity to write well-received books, to direct well-accepted movies and to be given and accept international awards and honors, however, when thinking of Arkansas I am immediately returned to the lonely little black girl on the red dirt yard in the broiling, mean sunshine. Ah, my dears, Thomas Wolfe said, 'You can't go home again.' How wrong he was. The truth is—no matter how slick and glossy the façade of sophistication one wraps around ones self, one can never leave home."

Bates had been Angelou's host on her recent visit to Arkansas. It was Angelou's first trip back to the state in thirty years, and it had not been a happy occasion. A relative had died, and Angelou and her mother, Vivian, had to travel to Pine Bluff to make sure affairs were in order. Bates had thrown Angelou a party and provided "total support," as well as "courage and strength."

"Joy!" Angelou concluded her letter. "Your Sister, Maya Angelou."[1]

Daisy Lee Gatson had been born in 1914 in the tiny sawmill town of Huttig, five hours or so away from Mississippi County but just a ninety-minute drive from Stamps. "The owners of the mill ruled the town," she later reflected. "Huttig may have been called a sawmill plantation, for everyone worked for the mill, lived in houses owned by the mill, and traded at the general store run by the mill."

The streets were red clay and mostly unnamed, with the Black residents—including little Daisy and her family—residing in drab shotgun houses, separated from the nicer homes of the white residents by the muddy Main Street. Daisy knew she was Black, but she did not really understand what that meant until one day when she was seven years old and she went to the market to pick up a pound of pork chops. The butcher repeatedly ignored her, serving white customers instead, and when he finally turned to her, he said, "[N-words] have to wait 'til I wait on the white people." She returned home and, crying, talked to her father, who "explained as best he could that a Negro had no rights that a white man respected." It was only a few years after the Elaine massacre, after all. Yet he also assured Daisy that he was not afraid of that white butcher. "I'm not afraid to die," he told her.[2]

A few months later, an older boy began bullying her. "You always act so uppity," he taunted. "If you knew what happened to your mother, you wouldn't act so stuck up."

"Nothing's wrong with my mother," Daisy said. "I just left her."

"I'm talking about your *real* mother, the one the white man took out and killed."

Daisy was confused, but she did not ask her parents what he might have meant. A few weeks later, an older cousin told her that when Daisy was just a baby, her mother had been lured away from her house and murdered, her body found the next day in a pond. Shortly after that, her father told her the full story. "He told me of the timeworn lust of the white man for the Negro woman—which strikes at the heart of every Negro man in the South," Daisy later wrote. Her father spoke plainly, in simple words that an eight-year-old could understand. "He wanted me to realize that my mother wouldn't have died if it hadn't been for her race—as well as her beauty, her pride, her love for my father."

"Your mother was not the kind to submit," he continued, his voice growing bitter, "so they took her. They say that three white men did it. There was some talk about who they were, but no one knew for sure, and the sheriff's office did little to find out."

Three white men had raped and murdered Daisy's biological mother. Her biological father, heartbroken, left town, and little Daisy was taken in by the man and woman she knew as her mother and father.

After that, dolls, games, even fishing had little allure for Daisy. "Young as I was, strange as it may seem, my life now had a secret goal—to find the men who had done this horrible thing to my mother," she later wrote. "So happy once, now I was like a little sapling which, after a violent storm, puts out only gnarled and twisted branches."[3]

Daisy quickly became an activist and an advocate for justice. While still a young woman, she moved to Little Rock with her new husband, Lucius Christopher "L. C." Bates, and together they started *Arkansas State Press,* a weekly newspaper that passionately promoted civil rights and the achievements of Black Arkansans. Daisy Bates also joined the Little Rock branch of the NAACP, making the fight against police brutality her "first crusade." Two years before *Brown v. Board of Education,* she became president of the Arkansas Conference of Branches. When Arkansas dithered in desegregating its schools in accordance with *Brown,* Bates sued the Little Rock school district; a year later she became nationally famous for guiding nine Black students into Little Rock Central High School. When Little Rock officials attempted to arrest her in retaliation, the NAACP appealed her case to the U.S. Supreme Court and won. When the backlash to her civil rights work starved her newspaper of revenue, Bates moved to New York and wrote a memoir. *The Long Shadow of Little Rock* was published in 1962.[4]

As the historian Danielle McGuire has noted, anti-rape activism was central to Bates's fight for justice. She "became known as the go-to person for victims of racial and sexual violence in Little Rock," McGuire wrote. "She listened to them and scribbled notes, then placed their stories on the front page of her newspaper." Bates's relentless public advocacy succeeded in activating the local Black community—and alerting white officials that "crimes against black women would not go unnoticed." In large part because of Bates's efforts, many assaults that in years past would have been met with official silence resulted instead in trials—"and, in some instances, even rare convictions of white assailants who attacked black women in Arkansas during the 1940s and early 1950s."[5]

The Arkansas historian Grif Stockley later found it impossible to verify many of the details of Bates's childhood and parentage, and some residents of Huttig disputed or complicated certain aspects of her recounting of her beginnings. But this is hardly surprising. The Huttig press routinely ignored the town's Black residents, and much of the violence directed against them was deliberately excised or omitted from official records.[6] As with *Caged Bird,* it is irrelevant whether every scene and line of dialogue that appears in *The Long Shadow of Little Rock* happened precisely as Bates rendered it. That is not how memoir works, nor where its power lies. The book gestures to a larger experiential truth. As Angelou wrote to Toni Morrison after reading *The Bluest Eye* in 1971, "The truths of our existence do depend upon us for revelation while the facts are being documented interminably in sociologists theses." A generation later, Morrison herself would write, in an essay on Black memoirists, "No matter how 'fictional' the account of these writers, or how much it was a product of invention, the act of imagination is bound up with memory.... It is emotional memory—what the nerves and the skin remember."[7]

At roughly eight years old, Angelou had been raped; at roughly eight years old, Bates had learned the stark realities of rape and racism. In later years, both women became internationally renowned writers and activists. Neither did so without remarkable role models: Angelou was fortified by the examples of Momma and Mrs. Flowers; Bates's father had been part of the local NAACP branch "when it was not popular to be a member."[8] And Bates's own work undoubtedly inspired some of Angelou's. Though less remembered now, Bates's memoir came out almost a decade before Angelou's, and the two books shared many commonalities: both featured Black girls in small-town Arkansas surviving bigotry and violence; both discussed pain and trauma with remarkable frankness; both spotlighted the centrality of sexual violence in the oppression of Black people—Black women in particular—and the maintenance of white supremacy and its attendant misogyny.

Throughout Angelou's lifetime, rape law evolved tremendously. In the years immediately after *Caged Bird* was published, the laws governing sexual assault became a subject of fervent public debate. They were rightly condemned as outdated and bigoted and based on sexist assumptions. In the early 1970s, civil rights activists, women's lib activists, incarcerated activists, and citizen-journalists launched a remarkable anti-rape movement, seeking to explode harmful myths and demanding long overdue change. By the mid-1970s, hundreds of rape crisis centers blanketed the United States; activists across the nation were teaching self-defense classes, recalling sexist judges, marching to Take Back the Night, and advocating for incarcerated rape survivors and against police violence. There were tensions within the anti-rape movement, as women of color were marginalized or ignored by prominent white feminists, but there was also astounding momentum and interracial collaboration. For so many activists, rape was personal, and—as many were proclaiming during these years—the personal was political.[9]

These activists began exposing and exploring the burdensome requirements of rape laws. As the scholars Julie Horney and Cassia Spohn have noted, they demanded a number of specific changes: (1) the replacement of a single definition to one with a series of offenses decreasing by seriousness, as well as a move toward gender-neutrality; (2) the elimination of the requirement that the victim exhibit resistance; (3) the elimination of the requirement that the victim's testimony be corroborated; and (4) the passage of rape shield laws, to restrict the defense's ability to introduce evidence of promiscuity or other sexual contact meant to impeach the victim's credibility. Over the next couple of decades, activists achieved nearly all these aims.[10]

By the mid-1980s, almost every state had eliminated the resistance and corroboration requirements, replaced its unitary, gendered definition of rape with a series of offenses framed in gender-neutral language, and passed early versions of rape shield laws.[11] By the mid-1990s, every state in the nation had criminalized spousal rape.[12] Yet while studies suggest that these reforms did increase the number of survivors who reported their assaults—at least those that authorities deemed well-founded—today that number remains painfully low, with only one in three or four or five or even six rape survivors reporting their assault (statistics vary). Fewer than one in ten make it to trial. In total, only a tiny fraction of sexual assailants are convicted.[13] Women of color are disproportionately likely to be sexually assaulted, and they are also disproportionately likely not to be believed.[14] Numerous studies found that the new rape laws did little to change popular or professional attitudes about rape.[15]

In large part, this is because of the inadequacies of legal reform as a tool for social change. The possibilities of progress were sharply limited by the durability and adaptability of white supremacy, patriarchy, and capitalism, with all their attendant rationalizations and ramifications. "The enactment of the first rape shield laws led to increased reporting of rape but not to higher conviction rates," the historian Estelle Freedman has written. "Defense attorneys continued to refer to women's past sexual behavior, and a majority of jurors expressed the belief that women's appearance and behavior provoked rape. Historical stereotypes about promiscuity continued to haunt women of color."[16] Further, officials across the country still seemed to tacitly rely on the old resistance and corroboration requirements. And an enhanced reliance on human caging—that is, the rise of mass incarceration—ultimately "conflicted with a progressive justice-based agenda," concluded Jacquet.[17] Between Angelou's birth in 1928 and her death in 2014, rape law underwent seismic changes. Rape trials changed too—but, undeniably, not enough.

Four months after penning her poignant thank-you note to Daisy Bates, Angelou returned to Arkansas, this time for a happier occasion. She was there to speak at the state's annual Poetry Day celebration, organized by the Poets

Roundtable of Arkansas. The theme for Poetry Day that year was "We know why a poet sings."

As she stepped off the plane in Little Rock, a throng of excited fans was there to meet her. Angelou spoke at an informal press conference at the airport—a press conference that had been organized by her friend Daisy Bates. Angelou told the crowd, "For many people in this state and in this region, the Civil War has not ended. I see it in the faces of people on the planes when I come to Arkansas."

"No one is free until all people are free," she continued. "One sees in the turbulence and turmoil of American society that no one is really free. By free . . . I mean the freedom of mind, of choice, and the freedom of spirit and hope."[18]

Later, in the car on the way to Poetry Day, she told an interviewer that *I Know Why the Caged Bird Sings* "just became. It became, not I. The work chose its own place on the shelf." Her memories of her childhood in Stamps had "refused to leave me. I didn't have to go anywhere but inside myself."

"I thought I had something to say," she added a moment later. "What it was, I still don't know. I have lived and am living an adventure. I know that I've tried to develop to increase my courage so that I can continue to say what I see."[19]

A year later, with *Roots* about to return to television, Daisy Bates and a number of other Little Rock friends "got busy on telephones," telling acquaintances to be sure not to miss the first episode, "because the lady from Stamps will be in the scene."

"Your visits here have not been forgotten," Bates wrote to Angelou.[20]

Perhaps, as she had written to Daisy Bates, Maya Angelou could never leave truly home. But in a literal sense she had. And she hadn't been back to Stamps for thirty years. Even after returning to Arkansas for family funerals, she had not ventured to her childhood home. Until, finally, something changed.

Not long after *Caged Bird* was released, the journalist Bill Moyers suggested that Angelou allow him to film her returning to Stamps. She refused, telling him there were "too many demons" back there. A dozen years later, Moyers asked again. Eventually, she agreed. But she soon found herself dreading the trip. "I started to really fear the ghosts who I was about to bestir," Angelou later reflected.[21]

The year was 1982. Ronald Reagan was president, "Ebony and Ivory" was a nationwide hit, and Alice Walker had just published *The Color Purple,* a book about racial violence, sexual violence, queer sexuality, and Black female solidarity set in the Jim Crow South. The latter was a celebrated, controversial novel by a Black, female author, another book that spoke powerfully to survivors of sexual assault—especially survivors of intraracial sexual assault, as Angelou was.[22] For her part, Angelou was moved by the novel. "Thank you for seeing. Thank you for saying," she wrote to Walker shortly after the book's publication. "Hallelujah for The Color Purple."[23] Perhaps the world was changing. The next year, *The Color Purple* would win the Pulitzer Prize.

As Moyers, Angelou, and a film crew from New York drove through Arkansas, east from Texarkana toward Stamps, Angelou was seized with a sudden fear. About three miles outside of town, she demanded that Moyers get in a different car, with the crew, and that she be allowed to take their car. "I suddenly was taken back to being twelve years old in a southern, tiny town where my grandmother told me, 'Sistah, never be on a country road with any white boys.' " Moyers, a white man, was a "brother-friend" to her, and she cared for him deeply. "But dragons, fears, the grotesques of childhood always must be confronted at childhood's door."[24]

A camera captured Angelou driving into town, smoking a cigarette. "I am a writer, and Stamps must remain for me in that nebulous, unreal reality, because I am a poet, and I have to draw from these shadows, these densities, these phantasmagories, for my poetry," she said, slowly. "I don't want it to become a place on the map. Because the truth is, you never can leave home. You take it with you everywhere you go." "I was terribly hurt in this town," she added, "and vastly loved."

A camera captured Angelou and Moyers in front of Momma's now-dilapidated Store. Angelou recalled the Black workers who used to gather there, to get picked up to go pick cotton. She recalled the white people that treated her and her grandmother with "such loathing." She recalled the odors of her childhood: "The earth smell was pungent, spiced with the smell of cattle manure," she said into the camera. "Flowers added their heavy aroma. And, above all, the atmosphere was pressed down with the smell of old fears, and hates, and guilt."[25]

Angelou described her years of silence in Stamps. "I'd had a difficulty in St. Louis when I was seven-and-a-half," she told Moyers. "I had been—" she paused. "I had been raped, and the person who had raped me was killed. I said he—I called his name—and he was killed. And I thought at the time that it was my voice that caused the man to be dead, and so I just refused to put my voice out and put anybody else in danger."

Moyers and Angelou walked toward the railroad tracks that divided Black and white Stamps, into the "no-man's-land" between. Angelou reflected on how she used to hate having to walk into the white side of town, feeling she had no protection there, away from her community. Nearly half a century later, as the pair neared the railroad tracks, preparing to walk from the Black territory into the white, Angelou paused.

It was a singular moment. Maya Angelou was one of the most celebrated authors in the country. She had survived so much violence, so much adversity, so many of the barriers her society had placed in her way, and she had done so in a way that moved so many others. Now she had returned to a site of so much happiness and so much pain. As she approached the railroad tracks—this literal crossroads—the author and activist appeared to come to some kind of decision.

Angelou stopped and turned to her friend. "Bill, I tell you, to show how much things don't change, I'm not even going to cross it with you now. I don't really—I really don't—I'm not doing it for any reason other than I really do not want to go across there. I really don't."

They turned back.[26]

Notes

Abbreviations

ABVS	Arkansas Bureau of Vital Statistics
AD	*Arkansas Democrat*
ADC	Arkansas Department of Corrections
AG	*Arkansas Gazette*
AHQ	*Arkansas Historical Quarterly*
BCN	*Blytheville Courier-News*
CB	Maya Angelou, *I Know Why the Caged Bird Sings* (1969)
CCOH	Columbia Center for Oral History
CHH	Charles Hamilton Houston
DW	*Daily Worker*
DHR	*Delta Historical Review*
HPP	Harvey Parnell Papers, Arkansas State Archives
HPPS	Harvey Parnell Papers Supplement, Arkansas State Archives
HS	*Hope Star*
JAH	John A. Hibbler
JM	Jessica Mitford
JMFP	J. M. Futrell Papers, Arkansas State Archives
LAR	Leon A. Ransom
LWCR	Lee Wilson & Company Records, University of Arkansas Libraries
MA	Maya Angelou
MAP	Maya Angelou Papers, Schomburg Center for Research in Black Culture, New York Public Library
NAACPLDFR	NAACP Legal Defense and Educational Fund Records
NAACPR	National Association for the Advancement of Colored People Records, Library of Congress

NAT	Northwest Arkansas Times
NYT	New York Times
OT	Osceola Times
RW	Roy Wilkins
SAJ	Scipio A. Jones
SLPD	St. Louis Post-Dispatch
STFUR	Southern Tenant Farmers' Union Records (microfilm)
TM	Thurgood Marshall
THM	The HistoryMakers (oral history collection)
WW	Walter White
WWIDC	United States World War I Draft Registration Cards, 1917–1918
WWIIDC	United States World War II Draft Registration Cards

Case Files Abbreviations

All case files are referred to as [name of case] [document], [page number]. For example, Bethel transcript, 10, refers to page 10 of the trial transcript in *Bethel v. State*. All are on file with the University of Arkansas at Little Rock.

Alford v. State, 266 S.W.2d 804 (Ark. 1954)
Allison v. State, 164 S.W.2d 442 (Ark. 1942)
Amos v. State, 189 S.W.2d 611 (Ark. 1945)
Bailey v. State, 219 S.W.2d 424 (Ark. 1949)
Bender v. State, 151 S.W.2d 668 (Ark. 1941)
Bethel v. State, 21 S.W.2d 176 (Ark. 1929)
Black v. State, 222 S.W.2d 816 (Ark. 1949)
Bradshaw v. State, 199 S.W.2d 747 (Ark. 1947)
Boyd v. State, 182 S.W.2d 937 (Ark. 1944)
Boyett v. State, 56 S.W.2d 182 (Ark. 1933)
Braswell v. State, 280 S.W. 367 (Ark. 1926)
Brock v. State, 270 S.W. 98 (Ark. 1925)
Brust v. State, 240 S.W. 1079 (Ark. 1922)
Burks v. State, 120 S.W.2d 345 (Ark. 1938)
Cabe v. State, 30 S.W.2d 855 (Ark. 1930)
Caldwell v. State, 168 S.W.2d 807 (Ark. 1943)
Cates v. State, 4 S.W.2d 952 (Ark. 1928)
Cauley v. State, 247 S.W. 772 (Ark. 1923)
Clack v. State, 212 S.W.2d 20 (Ark. 1948)
Clayton v. State, 89 S.W.2d 732 (Ark. 1935)
Comer v. State, 257 S.W.2d 564 (Ark. 1953)

Cook v. State, 276 S.W. 583 (Ark. 1925)
Cureton v. State, 174 S.W. 810 (Ark. 1915)
Cutts v. State, 288 S.W. 883 (Ark. 1926)
Daniels v. State, 53 S.W.2d 231 (Ark. 1932)
Davis v. State, 244 S.W. 750 (Ark. 1922)
DeVoe v. State, 97 S.W.2d 75 (Ark. 1936)
Doss v. State, 157 S.W.2d 499 (Ark. 1941)
Durham v. State, 16 S.W.2d 991 (Ark. 1929)
Fanning v. State, 136 S.W.2d 1040 (Ark. 1940)
Fields v. State, 159 S.W.2d 745 (Ark. 1942)
Franks v. State, 272 S.W. 648 (Ark. 1925)
Gann v. State, 141 S.W.2d 834 (Ark. 1940)
Gerlach v. State, 229 S.W.2d 37 (Ark. 1950)
Goodnaugh v. State, 85 S.W.2d 1019 (Ark. 1935)
Green v. State, 46 S.W.2d 8 (Ark. 1932)
Hamm v. State, 214 S.W.2d 917 (Ark. 1948)
Harrison v. State, 262 S.W.2d 907 (Ark. 1953)
Hawkins v. State, 267 S.W.2d 1 (Ark. 1954)
Hawthorne v. State, 204 S.W. 841 (Ark. 1918)
Hays v. State, 278 S.W. 15 (Ark. 1925)
Head v. State, 297 S.W. 828 (Ark. 1927)
Hedrick v. State, 279 S.W. 785 (Ark. 1926)
Hildreth v. State, 223 S.W.2d 757 (Ark. 1949)
Hodges v. State, 197 S.W.2d 52 (Ark. 1946)
Hogan v. State, 282 S.W. 984 (Ark. 1926)
Hogan v. State, 86 S.W.2d 931 (Ark. 1935) [Hogan II]
Houston v. State, 79 S.W.2d 999 (Ark. 1935)
Jackson v. State, 218 S.W. 369 (Ark. 1920)
James v. State, 188 S.W. 806 (Ark. 1916)
Kazzee v. State, 299 S.W. 354 (Ark. 1927)
Korsak v. State, 154 S.W.2d 348 (Ark. 1941)
Lewis v. State, 271 S.W. 708 (Ark. 1925)
Lindsey v. State, 209 S.W.2d 462 (Ark. 1948)
Lipsmeyer v. State, 266 S.W. 275 (Ark. 1924)
Martin v. State, 283 S.W. 29 (Ark. 1926)
Maxwell v. State, 225 S.W.2d 687 (Ark. 1950)
Maxwell v. State, 232 S.W.2d 982 (Ark. 1950) [Maxwell II]
McDonald v. State, 244 S.W. 20 (Ark. 1922)
McDonald v. State, 279 S.W.2d 44 (Ark. 1955)
McGee v. State, 223 S.W.2d 603 (Ark. 1949)
McGill v. State, 189 S.W.2d 646 (Ark. 1945)

McGlosson v. State, 286 S.W. 931 (Ark. 1926)
McLaughlin v. State, 174 S.W. 234 (Ark. 1915)
Morgan v. State, 76 S.W.2d 79 (Ark. 1934)
Mynett v. State, 18 S.W.2d 335 (Ark. 1929)
Needham v. State, 224 S.W.2d 785 (Ark. 1949)
Palmer v. State, 214 S.W.2d 372 (Ark. 1948)
Perkinson v. State, 172 S.W.2d 18 (Ark. 1943)
Powell v. State, 232 S.W. 429 (Ark. 1921)
Priest v. State, 163 S. W. 2d 159 (Ark. 1942)
Pugh v. State, 210 S.W.2d 789 (Ark. 1948)
Reed v. State, 299 S.W. 757 (Ark. 1927)
Reynolds v. State, 246 S.W.2d 724 (Ark. 1952)
Rose v. State, 184 S.W. 60 (Ark. 1916)
Rowe v. State, 244 S.W. 463 (Ark. 1922)
Sanders v. State, 296 S.W. 70 (Ark. 1927)
Sherman v. State, 279 S.W. 353 (Ark. 1926)
Smith v. State, 210 S.W.2d 913 (Ark. 1948)
Snetzer v. State, 279 S.W. 9 (Ark. 1926)
Sutton v. State, 122 S.W.2d 617 (Ark. 1938)
Taylor v. State, 297 S.W. 854 (Ark. 1927)
Terrell v. State, 2 S.W.2d 87 (Ark. 1928)
Thomas v. State, 11 S.W.2d 771 (Ark. 1928)
Thomas v. State, 116 S.W.2d 358 (Ark. 1938) [Thomas II]
Thornsberry v. State, 92 S.W.2d 203 (Ark. 1936)
Tugg v. State, 174 S.W.2d 374 (Ark. 1943)
Underdown v. State, 250 S.W.2d 131 (Ark. 1952)
Venable v. State, 5 S.W.2d 716 (Ark. 1928)
Wadlington v. State, 227 S.W.2d 940 (Ark. 1950)
Ward v. State, 160 S.W.2d 864 (Ark. 1942)
Warford v. State, 216 S.W.2d 781 (Ark. 1949)
Waterman v. State, 154 S.W.2d 813 (Ark. 1941)
Watt v. State, 261 S.W.2d 544 (Ark. 1953)
West v. State, 234 S.W. 997 (Ark. 1921)
West v. State, 192 S.W.2d 135 (Ark. 1946) [West II]
Whittaker v. State, 286 S.W. 937 (Ark. 1926)
Willis v. State, 252 S.W.2d 618 (Ark. 1952)
Wills v. State, 98 S.W.2d 72 (Ark. 1936)
Wilson v. State, 7 S.W.2d 969 (Ark. 1928)
Wise v. State, 164 S.W.2d 897 (Ark. 1942)
Young v. State, 221 S.W. 478 (Ark. 1920).

Introduction

1. Isabel Wilkerson, *The Warmth of Other Suns: The Epic Story of America's Great Migration* (2010), 294.
2. CB, 6.
3. Ibid.
4. Steven Teske, "Stamps (Lafayette County)," *Encyclopedia of Arkansas*, January 6, 2018, https://encyclopediaofarkansas.net/entries/stamps-lafayette-county-915/ [https://perma.cc/U342-ANEK]; A. E. Brown, "The Louisiana & Arkansas Railway: Structure and Operation in the Age of Steam," *Railroad History* 144 (Spring 1981), 51–59.
5. CB, 7.
6. Ibid., 13–14.
7. Bethel and Wallace prison files, ADC; "To Die for Attack," *Eau Claire Leader*, April 28, 1928, 12; "Mississippi County Youths under Sentence to Die in Electric Chair," AG, April 15, 1928, 5.
8. "Flowers Flourish within Grim Walls," AG, August 14, 1932, 18; "Notorious Killers Receive Clemency," AG, December 24, 1932, 9.
9. Story L. Matkin-Rawn, " 'We Fight for the Rights of Our Race': Black Arkansans in the Era of Jim Crow" (Ph.D. diss., University of Wisconsin, 2009), 11–12; *The WPA Guide to 1930s Arkansas* (1987), 330.
10. "Bethel and Wallace Get Furloughs," BCN, August 23, 1930, 1; "Mike Wallace Is Given Pardon," BCN, September 19, 1934, 1.
11. "Penitentiary Data Provided by Audit," AG, January 28, 1933, 15. The spelling of "Carruthers" varies considerably in surviving records (often appearing with one "r"). I have chosen this spelling at the request of his living descendants. Interview of Trina Nicholson and Gail Terry (May 30, 2024).
12. Clyde Crosley, *Unfolding Misconceptions: The Arkansas State Penitentiary, 1836–1986* (1986), 45–55.
13. TM to WW, May 18, 1939, f13, bD50, NAACPR.
14. Although this book builds on considerable existing scholarship, it is distinguishable from previous works by its sources, methodology, and geography. While Lisa Lindquist Dorr's incisive analysis looked at case files from early twentieth-century Virginia, she examined only "cases of Black-on-white rape." Lisa Lindquist Dorr, *White Women, Rape, and the Power of Race in Virginia, 1900–1960* (2004), 5. My analysis, by contrast, considers cases with white accusers, Black accusers, white defendants, and Black defendants. Patrick Lynn Rivers's study of sexual assault cases in turn-of-the-century North Carolina considered assaults across the racial spectrum but—unlike this book—it did not delve deeply into trial dynamics or mechanics. Patrick Lynn Rivers, "Race, Sex, Violence, and the Problem of Agency in North Carolina, 1889–1903," *Australasian Journal of American Studies* 28.1 (July 2009), 34–49. Other studies have been narrower—focusing only on sex crimes against children, for example—or considered other parts of the United States, such as Los Angeles, New York, Chicago, Nebraska, or Ingham County, Michigan. See Brian M. Trump, "Sex Crimes and Criminal Sexuality:

Legislating and Policing Community Boundaries in Nebraska, 1880–1980" (Ph.D. diss., University of Kansas, 2022); Stephen Robertson, *Crimes against Children: Sexual Violence in New York City, 1880–1960* (2005); Bonni Kay Cermak, "In the Interest of Justice: Legal Narratives of Sex, Gender, Race and Rape in Twentieth Century Los Angeles, 1920–1960" (Ph.D. diss., University of Oregon, 2005); Brian Donovan, *Respectability on Trial: Sex Crimes in New York City, 1900–1918* (2016); Dawn Rae Flood, *Rape in Chicago: Race, Myth, and the Courts* (2012); Kathleen Ruth Parker, "Law, Culture, and Sexual Censure: Sex Crime Prosecutions in a Midwest County Circuit Court, 1850–1950" (Ph.D. diss., Michigan State University, 1993). In this book, by contrast, I consider sex crimes against children as well as against adults and examine Jim Crow Arkansas. An earlier version of some of this research appeared in Scott W. Stern, "Shadow Trials, or A History of Sexual Assault Trials in the Jim Crow South," *UCLA Journal of Gender and Law* 29 (2022), 257.

15. An earlier version of some of this research appeared in Scott W. Stern, "The NAACP's Rape Docket and the Origins of Criminal Procedure," *University of Pennsylvania Journal of Law and Social Change* 24 (2021), 301.

16. See Danielle L. McGuire, *At the Dark End of the Street: Black Women, Rape, and Resistance—A New History of the Civil Rights Movement from Rosa Parks to the Rise of Black Power* (2010); Jeanne Theoharis, *The Rebellious Life of Mrs. Rosa Parks* (2013); Catherine O. Jacquet, *The Injustices of Rape: How Activists Responded to Sexual Violence, 1950–1980* (2019); Chana Kai Lee, *For Freedom's Sake: The Life of Fannie Lou Hamer* (1999). See also Christina Greene, *Free Joan Little: The Politics of Race, Sexual Violence, and Imprisonment* (2022); Kate Clifford Larson, *Walk with Me: A Biography of Fannie Lou Hamer* (2021); Keisha N. Blain, *Until I Am Free: Fannie Lou Hamer's Enduring Message to America* (2021).

17. See Cermak, "In the Interest of Justice," 8–11; Parker, "Law, Culture, and Sexual Censure," 68–69.

18. The theater analogy is discussed later in the book, especially at the start of chapter 12. See also Mary Frances Berry, "Judging Morality: Sexual Behavior and Legal Consequences in the Late Nineteenth-Century South," *Journal of American History* 78.3 (December 1991), 837 ("Everyone had a role to play.").

19. Examining Nebraska, Brian M. Trump argues that sex crime prosecutions reinforced the intriguing additional hierarchy of "mobility." Trump, "Sex Crimes and Criminal Sexuality," 2. See also ibid., 76–79.

20. See Christopher Waldrep, "Substituting the Law for the Lash: Emancipation and Legal Formalism in a Mississippi County Court," *Journal of American History* 82 (March 1996), 1425–51.

21. Suzette A. Henke, "Autobiography as Revolutionary Writing in *I Know Why the Caged Bird Sings*," in Mary E. Williams, ed., *Readings on Maya Angelou* (1997), 99 (autobiography of women of color "is, or at least has the potential to be, a revolutionary form of writing").

22. Susan Myers to MA, June 28, 1989, f8, b74, MAP.

23. MA to Susan Myers, July 25, 1989, f8, b74, MAP.

Chapter 1. The Making of a Cotton County, 1541–1927

1. Jeannie Whayne, *Delta Empire: Lee Wilson and the Transformation of Agriculture in the New South* (2011), 8–11.

2. Whayne, *Delta Empire*, 12–14; Joseph Patrick Key, "Indians and Ecological Conflict in Territorial Arkansas," *AHQ* 59 (Summer 2000), 127–46; James Penick Jr., *The New Madrid Earthquakes of 1811–1812* (1976), 33–35; M. L. Fuller, *The New Madrid Earthquake* (1912), 10–11; James M. Gardner, "Territorial Days in Mississippi County, Arkansas," *DHR* (Spring 1995), 41; Jay Feldman, *When the Mississippi Ran Backwards: Empire, Intrigue, Murder, and the New Madrid Earthquakes* (2005).

3. Mabel F. Edrington, *History of Mississippi County, Arkansas* (1962), 32–65; Whayne, *Delta Empire*, 8; Gardner, "Territorial Days in Mississippi County," 44, 46.

4. Fon Louise Gordon, "From Slavery to Uncertain Freedom: Blacks in the Delta," in Jeannie Whayne and Willard B. Gatewood, eds., *The Arkansas Delta: Land of Paradox* (1993), 98–103; Whayne, *Delta Empire*, 24–27.

5. Whayne, *Delta Empire*, 29–33, 50; Gordon, "From Slavery to Uncertain Freedom," 103–6; Matkin-Rawn, " 'We Fight for the Rights of Our Race,' " 12–13, 30–38; interview of Edward Bradley by Bernice Bowden (November to December 1938), in *Federal Writers' Project: Slave Narrative Project*, vol. 2, Arkansas, part 1, Abbott-Byrd, 229–30.

6. Bradley interview, 229–30; Whayne, *Delta Empire*, 60–86; Nan Elizabeth Woodruff, *American Congo: The African American Freedom Struggle in the Delta* (2003), 10–11, 17; A. F. Barham, "As I Saw It: The Story of the Development of Drainage and Flood Control in the St. Francis Basin of Arkansas" (1964), 7, Special Collections, University of Arkansas.

7. Whayne, *Delta Empire*, 72–74; Edrington, *History of Mississippi County*, 75–87; Woodruff, *American Congo*, 11–12; Barham, "As I Saw It," 5, 12–13.

8. "Judge S. L. Gladish," *OT*, June 3, 1909, 1; "Rich, Rare and Racy," *OT*, November 18, 1909, 1; Barham, "As I Saw It," 5, 13; Edrington, *History of Mississippi County*, 75–87; Whayne, *Delta Empire*, 57, 74–75, 86–87; Woodruff, *American Congo*, 11–12.

9. Edrington, *History of Mississippi County*, 33, 40–42, 111–13; Oscar Fendler, "Political History of Blytheville," *DHR* (Fall 1991), 28–29; Paul Cooley, "Some Recollections of Parts of the 19th and 20th Centuries," *DHR* (Winter 1990), 23–25; Paul Cooley, "A Brief History and Founding of Blytheville Arkansas," *DHR* (Winter 1990), 32; Oscar Fendler, *Chronicles: Incidents in the Life of Oscar Fendler, 1909 to 1926* (1991), 127–29, Northeast Arkansas Regional Archives.

10. *WPA Guide to 1930s Arkansas*, 131–32.

11. Matkin-Rawn, "We Fight for the Rights of Our Race," 76.

12. Whayne, *Delta Empire*, 50–52; Woodruff, *American Congo*, 25–29; Matkin-Rawn, "We Fight for the Rights of Our Race," 78–80.

13. Whayne, *Delta Empire*, 53; Woodruff, *American Congo*, 33–36; Matkin-Rawn, "We Fight for the Rights of Our Race," 38–39; TM to Homer S. Cummings, September 17, 1937, and attachments, f10, b107, NAACPLDFR.

14. Oscar Fendler, "Documentary TV," 4–5, f28, b356, LWCR.

15. Matkin-Rawn, "We Fight for the Rights of Our Race," 77; Whayne, *Delta Empire*, 117–18.

16. Matkin-Rawn, "We Fight for the Rights of Our Race," 225–26; Sammy L. Morgan, "Elite Dominance in the Arkansas Delta, from the New Deal to the New Millennium," (Ph.D. diss., University of Mississippi, 2005), 11.

17. Southern Tenant Farmers' Union, A Statement Concerning Farm Tenancy Submitted to the Governor's Commission on Farm Tenancy by the Executive Council (1936), 3–8, f10, b101, NAACPLDFR; Norman Thomas, *The Plight of the Share-Cropper* (1934), reel 1, STFUR; Howard Kester, *Revolt among the Sharecroppers* (1969), 40–52; Anthony P. Dunbar, *Against the Grain: Southern Radicals and Prophets, 1929–1959* (1981), 87; Matkin-Rawn, "We Fight for the Rights of Our Race," 123.

18. Woodruff, *American Congo*, 14–15, 22–23; Matkin-Rawn, "We Fight for the Rights of Our Race," 39–49, 155–56; Gordon, "From Slavery to Uncertain Freedom," 108–10; Whayne, *Delta Empire*, 136; Matthew Hild, *Arkansas's Gilded Age: The Rise, Decline & Legacy of Populism & Working-Class Protest* (2018), 58–59, 78–79, 106–8, 127, 137; M. Langley Biegert, "Legacy of Resistance: Uncovering the History of Collective Action by Black Agricultural Workers in Central East Arkansas from the 1860s to the 1930s," *Journal of Social History* 32.1 (Autumn 1998), 81–84.

19. W. A. Percy, *Lanterns on the Levee* (1941), 249–50; Matkin-Rawn, "We Fight for the Rights of Our Race," 212; William Downs Jr., *Stories of Survival: Arkansas Farmers during the Great Depression* (2011), 6–7.

20. Whayne, *Delta Empire*, ch. 6; Ethel C. Simpson, "Letters from the Flood," *AHQ* 55 (Autumn 1996), 277–83. See also Pete Daniel, *Deep'n as It Come: The 1927 Mississippi River Flood* (1977).

21. Morgan, "Elite Dominance in the Arkansas Delta," 13–19; Jeannie Whayne, "An Interview with Billy Lee Riley," *AHQ* 55 (August 1996), 303.

22. W. E. B. Du Bois, "The Black Belt of Arkansas," 2, n.d., f16, b1, W. E. B. Du Bois Collection, Beinecke Rare Book & Manuscript Library, Yale University.

23. Sue Thrasher and Leah Wise, "The Southern Tenant Farmers' Union," *Southern Exposure* 1 (Winter 1974), 8.

24. Matkin-Rawn, "We Fight for the Rights of Our Race," 74.

Chapter 2. The Law of Rape, 1820–1920s

1. Jerry Wayne Looney, " 'A Stronghold of Southern Legal Puritanism': The Arkansas Supreme Court and the Development of Criminal Law and Procedure, 1836–1874," (master's thesis, University of Arkansas, 2010), 4, 8; United States v. Dickinson, Hempstead's Reports 1 (January 1820). Dickinson's argument was not without precedent; it likely drew on centuries-old beliefs that women must experience orgasm to conceive.

2. *Laws of Arkansas Territory*, ed. J. Steele and J. M'Campbell (1835), 172.

3. Ark Rev. Stat. ch. 51, art. IV (1848); Florence R. Beatty-Brown, "Legal Status of Arkansas Negroes before Emancipation," *AHQ* 28.1 (Spring 1969), 10.

4. Charles (a Slave) v. State, 11 Ark. 389, 397, 404–5 (1850); Peter W. Bardaglio, "Rape and the Law in the Old South: 'Calculated to Excite Indignation in Every Heart,' " *Journal of Southern History* 60.4 (November 1994), 756.

5. Mary R. Block, " 'An Accusation Easily to Be Made': A History of Rape Law in Nineteenth-Century America" (Ph.D. diss., University of Kentucky, 2001), 42–44; Charles (a Slave) v. State, 11 Ark. 389, 401 (1850).

6. Bardaglio, "Rape and the Law in the Old South," 751.

7. Diane Miller Sommerville, *Rape & Race in the Nineteenth-Century South* (2004), 21, 28–29, 42, 72–73, 85, 103.

8. Jennifer Wriggins, Note, "Rape, Racism, and the Law," *Harvard Women's Law Journal* 6 (1983), 103, 106.

9. George (a Slave) v. State, 37 Miss. 316, 317 (1859); Hannah Rosen, *Terror in the Heart of Freedom: Citizenship, Sexual Violence, and the Meaning of Race in the Postemancipation South* (2009), 10.

10. Dorothy Roberts, "Race," in Nikole-Hannah Jones, ed., *The 1619 Project: A New Origin Story* (2021), 60.

11. Pleasant v. State, 15 Ark. 624, 644 (1855); Orville W. Taylor, " 'Jumping the Broomstick': Slave Marriage and Morality in Arkansas," *AHQ* 17.3 (Autumn 1958), 231.

12. Looney, " 'Stronghold of Southern Legal Puritanism,' " 5–11.

13. Edrington, *History of Mississippi County*, 33.

14. Sommerville, *Rape & Race in the Nineteenth-Century South*, 179; Madelin Joan Olds, "The Rape Complex in the Postbellum South" (Ph.D. diss., Carnegie Mellon University, 1989), 112–38.

15. Olds, "Rape Complex in the Postbellum South," 27–43, 139.

16. Elain Frantz Parsons, *Ku-Klux: The Birth of the Klan During Reconstruction* (2015), 29–30; Eric Foner, *Reconstruction: America's Unfinished Revolution, 1863–1877* (1988), 119, 342; Rosen, *Terror in the Heart of Freedom*, 159–75; Richard A. Buckelew, "Racial Violence in Arkansas: Lynchings and Mob Rule, 1860–1930" (Ph.D. diss., University of Arkansas, 1999), 22–27; Sommerville, *Rape & Race in the Nineteenth-Century South*, 148–49; Lisa Cardyn, "Sexualized Racism/Gendered Violence: Outraging the Body Politic in the Reconstruction South," *Michigan Law Review* 100 (2002), 675, 719–36.

17. See Nicholas Lemann, *Redemption: The Last Battle of the Civil War* (2006); Foner, *Reconstruction*, 550–63.

18. Foner, *Reconstruction*, 528; Thomas A. DeBlack, *With Fire and Sword: Arkansas, 1861–1874* (2003), ch. 7; Otis A. Singletary, "Militia Disturbances in Arkansas during Reconstruction," *AHQ* 15.2 (Summer 1956), 145–50; Earl F. Woodward, "The Brooks and Baxter War in Arkansas, 1872–1874," *AHQ* 30.4 (Winter 1971), 315–36;

Guy Lancaster, *Racial Cleansing in Arkansas, 1883–1924: Politics, Land, Labor, and Criminality* (2014), ch. 2.

19. Sommerville, *Rape & Race in the Nineteenth-Century South*, 83. This reform proved to "short lived. By the end of the nineteenth century, every state in the South allowed capital punishment, and some states required it, for those convicted of rape." Peter W. Bardaglio, *Reconstructing the Household: Families, Sex, and the Law in the Nineteenth-Century South* (1995), 190.

20. Ark. Code Ann. §§ 1300–1305 (1874).

21. Sommerville, *Rape & Race in the Nineteenth-Century South*, 124, 159.

22. Estelle B. Freedman, *Redefining Rape: Sexual Violence in the Era of Suffrage and Segregation* (2013), 89; "Rape," *The Crisis* (May 1919), 12; Ida B. Wells, "Eight Negroes Lynched since Last Issue of *Free Speech*," *Free Speech & Headlight* (May 21, 1892), 2; Ida B. Wells-Barnett, *Southern Horrors: Lynch Law in All Its Phases* (1892), ch. 2.

23. Wriggins, "Rape, Racism, and the Law," 107–8; Jacquelyn Dowd Hall, " 'The Mind That Burns in Each Body': Women, Rape, and Racial Violence," in Ann Smitow, Christine Stansell, and Sharon Thompson, eds., *Powers of Desire: The Politics of Sexuality* (1983), 330–31.

24. Freedman, *Redefining Rape*, 96; Bourke, *Rape*, 101–2; Buckelew, "Racial Violence in Arkansas," ch. 1; Kelly Houston Jones, " 'Doubtless Guilty': Lynching and Slaves in Antebellum Arkansas," in Guy Lancaster, ed., *Bullets and Fire: Lynching and Authority in Arkansas, 1840–1950* (2018).

25. Todd E. Lewis, "Race Relations in Arkansas, 1910–1929," (Ph.D. diss., University of Arkansas 1995), 4–12; Matkin-Rawn, " 'We Fight for the Rights of Our Race,' " 7, 67–73, 91–102; Guy Lancaster, " 'Leave Town and Never Return': Case Studies of Racial Cleansing in Arkansas, 1887–1937" (Ph.D. diss., Arkansas State University, 2010); Jacqueline Froelich and David Zimmermann, "Total Eclipse: The Destruction of the African American Community of Harrison, Arkansas, in 1905 and 1909," *AHQ* 58.2 (Summer 1999), 131–59; Kenneth C. Barnes, *Who Killed John Clayton? Political Violence and the Emergence of the New South, 1861–1893* (1998), 128.

26. Buckelew, "Racial Violence in Arkansas," ch. 2; Freedman, *Redefining Rape*, 92; Olds, "Rape Complex in the Postbellum South," 142; Randy Finley, "A Lynching State: Arkansas in the 1890s," in Lancaster, ed., *Bullets and Fire*; Grif Stockley, *Ruled by Race: Black/White Relations in Arkansas from Slavery to the Present* (2009), 126–28.

27. Quoted in Bourke, *Rape*, 103–6.

28. Lewis, "Race Relations in Arkansas," 17–18; Wriggins, "Rape, Racism, and the Law," 108.

29. Wriggins, "Rape, Racism, and the Law," 108; Sommerville, *Rape & Race in the Nineteenth-Century South*, 201; W. Fitzhugh Brundage, *Lynching in the New South: Georgia and Virginia, 1880–1930* (1993), 68, 264; Martha Hodes, *White Women, Black Men: Illicit Sex in the Nineteenth-Century South* (1997), 176; Stewart E. Tolnay and E. M. Beck, *A Festival of Violence: An Analysis of Southern Lynchings, 1882–1930* (1995), 48–49;

Wells-Barnett, *Southern Horrors*, 30; Terrence Finnegan, " 'At the Hands of Parties Unknown': Lynching in Mississippi and South Carolina, 1881–1940" (Ph.D. diss., University of Illinois, 1993), 167–68.

30. NAACP, *Seventh Annual Report* (1917), 6, bI:A25, NAACPR; NAACP, *Thirty Years of Lynching in the United States, 1889–1918* (April 1919), 7–10; Jonathan Markovitz, *Legacies of Lynching: Racial Violence and Memory* (2004), 11; Frederick Douglas, *Why Is the Negro Lynched?* (1895), 10; Freedman, *Redefining Rape*, 101.

31. Woodruff, *American Congo*, 1; Sommerville, *Rape & Race in the Nineteenth-Century South*, 202–7.

32. Freedman, *Redefining Rape*, 128–33; Block, " 'An Accusation Easily to Be Made,' " 154–55; Brian Donovan, *White Slave Crusades: Race, Gender and Anti-Vice Activism, 1887–1917* (2006), 18–22, 38–39; Robertson, *Crimes against Children*, 87–88; Jane E. Larson, " 'Even a Worm Will Turn at Last': Rape Reform in Late Nineteenth-Century America," *Yale Journal of Law & the Humanities* 9 (1997), 1.

33. Freedman, *Redefining Rape*, 127, 134–36; Carolyn Cocca, *Jailbait: The Politics of Statutory Rape Laws in the United States* (2004), 12–14; Mary E. Odem, *Delinquent Daughters: Protecting and Policing Adolescent Female Sexuality in the United States, 1885–1920* (1995), 30–31; Robertson, *Crimes against Children*, 88–92.

34. Ark. Code Ann. § 1865 (1893); Freedman, *Redefining Rape*, 135; Mara Keire, "Women and Sexual Assault in the United States, 1900–1940," *Oxford Research Encyclopedia of American History* (March 2019), 7, http://oxfordre.com/americanhistory/view/10.1093/acrefore/9780199329175.001.0001/acrefore-9780199329175-e-495?print=pdf [https://perma.cc/2W9T-NWYU].

35. Freedman, *Redefining Rape*, 128.

36. Biennial Report of the Attorney General for the Biennial Period 1925–1926 (State of Arkansas), 244.

Chapter 3. Vigilantism and Resistance, 1899–1930s

1. Lewis, "Race Relations in Arkansas," 10; Buckelew, "Racial Violence in Arkansas," 97–99.

2. Lewis, "Race Relations in Arkansas," 276–78, 292–95, 307; Buckelew, "Racial Violence in Arkansas," 99, 191–92.

3. Lewis, "Race Relations in Arkansas," 296; State v. Petit, 44 So. 848, 849 (La. 1907); Wriggins, "Rape, Racism, and the Law," 109.

4. Crystal Nicole Feimster, " 'Ladies and Lynching': The Gendered Discourse of Mob Violence in the New South" (Ph.D. diss., Princeton University, 2000), 129–30, 136–37, 148, 156.

5. Charles C. Alexander, "White-Robed Reformers: The Ku Klux Klan Comes to Arkansas, 1921–1922," *AHQ* 22.1 (Spring 1963), 8–23; Charles C. Alexander, "White Robes in Politics: The Ku Klux Klan in Arkansas, 1922–1924," *AHQ* 22.3 (Autumn

1963), 195–214; Charles C. Alexander, "Defeat, Decline, Disintegration: The Ku Klux Klan in Arkansas, 1924 and After," *AHQ* 22.4 (Winter 1963), 311, 317–18; Lewis, "Race Relations in Arkansas," 297–301; Whayne, *Delta Empire*, 123; Matkin-Rawn, "We Fight for the Rights of Our Race," 198.

6. Matkin-Rawn, "We Fight for the Rights of Our Race," 73–75; Downs, *Stories of Survival*, ch. 27.

7. Matkin-Rawn, "We Fight for the Rights of Our Race," 83–85, 94–96, 167.

8. John L. Crouthamel, "The Springfield Race Riot of 1908," *Journal of Negro History* 45 (July 1960), 164–77; Roberta Senechal de la Roche, *In Lincoln's Shadow: The 1908 Race Riot in Springfield, Illinois* (2008), 158–59; "Negro's Heinous Crime," *Illinois State Journal*, August 14, 1908, 1; "Dragged from Her Bed and Outraged by Negro," *Illinois State Register*, August 14, 1908, 1; William English Walling, "The Race War in the North," *The Independent*, September 3, 1908, 529–34; Patricia Sullivan, *Lift Every Voice: The NAACP and the Making of the Civil Rights Movement* (2009), 5–18; Freedman, *Redefining Rape*, 243.

9. Matkin-Rawn, "We Fight for the Rights of Our Race," 120–23.

10. Robert Whitaker, *On the Laps of Gods: The Red Summer of 1919 and the Struggle for Justice that Remade a Nation* (2008), 1; Matkin-Rawn, " 'We Fight for the Rights of Our Race,' " 123; Grif Stockley, "Elaine Massacre of 1919," *Encyclopedia of Arkansas* (November 5, 2019), https://encyclopediaofarkansas.net/entries/elaine-massacre-of-1919-1102/# [https://perma.cc/VK9R-BKZ3].

11. Ida B. Wells-Barnett, *The Arkansas Race Riot* (Chicago, 1920), 7–8, 48–55; "The Real Cause of Two Race Riots," *The Crisis*, December 1919, 56; Walter White, "The Race Conflict in Arkansas," *Survey*, December 13, 1919, 234; Matkin-Rawn, " 'We Fight for the Rights of Our Race,' " 107–11, 123–25; Steven Anthony, "The Elaine Riot of 1919: Race, Class, and Labor in the Arkansas Delta" (Ph.D. diss., University of Wisconsin at Milwaukee, 2019), chs. 2–3; Woodruff, *American Congo*, 74–79; Buckelew, "Racial Violence in Arkansas," 125–26; Jeannie M. Whayne, "Low Villains and Wickedness in High Places: Race and Class in the Elaine Riots," *AHQ* 58.3 (Autumn 1999), 294–97; Bessie Ferguson, "The Elaine Race Riot" (master's thesis, Peabody College for Teachers, 1927), chs. 1–2, in f16, b1, Subseries II, Series I, Grif Stockley Papers, Butler Center for Arkansas Studies.

12. Matkin-Rawn, " 'We Fight for the Rights of Our Race,' " 125–33; Buckelew, "Racial Violence in Arkansas," 123–25, 128; Woodruff, *American Congo*, 82–84; B. Boren McCool, *Union, Reaction, and Riot: A Biography of a Race Riot* (1970), 12–13, 21–23; Arthur I. Waskow, *From Race Riot to Sit-In: 1919 and the 1960s* (1967), 123–24; O. A. Rogers, "The Elaine Riots of 1919," *AHQ* 19.2 (Summer 1960), 144–47; Ferguson, "Elaine Race Riot," ch. 3; Stockley, *Ruled by Race*, 159.

13. Wells-Barnett, *Arkansas Race Riot*, 10–18, 25–27; Walter White, "Massacring Whites in Arkansas," *The Nation* (December 6, 1919), 715–16; White, "The Race Conflict in Arkansas," 233–34; "The Real Cause of Two Race Riots," 56; Matkin-Rawn,

" 'We Fight for the Rights of Our Race,' " 133–35, 289 n.56; Anthony, "Elaine Riot of 1919," ch. 4; Woodruff, *American Congo*, 86–88; Whitaker, *On the Lap of Gods*, 83–126; Grif Stockley, *Blood in Their Eyes: The Elaine Race Massacres of 1919* (2001), xxiii–xxv; Grif Stockley, Timeline of Elaine Race Riot, 1–2, f19, b1, Subseries II, Series I, Grif Stockley Papers, Butler Center for Arkansas Studies; Buckelew, "Racial Violence in Arkansas," 131–35, 142; Lewis, "Race Relations in Arkansas," 222–25; Cherisse Jones-Branch, "Women and the 1919 Elaine Massacre," in Guy Lancaster, ed., *The Elaine Massacre and Arkansas: A Century of Atrocity and Resistance, 1819–1919* (2018), 181–82, 187–89; Richard C. Cortner, *A Mob Intent on Death: The NAACP and the Arkansas Riot Cases* (1988), 5–8, 30, 121–25, 207–8; McCool, *Union, Reaction, and Riot*, 21–30; Waskow, *From Race Riot to Sit-In*, 129; Rogers, "Elaine Riots of 1919," 147–49; Ferguson, "Elaine Race Riot," 45–61.

14. Wells-Barnett, *Arkansas Race Riot*, 3, 15–18, 28–47, 55; Lewis, "Race Relations in Arkansas," 225–31, 233–35, 241–45; Woodruff, *American Congo*, 88–91; Todd E. Lewis, " 'Through Death, Hell, and the Grave': Lynching and Antilynching Efforts in Arkansas, 1901–1939," in Lancaster, ed., *Bullets and Fire*, 149; Whitaker, *On the Lap of Gods*, chs. 7 and 9; Stockley, *Blood in Their Eyes*, chs. 4–5; Stockley, Timeline of Elaine Race Riot, 2–5; Buckelew, "Racial Violence in Arkansas," 138, 144–48, 152–55; Matkin-Rawn, " 'We Fight for the Rights of Our Race,' " 135–38; Cortner, *A Mob Intent on Death*, 12–23; McCool, *Union, Reaction, and Riot*, 30–33; Waskow, *From Race Riot to Sit-In*, 131–38.

15. Whayne, *Delta Empire*, 122–24, 136; Lewis, "Race Relations in Arkansas," 69–70. See also William Pickens, *Lynching and Debt Slavery* (1921).

16. Matkin-Rawn, " 'We Fight for the Rights of Our Race,' " 138–42, 146–47; Walter White, *A Man Called White: The Autobiography of Walter White* (1948), 44–51; Whitaker, *On the Lap of Gods*, 146–58, 185–293; Stockley, *Blood in Their Eyes*, 92–222; Stockley, Timeline of Elaine Race Riot, 5–6; Lewis, "Race Relations in Arkansas," 238–40, 247, 251–56; Lewis, " 'Through Death, Hell, and the Grave,' " 149–50; Moore v. Dempsey, 261 U.S. 86 (1923); William H. Pruden III, "Cracking Open the Door: *Moore v. Dempsey* and the Fight for Justice," in Lancaster, ed., *Elaine Massacre and Arkansas*, 238–67; Buckelew, "Racial Violence in Arkansas," 155–76; Lewis, " 'Through Death, Hell, and the Grave,' " 150; Megan Ming Francis, *Civil Rights and the Making of the Modern American State* (2014), 27.

17. Lewis, "Race Relations in Arkansas," 281–83; Buckelew, "Racial Violence in Arkansas," 114–15; Matkin-Rawn, " 'We Fight for the Rights of Our Race,' " 164; Lewis, " 'Through Death, Hell, and the Grave,' " 151–52; Whayne, *Delta Empire*, 113–14, 118–19, 127–33.

18. Lewis, "Race Relations in Arkansas," 285–86; Matkin-Rawn, " 'We Fight for the Rights of Our Race,' " 186; Lewis, " 'Through Death, Hell, and the Grave,' " 153.

19. Lewis, "Race Relations in Arkansas," 286–89; Lewis, " 'Through Death, Hell, and the Grave,' " 154–55.

20. Brian Greer, "A Reign of Terror," *Arkansas Times*, August 4, 2000; Marcet Haldeman-Julius, "The Story of a Lynching—An Exploration of Southern Psychology," *Haldeman-Julius Monthly* 6.3 (August 1927); James Reed Eison, "Dead, but She Was in a Good Place, a Church," *Pulaski County Historical Review*—all in f24, b1, Subseries II, Series I, Grif Stockley Papers, Butler Center for Arkansas Studies; Lewis, "Race Relations in Arkansas," 290–91, 305–6; Buckelew, "Racial Violence in Arkansas," 199–209; Matkin-Rawn, " 'We Fight for the Rights of Our Race,' " 197–98; Lewis, " 'Through Death, Hell, and the Grave,' " 131–32; Stephanie Harp, "Stories of a Lynching: Accounts of John Carter, 1927," in Lancaster, ed., *Bullets and Fire*; Amy Louise Wood, *Lynching and Spectacle: Witnessing Racial Violence in America, 1890–1940* (2009), 42, 98.

21. Lewis, "Race Relations in Arkansas," 291; Buckelew, "Racial Violence in Arkansas," 184, 215; Matkin-Rawn, " 'We Fight for the Rights of Our Race,' " 165–66; Lewis, " 'Through Death, Hell, and the Grave,' " 154; Equal Justice Initiative, *Lynching in America: Confronting the Legacy of Racial Terror* (3d ed., 2017), tbls. 1 and 3, https://lynchinginamerica.eji.org/report/ [https://perma.cc/L8SR-9P6F]; Equal Justice Initiative, *Lynching in America: Confronting the Legacy of Racial Terror: Supplement: Lynchings by County* (3d ed., 2017), 2, https://eji.org/sites/default/files/lynching-in-america-third-edition-summary.pdf [https://perma.cc/B8UN-66UC]; Vincent Vinikas, "Thirteen Dead at Saint Charles: Arkansas's Most Lethal Lynching and the Abrogation of Equal Protection," in Lancaster, ed., *Bullets and Fire*, 107–8; Jessie Daniel Ames, *The Changing Character of Lynching: Review of Lynching, 1931–1941* (1942), 35. See also Michael Ayers Trotti, "What Counts: Trends in Racial Violence in the Postbellum South," *Journal of American History* 100.2 (September 2013), 375–400.

22. Matkin-Rawn, " 'We Fight for the Rights of Our Race,' " 186, 191–93; W. A. Singfield to NAACP, July 29, 1921, f8, bI:G12, NAACPR.

23. Matkin-Rawn, " 'We Fight for the Rights of Our Race,' " 154–58, 161.

24. Buckelew, "Racial Violence in Arkansas," 115–16; Matkin-Rawn, " 'We Fight for the Rights of Our Race,' " 164–65, 186–90; Lewis, " 'Through Death, Hell, and the Grave,' " 152.

25. Buckelew, "Racial Violence in Arkansas," 215; Cermak, "In the Interest of Justice," 6, citing Waldrep, "Substituting the Law for the Lash."

Chapter 4. A Jim Crow Childhood, 1930s

1. Bill Bowden, "Bones Depict Many Illnesses in Community," *AG*, July 21, 1984, 1B–2B; Thomas Wayne Copeland, "Good Neighbors: Agents of Change in the New Rural South, 1900 to 1940" (Ph.D. diss., University of Mississippi, 2011), 15–16.

2. Henry Louis Gates Jr., *In Search of Our Roots: How 19 Extraordinary African Americans Reclaimed Their Past* (2009), 27–28; *CB*, 47.

3. *CB*, 6–8; Jeffrey Elliot, "Author Maya Angelou," *Sepia*, October 1977, 22, f4, b346, MAP.

4. *CB*, 10–12.
5. Ibid., 60–61.
6. Gates, *In Search of Our Roots*, 29–30.
7. Ibid., 32–37.
8. *CB*, 170.
9. MA, Essay for *Lift Every Voice and Sing* Project (1999–2000), f25, b180, MAP.
10. *CB*, 64.
11. *Step Back in Time: Virgil and Sarah Flowers Family History: 1800–2002* (2d ed., 2002), 56, f3, b5, MAP.
12. "State Figures on Educational Expenditures Show Discrimination against Negro Schools," *Commonwealth College Fortnightly* (March 15, 1938), 4, Education—Arkansas—1938 f, bI:C270, NAACPR.
13. David Charles Deller, "Sing Me Home to Gloryland: Arkansas Songbook Gospel Music in the Twentieth Century" (Ph.D. diss., University of Arkansas, 1999), 59–61.
14. Cheryl Lynn Greenberg, *To Ask for an Equal Chance: African Americans in the Great Depression* (2009).
15. *CB*, 50–51.
16. Annie Henderson, Account Book, 1930s, f2, b1, MAP.
17. Annie Henderson, financial records, 1930s, f2, b1, MAP.
18. *CB*, 50–51.
19. Joanne M. Braxton, "Symbolic Geography and Psychic Landscapes: A Conversation with Maya Angelou," *in* Joanne M. Braxton, ed., *Maya Angelou's* I Know Why the Caged Bird Sings: *A Casebook* (1999), 8–10.
20. *CB*, 17–19.
21. Ibid., 49.
22. The HistoryMakers interview with Barbara Wright-Pryor, tape 1, September 24, 2006, THM.
23. *CB*, 25.
24. Ibid., 50–51.
25. John Reed Tarver, "The Clan of Toil: Piney Woods Labor Relations in the Trans-Mississippi South, 1880–1920 (Ph.D. diss., Louisiana State University, 1991), 395–96, 452.
26. Correspondence in f16, bG13, NAACPR.
27. "The Anti-Lynching Crusaders: 'A Million Women United to Suppress Lynching,'" n.d., 6 (on file with author).
28. *CB*, 47–48.
29. Mary Medearis, "Big Doc's Girl," in John Caldwell Guilds, ed., *Arkansas, Arkansas: Writers and Writings from the Delta to the Ozarks, 1541–1969*, vol. 1 (1999), 586.
30. MA, "A Clean Telling of a Dirty Story," *Los Angeles Times*, June 1975, f8, b171, MAP.
31. Undated fragment of a play, f4, b181, MAP.

32. Marguerite Johnson, composition book, 1930s, f3, b1, MAP.
33. Marguerite Johnson, Scrapbook, b3, MAP.

Chapter 5. Bethel and Wallace, 1928

1. Bethel transcript, 202; "The Sun Calendar," *Baltimore Sun*, classified section, April 1, 1928, 1; "Weather Forecast," *AG*, April 1, 1928, 1; Bethel transcript, 356; "Weekly Review of the Cotton Trade," *AG*, March 19, 1928, 9; "Trade Conditions Continue Spotted, Says Bradstreet's," *AG*, April 28, 1928, 17; "Three Persons Are Convicted in Dry Law Cases," *AG*, April 11, 1928, 7; Martha Jones Bolsterli, "Born in the Delta," in John Caldwell Guilds, ed., *Arkansas, Arkansas: Writers and Writings from the Delta to the Ozarks, 1541–1969*, vol. 2 (1999), 49.

2. Bethel transcript, 161, 213–15, 419; "For Sale," *BCN*, January 7, 1938, 7; "Poplar Corners Wins Sixth Straight Game," *BCN*, May 17, 1932, 3; "Jolliff's Supply Store, Manila, Arkansas, 1909," *DHR* (Spring 1995), 6.

3. Bethel transcript, 195, 476–84; Henry Thomas Bolin, *WWIDC*, Mississippi County, AR, FHL film number 1530561.

4. Bethel transcript, 153, 200–203, 216–17, 224–27, 265–67, 430–31, 460–61, 480.

5. "Lynching Near Warren," *Pine Bluff Daily Graphic*, July 20, 1903, 1; "Negro Lynched Near Warren," *AG*, July 21, 1903, 1; "Hanging from a Limb," *AD*, July 21, 1903, 1.

6. Delayed birth certificate, Guy Frank Bethel, January 20, 1934, ABVS; 1900 U.S. Census, Buffalo, Craighead, AR, 14, family 263, lines 32–38, June 14, 1900; 1910 U.S. Census, Paragould Ward 1, Greene, AR, 12A, family 502, lines 1–8, March 20, 1910; 1930 U.S. Census, Big Rock Township, Pulaski, AR, 1A; 1940 U.S. Census, Flint, Genesee, MI, 11B, family 210, lines 64–65, April 13, 1940; 1940 U.S. Census, Monette, Craighead, AR, 12A, family 259, lines 15–18, April 15, 1940; certificate of marriage, Frank Bethel and Gladys Shields, January 15, 1925, ABVS; Bethel transcript, 416; Bethel prison file, ADC; Thea Baker to Scott Stern, November 9, 2019. I am indebted to Ms. Baker's analysis of Bethel's delayed birth certificate.

7. Delayed birth certificate, Roy Thomas "Mike" Wallace, March 31, 1941, ABVS; Wallace prison file, ADC; Bethel transcript, 351–52; 1910 U.S. Census, Monette, Craighead, AR, 6A, family 103, lines 16–24, April 20, 1910; 1930 U.S. Census, Monette, Craighead, AR, 10A, family 214, lines 15–16, April 12, 1930; Roy Thomas Wallace, July 1, 1922, *Colorado Steelworks Employment Records, 1887–1979*; Thea Baker to Scott Stern, November 9, 2019. I am once again indebted to Ms. Baker's analysis.

8. Fendler, *Chronicles*, 94, 151–52; Eldon Fairley, "Depression Kids," *DHR* (Summer 1992), 49, 67; Eldon Fairley, "The Great Sutton Shows," *DHR* (Fall 1995), 23–26.

9. Bethel transcript, 142, 146.

10. Ibid., 146–52, 188–94.

11. Ibid., 210–13.

12. Fendler, *Chronicles*, 67.

13. Bethel transcript, 204–9, 218–19; Registration Form, Herman Davis Memorial, National Register of Historic Places, OMB No. 1024-0018.

14. "Recaptured Fugitive Pleads Guilty to Forgery," *AG*, April 10, 1928, 5; "Death Penalty Is Sought for Two," *AG*, April 11, 1928, 7; "Two Given Death on Assault Charge," *AG*, April 12, 1928, 12; "Two Executions Scheduled Friday," *AG*, May 27, 1928, 12; statement of Arthur L. Adams before the District Court for the Eastern District of Arkansas, Caruthers & Clayton v. Cogbill, December 1936, 30, f10, bD50, NAACPR.

15. "Two Sentenced to Be Killed June 1," *AG*, April 14, 1928, 22; "Few Executed on Assault Charges," *AG*, April 15, 1928, 5.

16. "Two Executions Scheduled Friday," *AG*, May 27, 1928, 12.

17. Bethel v. State, 10 S.W.2d 370 (Ark. 1928).

18. "Bethel and Wallace Win Chance for Life," *BCN*, November 5, 1928, 1; "Once Condemned, To Be Tried Again," *AG*, February 6, 1929, 11.

Chapter 6. Class War, 1929–1935

1. Woodruff, *American Congo*, 152–153; Whayne, *Delta Empire*, 163.

2. Gail S. Murray, "Forty Years Ago: The Great Depression Comes to Arkansas," *AHQ* 29 (Winter 1970), 291–312 (40 percent statistic from 306); Gavin Wright, *Old South, New South: Revolutions in the Southern Economy since the Civil War* (1986), 55–57; Whayne, *Delta Empire*, 5, 163; Jeannie Whayne, *A New Plantation South: Land, Labor, and Federal Favor in Twentieth-Century Arkansas* (1996), ch. 8; Oscar Fendler, "Memorandum: Southern Tenant Farmers Union," 1, f28, b356, LWCR (mentioning banks closing); Charles Morrow Wilson, "Famine in Arkansas," *Outlook*, April 29, 1931, 596–97; Matkin-Rawn, "We Fight for the Rights of Our Race," 213–14; Roger Lambert, "Hoover and the Red Cross in the Arkansas Drought of 1930," *AHQ* 29 (Spring 1970), 3–19; Nan Woodruff, "The Failure of Relief during the Arkansas Drought of 1930–1931," *AHQ* 39 (Winter 1980), 301–13 (30 to 50 percent statistic from 302); Downs, *Stories of Survival*, 8–11.

3. Morgan, "Elite Dominance in the Arkansas Delta," 16–17; Whayne, *New Plantation South*, 152–53, ch. 7, 216; Matkin-Rawn, "We Fight for the Rights of Our Race," 217–19; Woodruff, "Failure of Relief During the Arkansas Drought," 303–9; Woodruff, *American Congo*, 153–59; Downs, *Stories of Survival*, 11–13; Alison Collis Greene, *No Depression in Heaven: The Great Depression, the New Deal, and the Transformation of Religion in the Delta* (2015).

4. Woodruff, *American Congo*, 154–55; Whayne, *New Plantation South*, 187–88; Matkin-Rawn, "We Fight for the Rights of Our Race," 214; Fendler, "Documentary TV," 3–4; Lambert, "Hoover and the Red Cross," 10; Murray, "Forty Years Ago," 296–98.

5. Morgan, "Elite Dominance in the Arkansas Delta," 23; Woodruff, *American Congo*, 159; James D. Ross, " 'I Ain't Got No Home': The Rise and Fall of the Southern Tenant Farmers' Union in Arkansas" (Ph.D. diss., Auburn University, 2004), 26–27; Norman Thomas, *Human Exploitation in the United States* (1934), 5–6.

6. H. L. Mitchell, *Mean Things Happening in This Land: The Life and Times of H. L. Mitchell* (1979), 47–58; Woodruff, *American Congo*, 159–68; Kester, *Revolt among the Sharecroppers*, 55–59; Raymond F. Gregory, *Norman Thomas, The Great Dissenter* (2008), 111–16; Harry Fleischman, *Norman Thomas, A Biography: 1884–1968* (1969), 145; "Arkansas Fields Worse Than Slums, Says Thomas," *New York Herald Tribune*, February 18, 1934, 15; "Thomas Finds 'Forgotten Man,' " *Washington Post*, February 18, 1934, 3; H. L. Mitchell, "The Founding and Early History of the Southern Tenant Farmers Union," *AHQ* 32 (Winter 1973), 342–54; Whayne, *New Plantation South*, 190–99; Thrasher and Wise, "The Southern Tenant Farmers' Union," 6, 16–17; Southern Tenant Farmers Union, Constitution and By-Laws, reel 1, STFUR; Ross, " 'I Ain't Got No Home,' " 93–96; Biegert, "Legacy of Resistance," 73–76.

7. Kester, *Revolt among the Sharecroppers*, 60–61.

8. "Tenant Farmers Union Protested," *AG*, November 4, 1934, 14.

9. "FERA Instructor Gives His Side of Anarchy Arrest," *SLPD*, January 19, 1935, 1.

10. Dunbar, *Against the Grain*, 89; Mitchell, *Mean Things Happening in This Land*, 52–53; Report of the Executive Secretary, December 1, 1934, reel 1, STFUR.

11. Carey Wayne Rogers, "The Southern Tenant Farmers' Union as a Social Movement: Conflict in a Plantation Society" (master's thesis, University of Arkansas, 1975), 57; "Four Organizers of Tenants Held," *AG*, November 23, 1934, 14.

12. Woodruff, *American Congo*, 168.

13. Luther Moore to WW, June 26, 1935, f10, bD50, NAACPR; statement of John A. Hibbler before the District Court for the Eastern District of Arkansas, Caruthers & Clayton v. Cogbill, December 1936, 7, f10, bD50, NAACPR; "Launch Drive to End Robberies," *BCN*, December 7, 1941, 1.

14. Fendler, "Documentary TV," 2–4; John Herling, "Field Notes from Arkansas," *The Nation*, April 10, 1935, 419–20; Fleischman, *Norman Thomas*, 148; Gregory, *Norman Thomas*, 118–19; Mitchell, *Mean Things Happening in This Land*, 73.

Chapter 7. Clayton and Carruthers, 1935

1. "Weather Forecast," *AG*, January 12, 1935, 1; "Amelia Earhart in Pacific Flight," *AG*, January 12, 1935, 1; "Daily Weather Record," *AG*, January 12, 1935, 14; "Share-the-Wealth Huey in New Attack on President," *AG*, January 12, 1935, 14; "Cold Wave Due in Arkansas Tonight," *AG*, January 13, 1935, 1; "Amelia Earhart Lands at Oakland," *AG*, January 13, 1935, 1.

2. "Return from Arizona with Robbery Suspects," *BCN*, January 12, 1935, 1; Rex Pitkin, "Negroes' Death Verdict Upheld in Arkansas 'Rape' Frame-up," *DW*, November 25, 1935, f10, bD50, NAACPR; " 'Big Boy' Wilson Out for Sheriff," *BCN*, January 14,

1932, 1; "Pay Tribute to Wilson for Constructive Work," *BCN*, September 28, 1933, 1; "Sheriff Wilson Seriously Hurt," *OT*, January 18, 1935, 1; "Hold Negroes Who Wounded Sheriff," *BCN*, January 14, 1935, 1.

3. "Return from Arizona with Robbery Suspects," 1; Pitkin, "Negroes' Death Verdict Upheld in Arkansas 'Rape' Frame-up"; " 'Big Boy' Wilson Out for Sheriff," 1; "Pay Tribute to Wilson for Constructive Work," 1; "Sheriff Wilson Seriously Hurt," 1; "Hold Negroes Who Wounded Sheriff," 1.

4. Clayton statement, abstract, and brief of appellants, 41; Moore to WW, June 26, 1935, NAACPR; CHH, Handwritten notes, December 11, 1936, f2, bD51, NAACPR; statement of V. M. Townsend before the District Court for the Eastern District of Arkansas, Carruthers & Clayton v. Reed, March 1938, f3, bD51, NAACPR; "Sheriff Wilson Seriously Hurt," 1.

5. "Hold Negroes Who Wounded Sheriff," 1; "Physicians Confident of Saving Wilson's Eyes," *BCN*, January 15, 1935, 1; "Bits of News: Mostly Personal," *BCN*, January 15, 1935, 2; Clayton statement, abstract, and brief of appellants, 41–42; statement of R. F. Harris before the District Court for the Eastern District of Arkansas, Carruthers & Clayton v. Reed, March 1938, f3, bD51, NAACPR.

6. Clayton abstract, 31–32.

7. "Hold Negroes Who Wounded Sheriff," 1.

8. Clayton abstract, 30; "Hold Negroes Who Wounded Sheriff," 1; Matkin-Rawn, "We Fight for the Rights of Our Race," 191.

9. "Hold Negroes Who Wounded Sheriff," 1; Clayton statement, abstract, and brief of appellants, 29.

10. "Hold Negroes Who Wounded Sheriff," 1.

11. Interview of Trina Nicholson (January 7, 2020); Interview of Trina Nicholson and Gail Terry (May 30, 2024).

12. "Hold Negroes Who Wounded Sheriff," 1.

13. Clayton abstract, 19.

14. Marriage record for Edie Mitchell and Clear Clayton, April 16, 1898, Mississippi Compiled Marriage Index, 1776–1935; 1900 U.S. Census, DeSoto, MS, 11A-11B, family 202, lines 46–51, June 13, 1900; 1920 U.S. Census, Mississippi, AR, 7B, family 158, lines 71–78, March 9, 1920.

15. Clayton prison file, ADC; "Sheriff Takes Nine Prisoners to Pen," *Caruthersville Journal*, August 13, 1931, 1; Clayton transcript, 20–21.

16. Carruthers prison file, ADC; Clayton abstract 27.

17. Interview of Trina Nicholson (April 25, 2020); interview of Trina Nicholson (January 7, 2020); 1920 U.S. Census, Hickman Township, Mississippi, AR, 2A, family 20, lines 6–10, January 20, 1920; Clayton statement, abstract, and brief of appellants, 27; 1910 U.S. Census, Chickasaw, MS, 15A, family 270, lines 25–29, May 7, 1910.

18. "Mississippi County Jail," *DHR* (Fall 1995), 59; Edrington, *History of Mississippi County*, 173; "Rich, Rare and Racy," 1.

19. Statement of Bubbles Clayton before the District Court for the Eastern District of Arkansas, Carruthers & Clayton v. Reed, March 1938, f3, bD51, NAACPR; Clayton statement, abstract, and brief of appellants, 32; Pitkin, "Negroes' Death Verdict Upheld in Arkansas 'Rape' Frame-up." The deputy whom the transcript identifies here as "Ran Miller" appears to have been Deputy Rainmiller.

20. Statement of Jim X. Carruthers before the District Court for the Eastern District of Arkansas, Carruthers & Clayton v. Reed, March 1938, f3, bD51, NAACPR.

21. Statement of A. Lindsey before the District Court for the Eastern District of Arkansas, Carruthers & Clayton v. Reed, March 1938, f3, bD51, NAACPR.

22. Statement of C. H. Wilson before the District Court for the Eastern District of Arkansas, Carruthers & Clayton v. Reed, March 1938, f3, bD51, NAACPR; brief in support of petition for writ of certiorari to the Supreme Court of the United States, Carruthers & Clayton v. Reed, March 1938, f1, bD51, NAACPR.

23. "Remove Negroes as Crowd Threatens," *BCN*, January 15, 1935, 1; statement of A. Lindsey before the District Court for the Eastern District of Arkansas, Carruthers & Clayton v. Reed, March 1938, f3, bD51, NAACPR; statement of Jim X. Carruthers before the District Court for the Eastern District of Arkansas, Carruthers & Clayton v. Reed, March 1938, f3, bD51, NAACPR; statement of Bubbles Clayton before the District Court for the Eastern District of Arkansas, Carruthers & Clayton v. Reed, March 1938, f3, bD51, NAACPR; statement of John A. Hibbler before the District Court for the Eastern District of Arkansas, Caruthers & Clayton v. Cogbill, December 1936, 8–9, f10, bD50, NAACPR; Clayton statement, abstract, and brief of appellants, 29–30; "Sheriff Wilson Seriously Hurt," 1; "Negro Prisoners Saved from Mob," *AG*, January 16, 1935, 2; "Pemiscot Wants Negro Bandits," *BCN*, January 19, 1935, 1.

24. "Hearing for Mother of Negro Bandit Delayed," *BCN*, January 21, 1935, 1; "Hearing for Mother of Bandit Again Delayed," *BCN*, January 22, 1935, 1; "Woman Held in Robbery Case," *BCN*, January 22, 1935, 1; interview of Trina Nicholson (April 25, 2020); interview of Trina Nicholson and Gail Terry (May 30, 2024).

25. "Sheriff Wilson to Return Soon," *BCN*, January 18, 1935, 1; "Sheriff Wilson Back at Office," *BCN*, January 21, 1935, 1.

26. "Weather," *BCN*, January 15, 1935, 1.

27. "Remove Negroes as Crowd Threatens," 1.

28. Mitchell, "Founding and Early History," 354–56; Mitchell, *Mean Things Happening in This Land*, 59–61; Kester, *Revolt among the Sharecroppers*, 67–69; Ross, " 'I Ain't Got No Home,' " 144; Matkin-Rawn, "We Fight for the Rights of Our Race," 230–31; "Rodgers Denies That He Made Lynching Threat," *AG*, January 17, 1935, 2; "Accused of Having Incited Tenants," *AG*, January 17, 1935, 2; "FERA Instructor Gives His Side of Anarchy Arrest," *SLPD*, January 19, 1935, 1; Thomas Fauntleroy, "Anarchy Suit Stirs Arkansas," *NYT*, January 27, 1935, E6; Mitchell, *Mean Things Happening in This Land*, 48.

29. Mitchell, "Founding and Early History," 356; Thrasher and Wise, "Southern Tenant Farmers' Union," 19; Dunbar, *Against the Grain*, 85, 92–95; Mitchell, *Mean*

Things Happening in This Land, 56–58, 61–62; "Woman Sent to Clean Up Cotton War," *New York Daily News*, January 20, 1935, 30; "Tenant Farmers' Leader Sentenced in 'Anarchy' Trial," *Daily Worker*, January 23, 1935, 2; Lem Harris to All Farm Groups & Organizations, January 28, 1935, reel 1, STFUR.

30. Mitchell, *Mean Things Happening in This Land*, 63, 74–75; Ross, " 'I Ain't Got No Home,' " 140; Kester, *Revolt among the Sharecroppers*, 76–77; "Asserts Trouble Looms in Arkansas," *AG*, January 21, 1935, 1; "Sharecropper War Bitterness Grows," *Boston Globe*, February 3, 1935, A3; "Reign of Terror Faces Share-Croppers' Union," February 5, 1935, reel 1, STFUR; "Arkansas Tenant Farmers Union Speakers Attacked," February 8, 1935, reel 1, STFUR.

31. Thrasher and Wise, "Southern Tenant Farmers' Union," 19–22; Mitchell, *Mean Things Happening in This Land*, 70–71; Kester, *Revolt among the Sharecroppers*, 76–77.

32. Mitchell, *Mean Things Happening in This Land*, 66; Whayne, *New Plantation South*, 207–8; Ross, " 'I Ain't Got No Home,' " 137–38; Matkin-Rawn, "We Fight for the Rights of Our Race," 234.

33. Kester, *Revolt among the Sharecroppers*, 83; Dunbar, *Against the Grain*, 100–101.

34. Kester, *Revolt among the Sharecroppers*, 82.

35. "Sharecropper Rally Blocked by Arkansans," *New York Herald Tribune*, February 10, 1935, 9; "Union Speakers Escorted from Birdsong Rally," *BCN*, February 11, 1935, 1; Dunbar, *Against the Grain*, 99–101; Mitchell, *Mean Things Happening in This Land*, 69–70; Mitchell, "Founding and Early History," 357; Kester, *Revolt among the Sharecroppers*, 80–81; Fleischman, *Norman Thomas*, 147–48; Pitkin, "Negroes' Death Verdict Upheld in Arkansas 'Rape' Frame-up."

36. Herling, "Field Notes from Arkansas," 420.

37. Gregory, *Norman Thomas*, 121.

38. Matkin-Rawn, "We Fight for the Rights of Our Race," 234. See also Mitchell, *Mean Things Happening in This Land*, 75.

39. Clayton statement, abstract, and brief of appellants, 46–47; statement of Bubbles Clayton before the District Court for the Eastern District of Arkansas, Carruthers & Clayton v. Reed, March 1938, f3, bD51, NAACPR; statement of John A. Hibbler, before the District Court for the Eastern District of Arkansas, Carruthers & Clayton v. Cogbill, 9, December 1936, f10, bD50, NAACPR; "New Sanity Plea for Mark Shank," *HS*, November 16, 1934, 1; "Barnes Executed for Taxi Murder," *HS*, March 1, 1935, 1; "Negro Woman's Throat Slashed by Husband," *AG*, March 28, 1935, 5; "Long Hunt for Negro Slayer Ends at Cairo," *BCN*, June 13, 1934, 1.

40. Clayton statement, abstract, and brief of appellants, 20, 25–26. Petition for Writ of Certiorari to Eighth Circuit, Carruthers & Clayton v. Reed (October 1938), f1, bD51, NAACPR; " 'Petting Party' Bandits to Face Capital Charge," *BCN* (March 9, 1935), 1; brief on behalf of appellants, Carruthers & Clayton v. Reed (1938), 2, Case No. 11,210, RG 276, National Archives at Kansas City, Missouri.

41. Statement of Bubbles Clayton, NAACPR; Clayton abstract, 20, 28; Clayton statement, abstract, and brief of appellants, 25–26, 30–33, 39.

42. Clayton abstract, 8–11, 15, 18, 32; Clayton statement, abstract, and brief of appellants, 10–13, 16, 46–47. Cf. Hamm transcript, 21, 37–38, 47; Palmer transcript, 28–29, 34, 63.

43. Clayton abstract, 32.

44. Clayton supplemental brief for appellants, 15.

45. Clayton statement, abstract, and brief of appellants, 30.

46. Pitkin, "Negroes' Death Verdict Upheld in Arkansas 'Rape' Frame-up."

Chapter 8. Mr. Freeman, Mid-1930s

1. *CB*, 52–53.

2. Ibid., 54–55, Bailey Johnson, *WWIIDC*, San Diego, CA; Hilton Als, "Songbird," *New Yorker*, August 5, 2002, https://www.newyorker.com/magazine/2002/08/05/songbird [https://perma.cc/GWS8-CJ8H]; 1910 U.S. Census, Stamps, Lafayette, AR, 2B, family 27, lines 51–54, April 16, 1910; Bailey Johnson, *U.S. Army Transport Service, Passenger Lists, 1910–1939*, Military Unit 302 Co. H., December 4, 1917; Bailey Johnson, *U.S. Army Transport Service, Passenger Lists, 1910–1939*, Military Unit 807 Co. T.C., Service Number 230857, June 26, 1919; MA, *Mom & Me & Mom* (2013), 7; MA, draft, *The Caged Bird Sings*, 2, f2, b112, MAP.

3. Marcia Ann Gillespie, Rosa Johnson Butler, and Richard A. Long, *Maya Angelou: A Glorious Celebration* (2008), 14; 1920 U.S. Census, Stamps, Lafayette, AR, 24B, family 589, lines 57–60, January 19, 1920; Angelou, *Mom & Me & Mom*, 3–7; Walter Johnson, *The Broken Heart of America: St. Louis and the Violent History of the United States* (2020), 252.

4. Gillespie, Butler, and Long, *Maya Angelou*, 14–15; Angelou, *Mom & Me & Mom*, 7–8; *CB*, 55; 1930 U.S. Census, St. Louis, St. Louis, MO, 12B, family 280, lines 83–91, April 10, 1930; 1930 U.S. Census, St. Louis, St. Louis, MO, 2A, family 32, lines 45–48, April 2, 1930.

5. *CB*, 55–60; PBS Documentary, *Maya Angelou: And Still I Rise*, February 21, 2017, at 11:51.

6. Johnson, *Broken Heart of America*, 252–259; *CB*, 61–64.

7. *CB*, 66–69.

8. Ibid., 72–83.

9. See Orville W. Taylor, " 'Jumping the Broomstick': Slave Marriage and Morality in Arkansas," *AHQ* 17.3 (Autumn 1958), 225–28; Harriet Ann Jacobs, *Incidents in the Life of a Slave Girl* (Boston, 1861), 49–57; Darlene Clark Hine, "Rape and the Inner Lives of Black Women in the Middle West," *Signs* 14.4 (Summer 1989), 912; Elizabeth Keckley, *Behind the Scenes, or, Thirty Years a Slave, and Four Years in the White House* (1868), 24; Stephanie E. Jones-Rogers, *They Were Her Property: White Women as Slave*

Owners in the American South (2019), 107, 149; Sharon Block, *Rape & Sexual Power in Early America* (2006), especially ch. 1; Elizabeth Fox-Genovese, *Within the Plantation Household: Black and White Women of the Old South* (1988), 294–326; Ronald G. Walters, "The Erotic South: Civilization and Sexuality in American Abolitionism," *American Quarterly* 25.2 (May 1973), 181–83; Cardyn, *Sexualized Racism/Gendered Violence*, 716–19; Eugene D. Genovese, *Roll, Jordan, Roll: The World the Slaves Made* (1974), 414; Rachel A. Feinstein, *When Rape Was Legal: The Untold History of Sexual Violence during Slavery* (2018). After this book went into production, a new, comprehensive study, Shannon C. Eaves, *Sexual Violence and American Slavery: The Making of a Rape Culture in the Antebellum* (2024), was released.

10. Cardyn, *Sexualized Racism/Gendered Violence*, 719–36; Laura Edwards, *Gendered Strife and Confusion: The Political Culture of Reconstruction* (1997), 199; Freedman, *Redefining Rape*, 75–76; Wriggins, "Rape, Racism, and the Law," 106–7; Kidada E. Williams, *They Left Great Marks on Me African American Testimonies of Racial Violence from Emancipation to World War I* (2012), 107–11; Sommerville, *Rape & Race in the Nineteenth-Century South*, 147–48.

11. Audre Lorde, "Age, Race, Class, and Sex: Women Redefining Difference," in Beverly Guy-Sheftall, ed., *Words of Fire: An Anthology of African-American Feminist Thought* (1995), 288; Susan A. Mann, "Slavery, Sharecropping, and Sexual Inequality," *Signs* 14.4 (Summer 1989), 789 ("there are few data on the frequency" of "sexual and physical abuse [of Black women] by Black males").

12. Freedman, *Redefining Rape*, 83; Patricia Hill Collins, *Black Sexual Politics: African Americans, Gender, and the New Racism* (2004), 63–66; Dorothy Roberts, *Killing the Black Body: Race, Reproduction, and the Meaning of Liberty* (1997), 11; Paula Giddings, "The Last Taboo," in Toni Morrison, ed., *Race-ing Justice, En-Gendering Power* (1992), 443. See also Crystal N. Feimster, *Southern Horrors: Women and the Politics of Rape and Lynching* (2009), 117.

13. Deborah Gray White, *Too Heavy a Load: Black Women in Defense of Themselves, 1894–1994* (1999), 61–62.

14. Collins, *Black Sexual Politics*, 217.

15. Freedman, *Redefining Rape*, ch. 4; Sommerville, *Rape & Race in the Nineteenth-Century South*, 147–60.

16. Feimster, *Southern Horrors*, 92, 107–17; Patricia A. Schechter, *Ida B. Wells-Barnett and American Reform, 1880–1930* (2001), 123–24; Freedman, *Redefining Rape*, 105–8, 113–19; Leslie K. Dunlap, "The Reform of Rape Law and the Problem of White Men: Age-of-Consent Campaigns in the South, 1885–1910," in Martha Hodes, ed., *Sex, Love, Race: Crossing Boundaries in North American History* (1999), 352–72.

17. Freedman, *Redefining Rape*, 85, 123, 208; Rivers, "Race, Sex, Violence," 43; Laura F. Edwards, "Sexual Violence, Gender, Reconstruction, and the Extension of Patriarchy in Granville County, North Carolina," *North Carolina Historical Review* 68.3 (July 1991), 242, 246–48; Vivien M. L. Miller, *Crime, Sexual Violence, and Clemency: Florida's Pardon*

Board and Penal System in the Progressive Era (2000), 182. See also Flood, *Rape in Chicago*, ch. 3 (documenting the "proliferation of black victims appearing in Chicago courts during the 1950s").

18. Feimster, *Southern Horrors*, 113–20; White, *Too Heavy a Load*, 69–72; Freedman, *Redefining Rape*, 85, 108–10.

19. MA, "I'm on My Journey Now" (2003), f4, b179, MAP.

20. Jayne Millsap Stone, " 'They Were Her Daughters': Women and Grassroots Organizing for Social Justice in the Arkansas Delta, 1870–1970" (Ph.D. diss., University of Memphis, 2010), 23–24, 59, 77–83, 99–104, 107–18, 121–23; Matthew Placido, "Founding Mothers and Movement Mamas: African American Women in the Depression-Era Southern Tenant Farmers' Union" (master's thesis, Florida Atlantic University, 2013), ch. 4; Matkin-Rawn, " 'We Fight for the Rights of Our Race,' " 191, 194–96.

21. Matkin-Rawn, " 'We Fight for the Rights of Our Race,' " 192.

22. Robin D. G. Kelley, " 'We Are Not What We Seem': Rethinking Black Working-Class Opposition in the Jim Crow South," *Journal of American History* 80.1 (June 1993), 75–76 (citing James C. Scott).

23. Hine, "Rape and the Inner Lives of Black Women," 912, 914; Saidiya Hartman, *Scenes of Subjection: Terror, Slavery, and Self-Making in Nineteenth-Century America* (1997), 60; Saidiya Hartman, "The Anarchy of Colored Girls Assembled in a Riotous Manner," *South Atlantic Quarterly* 117.3 (July 2018), 467.

24. CB, 83.

Chapter 9. The Trial Begins, 1929

1. "Weather Forecast," *AG*, April 10, 1929, 1; "The Weather," *AG*, April 10, 1929, 13; *WPA Guide to 1930s Arkansas*, 131–32; "Over a Score Killed, More Than 100 Injured, in Series of Tornadoes in Northern and Northeastern Arkansas," *AG*, April 11, 1929, 1.

2. Registration Form, Mississippi County Courthouse, National Register of Historic Places, OMB No. 1024–0018; Jared Craig, "Mississippi County Courthouse, Chickasawba District," *Encyclopedia of Arkansas*, October 15, 2019, https://encyclopediaofarkansas.net/entries/mississippi-county-courthouse-chickasawba-district-9247/ [https://perma.cc/RXX8-NXYZ]; "Open Blytheville's New Courthouse Soon," *AG*, June 12, 1921, 18; photographs 26–110 through 26–112, Courthouse Photograph Collection, Butler Center for Arkansas Studies.

3. "Heavy Criminal Docket Faces Court in Blytheville," *AG*, March 27, 1929, 2; "Blytheville Lawyer May Be Disbarred," *OT*, March 22, 1929, 1; "Criminal Court Opens, Facing Heavy Docket," *BCN*, April 1, 1929, 1.

4. "Judge Keck Rites to Be Tomorrow," *BCN*, November 1, 1958, 1; "Keck for County Judge," *OT*, October 29, 1915, 4; "Landslide for Good Government and Brough," *OT*, March 31, 1916, 1; "Errors or Plain Stealing, Which?" *OT*, April 7, 1916, 1; "County Out of Debt First Time in History," *OT*, September 16, 1921, 4; "G. E. Keck for Circuit

Judge," *OT,* August 4, 1922, 7; "Late Session of Criminal Court Disposed of Big Docket," *OT,* April 6, 1923, 1; "New Courthouse for Blytheville," *AD,* May 8, 1919, 16; "Receive Bids for Courthouse," *AD,* September 27, 1919, 2; "Local and Personal," *OT,* October 5, 1917, 5.

5. Matkin-Rawn, "We Fight for the Rights of Our Race," 72–73; transcript of interview of Harry C. Martin, conducted by Constance A. Apostolou, February 12, 1992; March 7, 1992, J-0006, p15, Law School Oral History Project, Southern Oral History Program, University of North Carolina.

6. "Death Penalty Is Asked for Youths," *AG,* April 11, 1929, 5.

7. "Judge S. L. Gladish," 1; "The Town Election," *OT,* April 8, 1909, 1; "Mrs. Gladish Entertains," *OT,* July 9, 1920, 1; "Hon. S. L. Gladish for Circuit Judge," *OT,* May 3, 1922, 1; "Hon. SL. Gladish for Circuit Judge," *OT,* May 26, 1922, 1; "S. L. Gladish Announces for Prosecuting Attorney," *OT,* February 22, 1924, 1; "Mrs. S. L. Gladish Rites in Osceola; Rites Held Today," *BCN,* July 21, 1954, 1; Edrington, *History of Mississippi County,* 84; "Vote in Mississippi County Democratic Primary," OT (August 18, 1922), 1. For Gladish's appearance, see photograph on file with Mississippi County Historical Society.

8. Correspondence in f147, b59 and f1, b70, LWCR. Quotation from Lee Wilson & Company to S. L. Gladish, April 24, 1936, f110, b80, LWCR.

9. 1920 U.S. Census, Monette, Craighead, AR, 11, family 238, lines 63–66, January 31, 1920; "Prosecutor Names Deputies," *AG,* October 30, 1912, 2; "C. W. Stanley Tried and Dismissed in Justice's Court," *Jonesboro Evening Sun,* January 13, 1914, 1.

10. 1930 U.S. Census, Blytheville, Mississippi, AR, 10A, family 235, lines 39–41, April 8, 1930.

11. Photographs: "Sidelights on Solons," *AG,* February 7, 1915, 4; "Foes of Lobby Maintained to Fight University Removal," *AD,* February 7, 1917, 3.

12. "Sidelights on Solons," 4; "E. E. Alexander Succumbs Today," *BCN,* November 26, 1940, 1.

13. "Pistol Toating a Felony," *OT,* November 27, 1914, 1; "May Become Candidate," *AG,* May 22, 1915, 1; "Will Be a Candidate," *OT,* August 27, 1915, 1; "New Faces for Assembly Halls," *AD,* April 22, 1916, 1; "Eight Senators Out for Pro Tem Honor," *AD,* March 6, 1917, 3; "Ponder and Newton Expect Elections without Contests," *AD,* January 9, 1919, 1; "Hester Heads New Committee," *AD,* January 28, 1919, 1; "Building of Roads Is 'War Measure,'" *AD,* September 1, 1917, 8.

14. "Tables Resolution to Kill Commission," *Hot Springs New Era,* January 30, 1920, 1; "About Town," *Little Rock Daily News,* January 7, 1921, 3; Clio Harper, "The Political Pot Begins to Simmer," *Hot Springs New Era,* April 23, 1919, 8; "Sen. Alexander to Make Race," *AD,* May 30, 1919, 10; Clio Harper, "State Capital Gossip," *OT,* April 2, 1920, 6; "Interesting Congressional Races," *Hot Springs New Era,* August 2, 1920, 4; "Close Race in First," *AG,* August 11, 1920, 6; "State Convention Selects Electors to Vote for Cox," *Pine Bluff Daily Graphic,* September 15, 1920, 1; "Alexander to be Toney's

Manager," *Little Rock Daily News,* February 7, 1922, 1; "E. E. Alexander for Representative," *OT,* March 21, 1924, 1; "Roster of 1927 Legislature," *North Arkansas Star,* September 9, 1926, 1; "Arkansas Second State to Vote Ratification," *AD,* July 29, 1919, 9; "E .E. Alexander," 1.

15. "Sen. Alexander to Make Race," *AD,* May 30, 1919, 10; "Commends Spirit of Pine Bluff Elkdom," *Pine Bluff Daily Graphic,* December 22, 1915, 7; "County Court Has Very Light Docket," *OT,* October 22, 1915, 1; "Warning Order," *OT,* February 6, 1920, 12; "Warning Order," *OT,* January 16, 1925, 6; "Pardons Innocent Man," *Southern Standard* (Arkadelphia, AR), August 16, 1917, 6; "E. E. Alexander," 1.

16. Transcript of interview of Harry C. Martin, 6, 15; transcript of interview with James K. Dorsett Jr., conducted by H. George Kurani, March 3, 1993, J-0014, 43–46; transcript of interview with Robert Strange Cahoon, conducted by Michael Grossman, September 27, 29, 1994, J-0024, 60–61; transcript of interview with Joseph Williamson Grier, conducted by Allen C. Smith, March 13, 16, 1992, J-0032, 14–15—all in Law School Oral History Project, Southern Oral History Program, University of North Carolina.

17. Bethel transcript, 30–31.

18. William C. Griffin, *WWIDC,* Mississippi County, AR, FHL film number 1530562; William C. Griffin, *WWIIDC, 1942,* Mississippi County, AR; 1910 U.S. Census, Big Lake, Mississippi, AR, 17B, family 61, lines 77–81, May 21, 1910; 1930 U.S. Census, Big Lake, Mississippi, AR, 7B, family 133, lines 57–62, April 11, 1930; "William C. 'Dobe' Griffin," *Find a Grave,* December 14, 2015, https://www.findagrave.com/memorial/156036148 [https://perma.cc/GA4L-Q5U6].

19. See "Jurors Summoned for Criminal Court Term," *BCN,* October 4, 1934, 3.

20. Crawford & Moses Digest, §§ 6352, 6383 (1921); Holly J. McCammon et al., "Becoming Full Citizens: The U.S. Women's Jury Rights Campaigns, the Pace of Reform, and Strategic Adaptation," *American Journal of Sociology* 113.4 (January 2008), 1109; "Negroes on Arkansas Jury Panel Make Legal History in Dixie," 1947, on file at Arkansas State Archive, http://photos.ark-ives.com/spirit/PS24_13r.jpg [https://perma.cc/GV94-M4JW].

21. Bethel transcript, 31–32; "Bethel and Wallace Trial Finally Underway with Completion of Jury," *BCN,* April 10, 1929, 1.

22. Bethel transcript, 32.

23. Ibid., 40, 77; Crawford & Moses Digest, §§ 6366, 6381, 6384 (1921); "Bethel and Wallace Trial Finally Underway," 1.

24. Bethel transcript, 3–4, 7, 10, 14, 16, 20, 22–26, 58; Davis abstract and brief for appellant, 45; Brust transcript, 477–79. See also Bradshaw transcript, 10–38; Sutton transcript, 30–31; West II transcript, 32–52.

25. See Cabe abstract and brief of appellant, 2–20; Thornsberry brief of appellant, 17–19.

26. See Bethel transcript, 56–57.

27. Mose Smith, *WWIDC*, Mississippi County, AR, FHL film number 1530563; 1920 U.S. Census, Chickasawba, Mississippi, AR, 4A, family 69, lines 1–3, March 22, 1920; 1930 U.S. Census, Chickasawba, Mississippi, AR, 15B, family 367, lines 88–93, April 25, 1930; 1940 U.S. Census, Chickasawba, Mississippi, AR, 1A, lines 36–38, April 2, 1940; "Yarbro, Ark., District No. 29," *BCN*, May 4, 1931, 8; "Jury for June Term Selected," *BCN*, May 21, 1930, 1.

28. Bethel transcript, 58–61.

29. Ibid., 94.

30. "Death Penalty Is Asked for Youths," 5; "Bethel and Wallace Trial Finally Underway," 1.

31. Bethel transcript, 94–99, "Bethel and Wallace Trial Finally Underway," 1.

32. Bethel transcript, 99–100.

33. Ibid., 101.

34. Ibid., 101–9.

35. Ibid., 109–20.

36. Ibid., 120.

37. "50 Known Dead from Series of State Storms," *AG*, April 12, 1929, 1.

Chapter 10. The Trial Begins, 1935

1. "Alleged Negro Rapists Sentenced to Death," *OT*, April 12, 1935), 1; "Forecast of Frost as Mercury Falls," *AG*, April 8, 1935, 1; "The Weather," *AG*, April 8, 1935, 9; statement of Arthur L. Adams before the District Court for the Eastern District of Arkansas, Caruthers & Clayton v. Cogbill, December 1936, 20, 25, 30, f10, bD50, NAACPR.

2. Neil Killough, *WWIDC*, Mississippi County, AR, FHL film number 1523090; "Succumbs to Heart Attack in Houston," *AG*, October 6, 1945, 7; "Serve Subpoenas for Criminal Term, Dec. 29th," *BCN*, December 23, 1930, 3; "Maj. Killough Member of Well Known Family," *AG*, October 3, 1945, 1; "Court Adjourned but Docket Cleared," *OT*, March 27, 1931, 1; "Grand Jury Returns Sixty Indictments," *OT*, March 20, 1931, 1; "Criminal Court Meets Judge Gladish Presides," *OT*, March 22, 1935, 1.

3. "Crowd Listens to Candidates for Four Hours," *BCN*, August 6, 1932, 3; "Denver Dudley Enters Contest," *BCN*, March 26, 1932, 1; Denver Layton Dudley, *WWIDC*, Clay County, AR, FHL film number 1522733; "Officers Meet," *BCN*, February 11, 1935, 1

4. "Arthur Adams Dies in Little Rock Hospital," *NAT*, July 27, 1948, 1, 2; Arthur Lambert Adams, *WWIIDC*, Craighead County, AR.

5. Statement of Bubbles Clayton before the District Court for the Eastern District of Arkansas, Caruthers & Clayton v. Reed, March 1938, f3, bD51, NAACPR.

6. "Alleged Negro Rapists Sentenced to Death," *OT*, April 12, 1935, 1; statement of W. B. Moore before the District Court for the Eastern District of Arkansas, Caruthers & Clayton v. Reed, March 1938, f3, bD51, NAACPR.

7. Statement of Arthur L. Adams before the District Court for the Eastern District of Arkansas, Caruthers & Clayton v. Cogbill, December 1936, 16; "True Bills Are Found against Accused Negroes," *BCN*, April 2, 1935, 1.

8. "Arthur Adams Dies in Little Rock Hospital," 1, 2; 1930 U.S. Census, Jonesboro, Craighead, AR, 2A, family 25, lines 8–12, April 2, 1930; Local News, *OT*, May 2, 1919, 6.

9. Statement of John A. Hibbler before the District Court for the Eastern District of Arkansas, Caruthers & Clayton v. Cogbill, December 1936, 10; statement of Arthur L. Adams before the District Court for the Eastern District of Arkansas, Caruthers & Clayton v. Cogbill, December 1936, 16–17, 26, 28, 32—both in f10, bD50, NAACPR; statement of Neil Killough before the District Court for the Eastern District of Arkansas, Carruthers & Clayton v. Reed, March 1938, f3, bD51, NAACPR; S. R. McCulloch, "Miscarriage of Justice in Arkansas Alleged," *SLPD*, March 1, 1936, 3-I.

10. Statement of Arthur L. Adams before the District Court for the Eastern District of Arkansas, Caruthers & Clayton v. Cogbill, December 1936, 16–19, 34–35, f10, bD50, NAACPR.

11. Ibid., 29; McCulloch, "Miscarriage of Justice in Arkansas Alleged," 3-I; "Trial of Attack Case Will Open Monday Morning," *BCN*, April 4, 1935, 1.

12. Statement of Arthur L. Adams before the District Court for the Eastern District of Arkansas, Caruthers & Clayton v. Cogbill, December 1936, 19, f10, bD50, NAACPR; Crawford & Moses Digest, § 3087 (1921).

13. Statement of Adams, 19–20, 29; statement of John A. Hibbler before the District Court for the Eastern District of Arkansas, Caruthers & Clayton v. Cogbill, December 1936, 10, f10, bD50, NAACPR; McCulloch, "Miscarriage of Justice in Arkansas Alleged," 3-I.

14. Clayton statement, abstract, and brief of appellants, 41–42; McCulloch, "Miscarriage of Justice in Arkansas Alleged," 3-I. Motions for a change of venue were always an uphill struggle. See, e.g., Hays abstract and brief for appellant, 1–2; Hays transcript, 4, 6–13, 32–77; Davis transcript, 6–29; Davis abstract and brief for appellant, 43–44.

15. Statement of Arch Lindsey before the District Court for the Eastern District of Arkansas, Carruthers & Clayton v. Reed, March 1938, f3, bD51, NAACPR; Arch Lindsey, *WWIIDC*, Mississippi County, AR.

16. Statement of Neil Killough before the District Court for the Eastern District of Arkansas, Carruthers & Clayton v. Reed, March 1938, f3, bD51, NAACPR; brief in support of petition for writ of certiorari, Carruthers & Clayton v. Reed, May 24, 1939, f1, bD51, NAACPR.

17. "Death Penalty Given Negroes for Assault," *AG*, January 7, 1938, 24; "Negroes Charged with Attack to be Tried," *AG*, December 31, 1937, 2; "Negro Convicted to Die in Chair," *AG*, June 14, 1932, 2. See also "Quizzing of Negro Slayer in Delayed," *AG*, December 17, 1925, 5; "Negro Slayer Sane, Two Doctors Say," *AG*, January 10, 1926, 5; "Death Penalty Is Asked for Martin," *AG*, January 12, 1926, 1.

18. McCulloch, "Miscarriage of Justice in Arkansas Alleged," 3-I; statement of Arthur L. Adams before the District Court for the Eastern District of Arkansas, Caruthers & Clayton v. Cogbill, December 1936, 23–24, f10, bD50, NAACPR.

19. Norris v. Alabama, 294 U.S. 587, 588 (1932); statement of Neil Killough before the District Court for the Eastern District of Arkansas, Carruthers & Clayton v. Reed, March 1938, f3, bD51, NAACPR.

20. McCulloch, "Miscarriage of Justice in Arkansas Alleged," 3-I.

21. Statement of John A. Hibbler before the District Court for the Eastern District of Arkansas, Caruthers & Clayton v. Cogbill, December 1936, 11, f10, bD50, NAACPR.

22. Statement of V. M. Townsend before the District Court for the Eastern District of Arkansas, Carruthers & Clayton v. Reed, March 1938, f3, bD51, NAACPR.

Chapter 11. Pearl Testifies, 1929

1. Bethel transcript, 121; "Weather Forecast," *AG*, April 11, 1929, 1; "The Weather," *AG*, April 11, 1929, 22.

2. Bethel transcript, 121–23; "School Teacher State Witness in Bethel Trial," *BCN*, April 11, 1929, 1, 3.

3. 1910 U.S. Census, Grassy, Cleburne, AR, 7(4)A, family 4, lines 12–15, April 28–29, 1910; 1920 U.S. Census, Grassy, Cleburne, AR, pB, family 78, lines 74–78, January 10–12, 1920; "Dolly G. ––," *Find a Grave*, September 4, 2009, https://www.findagrave.com/memorial/41562156 [https://perma.cc/T3JT-6SU4]; Pearl –– and Onus E. ––, *Arkansas County Marriage Index*, July 4, 1925; "Onis ––," *AD*, December 28, 1956, 10; Bethel transcript, 122–123, 127, 165–66.

4. Willie Curtis Culp, *WWIIDC*, Mississippi County, AR; Bethel transcript, 122–23, 166.

5. Eldon Fairley, "Miss Blanche," *DHR* (Spring 1995), 13; Shirley Mastin Richards, "Memories of My Fifth Grade Teacher," *DHR* (Spring 1995), 17–18; Pat Moseley, "Mrs. Hattie Donaldon McCants," *DHR* (Spring 1995), 19; Eldon Fairley, "Mrs. Marie N. Moore," *DHR* (Spring 1995), 41–42; Eunice Wells, "Shady Bend," *DHR* (Summer 1992), 5; "My Two Years at Shady Bend," *DHR* (Summer 1992), 8–9; Fendler, *Chronicles*, 130, 148; Matkin-Rawn, " 'We Fight for the Rights of Our Race,' " 170–71; Downs, *Stories of Survival*, 135, 141.

6. Sonia Toudji, "Women in Early Frontier Arkansas: 'They Did All the Work except Hunting,' " in Cherisse Jones-Branch and Gary T. Edwards, eds., *Arkansas Women: Their Lives and Times* (2018), 5, 13; Elizabeth Anne Payne, " 'What Ain't I Been Doing?': Historical Reflections on Women and the Arkansas Delta," in Whayne and Gatewood, eds., *Arkansas Delta*, 128–29.

7. Bernadette Cahill, *Arkansas Women and the Right to Vote: The Little Rock Campaigns, 1868–1920* (2015); Downs, *Stories of Survival*, ch. 17; Minoa Dawn Uffelman, " 'Rite Thorny Places to Go Thro'': Narratives of Identities, Southern Farm Women of

the Late Nineteenth and Early Twentieth Century" (Ph.D. diss., University of Mississippi, 2003), 56, 88, 131–33, 143; Jeannie M. Whayne, Thomas A. DeBlack, George Sabo III, and Morris S. Arnold, *Arkansas: A Concise History* (2019), 246.

8. For women resisting "mashers" in northern cities, see Freedman, *Redefining Rape*, ch. 10.

9. Bethel transcript, 123–26, 155–57; "Weather Forecast," *AG*, April 1, 1928, 1.

10. Bethel transcript, 125–27, 131.

11. Ibid., 127–33, 135–36, 156, 161; Wallace prison file, ADC; "Mississippi County Youths Under Sentence to Die in Electric Chair," *AG*, April 15, 1928, 5.

12. Bethel transcript, 133–34.

13. Questions about inconsistencies: Reed transcript, 53–54; Rose transcript, 29–37; Sanders transcript, 29; Wills transcript, 18–19. Accusations of lying: Priest transcript, 59–60; Doss abstract and brief for appellant, 4–5. Underaged girls: Burks transcript, 47–50; Comer transcript, 28–42; Reynolds transcript, 33. See also Cermak, "In the Interest of Justice," 50.

14. See Brock transcript, 14; Boyd transcript, 60–64; Snetzer transcript, 34; Sherman transcript, 18.

15. DeVoe transcript, 24, 30, 44.

16. McDonald v. State, 244 S.W. 20, 23 (Ark. 1922). See also Davis v. State, 234 S.W. 482, 483 (Ark. 1921); Smith v. State, 119 S.W. 655, 656 (Ark. 1909).

17. Green transcript, 12–14; McGlosson transcript, 35; Thomas transcript, 27, 31; Bender transcript, 27–28; Caldwell transcript, 52; Doss abstract and brief for appellant, 27–29; James transcript, 23; Korsak transcript, 18; Lipsmeyer transcript, 22–23, 25–26; McGill transcript, 45; Rose transcript, 40; Rowe transcript, 20, 23, 25; Tugg transcript, 28–29; Waterman transcript, 26–27, 33; Willis transcript, 44–50.

18. Hedrick transcript, 52; Hedrick abstract and brief for appellant, 18; *McDonald*, 244 S.W. at 23.

19. Venable transcript, 22.

20. Fanning transcript, 62–63.

21. Morgan transcript, 27–29.

22. Sanders transcript, 45.

23. Brust transcript, 87.

24. Mynett transcript, 30–35, 39–40.

25. Green transcript, 16.

26. Flood, *Rape in Chicago*, 23, 89, 102, 116–25. But see ibid., 43 (noting defense attorneys "questioning women's sexual respectability" in cross-examination).

27. Bethel transcript, 167–68; "School Teacher State Witness in Bethel Trial," 1, 3.

28. Bethel transcript, 165–71, 178.

29. "School Teacher State Witness in Bethel Trial," 1, 3.

30. Bethel transcript, 135–37.

31. Ibid., 137–42, 187.

32. Ibid., 142–45.

33. Stephen Robertson, "Signs, Marks, and Private Parts: Doctors, Legal Discourses, and Evidence of Rape in the United States, 1823–1930," *Journal of the History of Sexuality* 8.3 (January 1998), 350–52, 361–62, 385; Charles Mapes, "Sexual Assault," *Urologic & Cutaneous Review* 21.8 (1917), 433–34; Smith transcript, 47–48. See also Elizabeth Anne Mills, "One Hundred Years of Fear: Rape and the Medical Profession," in Nicole Hahn Rafter and Elizabeth A. Stanko, eds., *Judge, Lawyer, Victim, Thief: Women, Gender Roles, and Criminal Justice* (1982), 45.

34. Bradley v. State, 32 Ark. 704, 710 (1878); Brock v. State, 270 S.W. 98, 99 (Ark. 1925); Parker, "Law, Culture, and Sexual Censure," 22–23.

35. Terrell transcript, 51.

36. Snetzer transcript, 21.

37. Donovan, *Respectability on Trial*, 72.

38. Snetzer transcript, 27.

39. Donovan, *Respectability on Trial*, 73; Freedman, *Redefining Rape*, 25; Susan Schwartz, "An Argument for the Elimination of the Resistance Requirement from the Definition of Forcible Rape," 16 *Loyola of Los Angeles Law Review* 16 (1983), 569; State v. Hoffman, 280 N.W. 357 (Wis. 1938); Davis v. State, 39 S.W. 356, 357 (Ark. 1897); Zinn v. State, 205 S.W. 704, 707 (Ark. 1918).

40. Whitaker transcript, 11.

41. Cook transcript, 33–34.

42. Cabe transcript, 80; Lewis transcript, 31; Snetzer transcript, 25; Whitaker transcript, 20; Reed transcript, 43–44.

43. Boyett transcript, 23; Lewis transcript, 31–32. See also Alford transcript, 35; Bailey transcript, 105, 109; Bradshaw transcript, 49–51; Brust transcript, 55–56; Davis transcript, 236–40, 252, 255; Harrison abstract and brief for appellant, 35–36; Lindsey transcript, 20–21; Smith transcript, 32–33.

44. Mynett transcript, 38.

45. Venable transcript, 17.

46. Daniels transcript, 38. See also Bradshaw transcript, 56–57.

47. Daniels transcript, 51.

48. Head transcript, 44–45.

49. Terrell transcript, 48. See also Sanders transcript, 36; Sherman transcript, 14; Korsak transcript, 20; McGuire, *At the Dark End of the Street*, 177.

50. Kindle v. State, 264 S.W. 856, 857 (Ark. 1924). See also Braswell v. State, 280 S.W. 367, 368 (Ark. 1926).

51. Sanders transcript, 26.

52. Crawford & Moses Digest, § 2718 (1921); Pope Digest, § 3404 (1937).

53. Poe v. State, 129 S.W. 292, 294 (Ark. 1910); Clayton statement, abstract, and brief of appellants, 13; Sutton transcript, 38; Terrell transcript, 24; Head transcript, 74. See also Bailey transcript, 97; Hodges transcript, 65; Perkinson transcript, 25; Sanders

transcript, 25; Sherman transcript, 116; Whitaker transcript, 11; Caldwell transcript, 44; McGill transcript, 32–33.

54. Sanders transcript, 40. See also Underdown transcript, 18–19.

55. Bethel transcript, 162–65, 172–73, 183–85.

56. "School Teacher State Witness in Bethel Trial," 1, 3.

57. Bethel transcript, 159–60.

58. Robertson, *Crimes against Children*, 76–78. See Bailey transcript, 115; Underdown transcript, 20.

59. See, e.g., Cabe transcript, 74; McDonald brief of appellant, 4; McGlosson transcript, 20; Doss abstract and brief for appellant, 2; McDonald transcript, 63. On Billie Holiday, see Stuart Nicholson, *Billie Holiday* (1996), 25–26.

60. *See* Karin L. Zipf, *Bad Girls at Samarcand: Sexuality and Sterilization in a Southern Juvenile Reformatory* (2016); Molly Ladd-Taylor, *Fixing the Poor: Eugenic Sterilization and Child Welfare in the Twentieth Century* (2017); Saidiya Hartman, *Wayward Lives, Beautiful Experiments: Intimate Histories of Riotous Black Girls, Troublesome Women, and Queer Radicals* (2020), 28–29.

61. Reed transcript, 29. See also Burks transcript, 25.

62. David J. Gottlieb, "Criminal Trials as Culture Wars: Southern Honor and the Acquittal of Frank James," *University of Kansas Law Review* 51 (2003), 409.

63. Wilson transcript, 27–28, 32.

64. Robertson, *Crimes against Children*, 76–78; Hogan transcript, 35–40; "Missing Witness in Trial Found," *AG*, January 23, 1926, 2; Comer transcript, 41.

65. See, e.g., Whitaker transcript, 11; Bailey transcript, 93; Lindsey transcript, 19; Willis transcript, 50–51.

66. Snetzer transcript, 18.

67. Cureton transcript, 38.

68. Priest transcript, 47.

69. Bethel transcript, 175–76.

Chapter 12. Virgie Testifies, 1935

1. Charles Staples Mangum, *The Legal Status of the Negro* (1940), 274; Rebecca West, "Opera in Greenville," *New Yorker*, June 14, 1947, 31–65; Robert L. Carter, *A Matter of Law: A Memoir of Struggle in the Cause of Equal Rights* (2005), 78; "Dowdy Recounts Rape Story in Lee Court," newspaper unknown, 1943, f10, bII:B129, NAACPR. See also Silvan Niedermeier, *The Color of the Third Degree: Racism, Police Torture, and Civil Rights in the American South, 1930–1955* (transl. Paul Cohen) (2019), 40–41 (discussing West's essay and the opera/theater analogy); Christopher Waldrep, *The Many Faces of Judge Lynch: Extralegal Violence and Punishment in America* (2002), 162 (also discussing West's essay); Dorr, *White Women, Rape, and the Power of Race*, 5 (comparing such trials to "public performances"); Gilbert King, *Devil in the Grove: Thurgood Marshall, the*

Groveland Boys, and the Dawn of a New American (2012), 168 (quoting an NAACP attorney comparing an interracial rape trial to "a Hollywood story"), 174 (quoting a reporter comparing an interracial rape trial to a "play").

2. Saidee Newcombe Ross, "Trial for Rape in Mississippi" (1944), f1, bII:B127, NAACPR.

3. Clayton statement, abstract, and brief of appellants, 11–12; Clayton abstract and brief for appellee, 13; Virgie Beatrice ——, *U.S. Social Security Applications and Claims Index, 1936–2007*; Robert L. Pigue, "Negro Dies in Electric Chair," *Nashville Banner*, July 13, 1916, 1, 13; "Death Chair's First Victim," *Nashville Banner*, July 13, 1916, 9; Margaret Vandiver, *Lynchings and Legal Executions in the South* (2006), 44–46, 96–98; "The Burning at Dyersburg," *The Crisis*, February 1918, 178–83.

4. Clayton statement, abstract, and brief of appellants, 12, 15, 17; Clayton abstract and brief for appellee, 5; 1920 U.S. Census, Clear Lake, Mississippi, AR, 8A, family 108, lines 1–4, January 31, 1920; 1930 U.S. Census, Hickman, Mississippi, AR, 16A, family 345, lines 7–12, April 16, 1930.

5. Clayton abstract and brief for appellee, 5, 13, 17; Clayton statement, abstract, and brief of appellants, 5–6; 1920 U.S. Census, Big Lake, Mississippi, AR, 7B, family 150, lines 70–74, February 23, 1920; 1930 U.S. Census, Clear Lake, Mississippi, AR, 13B, family 296, lines 85–88, April 18–19, 1930.

6. Clayton abstract and brief for appellee, 2–9, 13–15, 17–21; Clayton supplemental brief for appellants, 9; "Pastor and Wife Entertain Ladies," *OT*, Dec. 21, 1934, 1.

7. Clayton abstract and brief for appellee, 21–22.

8. Cutts transcript, 14–16; Daniels transcript, 21–28; Thomas II abstract and brief for appellants, 12.

9. Cutts transcript, 18; Thomas II brief for appellee, 16; Hodges transcript, 18–20.

10. Cutts transcript, 24.

11. McGee transcript, 13.

12. Clayton abstract and brief for appellee, 20. See also King, *Devil in the Grove*, 166 (white accuser calling the defendants [n-words]).

13. Cutts transcript, 25. See also Hawthorne transcript, 82, 95.

14. Cutts brief for appellee, 3; Cutts transcript, 4.

15. Hawthorne transcript, 31–34.

16. Dorr, *White Women, Rape, and the Power of Race*, 5.

17. Clayton abstract and brief for appellee, 15–16.

18. Ibid., 17–21, 23.

19. Ross, "Trial for Rape in Mississippi," NAACPR.

20. Thomas II abstract and brief for appellants, 13; Daniels transcript, 38.

21. Dorr, *White Women, Rape, and the Power of Race*, 5, 11. See also ibid., 129–32; Edwards, "Sexual Violence, Gender, Reconstruction," 250–51.

22. Brock transcript, 19–20; Morgan transcript, 90, 126–27; Parker brief for appellant, 34–35. See also Cook transcript, 92; McLaughlin transcript, 18–19.

23. DeVoe transcript, 73.

24. Sutton transcript, 79–81.

25. See, e.g., Kazzee abstract and brief for appellant, 6. See also Bender transcript, 41–43; Goodnaugh transcript, 26, 29; Lipsmeyer transcript, 53–54, 65; Wilson transcript, 52; Young transcript, 96–97.

26. Goodnaugh transcript, 33–34.

27. See Cates transcript, 12–14; Hedrick transcript, 43–45; Powell transcript, 61–69.

28. Fanning transcript. See also Terrell transcript, 48.

29. Braswell transcript, 73; Mynett transcript, 100.

30. Glenda Gilmore, *Defying Dixie: The Radical Roots of Civil Rights, 1919–1950* (2008), 120.

31. Dorr, *White Women, Rape, and the Power of Race*, 142–45, 150–51. See also McGuire, *At the Dark End of the Street*, 58–59.

Chapter 13. Marguerite Testifies, Mid-1930s

1. *CB*, 84. In *Caged Bird*, Angelou identified herself as eight at the trial, but later she suggested she was seven and a half, see Naomi Epel, *Writers Dreaming* (1993), 27, making an exact year difficult to estimate. See also Linda Wagner-Martin, *The Life of the Author: Maya Angelou* (2021), 31 (suggesting she was in Stamps for the 1936–37 school year).

2. McDonald transcript, c–f.

3. *CB*, 84–85.

4. Whitaker transcript, 8; "Man Given Life Term in Pen Files Appeal," *AG*, July 2, 1926, 10. For examples of rape cases involving Black children, see transcripts for Gerlach, Jackson, Pugh, and Watt.

5. McDonald transcript, 10, 13–15; Pugh transcript, 13–15. See also McGuire, *At the Dark End of the Street*, 175 (noting that the Black press cast one Black accuser "into the role of respectable ladyhood"); Flood, *Rape in Chicago*, 83 (noting that prosecutors had to cast "African American victims as respectable women" to succeed in court).

6. Cauley, appellant reply brief, 2–3; Cauley appellee brief on motion for rehearing, 4. See also McDonald transcript, 104–9. Cf. Edwards, "Sexual Violence, Gender, Reconstruction," 246–49 (similar questioning in late nineteenth-century intraracial sexual assault cases in North Carolina); Flood, *Rape in Chicago*, 85–88, 92–95 (similar questioning in mid-twentieth-century intraracial sexual assault cases in Chicago).

7. Freedman, *Redefining Rape*, 87.

8. *CB*, 85.

9. Ruth Thompson-Miller and Leslie H. Picca, " 'There Were Rapes!': Sexual Assaults of African American Women in Jim Crow," *Violence against Women* 23.8 (2017), 937.

10. Whitaker transcript, 11, 17–19. See also Gerlach transcript, 39–49.

11. Gerlach transcript, 36–39.

12. Jackson transcript, 15–16.

13. Cauley v. State, 247 S.W. 772, 772 (Ark. 1923); Cauley, appellant reply brief, 2–3; Cauley appellee brief on motion for rehearing, 4.

14. Cauley, appellant reply brief, 3–4.

15. Ibid., 2–3.

16. Dallas v. State, 79 So. 690 (Fla. 1918); Wriggins, "Rape, Racism, and the Law," 121.

17. Robertson, *Crimes against Children*, 47–49.

18. See, e.g., Burks transcript, 25; DeVoe transcript, 12–13; Durham transcript, 27; Needham appellant's abstract and brief, 24–25; Reynolds transcript, 16; Rose transcript, 22; Sherman transcript, 75; Sutton transcript, 66; Watt transcript, 8–9. See also Bradshaw transcript, 42; Cutts transcript, 32–34; Alex Heard, *The Eyes of Willie McGee: A Tragedy of Race, Sex, and Secrets in the Jim Crow South* (2010), 137.

19. Hogan II transcript, 32–46, 133–40.

20. Robertson, *Crimes against Children*, 48.

21. Durham transcript, 29; DeVoe transcript, 18–19; Sanders transcript, 25.

22. Sutton transcript, 38.

23. Burks transcript, 32, 42; Head transcript, 44.

24. Durham transcript, 31.

25. Crawford & Moses Digest, § 27120 (1921); Pope Digest, § 3406 (1937).

26. Kazzee abstract and brief for appellant, 4, 10–11, 15; Hedrick transcript, 11–20, 23–24, 43, 76–91, 99–101, 136; Jackson transcript, 17–21, 31–35; James transcript, 20–21, 35, 45–47, 54–56, 59–63. See also Lipsmeyer transcript, 31 (testifying to a birthdate but claiming to have lost the family Bible); McDonald transcript, 140–41, 154, 217, 230–37 (testifying about whether or not family Bible had been forged). Interestingly, genealogical research tools actually give modern scholars better resources for assessing accusers' ages than were available to lawyers at the time. Based on such genealogical research, for instance, it appears that one girl who claimed that she was fifteen was telling the truth, while marriage and census records strongly suggest that another was lying. Compare Matilda ––, certificate of death (Indiana State Department of Health, November 28, 1995); 1920 U.S. Census, Pocahontas, AR, sheet 17A, family 368, lines 47–50, January 19, 1920, with 1920 U.S. Census, Madison Township, AR, 4B, family 60, lines 72–76, January 10–12, 1920; 1910 U.S. Census, Clear Creek Township, AR, 15B, family 284, lines 86–91, May 12, 1910; Bessie ––, certificate of marriage, *Arkansas County Marriages Index, 1837–1957* (April 23, 1929).

27. Kazzee abstract and brief for appellant, 3; Bender transcript, 21.

28. Cook transcript, 43–44; Green transcript, 14; Young transcript, 19–22, 73–75.

29. Wilson transcript, 27–28, 32.

30. *CB*, 85

31. Gerlach transcript, 44; Cauley, appellant brief, 4–5.

32. *CB*, 85; Freedman, *Redefining Rape*, 86, 155. See also Flood, *Rape in Chicago*, 97–98.

Chapter 14. The Origins of an Advocate, 1908–1933

1. Juan Williams, *Thurgood Marshall: American Revolutionary* (1998), 15–23; Larry Gibson, *Young Thurgood: The Making of a Supreme Court Justice* (2012), 35–41.

2. Gibson, *Young Thurgood*, 41–42; NAACP, *First Annual Report* (January 1, 1911), 8–9, bA25, NAACPR; correspondence in f10–13, bD55, NAACPR; Sullivan, *Lift Every Voice*, 18–19.

3. Williams, *Thurgood Marshall*, 28–29, 34; Gibson, *Young Thurgood*, 56–73; Sullivan, *Lift Every Voice*, 19, 42–44; *The Crisis*, January 1914, 139; August Meier and Elliott Rudwick, "Attorneys Black and White: A Case Study of Race Relations within the NAACP," *Journal of American History* 62.4 (March 1976), 920, 923–24, 930–31.

4. Gibson, *Young Thurgood*, 79–80; Sullivan, *Lift Every Voice*, 43–48; NAACP, *Fifth Annual Report* (1914), 29–30, bA25, NAACPR.

5. Williams, *Thurgood Marshall*, ch. 4; Gibson, *Young Thurgood*, ch. 4.

6. Williams, *Thurgood Marshall*, 27, 52–53; Gibson, *Young Thurgood*, 107–8.

7. Williams, *Thurgood Marshall*, 53–56; Gibson, *Young Thurgood*, 109–13.

8. Sullivan, *Lift Every Voice*, 152–53, 159; Meier and Rudwick, "Attorneys Black and White," 932–34; Dan T. Carter, *Scottsboro: A Tragedy of the American South* (1979), 49–58, 106; James E. Goodman, *Stories of Scottsboro* (1994), ch. 4; Hugh T. Murray Jr., "The NAACP versus the Communist Party: The Scottsboro Rape Case, 1931-1932," *Phylon* 28 (Fall 1967), 277–83; Robin D. G. Kelley, *Hammer and Hoe: Alabama Communists during the Great Depression* (1990), 79–81; Kenneth W. Mack, "Law and Mass Politics in the Making of the Civil Rights Lawyer, 1931–1941," *Journal of American History* 93 (June 2006), 41.

9. Carter, *Scottsboro*, 78, 80–84, 210, 233–34, 448 and n.4; Gilmore, *Defying Dixie*, 120–21; NAACP, *22nd Annual Report* (1931), 11, bI:A25, NAACPR; Freedman, *Redefining Rape*, 256–57.

10. Williams, *Thurgood Marshall*, 56–58; Gibson, *Young Thurgood*, 120; oral history interview of TM, conducted by Mark Tushnet (May 23, 1989), 6, CCOH.

11. Helen Boardman, "The South Goes Legal," *The Nation*, March 8, 1933, 258–59; Butler Wilson to WW, March 2, 1933; WW to CHH, March 6, 1933—both in George Crawford March 1932 f, bD51, NAACPR; Report of the Secretary for the April Meeting of the Board, April 6, 1933; Report of the Secretary for the May Meeting of the Board, May 4, 1933—both in January 5, 1933 to December 31, 1933 f, bA17, NAACPR; Gibson, *Young Thurgood*, 120; Sullivan, *Lift Every Voice*, 162, 166. David Bradley, *The Historic Murder Trial of George Crawford: Charles H. Houston, the NAACP and the Case That Put All-White Southern Juries on Trial* (2014), 5–23.

12. CHH to Butler Wilson, March 10, 1933, George Crawford March 1932 f, bD51, NAACPR; Williams, *Thurgood Marshall*, 58.

13. TM oral history, 4–5, 9–10, CCOH.

14. Meier and Rudwick, "Attorneys Black and White," 939; Gibson, *Young Thurgood*, 122–23.

15. Sullivan, *Lift Every Voice*, 181, 184–87; Kenneth W. Mack, *Representing the Race: The Creation of the Civil Rights Lawyer* (2012), 96–107, 173–80; Genna Rae McNeil, *Groundwork: Charles Hamilton Houston and the Struggle for Civil Rights* (1983), 90–95; Martha Gruening, "The Truth about the Crawford Case: How the N.A.A.C.P. 'Defended' a Negro into a Life Sentence," *The Masses*, January 8, 1935, 9–15.

16. Meier and Rudwick, "Attorneys Black and White," 940–42; Sullivan, *Lift Every Voice*, 180–82, 188; Mack, *Representing the Race*, 108.

17. Gibson, *Young Thurgood*, 123; Williams, *Thurgood Marshall*, 58–59.

Chapter 15. The Witnesses Testify, 1929

1. Bethel transcript, 200–203.

2. "Native of Ireland Dies in Arkansas," *The Herald* (Jasper, IN), May 20, 1950, 7; "Virgil Reily Greene," *Find a Grave*, June 5, 2011, https://www.findagrave.com/memorial/70884806 [https://perma.cc/RNX7-R6K6]; 1920 U.S. Census, Monroe, Mississippi, AR, 5A, family 93, lines 3–14, 1920.

3. Bethel transcript, 212.

4. Ibid., 271.

5. Ibid., 251–53, 258; 1930 U.S. Census, Monroe, Mississippi, AR, 25A, family 472, lines 42–50, April 17, 1930.

6. Bethel transcript, 254–55, 259.

7. See, e.g., ibid., 246, 264–65.

8. Jackson v. State, 122 S.W. 101, 101 (Ark. 1909); Smith v. State, 233 S.W. 1081, 1082 (Ark. 1921).

9. Brust transcript, 268, 273, 280–81, 286–93, 301–18, 329, 334, 340–44, 365–67; Cook abstract and brief for appellee, 11, 14; Cureton transcript, 59, 92; Kazzee abstract and brief for appellant, 7–8; Powell transcript, 36; Rose transcript, 76, 83–84; Tugg transcript, 19; Warford transcript, 69–70; Willis transcript, 95–97, 100–4, 118–19.

10. Mynett transcript, 55–82, 111–13; Terrell transcript, 144–62, 194, 198.

11. Walton v. State, 75 S.W. 1 (Ark. 1903); Taylor transcript, 59, 64, 68, 78–79.

12. Bethel transcript, 279, 282, 287, 290–91, 294–95, 297–300.

13. Ibid., 307–10, 317, 319, 323, 475.

14. Ibid., 339.

15. Ibid., 480–81.

16. See ibid., 313–14, 334–35.

17. See ibid., 220–22, 228, 481.

18. DeVoe transcript, 95–104 (four witnesses); Whitaker transcript, 49–51, 71–75 (five witnesses).

19. Priest transcript, 110–12; Reed transcript, 65–66; Sherman transcript, 56–61, 78–79, 85–87; Wills transcript, 38; Bender transcript, 79; Bradshaw transcript, 93–95; Clack transcript, 54–58, 60–64; Smith transcript, 80, 82, 84, 87; Terrell transcript, 183–89; West II transcript, 189, 191, 194.

20. See Bender transcript, 61–64; Cook abstract and brief for appellee, 11; Reed transcript, 82–83.

21. Priest transcript, 144–47; Wills transcript, 32–33.

Chapter 16. The Witnesses Testify, 1935

1. Clayton supplemental brief for appellants, 10–11.

2. Martin transcript, 33, 36–37.

3. Cutts transcript, 48; Daniels transcript, 47.

4. Martin transcript, 34–35. See also West transcript, 116; Hamm transcript, 40, 45.

5. Clayton abstract and brief for appellee, 2–4, 8–10; Clayton statement, abstract, and brief of appellants, 6, 9; Clayton petition for rehearing and appellants' brief thereon, 6.

6. Clayton petition for rehearing and appellants' brief thereon, 5, 8–9.

7. Clayton abstract and brief for appellee, 5; Clayton statement, abstract, and brief of appellants, 5.

8. Claude F. Sparks, "Blytheville Personalities: Constable Arch Lindsey Helped Give Sheriff the Mulecollar during Prohibition 'Still-Raid,'" *BCN*, June 6, 1951, 6; "Arch Lindsey Rites Tomorrow," *BCN*, October 24, 1955, 1; Arch Lindsey, *WWIIDC*, Mississippi County, AR.

9. Clayton abstract and brief for appellee, 11–13; Clayton statement, abstract, and brief of appellants, 10–11; McCulloch, "Miscarriage of Justice in Arkansas Alleged," 3-I.

10. Clayton petition for rehearing and appellants' brief thereon, 5, 7.

11. Alford transcript, 46; Bailey transcript, 122; Burks transcript, 70; Franks transcript, 73–74; Hogan II transcript, 79–80, 92 (quotation from 92); Mynett transcript, 45; Priest transcript, 17–18; Warford transcript, 58–62. Cf. Flood, *Rape in Chicago*, 28–30 (finding similar use of medical testimony in midcentury Chicago).

12. Hogan II transcript, 82–83. See also Terrell transcript, 90.

13. Burks transcript, 71; Cabe transcript, 234; Caldwell transcript, 53; Lipsmeyer transcript, 80–85, 98–100; McGlosson transcript, 64–65; Reynolds transcript, 83–84; Sutton transcript, 76–77; Needham transcript, 163–66; Willis transcript, 61. See also Mills, "One Hundred Years of Fear," 38–39.

14. Head transcript, 148–153.

15. Sherman transcript, 43. See also Doss abstract and brief for appellant, 43; McGill transcript, 50.

16. Franks transcript, 75; Cabe transcript, 233, 235.

17. Mary Spongberg, *Feminizing Venereal Disease: The Body of the Prostitute in Nineteenth-Century Medical Discourse* (1997), 32–33.

18. Robertson, "Signs, Marks, and Private Parts," 376–78, 382. See, e.g., Fields transcript, 42–44.

19. Durham transcript, 37–38, 45–59. See also DeVoe transcript, 53; Fields transcript, 51.

20. Daniels transcript, 70, 75–76, 78, 82–90; Martin transcript, 191–209.

21. Clayton abstract and brief for appellee, 33.

22. Statement of Arthur L. Adams before the District Court for the Eastern District of Arkansas, Caruthers & Clayton v. Cogbill, December 1936, 18–20, f10, bD50, NAACPR.

23. 1930 U.S. Census, Blytheville, Mississippi, AR, 24B, family 604, lines 53–56, April 14, 1930; 1940 U.S. Census, Blytheville, Mississippi, AR, 4A, family 118, lines 21–24, April 8, 1940.

24. Clayton abstract and brief for appellee, 33–34.

25. Ibid., 34–37.

26. Ibid., 45–46.

Chapter 17. The Recovery, 1930s–1953

1. *CB*, 85–86.

2. Ibid., 87.

3. E. M. Beck and Stewart E. Tolnay, "When Race Didn't Matter: Black and White Mob Violence against Their Own Color," in W. Fitzhugh Brundage, ed., *Under Sentence of Death: Lynching in the South* (1997), 132–49.

4. *CB*, 88.

5. Suzette M. Henke, "Maya Angelou's *Caged Bird* as Trauma Narrative," in Mildred R. Mickle, *Critical Insights: I Know Why the Caged Bird Sings by Maya Angelou* (2010), 250.

6. *CB*, 88.

7. Ibid., 89; Wagner-Martin, *Life of the Author*, 28.

8. PBS Documentary, *Maya Angelou: And Still I Rise*, February 21, 2017, at 14:10.

9. *CB*, 90–92; Richard Ballad, "Maya Angelou Interview" (1971), in f4, b201, MAP; Maya Angelou, *And Still I Rise* (1978), 36; Dolly A. McPherson, *Order Out of Chaos: The Autobiographical Works of Maya Angelou* (1990), 147–48.

10. *CB*, 93–95; Bill Moyers, "Watch: Going Home with Maya Angelou," *HuffPost*, October 12, 2014, https://www.huffpost.com/entry/watch-going-home-with-may_b_5671660.

11. *Step Back in Time: Virgil and Sarah Flowers Family History: 1800–2002* (2d ed., 2002), 2–4, f3, b5, MAP.

12. Maya Angelou, "Greetings!" in *Step Back in Time*, MAP.

13. *CB*, 95–100; Moyers, "Watch: Going Home with Maya Angelou."

14. Mert Guswiler, " 'You Must Love Truth for Truth's Sake, and Right for Right's Sake': Maya Angelou, National Book Award Nominee," *Los Angeles Herald-Examiner*, March 12, 1971, A19.

15. *CB*, 100–101; PBS Documentary, *Maya Angelou: And Still I Rise*, February 21, 2017, at 16:08; Moyers, "Watch: Going Home with Maya Angelou."

16. MA, "For Years We Hated Ourselves," *NYT*, April 16, 1972, in f2, n171, MAP.

17. *CB*, 194–95, 199–200.

18. Ibid., 201–11, 220.

19. Ibid., 215–16; "Maya Angelou Returns to G.W.," *The Eagle* (George Washington High School), May 4, 1976, in f3, b346, MAP.

20. *CB*, 227–281; Gillespie, Butler, and Long, *Maya Angelou*, 26–28; DeNeen L. Brown, "Why Maya Angelou Wanted to Become a Street Car Conductor," *Washington Post*, March 12, 2014, https://www.washingtonpost.com/blogs/she-the-people/wp/2014/03/12/why-maya-angelou-wanted-to-become-a-street-car-conductor/ [https://perma.cc/NZ5E-KEUBU].

21. *CB*, 281–290; PBS Documentary, *Maya Angelou: And Still I Rise*, February 21, 2017, at 21:35; Clyde Bailey Johnson, *California Birth Index, 1905–1995*. Notably, in the mid-twentieth century, "black, single, pregnant women were not, in general, spurned by their families," as white unwed mothers routinely were. "For the most part, black families accepted the pregnancy and made a place for the new mother and child." Rickie Solinger, *Wake Up, Little Susie: Single Pregnancy and Race before* Roe v. Wade (1992), 6.

22. Richard Koch and Ray Lyman Wilbur, "Promiscuity as a Factor in the Spread of Venereal Disease," *Journal of Social Hygiene* 30.9 (December 1944), 521–25; Scott W. Stern, *The Trials of Nina McCall: Sex, Surveillance, and the Decades-Long Government Plan to Imprison "Promiscuous" Women* (2018), 215, 223, 230–32, 235, 239.

23. *CB*, 273.

24. MA, *Gather Together in My Name* (1974), 1–3.

25. Ibid., 4–28.

26. Ibid., 29–79, 120–166; Elliot, "Author Maya Angelou," 25, MAP.

27. See files in b57, Entry 3, RG 215, National Archives, College Park, Maryland; "Moral Conditions in City Approved by Authorities," *San Diego Union*, November 22, 1917, 13; W. F. Schwermeyer to Mayor and City Council Members of San Diego, September 15, 1917, doc. 8451, b6, Entry 393, RG 165, National Archives, College Park, MD. See generally Stern, *The Trials of Nina McCall*.

28. MA, *Gather Together in My Name*, 52, 137.

29. Scott W. Stern, "COVID-19 and Welfare Queens," *Boston Review*, April 17, 2020, https://bostonreview.net/class-inequality/scott-w-stern-covid-19-and-welfare-queens?fbclid=IwAR3HYFth1_J6YNt6HktLtI-t8E-wDozjREH28d9vpcw_LF-r-ppY-78uSkZg [https://perma.cc/9N2U-YXBN]; Josh Levin, *The Queen: The Forgotten Life behind an American Myth* (2019), 201–10.

30. Nicholson, *Billie Holiday*, 27, 32–33; Hartman, *Wayward Lives, Beautiful Experiments*, 223–24.

31. MA, *Singin' and Swingin' and Gettin' Merry Like Christmas* (1977), 1–38; Gillespie, Butler, and Long, *Maya Angelou*, 29.

32. Angelou, *Singin' and Swingin'*, 34, 42–78; Gillespie, Butler, and Long, *Maya Angelou*, 35–41; Barbara Bladen, "The Marquee," *San Mateo Times*, May 7, 1971, in f3, b347, MAP; Angelou, *Gather Together in My Name*, 100–03, 111–14.

33. Angelou, *Singin' and Swingin'*, 79–85.

Chapter 18. The Rape Docket, 1930s

1. Gibson, *Young Thurgood*, chs. 1 and 5; Williams, *Thurgood Marshall*, 59–61.

2. Williams, *Thurgood Marshall*, 62–68; Rawn James Jr., *Root and Branch: Charles Hamilton Houston, Thurgood Marshall, and the Struggle to End Segregation* (2010), 59–64; Gibson, *Young Thurgood*, 149–52.

3. Sullivan, *Lift Every Voice*, 181; McNeil, *Groundwork*, 131–32; King, *Devil in the Grove*, 22.

4. Sullivan, *Lift Every Voice*, 178–79; Kelley, *Hammer and Hoe*, 83–84; Paul Blanshard to WW, February 2, 1932; WW to Charles McPherson, February 1, 1932; WW to Will Alexander, February 5, 1932—all in Willie Peterson, February 1–16, 1932 f, bD65, NAACPR; "NAACP to Press Fight for Full Willie Peterson Freedom," *Philadelphia Tribune*, March 29, 1934, 1; WW to Charles McPherson, October 5, 1931, Willie Peterson, March–December, 1931 f, bD65, NAACPR.

5. Sullivan, *Lift Every Voice*, 171–72, 184, 187; Kelley, *Hammer and Hoe*, 89–90; WW to CHH, October 6, 1933, Willie Peterson, October 3–30, 1933 f, bD66, NAACPR; "Peterson, Who Cheated Death, Dies in Prison," *Pittsburgh Courier*, July 13, 1940, 5.

6. Roger W. Cummins, " 'Lily-White' Juries on Trial: The Civil Rights Defense of Jess Hollins," *Chronicles of Oklahoma* 63 (1985), 167–74; Charles H. Martin, "Oklahoma's 'Scottsboro' Affair: The Jess Hollins Rape Case, 1931–1936," *South Atlantic Quarterly* 79 (1980), 175–79; RW to Roscoe Dunjee, August 15, 1932, f7, bD59, NAACPR; WW to Roscoe Dunjee, October 10, 1932, f9, bD59, NAACPR.

7. Meredith Clark-Wiltz, "Persecuting Black Men and Gendering Jury Service: The Interplay between Race and Gender in the NAACP Jury Service Cases of the 1930s," in Carol Faulkner and Alison M. Parker, eds., *Gender and Race in American History* (2012), 168, 170, 174; 295 U.S. 394 (1935); McNeil, *Groundwork*, 121–22; Martin, "Oklahoma's 'Scottsboro' Affair," 182, 185; Paul Finkelman, "Not Only the Judges' Robes Were Black:

African-American Lawyers as Social Engineers," *Stanford Law Review* 47 (1994), 168. For the cases relying on *Hollins,* see Batson v. Kentucky, 476 U.S. 79, 84 (1986); Patton v. Mississippi, 332 U.S. 463, 465 (1947).

8. Sullivan, *Lift Every Voice,* 229–30; McNeil, *Groundwork,* 135; NAACP, *29th Annual Report* (1938), 16, bII:L269, NAACPR.

9. Martin, "Oklahoma's 'Scottsboro' Affair," 180–83; Cummins, " 'Lily-White' Juries on Trial," 181; Clark-Wiltz, "Persecuting Black Men and Gendering Jury Service," 173.

10. Blanshard to White, February 2, 1932, NAACPR; White to McPherson, October 5, 1931, NAACPR.

11. Freedman, *Redefining Rape,* 243–45; correspondence in f12–13, bC265, NAACPR; Stephen Weinberger, "*The Birth of a Nation* and the Making of the NAACP," *Journal of American Studies* 45.1 (February 2011), 77, 86–87; NAACP, *Sixth Annual Report* (1915), 11, bA25, NAACPR.

12. Jonathan Markovitz, *Legacies of Lynching: Racial Violence and Memory* (2004), 11; Thomas J. Edge, " 'An Arm of God': The Early History of the NAACP in Charleston, West Virginia, 1917–1925," *West Virginia History* 7 (2013), 20; Telegram from "Jim" to J. Rosamond Johnson, August 25, 1920, and other correspondence in Duluth f, bI:G103, NAACPR; John D. Bessler, *Legacy of Violence: Lynch Mobs and Executions in Minnesota* (2003), ch. 8; W. A. Singfield to NAACP, July 29, 1921, f8, bI:G12, NAACPR; Matkin-Rawn, " 'We Fight for the Rights of Our Race,' " 186; Sullivan, *Lift Every Voice,* 115; Freedman, *Redefining Rape,* 92, 246–47.

13. Collins v. State, 254 S.W. 805, 806–7 (Tex. Ct. App. 1923); "In Texas," *The Crisis,* August 1923, 165; NAACP, *17th Annual Report* (1926), 8–9, bA25, NAACPR; "Houston, Texas, N.A.A.C.P. Wins Fight Freeing Condemned Negro," *California Voice,* October 1, 1926, Houston, TX, February–December 1926 f, bI:G203, NAACPR.

14. WW to E. O. Smith, April 9, 1924, Houston, TX, January–November 1924 f, bI:G203, NAACPR; WW, *Rope and Faggot: A Biography of Judge Lynch* (2001), 261.

15. See "New 'Scottsboro' Case Hinted in Jersey Town," *Baltimore Afro-American,* October 12, 1935, 6; Clara Jordan to "Sir," July 9, 1939, f10, bII:B124, NAACPR; James Gannaway and Fred Alderson to WW, May 31, 1940, f6, bII:B122, NAACPR; Oscar Fields to "WHO IT MAY CONCERN," December 16, 1939, f1, bII:B123, NAACPR.

16. See RW to T. M. Alexander, December 29, 1939; A. T. Walden to T. M. Alexander, January 5, 1940—both in f1, bII:B123, NAACPR; Mark Tushnet, *Making Civil Rights Law: Thurgood Marshall and the Supreme Court, 1936–1961* (1994), 28–29; NAACP, *28th Annual Report* (1937), 17, bA25, NAACPR; "Branch News, *The Crisis,* May 1936, 153.

17. "Unusual Endings to the 'Usual Crime' Told by NAACP," *Atlanta Daily World,* August 1, 1934, 6.

18. WW to TM, November 11, 1934; TM to WW, November 23, 1934—both in Thurgood Marshall, September 1935 to May 1936 f, bI:C84, NAACPR.

19. TM to RW, December 18, 1934; TM, "Re: State vs William Carter," December 18, 1934—both in Thurgood Marshall, 1934–1935 f, bI:C84, NAACPR; TM to WW, December 12, 1934, Kater Stevens October–December 1934 f, bD85, NAACPR; Gibson, *Young Thurgood*, 208.

20. TM to Wilkins, December 18, 1934, NAACPR; TM, "Re: State vs William Carter," December 18, 1934, NAACPR; Gibson, *Young Thurgood*, 208; Williams, *Thurgood Marshall*, 68–69; Mack, *Representing the Race*, 120–21.

21. TM to Edward S. Lewis, December 19, 1934; RW to TM, December 20, 1934—both in Thurgood Marshall, 1934–1935 f, bI:C84, NAACPR; TM to WW, December 12, 1934; WW to TM, December 17, 1934—both in Kater Stevens October–December 1934 f, bD85, NAACPR; Gibson, *Young Thurgood*, 208–9, 373; Williams, *Thurgood Marshall*, 69.

Chapter 19. Bethel and Wallace Testify, 1929

1. "Testimony Heard in Assault Case at Blytheville," *AG*, April 12, 1929, 1.
2. Wallace prison file, ADC; "To Die for Attack," *Eau Claire Leader*, April 28, 1928, 12; "Mississippi County Youths under Sentence to Die in Electric Chair," *AG*, April 15, 1928, 5.
3. Bethel transcript, 351; "School Teacher State Witness in Bethel Trial," *BCN*, April 11, 1929, 1, 3.
4. "Daily Weather Record," *AG*, April 2, 1928, 8; "Weather Forecast," *AG*, April 1, 1928, 1.
5. Bethel transcript, 374–75, 433, 440–41.
6. Ibid., 352–56, 375–76, 383.
7. Ibid., 358.
8. Ibid., 383–84, 420.
9. Ibid., 437–38.
10. Ibid., 439.
11. Ibid., 400, 449.
12. Franks transcript, 178.
13. Promiscuity: Braswell transcript, 61–62; Clack transcript, 35–36; Davis transcript, 327–28; Morgan transcript, 109–10; Mynett transcript, 85. Prostitution: Fanning transcript, 87, 108, 125; Terrell transcript, 171. Interracial familiarity: Doss abstract and brief for appellant, 63–64. Frankness: Terrell transcript, 179.
14. Willis transcript, 151–52.
15. Young transcript, 95–96, 98.
16. Cabe transcript, 60, 288, 303.
17. "Bethel-Wallace Case Goes to Jury," *BCN*, April 12, 1929, 1, 3.
18. Bethel transcript, 358–59.
19. Ibid., 394, 421.
20. Ibid., 359–62.

21. Ibid., 363.
22. Ibid., 425.
23. Bethel prison file, ADC; "To Die for Attack," 12; "Mississippi County Youths under Sentence to Die in Electric Chair," 5.
24. Bethel transcript, 432–33.
25. Ibid., 433–34.
26. Clack transcript, 38–39; Lindsey transcript, 77; Powell transcript, 106–7; Rowe transcript, 58–59; Tugg transcript, 49.
27. Mynett transcript, 88.
28. Ibid., 88–90, 97–98.
29. Priest transcript, 142–43. See also Fanning transcript, 125.
30. Davis transcript, 228–29, 231–59, 266.
31. Fields transcript, 75.
32. Bethel transcript, 453.
33. Houston transcript, 63–64; Morgan transcript, 107–8; Sutton transcript, 106–8; Bradshaw transcript, 108; Caldwell transcript, 93–95; Davis transcript, 305–6; Hawthorne transcript, 177–79; McGill transcript, 83–86; Smith transcript, 71–74; Tugg transcript, 46.
34. Whitaker transcript, 46, 48.
35. Lewis transcript, 114, 116; Morgan transcript, 107–8; Sutton transcript, 108–9; Priest transcript, 130.
36. Whitaker transcript, 45.
37. Bethel transcript, 402–3.
38. Ibid., 390, 403, 405, 460, 465–66.
39. Ibid., 411–13.
40. Ibid., 363, 422–23.
41. Ibid., 455–56.
42. Ibid., 401.

Chapter 20. Clayton and Carruthers Testify, 1935

1. Clayton abstract and brief for appellee, 14.
2. Statement of Arthur L. Adams before the District Court for the Eastern District of Arkansas, Caruthers & Clayton v. Cogbill, December 1936, 20, f10, bD50, NAACPR.
3. Guy Johnson, "The Negro and Crime," *Annals of the American Academy of Political and Social Science* 217 (September 1941), 97.
4. Clayton abstract and brief for appellee, 23–24; Clayton statement, abstract, and brief of appellants, 19.
5. Clayton abstract and brief for appellee, 24–25, 37–38, 41. Cf. Flood, *Rape in Chicago*, 55 ("Attorneys in most interracial rape cases thus relied on alibis in an effort to defend their black clients.").
6. Clayton abstract and brief for appellee, 24–25.

7. Ibid., 37.

8. Ibid., 14; Carruthers prison file, ADC.

9. Clayton abstract and brief for appellee, 41–42.

10. Clayton abstract and brief for appellee, 42–43; Clayton statement, abstract, and brief of appellants, 31.

11. Clayton abstract and brief for appellee, 43.

12. Clayton statement, abstract, and brief of appellants, 22–24; Clayton abstract and brief for appellee, 32.

13. Daniels transcript, 76. See also Alford transcript, 93–94; Hodges transcript, 68–69; Maxwell transcript, 180–81; Palmer transcript, 35–36, 116–20; Pugh transcript, 60, 63, 77–78.

14. Cermak, "In the Interest of Justice," 11–12, 86, 88–89, 92–94.

15. Clayton statement, abstract, and brief of appellants, 22.

16. Clayton abstract and brief for appellee, 37.

17. Cutts transcript, 49–50.

18. West transcript, 458, 464.

19. White defendants, too, sometimes asserted their respectability. Clack transcript, 32–33, 46; Bradshaw transcript, 101; Bradshaw statement, abstract, and brief of appellant, 23.

20. Clayton abstract and brief for appellee, 40–41, 44.

21. Clayton abstract and brief for appellee, 27–28; Clayton supplemental brief for appellants, 21. See also Hodges transcript, 75.

22. Clayton supplemental brief for appellants, 21.

23. Clayton abstract and brief for appellee, 28–29.

24. S. R. McCulloch, "Miscarriage of Justice in Arkansas Alleged," *SLPD*, March 1, 1936, 3-I.

25. Clayton abstract and brief for appellee, 31–32.

26. Clayton supplemental brief for appellants, 22.

27. Cutts transcript, 49.

28. Clayton statement, abstract, and brief of appellants, 20–21; Clayton abstract and brief for appellee, 26.

29. Clayton abstract and brief for appellee, 40.

Chapter 21. The Ascent, 1954–1968

1. Purple Onion advertisement, *San Francisco Examiner*, January 20, 1954, 20; MA, *Singin' and Swingin,'* 87–89, 112–228; Gillespie, Butler, and Long, *Maya Angelou*, 43–47; Stephanie Caruana, "Maya Angelou: An Interview," *Playgirl*, 1974, in f6, b347, MAP; "Porgy Is Complete Art," *Jerusalem Post*, 1955, in Scrapbook, b3, MAP; Program, Porgy and Bess, Théâtre de l'Empire, 1955, f5, b1, MAP; MA, "Imitations of Life," *NYT*, December 17, 1972, f4, b171, MAP; foreign reviews in f1, b346, MAP.

2. Gillespie, Butler, and Long, *Maya Angelou*, 47–48; Hazel Washington, "This... Is Hollywood," *Chicago Defender*, March 26, 1957, 7; Edwin Schallert, "Calypso Craze Inspires Tide of New Films," *Los Angeles Times*, April 14, 1957, E1, E3; Gertrude Gipson, "Candid... Comments," *Los Angeles Sentinel*, May 2, 1957, B11; "On the Town with Will Leonard," *Chicago Tribune*, December 16, 1958; Chuck Foster, "The Exception Rules," *The Beat* 12.4 (1993), 12–19; MA, *The Heart of a Woman* (1982), 1–21.

3. MA, *Heart of a Woman*, 21–52; William Banks Jr., *Beloved Harlem: A Literary Tribute to Black America's Most Famous Neighborhood, from the Classics to the Contemporary* (2005), 155–56, 297–98; C. Gerald Fraser, "John Oliver Killens, 71, Author and Founder of Writers' Group," *NYT*, October 30, 1987, D22; Wagner-Martin, *Life of the Author*, 69–71.

4. MA, *Heart of a Woman*, 52–57; MA, "Martin Luther King" KQED, March 1973, f6, b180, MAP; PBS Documentary, *Maya Angelou: And Still I Rise*, February 21, 2017, at 38:05; MA, *Even the Stars Look Lonesome* (1998), 27–31.

5. MA, *Heart of a Woman*, 58–71; Jesse Walker, "Theatricals," *New York Amsterdam News*, October 29, 1960, 17; "'Cabaret for Freedom' New Theatre Movement," *New York Amsterdam News*, November 19, 1960, 18.

6. MA, *Heart of a Woman*, 71–72, 85–89; Jackie Kay, "The Maya Character," in Jeffrey M. Elliot, ed., *Conversations with Maya Angelou* (1989), 196; Martin Luther King Jr. to Eleanor Roosevelt, October 6, 1960, in Martin Luther King Jr. Papers (digitized and provided online by the King Institute at Stanford University), https://kinginstitute.stanford.edu/king-papers/documents/eleanor-roosevelt-3 [https://perma.cc/L8YW-NZV5]; Stanley D. Levison to Martin Luther King Jr., October 13, 1960, in King Papers, https://kinginstitute.stanford.edu/king-papers/documents/stanley-d-levison-3 [https://perma.cc/4FEB-LZW4]; John Nichols, "Maya Angelou's Civil Rights Legacy," *The Nation*, May 28, 2014, https://www.thenation.com/article/archive/maya-angelous-civil-rights-legacy/.

7. MA, *Heart of a Woman*, 89–97, 104–5; Ballad, "Maya Angelou Interview," MAP; Levison to King, October 13, 1960, King Papers.

8. MA, *Heart of a Woman*, 133, 139–70; Gillespie, Butler, and Long, *Maya Angelou*, 59; "Mob Invades U.N.; 21 Hurt!" *Chicago Tribune*, February 16, 1961, 1; "Blame Reds for Howling UN Riot," *Chicago Defender*, February 16, 1961, 1, 3; "Americans Active in Demonstration at U.N. Meeting," *Alabama Tribune*, February 17, 1961, 1.

9. Angelou, *Heart of a Woman*, 170–83; Howard Taubman, "Theatre: 'The Blacks' by Jean Genet," *NYT*, May 5, 1961, 23; Susan Berman, "Involvement in Black and White: Interviewing Author, Actress Results in Fascinating Afternoon," *Oregonian*, February 17, 1971, f3, b347, MAP; Curt Davis, "Maya Angelou: And Still She Rises," in Elliot, *Conversations with Maya Angelou*, 71–72.

10. MA, "A Brother's Love," *NYT*, December 20, 1987, 29–30; Carol Benson, "Out of the Cage and Still Singing: A Short but Sweet Interview with Maya Angelou," *Writer's Digest*, January 1975, f7, b347, MAP; MA, *Heart of a Woman*, 22, 180.

11. James Baldwin to MA, November 27, 1970, f6, b13, MAP.

12. MA, *Heart of a Woman*, 185–211; Gillespie, Butler, and Long, *Maya Angelou*, 64–65.

13. Kimmis Hendrick, "Ingathering and Ongoing: Two Views," *Christian Science Monitor*, October 13, 1970, f2, b180, MAP.

14. Bob Robertson, " 'Where My Dream Is': Last Song in S.F.—A Life in Africa," *San Francisco Chronicle*, January 28, 1962, 3, f2, b346, MAP; MA, *Heart of a Woman*, 211–56; Joseph Williamson to E. Reginald Townsend, July 10, 1963, f7, b1, MAP.

15. MA, *Heart of a Woman*, 254–72; Joseph Williamson to Ellen Mills-Scarbrough, July 10, 1963, f7, b1, MAP; Exchange Control Act form no. 228115, f8, b1, MAP; correspondence in f7–8, b1, MAP; MA, *All God's Children Need Traveling Clothes* (1986), 1–17; Jane Julianelli, "Maya Angelou," *Harper's Bazaar*, November 1972, f4, b347, MAP.

16. MA, *All God's Children*, 17–29; Bill Moyers, "A Conversation with Maya Angelou," in Elliot, *Conversations with Maya Angelou*, 22; The HistoryMakers interview with Alice Windom, tape 8, October 17, 2007, THM.

17. MA, *All God's Children*, 32–119; Caruana, "Maya Angelou," MAP; Gillespie, Butler, and Long, *Maya Angelou*, 75–78; Vus Make to MA, February 28, 1964; Vus Make to MA, July 23, 1964—both in f19, b33, MAP; Alice Windom to MA, March 23, 1967, f19, b40, MAP; David Tyroler Romine, " 'Into the Mainstream and Oblivion': Julian Mayfield's Black Radical Tradition, 1948–1984" (Ph.D. diss., Duke University, 2018), 196–97.

18. Angelou, *Singin' and Swingin,'* 98–99; MA, *Heart of a Woman*, 85, 91–97.

19. Both articles are Maya Make, "News Talk," early 1960s, f2, b180, MAP.

20. Maya Angelou Make, "The Long March . . . A Stand Still?" *Ghanaian Times*, 1963; MA, "Le Théâtre Africain," *Ghanaian Times*; Maya Angelou Make, "Women in the Public Eye," *Ghanaian Times*; Maya Make, "Women and Ghana's Moral Code," *Ghanaian Times*; Maya Angelou Make, "Women as Educators," *Ghanaian Times*; Maya Make, "Women as Preventive First-Aiders," *Ghanaian Times*; MA, untitled draft article (possibly for *Ghanaian Times*)—all in f3, b180, MAP.

21. Bailey Johnson Jr. to John F. Kennedy, July 13, 1963; William Price to Maya Make, October 16, 1963; Bailey Johnson Jr. to MA, April 17–June 28, 1964—all in f5, b5, MAP.

22. Alice Windom to [unclear], September 11, 1963, f19, b40, MAP; MA, *All God's Children*, 119–28; The HistoryMakers interview with Alice Windom, tape 8, October 17, 2007, THM.

23. Windom to [unclear], MAP; MA, *All God's Children*, 119–28; Windom interview.

24. Windom to [unclear], MAP; MA, *All God's Children*, 119–28; Windom interview.

25. Manning Marable, *Malcolm X: A Life of Reinvention* (2011), 189–90, 314–19; MA, *All God's Children*, 128–46; Alice Windom to Christine, May 21, 1964, f19, b40, MAP; MA, *Heart of a Woman*, 166–70; The HistoryMakers interview with Alice Windom, tape 8, October 17, 2007, THM; Rosa Guy, "A Conversation between Rosa Guy and Maya Angelou," in Elliot, *Conversations with Maya Angelou*, 228.

26. Malcolm X to Maya Maki, June 1, 1964; MA to Malcolm X, July 11, 1964, both in f1, b43, MAP.

27. MA, *All God's Children*, 152, 193–96; "Maya Angelou Returns to G.W.," MAP; Maya Angelou, *A Song Flung Up to Heaven* (2002), 4–10.

28. MA, *Song Flung Up to Heaven*, 11–26; Caruana, "Maya Angelou," MAP; Mildred Schroeder, "Wine, Words and Song of Ghana," *San Francisco Examiner*, March 15, 1965, 31.

29. MA, *Song Flung Up to Heaven*, 26–83, 115; Gillespie, Butler, and Long, *Maya Angelou*, 85–91; MA to Julian Mayfield and Ana Livia Cordero, 1965, f4, b4, Julian Mayfield Papers, Schomburg Center for Research in Black Culture, New York Public Library; Caruana, "Maya Angelou," MAP; Alice Windom to MA, March 3, 1966, f19, b40, MAP.

30. MA to Mayfield and Corder, 1965, Mayfield Papers; MA, *Song Flung Up to Heaven*, 114, 124–49; Maggie Savoy, "Faith of a Black Woman in a World Full of Conflict," *Los Angeles Times*, April 16, 1970, IV-1; Terry Yermon, "Tele-Vues," *Long Beach Independent*, November 19, 1966, C12; "Your Calendar of Lively Arts," *San Bernardino Sun-Telegram*, November 27, 1966, C13; Malcolm X to Maya Maka, January 15, 1965, f1, b43, MAP. For Angelou's poetry, see f1-f3, b179, MAP.

31. MA, Comment on "The Second Civil War" by Gary Wills, 1968, f4, b180, MAP; MA, Review of the poetry of Gwendolyn Brooks, late 1960s, f5, b180, MAP.

32. MA, *Song Flung Up to Heaven*, 172–77.

Chapter 22. The Anti-Rape Docket, 1930s

1. Mack, *Representing the Race*, 121–22; "Weather Forecast," *The News* (Frederick, MD), June 4, 1935, 1; "Weather Forecast," *The News* (Frederick, MD), June 5, 1935, 1.

2. TM, "Re: STATE VS. JAMES POINDEXTER," June 7, 1935, f2, bI:C85, NAACPR; Mack, *Representing the Race*, 119; "Rockville Case Attack Suspect Seized at Last," *Washington Post*, April 14, 1935, 18; "Man Arraigned in Chevy Chase Attack on Girl," *Washington Post*, April 21, 1935, 8; "Held in Jail, 'Innocent' Man Asks Aid," *Pittsburgh Courier*, April 20, 1935, 8; "Negro Denies Charge of Attacking White Girl," *Baltimore Sun*, April 21, 1935, 3; James Poindexter to NAACP, May 20, 1935, Cases rejected by the Montgomery County branch f, bI:D32, NAACPR.

3. CHH to James Poindexter, May 21, 1935, f2, bI:C85, NAACPR.

4. RW to TM, June 3, 1935, f2, bI:C85, NAACPR.

5. TM to Emmitt Poindexter, June 7, 1935; TM to RW, June 7, 1935; Marshall, "Re: STATE VS. JAMES POINDEXTER"—all in f2, bI:C85, NAACPR.

6. RW to TM, June 20, 1935, f2, bI:C85, NAACPR; Williams, *Thurgood Marshall*, 69–74.

7. Gibson, *Young Thurgood*, 209; Maryland v. George Clark, No. 3504 (Md. Crim. Ct. of Balt. Nov. 13, 1935), https://msa.maryland.gov/megafile/msa/speccol/sc5300/

sc5339/000123/000000/000001/restricted/1935_criminal.pdf; Maryland v. James E. Judley, No. 102 (Md. Crim. Ct. of Balt. Jan. 15, 1936), https://msa.maryland.gov/megafile/msa/speccol/sc5300/sc5339/000123/000000/000001/restricted/1936_criminal.pdf.

8. Feimster, *Southern Horrors*, 120–23; Schechter, *Ida B. Wells-Barnett and American Reform*, 122; Paula J. Giddings, *Ida: A Sword among Lions: Ida B. Wells and the Campaign Against Lynching* (2008), 7; Hazel Carby, *Reconstructing Womanhood: The Emergence of the Afro-American Woman Novelist* (1987), 39.

9. Peter Lau, *Democracy Rising: South Carolina and the Fight for Black Equality Since 1865* (2006), 42; Theresa Napson-Williams, "Violating the Black Body: Black Women, White Men and Sexual Violence, 1920–1952" (Ph.D. diss., Rutgers University, 2007), 14–15, 75; WW to Mrs. L. A. Houston, February 10, 1926; NAACP press release, "Defense Fund Enables N.A.A.C.P. to Join in Prosecution of White Rapists," February 5, 1926—both in f3, bI:D55, NAACPR.

10. Napson-Williams, "Violating the Black Body," 14–15, 78–81.

11. NAACP, *A Year's Defense of the Negro's American Citizenship Rights: Being the 19th Annual Report* (1928), 10, bI:A25, NAACPR; Michelle Grigsby Coffey, "The State of Louisiana v. Charles Guerand: Interracial Sexual Mores, Rape Rhetoric, and Respectability in 1930s New Orleans," *Louisiana History* 54 (Winter 2013), 37, 55.

12. Napson-Williams, "Violating the Black Body," 76–77, 81–83; Alan Dingle to WW, March 23, 1926; Alan Dingle to WW, March 24, 1926; NAACP press release, "N.A.A.C.P. Reports on Bronx Assault Case," April 2, 1926—all in f4, bI:D55, NAACPR. Penetration requirement: N.Y. Penal Law §§ 2010–11 (Birdseye 1925); People v. Seaman, 137 N.Y. Supp. 294 (App. Div. 1912); People v. Kline, 137 N.Y. Supp. 296 (App. Div. 1912). Corroboration requirement: N.Y. Penal Law § 2013 (Birdseye 1925); People v. Page 56 N.E. 750 (N.Y. 1900).

13. Coffey, "The State of Louisiana v. Charles Guerand," 53–54; Althea Hart to W. E. B. Du Bois, February 11, 1930; G.W. Lucas to WW, February 21, 1930—both in New Orleans, LA, January–April 1930 f, bI:G82, NAACPR; White, *Rope and Faggot*, 260 (quoting James Weldon Johnson).

14. Memorandum from Frank D. Reeves, "Re: Case of Gwendolyn Smith," December 12, 1940, f6, bII:B123, NAACPR; "Cleveland WPA Boss Accused of 3 Attempted Rapes on Race Women; No Arrest," *Kansas City Star*, November 13, 1936, 6; NAACP Press Release, "White Man's Attempted Assault on 16-Year-Old Girl Nets Sentence of Fifteen Years in N.C.," March 22, 1940, f6, bII:B123, NAACPR; "Watch Rape Crisis," *The Crisis*, March 1937, 88; "N.A.A.C.P. Will Fight Rape Case against Judge's Nephew," *Pittsburgh Courier*, December 19, 1936, 4; "NAACP Takes Case of N.J. Rape Victim," *Baltimore Afro-American*, December 19, 1936, 20.

15. Sullivan, *Lift Every Voice*, 18–19; McNeil, *Groundwork*, 88–89; TM to E. L. Sullinger, March 28, 1940, f6, bII:B123, NAACPR; Fritz Cansler, "Gets $354 for Girl's Defense," *Baltimore Afro-American*, February 27, 1937, 16; Alexander Miller to WW, October 16, 1940, f7, bII:B125, NAACPR.

16. "From the Press of a Nation," *The Crisis*, June 1937, 179 (reprinting editorial); H. A. Merchant to TM, April 11, 1940, f2, bII:B123, NAACPR.

17. Joy B. Jones to Arthur Spingarn, 1947, f6, bII:B123, NAACPR; McGuire, *At the Dark End of the Street*, xv–xxiii, 3–47, 79–83; Napson-Williams, "Violating the Black Body," 92–97.

Chapter 23. The Trial Ends, 1929

1. Bethel transcript, 494–505; "Bethel-Wallace Case Goes to Jury," *BCN*, April 12, 1929, 1, 3.

2. Force: Cook abstract and brief for appellee, 34; Franks abstract and brief for appellant, 22–23; Cabe abstract and brief for appellant, 43. Resistance: Boyd appellant's brief and argument, 45; Cook abstract and brief for appellee, 33–34; Franks abstract and brief for appellee, 23, 25; Bethel abstract and brief for appellant, 30; Head transcript, 161; Sanders transcript, 237.

3. Allison transcript, 86.

4. Reed transcript, 99; Franks abstract and brief for appellant, 27–28; Snetzer transcript, 90; Cook abstract and brief for appellee, 31–32; Whitaker transcript, 76; Durham transcript, 73; Cook abstract and brief for appellee, 30.

5. Terrell transcript, 206.

6. Underdown transcript, 90.

7. Caldwell transcript, 107. See also Fields transcript, 113.

8. "Bethel-Wallace Case Goes to Jury," 1; "Bethel and Wallace Get 18 Years," *BCN*, April 13, 1929, 1, 8.

9. See Lewis transcript, 129–30; Reed transcript, 11; Wills transcript, 47; Durham abstract and brief for appellant, 40.

10. "Bethel and Wallace Get 18 Years," 1, 8; "Pair Convicted of Attacking Teacher," *AG*, April 13, 1929, 14.

11. Bethel transcript, 506; "Bethel and Wallace Freed under Bond Pending Appeal," *BCN*, April 15, 1929, 1.

12. Bethel transcript, 506–10; "Highway Commission Appeals License Fee Case," *AG*, June 4, 1929, 10.

13. "Sheriff's Fees for April Court Term $800," *BCN*, June 20, 1929, 1; "County's Funds Are Nearly Out Report Reveals," *BCN*, September 10, 1929, 3. For Wallace's marriage, see "Bethel-Wallace Case Closes as Men Enter Pen," *BCN*, November 20, 1929, 1; Wallace prisoner file, ADC; 1930 U.S. Census, Monette, Craighead, AR, 10A, family 214, lines 15–16, April 12, 1930; certificate of marriage, Roy Wallace and Elly Jurasin Meurer, April 27, 1929, ABVS; 1920 U.S. Census, Black Oak, Craighead, AR, 16B, family 297, lines 71–75, February 18, 1920.

14. "Brother of Frank Bethel Sought on Attack Charge," *BCN*, June 17, 1929, 1; "Brother of Convict Arrested on Assault Charge," *AG*, January 2, 1930, 2; "Bethel Boy

Waives Preliminary Hearing," *BCN,* January 3, 1930, 1; "Daily Weather Report," *AG,* June 11, 1929, 12.

15. "Bethel-Wallace Case Closes as Men Enter Pen," *BCN,* November 20, 1929, 1; "Sheriff-Elect Names Deputies at Blytheville," *AG,* December 30, 1928, 2; "Sheriffs End Meet with Pistol Shoot," *AG,* November 17, 1929, 16.

16. Thanks to Thea Baker for images of The Walls, which apparently came from Darrell McHenry at the ADC.

17. Lewis Barnard, "Old Arkansas State Penitentiary," *AHQ* 13.3 (Autumn 1954), 321; Crosley, *Unfolding Misconceptions,* 11–12.

18. Joe Wirges, "The Penitentiary, 1864–1961," 2 (on file with Thea Baker).

19. Barnard, "Old Arkansas State Penitentiary," 321–22; Wirges, "Penitentiary," 2–5; Crosley, *Unfolding Misconceptions,* 12–16.

20. Barnard, "Old Arkansas State Penitentiary," 322–23; Crosley, *Unfolding Misconceptions,* 32–33; Wirges, "Penitentiary," 6–7; "Arkansas Department of Corrections," *Encyclopedia of Arkansas,* November 18, 2019, https://encyclopediaofarkansas.net/entries/arkansas-department-of-correction-5704/; Hiram U. Ford, "A History of the Arkansas Penitentiary to 1900" (master's thesis, University of Arkansas, 1936).

21. Wirges, "Penitentiary," 7; William Newton Hill, *Story of the Arkansas Penitentiary* (1912), 1–26; Crosley, *Unfolding Misconceptions,* 14.

22. Wirges, "Penitentiary," 7; "Flowers Flourish within Grim Walls," *AG,* August 14, 1932, 18; "Notorious Killers Receive Clemency," *AG,* December 24, 1932, 9; "Penitentiary Population March 31 Was 1,101," *Star Progress* (Berryville, AR), April 18, 1929, 2. See also M. C. Blackman, "Little Rocking Along," *AG,* August 3, 1930, 9.

23. For evidence that Bethel and Wallace remained in The Walls for the bulk of their sentences, see their prison files (listing both their intake and release sites as The Walls) and their entries in the 1930 census (listing their continued presence at The Walls, many months after arriving).

24. "Bass Will Be Given Sanity Test," *Camden News,* May 27, 1930, 1.

25. Elmer Mikel to Winthrop Rockefeller, March 24, 1968, in Elmer Mikel, *Uncle Tom's Prison* (self-published, 1970). Note that the page numbers in this book are highly irregular.

Chapter 24. The Trial Ends, 1935

1. Arthur L. Adams, Motion for a New Trial, 1935, f3, bD51, NAACPR; statement of Arthur L. Adams before the District Court for the Eastern District of Arkansas, Caruthers & Clayton v. Cogbill, December 1936, 30–31, f10, bD50, NAACPR; statement of Neil Killough before the District Court for the Eastern District of Arkansas, Carruthers & Clayton v. Reed, March 1938, f3, bD51, NAACPR; S. R. McCulloch, "Miscarriage of Justice in Arkansas Alleged," *SLPD,* March 1, 1936, 3-I.

2. Adams, Motion for a New Trial, NAACPR; statement of Adams, December 1936, 30–31, NAACPR; statement of Killough, March 1938, NAACPR; McCulloch, "Miscarriage of Justice in Arkansas Alleged," 3-I.

3. Clayton statement, abstract, and brief of appellants, 33–37.

4. Daniels transcript, 100; Cutts transcript, 68.

5. Wriggins, "Rape, Racism, and the Law," 111; McQuirter v. State, 63 So.2d 388, 390 (Ala. 1953); Pumphrey v. State, 47 So. 156, 158 (Ala. 1908); Dorsey v. State, 34 S.E. 135 (Ga. 1899); Story v. State, 5 So. 480 (Ala. 1912).

6. McCulloch, "Miscarriage of Justice in Arkansas Alleged," 3-I; Adams, Motion for a New Trial, NAACPR; "Negroes Sentenced to Electric Chair," *AG*, April 11, 1935, 2.

7. McCulloch, "Miscarriage of Justice in Arkansas Alleged," 3-I; Adams, Motion for a New Trial, NAACPR; "Negroes Sentenced to Electric Chair," 2; statement of Neil Killough, Carruthers & Clayton v. Reed, NAACPR.

8. "Dust Storm Here," *OT*, April 12, 1935, 1.

9. Stern, "Shadow Trials," 317–18.

10. Ibid., 318–19; Cutts transcript, 14–16; Jeffrey J. Pokorak, "Rape as a Badge of Slavery: The Legal History of, and Remedies for, Prosecutorial Race-of-Victim Charging Disparities," *Nevada Law Journal* 7 (2006), 32–33 (2006). See also Miller, *Crime, Sexual Violence, and Clemency*, 181; Donald H. Partington, "The Incidence of the Death Penalty for Rape in Virginia," *Washington & Lee Law Review* 22 (1965), 43. Lisa Lindquist Dorr has complicated the neat racial disparities by noting that the class status of white accusers could diminish the sentences juries imposed on Black defendants. See Dorr, *White Women, Rape, and the Power of Race*, 129.

11. Stern, "Shadow Trials," 320. See also West v. State, 192 S.W.2d 135 (Ark. 1946); Hogan v. State, 86 S.W.2d 931 (Ark. 1935); Burks v. State, 120 S.W.2d 345 (Ark. 1938); Franks v. State, 272 S.W. 648 (Ark. 1925); Sutton v. State, 122 S.W.2d 617 (Ark. 1938); Cook v. State, 276 S.W. 583 (Ark. 1925); Thornsberry v. State, 92 S.W.2d 203 (Ark. 1936).

12. Adams, Motion for a New Trial, NAACPR; McCulloch, "Miscarriage of Justice in Arkansas Alleged," 3-I; Hodges brief for appellant, 3; "Death Penalty Given Negroes for Assault," *AG*, January 7, 1938, 24; "Spectators Cheer as Negro Gets Death Sentence in Rape," *AG*, March 18, 1949, 6.

13. Adams, Motion for a New Trial, NAACPR.

14. Ibid.; Hamm transcript, 6.

15. Statement of Bubbles Clayton before the District Court for the Eastern District of Arkansas, Carruthers & Clayton v. Reed, March 1938, f3, bD51, NAACPR.

16. Crosley, *Unfolding Misconceptions*, 54–55, 70; Mikel, *Uncle Tom's Prison*, 50; Wirges, "Penitentiary," 7.

17. Matthew J. Mancini, *One Dies, Get Another: Convict Leasing in the American South, 1866–1928* (1996), 24–41 (quoting James L. Roark and Pete Daniel).

18. Crosley, *Unfolding Misconceptions*, 16–19, 27–32; Hill, *Story of the Arkansas Penitentiary*, 30–32; Calvin R. Ledbetter Jr., "The Long Struggle to End Convict Leasing in Arkansas," *AHQ* 52.1 (Spring 1993), 1–11; Jane Zimmerman, "The Convict Lease System in Arkansas and the Fight for Abolition," *AHQ* 8.3 (Autumn 1949), 172–78.

19. Crosley, *Unfolding Misconceptions*, 33–46; Ledbetter, "Long Struggle," 11–27; Zimmerman, "Convict Lease System in Arkansas," 178–88; Thomas Baxley, "Prison Reforms during the Donaghey Administration," *AHQ* 22.1 (Spring 1963), 76–84; George W. Donaghey, *Autobiography of George W. Donaghey* (1939), 286–90.

20. Crosley, *Unfolding Misconceptions*, 47–53; statement of Thomas Slaughter to Arkansas State Penitentiary Commission, September 21, 1921, f5, b1, Laura Cornelius Conner Papers, University of Arkansas Libraries.

21. M. C. Blackman, "Little Rocking Along," *AG*, August 3, 1930, 9; "The Truth Will Out," *Camden Times*, February 15, 1934, 1.

22. "Todhunter Dismissed, Penitentiary Abandoned," *Madison County Record*, July 20, 1933, 1; "The Truth Will Out," 1; Crosley, *Unfolding Misconceptions*, 48.

23. Hill, *Story of the Arkansas Penitentiary*, 33; "State Prison Survey Made," *Star Progress* (Berryville, AR), November 17, 1927, 4; Crosley, *Unfolding Misconceptions*, 55; Mikel, *Uncle Tom's Prison*, 83–84.

24. M. C. Blackman, "Little Rocking Along," *AG*, August 3, 1930, 9.

25. Affidavit of Susie Smith, Pennie Scott, and Frank Atkinson, 1946, f17, b63, NAACPLDFR.

26. Smith, "Laura Conner and the Limits of Prison Reform," 57–58; interview of Torressia Dancler McDowell by Laura Conner, October 8, 1921, f5, b1, Laura Cornelius Conner Papers, University of Arkansas Libraries.

27. Mikel, *Uncle Tom's Prison*, 44–46.

28. Woodruff, *American Congo*, 169; Mitchell, *Mean Things Happening in This Land*, 81; Mitchell, "The Founding and Early History," 356; Kester, *Revolt among the Sharecroppers*, 66.

29. Woodruff, *American Congo*, 169–70; Mitchell, *Mean Things Happening in This Land*, 81–83; Mitchell, "The Founding and Early History," 356–57; Kester, *Revolt among the Sharecroppers*, 95–96.

30. Woodruff, *American Congo*, 170; Mitchell, "Founding and Early History," 357; Kester, *Revolt among the Sharecroppers*, 96.

Chapter 25. Taking Flight, 1968–1969

1. MA, *Song Flung Up to Heaven*, 187–93; Gillespie, Butler, and Long, *Maya Angelou*, 97; Mary Jane Lupton, *Maya Angelou: A Critical Companion* (1998), 10.

2. MA, *Song Flung Up to Heaven*, 194–97; Jane Julianelli, "Maya Angelou," *Harper's Bazaar*, November 1972, f4, b347, MAP; PBS Documentary, *Maya Angelou: And Still I Rise*, February 21, 2017, at 1:04:15; Gerald Gladney, " 'Touch Me, Life, Not Softly':

An Interview with Maya Angelou," *UPTOWN: The Voice of Central Harlem*, 1979, f4, b346, MAP.

3. Wayne Warga, "Maya Angelou: One-Woman Creativity Cult," *Los Angeles Times*, January 9, 1972, f4, b347, MAP; Gladney, " 'Touch Me, Life, Not Softly,' " MAP; Dinitia Smith, "A Career in Letters, 50 Years and Counting," *NYT*, January 23, 2007, https://www.nytimes.com/2007/01/23/books/23loom.html [https://perma.cc/54RK-Y9VV]; Carol Benson: "Out of the Cage and Still Singing: A Short but Sweet Interview with Maya Angelou," *Writer's Digest*, January 1975, f7, b347, MAP; Gillespie, Butler, and Long, *Maya Angelou*, 100; MA, *Song Flung Up to Heaven*, 206–09.

4. MA, *Song Flung Up to Heaven*, 210–12; Gillespie, Butler, and Long, *Maya Angelou*, 100–01.

5. Julianelli, "Maya Angelou," MAP.

6. Braxton, "Symbolic Geography and Psychic Landscapes," in Braxton, *Maya Angelou's I Know Why the Caged Bird Sings*, 12.

7. Handwritten drafts in f1, b112, MAP.

8. MA, "Perspectus," f2, b112, MAP.

9. Claudia Tate, "Maya Angelou: An Interview," in Braxton, *Maya Angelou's I Know Why the Caged Bird Sings*, 154.

10. Linda Wagner-Martin, *Maya Angelou: Adventurous Spirit* (2016), 35. See also ibid., 38.

11. Tate, "Maya Angelou," 154.

12. Mary Ann Seawell, "Memories of Black Childhood Full of Beauty and Terror," *Palo Alto Times*, May 18, 1970, b348, MAP.

13. MA to Dolly McPherson, November 20, 1968, f13, b33, MAP.

14. MA to Dolly McPherson, December 3, 1968, f13, b33, MAP.

15. Cover of notebook in f3, b112, MAP.

16. Handwritten drafts in f1, 2, and 7, b112, MAP. Benson, "Out of the Cage and Still Singing," MAP.

17. Sheila Weller, "Work in Progress: Maya Angelou," *Intellectual Digest* (June 1973), 11–12, f5, b347, MAP.

18. MA to James Baldwin, May 1, 1973, f6, b13, MAP.

19. Mert Guswiler, " 'You Must Love Truth for Truth's Sake, and Right for Right's Sake': Maya Angelou, National Book Award Nominee," *Los Angeles Herald-Examiner*, March 12, 1971, A19.

20. Hollie I. West, " 'That's the Kind of Meaning I Want This Book to Have,' " *Oregonian*, May 16, 1970, f2, b347, MAP. See also Braxton, "Symbolic Geography and Psychic Landscapes," in Braxton, *Maya Angelou's I Know Why the Caged Bird Sings*, 6–7.

21. Weller, "Work in Progress," 11; Rudy Maxa, "Maya Angelou: A Caged Bird She's Not," *Washington Post Magazine*, April 9, 1978, 5; MA, draft of essay on writing, January 10, 1991, f20, b180, MAP; George Plimpton, "Maya Angelou, The Art of Fiction No.

119," *Paris Review* (Fall 1990), https://www.theparisreview.org/interviews/2279/the-art-of-fiction-no-119-maya-angelou [https://perma.cc/U4NR-RXG7]; Walter Blum, "Listening to Maya Angelou," in Elliot, *Conversations with Maya Angelou*, 40.

22. Bette Tambling, "Maya Angelou 'Celebrates Life' in Both Fact and Fiction," *Fresno Bee*, March 1, 1972, C1.

23. Drafts in f1–2, b112, MAP.

24. Early handwritten draft in f3 and early typed draft in f6—both in b112, MAP; *CB*, 78. See also Lupton, *Maya Angelou*, 56, 67.

25. Lupton, *Maya Angelou*, 34–35; Plimpton, "Maya Angelou."

26. MA, draft of essay on writing, January 10, 1991, f20, b180, MAP.

27. Lupton, *Maya Angelou*, 35.

28. *CB*, 180.

29. Mary Vermillion, "Reembodying the Self: Representations of Rape in *Incidents in the Life of a Slave Girl* and *I Know Why the Caged Bird Sings*," in Mickle, *Critical Insights*, 142.

30. Ibid., 138.

31. Mildred R. Mickle, "On *I Know Why the Caged Bird Sings*," in Mickle, *Critical Insights*, 5.

32. Christine Froula, "The Daughter's Seduction: Sexual Violence and Literary History," *Signs* 11.4 (Summer 1986), 636–37.

33. Drafts in f1–2, b112, MAP.

34. Quoted in Tate, "Maya Angelou," 158; Lyman B. Hagen, *Heart of a Woman, Mind of a Writer, and Soul of a Poet: A Critical Analysis of the Writings of Maya Angelou* (1997), 54.

35. Lupton, *Maya Angelou*, 66.

36. Elizabeth Fox-Genovese, "Myth and History: Discourse of Origins in Zora Neale Hurston and Maya Angelou," *Black American Literature Forum* 24.2 (Summer 1990), 221–22; Colette S. Mongeau-Marshall, "The Masks of Maya Angelou: Discovered, Discarded, and Designed" (master's thesis, University of Alaska at Anchorage, 1994), 7–8.

37. Myra K. McMurry, "Role-Playing as Art in Maya Angelou's 'Caged Bird,'" *South Atlantic Bulletin* 41.2 (May 1976), 106.

38. Emily Rovetch, ed., *Like It Is: Arthur E. Thomas Interviews Leaders on Black America* (1981), 6–7.

39. Gladney, "'Touch Me, Life, Not Softly,'" MAP.

40. MA to unknown recipient, 1964, f8, b1, MAP.

41. MA to unknown recipient, n.d., f8, b1, MAP.

42. Malcolm X to Maya Maka, January 15, 1965, f1, b43, MAP.

43. MA, "They Outlasted the Slaver's Whip," *Life*, May 5, 1972, f3, b171, MAP.

44. Weller, "Work in Progress," MAP.

45. Richard Ballad, "Maya Angelou Interview," 1971, f4, b201, MAP. See also Wagner-Martin, *Maya Angelou*, 17–18.

46. Doug McClelland, "Maya's GWP LP More Than Half a Lifetime's Work," *Record World*, 1968, f1, b347, MAP; Dwight Newton, "Will Blacks Still Like Her Next Week?"

San Francisco Examiner, July 21, 1968, B5; John Stanley, "Blacks, Blues, and 24 Robbers," *San Francisco Examiner,* August 4, 1968, 16; "Afro-American Seminar Will Be Held Saturday," *Minneapolis Star,* November 1, 1968, 7B; "Maya Angelou Teaches Black History on TV," *New Pittsburgh Courier,* March 8, 1969, 6; Dianne Thompson, "A Woman of Many Talents . . . and Now She's a Poet," *New York Amsterdam News,* May 10, 1969, 19; MA to Dolly McPherson, July 21, 1969, f13, b33, MAP.

47. Cf. Amy Sickels, "*I Know Why the Caged Bird Sings:* African American Literary Tradition and the Civil Rights Era," in Mickle, *Critical Insights,* 22.

48. Alice Echols, *Daring To Be Bad: Radical Feminism in America, 1967–1974* (1989), 141–43, 193; Lucinda Cisler, "Unfinished Business: Birth Control and Women's Liberation," in Robin Morgan, ed., *Sisterhood Is Powerful: An Anthology of Writings from the Women's Liberation Movement* (1970), 274–75; Edith Evans Asbury, "Women Break Up Abortion Hearing," *NYT,* February 14, 1969, 42; Brian Barrett and Lewis Grossberger, "Women Invade Abortion Hearing," *NYT,* February 14, 1969, 4; Margie Stamberg, "The New Feminism," *Guardian,* April 19, 1969, 11; Ellen Willis, "Up from Radicalism: A Feminist Journal," *US Magazine,* October 1969, 4–5; "Speaking Out on Abortion," *Washington Post,* June 14, 1969, C1; "Abortion Topic of 'Speak-Out,' " *Chicago Tribune,* February 26, 1970, 3; Judith Hole and Ellen Levine, *Rebirth of Feminism* (1975), 298–99; Meg Gillette, "Modern Abortion Narratives and the Century of Shame," *Twentieth Century Literature* 58 (2012), 664.

49. Plimpton, "Maya Angelou"; Hagen, *Heart of a Woman,* 4–5, 8–9; McPherson, *Order Out of Chaos,* ch. 6; Mickle, "On *I Know Why the Caged Bird Sings,*" in Mickle, *Critical Insights,* 6; Selwyn R. Cudjoe, "Maya Angelou and the Autobiographical Statement," in Mari Evans, ed., *Black Women Writers, 1950–1980: A Critical Evaluation* (1984), 6; Joanne M. Braxton, *Black Women Writing Autobiography: A Tradition within a Tradition* (1989), 181–84, 191; Susan Gilbert, "Paths to Escape," in Braxton, *Maya Angelou's* I Know Why the Caged Bird Sings, 102; Cherron A. Barnwell, "Singin' de Blues, Writing Black Female Survival in 'I Know Why the Caged Bird Sings,' " *Langston Hughes Review* 19 (Spring 2005), 49; Pierre A. Walker, "Racial Protest, Identity, Words, and Form," in Braxton, *Maya Angelou's* I Know Why the Caged Bird Sings, 79; Lupton, *Maya Angelou,* ch. 2; Wagner-Martin, *Maya Angelou,* 3–4.

50. MA interview, f1155, b139, Jessica Mitford Collection, Ohio State University; Susan Berman, "Involvement in Black and White: Interviewing Author, Actress Results in Fascinating Afternoon," *Oregonian,* February 17, 1971, f3, b347, MAP; Natasha Walter, "Decca Mitford Liked a Good Sing-Song. 'Right Said Fred' Was a Favourite," *The Observer,* February 16, 1997, 9; Hagen, *Heart of a Woman,* 57.

Chapter 26. The Appeal, 1935–1936

1. "The Weather," *Baltimore Sun,* January 24, 1936, 23; "The Weather," *Evening Sun,* January 24, 1936, 2; Mack, *Representing the Race,* 126–28.

2. "Four Accused Cheltenham Boys Freed," *Baltimore Afro-American*, February 1, 1936, 3; "Baltimore Has Its 'Scottsboro' Farce," *Norfolk Journal & Guide*, February 8, 1936, 5; TM, "Memorandum Re: Four Boys from Cheltenham Held for Questioning at Upper Marlboro," January 25, 1936, TM 1936 f, bI:C84, NAACPR; Gibson, *Young Thurgood*, 214; Mack, *Representing the Race*, 128.

3. Spencer Clayton to NAACP, March 12, 1935, f10, bD50, NAACPR.

4. SAJ to WW, April 12, 1935, f10, bD50, NAACPR.

5. Arthur L. Adams to SAJ, April 11, 1935, f10, bD50, NAACPR.

6. RW to SAJ, April 25, 1935, f10, bD50, NAACPR.

7. RW to Spencer Clayton, May 13, 1935, f10, bD50, NAACPR.

8. Luther Moore to I. A. Clark, June 18, 1935; Luther Moore to CHH, July 18, 1935—both in f10, bD50, NAACPR; "Death Sentences against Two Negroes to Be Appealed," *AG*, May 11, 1935, 2; "Stay Given Negroes Sentenced to Die," *HS*, May 13, 1935, 1; "Execution of Negroes in Arkansas Is Stayed," *Morning Advocate* (Baton Rouge), May 14, 1935, 1; "Pair, Condemned to Death, Appeal," *AG*, May 14, 1935, 20; "Arkansas Youths Face Legal Lynching," *Pittsburgh Courier*, September 28, 1935, 3; "Execution Stay Is Won for Negroes in Eastern Arkansas," *DW*, May 23, 1935, 3.

9. Notes in f34, b5, Series I, Tom W. Dillard Black Arkansiana Materials, Butler Center for Arkansas Studies; Judith Kilpatrick, "John A. Hibbler," *Arkansas Black Lawyers*, 2003, https://arkansasblacklawyers.uark.edu/lawyers/jahibbler.html; Stockley, *Blood in Their Eyes*, 198; Whitaker, *On the Lap of Gods*, 197–98, 305; Darlene Clark Hine, *Black Victory: The Rise and Fall of the White Primary in Texas* (2003), 132–35; "To Encourage Race Hatred Is Dangerous," *Hot Springs New Era*, June 26, 1914, 8.

10. Correspondence in f10, bD50, NAACPR; "Two Innocent Negro Boys Face Chair in Little Rock," *DW*, August 1, 1935, 4; S. R. McCulloch, "Miscarriage of Justice in Arkansas Alleged," *SLPD*, March 1, 1936, 3-I.

11. CHH to Luther Moore, July 22, 1935; CHH to Luther Moore, September 6, 1935—both in f10, bD50, NAACPR; draft supplemental brief, Carruthers & Clayton v. Reed, September 6, 1935, f2, bD51, NAACPR.

12. CHH to Luther Moore, September 13, 1935; Luther Moore to CHH, September 16, 1935; CHH to WW, September 27, 1935—all in f10, bD50, NAACPR.

13. CHH to Moore, September 13, 1935; SAJ to CHH, October 21, 1935; SAJ to CHH, October 30, 1935—all in f10, bD50, NAACPR; Whitaker, *On the Laps of Gods*, 185.

14. Tom Dillard, "Scipio A. Jones," *AHQ* 31.3 (Autumn 1972), 201–19; correspondence/notes in b9, Series I, Tom W. Dillard Black Arkansiana Materials, Butler Center for Arkansas Studies; correspondence/notes in f9, b1, Subseries I, Series I, Grif Stockley Papers, Butler Center for Arkansas Studies; Judith Kilpatrick, "Scipio Africanus Jones," *Arkansas Black Lawyers* (2003), https://arkansasblacklawyers.uark.edu/lawyers/sajones.html; Steven Teske, "Scipio Africanus Jones, 1863–1943," *Encyclopedia of Arkansas*, November 13, 2019, https://encyclopediaofarkansas.net/entries/scipio-

africanus-jones-2427/; Whitaker, *On the Laps of Gods*, 185–208; Stockley, *Blood in Their Eyes*, 92–100; Cortner, *A Mob Intent on Death*, 51; SAJ to Robert E. Lee Wilson, May 25, 1932; Robert E. Lee Wilson to SAJ, May 27, 1932—both in f65, b49, LWCR; Whayne, *Delta Empire*, 137.

15. "Execution Stay Is Won for Negroes in Eastern Arkansas," 3; "Two Innocent Negro Boys Face Chair in Little Rock," 4.

16. "Framed Youth Faces Death In Arkansas," *Cleveland Call and Post*, August 15, 1935, 6; H. T. Sims, "World's Flashlight," *Negro Star*, September 20, 1935, 1; "Scottsboro Case Parallel Fought in Ark. Courts," *Morning Advocate* (Baton Rouge), September 27, 1935, 14; "Arkansas Youths Face Legal Lynching," *Pittsburgh Courier*, September 28, 1935, 3; "N.A.A.C.P. Aid Enlisted," *Omaha Guide*, September 28, 1935, 2; "Another Scottsboro Case Is Unearthed in Arkansas; Two Boys Face Legal Lynching," *Atlanta Daily World*, October 1, 1935, 2; "New 'Scottsboro Case' Brought to Light in Arkansas," *Baltimore Afro-American*, October 5, 1935, 10.

17. Williams, *Thurgood Marshall*, 82–83; Gibson, *Young Thurgood*, 295–99; correspondence in bI:C84, NAACPR.

18. Gibson, *Young Thurgood*, 231–37; Sullivan, *Lift Every Voice*, 207–11.

19. Gibson, *Young Thurgood*, 238–46; TM oral history, 11–14, CCOH; McNeil, *Groundwork*, 138–39.

20. CHH to JAH, November 1, 1935; CHH to JAH, November 8, 1935—both in f10, bD50, NAACPR.

21. SAJ to CHH, November 8, 1935, f10, bD50, NAACPR.

22. W. W. Satterfield, "Edgar Lafayette McHaney, 1876–1948," *Encyclopedia of Arkansas*, May 18, 2019, https://encyclopediaofarkansas.net/entries/edgar-lafayette-mchaney-8952/; Stockley, *Blood in Their Eyes*, 103–4; "Mr. E. L. M'Haney, Miss Gail Myers," *AD*, April 21, 1904, 1; "Diplomas for Ten Lawyers," *AD*, June 15, 1904, 2.

23. Stockley, *Blood in Their Eyes*, 103–4, 174–77, 188–94; Whitaker, *On the Lap of Gods*, 231–32, 248–49, 256–65; W. W. Satterfield, "Edgar McHaney: Supreme Court Justice and Elaine Attorney," *Pulaski County Historical Review* 67 (Summer 2019), 32–40.

24. Satterfield, "Edgar Lafayette McHaney"; Stockley, *Blood in the Water*, 227; Robinson v. Holman, 26 S.W.2d 66 (Ark. 1930), cert. denied, 282 U.S. 804 (1930).

25. Clayton v. State, 89 S.W.2d 732 (Ark. 1935).

26. SAJ to CHH, November 18, 1935, f10, bD50, NAACPR.

27. JAH to CHH, November 18, 1935; CHH to JAH, December 5, 1935; JAH to CHH, December 9, 1935—all in f10, bD50, NAACPR; "Petition Seeks Rehearing for Condemned Negroes," *AG*, December 6, 1935, 15.

28. "Death Sanctioned for 2 in Arkansas," *Baltimore Afro-American*, November 30, 1935, 11; "Arkansas High Court Ignores Race Jury Issue," *Pittsburgh Courier*, November 30, 1935, 2; "Scottsboro Plea Fails Doomed Ark. Negroes," *Morning Advocate* (Baton Rouge), November 19, 1935, 6; "Negroes Lose in Arkansas Court," *Birmingham News*,

November 18, 1935, 9; "Death Sentence of 2 Negroes in Attack Conviction Upheld," *Beaumont Enterprise*, November 19, 1935, 5; "Court Affirms Death Sentence for Negroes," *Jefferson City Post-Tribune*, November 18, 1935, 2; "Death of Pair for Assault Is Upheld," *New York Daily News*, November 19, 1935, 37; Robert Wood, "Scores of Lynchings and Strike Killings Mark New Terror in South," *DW*, November 23, 1935, 5.

29. "The Weather," *AG*, January 20, 1936, 10; Clayton v. State, 89 S.W.2d 732, 734–35 (Ark. 1935).

30. West v. State, 192 S.W.2d 135, 136 (Ark. 1946) (Smith, C.J., dissenting).

31. Stern, "Shadow Trials," 321–22; DeVoe abstract and brief for appellant, 19; Braswell abstract and brief for appellant, 39; Thornberry reply brief of appellant, 16; DeVoe v. State, 97 S.W.2d 75 (Ark. 1936); Braswell, 280 S.W. 357; Thornsberry v. State, 92 S.W.2d 203 (Ark. 1936).

32. Boyd appellant's brief and argument, 52, 55; DeVoe abstract and brief for appellant, 19; Rose abstract and argument for appellant, 71–74; Brust abstract and brief of appellant, 12–18.

33. Kazzee abstract and brief for appellant, 16. See also Boyd appellant's brief and argument, 47; Thomas v. State, 11 S.W.2d 771, 771–72 (Ark. 1928); Young v. State, 221 S.W. 478–80 (Ark. 1920).

34. Thomas II abstract and brief for appellants, 3–4; Maxwell II abstract and brief for appellant, 2, 5, 7–16; Palmer brief for the appellant, 1–7; West abstract and brief of appellant, 117–18.

35. Clayton statement, abstract, and brief of appellants, 38, 42; Clayton supplemental brief for appellants, 10–15. For similar arguments as to race discrimination, see Cutts transcript, 10–11; Daniels transcript, 18; Hodges brief for appellant, 3; Maxwell abstract and brief for appellant, 23; McGee abstract and brief for appellant, 13

36. Clayton supplemental brief for appellants, 2–6. See also Maxwell abstract and brief for appellant, 22–23; Thomas II abstract and brief for appellants, 25; Dorr, *White Women, Rape, and the Power of Race*, chs. 2 and 4.

37. "Execution Stay Is Won for Negroes in Eastern Arkansas," 3; Priest v. State, 163 S. W. 2d 159, 160 (Ark. 1942).

38. JAH to CHH, January 20, 1936, f11, bD50, NAACPR.

39. CHH to JAH, February 7, 1936; JAH to Carol King, February 10, 1936—both in f11, bD50, NAACPR; "Doomed Pair's Lawyers Seek to Delay Mandate," *AG*, January 25, 1936, 8.

40. The newspapers later stated that Clayton and Carruthers's attorneys failed to file their appeal at this time, but this is not reflected in the correspondence or legal records that survive in the NAACPR. Sid B. Redding to JAH, November 19, 1936; Luther Moore to WW, November 23, 1936—both in f11, bD50, NAACPR; McCulloch, "Miscarriage of Justice in Arkansas Alleged," 31.

41. "Doomed Pair Lets Time for New Plea Pass," *AG*, May 5, 1936, 7; "Chair for 4 at Once," *New Orleans Item*, May 7, 1936, 5; "Doomed Pair Given Writ in U.S. Court," *AG*,

May 15, 1936, 18; "U.S. Court Hears Arkansas Mob Law Case Monday," *SLPD*, June 16, 1936, 8; "Condemned Pair Gets New Delay in U.S. Court," *AG*, June 19, 1936, 8; "Hearing for Two Negroes December 10," *AG*, November 27, 1936, 5; "Carruthers-Clayton Hearing December 10," *BCN*, November 27, 1936, 1.

42. S. R. McCulloch, "Miscarriage of Justice Alleged in Trial and Death Sentences of Two Negroes in Arkansas," *SLPD*, March 1, 1936, 1I, 3I.

43. Telephone call for Mr. Wilkins, December 4, 1936, f11, bD50, NAACPR.

44. Redding to JAH, November 19, 1936, NAACPR.

45. Gibson, *Young Thurgood*, 291–95, 305–6; Williams, *Thurgood Marshall*, 83–84.

46. Gibson, *Young Thurgood*, 306–8; Williams, *Thurgood Marshall*, 84–87; McNeil, *Groundwork*, 144–45; "Thurgood Marshall Joins NAACP Legal Staff," *Norfolk Journal & Guide*, October 31, 1936, 4.

47. Gibson, *Young Thurgood*, 254–55, 314–16; "Maryland Bar Hears Jim-Crow School Charges," *Chicago Defender*, November 16, 1935, 1; Sullivan, *Lift Every Voice*, 229–30.

48. TM to Luther Moore, November 28, 1936, f11, bD50, NAACPR.

49. Woodruff, *American Congo*, 170–77; Donald Grubbs, *Cry from the Cotton: The Southern Tenant Farmers' Union and the New Deal* (1971), chs. 5–6; Dunbar, *Against the Grain*, ch. 5; Mitchell, *Mean Things Happening in This Land*, 86–92; Ross, " 'I Ain't Got No Home,' " 139–41.

50. Rex Pitkin, "Planter Justice Speeds Two Negroes to Death," *DW*, January 31, 1936, 6. Pitkin believed the "one last resort" would be an appeal to the U.S. Supreme Court, but Clayton's and Carruthers's lawyers instead decided to seek a writ of habeas corpus in federal district court.

51. Statement of JAH before the District Court for the Eastern District of Arkansas, Caruthers & Clayton v. Cogbill, December 1936, 6, f10, bD50, NAACPR.

52. "U.S. Judge Defers Case of Negroes Condemned to Die," *SLPD*, December 10, 1936, 13A; "Many Witnesses to Little Rock," *BCN*, December 10, 1936, 12; CHH to RW, December 10, 1936, f11, bD50, NAACPR.

53. Luther Moore to WW, November 23, 1936, f11, bD50, NAACPR; "Hearing on Writ for Two Negroes in Mob Law Case," *SLPD*, December 8, 1936, 3C;

54. "Bailey's Assistants to Question Local Negroes," *BCN*, June 9, 1936, 1; "Seek Facts for Negroes' Appeal," *BCN*, June 12, 1936, 3; "Many Witnesses to Little Rock," 12.

55. Statement of JAH, 6–12, NAACPR.

56. Statement of Hugh Wharton before the District Court for the Eastern District of Arkansas, Caruthers & Clayton v. Cogbill, December 1936, 13–15, f10, bD50, NAACPR.

57. Statement of Arthur Adams before the District Court for the Eastern District of Arkansas, Caruthers & Clayton v. Cogbill, December 1936, 15–25, f10, bD50, NAACPR.

58. Ibid., 34–36.

59. Ibid., 34.

60. "U.S. Judge Defers Case," 13A.

61. Record of hearing before the District Court for the Eastern District of Arkansas, Caruthers & Clayton v. Cogbill, December 1936, 37–43, f10, bD50, NAACPR.

62. "U.S. Judge Defers Case," 13A; "Refuses to Take Action for Negroes," *BCN*, December 10, 1936, 1; "Negroes Will Renew Fight for Lives," *AG*, December 11, 1936, 20.

63. "The Law's Delays," *BCN*, December 11, 1936, 3.

64. CHH, "Memorandum on the Clayton Caruthers Hearing," December 18, 1936, f2, bD51, NAACPR.

65. Ibid.

Chapter 27. Seeking Mercy, Seeking Clemency, 1929–1936

1. Bethel appellant's brief, 1–5; "Highway Commission Appeals License Fee Case," *AG*, June 4, 1929, 10.

2. Stern, "Shadow Trials," 321.

3. See, e.g., Hays v. State, 278 S.W. 15, 16 (Ark. 1925); Hogan v. State, 86 S.W.2d 931, 933–34 (Ark. 1935); Sanders v. State, 296 S.W. 70, 71 (Ark. 1927).

4. Bethel appellant's brief, 5–9.

5. "Bethel-Wallace Case Submitted," *BCN*, October 29, 1929, 1.

6. Young appellant's brief, 26, 31–32; Young v. State, 221 S.W. 478 (Ark. 1920).

7. Bethel v. State, 21 S.W.2d 176, 177 (Ark. 1929).

8. "Bethel and Wallace Must Serve Terms," *BCN*, November 4, 1929, 1.

9. Colin Edward Woodward, "Elmer Wayne Mikel, 1905–1988," *Encyclopedia of Arkansas*, April 20, 2017, https://encyclopediaofarkansas.net/entries/elmer-wayne-mikel-7940/; Elmer Mikel to Winthrop Rockefeller, March 24, 1968, in Elmer Mikel, *Uncle Tom's Prison* (self-published, 1970); Mikel, *Uncle Tom's Prison*, 5, 7. Note that the page numbers in this book are highly irregular.

10. Report of Superintendent S. L. Todhunter, July 30, 1934, f484, b19, JMFP.

11. Report of Superintendent S. L. Todhunter, April 3, 1935, f484, b19, JMFP.

12. See "Tucker State Farm, Men on Short Furlough," September 24, 1932, f168, b6, HPP; Crosley, *Unfolding Misconceptions*, 63.

13. George Washington Donaghey to Duvall Purkins, June 8, 1933, f134, b4, JMFP.

14. George W. Hays, "The Motives That Guided Me in Exercising the Pardon Power," *Dearborn Independent*, September 25, 1926, 3, 4, 18, f4, b2, George Washington Hays Miscellaneous Papers, University of Arkansas Libraries.

15. This policy was once undermined in spectacular fashion when Terral left town. "Governor Gone, Hamp Hall Set Free by M'Call," *AG*, October 29, 1925, 1; "Terral Denounces Freeing of Hall," *AG*, October 29, 1925, 1; "M'Call Is Busy While Governor Hastens Home," *AG*, October 30, 1925, 1; "Terral Returning in an Angry Mood," *AG*, October 30, 1925) 1; "Terral Orders Arrest of All of Pardonees," *AG*, November 4, 1925, 1; "Futrell Requires Full Publicity on Pardon Petitions," *HS*, April 4, 1933, 4.

16. See "Choose You This Day Whom You Will Believe," *Nashville News*, July 28, 1926, 3.

17. J. M. Futrell to S. L. Todhunter, December 21, 1934, f133, b4, JMFP.

18. J. M. Futrell to George I. Brandon, March 28, 1934, f134, b4, JMFP; "Futrell Requires Full Publicity on Pardon Petitions," *HS*, April 4, 1933, 4.

19. "Bethel and Wallace Get Furloughs," *BCN*, August 23, 1930, 1.

20. S. L. Todhunter to J. M. Futrell, December 12, 1934, f133, b4, JMFP.

21. "Bethel and Wallace Get Furloughs," 1.

22. Private Secretary of J. M. Futrell to A. O. Colburn, March 18, 1935, f133, b4, JMFP.

23. Harvey Parnell to William Edgar Kniep, March 12, 1930, f472, b16, HPP; J. M. Futrell to Barnett Brothers, November 19, 1934, f133, b4, JMFP.

24. Private Secretary to Colburn, March 18, 1935, JMFP.

25. E. E. Alexander to Harvey Parnell, June 27, 1929, f465, b16, HPP.

26. Transcript of interview with Torressia Dancler McDowell, October 8, 1921, f5, b1, Laura Cornelius Conner Papers, University of Arkansas Libraries.

27. Furlough records in f470, b16, HPP.

28. Record of indefinite furlough granted to Robert James (Prisoner No. 23317), December 23, 1929, f471, b16, HPP.

29. J. C. White and Anniston Branch to NAACP Legal Department, December 23, 1946, f7, bII:B123, NAACPR.

30. M. B. Burns to Harvey Parnell, September 1929, f465, b16, HPP.

31. Luke Winters to Harvey Parnell, July 3, 1929, f478, b16, HPP.

32. "Nine Pardons Issued by Governor," *AG*, November 22, 1940, 15; Fanning transcript, 20–28.

33. J. A. Bass to Harvey Parnell, n.d., f465, b16, HPP.

34. Mrs. M. J. Greer to J. M. Futrell, July 16, 1935, f434, b17, JMFP.

35. Bob Bailey to Carl Bailey, Re: O. D. Stokes, Negro, No. 32105, n.d., f5, b11, Carl E. Bailey Personal and Political Papers, Center for Arkansas History and Culture.

36. Dorr, *White Women, Rape, and the Power of Race*, 137; Miller, *Crime, Sexual Violence, and Clemency*, 186, 191–92, 194–96.

37. "Bethel, Wallace Back to Prison," *BCN*, November 28, 1930, 1.

38. "Officers Did Not Request Furlough," *AG*, March 31, 1931, 2.

39. "Indefinite Furloughs for Two Convicted of Attack," *AG*, October 10, 1931, 24.

40. "Futrell Requires Full Publicity on Pardon Petitions," *HS*, April 4, 1933, 4.

41. "Futrell Admits Mistake," *HS*, July 3, 1934, 1, 3; "Henley's Capture Asked by Barnett to Stop Killings," *HS*, July 3, 1934, 1.

42. "Holiday Leaves Given Prisoners by Grady M'Call," *BCN*, December 27, 1933, 1

43. "Mike Wallace Is Given Pardon," *BCN*, September 19, 1934, 1.

44. William Newton Hill, *Story of the Arkansas Penitentiary* (1912), 62–63.

45. "Frank Bethel Given Pardon," *BCN*, August 15, 1936, 1.

Chapter 28. The Appeal, 1937–1939

1. "Dobbs Goes to Death Claiming Another Guilty," *AG*, November 2, 1935, 3; "Points Out Dobbs Brutal Killer," *AG*, March 14, 1935, 13; "Dobbs to Pay for Murder with Life," *AG*, March 15, 1935, 28; "Dobbs Due to Atone for His Crime Today," *AG*, November 1, 1935, 3.

2. Handwritten notes on Clayton-Carruthers case, January 1, 1937; memorandum from CHH to JAH and SAJ, "Re Clayton and Caruthers—Writ of Error Coram Nobis," January 15, 1937—both in f2, bD51, NAACPR; CHH to JAH, January 5, 1937; JAH to CHH, January 6, 1937; TM to CHH—all in f11, bD50, NAACPR.

3. Crosley, *Unfolding Misconceptions*, 62.

4. "Garland Salary Suit Remanded by High Court," *AG*, January 12, 1937, 7; "Permission to File Writ in Rape Case Denied," *AG*, January 19, 1937, 9; "Permission for Writ Is Denied," *BCN*, January 19, 1937, 1; SAJ to CHH, January 19, 1937; CHH to JAH and SAJ, January 21, 1937; JAH to CHH, January 25, 1937—all in f11, bD50, NAACPR.

5. "Case of Two Condemned Negroes Postponed," *AG*, June 27, 1937, 8; CHH to JAH, September 24, 1937; JAH to CHH, October 13, 1937—both in f11, bD50, NAACPR; JAH to TM, January 20, 1938, f12, bD50, NAACPR; "Another Delay in Condemned Negroes' Case," *AG*, January 19, 1938, 2; "Negroes Case Again Delayed," *BCN*, January 18, 1938, 1.

6. Woodruff, *American Congo*, 178–81; Ross, " 'I Ain't Got No Home,' " 145.

7. McNeil, *Groundwork*, 97; Robert L. Zangrando, "The NAACP and a Federal Antilynching Bill, 1934–1940," *Journal of Negro History* 50 (1965), 107–8; TM to Charles A. Chandler, January 6, 1937, bI:C69, NAACPR.

8. August Meier, untitled notes, 1937, f11, b144, August Meier Papers, Schomburg Center for Research in Black Culture, New York Public Library.

9. JAH to TM, January 20, 1938, NAACPR; letter JAH to TM, January 21, 1938; SAJ and JAH to NAACP, February 19, 1938; CHH to SAJ and JAH, February 24, 1938; JAH to CHH, March 4, 1938; CHH to JAH, March 5, 1938—all in f12, bD50, NAACPR; McNeil, *Groundwork*, 145–46.

10. "Weather Forecast," *AG*, March 9, 1938, 1; "The Weather," *AG*, March 9, 1938, 15.

11. "Motion to Summon Witnesses in Assault Case Filed," *AG*, March 3, 1938, 14; "Three Witnesses Summoned to Habeas Corpus Hearing," *AG*, March 5, 1938, 8; "Negroes' Case before Trimble," *BCN*, March 7, 1938, 1; "Call Witnesses in Attack Case," *BCN*, March 8, 1938, 1; "Habeas Corpus Hearing for Condemned Negroes Today," *AG*, March 9, 1938, 5; "Negroes' Plea Is Heard Today," *BCN News*, March 9, 1938, 1.

12. Judith Kilpatrick, "Joseph Robert (J. R.) Booker," *Arkansas Black Lawyers*, 2003, https://arkansasblacklawyers.uark.edu/lawyers/jrbooker.html; Judith Kilpatrick, "Extraordinary Men: African-American Lawyers and Civil Rights in Arkansas Before 1950," *Arkansas Law Review* 53 (2000), 371, 384; NAACP Report, "Arkansas White

Primary Case," September 30, 1929, f11, b142, August Meier Papers, Schomburg Center for Research in Black Culture, New York Public Library.

13. "T. C. Trimble of Lonoke Will Be New U.S. Judge," *AG*, June 18, 1937, 6.

14. Statements of W. B. Moore, V. M. Townsend, and C. J. Little before the District Court for the Eastern District of Arkansas, Carruthers & Clayton v. Reed, March 1938, f3, bD51, NAACPR; "Trimble Hears Testimony in Negroes' Case," *BCN*, March 10, 1938, 1.

15. Statements of R. F. Harris, R. L. Atkinson, M. Fitzsimmons, Lon Moore, J. S. Sudberry, L. W. Haraway, A. Bradford, C. E. Tate, R. A. Greenaway, C. H. Wilson, and A. Lindsey before the District Court for the Eastern District of Arkansas, Carruthers & Clayton v. Reed, March 1938, f3, bD51, NAACPR; JAH to CHH, March 19, 1938, f12, bD50, NAACPR.

16. Statement of N. Killough before the District Court for the Eastern District of Arkansas, Carruthers & Clayton v. Reed, March 1938, f3, bD51, NAACPR.

17. "Trimble Hears Testimony," 1.

18. Statement of Bubbles Clayton before the District Court for the Eastern District of Arkansas, Carruthers & Clayton v. Reed, March 1938, f3, bD51, NAACPR.

19. Statement of Jim X. Carruthers before the District Court for the Eastern District of Arkansas, Carruthers & Clayton v. Reed, March 1938, f3, bD51, NAACPR.

20. JAH to CHH, March 19, 1938, NAACPR; "Trimble Hears Testimony," 1; "Mob Issue Raised in Plea for Pair Facing Execution," *SLPD*, March 10, 1938, 14A.

21. "Clayton and Caruthers Pace Their Cell as Brockelhurst and Sims Die," *BCN*, March 19, 1938, 1.

22. Ibid.

23. "Two Arkansas Men Again Lose Fight for Life," *SLPD*, March 30, 1938, 6.

24. "Arkansas Men Lose Fight to Escape Chair," *Chicago Defender*, April 9, 1938, 11; "Scottsboro Case in Ark up for Appeal," *Norfolk Journal & Guide*, April 9, 1938, 10; "Almost Same as Scottsboro," *New York Amsterdam News*, April 9, 1938, 16; "Another 'Scottsboro Case' Headed for Supreme Court," *Pittsburgh Courier*, April 9, 1938, 22; "Lawyers for Condemned Pair Take Appeal," *AG*, April 12, 1938, 6; "Denial of Writ Basis of Appeal," *BCN*, April 12, 1938, 1.

25. "Two Arkansas Men Again Lose," 6; "Denial of Writ Basis of Appeal," 1; brief on behalf of appellants, Carruthers & Clayton v. Reed, 1938, Case No. 11,210, RG 276, National Archives at Kansas City, Missouri.

26. See correspondence in f12, bD50, NAACPR.

27. TM to A. Maurice Mackel, January 21, 1941, f2, bII:B128, NAACPR; TM to H. A. Merchant, December 24, 1940, f2, bII:B123, NAACPR; TM to Leon P. Miller, December 1, 1939, f10, bII:B124, NAACPR; TM to John D. Stith, May 29, 1940, f10, bII:B124, NAACPR; August Meier, untitled notes, 1934, f21, b143, August Meier Papers, Schomburg Center for Research in Black Culture, New York Public Library; Joseph Murray to RW, September 29, 1941, f8, bII:B128, NAACPR.

28. McNeil, *Groundwork*, 147–49; Williams, *Thurgood Marshall*, 99–101; Sullivan, *Lift Every Voice*, 233–34.

29. JAH to TM, August 15, 1938, f12, bD50, NAACPR.

30. "CME Conference Gives $164 for a Defense Fund," *Kansas City Plaindealer*, May 13, 1938, 1; Luther Moore and Mrs. E. I. Copeland to Annie Gillam, January 10, 1939, f13, bD50, NAACPR; "Commonwealth College Pleads for Negro Pair," *BCN*, April 20, 1938, 1; Commonwealth College, "We Are Not Alone: A One Act Dramatization of the Case of Bubbles Clayton and Jim X. Caruthers Now in the Death Cell at Tucker Farm" (Mena, AR: May 4, 1938); JAH to W. H. Smith, March 29, 1939, f13, bD50, NAACPR.

31. "Arkansas Negroes Court Fight to St. Louis," *NAT*, December 15, 1938, 10; "Two Arkansas Negro Rapists' Appeal Heard," *AG*, December 15, 1938, 12; "Two Arkansas Negro Rapists' Appeal Heard," *AG*, December 16, 1938, 3; "Seek Appeals for 2 Arkansas Men Held under Death Penalty for Attacks," *Chicago Defender*, December 24, 1938, 10; " 'Jury Exclusion' Used to Save Doomed Men," *Pittsburgh Courier*, December 24, 1938, 4.

32. Carruthers v. Reed, 102 F.2d 933 (8th Cir. 1939); opinion of Judge Woodrough, Carruthers & Clayton v. Reed, May 24, 1939, f1, bD51, NAACPR; "Arkansas Negroes, Facing Death Penalty, Lose Appeal," *SLPD*, February 26, 1939, 3; "Condemned Negroes' Case May Go to U.S. Supreme Court," *AG*, February 26, 1939, 2.

33. Hibbler and the other lawyers did immediately seek a rehearing from the Eighth Circuit, but this quickly proved to be futile. Petition for Rehearing, Carruthers & Clayton v. Reed, 1939, Case No. 11,210, RG 276, National Archives at Kansas City, Missouri; "Condemned Pair Denied Rehearing," *AG*, March 29, 1939, 10; JAH to TM, March 29, 1939, f13, bD50, NAACPR.

34. TM to JAH, April 28, 1939, f13, bD50, NAACPR.

35. Pierce Butler, Stay, Carruthers & Clayton v. Reed, May 24, 1939, f1, bD51, NAACPR; Leon A. Ransom to WW, May 15, 1939, f13, bD50, NAACPR; Buck v. Bell, 274 U.S. 200 (1927); Palko v. Connecticut, 302 U.S. 319 (1937); Ashley K. Fernandes, "The Power of Dissent: Pierce Butler and *Buck v. Bell*," *Journal of Peace and Justice Studies* 12.1 (2002), 115–34.

36. TM to WW, May 18, 1939; TM to CHH, May 25, 1939—both in f13, bD50, NAACPR; petition for writ of certiorari, Carruthers & Clayton v. Reed, May 24, 1939; affidavit and motion for leave to proceed in forma pauperis, Carruthers & Clayton v. Reed, May 24, 1939—both in f1, bD51, NAACPR.

37. LAR to JAH, May 26, 1939, f13, bD50, NAACPR.

Chapter 29. The End, 1939

1. Oral history interview of Thurgood Marshall, conducted by Mark Tushnet, May 23, 1989, 7, CCOH.

2. LAR to TM, May 25, 1939, f13, bD50, NAACPR ("No Good"); TM to LAR, March 7, 1939, f13, bD50, NAACPR.

3. LAR to TM, June 5, 1939, f14, bD50, NAACPR.

4. William Pickens to TM, May 28, 1939, f14, bD50, NAACPR.

5. JAH to LAR, June 5, 1939, f14, bD50, NAACPR.

6. JAH to TM, June 13, 1939, f14, bD50, NAACPR.

7. Secretary to TM to JAH, June 15, 1939, f14, bD50, NAACPR; expense account, June 14–17, 1939, bC69, NAACPR.

8. TM to LAR, June 17, 1939, f14, bD50, NAACPR.

9. JAH to TM, June 22, 1939, f14, bD50, NAACPR.

10. Ibid.

11. See correspondence in f1–3, b11, Carl E. Bailey Personal and Political Papers, Center for Arkansas History and Culture.

12. JAH to TM, June 22, 1939, NAACPR.

13. "Tourists Back, Praise New York Trip," *AG*, June 20, 1939, 12; John L. Fletcher, "State Finances in Good Shape, Says Governor," *AG*, June 20, 1939, 1, 7; JAH to TM, June 22, 1939, NAACPR.

14. "Arkansas Governor Ends Preliminary Parleys," *Evening Star*, June 22, 1939, 22; TM, "Re: Telephone Conversations with Office of Governor Bailey of Arkansas," June 23, 1939, f14, bD50, NAACPR.

15. TM, "Re: Telephone Conversations with Office of Governor Bailey of Arkansas," NAACPR.

16. Ibid.

17. TM to JAH, June 23, 1939, f14, bD50, NAACPR.

18. Ibid.; expense account, June 24–July 2, 1939, bC69, NAACPR.

19. "Two in Arkansas Death House May Get Hearing Says Governor's Secretary," June 23, 1939, f14, bD50, NAACPR.

20. Donald Holley, "Carl Edward Bailey, 1937–1941," in Timothy P. Donovan et al., *The Governors of Arkansas: Essays in Political Biography* (2d ed., 1995), 190–97; "Qualified . . . Experienced . . . Hal Norwood for Attorney General," *AG*, July 29, 1934, 12.

21. Crosley, *Unfolding Misconceptions*, 60.

22. JAH to TM, June 27, 1939, f14, bD50, NAACPR.

23. Catherine T. Freeland to TM, June 28, 1939, f14, bD50, NAACPR.

24. TM to Carl Bailey, June 28, 1939, f14, bD50, NAACPR.

25. TM to Catherine T. Freeland, June 28, 1939; TM to Charles Irvin, June 28, 1939; A. Philip Randolph to TM, June 28, 1939; TM to JAH, July 14, 1939—all in f14, bD50, NAACPR; expense account, June 24-July 2, 1939, bC69, NAACPR.

26. Catherine T. Freeland to TM, June 29, 1939, f14, bD50, NAACPR.

27. TM to JAH, June 29, 1939, f14, bD50, NAACPR.

28. J. B. Luck to Harvey Parnell, n.d., f476, b16, HPP.

29. Petition to Harvey Parnell, 1931, f466, b16, HPP.

30. George Cherry to Freed Hutto, April 16, 1934, f134, b4, JMFP.

31. For the conventional narrative of the end of convict-leasing: Calvin R. Ledbetter Jr., "The Long Struggle to End Convict Leasing in Arkansas," *AHQ* 52 (1993), 1; Jane Zimmerman, "The Convict Lease System in Arkansas and the Fight for Abolition," *AHQ* 8 (1949), 171.

32. Office of Governor Harvey Parnell to T. C. Cogbill, December 4, 1929, f12, b2, HPPS.

33. Office of Governor Harvey Parnell to T. C. Cogbill, July 29, 1931, f12, b2, HPPS.

34. Office of Governor Harvey Parnell to T. C. Cogbill, March 28, 1930, f12, b2, HPPS.

35. Tom Davis to Harvey Parnell, January 10, 1931, f480, b16, HPPS; I. E. Moore to Harvey Parnell, April 5, 1929, f473, b16, HPPS.

36. Oral history interview of R. Robert Bailey, interviewed by Kaye M. Lundgren, January 22, 2013, f4, b40, Carl E. Bailey Personal and Political Papers, Center for Arkansas History and Culture.

37. Hillary Clinton, *It Takes a Village: And Other Lessons Children Teach Us* (1996), 61–62.

38. "Execution of Two Rapists Set Today," *AG*, June 24, 1938, 7.

39. JAH to TM, July 7, 1939; TM to WW, "Clayton and Carruthers Case," June 21, 1939; David Dubinsky to Carl Bailey, June 23, 1939—all in f14, bD50, NAACPR; "An Arkansas 'Scottsboro,'" *DW*, June 24, 1939, 6; "Arkansas Gov. Dodges Lynch Quiz Here," *DW*, June 27, 1939, 5.

40. Joint Action Committee, Commonwealth College, to WW, June 16, 1939; David Beardsley to TM, June 17, 1939—both in f14, bD50, NAACPR; "Letters to Save Lives of 2 Negro Boys Urged Now," *DW*, June 20, 1939, 5.

41. TM to WW, "Clayton and Carruthers Case," June 21, 1939, NAACPR; WW to David Beardsley, June 22, 1939, f14, bD50, NAACPR.

42. TM to JAH, June 22, 1939, f14, bD50, NAACPR.

43. Cassandra E. Maxwell to TM, June 29, 1939, f14, bD50, NAACPR.

44. "Acting Governor Relieved by Carruthers' Confession," *AG*, July 4, 1939, 3.

45. "The Weather," *AG*, June 30, 1939, 25; "Three Negroes Put to Death for Rape of Two White Girls," *Corpus Christi Times*, June 30, 1939, 1.

46. "Carruthers Confesses as He Dies," *AG*, July 1, 1939, 7; "Three Negroes Put to Death for Rape of Two White Girls," 1.

47. Gilbert King, *The Execution of Willie Francis: Race, Murder, and the Search for Justice in the American South* (2008), 23–26.

48. "Ark. Governor Fails to Act; 3 Go to Chair," *Chicago Defender*, July 15, 1939, 7.

49. JAH to TM, July 7, 1939, f14, bD50, NAACPR; "Carruthers Confesses as He Dies," 7; "Three Negroes Put to Death for Rape of Two White Girls," 1; "Ark. Governor Fails to Act; 3 Go to Chair," 7.

50. "Acting Governor Relieved by Carruthers' Confession," *AG*, July 4, 1939, 3; "Three Negroes to Chair," *Kansas City Times*, June 30, 1939, 8.

51. JAH to TM, July 7, 1939, NAACPR; "Arkansas Governor Electrocutes Negro Boys over Protests," *DW*, July 7, 1939, 3 ("No newspaper men heard Carruthers's alleged statement.").

52. "Wash Martin Evasive in Final Statement," *Nashville News*, June 12, 1926, 1.

53. "Cigarettes Last Request of Negro," *AG*, November 25, 1932, 13.

54. JAH to TM, July 7, 1939, NAACPR.

55. TM to Carl Bailey, July 14, 1939; TM to JAH, July 14, 1939; Carl Bailey to TM, August 18, 1939; JAH to TM, September 5, 1939—all in f14, bD50, NAACPR; "Ark. Governor May Save 2 Youths in Death Row," *Chicago Defender*, July 1, 1939, 4; "Two in Arkansas Death House May Get Hearing," *Pittsburgh Courier*, July 1, 1939, 5.

56. JAH to TM, July 7, 1939, NAACPR.

Chapter 30. Maya Angelou, 1970s

1. "New Books Today," *NYT*, February 25, 1970, 44; Thompson, "A Woman of Many Talents . . . and Now She's a Poet," 19; McClelland, "Maya's GWP LP More Than Half a Lifetime's Work," MAP; Mert Guswiler, " 'You Must Love Truth for Truth's Sake, and Right for Right's Sake': Maya Angelou, National Book Award Nominee," *Los Angeles Herald-Examiner*, March 12, 1971, A19; MA, "I Know Why the Caged Bird Sings," *Harper's*, February 1970; MA, "I Know Why the Caged Bird Sings," *Ebony*, April 1970—both in f2, b347, MAP; "Announcing a Special Spring 1970 Selection," *Book-of-the-Month Club News*, 1970, in b348, MAP.

2. Roland Forte, "Poetry Corner: The Poetry of Maya Angelou," *Muntu Drum*, November 1, 1971, 2, f3, b347, MAP; Elliot, "Author Maya Angelou," 26; Barbara Bladen, "The Marquee," *San Mateo Times*, May 7, 1971, f3, b347, MAP.

3. George Goodman Jr., "Maya Angelou: Prolific Spokesman for Black Women," *San Francisco Chronicle*, April 1, 1972, 32; Mildred Hamilton, "Mighty Pen of Maya . . .," *San Francisco Examiner*, March 24, 1970, 20; Forte, "Poetry Corner: The Poetry of Maya Angelou," MAP; Jim Cleaver, "Maya Angelou: One of Most Beautiful Women in World," *Los Angeles Sentinel*, April 15, 1971, A7. See also Blum, "Listening to Maya Angelou," 38.

4. Wade Hall, "Maya Angelou Autobiography Has Soul," *Courier-Journal & Times*, 1970, in b348, MAP; Robert A. Gross, "Growing Up Black," *Newsweek*, March 2, 1970; Christopher Lehmann-Haupt, "Books of the Times: Masculine and Feminine," *NYT*, February 25, 1970; Diane Monk, "Why Maya Angelou Sings," *Chicago Daily News*, March 12, 1970—all in f2, b347, MAP.

5. Ward Just, "Personal, Not Propaganda: A Black Woman's Story: Grace, Tragedy, and Wit," *Toledo Blade*, April 27, 1970, G5; Rosemary Yardley, "A 'Caged Bird' Struggling for Release," *Greensboro News*, March 29, 1970; Grace Kennan Warnecke, "Beyond Eldridge Cleaver," *San Francisco Magazine*, May 1970—both in b348, MAP.

6. West, " 'That's the Kind of Meaning I Want This Book to Have,' " MAP; Ballad, "Maya Angelou Interview," MAP. See also Julianelli, "Maya Angelou," MAP; Judith

Rich, "Westways Women: Life Is for Living," in Elliot, *Conversations with Maya Angelou*, 83; MA, "Shades and Slashes of Light," in Evans, *Black Women Writers*, 3–4.

7. Goodman, "Maya Angelou," 32; Curt Davis, "Maya Angelou: Living a Good One," f4, b201, MAP.

8. Bladen, "Marquee," MAP; Bunny Gillespie, "Between Us Gals," *Daly City Record & West Lake Times*, 1971, in f3, b347, MAP; Bladen, "Marquee," MAP; Wayne Warga, "Maya Angelou: One-Woman Creativity Cult," *Los Angeles Times*, January 9, 1972, in f4, b347, MAP.

9. Bladen, "Marquee," MAP; Selma Shapiro to Joan Cook (*NYT*), April 22, 1970, Angelou, Maya, I Know Why the Caged Bird Sings f, b994, Random House Records, Columbia University (similar letters were sent to the Associated Press and many other publications, held in the same folder); Ballad, "Maya Angelou Interview," MAP.

10. Douglas Des Verney to Selma Shapiro, March 15, 1970, Angelou, Maya, I Know Why the Caged Bird Sings f, b994, Random House Records, Columbia University; Alice Windom to MA, May 6, 1970, f19, b40, MAP; advertisement, *NYT*, March 20, 1970, f2, b347, MAP; James Baldwin to Robert Loomis, February 22, 1970, f6, b13, MAP.

11. The HistoryMakers interview with Barbara Wright-Pryor, tape 2, September 24, 2006, THM.

12. Jimmy Jones, "Author's Memory of Stamps: Total Segregation," *AG*, July 19, 1970, 4A.

13. Lee Stanfield to MA, February 3, 1985, f10, b261, MAP; Christopher Swan, "Writer Maya Angelou, A 'Hunter of the Heart,' " *Christian Science Monitor*, February 1, 1985, 23. Stanfield's background: Ron Franck, "Citizens Angry Over Dropping of Sex Charges," *Casper Star-Tribune*, October 14, 1981, B1; Joan Barron, "Recanting Rape Is News, but Odd Exception," *Casper Star-Tribune*, April 10, 1985, A10.

14. Stanfield to MA, February 3, 1985, MAP; Maria Bevacqua, *Rape on the Public Agenda: Feminism and the Politics of Sexual Assault* (2000), 86–87; Janis Kelly, "Anti-Rape Coalition," *Off Our Backs* 9.9, October 1979, 11; Jane Mildred, "Band-Aid Approach to Violence," *Off Our Backs* 9.11, December 1979, 29; Pauline Bart, "On Sexual Assault Conference," *Off Our Backs* 16.10, November 1986, 24.

15. Stanfield to MA, February 3, 1985, MAP.

16. MA to Lee Stanfield, June 26, 1985, f10, b261, MAP.

17. Program, National Coalition Against Sexual Assault, 7th Annual Conference, Knoxville, Tennessee, 1985, f10, b261, MAP; "Mens' Magazines Questioned," *Kingsport Times-News*, August 4, 1985, 8.

18. PBS Documentary, *Maya Angelou: And Still I Rise*, February 21, 2017, at 1:08:57.

19. Lennie Goodings, "My Hero: Maya Angelou by Her Publisher Lennie Goodings," *The Guardian*, May 29, 2014, https://www.theguardian.com/books/2014/may/29/my-hero-maya-angelou-by-lennie-goodings.

20. Stephanie Caruana, "Maya Angelou: An Interview," *Playgirl*, 1974, f6, b347, MAP; MA, "Nina Simone: High Priestess of Soul," *Redbook*, November 1970, f1, b171,

MAP; Bladen, "Marquee," MAP; Ballad, "Maya Angelou Interview," MAP; advertisement for *Just Give Me a Cool Drink of Water, At Random* 5.8, September 1971, f3, b347, MAP; Davis, "Maya Angelou," MAP.

21. Caruana, "Maya Angelou," MAP; MA, "The Black Woman as Legend," 1975 or 1976, f12, b180, MAP; Ballad, "Maya Angelou Interview," MAP.

22. Rosa Guy, "A Conversation between Rosa Guy and Maya Angelou," in Elliot, *Conversations with Maya Angelou*, 238–39; MA, *Wouldn't Take Nothing for My Journey Now* (1994), 108–11; JM to MA, February 27, 1971, f21, b33, MAP; Wayne Warga, "Maya Angelou: One-Woman Creativity Cult," *Los Angeles Times*, January 9, 1972, f4, b347, MAP; Weller, "Work in Progress," MAP.

23. bell hooks, *ain't i a woman: black women and feminism* (1981), 6.

24. MA to Toni Morrison, June 4, 1971; MA to Toni Morrison, October 25, 1987—both in f31, b33, MAP; MA to Alice Walker, September 28, 1982, f1, b40, MAP; Maxine Waters to MA, August 14, 1992, f8, b40, MAP; correspondence in f1, b40, MAP (Walker); f7, b30, MAP (King); Jackie Kay, "The Maya Character," in Elliot, *Conversations with Maya Angelou*, 197; Lupton, *Maya Angelou*, 49.

25. Sickels, "*I Know Why the Caged Bird Sings*," 20–21; McPherson, *Order Out of Chaos*, 23; Sondra O'Neale, "Reconstruction of the Composite Self: New Images of Black Women in Maya Angelou's Continuing Autobiography," in Evans, *Black Women Writers*, 26. See also Braxton, *Black Women Writing Autobiography*, 143; Regina Blackburn, "African-American Women's Autobiography," in Williams, *Readings on Maya Angelou*, 43; Mary Burgher, "Images of Self and Race in the Autobiographies of Black Women," in Roseanne P. Bell, Bettye J. Parker, and Beverly Guy-Sheftall, eds., *Sturdy Black Bridges: Visions of Black Women in Literature* (1979), 113.

26. MA, "Rehearsal for a Funeral," *Black Scholar*, June 1975, f7, b171, MAP; Curt Davis, "Maya Angelou: And Still She Rises," in Elliot, *Conversations with Maya Angelou*, 68; MA, "I'm on My Journey Now," 2003, f4, b179, MAP.

27. MA, "Black Woman as Legend," MAP.

28. MA, *And Still I Rise*, 11–12; MA, "No No No No," *Just Give Me a Cool Drink of Water 'fore I Diiie* (1971), 39; MA, *Now Sheba Sings the Song* (1987), 31; Yasmin Y. DeGout, "The Poetry of Maya Angelou: Liberation Ideology and Technique," *Langston Hughes Review* 19 (Spring 2005), 42.

29. Goodman, "Maya Angelou," 32.

30. Tate, "Maya Angelou," 158.

31. Tricia Crane, "Maya Angelou," in Elliot, *Conversations with Maya Angelou*, 175. But see MA, *Letter to My Daughter* (2008), 45–47.

32. Ballad, "Maya Angelou Interview," MAP; Maggie Savoy, "Faith of a Black Woman in a World Full of Conflict," *Los Angeles Times*, April 16, 1970, F1; Julianelli, "Maya Angelou," MAP; Vivian Ross, "She Predicts 'More Doors' to Be Opened," *Charlotte Observer*, February 17, 1972, f4, b347, MAP; Bill Moyers, "A Conversation with Maya Angelou," in Elliot, *Conversations with Maya Angelou*, 21; tape of opening ceremo-

nies, side 1, Series 1, Audiotape Collection of the National Women's Conference, 1977, Schlesinger Library, Radcliffe Institute; "Harlem's Maya Angelou and Gloria Steinem Marching Arm in Arm, 1983," *Harlem World Magazine*, January 21, 2017, https://www.harlemworldmagazine.com/harlems-maya-angelou-gloria-steinem-marching-arm-arm-1983/ [https://perma.cc/7XWR-5P7D]. See also Robert Chrisman, "The Black Scholar Interviews Maya Angelou," in Elliot, *Conversations with Maya Angelou*, 65; Judith Pateson, "Interview: Maya Angelou," in Elliot, *Conversations with Maya Angelou*, 116–17.

33. MA to Alice Windom, September 6, 1974, f19, b40, MAP; MA to JM, September 25, 1974, f21, b33, MAP.

34. Paul du Feu to MA, n.d.; birthday cards; MA, untitled press release—all in f2, b5, MAP; "Couples: On Her Third Attempt, Maya Angelou Finds the Ideal Husband, Germaine Greer's Ex," 1975, f7, b347, MAP; James Baldwin to MA, 1971, f6, b13, MAP; Stephanie Stokes Oliver, "Maya Angelou: The Heart of the Woman," in Elliot, *Conversations with Maya Angelou*, 138.

35. Judy Stone, "How Maya Angelou Looks at Life," *San Francisco Chronicle*, August 17, 1976, 40; Rudy Maxa, "Maya Angelou: A Caged Bird She's Not," *Washington Post Magazine*, April 9, 1978, 5; Rovetch, ed., *Like It Is*, 9–10.

36. Julianelli, "Maya Angelou," MAP; Gillespie, Butler, and Long, *Maya Angelou*, 138–42; Kate Kellaway, "Poet for the New America," *The Guardian*, January 24, 1993, https://www.theguardian.com/books/1993/jan/24/poetry.mayaangelou.

37. Plimpton, "Maya Angelou."

38. Gerald Gladney, " 'Touch Me, Life, Not Softly': An Interview with Maya Angelou," *UPTOWN: The Voice of Central Harlem*, 1979, f4, b346, MAP.

39. JM to MA, August 4, 1973, f21, b33, MAP; Carol Benson "Out of the Cage and Still Singing: A Short but Sweet Interview with Maya Angelou," *Writer's Digest*, January 1975, f7, b347, MAP; Annie Gottlieb, "Growing Up and the Serious Business of Survival," *NYT*, June 16, 1974, f6, b347, MAP; JM to MA, August 28, 1974, f21, b33, MAP; Lupton, *Maya Angelou*, 14; John McWhorter, "Saint Maya," *New Republic*, May 20, 2002, https://newrepublic.com/article/66279/saint-maya# [https://perma.cc/9A6M-EG72]; Moyers, "Conversation with Maya Angelou," 23; Rich, "Westways Women," 84.

40. The HistoryMakers interview with Alice Windom, tape 8, October 17, 2007, THM.

41. Peaches M. Henry, "Maya Angelou," in Derek Jones, ed., *Censorship: A World Encyclopedia* (2001), 60; Lupton, *Maya Angelou*, 69; Opal Moore, "Learning to Live: When the Bird Breaks from the Cage," in Braxton, *Maya Angelou's I Know Why the Caged Bird Sings*, 49; Joyce L. Graham, "Freeing Maya Angelou's 'Caged Bird' " (Ed.D. diss., Virginia Polytechnic Institute, 1991).

42. Goodman, "Maya Angelou," 32; Weller, "Work in Progress," MAP; Howard Rosenberg, "Angelou and Baldwin Speaking Out Again," *Los Angeles Times*, April 27, 1979, IV-1; Gillespie, Butler, and Long, *Maya Angelou*, 122; reprint of script in f4, b346, MAP.

43. JM to MA, April 29, 1979, f21, b33, MAP.

44. Diane Monk, "Why Maya Angelou Sings," *Chicago Daily News*, March 12, 1970, b348, MAP; Maxa, "Maya Angelou: A Caged Bird She's Not," 5; Alice Windom to MA, July 4, 1976, f19, b40, MAP; Gary Younge, "No Surrender," *The Guardian*, May 25, 2002, https://www.theguardian.com/books/2002/may/25/biography.mayaangelou; MA, "I Dare to Hope," *NYT*, August 25, 1991, https://archive.nytimes.com/query.nytimes.com/gst/fullpage-9D0CE1DE173FF936A1575BC0A967958260.html [https://perma.cc/CLY8-N5GY]. See also Blum, "Listening to Maya Angelou," 43–44; Sal Manna, "The West Interview: Maya Angelou," in Elliot, *Conversations with Maya Angelou*, 159.

45. Caruana, "Maya Angelou," MAP; Ballad, "Maya Angelou Interview," MAP; MA, *Song Flung Up to Heaven*, 153–54; Ross Murray, "Maya Angelou Dies at 86," *GLAAD Blog*, May 28, 2014, https://www.glaad.org/blog/maya-angelou-dies-86 [https://perma.cc/ER44-3SNN].

46. Elliot, "Author Maya Angelou," 27.

Chapter 31. Frank Bethel, 1931–1952

1. Certificate of marriage, Frank Bethel and Gladys Shields, January 15, 1925, ABVS; divorce petition coupon, Frank Bethel and Gladys Bethel, August 11, 1930, ABVS; divorce decree coupon, Frank Bethel and Gladys Bethel, August 11, 1930, ABVS.

2. *Polk's Flint City Directory* (1934), 102.

3. Compare "Boys, 7 and 11, Sentenced to Industrial School," *AG*, August 9, 1937, 2 ("Frank Bethel Jr."), with 1930 U.S. Census, Buffalo, Craighead, AR, 13A, family 206, lines 10–12, April 11, 1930 ("John J. Bethel").

4. 1910 U.S. Census, Jonesboro, Craighead, AR, 14A, family 263, lines 38–44, May 9, 1910; 1920 U.S. Census, Jonesboro, Craighead, AR, 10A, family 188, lines 15–25, January 29, 1920; 1930 U.S. Census, Flint, Genesee, MI, 3A, family 70, lines 21–26, April 3, 1930; *Polk's Flint City Directory* (1931), 296; *Polk's Flint City Directory* (1932), 263.

5. 1930 U.S. Census, Buffalo, Craighead, AR, 13A, family 206, lines 10–12, April 11, 1930; 1940 U.S. Census, Monette, Craighead, AR, 12A, family 259, lines 15–18, April 15, 1940; "Boys, 7 and 11, Sentenced to Industrial School," *AG*, August 9, 1937, 2.

6. "Bound Over for Assault to Kill," *BCN*, October 20, 1932, 1; "Try Farmer for Attack to Kill," *BCN*, November 10, 1932, 3; "Negro Attacker Given 21 Years," *BCN*, November 12, 1932, 1; "13 Face Terms in Penitentiary," *BCN*, November 15, 1932, 1.

7. Certificate of marriage, Fred Bethel and Maxine Thornton, April 28, 1934 (on file with Michigan Division of Vital Records and Health Statistics); 1940 U.S. Census, Monette, Craighead, AR, 12A, family 259, lines 15–18, April 15, 1940; "Monette," *AG*, December 13, 1977, 8; Fred E. Bethel, *U.S. Social Security Death Index, 1956–2014*.

8. See city directories for their frequent movement. *Polk's Flint City Directory* (1937), 98; *Polk's Flint City Directory* (1938), 96; *Polk's Flint City Directory* (1939), 92; 1940 U.S. Census, Flint, Genesee, MI, 11B, family 210, lines 64–65, April 13, 1940; *Polk's Flint City Directory* (1942), 84; *Polk's Flint City Directory* (1947), 69; *Polk's Flint City Directory* (1949), 71; *Polk's Flint City Directory* (1950), 72; *Polk's Flint City Directory* (1952), 61; 1950 U.S. Census, Venice, Shiawassee, MI, 17, dwelling 181, lines 13–14, April 14, 1950; death record, Guy Frank Bethel, December 6, 1952 (on file with Michigan Division of Vital Records and Health Statistics); "Guy Frank Bethel," *Find a Grave*, March 27, 2011, https://www.findagrave.com/memorial/67508894/guy-frank-bethel; "Flossie Mae Gambill Bethel," *Find a Grave*, March 27, 2011, https://www.findagrave.com/memorial/67508852/flossie-mae-bethel.

9. "John J. (Honest John) Bethel," *Akron Beacon Journal*, May 18, 1990, C10; John Bethel Jr., *WWIIDC*, Detroit, Montclair County, MI; John Franklin Bethel, *U.S. Social Security Applications and Claims Index, 1936–2007*; certificate of marriage, John Junior Bethel and Bernice Hazel Bauknecht, August 20, 1971 (on file with Ohio Department of Health, Office of Vital Statistics).

Chapter 32. Mike Wallace, 1931–1983

1. 1940 U.S. Census, Buffalo, Craighead, AR, 4B, family 68, lines 51–52, April 10, 1940; Roy Thomas Wallace, *WWIIDC*, Black Oak, Craighead County, AR; "Father Gets Death Penalty; Son Wins Mistrial," *BCN*, November 7, 1934, 1.

2. "Mrs. Pruitt Is Freed on Bond," *BCN*, October 21, 1933, 1; "Alexander Will Oppose Driver," *BCN*, April 12, 1934, 1; "Still a Chance for Alexander," *BCN*, May 29, 1934, 1; "History of Bar Here Parallels North District's," *BCN*, July 1, 1936, F6; "E. E. Alexander Succumbs Today," *BCN*, November 26, 1940, 1.

3. "Blytheville Bar Elects Officers," *BCN*, June 19, 1947, 1; "Judge Keck Rites to Be Tomorrow," *BCN*, November 1, 1958, 1.

4. "Jackson, Gladish Win County Races," *BCN*, August 12, 1936, 1; "Judge Gladish Will Hear Lee Wilson Case Tomorrow," *BCN*, March 8, 1938, 1; "Election Contest," *NAT*, August 20, 1938, 6; "Gladish Declared Winner," *NAT*, October 6, 1938, 7; "State Jurists Reverse Stand on Poll Taxes," *NAT*, May 8, 1939, 1; "Supreme Court Mandate Filed," *BCN*, June 6, 1939, 1; "Gladish Appointed by Bailey," *BCN*, June 14, 1939, 1; "The Governor Acts," *BCN*, June 15, 1939, 8; "$250,000 Fire Guts Building in Osceola," *BCN*, December 21, 1953, 1; "Mrs. S. L. Gladish Rites in Osceola; Rites Held Today," *BCN*, July 21, 1954, 1; "Gladish Rites Will Be Sunday," *BCN*, March 11, 1955, 1; "Contest Brings to Mind Court Battles of Past," *BCN*, December 1, 1955, 1, 6; Henderson v. Gladish, 128 S.W.2d 257 (Ark. 1939).

5. 1950 U.S. Census, Buffalo, Craighead, AR, 26, dwelling 205, lines 5–6, April 14, 1950; "Roy Thomas 'Mike' Wallace," *Find a Grave*, May 30, 2009, https://www.findagrave.com/memorial/37716573/roy-thomas-wallace; "Elly Julia Wallace," *Find a Grave*,

June 24, 2009, https://www.findagrave.com/memorial/38688796/elly-julia-wallace; Roy Wallace, *U.S. Social Security Death Index, 1956–2014;* Elly J. Wallace, *U.S. Social Security Death Index, 1956–2014.*

Chapter 33. Pearl, 1929–

1. 1930 U.S. Census, Black River, Lawrence, AR, 5A, family 106, lines 32–35, April 23, 1930; certificate of marriage, Pearl —— and F. O. ——, August 27, 1932, ABVS; Thea Baker to Scott Stern, September 20, 2019.

2. 1950 U.S. Census, Oakland, Alameda, CA, 3, dwelling 39, line 16, April 1, 1950; Petition for Naturalization, Arnold Martin ——; Barton Earl ——, *WWIIDC,* Oakland, Alameda, CA; Barton Earl ——, *U.S. Social Security Applications and Claims Index, 1936–2007; Polk's Reno City Directory* (1946), 704; *Polk's Reno City Directory* (1964), 566; Thea Baker to Scott Stern, September 20, 2019.

Chapter 34. Virgie, 1936–2005

1. Certificate of marriage, Virgie —— and Henry ——, December 21, 1936, ABVS; Henry Clifton ——, *WWIIDC,* Marianna, Lee County, AR; 1920 U.S. Census, Goodwin, St. Francis, AR, 4A, family 76, lines 21–27, January 28, 1920; 1930 U.S. Census, Goodwin, St. Francis, AR, 3B, family 64, lines 67–73, April 10, 1930; divorce petition coupon, Henry —— and Clelar ——, September 24, 1936, ABVS.

2. Dorr, *White Women, Rape, and the Power of Race,* 140.

3. 1940 U.S. Census, Independence, Lee, AR, 4A, family 60, lines 31–32, April 9, 1940; 1950 U.S. Census, Eastman, Pulaski, AR, 21, dwelling 162, lines 19–21, April 11, 1950; *Polk's Little Rock-North Little Rock City Directory* (1951), 339; Henry C. ——, *U.S. Social Security Death Index, 1935–2014;* Pat Isabel Brown, "Henry Clifton ——," *Find a Grave,* October 20, 2015, https://www.findagrave.com/memorial/153995014/henry-clifton-isabel; Teddy, "Virgie Beatrice ——," *Find a Grave,* January 9, 2011, https://www.findagrave.com/memorial/63981197/virgie-beatrice-isabel.

Chapter 35. Bubbles Clayton, 1939–

1. "Torture of Youths, Draw Nationwide Protests," *Omaha Guide,* August 26, 1939, 3.

2. See Mikel, *Uncle Tom's Prison,* 11–12. Note that the page numbers in this book are highly irregular.

3. 1920 U.S. Census, Mississippi, AR, 7B, family 158, lines 71–78, March 9, 1920; 1930 U.S. Census, Pemiscot, MO, 10A, family 178, lines 27–31, April 16, 1930; 1940 U.S. Census, Helena, Phillips, AR, 5B, family 133, lines 75–77, April 5, 1940; 1950 U.S. Census, Helena, Phillips, AR, 16, dwelling 171, lines 1–2, April 6, 1950.

4. Thea Baker to Scott Stern, December 4, 2019; Thea Baker to Scott Stern, December 3, 2019; "Clarence Clayton," *Southern Illinoisan,* August 2, 1989, 11.

5. Certificate of death, Clarence Wilson, September 22, 1945 (on file in Arkansas Department of Vital Records); "Clarence H. Wilson Dies at Blytheville," *AG*, September 23, 1945, 14A; certificate of death, Arch Lindsey, October 23, 1955 (on file in Arkansas Department of Vital Records); "Arch Lindsey Rites Tomorrow," *BCN*, October 24, 1955, 1; "Arch Lindsey, 64, Veteran Lawman of Blytheville, Dies," *AG*, October 25, 1955, 7; Bill Sullivan, "Clarence H. Wilson," *Find a Grave*, July 14, 2014, https://www.findagrave.com/memorial/132795445/clarence-h-wilson; Kathy Jennings Brown, "Archie H. Lindsey," *Find a Grave*, September 11, 2014, https://www.findagrave.com/memorial/135755690/archie-h.-lindsey.

6. "Bulk of E. L. McHaney Estate Left to Widow," *AD*, June 4, 1948, 18; "Services for Mr. McHaney at 3:30 Today," *AG*, May 26, 1948, 12; W. W. Satterfield, "Edgard Lafayette McHaney, 1876–1948," *Encyclopedia of Arkansas*, May 8, 2019, https://encyclopediaofarkansas.net/entries/edgar-lafayette-mchaney-8952/; W. W. Satterfield, "James Monroe McHaney, 1918–1995," *Encyclopedia of Arkansas*, February 3, 2020, https://encyclopediaofarkansas.net/entries/james-monroe-mchaney-13843/.

7. "Arthur Adams Dies in Little Rock Hospital," *NAT*, July 27, 1948, 1; "Arthur Adams Dies; Sought Court Office," *AG*, July 30, 1948, 5.

8. "Scipio Jones, State Negro Leader, Dies," *AG*, March 29, 1943, 2; Steven Teske, "Scipio Africanus Jones, 1863–1943," *Encyclopedia of Arkansas*, November 13, 2019, https://encyclopediaofarkansas.net/entries/scipio-africanus-jones-2427/.

9. Judith Kilpatrick, "John A. Hibbler," *Arkansas Black Lawyers*, 2003, https://arkansasblacklawyers.uark.edu/lawyers/jahibbler.html; "Prominent Atty. Passes," *Arkansas State Press*, March 15, 1946, 1; "Dr. Hibbler Passes in Kansas City," *Arkansas State Press*, March 15, 1956, 1; "Hibbler Began Singing Career with Orchestra at Little Rock," *AG*, April 11, 1963, 3; Ben Ratliff, "Al Hibbler, a Singer with Ellington's Band, Dies at 85," *NYT*, April 26, 2001, C13. In later years, John Hibbler continued to work on the cases of Black men accused of rape. See, e.g., Pugh v. State, 210 S.W.2d 789 (Ark. 1948); Allison v. State, 164 S.W.2d 442 (Ark. 1942).

10. Morgan, "Elite Dominance in the Arkansas Delta," 167–79.

11. Mitchell, "Founding and Early History," 359–61; Ross, " 'I Ain't Got No Home in This World," 135–36, 169–70; Grubbs, *Cry from the Cotton*, 187–92; Dionicio Nodín Valdés, *Organized Agriculture and the Labor Movement before the UFW: Puerto Rico, Hawai'i, California* (2011), ch. 5; Matkin-Rawn, " 'We Fight for the Rights of Our Race,' " 245–46. Cf. Andrew J. Hazelton, *Labor's Outcasts: Migrant Farmworkers and Unions in North America, 1934–1966* (2022).

12. Grubbs, *Cry from the Cotton*, 192.

Chapter 36. Jim X. Carruthers, 1939–

1. "Death Penalty Paid by Three," *Reno Gazette-Journal*, June 30, 1939, 1; "Three Negroes Executed for Assaulting Girls," *Hazleton Plain Speaker*, June 30, 1939, 1; "3

Negroes Die for Assaulting Girls," *Fort Worth Star-Telegram*, June 30, 1939, 17; "Three Who Assaulted 2 Girls Die in Chair," *Washington Post*, July 1, 1939, 14; "Three Men Electrocuted for Attacking Women," *SLPD*, June 30, 1939, 7; "3 Electrocuted; 2 Admit Charges," *Atlanta Daily World*, July 3, 1939, 1; "Ark. Governor Fails to Act," *Chicago Defender*, July 15, 1939, 7.

2. Interview of Trina Nicholson, April 25, 2020; interview of Trina Nicholson, January 7, 2020; interview of Trina Nicholson and Gail Terry, May 30, 2024.

3. Interviews of Trina Nicholson; 1940 U.S. Census, Chickasawba, Mississippi, AR, 22A, dwelling 451, lines 27–29, 1940; 1950 U.S. Census, Blytheville, Mississippi, AR, 36, dwelling 378, lines 22–26, May 3, 1950.

4. Interviews of Trina Nicholson.

5. Ibid.

6. Clayton abstract and brief for appellee, 39.

7. Ibid.

8. Ibid., 40.

9. Interviews of Trina Nicholson and Gail Terry.

Chapter 37. Thurgood Marshall, 1977

1. Oral argument, *Coker v. Georgia*, March 28, 1977, Oyez database, https://www.oyez.org/cases/1976/75-5444.

2. Ibid.

3. Williams, *Thurgood Marshall*, 99, 104; McNeil, *Groundwork*, 151–52.

4. Daniel J. Sharfstein, "Saving the Race," *Legal Affairs*, March/April 2005, 50; "Probe Casts Doubt on Socialite's Rape Story," *Chicago Defender*, December 28, 1940, 1.

5. Sullivan, *Lift Every Voice*, 238–39, 267–70.

6. NAACP, *Annual Report for 1942*, 11–12, f2, bII:B124, NAACPR; "Army's Death Penalty for Race Mixing Withdrawn," *Pittsburgh Courier*, January 10, 1942, 1.

7. Mary Louise Roberts, *What Soldiers Do: Sex and the American GI in World War II France* (2013), 195–96, 220; Stephanie Lauren De Paola, "Sexual Violence, Interracial Relations, and Racism during the Allied Occupation of Italy: History and the Politics of Memory" (Ph.D. diss., Fordham University, 2018), 91; Jennifer Dominique Jones, " 'To Stand upon My Constitutional Rights': The NAACP and World War II-Era Sexual Exclusion," *Journal of Civil & Human Rights* 2 (2016), 127.

8. Edward Lane to TM, February 27, 1945, f2, bII:B164, NAACPR; Rosie Murry to WW, August 13, 1945, f10, bII:B165, NAACPR; Earnest Shakespeare to NAACP, August 21, 1945, f22, bII:B167, NAACPR.

9. This lawyer was Franklin H. Williams. Marian Wynn Perry to Bernice Easley, September 5, 1947, f11, bII:B157, NAACPR; "Clemencies and Discrimination," *The Crisis*, June 1946, 183.

10. De Paola, "Sexual Violence, Interracial Relations," 109; "NAACP Petitioned Sentence Reduced," *Alabama Tribune*, August 8, 1947, 5; Robert Carter to TM, December 12, 1944, f1, bII:B156, NAACPR.

11. "Soldier Found Guilty in R.I. Assault Case," *Baltimore Afro-American*, January 29, 1944, 3; "Black and White Rape," *The Crisis*, July 1944, 217; "Seek Immediate Release of Two Men in Army 'Scottsboro' Affair," *Atlanta Daily World*, May 4, 1945, 1.

12. Constance Baker Motley to Robert Carter, November 10, 1945, f8, bII:B163, NAACPR.

13. Sullivan, *Lift Every Voice*, 272–73; Tushnet, *Making Civil Rights Law*, 64–66; TM oral history, 1–2, CCOH; Adams v. United States, 319 U.S. 312 (1943); "Soldiers Sentenced to Death Get New Trial," *Pittsburgh Courier*, July 31, 1943, 16; NAACP, *Annual Report for 1943* (1943), 10, bII:K1, NAACPR.

14. Williams, *Thurgood Marshall*, 113; Curtis Robinson to WW, November 27, 1941, f3, bII:B127, NAACPR; Maggie Alexander to NAACP, September 29, 1949, f6, bII:B122, NAACPR; Marie Swisher to "Dear Friends," October 18, 1941, f2, bII:B127, NAACPR; John Williams to WW, 1941, f12, bII:B129, NAACPR; Bethel A.M.E. Church of Reidsville, NC, to WW, October 27, 1942, f8, bII:B123, NAACPR; C. J. Gates to Constance Baker Motley, August 6, 1948, f11, bII:B123, NAACPR; Maurice Weaver to P. A. Stephens, May 6, 1947, f5, bII:B123, NAACPR; Moses Riddick et al., to NAACP, March 15, 1945; P. W. Gildewell Sr. to Men's Progressive Club, January 13, 1943—both in f8, bII:B123, NAACPR.

15. Victor Vollman to NAACP, July 24, 1946, f2, bII:B125, NAACPR.

16. Jack Greenberg to S. T. Cooper, June 25, 1954; Jack Greenberg to Utillus Phillips, April 14, 1954—both in f12, b65, NAACPLDFR; Robert Carter to F. L. Roberson, April 1, 1946, f6, bII:B122, NAACPR; TM to J. M. Hinton, October 28, 1942; P. A. Stephens to WW, November 16, 1945—both in f8, bII:B123, NAACPR; Frank D. Reeves to J. M. Jackson, December 9, 1941, f3, bII:B127, NAACPR; Frank D. Reeves to T. T. Allen, August 25, 1941, f10, bII:B123, NAACPR; J. L. LeFlore to TM, January 10, 1942, f3, bII:B127, NAACPR.

17. Gloria Samuels to Maurice Weaver, June 3, 1947; TM to Maurice Weaver, June 13, 1947—both in f5, bII:B123, NAACPR; Williams, *Thurgood Marshall*, 113.

18. Jack Greenberg, *Crusaders in the Courts: How a Dedicated Band of Lawyers Fought for the Civil Rights Revolution* (1994), 101–2, 256–57; TM to Herb Nipson, September 13, 1951, and other files in f2, b66, NAACPLDFR.

19. King, *Devil in the Grove*; Williams, *Thurgood Marshall*, 113, 152–57.

20. Stern, "NAACP's Rape Docket."

21. See Eric Rise, *The Martinsville Seven: Race, Rape, and Capital Punishment* (1995), 63–69, 99, 118, 136, 155–57; Eric Rise, "Race, Rape, and Radicalism: The Case of the Martinsville Seven, 1949–1951," *Journal of Southern History* 58 (1992), 462; Marvin Caplan, "Virginia's Black Justice," *New Republic*, January 29, 1951, 17; Hampton v. Virginia, 58 S.E.2d 288 (Va. 1950), cert. den. 339 U.S. 989 (1950); NAACP, *The Fight for*

Freedom in a Transition Year: NAACP Annual Report, 44th Year (1952), 66, bII:K1, NAACPR.

22. Rudolph v. Alabama, 375 U.S. 889, 889–91 (Goldberg, J., dissenting); Greenberg, *Crusaders in the Courts*, 441.

23. Greenberg, *Crusaders in the Courts*, 441–45; Barrett Foerster, *Race, Rape, and Injustice: Documenting and Challenging Death Penalty Cases in the Civil Rights Era* (2012), 9–10; Evan Mandery, *A Wild Justice: The Death and Resurrection of Capital Punishment in America* (2013), 38–39; Maxwell v. Bishop, 398 F.2d 138, 147 (8th Cir. 1968).

24. Adderly v. Wainwright, 272 F. Supp. 530 (M.D. Fla. 1967); Greenberg, *Crusaders in the Courts*, 446–50 (citing Furman v. Georgia, 408 U.S. 238 [1972]); Branch v. Texas, No. 69-5031; Jackson v. Georgia, No. 69-5030; Aikens v. California, No. 68-5027; Mandery, *Wild Justice*, 49, 52.

25. Furman v. Georgia, 408 U.S. 238, 314–74 (1972) (Marshall, J., concurring) and 240–57 (Douglas, J., concurring) (also citing statistics); David M. Oshinsky, *Capital Punishment on Trial: Furman v. Georgia and the Death Penalty in Modern America* (2010).

26. Robert Burt, "Disorder in the Court," *Michigan Law Review* 85 (1987), 1741; Robert Weisberg, "Deregulating Death," *Supreme Court Review* (1983), 315–16.

27. *Furman*, 408 U.S. at 251 n.21 (Douglas, J., concurring) (quoting E. Barrett Prettyman Jr., *Death and the Supreme Court* [1961]) and 287 n.34 (Brennan, J., concurring) (citing Powell v. Alabama, 287 U.S. 45 [1932]).

28. Mandery, *A Wild Justice*, 247–371; 428 U.S. 153 (1976); Greenberg, *Crusaders in the Courts*, 453–54; Williams, *Thurgood Marshall*, 359–60.

29. Greenberg, *Crusaders in the Courts*, 453–54; Jacquet, *Injustices of Rape*, 176–77.

30. Oral argument, *Coker v. Georgia*, Oyez database.

31. Jacquet, *Injustices of Rape*, 41. See also McGuire, *At the Dark End of the Street*, 241–42.

32. Harry Blackmun, notes from deliberations (March 30, 1977), f75-5444, b249, Harry A. Blackmun Papers, Library of Congress.

33. 433 U.S. 584, 592–96, 599 (1977), 604–22 (Burger, C.J., dissenting), 600 (Brennan, J., concurring), 600–01 (Marshall, J., concurring); Jacquet, *Injustices of Rape*, 181–82; Richard Kluger, *Simple Justice: The History of Brown v. Board of Education and Black America's Struggle for Equality* (1975), 605–9, including his epic footnote.

34. *Coker*, 433 U.S. at 600–01 (Marshall, J., concurring). The draft of Marshall concurrence in f75-5444, b193, Thurgood Marshall Papers, Library of Congress, is identical to the one that was ultimately published.

35. Maxwell v. Bishop, 398 F.2d 138, 147 (8th Cir. 1968).

36. Harry Blackmun to Charles Vogel and M. C. Matthes, June 21, 1968; Harry Blackmun, untitled notes, October 3, 1967—both in f652, b40, Harry A. Blackmun Papers, Library of Congress.

37. See Callins v. Collins, 510 U.S. 1141, 1153–57 (1994) (Blackmun, J., dissenting) (discussing statistical evidence of race discrimination).

38. "Female Groups Laud Rape Ruling," *Alabama Journal*, June 30, 1977, 8.

39. Adra J. Ruggles to Harry Blackmun, July 1, 1977; Mrs. John P. Stanford to Harry Blackmun, June 29, 1977; and other correspondence—all in f75–5444, b249, Harry A. Blackmun Papers, Library of Congress.

40. *Callins*, 510 U.S. at 1145; Mandery, *Wild Justice*, 434–35.

Epilogue

1. MA to Daisy and L. C. Bates, June 16, 1976, f13, b13, MAP; "Weather: NorCal," *Petaluma Argus-Courier*, June 16, 1976, 3A; Beti Gunter, "For Maya Angelou Poetry Is a Way of Life," *AG*, October 24, 1976, 1D.

2. Daisy Bates, *The Long Shadow of Little Rock: A Memoir* (1962), 6–9.

3. Ibid., 9–15.

4. Ibid., 32–225; John A. Kirk, *Redefining the Color Line: Black Activism in Little Rock, Arkansas, 1940–1970* (2002), 47–49; John Lewis Adams, " 'Time for a Showdown': The Partnership of Daisy and L. C. Bates and the Politics of Gender Protest and Marriage" (Ph.D. diss., Rutgers University, 2014).

5. McGuire, *At the Dark End of the Street*, 139, 315 n.11.

6. Grif Stockley, *Daisy Bates: Civil Rights Crusader from Arkansas* (2005), ch. 1.

7. MA to Toni Morrison, June 4, 1971, f31, b33, MAP; Toni Morrison, "The Site of Memory," in William Zinsser, ed., *Inventing the Truth: The Art and Craft of Memoir* (1995), 98–99.

8. Transcript of interview of Daisy Bates, conducted by Elizabeth Jacoway, October 11, 1976, 4, G-0009, Southern Oral History Program, University of North Carolina.

9. Freedman, *Redefining Rape*, 276–80. See also Arkansas People's History Project, "Violence & Control," *Women's Project*, 2022, https://www.womensprojectstory.org/chapter/chapter-one-violence-and-control.

10. Julie Horney and Cassia Spohn, "Rape Law Reform and Instrumental Change in Six Urban Jurisdictions," *Law and Society Review* 25 (1991), 118–19. See also Leigh Bienen, "Rape I," *Women's Rights Law Report* 3 (1976), 45; Leigh Bienen, "Rape II," *Women's Rights Law Report* 3 (1977), 90; Leigh Bienen, "Rape III," *Women's Rights Law Report* 6 (1981), 170. See also Freedman, *Redefining Rape*, 280–81.

11. Horney and Spohn, "Rape Law Reform," 118–19; Myka Held and Juliana McLaughlin, "Rape & Sexual Assault," 15 *Georgetown Journal of Gender and the Law* (2014), 159; David P. Bryden, "Redefining Rape," *Buffalo Criminal Law Review* 3 (2000), 319, 321.

12. Raquel Kennedy Bergen, *Marital Rape: New Research and Directions*, February 2006, http://www.ilcdvp.org/Documents/Marital%20Rape%20Revised.pdf; Held and McLaughlin, *Rape & Sexual Assault*, 159–60; Freedman, *Redefining Rape*, 281–82.

13. Kathleen Daly and Brigitte Bouhours, "Rape and Attrition in the Legal Process: A Comparative Analysis of Five Countries," *Crime and Justice* 39 (2010), 572, 583

(2010); "The Criminal Justice System: Statistics," *RAINN*, https://www.rainn.org/statistics/criminal-justice-system. Reliable statistics for sexual violence are difficult to gather and famously contested, as RAINN acknowledges.

14. "National Intimate Partner and Sexual Violence Survey: 2010 Summary Report," *Centers for Disease Control and Prevention*, 2011, https://www.cdc.gov/violenceprevention/pdf/nisvs_report2010-a.pdf [https://perma.cc/RYB5-SQWZ]; Roxanne A. Donovan, "To Blame or Not to Blame: Influences of Target Race and Observer Sex on Rape Blame Attribution," *Journal of Interpersonal Violence* 22 (2007), 722.

15. Jeanne C. Marsh, Alison Geist, and Nathan Caplan, *Rape and the Limits of Law Reform* (1982), 105–6; Cassia Spohn and Julia Horney, *Rape Law Reform: A Grassroots Revolution and Its Impact* (1992), 159–75.

16. Freedman, *Redefining Rape*, 284.

17. Jacquet, *Injustices of Rape*, 185.

18. Daisy Bates to MA, October 7, 1976, f13, b13, MAP; "Poets to Hear Ex-Arkansan," *AD*, September 30, 1976, 3A; Gunter, "Poetry Is a Way of Living," 1D, 12D.

19. Ibid.

20. Daisy Bates to MA, September 28, 1978, f13, b13, MAP.

21. Moyers, "Watch: Going Home with Maya Angelou."

22. Salamishah Tillet, *In Search of The Color Purple: The Story of an American Masterpiece* (2021).

23. MA to Alice Walker, September 28, 1982, f1, b40, MAP. See also Manna, "West Interview," 159.

24. Plimpton, "Maya Angelou"; Esther Hill, "Maya Angelou: Resolving the Past: Embracing the Future," in Elliot, *Conversations with Maya Angelou*, 110.

25. Moyers, "Watch: Going Home with Maya Angelou."

26. Ibid.

Acknowledgments

Looking back on the debts I incurred while writing this book, I am staggered. *There Is a Deep Brooding in Arkansas* began as a law school paper, so I will start there. Judith Resnik very kindly supervised the paper that later became this book, providing guidance throughout my time in law school and sharing insights from her own exploration of Arkansas history. Without the extraordinary generosity and hard work of Kathryn Fitzhugh and Curtis Williams at the University of Arkansas at Little Rock, I would never have been able to get through all the case files I wanted to see in Little Rock. This book also draws on another paper I wrote during law school, on the NAACP's rape docket, and I am deeply grateful to John Witt for supervising that project and for his good-humored counsel throughout my years at Yale. The *Yale Law Journal* and Yale Law School generously provided funding for my trips to Arkansas.

It would have been impossible to write this book without the archivists and librarians who did truly heroic work both before and, especially, during a global pandemic. I am appreciative of the staffs of: the Schomburg Center for Research in Black Culture (especially Bridgett Johnson-Pride); the Library of Congress (especially Loretta Deaver and Patrick Kerwin); the University of Arkansas's Special Collections (especially Geoffery Stark and Joshua Youngblood); the Center for Arkansas History and Culture (especially Cody Besett, Laura McClellan, and Henry Stotts); the Butler Center for Arkansas Studies; the Arkansas State Archives; the Northeast Arkansas Regional Archives (especially Fatme Myuhtar-May); the Mississippi County Circuit Clerk's office (especially Henrietta Watt); the Mississippi County Historical and Genealogical Society (especially Glynda Thompson and Sandra Carpenter); the St. Louis, Missouri, Circuit Clerk's office (especially Kathy Grillo); The HistoryMakers (especially Josie Walters-Johnston); the Maryland State Archives (especially Jennifer Abbott); the National Archives at Kansas City, Missouri (especially Joyce Burner); Columbia University's Rare Book & Manuscript Library (especially Tara Craig and Melina Moe); Ohio State University's Thompson Special Collections; and Yale University's Beinecke Rare Book & Manuscript Library.

I would never have finished this book without the generosity and fortitude of many friends. Sarah Finegold, Matthew Glover, Sara Samuel, and Justin Young hosted me when I visited New York to see archival documents; Cody Pomeranz did the same in Washington, D.C. Gordon McCambridge made a special trip to Little Rock to share bad fajitas while I was in town. Numerous friends from law school allowed me to drone on about this project, including Joshua Blecher-Cohen, Leanne Gale, Lisset Pino, and Soren Schwab. Mere hours before the pandemic indefinitely shut down Yale's libraries, Gabe Lewin heroically rescued an entire car trunk's worth of library books from my carrel, literally saving the project.

Many scholars generously shared their time, expertise, and/or unpublished documents with me as I was writing this book, and some even read my drafts. I am so grateful to Mara Keire, Estelle Freedman, Glenda Gilmore, Monica Bell, Brian M. Trump, Justin Randolph, and Alexander Zhang. When I visited Fayetteville, Jeannie Whayne patiently answered my questions and imparted insights about the history of the Delta. The genealogical portraits of many of the figures depicted in this book would not be nearly as rich without the astonishingly generous and dogged work of Thea Baker. Trina Nicholson spoke with me many times over the years, entrusting me with her family's remarkable history, and for this I am appreciative beyond words. I am also so grateful to Gail Terry.

Some of the research for this book and scattered passages first appeared in Scott W. Stern, "Shadow Trials, or A History of Sexual Assault Trials in the Jim Crow South," *UCLA Journal of Gender and Law* 29 (2022), 257, and Scott W. Stern "The NAACP's Rape Docket and the Origins of Criminal Procedure," *University of Pennsylvania Journal of Law and Social Change* 24 (2021), 301. I am grateful to the editors of those journals for their insights and careful fact-checking.

This book traveled a long, winding road to publication, and this too is a path dotted with my debts. My agent, Susan Lee Cohen, patiently and expertly helped me shape the manuscript, refine my pitch, and shepherd the book through acquisition with two editors and three publishing houses. Jessie Kindig was my dream editor for this project—an eminent historian, master word-smith, and compassionate person—and the present book most definitely would not exist without her. I am grateful to the entire staff at Yale University Press, including Ash Lago, Eliza Childs, Margaret Otzel, and Bill Frucht, as well as to the anonymous readers that helped me ensure that this book was the best I could make it. Sherri Marmon generously assisted me in securing permissions from Penguin Random House. Jacqui Lipton and Jacob Schriner-Briggs kindly answered my many questions about fair use.

Finally, my family sustained and supported me over the many years I worked on this book. My brothers, Eric and Benny Stern, were consistent sources of encouragement and good cheer. My father, Howard Stern, remains my most enthusiastic and optimistic fan, never failing to provide a boost when I most need one. My mother, Rhonda Wasserman, was generous beyond belief with her time and her wisdom, reading and rereading my drafts, providing sober advice and loving reassurances every step along the way. Endless thanks to other family members—Deborah and Marvin Wasserman, Evan Zuzik, Cynthia and Brian O'Malley, to name just a few. And Charlie O'Malley—I don't even know where to begin, so instead I will end with you. Your love, your patience, your help, your steadiness—you are my north star, my every metaphor, my quarantine companion. This book is for you.

Index

Abernathy, Ralph, 202
Adams, Arthur L.: background, 105–6; and Carruthers's car, 333; closing argument, 227; death of, 329; failure to request change of venue, 260–61, 284, 287; representing Clayton and Carruthers, 105–8, 109, 110, 132, 134, 158, 163, 164, 193, 198, 199, 229, 231; requesting appeal, 231–32, 253–54, 268–69, 282
African Americans. *See* Black people
age of consent, 31–32, 118, 142
Alexander, Edward Everett "E. E.": appealing verdict, 223, 224, 271; background, 96; jury selection, 98, 100; late career and death, 321–22; questioning Pearl, 125–26; questioning Wallace, 183–84, 191; representing Bethel and Wallace, 94–96, 101, 102–3, 106, 117, 154–57, 273; requesting clemency, 275, 276
Alexander, Michelle, 343
Ali, Muhammad, 210
All Day Long (Angelou), 212
Amalgamated Clothing Workers Union, 294, 297
American Bar Association, 29, 150

American Civil Liberties Union (ACLU), 255, 296; Women's Rights Project, 342
Anderson, Tommy, 164, 194
Angelos, Enistasious "Tosh," 174
Angelou, Maya: as activist, 5, 8–9, 202–4, 208–12, 311–12, 316–17, 346–51; in Africa, 205–11, 250; after the trial, 165–75; at Arkansas Poetry Day, 348–49; battle with depression, 309–10; birth in California, 83; birth of son, 171; in California, 170–73; ceasing to speak, 166–70; as dancer, 174–75; education, 45, 48–49, 84, 170–71; family background, 44–45, 83; and the feminist movement, 251; journey from California to Arkansas, 1–3; and Martin Luther King Jr., 9, 202, 203, 204, 208, 213, 241, 311; letter to Daisy Bates, 344; and Malcolm X, 9, 207, 210–11, 212, 304, 311, 315; marriage to and divorce from "Tosh," 174–75; marriage to Paul du Feu, 313; memoirs, 242, 243, 313–15; at the National Coalition Against Sexual Assault, 307–8; as performer, 201–2, 204–5, 308–9, 313; personal

437

Angelou, Maya: (*continued*)
papers of, 6; as professor, 313; and the SCLC, 202–4; sexual assault of, 85, 90; in St. Louis, 84–85, 90, 137–38, 140, 165–67; in Stamps, 44, 46–48, 82, 167, 306–7, 349–51; testimony at Freeman's trial, 137–42, 144–45; various employments, 171–73, 174; as writer, 202, 207–8, 212–13, 303–7, 310–11, 313–15; writing process, 244–45, 249

Angelou, Maya, works of, 88–89; *All Day Long* (play), 212; *All God's Children Need Traveling Shoes*, 314–15; *And Still I Rise*, 307; "The Black Woman as Legend," 309, 311; *Down in the Delta* (film), 313; "For Years We Hated Ourselves," 169–70; fragment of a play, 48; *Gather Together in My Name*, 314; *Give Me a Cool Drink of Water 'fore I Diiie*, 308–9; *The Heart of a Woman*, 314; *I Know Why the Caged Bird Sings*, 8, 242–51, 303–7, 308, 310, 315, 349; *In the Presence of Mine Enemies*, 250; *Mom & Me & Mom*, 314; poetry, 250; *Singin' and Swingin' and Gettin' Merry Like Christmas*, 314; *A Song Flung Up to Heaven*, 314

Arkansas Delta: Black community, 254–55; convict labor in, 19–20; cotton in, 48–49; county seats, 17–18; current state of, 330; demand for welfare relief, 63–64; Depression in, 62–63; disease in, 15; draining the swamps, 16–17; drought and famine, 63; flooding in, 21–22, 279; Phillips County, 36–39, 41; plantations in, 18–19, 22; sharecropping in, 18–21; STFU in, 65–66, 236–37, 279–80 women's daily experience, 114; 13–22, 42

Arkansas Larceny Act, 233

Arkansas State Press, 346

Arkansas Supreme Court: and the Bethel-Wallace case, 60, 272; and the Clayton-Carruthers case, 254, 255, 256, 257, 258–61, 263, 264, 269, 279; McHaney on, 260, 349; rulings on rape cases, 24, 118, 122, 124, 125, 155, 156, 262–63, 271; stay of execution by, 259–60

Atkins, Harry, 222

Autobiography of Malcolm X, The, 308, 309

Bailey, Bob, 290, 291, 294, 297, 299
Bailey, Carl E., 290, 291–93, 295, 296, 300
Baker, Josephine, 84
Baldwin, James, 86, 202, 205, 208, 213, 242, 244, 305–6, 309, 313, 316
Baldwin, Roger, 255
Bambara, Toni Cade, 310
Barden, Roosevelt, 332
Barden, Roosevelt Jr., 332
Barnes, Frank, 78
Bates, Daisy Lee Gatson, 344–46, 349
Bates, Lucius Christopher "L. C.," 346
Baxter (Grandmother), 44, 90, 139, 165–66
Baxter, Vivian, 83, 84–85, 89, 172, 316, 344
Beardsley, David, 296, 297
Beck, E. M., 166
Belafonte, Harry, 202
Bell, James "Cool Papa," 84
Bennett, Tony, 203
Berry, Chuck, 84
Bethel, Florence, 56
Bethel, Flossie Gambill, 318–19
Bethel, Frank (Guy Frank): after prison, 318–20; arrest of, 53–59, 62, 153; con-

clusion of second trial, 220; family background, 56; furlough for, 276–77; pardon for, 3–4, 274–75, 277; Pearl's accusations against, 54–55, 57–58, 101, 112, 115–21, 125–26, 128; at second trial, 183, 184–86, 185, 188, 190; sentencing, 60, 222–23; in The Walls, 224–26, 272–73. *See also* Bethel-Wallace trial

Bethel, Frank Jr. (John Junior/Jackie), 318–20

Bethel, Fred, 224, 272, 319

Bethel, Gladys, 56, 318–19

Bethel, John Warren, 56

Bethel, Minnie, 56

Bethel-Wallace trial: appeal and pardon, 271–77; conclusion of second trial, 220–26; conviction overturned, 3–4, 60–61; instructions to the jury, 220–21; jury selection, 97–100; jury's deliberations, 222–23; media coverage of, 80, 272, 274, 277, 321; other witnesses, 153–57; Pearl's testimony, 54–55, 57–58, 101, 112, 115–21, 125–26, 128; sentencing, 59–60; significance of, 5, 8; start of second trial, 93–103; Virgie's testimony, 132–36

Bethune, Mary McLeod, 311

"Black, Blues, Black!" (NET series), 250

Black people: in all-Black towns, 35; analysis of graveyard remains, 43; in Arkansas, 29, 344–47; in the Arkansas penal system, 235; autobiographies and memoirs of, 246, 346–47; and the Depression, 46; education for, 45–46; exclusion from juries, 178, 232, 257, 268, 287; in government positions, 29; and the Great Migration, 1, 36, 90, 328; leaving southeastern Arkansas, 39; resistance to oppression and violence,

35–37, 41, 77–78, 81, 87, 89–90; in Stamps, 47, 350–351

Blackmun, Harry, 341–42, 343

Blacks, The (Genet), 203–4

Bloom, Willie, 57

Bluest Eye, The (Morrison), 310, 346

Bolin, Henry T., 54, 55, 59

Booker, Joseph R., 281, 283, 285, 291

Boyon, Evelyn, 164

Bradley, Edward, 15

Brennan, William J., 339, 341

Brockelhurst, Lester, 283

Brooks, Gwendolyn, 212

Brown, Naomi, 71

Brown v. Board of Education, 258, 341, 346

Browne, Roscoe Lee, 315

Bruckner, Mina, 150

Bryals, W. J., 222

Bryant, Wiley, 79–80, 131–32, 134, 158, 159–60

Bryney, Clarence, 189

Buck v. Bell, 288

Buckelew, Richard A., 41, 42

Bunch, Spencer, 222

Burey, Vivian "Buster," 147

Burger, Warren, 340–41

Buster, Frank, 231

Butler, Pierce, 287–88

"Cabaret for Freedom," 203

Cabe, J. G., 162

California State University at Sacramento, 313

Cambridge, Godfrey, 202

capital punishment. *See* death penalty

capitalism, 6, 207, 316, 348

Carmichael, Stokely, 205, 250

Carson, Joel, 298

Carter, Frank, 296

Carter, John, 41

Carter, Robert L., 129
Carter, William, 181–82, 215
Carruthers, Adline, 71
Carruthers, Dora, 70, 72, 331–32
Carruthers, James (Jim X's father), 71, 253, 331
Carruthers, James (Jim X's grandfather), 71
Carruthers, Jim X: accusation of rape against, 73–74; arrest and escape, 62, 69, 73; beating by police, 73, 283; Chevrolet belonging to, 72, 164, 195, 332–33; Clayton's testimony about, 193–94; execution, 297–98; family background, 71–72; legacy of, 331–34; at the motion for new trial, 283; testimony of, 194–200; transfer to Memphis, 73–75; at Tucker Prison Farm, 78–80, 234–36, 264, 277, 283. *See also* Clayton-Carruthers trial
Carruthers, Kate/Katie, 71, 164
Carruthers, Lorraine, 70, 72, 331–32
Carruthers, Samuel, 71
Carruthers, Simon, 71
Carruthers, Sue Willie, 70, 71, 331
Carruthers, Virgie (Vergie), 71, 74, 331, 333
castration, 23, 130
Cauley, Otis, 140–41, 144
Chavez, Cesar, 330
child labor, 31
Childress, Alice, 305
Chisholm, Shirley, 305, 312
Civil Rights Congress, 337
Civil Rights Movement, 6, 203, 250–51, 327
Civil War, 15, 25, 146, 207
Clark, G. S., 156
Clark, Paul, 275–76
Clayton, Clear "Bubbles" (Bubber): accusation of rape against, 73–74; arrest of, 62, 70, 72; beating by police, 72–73, 282–83; education, 71; execution, 297–98, 327; family background, 70–71, 327–28; at the motion for new trial, 269, 282–83; prior conviction, 71; testimony of, 193–94, 196–99; transfer to Memphis, 73–75; at Tucker Prison Farm, 78–80, 234–36, 253, 264, 277, 278, 283. *See also* Clayton-Carruthers trial
Clayton, Clarence, 327–28
Clayton, Clay, 70, 327–28
Clayton, Edie/Edith Mitchell, 70, 327–28
Clayton, Isabella (Bell), 71
Clayton, Missouri Lucile, 71
Clayton, Nathan, 293–94
Clayton, Spencer, 253, 254
Clayton-Carruthers trial: appeal, 258, 260, 262, 267, 278–88; appeal denied, 284–85; appeal for clemency, 293–95; appeal to Supreme Court, 287–88; appeal to Supreme Court denied, 260–62, 289; commutation request, 290; conclusion of, 227–32; dramatization of, 286–87; execution, 290, 297–98; grand jury indictment, 105; Hibbler's brief, 255; Houstin and King's supplemental brief, 255–56; jury selection, 109–10; jury's deliberations, 229; legacy of, 327–30; media coverage of, 80, 257–58, 261, 264, 266–67, 269–70, 279, 283–84, 287, 298–99; motion for change of venue denied, 107–8; motion for new trial, 231–32; NAACP interest in, 149, 179, 253–70, 285–86, 289–90, 296–97; new hearing, 264; request for stay of execution, 290–94; second appeal (Eighth Circuit court), 285; significance of, 4–5, 8; start of

the trial, 104–11; stay of execution, 254, 259, 264, 287; threat of lynchings, 108–9; witness testimony, 158–64; writ of error coram nobis, 269–70, 279. *See also* Adams, Arthur L.; Jones, Scipio Africanus
Clayton-Carruthers Defense Committee, 254, 286
Cleaver, Eldridge, 250, 304
clemency, 178, 273–77, 280, 290, 292, 294–95
Clifton, Lucille, 310
Clinton, Hillary, 295
Clinton, William "Bill," 295, 313
Coker, Ehrlich Anthony, 334–35, 337, 339–40
Coker decision, 339–40, 341, 343
Cole, Johnetta, 311
Collins, Luther, 180
Collins, Patricia, 87
Color Purple, The (Walker), 349–50
Committee on Negro Organizations, 168
communism, 149, 178, 207, 316
Communist Party, 296, 297
convict leasing, 19–20, 232–33, 257, 295
Crawford, George, 150–51, 177
Crisis, The (Hart), 217
Culp, Ida, 154
Cultural Association for Women of African Heritage, 204
Cummins, 234, 235, 273
Cutts, William, 132–33, 197, 199, 228, 230

Daniels, Freeling, 109, 196, 228, 300
David, Eddie B., 164
Davis, Angela, 310
Davis, Jeff, 30
Davis, John, 190

Davis, Miles, 84
Davis, Sammy Jr., 203
de Soto, Hernando, 13
death penalty: for Clayton and Carruthers, 228–30, 278, 283, 296–300; screening jurors for objections to, 98, 99; for rape, 23–25, 27, 60, 94, 130, 182, 220, 222, 231, 337–43; and the U.S. Supreme Court, 334–35, 338–43
Debs, Eugene V., 233
DeGout, Yasmin Y., 311
Democratic National Convention (1968), 250–51
Depression, 46, 62–63, 148, 223
DeVoe, Bill, 117–18, 135
Dickinson, Thomas, 23
Dismukes, W. L., 54, 55, 59, 153, 154
Dobbs, Frank, 278
Dodson, Elma, 164
Dodson, Myrtle, 163–64
Donaghey, George Washington, 233, 274
Donovan, Brian, 122
Dorr, Lisa Lindquist, 133, 134, 263, 325
Douglas, William O., 339
Douglass, Frederick, 30, 251, 311
Down in the Delta (film), 313
Du Bois, Shirley Graham, 210
Du Bois, W. E. B., 2, 22, 28, 208, 209, 213
du Feu, Paul, 313
Dudley, Denver L., 105, 110, 132, 164, 229, 267, 277, 333; closing argument, 227; questioning Carruthers, 195–96, 199–200; questioning Clayton, 196, 198–99
Dunbar, Paul Lawrence, 2, 247–48
Durham, Dan, 174

earthquakes, 14
Edward VII (king of England), 261, 267

Edwards, Laura, 86
Eighth Amendment, 341
Elaine massacre, 36–39, 255, 259, 281
Elaine Twelve, 39, 257, 259, 260, 263–64, 272, 281, 288
Elmina Castle, 206
Equal Justice Initiative (EJI), 41
execution. *See* death penalty

Fanning, Leon, 275–76
Fanon, Frantz, 249
Feiffer, Judy, 242
Feiffer, Jules, 242
Feimster, Crystal, 34
feminism, 251, 312
Flood, Dawn Rae, 119
flooding, 21–22
Florida Supreme Court, 142
Flowers, Alonzo, 168
Flowers, Beulah Sampson, 168–69, 347
Flowers, Harold, 168
Floyd, Sam, 248–49
For the Love of Ivy (film), 250
Ford, Gerald, 316
Fourteenth Amendment rights, 110, 262, 279, 288, 341
Fowler, L. A., 222
Francis, Willie, 298
Freedman, Estelle B., 28, 32, 87, 88, 139, 145, 348
Freedom Rides, 205
Freeland, Catherine, 294
Freeman (Mr.), 85, 90, 246, 312; conviction and murder, 145, 165; trial of, 137–45, 246
Friedan, Betty, 312
Froula, Christine, 247
Furman v. Georgia, 338–39, 341, 343
Futrell, J. M., 274, 277, 293

Garrison, William Lloyd, 86
Garvey, Marcus, 89
Garvin, Vicki, 206
Genet, Jean, 203–4
Georgia, Georgia (film), 308
Ghana, 206–11
Gibson, Larry S., 176, 182
Gilmore, Glenda, 136
Giovanni, Nikki, 310
Gladish, Silas Lee "S. L.," 17, 94, 97, 98, 101, 104–5, 152, 157, 271, 276, 322; questioning Bethel, 185–86, 188, 190; questioning Wallace, 191–92
Goldberg, Arthur, 338
Good, Constance, 315
Good, Thorney, 146
Gossett, Lou Jr., 205
Gottlieb, David J., 127
Grant, Ulysses S., 26
Gray, Charles, 109
Great Migration, 1, 36, 90, 328
Great Society, 330
Green, Crane, 55
Greenberg, Jack, 338
Greene, Virgil, 100–102, 105, 112, 117, 121, 153, 157, 271
Greer, Germaine, 312, 313
Gregg v. Georgia, 339
Gregory, Dick, 84
Griffin, W. C. "Dobe," 97–98, 99
Grindle, B. Dean Jr., 334–35
Groveland Boys, 337
Guy, Rosa, 305
Gwaltney (Mr.), 72

Hale, Matthew, 262
Haley, Alex, 313
Hamer, Fannie Lou, 6
Hamm, Charles, 232
Hansberry, Lorraine, 38, 202

Haraway, L. W., 111
Harlem Writers Guild, 202, 205, 212, 305
Harris, Jack, 194
Hart, Althea, 217–18
Hastie, William, 149
Hayes, Brooks, 296
Hays, George Washington, 274
Henderson, Annie "Momma," 44, 46, 47, 89, 167, 170, 173, 347, 350
Henderson, Willie, 44, 46, 47, 170, 243, 306
Henke, Suzette A., 167
Henry, Callie, 89
Henslee, Lee, 298
Hibbler, John, 260
Hibbler, Al, 329–30
Hibbler, John A.: appeal for Clayton and Carruthers, 255, 256, 261, 263–64, 267–70, 279, 280, 282–83; appeal to Supreme Court, 284–86, 289; commutation attempt, 290–92, 294, 297, 300; and the Elaine Twelve, 255, 257, 259; later career, 329; questioning Carruthers's confession, 299
Hinds, James, 26
Hine, Darlene Clark, 86, 90
Hitler, Adolf, 167
Holiday, Billie, 126, 174
Holley, Donald, 293
Hollins, Jess, 178–79
Hollins v. Oklahoma, 178
hooks, bell, 310
Horney, Julie, 347
Houston, Charles Hamilton: and the Clayton-Carruthers trial, 255, 256, 258, 261, 263, 264, 267, 270, 279; and the Crawford case, 151; and the Hollins case, 178; at Howard University, 148, 150–51; and Marshall, 150, 176–77, 265; and the NAACP, 151–52, 176–77, 178, 181, 182, 215, 280; leaving the NAACP, 286, 335
Howard University, 148
Hughes, Langston, 2, 147, 203
Hurst, O. H., 94

Ilsley, Agnes Boeing, 150
Ingram, Mack, 337
International Labor Defense (ILD), 148–49, 150, 177–78, 182, 255, 296, 297
International Ladies' Garment Workers Union, 296
interracial marriage, 26
Irvin, Charles, 294, 297

Jackson, George, 305, 311
Jackson, Hale, 72, 74
Jackson, W. A., 94
Jacobs, Harriet, 86
Jacquet, Catherine, 340
Johnson, Bailey Jr.: in California, 83, 170; calling Marguerite "Maya," 175; letter to Kennedy, 208; in the Merchant Marine, 171, 172, 173; in prison, 204; in St. Louis, 84, 85, 90, 137, 138, 140, 165–66; in Stamps with Marguerite, 1–2, 44, 46, 82, 83, 167
Johnson, Bailey Sr., 82–84, 171
Johnson, C. F., 190
Johnson, Clyde Bailey "Guy," 171, 172, 173, 206, 207, 209, 316
Johnson, Ed, 78
Johnson, Henry, 195
Johnson, James Weldon, 2, 260
Johnson, Lyndon, 330, 338
Johnson, Marguerite. *See* Angelou, Maya
Johnson, Vivian Baxter. *See* Baxter, Vivian

Johnson, Walter, 84
Joint Action Committee of Commonwealth College, 296
Jones, Alexander, 214
Jones, James Earl, 205, 308
Jones, Ozzie, 337
Jones, Scipio Africanus: and the Clayton-Carruthers appeal, 258, 259–60, 261, 263, 264, 267, 270, 279, 280, 283, 285, 290–91; death of, 329; and the Elaine Twelve, 257, 259; family and education, 256–57; letter to White, 253
Jordan, June, 310
jury discrimination, 178, 257, 268, 287

Keck, Grover Elias, 94, 97, 98–99, 100, 101, 103, 183, 277, 322; addressing the jurors, 220–22
Keck, Nannie Boyles, 94
Kees, Willie, 41
Keith, (Dr.), 270
Kellaway, Kate, 313
Kelley, Robin D. G., 89–90
Kendall, David, 334, 339–40
Kennedy, Florynce, 312
Kennedy, John F., 208, 337
Kester, Howard, 78
Killough, Neil, 104, 106, 107, 108, 109, 110, 132, 164, 198, 199, 227, 282, 333; instructions to the jury, 227–28
King, B. B., 250
King, Carol, 255, 261, 263, 264
King, Coretta Scott, 310
King, Gilbert, 298
King, Martin Luther Jr., 9, 202, 203, 204, 208, 210, 213, 311; assassination of, 241–42, 250
Ku Klux Klan (KKK), 15, 26, 34–35, 41–42, 46, 86

Lange, Dorothea, 167
Lewis, Earl, 84
Lewis, Todd E., 33–34
"Lift Every Voice and Sing," 45, 203
Lincoln, Mary Todd, 309
Lincoln University, 147
Lindsey, Arch, 67–68, 72, 73, 79–80, 108, 135, 160, 196, 227, 267, 282, 328
Liston, Sonny, 85
Little Rock Central High School, 346
Long Shadow of Little Rock, The (Bates), 346
Look Away (play), 309
Loomis, Robert, 242, 248–49, 305, 314
Lorde, Audre, 86, 202, 310
Louis, Joe, 285
Louisiana Purchase, 13
Love, Herbert, 194
Lowery, Henry, 39–40, 42
Luciano, Lucky, 293
Lumumba, Patrice, 204
Lupton, Mary Jane, 246
Lyman, E. B., 222
Lynch, Charles, 28
lynch mobs, 24, 34, 40, 41, 42, 55, 70, 74, 76, 77, 87, 89, 108–10, 130, 164
lynchings, 29, 33, 37, 86; anti-lynching efforts, 41, 42, 87, 179, 181, 257, 280, 335, 337; by Black people, 166; legal, 214, 300, 327, 332; in response to rape allegations, 28, 30, 31, 36, 40, 47, 55, 110, 130, 147, 151, 160, 164, 166, 176, 180, 181, 196, 218–19, 231, 269, 280, 286; as social affairs, 34, 41; threat of, 108–9; of white people, 29; women's participation in, 34

Mack, Kenneth, 214, 253
Makeba, Miriam, 250
Manuel, Willie, 163, 164, 194

March on Washington, 207, 208, 312, 327
Marshall, Aubrey, 147
Marshall, Buster, 264, 265
Marshall, Norma, 146, 264
Marshall, Paule, 202, 305
Marshall, Thurgood: and the Clayton-Carruthers trial, 265, 285–94, 296–97, 299–300; education, 147–52; family background, 146; and the NAACP, 19, 258, 264–65, 280, 285, 286, 290, 335, 335–40; practicing law, 176–77, 181–82, 258, 264, 338; on the Supreme Court, 334–35, 338–43; work on rape trials, 214–19, 252–53, 334–35, 337
Marshall, William, 146, 264
Martin, Willie, 158–59, 299–300
Martineau, John E., 259–60, 263, 264, 267–70, 274, 279
Matkin-Rawn, Story, 18, 35, 37, 42, 94
Maxwell, William, 338, 341–42
Mayfield, Ana Livia, 209
Mayfield, Julian, 206, 208, 209, 210
McGuire, Danielle, 346
McHaney, Edgar Lafayette, 254, 258–61, 263, 264, 272, 328–29
McMurry, Myra K., 248
McPherson, Dolly A., 241, 244, 310
McWhorter, John, 314
Meriwether, Louise, 305, 310
Meurer, Elly Julia (Wallace), 223
Mickle, Mildred R., 247
Mikel, Elmer, 272–73
Miller, Ike, 227, 231
Miller, Ran, 72
Mississippi County (Arkansas). See Arkansas Delta
Mississippi Supreme Court, 25
Mitchell, Margaret, 167
Mitford, Jessica, 251, 309, 314, 316
Montgomery Bus Boycott, 327
Moore, Lon, 111
Moore v. Dempsey, 39, 260
Morgan, Sammy L., 20, 22, 63, 330
Morris, Harvey, 222
Morrison, Toni, 310, 346–47
Mother Cleo, 172–73
Motley, Constance Baker, 336
Moyers, Bill, 349–51
Murphy, George, 259
Murray, Donald, 265

Napson-Williams, Theresa, 216, 217
Nasser, Gamal Abdel, 207
National Association for the Advancement of Colored People (NAACP): archives, 6; Arkansas Conference of Branches, 346; attention to rape trials, 30, 129, 134, 178–79, 214–15, 252–53, 280, 335–41; and the Clayton-Carruthers trial, 5, 149, 179, 253–70, 285–86, 289–90, 296–97; and the Crawford trial, 150–51; and the Elaine Twelve, 39; Houston's work with, 150–52, 178–79; investigating convict leasing, 19; investigating prison violence, 235; Legal Defense and Educational Fund (LDF), 335–40; Legal Redress Committee, 147; legal department, 177–82; letter from Spencer Clayton, 253; Little Rock branch, 36, 42, 89, 254, 255, 256, 263, 265, 346; local branches, 42, 47, 347; Marshall's work for, 19, 258, 264–65, 280, 285–86, 290, 335, 335–40; and the Scottsboro Boys, 148–49; seeking financial assistance, 263, 285–86; using Black lawyers, 151–52; women's criticism of, 215–19
National Bar Association, 150

National Coalition Against Sexual Assault, 307–8
National Farm Labor Union (NFLU), 330
National Negro Congress, 296
National Women's Conference (Houston, 1977), 312
Native Americans, 13–14
Neeley, A. C., 222
Negro Womanhood Defense Committee, 219
Newton, Huey, 305
Nicholson, Trina, 332–33
Nkrumah, Kwame, 206, 208, 210, 211, 212
nonviolence, 202, 208, 213
Norwood, Hal N., 293

O'Neale, Sondra, 310
Organization of Afro-American Unity, 211
Orwell, Sonia, 251

Painter, Nell Irvin, 307
Palko v. Connecticut, 288
Pan-African Cultural Festival, 250
Parks, Rosa, 6, 219
Parnell, Harvey, 274, 276
paternalism, 35, 257, 295
patriarchy, 6, 28, 170, 348; Black, 87; racist, 86
Patterson, W. H., 222
Payne, Elizabeth Anne, 114
Pearl (accuser): accusations against Bethel and Wallace, 54–55, 57–58; after the trial, 323–24; family background, 112–15; testimony at the trial, 112, 115–21, 125–26, 128
Peterson, Willie, 177
Phillips, Green, 78–79
Pillows, Gus, 54

Pillows, J. C., 54
Pleasant (enslaved man), 25
Poetry Roundtable of Arkansas, 348–49
Poindexter, James, 214
poll taxes, 29
Poor People's Campaign, 213, 241
Porgy and Bess, 201, 205, 316
post-traumatic stress disorder, 167
Primus, Pearl, 174
Progressive Farmers and Household Union of America, 37
public schooling, 31

railroad travel, 1–2
Randolph, A. Philip, 294
Ranson, Leon A., 289
rape. *See* sexual assault
rape laws: age-of-consent laws, 31–32; debate surrounding, 347–48; inadequacy of, 217; and legal reform, 348; race-neutral, 26–27, 86; rape shield laws, 348; sexist aspects of, 217. *See also* rape trials
rape myth, 30, 179
Rape of Lucrece, The (Shakespeare), 247
rape trials: and Black defendants, 262–63; Black men accused by white women, 24, 26, 27–30, 33, 34, 36, 42, 110, 149, 177–82, 214–15, 228, 232, 263, 296, 298–300, 325, 327, 335–36, 337, 340, 342; Black men accused of assaulting Black women, 139, 140–41; instructions to the jury, 220–22, 227–28; interracial, 149, 177–78, 182, 214, 335–36, 342; in the Jim Crow South, 7–8; jury deliberations, 222–23, 229, 231; Marshall's work on, 214–19, 252–53, 334–35, 337; medical testimony at, 160–63, 262; and the morality of the defendant,

157; NAACP's attention to, 30, 129, 134, 178–79, 214–15, 252–53, 280, 335–41; as public theater, 7; question of resistance, 262–63, 348; shaming of women, 118, 125, 139, 162; for statutory rape, 31, 118–19, 138–39, 142–45, 161, 162, 166, 186; use of racist tropes, 140, 141, 158–59, 163; white men, 275–76; white men accused of assaulting Black women, 138–39, 190, 216–18, 218–19, 275, 340; white men accused of assaulting white women, 24, 28; and the accuser's reputation/character, 25, 60–61, 88, 118, 126–27, 134, 136, 139, 145, 155–57, 179, 180, 186, 190, 216–17, 218, 221–22, 262–63, 263, 272, 276, 336, 348. *See also* Bethel-Wallace trial; Clayton-Carruthers trial; death penalty; rape laws; sexual assault
Readye, Mrs. F. C., 48
Reagan, Ronald, 315, 349
Reconstruction, 25–27
redemptive suffering, 204
Reeves, Peter, 25
Rehnquist, William, 341
Rhoton, Lewis, 263, 264
Riley, Billy Lee, 22
Roberts, Dorothy, 25
Roberts, (Dr.), 270
Robertson, Stephen, 142, 174
Robinson, B. E., 111
Robinson, Jo Ann, 6
Robinson, Marvin, 197
Robinson, Sugar Ray, 304
Rodgers, Ward, 75–76
Rolle, Esther, 315
Roosevelt, Franklin Delano, 167, 170, 288, 336
Roosevelt, Theodore, 233
Roots (Haley), 313, 349

Ross, James D., 280
Russell, Nipsey, 203
Rustin, Bayard, 203

Sanchez, Sonia, 310
Sanders, Dock, 124
Scottsboro Boys, 42, 110, 136, 148–49, 150, 177, 267, 288, 339
Scottsboro motion, 110, 268–69, 284
Seale, Bobby, 305
segregation, 29, 47, 84, 147, 256–57, 281; in education, 258, 265, 346
sexual assault: accusations based on failure to marry or support a child, 135–36; accusers allegedly motivated by money, 135–36; advocacy for survivors, 346; age of consent, 31–32, 118, 142; in Angelou's writing, 243–44, 246, 247, 311–312; Black men accused by white women, 40–41, 55, 134, 159, 176, 230; Black men accused by Black children, 166; Black men accused by Black women, 24–25, 85–88; against Black women and girls, 25, 85–88; of children, 161, 162, 166, 186; consequences for women, 126–28; interracial, 25, 139; involving potions or drugs, 23, 27; penalties for, 3–4, 23–24, 26–27, 28, 60, 166, 220, 222, 228, 229–31; question of resistance, 121–25, 140, 187, 220–21; slave owners against enslaved women, 45; "speak-outs" about, 251; spousal rape, 348; use of force, 121–25; white men accused by white women, 54–55; white men accused by Black women, 24–25, 26, 85–86, 345, 346; white men accused by children, 66, 230–31. *See also* rape trials
Shakespeare, William, 2, 248; *The Rape of Lucrece*, 247

Shank, Mark, 78
sharecroppers and sharecropping, 18–21, 64, 76, 77, 80; Black female, 89; and the STFU, 236–37, 266
Shaver, W. W., 276
Short, Charley, 195
Shuttlesworth, Fred, 202
Sigman, Mrs. M. L., 295
Simone, Nina, 308
Simpson, Wallis, 267
Sims, Newt, 284
Sinatra, Frank, 203
Sinclair, Madge, 315
slave narratives, 251
slavery, 14–15, 170
Smith, Mose, 100, 222
Snetzer, Bill, 122
socialism/socialists, 63–65, 206, 207
Society for the Prevention of Cruelty to Children, 31
Sommerville, Diane Miller, 24, 30
Southern Christian Leadership Conference (SCLC), 202–4
Southern Conference on Human Welfare, 296
Southern Tenant Farmers' Union (STFU), 37–38, 64–66, 75–78, 80–81, 89, 105, 130, 167, 255, 330; organizing strikes, 236–37, 265–66, 279–80
Spohn, Cassia, 347
Stanfield, Lee, 307–8
Steinem, Gloria, 312
Stewart, Potter, 341
Stockley, Grif, 346
Stonewall riots, 251
Student Nonviolent Coordinating Committee (SNCC), 205, 330

Take Back the Night, 9, 347
Taylor, Beloit, 296

Taylor, Bert, 54, 59
Taylor, Guy, 156
Taylor, Linda, 174
Taylor, Lucien, 164
Taylor, Recy, 6, 219
tenant farmers, 19–21, 236–37
Terral, Tom, 35, 274
Terrell, Tug, 122
The Walls, 3–4, 224–26, 234, 272–73, 274
Thomas, Clarence, 316
Thomas, Howard, 246
Thomas, Norman, 64, 66, 78
Thomas, Theo, 231, 296
Thompson, John R., 254
Thompson, Wash, 222
Thornton, H. H., 111
Tolen, A. D., 222
Tolnay, Stewart E., 166
Trimble, Thomas C. III, 281–82, 284, 285
Tubman, Harriet, 89
Tucker Prison Farm, 4–5, 78, 226, 232–36, 264, 295, 297; furloughs from, 273, 274–75
Tyson, Cicely, 205, 315

Universal Negro Improvement Association (UNIA), 89
University of Maryland Law School, 258
University of North Carolina, 150
U.S. Supreme Court: *Brown v. Board of Education*, 258, 341, 346; *Buck v. Bell*, 288; on capital punishment, 334–35, 338–43; Clayton-Carruthers case appealed to, 258, 261, 263, 284, 285, 278–79; *Coker* decision, 334–35, 339–40, 341, 343; Crawford case, 151; and the Elaine Twelve, 257; *Furman v. Georgia*, 338–39, 341, 343; *Gregg v.*

Georgia, 339; *Hollins v. Oklahoma*, 178; Scipio Jones's cases, 260; Little Rock case, 346; Marshall on, 334–35, 337, 338; *Moore v. Dempsey*, 39, 260; *Palko v. Connecticut*, 288; rape cases heard by, 336, 337, 340; Scottsboro decision, 110, 267; Clarence Thomas on, 316; Thomas-Carter case, 296

venereal disease, 149, 162, 174, 336
Vermillion, Mary, 247
Virgie (accuser), 79–80, 158, 263, 268, 283; after the trial, 325–26; background and family, 130; Bryant's testimony about, 159–60; sexual assault of, 132; testimony at the trial, 132–36

Wafford, Mary "Kentucky," 44–45
Wagner-Martin, Linda, 243–44
Walker, Alice, 310, 349–50
Walker, Wyatt, 202
Wallace, C. A., 223
Wallace, Elly, 321, 322
Wallace, Henry, 76–77
Wallace, J. D., 223
Wallace, Mike (Roy Thomas/R. T.): after prison, 321–22; arrest of, 53–59, 62, 153; conclusion of second trial, 220; family background, 56–57; furlough for, 276–77; marriage, 223–24; pardon for, 3–4, 274–75, 277; Pearl's accusations against, 54–55, 57–58, 101, 115–21, 125–26, 128; sentencing, 60, 222–23; testimony at second trial, 183–88, 191–92; in The Walls, 224–26, 272–73. *See also* Bethel-Wallace trial
Wallace, T. R., 223
Washington, Booker T., 257
Waters, Maxine, 310

Watts riot, 212
We Are Not Alone (play), 286–87
Webb, Frank, 109
Wells (Wells-Barnett), Ida B., 28, 30, 39, 87–88, 89, 216
West, Emmanuel, 40, 42, 197
West, R. A., 154–55
West, Rebecca, 129
Whayne, Jeannie, 14–15, 21, 22, 40, 62
Whitaker, James, 138
Whitaker, Robert, 259–60
White, Byron, 341
White, Deborah Gray, 88
White, Martha Louise, 174
White, Walter: anti-lynching bill, 280; in Arkansas, 39; and the Clayton-Carruthers case, 253, 256, 288, 296–97; and the Crawford case, 150, 151; and the NAACP, 148–49, 177, 178, 179, 180, 181, 182, 265
white supremacy, 6, 26–27, 29, 33, 34, 35, 41, 42, 78, 89, 146, 159, 197, 205, 211, 269, 331, 348; as sexual violence, 247; all-white primaries, 257, 329
Wilkerson, Isabel, 1
Wilkins, Roy, 254, 261, 264
Williams, Claude C., 296
Williams, Juan, 182, 258, 339
Williams, Robert F., 205
Williams, Sylvester, 298–99
Wilson, Clarence H., 67–68, 70, 73, 74, 78, 79, 108, 135, 196, 198, 229, 268, 282, 283, 328, 333
Wilson, Robert E. Lee "Boss Lee," 16–17, 22, 39, 40, 42, 67, 94, 257, 279, 322
Windom, Alice, 206, 209, 210, 305, 313, 315
Winfrey, Oprah, 308, 313

Women Against Rape (WAR), 342
Women's Christian Temperance Union, 31
women's liberation movement, 312
Woodruff, Nan, 19, 63, 66, 237, 266, 279
World War II, 170, 172
Wriggins, Jennifer, 228
Wright, Richard, 37
Wright, Sarah, 305
Wright-Pryor, Barbara, 306

X, Malcolm, 9, 203, 207, 209–11, 212, 249, 304, 311, 315

Young, J. H., 222
Young Women's Christian Association (YWCA), 89, 296
Younge, Gary, 316